The Spoils of War

The Politics, Economics, and Diplomacy of
Reparations
1918–1932

BRUCE KENT

CLARENDON PRESS · OXFORD
1989

Oxford University Press, Walton Street, Oxford OX2 6DP
Oxford New York Toronto
Delhi Bombay Calcutta Madras Karachi
Petaling Jaya Singapore Hong Kong Tokyo
Nairobi Dar es Salaam Cape Town
Melbourne Auckland
and associated companies in
Berlin Ibadan

Oxford is a trade mark of Oxford University Press

Published in the United States
by Oxford University Press, New York

British Library Cataloguing in Publication Data
Kent, Bruce
The spoils of war: the politics, economics and diplomacy of reparations 1918–32
I. World War   II. Reparation for Germany
I. Title
940.3'1422
ISBN 0–19–822738–8

Library of Congress Cataloging in Publication Data
Kent, Bruce, 1932–
The spoils of war: the politics, economics, and diplomacy of
reparations, 1918–1932/Bruce Kent.
Revision of the author's thesis
Bibliography: p.   Includes index.
1. World War, 1914–1918—Reparations.   I. Title
D648.K36   1989   940.3'1422—dc19   88–38795
ISBN 0–19–822738–8

Set by Butler & Tanner Ltd, Frome and London
Printed in Great Britain by
Biddles Ltd., Guildford and King's Lynn

For my parents
Eric and Beatrice Kent

Who have never ceased to strive for
a fit country for heroes

Acknowledgements

THOSE who are versed in the archaeology of texts may discern that this work has grown out of a doctoral dissertation about reparations and German financial policy in the early post-war years. Because of my increasing awareness that the major parties to the reparation dispute behaved in a similar manner, this dissertation was gradually incorporated into a study of the interaction of British, French, German, and American policies up to the inauguration of the Dawes Plan in 1924. In recent years this study has in turn been extended to cover the period of the Dawes and Young Plans up to the effective abandonment of the reparation scheme in mid-1932. It is hoped that a treatment of both the early and later phases of the reparation dispute will pinpoint continuities and significant changes in the roles of the powers involved.

This work is based on published and unpublished papers of the Reparation Commission and on the American, British, French, and German government archives referred to in the bibliography. The following private collections of documents have also been used: the Bonar Law and Lloyd George Papers in the Beaverbrook Library, London; the Crewe Papers in the Cambridge University Library; the Keynes Papers in the Marshall Library, Cambridge; the Stuart M. Crocker, David E. Finley, and Ogden Mills Papers in the Library of Congress, Washington; the Stephane Lauzanne, James A. Logan, Louis Loucheur, and Arthur N. Young Papers in the Hoover Institution, Stanford; the Bernard M. Baruch and John Foster Dulles Papers in the Princeton University Library; and typescript copies of papers in the Smuts Archive formerly in the possession of the late Sir Keith Hancock.

My forays in search of archival and other materials have been made pleasant and fruitful by the co-operation of the officers of Archives de l'Assemblée Nationale, Paris; Archives Économiques et Financières, Ministère du Budget, Paris; Archives Nationales, Paris; Archives du Sénat, Paris; Archives du Ministère des Affaires Étrangères, Paris; the Australian National Library, Canberra; the Australian National University Library, Canberra; the Beaverbrook Library, London; the British Museum, London; the Cambridge University Library; the Deutsche Zentralarchiv, Potsdam; the Foreign Office Library, London; the Heidelberg University Library; the Hoover Institution on War,

Revolution, and Peace, Stanford; the Humboldt University Library, Berlin; the Library of Congress, Washington; the Library of the Institut für Soziologie, Heidelberg; the Marshall Library, Cambridge; the National Archives, Washington; the Princeton University Library; the Public Record Office, London; the Stanford University Library; and the La Trobe Library, Melbourne. I am indebted to the Trustees of the Smuts Archive and to the Dulles Committee for permission to study and cite papers in their custody.

In the course of such a wide-ranging study I have accumulated massive scholarly debts. My task would have been impossible had it not been for the labours of the compilers of the official collections of American, British, and German diplomatic documents—*Papers Relating to the Foreign Relations of the United States, Documents on British Foreign Policy, 1919–1939*, and *Akten zur deutschen auswärtigen Politik, 1918–1945*. I have also received invaluable assistance from the superb volumes of German documents edited by Gunter Abramowski, Karl Dietrich Erdmann, Anton Golecki, Karl-Heinz Harbeck, Tilman Koops, Ilse Maurer, Hagen Schulze, Ingrid Schulze-Bidlingmaier, Martin Vogt, Udo Wengst, and Peter Wulf. Other scholars who have published monographs and articles or edited materials in the field have been a source of enlightenment and stimulation. Some, who have written recently about the early years of the reparation dispute, are mentioned in the Introduction. Others whose work has been particularly helpful are E. W. Bennett, R. Bunselmeyer, P. M. Burnett, K. E. Born, W. J. Helbich, C.-D. Krohn, E. Laubach, W. Link, R. E. Lüke, A. J. Mayer, A. S. Milward, H. J. Rupieper, G. Schulz, F. Siebert, E. Wandel, E. Weill-Raynal, and P.-C. Witt. The extent of my indebtedness to each and all of them will be obvious to any reader of the pages that follow.

The research for this book could not have been undertaken without travel grants from the Australian National University and from the Australian–American Educational Foundation. Nor would it have been possible without the encouragement and help of Professor Manning Clark and my colleagues in the History Department of the Australian National University's Arts Faculty. I am particularly indebted to the late David Johanson, formerly of La Trobe University, Victoria, and Daphne Gollan for shouldering extra teaching burdens during my absences on study leave. For their cheerful and meticulous assistance in typing and keying in successive drafts of the manuscript my sincere thanks are due to Shirley Bradley, Faye Dockrill, Barbara Hutchinson,

June Murray, Paddy Maughan, Marian Robson, Robyn Rochford, Pat Romans, Doreen Whitfield, Bea Willcock, and, above all, Deborah Sprigg. Jennifer Lee, Janet McCalman, and Bill Fox also provided invaluable help in checking the footnotes and bibliography.

I have derived great benefit from contact with the following scholars: Professor R. D. Challener of Princeton University; L. F. Fitzhardinge, formerly of the Australian National University; J. M. Garland, formerly of the Reserve Bank of Australia; D. B. Goldey, of Lincoln College, Oxford; the late Professor Agnes Headlam-Morley, of St Hugh's College, Oxford; Emeritus Professor James Joll, of the University of London; Franz Lassner and Agnes Peterson, formerly of the Hoover Institution, Stanford; H. O. Pappe, formerly of the University of Sussex; Professor E. A. G. Robinson of Cambridge; Ted Sieper, of the Australian National University; A. J. P. Taylor, formerly of Magdalen College, Oxford; the late Ken Tite, of Magdalen College, Oxford; the late Professor G. S. L. Tucker, of the Australian National University; and Sir Edgar Williams, formerly of Rhodes House, Oxford. I am particularly grateful to Professor Arno J. Mayer, of Princeton University, for commenting some years ago on my first chapter and for helping with a travel grant; to Professor Alan S. Milward, of the London School of Economics and Political Science, for saving me from some economic solecisms; and, more recently, to Sir Harry Hinsley of St John's College, Cambridge for reading and criticizing an earlier version of the manuscript. My greatest debts are to the late Sir Keith Hancock, Emeritus Professor of History at the Australian National University, for his wisdom and encouragement; and to Ann, for her criticism and patience.

B.K.

Australian National University
January 1988

Contents

Illustrations

Illustrations are reprinted by permission of the *London Standard*

Tables

Abbreviations

A. Amt	Auswärtiges Amt
ADAP	*Akten zur deutschen auswärtigen Politik, 1918–1945,* Series B
ADGB	Allgemeiner Deutscher Gewerkschaftsbund
AEF	Archives Économiques et Financières
AF	*L'Action française*
AN	Archives Nationales
Annals	*Annals of the American Academy of Political and Social Science*
Archiv	*Archiv für Sozialwissenschaft und Sozialpolitik*
Bäy. VP	Bäyerische Volkspartei
BIS	Bank for International Settlements
BLA	*Berliner Lokal-Anzeiger*
BT	*Berliner Tageblatt*
CAE	Commission des Affaires Étrangères
CD	*Annales de la Chambre des Députés: Débats parlementaires*
CEH	*Central European History*
CFAE	Commissions des Finances et des Affaires Étrangères
CORC	Commission on the Organization of the Reparation Commission
DAZ	*Deutsche Allgemeine Zeitung*
DBFP I	*Documents on British Foreign Policy, 1919–1939,* Series I
DBFP IA	*Documents on British Foreign Policy, 1919–1939,* Series IA
DBFP II	*Documents on British Foreign Policy, 1919–1939,* Series II
DDP	Deutsche Demokratische Partei
DNVP	Deutschnationale Volkspartei
Doc. parl.	*Documents parlementaires*
DT	*Deutsche Tageszeitung*
DVP	Deutsche Volkspartei
EJ	*Economic Journal*
FBI	Federation of British Industries

FO	Foreign Office
FR	*Papers Relating to the Foreign Relations of the United States*
FRPPC	*Papers Relating to the Foreign Relations of the United States: Paris Peace Conference*
FZ	*Frankfurter Zeitung*
HC	*House of Commons Debates. Fifth Series*
HJ	*The Historical Journal*
HL	*House of Lords Debates. Fifth Series*
HMSO	His/Her Majesty's Stationery Office
HZ	*Historische Zeitschrift*
IC	International Conference Series, British Cabinet Papers
IWC	Imperial War Cabinet
JMH	*Journal of Modern History*
JPE	*Journal of Political Economy*
KAPD	Kommunistische Arbeiterpartei Deutschlands
KPD	Kommunistische Partei Deutschlands
KZ	*Kreuz-Zeitung*
LA	Leading Article
MAE	Ministère des Affaires Étrangères
MG	*Manchester Guardian*
MGCRE	*Manchester Guardian Commercial: Reconstruction in Europe*
MICUM	Mission Interalliée de Contrôle des Usines et des Mines
MP	*Morning Post*
NSDAP	Nationalsozialistische Deutsche Arbeiterpartei
NV	*Verhandlungen der verfassungsgebenden deutschen Nationalversammlung*
NYT	*New York Times*
PC	Plenary Commission
QJE	*Quarterly Journal of Economics*
RC	Reparation Commission
RDI	Reichsverband der Deutschen Industrie
RES	*Review of Economics and Statistics*
RH	*Revue historique*
RHMC	*Revue d'histoire moderne et contemporaine*
RT	*Verhandlungen des Reichstags*
RWR	Reichswirtschaftsrat

Sec. State	Secretary of State
Sénat	*Annales du Sénat: Débats parlementaires*
SPD	Sozialdemokratische Partei Deutschlands
USPD	Unabhängige Sozialdemokratische Partei Deutschlands
VfZ	*Vierteljahrsheft für Zeitgeschichte*
VKP	Vereinigte Kommunistische Partei
VSP	Vereinigte Sozialdemokratische Partei
VZ	*Vossische Zeitung*
Zentrum	Zentrumspartei Deutschlands

FIG. I. The *Evening Standard*, 29 April 1929.

Introduction

A CORNERSTONE assumption of this study is that Germany was incapable of fulfilling the reparation demands of the victors in the conditions which prevailed after the war of 1914–18. Strictly speaking, any effort to make a belligerent pay *subsequently* for the cost of a major war is ill conceived, since all wars, in so far as they are not financed by foreign loans, are paid for *immediately* by the diversion of human and material resources to the business of destruction.[1] The nations which emerged victorious in 1918 could have made Germany defray the cost of their war effort to a meaningful extent only if they had conquered an economically significant part of her territory soon after the outbreak of hostilities and forced its inhabitants to advance credits or donate goods and services to them for the remainder of the conflict. This method of shifting the economic burden of warfare, which was used with such devastating effect by Nazi Germany at the expense of France and other European countries during the war of 1939–45, was not available to the Entente powers because they never succeeded in carrying the war onto German soil.[2] All that they could realistically hope for after the war was that Germany might be required to ease the burden of reconstruction and assist the repayment of their domestic and foreign debts by transfers of foreign exchange, bullion, labour, and goods. Yet, because they did not assume economic control over Germany or even retain their own command economies after the war, two formidable preconditions had to be satisfied before this procedure could yield significant results. The first was that, in the absence of a sharp rise in her domestic productivity or a dramatic upsurge in world trade, it was necessary for Germany to regulate and restrict her capital expenditure and domestic consumption; and the second was that the victors, who happened to be Germany's major

---

[1] Any beneficial short-term side effects deriving from fuller employment and more rational economic organization are likely to be outweighed by the economic and social disruption caused by war and its aftermath. This was clearly so in the case of the war of 1914–18.

[2] The depredations of the Nazis have been lucidly analysed in A. S. Milward, *The New Order and the French Economy* (Oxford, 1970); *War, Economy and Society, 1939–1945* (London, 1977).

trade competitors, had to be prepared to facilitate a flood of her exports onto the world market.

Neither of these developments were likely to occur during the inter-war years. Post-war Germany was so economically exhausted and politically polarized that she was hard pressed even to accommodate the competing demands of her own capital and labour in a period when industrial reconstruction and better living conditions were both the order of the day. This, as Keynes proclaimed throughout the 1920s, made it highly unlikely that a substantial amount of wealth could be transferred by adjusting the conditions of supply within Germany, unless those who made such adjustments were prepared, like the Brüning government of 1930–2, to run the risk of serious social upheaval. The creditors, on the other hand, were reluctant to ease the transfer problem by regulating demand conditions outside Germany because the war had encouraged them to adopt autarkic and pro-tectionist policies which were to be strengthened by the recurrent recessions of the post-war period. The barriers which were erected against German goods reduced the practical validity of the theoretically unimpeachable assertion of Bertil Ohlin and other critics of Keynes that the transfer problem could be resolved via the demand generated by an initial monetary transfer from Germany to her creditors. Ohlin was correct to point out in 1929 that the purchasing power which had been transferred to Germany by the influx of foreign loans in the late 1920s had helped to increase her imports and diminish her exports. Yet he was unable to establish that a similar process would occur in the rest of the world if Germany somehow managed to defy the laws of economic gravity and reverse the net flow of funds. Apart from conceding to Keynes that there could be difficulties on the supply side of the transfer process because of the stickiness of German wages, Ohlin stressed that if the creditors reacted to increased German exports by intensifying their protectionist policies reparation payments would become 'virtually impossible'.[3]

It is important to note that Ohlin was pessimistic even about the practical scope of schemes for deliveries in kind, which he regarded as

---

[3] The monographs and articles by Keynes on the reparation problem are listed in the bibliography. See particularly his exchange with Ohlin: J. M. Keynes, 'The German Transfer Problem'; B. G. Ohlin, 'The Reparation Problem: A Discussion. I. Transfer Difficulties, Real and Imagined'; J. M. Keynes, 'The Reparation Problem: A Discussion. II. A Rejoinder'; B. G. Ohlin, 'Mr. Keynes' Views on the Transfer Problem. II. A Rejoinder from Professor Ohlin'; J. M. Keynes, 'Views on the Transfer Problem', *EJ* 39 (1929), 1–7, 172–82, 400–8.

the best means of orchestrating the required shift in demand from Germany to her creditors. Ideally, he argued, such deliveries should go to France or to South America, where the United States, which had by this time become the major recipient of reparations in the form of allied debt repayments, was funnelling a great deal of its surplus funds. In practice, however, such a solution was impossible. 'The inevitable opposition of powerful American and British export industries to any such plan', he concluded, 'is one of the real obstacles, perhaps the greatest of them all, which lie in the way of an organized solution of the reparation problem.' Even as Ohlin wrote, his pessimism was vindicated by the recommendation of the Young Committee, in response to British pressure, that deliveries in kind should be phased out within ten years. A year earlier a conference convened at Pyrmont on the reparation problem by the Friedrich List Society had seen similar writing on the wall. In summing up the views of leading German academic economists, bankers, businessmen, and statesmen, the chairman, Professor Bernhard Harms, a liberal international economist from the University of Kiel, had admitted that Germany could do somewhat more to raise productivity, reduce consumption, and encourage the export of capital goods rather than consumer goods. The major constraint upon her ability to pay reparations was, however, the unwillingness of the rest of the world to receive her goods. The theory of 'a more or less friction-free transfer of purchasing power' which had been expounded at the conference by Professors Walter Eucken and Wilhelm Röpke contained 'a kernel of truth'. Yet, the more closely it was applied to the real world, the more it needed modification. The greater the artificial stimulus given to German exports, Harms concluded, 'the more stringent the countermeasures which are to be expected in the form of tariffs and import restrictions'.[4]

Despite the evident inelasticity of world demand for German goods, an authority as eminent as Fritz Machlup has gone to the lengths of arguing that Germany's capacity to pay the reparations demanded of her was demonstrated by the way in which her virtually chronic visible trade deficit of the 1920s was temporarily converted into a sizeable surplus in the early 1930s. In an article which appears to have had an untoward influence on recent historians, Machlup observed that the German export surplus of 1929–32 was 'just about equal' to reparation

---

[4] The proceedings of the Pyrmont Conference of June 1928 are to be found in E. Salin (ed.), *Das Reparationsproblem* (2 vols.; Berlin, 1929). See particularly i. 280–91 (Harms).

payments and that reparations were only 7.9 per cent of the total value of foreign trade in these years. After pointing out that the latter ratio was 'relatively modest' and much lower than the indemnity/trade ratio of the reparations paid by France after the war of 1870–1, Machlup professed puzzlement about 'why some economists in the late 1920s made such a fuss about the supposed severity of the German transfer problem'. He failed, however, to make clear that this surplus was not achieved by the rise in German exports which he and other monetarist theorists of the late 1920s had predicted would follow from cash reparation transfers. What in fact happened was that a drop in the value of exports from 12.7 billion marks in 1929 to 5.7 billion in 1932 was outstripped by an even more traumatic fall in imports from 13.4 billions to 4.7 billions over the same period. Germany's export surplus was not therefore the result of an expansion in world demand for her goods but of the savage reduction in domestic production and consumption which had been induced by the withdrawal of foreign investment and the world depression. Far from demonstrating her long-term capacity to make substantial reparation transfers, this development merely signalled the short-term intolerability of her burdens. The shrinkage of German national income from 71 billion marks to 41 billion marks between 1929 and 1932 and the simultaneous decline of the value of German foreign trade from 26.1 billion to 10.4 billion had, in fact, made the continuation of substantial reparation payments socially and politicially insupportable. Apart from failing to make this obvious point, Machlup, in his anxiety to settle old academic scores, omitted to distinguish the financial situation of France in the 1870s from that of Germany in the 1930s. The most obvious difference was, of course, that France was able to cushion the financial impact of her indemnity payments substantially by resorting to foreign borrowing and selling foreign securities, whereas neither of these expedients was available to Germany after the 1920s. It is clearly unwise to use the tragic events of the depression years as evidence of Germany's long-term ability to shoulder the financial burdens which had been imposed on her.[5]

A second contention of this book is that the leaders of the four

<hr />

[5] F. Machlup, 'The Transfer Problem: Theme and Four Variations', in id., *International Payments, Debts and Gold* (New York, 1964), ch. 14. Note Machlup's influence on the conclusions of W. Link, *Die amerikanische Stabilisierungspolitik in Deutschland, 1921–1932* (Düsseldorf, 1970), 472. For references to more recent discussion of Germany's capacity to pay: see below, nn. 7 and 8.

major powers involved in the reparation imbroglio[6] were well aware from the outset that payments on the scale that they demanded were precluded by the inelasticities of supply and demand which have been described. There was no prima-facie reason for them to believe that the German government would be capable of achieving the deflationary budgets and Draconian social policies which they themselves sought to avoid, particularly when these sacrifices were for the benefit of former enemies. The financial and political strain imposed upon the victors when they reluctantly began to honour their much smaller debts to each other soon became apparent. The British government felt oppressed by the Anglo-American debt funding agreement of January 1923, which involved annuities only a third as high as those demanded from Germany by the relatively moderate Young Plan of 1929; and the Chamber of Deputies refused point-blank for a number of years to ratify the Mellon–Bérenger Agreement which provided for French repayments to the United States amounting to only a fifth of those undertaken by Britain. As for the belief of the creditors in their capacity to benefit from a large-scale reparation scheme, even the French, with their extensive devastated regions, soon found themselves weighing short-term budgetary gains against the damage that reparation deliveries could inflict on local industry. The economic absurdity of a haphazard attempt to extract a sizeable indemnity was most obvious for Britain, whose commerce was immediately jeopardized by the large quantities of coal and other German goods which the reparation scheme unleashed onto the markets of the world. The United States, although seemingly standing to gain much from the flow of war-debt repayments which Germany's annuities to the continental creditors made possible, was also acutely conscious of the threat posed by reparations to American trade and investment in Europe. For this reason the wilful optimism about Germany's capacity to pay which prevailed in certain sections of the United States Treasury, particularly in election years, tended to be counterbalanced by the opposition of the bankers and businessmen of Wall Street to excessive reparation demands.

The central question which confronts any student of the reparation problem is why the statesmen of Europe and North America knowingly allowed this exercise in economic self-destruction to continue for so

[6] The policies of the minor parties to the reparation dispute have not been systematically explored. The roles of the Italian and Belgian governments have, however, been described wherever they impinge on the main narrative.

long. An answer commonly suggested is that impossible reparation claims were fabricated by the European victors, in spite of American opposition, as part of a Carthaginian peace designed to eliminate Germany as a trade rival of Britain and a threat to the future security of France. Adherents of this view usually go on to observe that this stratagem merely undermined the British economy and generated the turmoil and revanchism which gave rise to Nazism in Germany and led eventually to the war of 1939–1945. This school of thought has, of course, been criticized by those who, eager to assign domestic causes to Hitler and his expansionism, assert that the treaty was not as Carthaginian, or Napoleonic, as the Germans claimed, that the financial wounds of the Weimar Republic were self-inflicted, and that the outbreak of war in 1939 was due if anything to the guilt complex of the peacemakers and their consequent appeasement of Hitler. Scholars of one or other of these persuasions have regarded reparations as a pawn in a wider power struggle between victors and vanquished and have not therefore been concerned to subject the origins and development of the reparation dispute to rigorous historical scrutiny. They have instead tended to rely on the more polemical writings of Keynes, which were designed to secure the prompt revision of the peace terms by predicting the effect of their strict implementation, or to emulate the casuistry of Keynes's celebrated critic, Étienne Mantoux, whose book, *The Carthaginian Peace, or the Economic Consequences of Mr Keynes*, was written in 1944 in an effort to overcome Allied reluctance to embark upon another reparation scheme. Apart from the ahistorical, albeit interesting, economic analysis upon which they have usually been based,[7] the main weakness of the contending Carthaginian

[7] Keynes stressed in *The Economic Consequences of the Peace*, which was published in December 1919 before the Versailles Treaty had even been ratified, that he was 'only concerned with tracing the consequences, *per impossibile*, of carrying out the Treaty *au pied de la lettre*' (p. 89). Although *A Revision of the Treaty*, the sequel published early in 1922, summarized developments up to the autumn of 1921, it was similarly intended to deliver what the author fondly hoped would be the *coup de grâce* to the problem. Mantoux, a young French economist who was killed in action in 1945, was justified in pointing out in his book that the liberal Keynesian notion of transfers being limited by the 'natural level' of exports of the debtor had become outdated by the Second World War when occupied countries were being systematically exploited by centrally planned invaders. Yet one is left with the impression that, although both men were special pleaders rather than historians, the conclusions arrived at by Keynes were closer to the confused reality of a post-1918 world which was formally committed to free enterprise and national self-determination while in practice condoning an increasing amount of protectionism. Note, in this context, a trenchant discussion of the views of some more recent scholars who consider that Allied reparation demands were realistic and that

and Germanophobe interpretations of the reparation dispute is that they make the policies of the European victors and vanquished appear too Machiavellian and those of the United States too disinterested. Although there were plenty of influential people in France and Britain who were worried about the possibility of Germany's political and economic resurgence, reparations were never systematically used, or even originally devised, as an instrument for preventing her recovery. Valuable research into French reparation policy in the early post-war period by Georges Soutou, Walter A. McDougall, and Marc Trachtenberg has recently confirmed that it was neither as relentless nor as strategically motivated as has been claimed in the past. The condemnatory tone of previous historians has perhaps prompted McDougall to over-compensate by attempting to dignify French policy as a premature and tortuous attempt to achieve Franco-German economic integration; and Trachtenberg, not content with exonerating the French from the major responsibility for the harshness of the financial terms of the Versailles Treaty, may have erred in imputing *vindictive* motives to the British, whom most scholars would now agree were the villains of the piece during the reparation negotiations at Paris in 1919. Yet the majority of recent studies, such as those of Albertin, Laubach, and Feldman, which throw light on the German response to Allied reparation demands have avoided speaking of either deliberate sabotage or inevitable collapse under the weight of intolerable burdens. The emerging consensus seems to be that, even during its most traumatic phase in the early 1920s, the reparation dispute cannot adequately be described in terms of Allied Carthaginianism or deliberate German default. Such a conclusion is also encouraged by Denise Artaud's study of the inter-Allied debt problem, which demonstrates the constraints which were imposed on the European powers by the short-sighted and self-interested financial policies of the United States.[8]

Germany deliberately evaded her obligations: P. Krüger, 'Das Reparationsproblem der Weimarer Republik in fragwürdiger Sicht: kritische Überlegungen zur neuesten Forschung', *VfZ* 29 (1981), 26–30.

[8] For a well-argued 'strategic' interpretation of French reparation policy: J. Bariéty, 'Les Réparations allemandes après la première guerre mondiale: Objet ou prétexte à une politique Rhénane?', *Bulletin de la Société d'Histoire Moderne*, Ser. 15, No. 6 (May 1973), 21–35. Cf. G. Soutou, 'Problèmes concernant le rétablissement des relations économiques franco-allemandes après la première guerre mondiale', *Francia*, 2 (1974), 580–96; 'Die deutschen Reparationen und das Seydoux-Projekt 1920/21', *VfZ* 23 (1975), 237–70; W. A. McDougall, *France's Rhineland Diplomacy, 1914–1924: The Last Bid for a Balance of Power in Europe* (Princeton, 1978); M. Trachtenberg, *Reparation in World Politics: France and European Economic Diplomacy, 1916–1923* (New York, 1980). The

The most fruitful way of explaining both the demands of the creditors, among whom the United States must emphatically be numbered, and the reaction of the debtor is that they were a series of improvisations by conservative liberal democracies which were designed primarily to pre-empt any socially radical solution of the unprecedented and seemingly intractable post-war problems of national and international indebtedness. To put it another way, the preoccupations of the statesmen who were responsible for generating and prolonging the reparation dispute were neither strategic nor even genuinely financial, in that no appreciable financial dividends could be expected, but demagogic and diversionary. As far as the European victors were concerned, this behaviour was not simply, as the statesmen of the day encouraged everyone to believe, a reluctant response to popular nationalistic passions which had been inflamed by the war. It was, in the first place, the product of anxiety among the upper classes about the social tensions which had been generated by the war. The political polarization which occurred in all the belligerent countries, particularly after the Bolshevik victory in October 1917, was a profound source of concern among the well-to-do. From 1917 onwards discussion among academic economists and left-wing politicans about the desirability of a levy on capital to defray war costs deepened the apprehension of

distilled views of McDougall and Trachtenberg, together with a judicious critical appraisal of them by Charles Maier, are to be found in a symposium on the early years of the reparation problem in the March 1979 issue of the *Journal of Modern History*: W. A. McDougall, 'Political Economy versus National Sovereignty: French Structures for German Economic Integration after Versailles', *JMH* 51 (1979), 4–23; M. Trachtenberg, 'Reparation at the Paris Peace Conference', ibid. 24–55; C. S. Maier, 'The Truth about the Treaties?', ibid. 56–67. For the most recent attempt to read a pattern into French policy: J. Jacobson, 'Strategies of French Foreign Policy after World War I', ibid. 55 (1983), 78–95. For scholars who argue that Germany manipulated her financial system to evade reparations: S. Marks, 'The Myths of Reparations', *CEH* 11 (1978), 231–55 at 238, 248; S. A. Schuker, 'Finance and Foreign Policy in the Era of the German Inflation: British, French, and German Strategies for Economic Reconstruction after the First World War', in O. Busch and G. D. Feldman (edd.), *Historische Prozesse der deutschen Inflation, 1914 bis 1924* (Berlin, 1978), 343–61; 'American "Reparations" to Germany, 1919–1933', in G. D. Feldman and E. Müller-Luckner (edd.), *Die Nachwirkungen der Inflation auf die deutsche Geschichte, 1924–1933* (Munich, 1985), 335–84, at 336, 340. For less Machiavellian explanations of German policy in the early 1920s: L. Albertin, 'Die Verantwortung der liberalen Parteien für das Scheitern der Grossen Koalition im Herbst 1921', *HZ* 205 (1967), 566–627; E. Laubach, *Die Politik der Kabinette Wirth, 1921–22* (Lübeck, 1968); G. D. Feldman, *Iron and Steel in the German Inflation, 1916–1923* (Princeton, 1977); H. J. Rupieper, 'Politics and Economics: The Cuno Government and Reparations', Ph.D. thesis (Stanford, 1974); C.-L. Holtfrerich, *Die deutsche Inflation, 1914–1923* (Berlin, 1980). For American war-debt policy: D. Artaud, *La Question des dettes interalliées et la reconstruction de l'Europe (1917–1929)* (2 vols.; Paris, 1978).

men of property. By the end of 1918 there were, therefore, many powerful people who welcomed any proposal, however ill conceived, which might postpone the seemingly imminent day of reckoning. Another problem for conservative politicans to contend with was the widespread hope of social betterment among the long-suffering masses. It would have required courage to admit that a 'fit country for heroes' was beyond the immediate reach of economies dislocated and distorted by prolonged total war. Vague assertions that the enemy should 'pay' were therefore exceedingly useful. Finally, extravagant reparation claims recommended themselves for tactical reasons to belligerents which had suffered relatively little damage but had accumulated large domestic and foreign debts. It was distributive manœuvring, not vindictiveness, which made the British Empire the most strenuous advocate of an indemnity to cover war costs during the peace negotiations of 1919. Even France, whose underlying tactical interest was in a more restricted claim for purely physical reparation, toyed briefly with the idea of using inflated reparation claims as bargaining counters in negotiations about the settlement of inter-Allied debts.

The central theme of what follows is that, once the indemnity cry had been raised, the reparation problem continued to be a running sore because the creditor powers did not dare dispel the financial illusions they had created and steadfastly refused to make financial concessions to each other. The burden of guilt for this behaviour lies most heavily on the shoulders of Great Britain and the United States, which had most to lose from lunatic claims and enjoyed sufficient financial stature to engineer a sane settlement. The Lloyd George government, having made the early running in the campaign for a wider indemnity as opposed to a more restricted demand for physical reparation, lacked the nerve to reverse its policy before the arteries of inter-governmental indebtedness had hardened. Although it is impossible to gauge accurately in retrospect what the impact on American opinion would have been, Britain was well placed to make an effective gesture of unilateral financial renunciation in the early post-war years because London was still regarded, albeit with decreasing justification, as the financial centre of the world. Yet Lloyd George refused at the end of 1921 to heed the advice of the British Treasury that he should resolve the reparation problem and promote European recovery by writing off Britain's claims on Germany and the continental Allies. Because the British Prime Minister refused to set an example of financial statesmanship, the initiative passed, by default, to the United

States, a nation which was still unattuned to the responsibility of financial power and proved, especially after the Republicans took over the helm in 1921, even less ready than Britain to usher in any settlement which might seem to jeopardize the short-term interests of its taxpayers. The immediate result was that, after an ineffectual Anglo-French flirtation with co-operative European reconstruction at the Genoa Conference in April 1922, the fate of western Europe came to depend on M. Raymond Poincaré, a politician who had given himself very little room to manœuvre in French financial politics. To give the French premier his due, it was only after the repeated failure of his efforts to arrive at some financial arrangement with the Anglo-Saxon powers that he embarked on his disastrous Ruhr invasion. Although this operation was launched for short-term face-saving reasons, it eventually produced sufficient economic chaos and political unrest to induce Anglo-Saxons and continentals to collaborate briefly in restoring economic order and patching up a very moderate temporary reparation scheme with the aid of international loans. Yet the ultimate aim of both the Dawes Plan of 1924 and the Young Plan which succeeded it in 1929 was not to produce a financially viable settlement but merely to ensure a flow of German annuities which was sufficiently large to enable the European victors to repay their war debts to the United States. It was hardly surprising that this rickety financial structure, the maintenance of which depended on a vigorous expansion of world trade and a buoyant international credit system, should have been shaken to its foundations by the economic contraction and financial pandemonium of the early 1930s. French and American political leaders, nevertheless, went to inordinate lengths to prop up their house of cards. The twelve-month moratorium on inter-government debt repayments which was initiated by Herbert Hoover in June 1931 was not intended by either the United States or France as a prelude to the cancellation or substantial reduction of those debts but as a means of preserving them intact until conditions improved. The measures which were subsequently improvised to shore up Germany's sagging external credit after the collapse of her banking system in the summer of 1931 were also predicated on the assumption that reparations and war debts would not be tampered with. Reparations were finally dismantled only after the swing to the left at the French elections of May 1932 enabled the revisionist MacDonald government to persuade the moderate administration of Eduard Herriot to ignore the opposition of the Americans and put an end to a system which was now regarded not as a financial or strategic panacea but as an obstacle to international economic recovery and a threat to peace. It was, however, typical that the Lausanne settlement, which effectively put an end to reparations in July 1932, was designed to convey the misleading impression that Germany would make a token final payment at a later date. The United States administration also pandered to the illusions of the American taxpayer by refusing to admit publicly that its war loans would never be repaid.

In view of the domestic and international obstacles to an effective reparation scheme, it may appear remarkable that up to June 1931 Germany actually paid, even according to the most conservative reckoning, about 23 billion marks (upwards of $5 billion), or approximately 15 per cent of the 152 billions formally demanded by the victors.[9] Yet the transfer of a significant proportion of this sum was achieved either by selling depreciating paper marks to foreign speculators in the early 1920s or by borrowing abroad in later years. The debtor's less than dynamic response to post-war financial problems was, like that of her creditors, heavily influenced by the privileged position of right-wing groups within her body politic. The inordinate power of conservative states-righters in the Second Reich was largely responsible for the indifferent fiscal performance of the federal government during the war; and the obstructive behaviour of these elements after they were temporarily displaced by the revolution of 1918 made it difficult for Republican statesmen to implement an effective budgetary policy in the troubled early post-war years before large-scale reparation payments

[9] Global estimates of the amount that Germany paid vary considerably because of differing valuations of property in ceded territories and transfers of capital goods and goods from current output. They are of marginal relevance to this study, which seeks, among other things, to unravel the year-by-year, and sometimes the month-by-month, economic, financial, and political impact of the reparation problem on the debtor. For a recent low estimate of Germany's payments and a discussion of how far these were unwittingly financed by foreigners (particularly Americans) who bought mark notes or subscribed to German loans that were never repaid: Schuker, 'American "Reparations" to Germany', at 364–71, 382–3. Schuker points out (at 364) that about 6 billion of his total of 23 billions was not transferred over the exchanges, since it represented credits for items such as state property in ceded territories and the costs of Allied armies of occupation and commissions. For somewhat higher totals: Holtfrerich, 144–54. The figure of 152 billions is the sum of the 20 billion mark preliminary payment demanded by Article 235 of the Versailles Treaty and the total obligation of 132 billions fixed by the Reparation Commission in April 1921. Since Germany's alleged 12 billion mark default on the preliminary payment was tacitly 'assimilated' into the figure of 132 billions, it could be argued that the amount officially demanded by the victors was only 140 billions.

began. After the inauguration of the London Schedule of Payments in May 1921 the course of German financial history was determined not only by pressure from the creditor powers but also by the brittle relations between the left-centre government of Joseph Wirth and the captains of German industry. The support of business leaders for the government's policies of financial reform and treaty fulfilment would, in fact, have been vouchsafed only if Wirth had succumbed to right-wing pressure for a longer working day and denationalization of the railway system and if the victors had either orchestrated a favourable settlement of the future of Upper Silesia in 1921 or arranged a Wall Street loan for Germany in 1922. When these conditions were not met significant members of the German propertied classes not only withdrew their political support but also had no compunction in indulging in practices such as tax evasion and capital flight, which did so much to undermine the German currency. Although the Franco-Belgian occupation of the Ruhr prompted Cuno's 'business cabinet' (which had replaced the hamstrung Wirth administration in November 1922) to make a brief gesture towards financial reform, the federal budget had degenerated by the summer of 1923 into little more than a conduit pipe for hyper-inflationary subventions to the beleaguered Ruhr district. Even after this process had paralysed the German economy, wiped out the value of government bonds, impoverished thousands of small savings-bank depositors, and driven the nation to the brink of political disintegration, the German financial élite still contrived that the short-term measures which were taken to stabilize the mark in 1923 and 1924 would be socially regressive. The extreme right wing was, it is true, embarrassed and divided in the summer of 1924 about whether to swallow its patriotism and vote for the Dawes Plan for the sake of American loans. Yet the more moderate diplomatic position which the Nationalist Party was to adopt in the mid-1920s paid dividends by enabling it to participate in two of the cabinets of Luther and Marx and hence to ensure that the German fiscal system retained its conservative anti-centralist bias. Although right-wing influence receded briefly during the period of Hermann Müller's *Grosse Koalition*, which was formed after the gains of the SPD in the May 1928 elections, it reasserted itself when Heinrich Brüning came to power in March 1930. The rigidly deflationary policies of the early 1930s were not, as Brüning frequently proclaimed at the time and some historians have subsequently asserted, the product of an overriding preoccupation with ridding Germany of reparations. Just as the inflationary behaviour of the Cuno government eight years earlier had reflected the interests of heavy industry, so Brüning's policies of savage retrenchment and wage reduction were designed to benefit Germany's export industries. In each case added justification was sought for policies which were already in place by alleging that they would unleash a flood of paper marks or German goods onto world markets and thereby free Germany from her external burdens. Yet in neither case is it correct to speak of the primacy of foreign policy. There was, on the contrary, a remarkable correspondence between the diplomatic strategy adopted and the economic interests of different sections of the right-wing establishment.

The following account seeks to distinguish between four different phases of the reparation problem and to weigh the changing con- tribution of the parties to each stage of the dispute. Part One discusses Allied reparation and war debt policies and the condition of Germany in the thirty months between the end of the war and the formal presentation of Allied demands in the London Schedule of Payments of May 1921. The first chapter of this Part attributes the clamour for indemnities in general terms to the financial delinquency of all the belligerents, and shows how the short-term diversionary pre- occupations and distributive rivalries of conservative political leaders prompted them to create the impression that their post-war financial problems could be off-loaded onto Germany without any regard for her short-term prostration or long-term economic capacity. Chapter 2 discusses the reluctance of the peacemakers to commit themselves to a definitive reparation scheme in 1919 and early 1920 and examines why the moderate German governments of this period were unable to cope even with their domestic financial difficulties. The third chapter describes the twelve months of negotiations between the creditors and the more conservative and less malleable Fehrenbach cabinet which eventually led to the unilateral imposition of the London Schedule by the victors. Part Two covers the next thirty months (to the end of 1923) when the creditors made an ineffectual attempt to dun Germany and the debtor's financial system disintegrated in response both to external pressures and the growing dereliction of government policy. Chapter 4 explains the premature breakdown of the Wirth government's 'offensive of fulfilment' at the end of 1921 and discusses the failure of the victors to make a realistic adjustment of Germany's obligations at this crucial stage. The next chapter analyses the increas- ing passivity and conservatism of German policy in 1922 and discusses the various expedients which the creditors canvassed—the British initiative for general European reconstruction, an American international loan proposal, and, finally, Franco-Belgian schemes for imposing sanctions and economic controls on Germany—in an effort to make some sort of sense of their policies. The sixth chapter assesses the disappointing yield and dire repercussions of the Ruhr struggle which occurred in 1923 when France and Belgium resorted to the last option; and it discusses the way in which the Anglo-Saxon powers helped to precipitate, prolong, and ultimately resolve the conflict. Part Three deals with the last two phases of the reparation dispute during which it was partially depoliticized and internationalized and then adjourned *sine die*. Chapter 7 treats the American-backed Dawes Plan as an evasion, rather than resolution, of the reparation problem; and it goes on to show how the underlying dispute resurfaced when the question of a 'final' settlement was broached again in 1928 and 1929. The following chapter brings out the overwhelmingly political character of the reparation and war debt scheme which was recommended by the American-dominated Young Committee and adopted by the Hague Conferences of August 1929 and January 1930. The ninth and final chapter demonstrates how, in the concluding phase of the reparation dispute, the fair-weather Young Plan became increasingly vulnerable to the world economic depression and financial crisis of 1930–2. It then relates how, despite a determined Franco-American rearguard action, the Lausanne Conference of July 1932 finally rang down the curtain on the reparation and war debt charade.

PART ONE
The Origins of the Reparation Problem

I

Between Rhetoric and Reality

Allied Reparation Claims and the Condition of Germany

SOME years ago a distinguished historian, echoing Arthur Balfour's explanation of the Liberal victory in the British elections of 1906, suggested that the peacemakers of 1919 were 'mere corks dancing on a torrent they could not control'.[1] Such an image is misleading when explaining the reparation demands of the victors. The popular passions aroused by the war certainly helped to underpin a demand for reparations. Yet the poisonous financial dispute which the Paris Peace Conference was to inject into the veins of Europe and North America was not a product of spontaneous mass hysteria.

A tendency for historians to blame the masses and exonerate political leaders has been encouraged by the exemplary moderation of official Allied reparation policy during the war. This restraint was not for want of precedents for large indemnities. Although the Hague Conventions of 1899 and 1907 provided only for the compensation of individuals who had suffered at the hands of invading armies, punitive levies had been imposed by Prussia on France in 1871 and by the Second Reich on Bolshevik Russia in 1918. German politicians had also declared that there would be an indemnity if the Central Powers won the war. The reluctance of the Allies to envisage anything more than limited reparation to a certain extent reflected misgivings about the outcome of the war and sensitivity to mounting radical, socialist, and American pressure for a peace 'without annexations and indemnities'. Yet it was founded chiefly, as we shall see, upon a realistic appraisal of national interest. French politicians were preoccupied with the practical problem of making good the physical devastation of their country rather than with the will-o'-the-wisp of general war costs; and the British government believed that a large indemnity would be difficult to collect and prejudicial to trade.[2]

[1] Balfour's image is used in R. J. Sonntag's review of A. J. Mayer, *The Politics and Diplomacy of Peacemaking: CEH* 1 (1968), 388–91.
[2] The texts of the Conventions of 1899 and 1907 (particularly Articles 3 and 47–56

The clamour for indemnities which supplanted this realism at the end of 1918 was partly the product of a desire to cripple Germany. It was also tactical: some British statesmen saw inflated reparation demands as a means of guaranteeing a 'fair share' of the spoils for the British Empire; and a few Frenchmen regarded them as a way of bludgeoning the United States and Britain into a scheme of co-operative post-war reconstruction. Yet the underlying reason for the excessive claims that were canvassed was the concern of conservative interest groups about the domestic financial implications of the war. None of the belligerents had imposed heavy taxation to offset swollen government expenditure or to dampen inflationary demand for consumer goods. The United States covered only 22 per cent of its war expenditure out of current revenue during its brief involvement in hostilities. Britain did rather worse; and France, which bore the brunt of the fighting on the western front, failed to maintain even its peacetime level of tax receipts. Such behaviour was originally encouraged by the widespread belief that the war would be short: but it persisted because of the unwillingness of political leaders to make harsh financial demands on their electorates. There was, in fact, no technical reason why the bulk of expenditure should not have been borrowed from the wealthy, from the banking system, and from abroad. Nor, in view of the remarkable recuperative powers of modern industrial states, were the belligerents necessarily doomed to prolonged economic privation after the war. Yet their previous lack of candour and the concern of conservatives about the radical financial programmes of the left wing prompted British and French statesmen to raise the cry that Germany should pay the whole cost of the war. The campaign of the European victors for indemnities as opposed to reparation was intensified when the United States government, which was also eager to save face with its taxpayers, indicated that it would cut off, and possibly reverse, the

of the latter) are in *Rapports faits aux Conférences de la Haye de 1899 et 1907 ... avec une Introduction de James Scott Brown* (Publication de la Dotation Carnegie pour la Paix Internationale, Division de Droit International, Oxford, 1920), 128–37, 509–20. See also A. Weiss, 'Le Droit international et les dommages de guerre', in F. Larnaude, H. Barthélemy, *et al.* (edd.), *La Réparation des dommages de guerre: Conférences faites à l'école des hautes études sociales, novembre 1915 à janvier 1916* (Paris, 1917), 163–8. For the indemnities of 1871 and 1918: Ministère des Affaires Étrangères, *Documents diplomatiques français, 1871–1914* (Paris, 1929–59), i. 7–8; *Papers Relating to the Foreign Relations of the United States* (henceforth FR), 1918, Russia, i. 604–5. For Allied moderation and German declarations: see below, 19–25, 28–32, 50–2.

flow of funds which had thus far cushioned the financial impact of the war on the Allies.[3]

The unreality of Allied reparation demands was emphasized by the condition of Germany at the end of 1918. On the eve of the armistice the Second Reich was approaching economic, financial, and political collapse. Germany's plight was due to the determination of her rulers to stake their political future, along with the fortunes of the country, on total victory. Her financial difficulties were compounded by the reluctance of conservative particularists (states-righters) to grant the federal government adequate powers of direct taxation and by the insistence of the commercial classes that the war should be financed as far as possible by loans rather than Draconian imposts. During the war, the indemnity illusion was used far more in Germany than elsewhere as an excuse for fiscal inertia. In the first year of the conflict much was made of the indemnity which had been imposed on France after the *Blitzkrieg* of 1870–1. By early in 1918, however, conservative politicians, whose hopes of victory had been rekindled by the military collapse of Russia, were providing a foretaste of subsequent Allied demagoguery by demanding indemnities so as to defuse agitation for increased direct taxation. Their stonewalling was so effective that by the end of the war the German financial system was singularly ill-equipped to withstand the strain of defeat, revolution, and the transition to peace. Even if Germany had willingly assumed her allotted role as the financial scapegoat of the western world, she would clearly have been unable to sustain it.[4]

FRANCE: PHYSICAL REPARATION OR WAR COSTS?

The demand that Germany should compensate her conquerors for the entire cost of the war was rarely heard in France until the armistice of November 1918. The most important reason for this moderation was, paradoxically, the extensive physical devastation of French territory. In the ten *départements* which were the scene of the heaviest fighting

---

[3] Allied financial policies are treated by E. V. Morgan, *Studies in British Financial Policy, 1914–1925* (London, 1952), 94; E. R. Seligman, *Essays in Taxation* (10th edn., rev., New York, 1931), 760–7; C. Gilbert, *American Financing of World War I* (Westport, Conn., 1970), 222–3. See below, 26–8, 33–44.

[4] The condition of Germany will be analysed at length in the final section of this chapter.

approximately 600,000 houses, 20,000 factories, and 6,500 schools were either partially or totally destroyed; some 4,000 villages were devastated; and almost three million people were driven from their homes. The *départements* in question were, moreover, the centre of the French iron, coal, woollen, and cotton industries. This destruction, vast even by modern standards, caused the French public to be preoccupied with physical damage, particularly when any ebb in the tide of war revealed the full extent of the havoc. When, moreover, the question of reparation was first raised in the Chamber of Deputies after the Battle of the Marne, in December 1914, the main concern was to determine the conditions under which the *sinistrés* (disaster victims in the devastated areas) were to be compensated by the French government for the material damage which they had suffered. The same was true in October 1916 when a law for the reparation of war damage, which had been drawn up by a forty-four-man committee appointed in 1915, was laid before the Chamber. Desplas, the *rapporteur* for the committee, did prophesy that Germany would one day be confronted with the bill for all the damage, but stressed that the proposed legislation merely established the right of the *sinistrés* to claim compensation from the French government.[5]

Two weeks later the ruins revealed and hopes aroused by Allied gains on the western front prompted Pierre Forgeot, who represented the battered city of Reims, to voice one of the earliest demands that 'Germany should pay'. The slogan was taken up by Louis Barthou, the veteran French conservative statesman, in an article in *Le Matin* a few days later. While conceding that it was still premature to discuss the post-war territorial settlement, Barthou challenged anyone 'to deny the necessity of exacting from Germany reparations, which would be an act of strict justice, and guarantees, which would be an elementary measure of prudence'. But the cry failed to gain the currency that it attained two years later. And, in any case, Forgeot, Barthou, and others who echoed them still regarded reparation only as the making good of physical damage in the devastated territories.[6]

---

[5] Details of damage: A. Tardieu, *The Truth about the Peace Treaties* (London, 1921), 377–8. On *sinistrés*: *Annales de la Chambre des Députés. Débats parlementaires* (henceforward *CD*), 23 Dec. 1914, 936; 11 May 1915, 590–7; 3 Oct. 1916, 1883. For comment: *Le Petit Parisien*, 9 June 1916, 2.

[6] *CD*, 5 Oct. 1916, 1936 (Forgeot); *Le Matin*, 14 Oct. 1916 (LA, Barthou). Neither Forgeot's speech nor Barthou's article was the subject of editorial comment in either *Le Petit Parisien*, a moderate republican journal with a circulation of over three million, or *Le Temps*, the mouthpiece of the government. Note, however, the reference to

To judge from the proceedings of the Paris Economic Conference a few months earlier, the approach of the French government to the problem of post-war reconstruction was still more co-operative than retributive. The concern of Étienne Clémentel, the French Minister of Commerce, who preconcerted the resolutions of the conference with Walter Runciman, the British president of the Board of Trade, was to prolong inter-allied economic collaboration into peacetime so as to ensure that, whoever won the war, France should have access to the raw materials, plant, and transport facilities she needed in order to rebuild her economy. His purpose was, it is true, to prevent Germany from gaining undue commercial advantage after the war over those belligerents which, like France, had suffered extensive devastation. Yet the moderate attitude of the conference towards reparations, which were envisaged only for material damage, indicates that France's economic concerns were defensive rather than offensive.[7]

Although there was increased discussion in the right-wing press and government circles during the autumn and winter of 1916–17 about an annexationist peace which would either secure or neutralize the Rhineland, there was little mention of indemnities until the following spring. Perhaps in response to fresh evidence of German depredations brought to light by the advance of the Allied armies, *Le Matin* published a series of articles in April 1917 by Louis de Verneuil, a member of the French stock exchange, who asserted that Germany was capable of reimbursing France's general war expenditure as well as the cost of physical reparation. A similar claim was made during the secret debate on war aims in the Chamber of Deputies in June 1917 by André Lefèvre, who had been an Under-Secretary of State in the Finance Ministry in 1910–11. However, despite this pressure from the right

physical reparations in a declaration of the Radical Party: *Le Matin*, 23 Oct. 1916, 2. Figures of $10,000,000,000–$20,000,000,000 were being mooted in the North American press at this time by Stephane Lauzanne, the editor of *Le Matin*, who had been sent to the United States in October 1916 on a propaganda mission by the French Foreign Office. However, even Lauzanne seems to have envisaged reparations only for physical damage. Stephane Lauzanne Papers, Scrap Book, vi. 57–66.

[7] The best treatment of the Paris Economic Conference is provided by Robert E. Bunselmeyer, *The Cost of the War, 1914–1919: British Economic War Aims and the Origins of Reparation* (Hamden, Conn., 1975), 35–47. See also M. Trachtenberg, 'A New Economic Order: Étienne Clémentel and French Economic Diplomacy during the First World War', *French Historical Studies*, 10 (1977), 315–41. For the Clémentel–Runciman discussions: Notes of a Conference at Paris on 6th May (1916) ..., Crewe papers (Cambridge University Library), M/6(4). For the published minutes of the conference: *Conférence économique des gouvernements alliés tenue à Paris, les 14, 15, 16 et 17 juin 1916* (Paris, 1916). For the resolutions: *FR*, 1916, Supplement, 975–7.

wing and the prodding of Raymond Poincaré, the President of the Republic, who was agitating from the end of 1916 for a clearer, and more ambitious, definition of French war aims, the successive governments of Briand, Ribot, Painlevé, and Clemenceau remained moderate or imprecise in both their territorial aims and their reparation policy. This reticence was a response to the less favourable trend of the war and the moral pressure exerted by President Wilson, first as a potential mediator and then as an ally. It was also encouraged by the mounting agitation of the French socialist movement for a peace without 'annexations and indemnities'.[8]

In 1918 the successful German spring offensive precluded any French illusions, either official or popular, about reparations until just before the armistice. As in 1916 and 1917, popular attitudes hardened when the advance of the Allied armies revealed the devastation which lay in the wake of the retreating Germans. In September and October the French press was outraged at the manner in which the enemy had fired towns such as Cambrai and had flooded coal mines in the Pas-de-Calais. Resentment at the plight of the liberated areas was also heightened by an emotional demonstration of national solidarity with the *sinistrés* in the Senate on 15 October. But at no time before the armistice did this indignation inspire either parliamentarians or journals such as *Le Temps, Le Figaro*, and *Le Petit Parisien* to suggest that Germany should do more than restore physical damage. *Le Matin* was by

[8] On French war aims: P. Renouvin, 'Les Buts de guerre du gouvernement français, 1914–1918', *RH* 235 (1966), 10–11; McDougall, *France's Rhineland Diplomacy*, 15–25; D. Stevenson, 'French War Aims and the American Challenge, 1914–1918', *HJ* 22 (1979), 877–94; R. A. Prete, 'French Military War Aims, 1914–1916', ibid. 28 (1985), 887–99. For discussions in the spring of 1917: *Annales du Sénat. Débats parlementaires* (henceforward *Sénat*), 31 Mar. 1917, 433–9. See also *Le Matin*, 1 Apr. 1917, 1; *AF*, 1 Apr. 1917 (Maurras); *Le Matin*, 3, 7, 14, 21 Apr. 1917, 1 (Verneuil). Verneuil's assertion was at that time not as unrealistic as at the end of 1918. For the secret debate: Chambre des Députés: Comité secret du 1er juin, *Journal officiel*, 16 May 1925, 530–1. On Poincaré: G. Wright, *Raymond Poincaré and the French Presidency* (Stanford, 1942), 165–6. For government policy: *CD*, 19 Jan. 1917, 108 (Briand); 21 Mar. 1917, 779–80 (Ribot); 22 May 1917, 1179 (Ribot); 19 Sept. 1917, 2440 (Ribot); 19 Oct. 1917, 2845–6 (Painlevé); *Sénat*, 6 June 1917, 589–90 (Ribot). It was in response to a demand by Pierre Forgeot for an official statement of war aims that Clemenceau replied with his famous evasion: '... Quand vous me demandez mes buts de guerre, je vous réponds: mon but, c'est d'être vainqueur.' During his speech he had referred, in what may have been an oblique demand for war costs, to 'l'indemnité que le temps et les dommages aggravent chaque jour': *CD*, 20 Nov. 1917, 3062 (Forgeot): 3066–7 (Clemenceau). For Socialist pressure: Chambre des Députés: Comité secret du 1er juin 1917, 503 (Cachin); 519–20 (Augagneur). See also: *CD*, 2 Aug. 1917, 2363–4 (Moutet). Note the specific exclusion of penal indemnities from the peace terms which Briand drew up in Sept. 1917 after consulting Ribot: *Sénat, CAE*, 14 Nov. 1917, 1171–2.

this time drawing a clear distinction between financial and physical reparation. 'What we need', it proclaimed on 14 October, 'is vengeance for our martyrs, labour and materials for our reconstruction, and billions to save us from being crushed under the weight of our debt.' Yet even this conservative journal espoused the relatively moderate reparation policies of the English press baron, Lord Northcliffe, and of the Parisian deputy, Henri Galli, in the early weeks of November.[9]

The restraint of the Parisian press was an accurate reflection of French reparation policy when Allied leaders met in Paris at the end of October to discuss their reservations about the Fourteen Points and other Wilsonian declarations as a basis for the coming peace settlement.[10] Clemenceau, the French premier, had a few weeks earlier endorsed a proposal by Clémentel for co-operative reconstruction similar to that which had been suggested by the Paris Economic Conference of 1916; and he made no recorded protest against the restricted reparation proposals which were to be incorporated in the Lansing Note. Nor is there any real evidence, despite subsequent French allegations to the contrary, that either Clemenceau or Klotz, his Finance Minister, were trying to establish the legality of a claim for total war costs during the inter-Allied discussions of the next few days about the terms of the impending armistice with Germany. Clemenceau's criticism of the draft armistice terms was solely that they contained no reference to Germany's obligation to repair the damage she had done. As he complained to the Supreme War Council on 2 November, 'France would not be able to understand why there was not a single line in the text on this subject. . . . It was a matter of giving moral satisfaction to the French population which had suffered so much.' Despite the initial opposition of Lloyd George, Bonar Law, Sonnino, and even Foch, all of whom considered that the question of reparations should be dealt with in the peace treaty rather than in the

---

[9] On Cambrai and coal mines: Le Figaro, 10, 15 Oct. 1918, 1; Le Temps, 16 Oct. 1918, 1; Le Matin, 15 Sept. 1918 (LA); 16 Oct. 1918, 1. On the sinistrés: Sénat, 15 Oct. 1918, 779–80. Cf. Le Figaro, 21 Oct. 1918, 1. Note the poignant series of articles by Gabriel Hanotaux, the historian, who was a resident of the devastated département of the Aisne: ibid. 31 Oct. 1918, 1; 2, 25 Nov. 1918, 1. See also Le Matin, 14 Oct. 1918, 1; 3, 7, 15 Nov. 1918, 1.

[10] The German government had, in an exchange of notes with Wilson early in October, agreed that the peace settlement should be based on the declared war aims of the American President. The European Allies were not, however, formally invited to comment on these aims until late in October. On the German–American note exchange, see below, ch. 2 n. 16 and text thereat.

armistice, the phrase 'réparation des dommages' was inserted, at the request of Clemenceau, in the financial section of the terms which were transmitted to Germany. These words were, however, clearly regarded by Clemenceau not as a claim for war costs but as a sop to the *sinistrés*.[11]

The preoccupations of Klotz were also narrow. As Finance Minister his immediate concern was to obtain prompt restitution of all circulating media which Germany had confiscated in the occupied territories and to prevent the liquidation of German assets which could be used for reparations. It was because he was apprehensive lest Article XIX, which embodied these specific objectives, should prejudice a general Allied claim for reparations that he moved the insertion of the preamble 'with the reservation that any subsequent concessions and claims by the Allies and United States remain unaffected'. Neither the minutes of the meeting of 2 November, at which this preamble was inserted, nor the reminiscences subsequently published by its author suggest that this was a positive claim for war costs rather than a negative safeguard against the undue restriction of Allied demands.[12]

If Klotz was, in fact, being devious he was well in advance of French press opinion and government policy in the first half of November. *Le Figaro*, *Le Temps*, and *Le Petit Parisien* made no unfavourable comment in the days before the armistice about the restrictions imposed by the Lansing Note on Allied reparation claims. *Le Temps* remarked on 12 November that the Klotz preamble to the financial clauses of the armistice 'left open the question of payments which are more in the nature of an indemnity than of reparations'. But the continuing preoccupation of this journal with the repair of physical damage was revealed when it went on to observe that the reservation

[11] On Clémentel's proposal: Trachtenberg, 'A New Economic Order', 329–31. For inter-Allied discussions: Conversations au MAE, 29 Oct. 1918, 3 p.m.; 30 Oct. 1918, 3 p.m.; Séance du Conseil Supérieur de Guerre à Versailles, 1 Nov. 1918, 3 p.m., 8–9; 2 Nov. 1918, 3 p.m., 2–3; Louis Loucheur Papers, Box 12, Folder 33. Paul Mantoux's minutes of this and other meetings of the Allied leaders between 29 Oct. and 4 Nov. 1918 have been published in J. de Launay, *Secrets diplomatiques, 1914–1918* (Brussels, 1963), 83–153. For the British minutes: Cabinet Papers IC 84, 85, 91, PRO CAB 28/5. See also Mermeix (Gabriel Terrail), *Les Négociations secrètes et les quatres armistices, avec pièces justificatives* (Paris, 1919), 232–3, 241–2.

[12] The Mantoux minutes of this meeting, which are more compressed than the British minutes and those published by Gabriel Terrail (Mermeix), make no reference to the adoption of the Klotz preamble. This occurred, according to the British minutes, which in other respects corroborate the Mantoux version, at the close of the meeting of 2 Nov. See Louis Loucheur Papers, Box 12, Folder 33, 3–4; Mermeix, 24–250; de Launay, 129; IC 91, at 36, CAB 28/5. Cf. L.-L. Klotz, *De la guerre à la paix* (Paris, 1924), 94–7.

enabled the Allies to choose whether they wanted losses of this type to be made good by replacement, by restoration, or by payment. Even a French memorandum on peace terms transmitted to the United States government late in November 1918 referred only to 'reparation for war damage on land and at sea, restitution, reconstruction, compensation in kind, reimbursement of expenses unlawfully imposed'. It stated, moreover, that the question of indemnity affected only a few nations since 'outside of the torpedoing from which the British government mainly suffered, Belgium and France alone are entitled to indemnities on account of the systematic devastation suffered by them'.[13]

This restraint, which was based on the assumption that reparations would be paid only for physical damage and that France would be the main beneficiary, was soon challenged by a powerful movement in favour of debiting the whole cost of the war to Germany. One of the first prominent Frenchmen to make an unequivocal demand of this sort was Fernand Faure, the editor of *Revue politique et parlementaire* and sometime Professor of Financial Legislation at Paris, whose views were published on 10 November 1918. Faure, who was an admirer of another advocate of war costs, the Australian Prime Minister, W. M. Hughes, couched his argument for a comprehensive indemnity in a way which reflected the previous narrowness of French reparation policy. The sums to be demanded from Germany were not, he stressed, to be restricted to the reparations which were being claimed by the *sinistrés* from the French government. 'No matter how high the figure', he wrote, 'which France has promised to pay to our unfortunate *sinistrés* from the invaded *départements*, it will certainly be much lower than the total indemnity which Germany ought to pay us.' Professor Faure's proposal that Germany should pay for indirect as well as direct war damage, which was cited approvingly by *Le Temps* on 15 November, signalled, if it did not precipitate, the dramatic development of French opinion in the days that followed the armistice. Although most Frenchmen could not have been either as extravagant or as specific in their financial expectations as *Le Matin*, which on 16 November estimated Germany's total debt to France at 340,000,000,000 francs, the feeling now became widespread that Germany should assume the responsibility for France's post-war budgetary problems. This conviction was encouraged by conservative groups who advocated an indemnity in the hope that it would lighten

---

[13] Jusserand to Lansing, 29 Nov. 1918, in R. S. Baker, *Woodrow Wilson and the World Settlement* (5 vols.; New York, 1921), iii. 56–63. See also, Tardieu, 88–93.

the burden of direct taxation after the war. It was also fostered by a press campaign in support of the Fourth French Liberation Loan, which stressed the prospect of German reparations as an inducement to subscribers. Further stimulus was provided by the loose language and loose thought which was prevalent at this time across the Channel; and by apprehension lest Germany should emerge economically unscathed from the conflict.[14]

The vulnerability of the French government to these currents of

TABLE 1. *French Government Revenue and Expenditure, 1914–1919* (million francs)

Year	Expenditure	Revenue	Deficit
1914	10,371	4,196	6,175
1915	22,120	4,130	17,990
1916	36,848	4,932	31,916
1917	44,661	6,186	38,475
1918	56,649	6,791	49,858
1919	54,213	11,586	42,627
TOTAL	224,862	37,821	187,041

Source: G. Jèze and H. Truchy, *The War Finance of France* (New Haven, 1927), 334–5.

opinion was increased by the weakness of its wartime financial policy. During the war years an enormous gap of 187 billion francs (Table 1) had been allowed to develop between revenue and expenditure. The fundamental reason for this discrepancy was that revenues had remained at, or below, their 1913 level of 4.9 billion francs until 1917. M. Henri Truchy, an apologist for his government's performance, has

---

[14] F. Faure, 'La Fin de la guerre et les responsabilités de l'Allemagne', *Revue politique et parlementaire*, 97 (Nov. 1918), 113–41. See Faure's encomium on Hughes, and the verbatim reports of two of Hughes's speeches: ibid. 97 (Oct. 1918), 101–10, 138–43. The role of Hughes in generating the demand for war costs in Great Britain will be discussed in the next section of this chapter. On pressure from conservatives: A. J. Mayer, *The Politics and Diplomacy of Peacemaking: Containment and Counter-revolution at Versailles, 1918–1919* (New York and London, 1968), 648–52. On the loan campaign: *Le Temps*, 18 Nov. 1918, 3 (financial column); *Le Figaro*, 21 Nov. 1918, 1. Note the statement of Klotz in the Chamber of Deputies that 'subscribers will accept more readily the financial sacrifices that are demanded of them if they feel that everything is being done to extract the necessary reparations and restitution from the enemy': *CD*, 3 Dec. 1918, 2867. For British influence: *Le Temps*, 1 Dec. 1918 (LA). For vindictive feelings: *Le Figaro*, 1 Dec. 1918 (Capus).

emphasized 'the profound disturbance of the country's administrative, economic, and financial system' caused by the invasion of France and 'the belief, only slowly dispelled, that the war would be of short duration'. But he admits that French political leaders 'showed a lack of confidence in the country's financial courage' during the war; that they concealed from the civilian population 'the rough side of the war' in order to spare its nerves; and that they were guilty of 'not telling the electorate the naked truth, but of window-dressing'. This deception was achieved principally by refusing to impose heavy taxes; but it was reinforced by the presentation of budgets in a manner which tended to conceal the growth of the floating debt. Between 1915 and 1917 the unpredictable expenditure occasioned by the conflict and the unsettled state of tax receipts prompted the French Finance Ministry to inaugurate a system of *ad hoc* quarterly credits which bore no relation to revenues. Even when an annual budget was reintroduced in 1918 the true state of affairs continued to be obscured by the practice of distinguishing between the 'ordinary' budget, which included recurring expenditures on the public service, on pensions, and on the public debt, and the 'extraordinary' budget, which comprehended all outlays in any way occasioned by the war. Emphasis on the unavailing struggle to balance the 'ordinary' budget out of current revenue tended to divert public attention from the uninhibited resort to borrowing to cover all 'extraordinary' expenditures. On 3 December 1918 Klotz prolonged the subterfuge when he addressed the Chamber of Deputies on the embarrassing topic of the budget for 1919. 'Since the armistice', he declared, 'the question of balancing the budget has assumed a new character. My essential duty as Finance Minister is simply to draw up the list of items which the enemy must be asked to restore and make good. That is my sacred duty ... If, after that, it appears that new taxes are unavoidable, if it appears that the French people, who did not provoke the war, have still to tax themselves, either directly or indirectly, I will take the necessary steps.' Although Klotz stopped short of a claim for general war costs, which he knew would merely reduce France's share of reparations, his insistence on deferring discussion of increased taxation until Germany's reparation bill had been fixed aroused extravagant hopes about the size of the indemnity which could be obtained. The fiscal irresponsibility which underlay his behaviour was apparent when he testified late in February to a joint sitting of the Foreign Affairs and Finance Committees of the Senate. Although he had by this time mooted an extraordinary levy on capital in order to impress upon the other victors the seriousness of France's financial plight, Klotz made it clear that he preferred to resort to inflationary deficit financing rather than increase regular taxation. New indirect taxes would, he declared, be a ticklish (*délicat*) matter because of the difficulty which had been experienced in getting such imposts approved in the preceding year; and he was reluctant 'to give the tax-payer further cause for concern by increasing the income tax'. The false expectations which he aroused about reparations in order to side-step France's immediate budgetary problems were to prove a formidable obstacle to budgetary reform and a menace to the peace of Europe for a number of years.[15]

GREAT BRITAIN: TRADE VERSUS INDEMNITY

British reparation policy was imprecise and, like that of France, restricted for most of the war. Until as late as October 1916 Asquith's vague formulation of British war aims as 'adequate reparation for the past and adequate security for the future' occasioned little comment. Reparations were initially identified with compensation for the wrong done by Germany to Belgium—an association of ideas sedulously fostered by the press of the Belgian *émigrés* who had taken refuge in Britain during the war. By December 1916 mounting British shipping losses and the 'ton for ton' resolutions of the Navy League had prompted Lloyd George to declare in his first speech to the Commons as Prime Minister that Germany's 'outrages against humanity on land and sea' could not be expiated by 'a few pious phrases about humanity'. Yet specific demands such as that of the 'independent nationalist' demagogue, Horatio Bottomley, that Germany should pay Britain 'the pretty little figure' of five billion pounds sterling appear to have been rare even on the lunatic fringe of British politics.[16]

[15] G. Jèze and H. Truchy, *The War Finance of France* (New Haven, 1927), 187–227, 334–6; R. M. Haig, *The Public Finances of Post-War France* (New York, 1929), 51–3; Klotz, 3 Dec. 1918, CD, 2868; Sénat, CFAE, Audition de M. L. Klotz, Ministre des Finances, 27 Feb. 1919, 1683–6, 1750–1. For the extremism of Klotz late in 1918: D. Stevenson, *French War Aims Against Germany, 1914–1919* (Oxford, 1982), 152–3.

[16] Although its conclusions differ from my own (see below, n. 22 and text thereat),

The moderation of the British government was due primarily to its overriding concern with trade. The first official investigation of the indemnity question occurred when the Board of Trade commissioned an inquiry into 'the probable economic effect on British trade and industry of an indemnity ... paid by the enemy ... to make good damage in the territories over-run'. The memorandum submitted to the board by Sir William Ashley and J. M. Keynes on 2 January 1916 makes it clear that interest centred on whether an indemnity would act as 'a stimulus to the trade of the defeated enemy and a corresponding hindrance to the trade of the victorious Alliance'. The anxiety which prevailed on this subject—intensified, no doubt, by the celebrated demonstration of Sir Norman Angell's *The Great Illusion* in 1910 that, far from being a source of aggrandizement, wars and indemnities were commercially counter-productive—prompted the two economists to attempt to allay fears by arguing that a moderate indemnity would not necessarily be damaging to the recipients. Their analysis of the Franco-Prussian indemnity of 1871 demonstrated that its evil effect on the German financial system had been exaggerated and would, in any case, have been reduced if payments had included transfers of capital equipment and been made over an extended period. They also denied the allegation that an indemnity would necessarily involve 'a stream of ordinary commercial commodities' which would cause unemployment in the recipient nations. This does not, however, make Ashley and Keynes vulnerable to the capricious charge of Lloyd George in his memoirs that their memorandum was the source of 'all the extravagant estimates formulated after the war as to Germany's capacity to pay'. As Keynes observed in a letter to the *Sunday Times* in 1938, the memorandum was concerned with assessing the effects on Britain of an indemnity paid to France and Belgium in respect of their devastated areas and was based on the assumption that Britain would make no reparation claim. It was clear that the

Robert E. Bunselmeyer's *The Cost of the War* (see n. 7 above) provides a stimulating analysis of British financial war aims. For early British policy: Asquith, *House of Commons Debates*, 5th Ser. (henceforward *HC*), 11 Oct. 1916, lxxxvi. 103. For the Belgian reparation claim see the interview of Baron de Broqueville, the Belgian Prime Minister in exile, with the *Daily Chronicle*: *L'Indépendance belge*, 25 Sept. 1916, 3. Note also the activities of the Union pour la Sauvegarde des Intérêts Belges: ibid. 1 July 1916, 2; 11 Aug. 1916, 1; 27 Oct. 1916, 1. For the 'ton for ton' resolutions: *HC*, 20 Nov. 1917, xcix. 1030–1. Cf. Lloyd George, 19 Dec. 1916, lxxxviii. 1336. For Horatio Bottomley: *Sunday Pictorial*, 27 Aug. 1916; and other early lunatic claims: Bunselmeyer, 64–5.

reparation scheme which its authors envisaged was very limited in scope.[17]

The continuing preoccupation of Britain with trade rather than indemnities was evident at the Paris Economic Conference of June 1916, which was a field day for protectionists and advocates of imperial preference who wished to ensure that the Central Powers did not derive any commercial advantage from the devastation and dislocation caused by the war. The conference resolved on joint action after the war to restore countries which had suffered from 'acts of destruction, spoliation, and unjust requisition'. It also foreshadowed a programme of post-war commercial discrimination against Germany; and concluded a secret agreement 'relating to the collection and interchange of information as to stocks of raw materials and manufactured goods collected and secured by the enemy for use at the end of the war'. No undue emphasis was placed on reparations, which were, as we have seen, to be limited to the making good of material damage.[18]

The attitude of the British government remained moderate in 1917. Lord Milner's Committee on Peace Terms, which was set up by Lloyd George in April after discussion of war aims had arisen in the Imperial War Cabinet, was even critical of the proposals of the Paris Economic Conference for economic discrimination against Germany. The committee also echoed the opinion of the Board of Trade (which had submitted its report on indemnities early in the year) by declaring that 'anything like complete reparation for the losses imposed by the war was manifestly impossible', and that any attempt to impose a large tribute was 'undesirable as being likely to lead to many difficulties and to retard the gradual reestablishment of a pacific spirit throughout the world'. The only dissenting voice was that of Sir Joseph Ward, the New Zealand Finance Minister, who urged that a claim should be made both for a large indemnity and for the surrender of the German navy. While the committee resolved in the end that the possibility of a money indemnity should not be excluded, it observed that the size of this would 'depend upon the completeness of the victory gained and

---

[17] On Angell's impact: Bunselmeyer, 59–63. See also W. J. Ashley and J. M. Keynes, 'Memorandum on the Effect of an Indemnity', 2 Jan. 1916, in E. Johnson (ed.), *The Collected Writings of John Maynard Keynes, xvi: Activities 1914–1919* (London, 1971), 313–34; Keynes to the editor of the *Sunday Times*, 30 Oct. 1938, ibid. 335–6; D. Lloyd George, *The Truth about the Peace Treaties* (2 vols.; London, 1938), i. 445–9. For a different interpretation of the Ashley–Keynes Memorandum: H. Elcock, 'J. M. Keynes at the Paris Peace Conference', in M. Keynes (ed.), *Essays on John Maynard Keynes* (Cambridge, 1975), 163.   [18] See above, n. 7.

on the ability of the Enemy Powers to pay'. A few days later the Imperial War Cabinet, after considering the committee's report, concluded that insufficient stress had been laid on the idea of an indemnity in cash which 'though perhaps not the most useful from the point of view of the Allies, would be very effective in crippling Germany'. Yet it was understood that 'the amount of pecuniary indemnities payable by Germany was relatively small inasmuch as the over-whelming bulk of her capital was fixed in the shape of industrial plant and other means of production . . .'.[19]

Despite the violent Germanophobia of such journals as the *Morning Post* and *National Review*, British reparation policy was unimpeachable until the end of the war. As in France, moderation was encouraged by pressure from left-wing groups who denied that Germany should make reparation to any country except Belgium and advocated that war damage should be made good by an international commission financed by all the belligerents. Another source of restraint was the sobering reflection that the war might not end in an Allied victory. Opposition spokesmen also claimed in the House of Commons in December 1917 that the government's policy was affected by the emergence of the United States as 'the controlling power in peace terms'. It is, however, noteworthy that Lloyd George's speech to the Trade Union Congress on 5 January 1918, in which he expressly repudiated penal indemnities and insisted only on reparation for damage in the invaded territories and on the high seas, was delivered largely to combat domestic war-weariness three days before Woodrow Wilson laid down similar guide-lines in his Fourteen Points.[20]

[19] Imperial War Cabinet (henceforward IWC), Minutes, 3, 23 Mar. 1917, Min. 6; 4, 27 Mar. 1917, Min. 6; 12, 27 Apr. 1917, Min. 18, CAB 23/40; Committee on Terms of Peace, Minutes, 20 Apr. 1917, Min. 2, CAB 21/71. See also T. Jones, *Whitehall Diary* (2 vols.; London, 1969), i. 29–30. For a perfunctory reference to the work of the Milner Committee: D. Lloyd George, *War Memoirs* (2 vols.; London, 1938), i. 1036–7, 1066–7.

[20] See the complaint of Ramsay MacDonald about press Germanophobia during a debate on war aims: *HC*, 26 July 1917, xcvi. 1487–8. Note the vendetta between MacDonald and the jingo press: *MP*, 17 July 1917 (LA). For left-wing opposition to reparations: *HC*, xcvi. 1528. Cf. the official war aims of the Labour Party: *The Times*, 18 Dec. 1917, 3. British 'nationalists' opposed co-operative reconstruction on the grounds that it implied admission of joint war guilt: Viscount Esher, 'Pax Mundi', *The National Review*, Aug. 1917, 704. For doubts about the outcome of the war: Runciman, *HC*, 13 Feb. 1918, ciii. 181. For claims of American influence on war aims: ibid. 19 Dec. 1917, c. 2020–1 (Wedgwood); 2084–5 (Runciman). For texts of Lloyd George's speech of 5 Jan. 1918 and Wilson's Fourteen Points: *FR*, 1918, Suppl. I, i. 4–17. On Lloyd George's motives: Cate Haste, *Keep the Home Fires Burning: Propaganda in the First World War* (London, 1977), 175.

Even in the autumn of 1918, when the tide of war had turned in favour of the Allies, government spokesmen were reluctant to tarnish their war aims. The language of Lord Northcliffe, the Director of Propaganda in Enemy Countries, had become highly coloured by September. 'We must see to it', he declared in Scotland, 'that Prussia pays town for town, village for village, ship for ship, jewel for jewel, picture for picture, dollar for dollar. That is, she must pay full compensation for all that she has gorged and stolen, sacked and burnt.' Yet in what the *Manchester Guardian* dubbed as his 'Peace Encyclical' on the eve of the armistice, Northcliffe continued to link reparation claims to physical damage. The same restraint characterized the demand for reparations in a town like Liverpool, which, as Britain's main trans-Atlantic seaport, was highly sensitive to the human and physical losses inflicted by German submarine warfare. From October 1918, particularly after the torpedoing of the Irish mail steamer *Leinster* with the loss of five hundred lives, there was an outcry that Germany should replace the shipping that had been sunk and pay pensions to the dependents of civilians who had been 'murdered'. Yet there was still no talk of a wider indemnity. It was hardly surprising that a similar spirit pervaded the Lansing Note which was, as we have seen, drafted by the European Allies in Paris on 30 October and transmitted by the United States to Germany on 5 November to clarify the terms of the coming peace settlement. Here a reference in Wilson's Fourteen Points to the restoration of invaded territories was restrictively construed to mean that 'compensation [would] be made by Germany for all the damage done to the civilian population of the Allies and their property by the aggression of Germany by land, by sea, and from the air'. The word 'aggression', it should be noted, was only substituted for 'invasion' at British instigation so that the physical reparation claims of those victors whose territory had not actually been violated would be covered. Contrary to what was later alleged at the Paris Peace Conference, there was no implication at this stage of Germany's war guilt or her consequent liability for general war costs.[21]

The received wisdom is that the immoderate demands which swamped this restraint in the next few weeks were the product of a

---

[21] For Northcliffe: *The Times*, 20 Sept. 1918, 3; 23 Oct. 1918, 7; 4 Nov. 1918, 9 (text of 'encyclical'). See the report of a mass meeting of seamen in Liverpool: *Liverpool Daily Post and Mercury*, 15 Oct. 1918, 5; and 22 Oct. 1918 (LA). See also a resolution of the Liverpool Steam Ship Owners' Association on the terms of peace: ibid. 31 Oct. 1918, 3. Text of Lansing Note: *FR*, 1918, Suppl. I, i. 468–9. For its origins: see above, n. 11.

sudden upsurge of vindictive Germanophobia, which British political leaders either induced or were powerless to control. Robert E. Bunselmeyer, for instance, has concluded that 'fear of Germany's economic and military strength, and hatred of her arrogance ... were the origins of reparation and war guilt in Britain.' Although there was certainly a strong xenophobic element in the cry for reparations, such an interpretation tends to obscure the financial demagoguery which underlay the reparation problem. The clamour for a punitive indemnity by jingo extremists such as the National Party's Brigadier-General Page-Croft had a considerable impact in the closing months of the war. Yet the idea of an immense reparation claim only really took hold when it was touted by men of property and dominion statesmen as a solution to the British Empire's post-war budgetary and commercial problems.[22]

The readiness of British political leaders to condone and even to encourage a campaign for extracting the whole cost of the war from Germany flowed naturally from their budgetary delinquency during the war. It was not just that in the financial years 1914–19 only £2,733,000,000 of a total expenditure of £9,593,000,000 had been recouped from taxation, or that by 31 March 1919 the British national debt stood at £7,434,000,000. Even more important was the complacency which had been allowed to develop. The lightweight budgets introduced by Lloyd George, the then Chancellor of the Exchequer, in November 1914 and May 1915 were excusable because of the expectation that the war would be short. It was far more significant that Reginald McKenna, the 'new broom' Chancellor who replaced Lloyd George, should have been so timid in the fiscal demands he made upon the British people. According to the so-called 'McKenna principle' which was enunciated in 1916, permanent revenues were limited during the war to the amount necessary to cover normal peacetime expenditure *plus* the interest and sinking fund on the rapidly rising public debt. In justifying such a procedure McKenna was able to emphasize the even feebler fiscal performance of the German government: but he was motivated primarily by reluctance 'to drive the spirit of public sacrifice too hard'. Although Bonar Law, McKenna's successor as Chancellor, was candid enough to make gloomy predictions in 1917

---

[22] Bunselmeyer, 183. Cf. the conclusion of Haste, 179, that the peace terms were 'the harvest of four and a half years of anti-German propaganda'. For Page-Croft: *MP*, 7 Oct. 1918, 3; 10 Oct. 1918, 7; R. B. McCallum, *Public Opinion and the Last Peace* (London, 1944), 30. Cf. L. J. Maxse, 'Can Downing Street Save Germany?', *The National Review*, Nov. 1918, 345.

and 1918 about the long-term financial effect of the war, he never departed from the guide-lines established by McKenna. As E. V. Morgan, a student of British financial policy, has observed, the governments of the day took no practical steps during the war to bring home to the British people 'the basic fact that, if the government was to purchase more of the real product of the nation, then private citizens must purchase less'.[23]

Political leaders who were so reluctant to trouble the British taxpayer were put under added pressure to indulge in diversionary financial behaviour by the increasing discussion in radical and academic circles about the desirability of confiscatory taxation to reduce the public debt. Proposals for a capital levy had been mooted in both houses of parliament and discussed at length in the June and September 1918 issues of the *Economic Journal*; and they were soon to be embodied in the election manifesto of the Labour Party. The fears of the well-to-do, which had been aroused by rumours that 'the conscription of wealth' was regarded sympathetically by Bonar Law, would hardly have been allayed when the Chancellor, after ruling out an early repeal of the wartime Excess Profits Duty, reaffirmed to the House of Commons on 18 November his long-standing conviction that Britain's financial difficulties would be 'far greater when the war ended than they were even during the continuance of the war'.[24]

It was no accident that the cry for an indemnity to cover war costs was first raised by dominion statesmen, whose countries had sustained little or no physical damage but had incurred heavy government expenditure during the conflict. One of the earliest coherent demands for an indemnity for budgetary rather than retributive purposes was made in a speech delivered in Trafalgar Square in mid-October 1918 by Lord Morris, the ex-premier of Newfoundland. The Canadian government was next in the field with a demand that it should be 'at least partially indemnified for the cost of the war'. The most vocal advocate of a

[23] For figures: F. W. Hirst, *The Consequences of the War to Great Britain* (London, 1934), 144–67, 251; Morgan, 90–5. Although these figures indicate that revenue amounted to 28% of expenditure, a much lower percentage can be derived if war expenditure and war revenue are more rigorously defined. See also McKenna, *HC*, 4 Apr. 1916, lxxxi. 1052, 1055, 1065; Bonar Law, 2 May 1917, xciii. 378; 3 June 1918, cvi. 1332. The fiscal policy of the German government will be discussed in the final section of this chapter.

[24] On the capital levy: *HC*, 23 Apr. 1918, cv. 890; 14 May 1918, cvi. 226; *House of Lords Debates*, 5th Ser. (henceforward *HL*), 5 Aug. 1918, xxxi. 477–8; *EJ* 28 (1918): see particularly the favourable comments by Professor A. C. Pigou at 135–56. On its origin: P. Snowden, *Labour and National Finance* (London, 1920), 160. For Bonar Law's attitude: *HC*, 21 Nov. 1917, xcix. 1187; 18 Nov. 1918, cx. 3292–3.

wider indemnity proved to be W. M. Hughes, the Prime Minister of Australia. Hughes had kept himself in the British and French public eye since 1916 by advocating, without much success, a policy of post-war economic discrimination against the 'German commercial octopus'. He had also earned the applause of the conservative *Morning Post* in October 1918 by demanding retribution for Germany's 'crimes against civilization'. But he made his greatest impact when, a few days before the armistice, he protested on budgetary grounds against the restrictive reparation provisions of the Lansing Note.

While provision is made in some fashion for restoration and reparation, none is made for indemnity. Why? ... Do the citizens of the Empire understand that for generations we shall be staggering under a load of debt that will impose upon us a burden of taxation which it was not imagined before the war could be borne? And is Germany to escape bearing at least some share of these frightful burdens?[25]

The entry of Hughes into the lists on behalf of the British taxpayer coincided with that of the local jingoes. A National Party advertisement advocating an indemnity to defray the national debt appeared in *The Times* on 28 October; and a few days later Horatio Bottomley was to be heard at the Albert Hall demanding a good round sum of £10,000,000,000 sterling because 'no indemnities meant that for generations to come we should have around our necks financial claims which would ruin our industries'. The *Daily Express* and the *Evening Standard* also took up the cry in the first week of November. Soon anxiety began to be expressed by men of substance in the House of Commons. On 12 November the Yorkshire coal owner, Sir Joseph Walton (Coalition Liberal) asked why, despite the prospect of huge post-war taxation, there was no mention in the armistice terms of any intention 'to enforce the payment of indemnities'; and Mr R. P. (later Sir Robert) Houston, of the Houston Shipping Line, who was the Conservative member for the West Toxteth Division of Liverpool, enquired even more specifically whether the victors were determined to make Germany 'pay in full' for all the expenditure she had 'inflicted on the peoples of the Allied countries, including all pensions to sailors and soldiers and their dependents'.[26]

[25] *The Times*, 15 Oct. 1918, 8 (Morris); 21 Oct. 1918, 8 (Canada); 8 Nov. 1918, 8 (Hughes); *MP*, 26 Oct. 1918 (LA). For a comprehensive account of the activities of Hughes in Britain: L. F. Fitzhardinge, *William Morris Hughes: A Political Biography* (2 vols.; Sydney, 1964, 1979), ii. *The Little Digger, 1914–1952*, chs. 4–5, 14.

[26] Bunselmeyer, 115–16. *The Times*, 4 Nov. 1918, 3 (Bottomley). On the relations of

Although there was no immediate reaction from the government, the election campaign of November–December 1918 increased its vulnerability to such agitation. The case for an indemnity appeared to be bolstered by the budgetary implications of the ambitious programme of reconstruction and social reform which Lloyd George proclaimed in his 'fit country for heroes' speech at Wolverhampton on 23 November. The *Morning Post*, which was to set the pace in the indemnity campaign, extended a sardonic welcome to the government's plans for higher wages, increased agricultural production, improved housing, transportation, education, and social welfare. Having observed that 'all these things cost a great deal of money, and that the whole of their cost would be extraneous to the immense obligations incurred during the war', it went on to ask why, 'in these rather terrifying circumstances ... the Government [had] preserved total silence with regard to the question of demanding an indemnity from Germany'. The electorate should, it concluded, 'first of all ... ask every candidate whether he is or is not in favour of demanding an indemnity and ... insist upon a plain answer'. Two days later the *Morning Post* was trying to put Lloyd George himself on the spot. 'The Prime Minister', it declared, 'is to deliver a speech in Newcastle today, and he will perhaps—and perhaps not—refer to what is in fact the main issue of the election ... the terms of peace.'[27]

Even before the *Morning Post* had begun to needle Lloyd George, the Prime Minister had conceded ground to Hughes and Bonar Law within the Imperial War Cabinet. On 26 November Hughes reiterated his earlier public complaint that the Lansing Note had not mentioned an indemnity. 'If this [omission] was intended', he said, 'an invidious distinction would be made between a country like Belgium, or even England, and Australia. Australia would get no reparation for damage incurred during the war.' Lloyd George's initial reaction was unfavourable; and he parried with the responsible observation that, since Germany had very little gold, she could pay an indemnity only by dumping manufactured goods. But Hughes received strong support from Conservatives in the cabinet. Bonar Law, who had in April 1918 quashed debate about indemnities in the Commons, now expressed concern about Britain's £8,000,000,000 public debt and announced

Bottomley with the National Party: H. P. Croft, *My Life of Strife* (London, 1948), 139–40. See also *HC*, 12 Nov. 1918, cx. 2633–4 (Walton); 2511 (Houston).

[27] *The Times*, 25 Nov. 1918, 13 (Lloyd George); *MP*, 27 Nov. 1918 (LA); 29 Nov. 1918 (LA).

that he disagreed (he did not divulge by how much) with a Treasury Committee, headed by J. M. Keynes, which had just estimated that Germany could not pay more than £2,000,000,000. It was, therefore, decided, after 'a discussion of some length', to invite Hughes and Bonar Law to set up a special committee under the chairmanship of the former which was to investigate 'the amount of indemnity which it would be possible to exact; the means by which payment could be made; and the subsequent effect on the Allied countries of Germany having to pay such an indemnity'.[28]

Although Lloyd George had stressed that the purpose of the Hughes Committee was to find out 'whether we could get an indemnity out of Germany without doing ourselves harm in the future', the composition and outlook of the committee ensured that it would be little more than a platform for fiscal demagogues. Hughes later reported to the Imperial War Cabinet that its deliberations had been dominated by Lord Cunliffe, an erratic former governor of the Bank of England, and Herbert Gibbs, the chairman of the City of London Conservative Association. These men, according to another committee member, Walter Long, the Conservative Secretary of State for the Colonies, represented the views of the Federation of British Industries and the Associated Chambers of Commerce, both of which had expressed alarm about the prospect of confiscatory post-war taxation. The fiscal qualms of Cunliffe and Gibbs would have been compounded by their anxiety about the impact of Britain's huge public debt upon her already precarious international financial standing. Both men had been party four months earlier to the Cunliffe Committee's *Report on Currency and Foreign Exchanges after the War*, which had warned that, unless a drastic reduction of government indebtedness permitted a return to the gold standard, the uncertainty of the monetary situation would handicap Britain's industry, damage her 'position as an international financial centre', and lower her 'general commercial status in the eyes of the world'. The concern of leading members of the Hughes Committee to restore something of London's financial prestige helps to explain the cursory nature of its inquiry into Germany's capacity and the recklessness of its recommendation that she should be asked to pay the

---

[28] IWC, 38, 26 Nov. 1918, Min. 12, CAB 23/42. See 'Memorandum by the Treasury on the Indemnity Payable by the Enemy Powers for Reparation and Other Claims': Johnson, 344–83. See also Bonar Law, *HC*, 29 Apr. 1918, cv. 1284. For his somersault compare his speeches at Glasgow on 25 Nov. and Bootle on 3 Dec.: *The Times*, 26 Nov. 1918, 7–8; 4 Dec. 1918, 12. See also R. Blake, *The Unknown Prime Minister* (London, 1955), 404.

whole cost of the war, which it reckoned at £24,000,000,000, or annual payments of £1,200,000,000. Sir George Foster, the Canadian Minister of Trade and Finance, who was one of the more detached members of the committee, subsequently observed to the Imperial War Cabinet that he and his colleagues had neither 'the time nor the sources of information' at their disposal to enable them to determine 'what Germany could pay without injury to her or to us'. Cunliffe himself either misunderstood or chose to ignore the remark of Keynes (who attended three of the committee's meetings as Treasury spokesman) that Germany could not pay even £100,000,000 a year (one-twelfth of the sum eventually recommended by the committee) without privileged access to raw materials and artificial stimulus for her exports. This made it easier for him to propose on 2 December the impossible figure—apparently revealed to him in church on the preceding day— which was to form the basis for the committee's recommendations.[29]

The Hughes Committee's tactic of skirting its terms of reference by simply totting up Allied claims against Germany rather than investigating her capacity to pay was strongly supported by the influential Northcliffe press from the end of November. First the *Daily Mail* and then the hitherto restrained Northcliffe flagship, *The Times*, argued that Britain should not at this stage concern herself with Germany's capacity but should simply draw up her claims and present the bill. They adopted this attitude partly because their proprietor desired for personal reasons to embarrass Lloyd George, who had referred hopefully to the moderating role of the Hughes Committee when he broached the subject of an indemnity for war costs in a highly qualified and equivocal speech at Newcastle on 29 November. Yet Northcliffe had other motives, one of which was probably crystallized by the renewed demand of the Labour Party for a levy on capital in its election

[29] For a thorough appraisal of the Hughes Committee: Bunselmeyer, ch. 6. See also the comments of Hughes, Long, and Foster: IWC, 46, 24 Dec. 1918, Min. 3, CAB 23/42. Cf. Lloyd George, *The Truth about the Peace Treaties*, i. 457–61, 475–83. On Cunliffe: A. Boyle, *Montagu Norman: A Biography* (London, 1967), 118–23. Cunliffe's behaviour may also have been influenced by his dislike of the Treasury, with which he had very bad relations in 1917–18, his stormy final year as governor. For the Cunliffe Committee: *First Interim Report of the Committee on Currency and Foreign Exchanges after the War*, 15 Aug. 1918, *House of Commons Papers*, 1918, vii. Cd. 9182, at 5–6. For fears of businessmen about post-war taxation: *The Times*, 11 Dec. 1918, 10. See also Bunselmeyer, 139–40. Note the continuing opposition of Gibbs to the taxation of war fortunes a year later: *The Times*, 27 Feb. 1920, 19. For Keynes and Cunliffe: Committee on Indemnity, 2, 28 Nov. 1918, 8–10 (Keynes); 4, 2 Dec. 1918, 1 (Cunliffe), CAB 27/43. On the divine source of Cunliffe's inspiration: Fitzhardinge, 381.

manifesto of 28 November. The press baron not only feared for his personal fortune—he subsequently remarked to his brother, Rother-mere, that he did not intend to spend the rest of his life 'swotting to pay excess profits tax and supertax for the benefit of Germany'—but was also concerned that heavy taxes might cause unemployment and increase the risk of social revolution in Britain. A further justification for extremism in the eyes of Northcliffe and his press early in December was the possibility that Britain would lag behind France and the other Allies in registering her claims. His fears appear to have been aroused by a conference of Allied leaders in London at the beginning of December at which it was decided to establish an inter-Allied Com-mission on Reparation and Indemnity. Lloyd George tried, as he had with the Hughes Committee, to limit the function of this body to assessing Germany's capacity to pay. However, as a result of French and Italian pressure, it was decided that each government should first of all 'enumerate its claims' and that these should subsequently be referred to the commission which was to be set up. This encouraged *The Times* to demand in the second week of December that the Hughes Committee should stop 'wasting its time' by trying to determine Ger-many's capacity. 'Our business', it declared, 'is simply to assess our own bill of damages, as the French have already done, and then to present it for payment.' Although Lloyd George reproved Northcliffe for 'making mischief' by suggesting that the other Allies were stealing a march on Britain, the idea that the British Empire should ensure its 'fair share' of reparations by rushing in with an extravagant claim was henceforth to have a profound influence on British policy.[30]

Lloyd George and Bonar Law were fully aware of the disastrous effect which a large indemnity would have on British trade; and neither of them were susceptible to the illusions which the Hughes Committee and its Conservative supporters sought to encourage about massive tribute as a panacea for post-war budgetary and commercial problems. Yet, instead of playing down the committee's recommendations, which

[30] For an account which emphasizes the importance of the vendetta between Lloyd George and Northcliffe over the latter's exclusion from office after the war: Bunselmeyer, 131–2, 140–2. Cf. Northcliffe to Rothermere, 10 Apr. 1919, R. Pound and G. Harmsworth, *Northcliffe* (London, 1959), 712; *The Times, The History of The Times* (4 vols.; London, 1935–52), IV. i. 366–8. Note the transition of *The Times* from moderation (25 Nov. 1918, 10; 30 Nov. 1918 (LA)) to extremism (7, 9 Dec. 1918 (LA)); and its disapproval of Labour's capital levy proposal (29 Nov. 1918 (LA)). For Lloyd George's views on the role of the committees: ibid. 30 Nov. 1918, 6 (Newcastle speech); Notes of an Allied Conversation . . ., 2 Dec. 1918, at 11.00 a.m., 3–8; Notes of an Allied Conversation . . ., 3 Dec. 1918, at 11.15 a.m., 1, IC 98, 100, CAB 28/5.

they both regarded as a 'wild and fantastic chimera', they proceeded to cite them approvingly in the closing stages of the election campaign. After dwelling at length on the great financial burden which Britain would have to bear in the coming years, the Prime Minister reproduced almost word for word in a speech he delivered at Bristol on 11 December the findings of the committee about the propriety of demanding the whole cost of the war *and* the viability of such a claim. Although he may have been sensitive to the tactical argument of Conservatives and colonials for an inflated British reparation claim, his behaviour was also dictated by a narrow partisan preoccupation with dishing the Labour Party. As one would expect, several of the Prime Minister's speeches in the last two weeks of the campaign were delivered at towns which contained marginal constituencies. At Newcastle and Bristol, where he made his most extreme statements on the indemnity question, the threat came from a well-organized local Labour Party, which had been a force to be reckoned with before the war and had become even more menacing with the extension of the franchise. An added cause for concern was that the pre-war arrangement whereby the Liberal and Labour Parties had divided the constituencies between them had been discontinued, and that, as a result, there was to be a straight fight between Labour and Lloyd George's Coalition Liberals in five of the nine seats in the two centres. The temptation for the Prime Minister to indulge in a little well-hedged financial jingoism in order to discredit his Labour anti-indemnity opponents appears to have been too great. It is ironical that within five years of attempting to win votes by espousing policies which threatened the peace and prosperity of the world Lloyd George was a political outcast and Bonar Law was dead.[31]

THE UNITED STATES: FROM INVOLVEMENT TO ISOLATIONISM

If the reparation problem, in its intractable form, was created by British and French statesmen, it was compounded by Americans. Although the wartime moderation of the Entente had its own logic, it was underpinned by an enormous flow of American government loans

---

[31] *The Times*, 12 Dec. 1918, 6 (Bristol speech); Lloyd George, *The Truth about the Peace Treaties*, i. 461–7 (for the most restrained passages of the speech). On the Labour Party's challenge to the Coalition in Newcastle and Bristol: *The Times*, 29 Nov. 1918, 9–10; 11 Dec. 1918, 10.

(totalling over $8 billion) into the coffers of the European belligerents in 1917 and 1918, and by an unstated assumption that international financial co-operation would be maintained after the war. Even if such an idea had been laughed down when it was suggested by the Labour Party in the House of Commons in July 1917, it was taken seriously in influential circles in Britain and France by December 1918. Projects mooted at this time included proposals by Bonar Law and Klotz for the cancellation of inter-Allied debts, and French suggestions for the pooling of war costs and for the formation of a Financial League of Nations to underwrite German reparation payments.[32]

The viability of all these schemes depended on the United States, the major creditor of the Allies. Some American initiative seemed called for at the end of 1918, if only because of the enormous profits which the American people had reaped from Europe during the war. The loans initially advanced by the United States government to the Allies in 1917 were, moreover, in a very real sense a substitute for American troops who did not arrive in France until 1918. In her treatment of the origins of the war-debt problem Denise Artaud has attributed the parsimonious attitude of the American government at this stage to Anglo-American commercial rivalry. Influential Americans certainly entertained groundless fears that Britain would reassert her international financial hegemony if her debts were waived or reduced. Yet the budgetary history of the United States is sufficient to explain the behaviour of its leaders. The remarkable vigour with which the Wilson administration attacked the problem of war finance in 1917 and 1918 was bound to create tension within a federal financial system in which Washington had normally played second fiddle to the states. The United States was, in fact, only slightly better equipped to face the financial challenge of the war than Germany where, as we shall see, the states rather than the central government controlled direct

---

[32] For American loans: Artaud, *Question des dettes interalliées*, i, ch. 1. For Labour Party's proposal: *HC*, 26 July 1917, xcvi. 1528. For Bonar Law's: D. H. Miller, *My Diary at the Conference of Paris* (21 vols.; New York, 1924), i. 25. For Klotz's: B. D. Rhodes, 'Reassessing "Uncle Shylock": The United States and the French War Debt, 1917–1929', *J. of American History*, 55 (1969), 789. For the pooling of war costs: Ribot (former President of the Council, Finance Minister, and Minister for Foreign Affairs), *Sénat*, 17 Dec. 1918, 915. The proposal was formally embodied in a report of 27 Feb. 1919 by the Budget Commission: *Le Temps*, 1 Mar. 1919, 2. For the Financial League of Nations: Letter from Jacques Stern, the French banker: ibid. 22 Dec. 1918, 2–3. Klotz tabled a proposal for such a body at the Preliminary Peace Conference in Jan. 1919: Plenary Session of 25 Jan. 1919, *FR, Paris Peace Conference, 1919* (henceforward *FRPPC*), iii. 199. For French press discussion: Pierre Miquel, *La Paix de Versailles et l'opinion publique française* (Paris, 1972), 460–70.

taxation until 1919. The ratification of the Sixteenth Amendment to the United States Constitution early in 1913 had given Congress the formal power 'to lay and collect taxes on incomes, from whatever sources derived'. Yet the continuing power of conservative states-righters and the underdevelopment of the federal income tax system were such that, in order to redress the fall in revenue occasioned by the commercial dislocation of the early months of the war, Wilson and his colleagues resorted to higher indirect levies rather than direct taxes. Because the federal government's expenditure made up a mere 2 per cent of the American gross national product in 1913 the massive outlays occasioned by the war were even more difficult to justify to

TABLE 2. *United States: GNP and Federal Government Revenue and Expenditure, 1913 and 1917–1919 ($ billion)*

	GNP	Expenditure		Revenue	
		War	Total	War	Total
1913	40.6[a]	—	0.96	—	0.97
1917	49.9	1.34	2.09	0.38	1.12
1918	61.6	13.05	13.79	3.44	4.18
1919	65.7	18.21	18.95	3.91	4.65

[a] (av. 1912–16).

Source: United States Department of Commerce, *Historical Statistics of the United States: Colonial Times to 1957* (Washington, 1961), 139, 724. Cf. Gilbert, 225.

the public than they were in Britain, whose central government spending had risen to 8 per cent of national income by the last year of peace. From its low 1913 base American federal expenditure (Table 2) had increased twenty-fold and ballooned to just under 30 per cent of GNP by 1919.[33]

---

[33] US exports to Europe increased from $6.8 billion in the five years before the war to $19.5 billion during the five war years. P. Snowden, 'The Debt Settlement: The Case for Revision', in J. T. Gerould and L. S. Turnbull (edd.), *Selected Articles on Interallied Debts and Revision of the Debt Settlements* (New York, 1928), 445–6. On loans versus troops: ibid. 443–4. For Anglo-American rivalry: Artaud, *Question des dettes interalliées*, i. 79–104. For the fullest study of American fiscal politics: S. Ratner, *Taxation and Democracy in America* (New York, 1967 edn.), espec. chs. 14–18. Cf. R. E. Paul, *Taxation in the United States* (Boston, 1954), chs. 3–4. For war finance: Gilbert, chs. 7–8. For British figures: B. R. Mitchell and Phyllis Deane, *Abstract of British Historical Statistics* (Cambridge, 1962), 394, 398; C. H. Feinstein, *Statistical Tables of National*

Although tax revenues only quintupled because of the remarkable, if transient, fervour which was whipped up in support of a succession of government war loans, it was most unlikely that the Republican majority which was returned in the elections of November 1918 would sanction the further tax increases necessary for any renunciation or extension of inter-Allied loans. Some Americans, such as Thomas W. Lamont, of the firm of J. P. Morgan, and Paul M. Warburg, the German-American banker, were aware of their country's crucial financial role at this time; and they pleaded for the prolongation of the financial aid which the government had proffered during the war. Yet even the efforts of McAdoo to divert to European reconstruction the unexpended portion of the government's war credits to its allies met with formidable opposition in the Ways and Means Committee of the Senate. 'Secretary McAdoo's request', declared Senator Charles Sloan (Republican, Nebraska), '..., is certainly the *ne plus ultra* of spectacular financial legislation. The American people submitted to loans being made to the Allies during the war, solely on the grounds of its being a war measure. I doubt if the American people are prepared to approve the Federal Treasury becoming the international banker of the world.' Secretary McAdoo was, therefore, constrained to instruct the American Commission to Negotiate Peace on 11 December that 'the cancellation of our foreign loans or any action which would diminish their value would not meet with the approval of Congress or of our people who would thereby be subjected to heavy additional taxation'. He also forecast that the American government's foreign lending would henceforth be very much reduced.[34]

The refusal of the United States government to assist with international reconstruction and its evident determination to dun the Europeans for their debts were to ensure that the reparation problem would

Income, Expenditure and Output of the U.K., 1855–1965 (Cambridge, 1972), Table I. The British government's peak war expenditure (in 1918) was between 14 and 15 times its 1913 outlay and amounted to 57% of GNP.

[34] For Lamont's appeal: *The Times*, 13 Dec. 1918, 12. Lamont had organized American loans to the Allies before the US entered the war. He later became chairman of a committee appointed by the Investment Bankers' Association to protect the interests of American investors in these loans: ibid. 23 Aug. 1918, 10. His role in the American financial delegation at the Paris Peace Conference will be discussed in the next chapter. Cf. 'Some Phases of Financial Reconstruction, An Address Delivered to the United States Chamber of Commerce ... on 6 December 1918', in Paul M. Warburg, *The Federal Reserve System* (2 vols.; New York, 1930), ii. 547–88. For the Ways and Means Committee: *NYT*, 10 Dec. 1918, 6; 13 Dec. 1918, 14. For McAdoo: *FRPPC* ii. 538–9. This policy was endorsed a week later by McAdoo's successor, Carter Glass: ibid. 544–6. Cf. Artaud, *Question des dettes interalliées*, i. 84–6.

remain a running sore for more than a decade. Yet the extravagance of the sums that were originally envisaged must be sheeted home to political leaders on the other side of the Atlantic. The popularity of Lloyd George and Clemenceau at the end of the war and the widespread support for the idea of a negotiated peace suggest that a much greater effort could have been made to guide public opinion, despite the suddenness and completeness of Germany's collapse. The natural tendency of politicians to conceal unpleasant facts may have been accentuated because the British and French Prime Ministers had thrown in their lot with conservative groups and were thus over-sensitive to right-wing pressures. This could help to explain why Lloyd George, who had shown such scant respect for the House of Lords a decade earlier, should have made public what he knew to be bad advice from special pleaders; and why Clemenceau should have tolerated the irresponsible utterances of his Finance Minister, Klotz, in December 1918. The uneasy conscience of the two former radicals was reflected in their subsequent attempts to blame their colleagues and advisers for what had occurred. Clemenceau even descended to the jibe that Klotz was the only Jew of his acquaintance who knew nothing about finance; and Lloyd George stooped to attributing the inflated reparation claims of the British Empire to the suggestion of Ashley and Keynes in 1916 that an indemnity might be collected in instalments. Both men had received clear advice during the war that huge demands for war costs were neither practicable nor in the interests of their respective countries; and their decision to air fantastic figures was clearly a political one for which they bore the ultimate responsibility. Financial demagoguery was, in both cases, tinged with vindictiveness and a desire to impede Germany's post-war recovery. Also important was the desire of the British Empire, which had sustained relatively little physical damage, to swell its theoretical share of the spoils by claiming general war costs. The reluctance of the United States to waive its war loans was an added reason for large reparation claims. Yet the mainspring of the reparation problem was the diversionary fiscal rhetoric employed by the political spokesmen of the wealthy classes of the European victors.[35]

---

[35] For Clemenceau on Klotz: D. W. Brogan, *The Development of Modern France* (*1870–1939*) (London, 1953), 589. For Lloyd George's claim and the reply of Keynes: Johnson, 311–13, 334–6.

THE GERMAN BALANCE SHEET

The irresponsibility of the victors is thrown into relief by the prostration of Germany at the end of 1918. Although economic historians have been reluctant to attempt an assessment of the German gross national product during the conflict, it is clear that the diversion of human and material resources from normal economic activity to the business of destruction had a traumatic effect. The mobilization of the German economy for war led to lower investment in many sectors of the economy, the disruption of international trade, reduced production of consumer goods, and the slaughter, maiming, or prolonged relocation to unproductive work of a significant proportion of the work force. This economic mayhem caused a rapid diminution of wealth and welfare. Even the output of strategically important enterprises such as coal mining, the iron and steel industry, and agriculture fell sharply between 1914 and 1918. Black coal production, which was 190 million tons in 1913, declined to 160 million tons by 1918. Over the same period output of pig iron fell from 12.9 to 9.2 million tons; and production of crude steel, which had been 15.3 million tons in 1913, dropped to 12.9 million in the last year of the war. In the agricultural sector the yield of major crops and holdings of livestock slumped alarmingly. It is hardly surprising that one scholar has estimated Germany's national income and consumer spending in 1918 at 57 per cent and 42 per cent respectively of their 1913 level.[36]

This fall in production and consumption was partly the result of the deployment of almost 11 million Germans (16.4 per cent of the population) into the armed services by 1918. Falling output was also caused by declining productivity, which in turn stemmed partly from insufficient capital investment and the consequent deterioration of industrial plant and land, and partly from the widespread employment of underfed, ill-clothed, and badly trained workers. By 1918 there had been a considerable decline in the output of coal and iron per miner and foundry worker and in the agricultural yield per hectare. It is also noteworthy that the productivity of the German railway system measured in terms of the availability of rolling stock had decreased considerably. The process of deterioration and dislocation was accelerated

[36] For the German GNP: K. Laursen and J. Pedersen, *The German Inflation, 1918–1923* (Amsterdam, 1964), 75 n. 1. For national income and consumer spending in 1918: K. Roesler, *Die Finanzpolitik des deutschen Reiches im ersten Weltkrieg* (Berlin, 1967), 154. See below, Appendix I, for: coal, iron, and steel figures, Table A; livestock, Table B; crops, Table C.

by the National Service Law of 5 December 1916 which inaugurated a period of intensified production of war materials through the intro-duction of civilian forced labour. Although this law (the so-called Hindenburg Programme) temporarily increased the volume of war production, it only did so by impoverishing the German economic system. In the words of one historian of the German war economy 'anything and everything that seemed of any possible use for war purposes—factories, machinery, laboratories, and every kind of insti-tution—was forced into the compass of this, the last mobilization of all available forces and was used up in it.' By September 1918 the scarcity of food, the shortage of manpower, and the lack of raw materials and machinery were so acute that Germany was close to economic collapse, starvation, and social disintegration.[37]

Internal disruption was matched by the dislocation of foreign trade. Despite the absence of complete figures, it is clear that German exports declined to well below their 1910–13 average of 8.9 billion gold marks. This was largely because over half of the German goods sold abroad in 1913 had found their market in Allied countries. Another important reason was the Allied naval blockade, which seriously reduced Ger-many's trade with overseas neutrals. Finally, although exports of coal, metallurgical products, and chemicals were still made to neutral neighbours, most of what had in the past been an exportable surplus was absorbed in the war effort. Walther Rathenau, who was head of Germany's wartime Department of Raw Materials in 1915, interpreted this as a trend towards economic autarky or towards the 'protection of raw materials', which, he predicted hopefully, would continue after the war. However, with the coming of peace and the cessation of war production, it was clear that Germany had not become economically

[37] For the deployment of German labour to the armed services and war industries: Roesler, p. 156; J. Kocka, *Klassengesellschaft im Krieg: deutsche Sozialgeschichte, 1914–1918* (Göttingen, 1973), 12–13. For the food shortage: ibid. 19–20; C. P. Vincent, 'The Post-World War I Blockade of Germany: An Aspect in the Tragedy of a Nation', Ph.D. thesis (Univ. of Colorado, 1980), ch. 2. On productivity: *Statistisches Jahrbuch für das deutsche Reich*, 1919, 70 (agriculture); 1926, 80 (mining). Cf. G. Lübsen, 'The German Coal Situation and the Reparation Coal Deliveries', *Manchester Guardian Commercial: Reconstruction in Europe* (henceforward *MGCRE*), 7 Sept. 1922, 427; G. Francke, 'The German Railway System after the War', *MGCRE*, 7 Sept. 1922, 405. Cf. Hue (SPD), 15 Aug. 1919, *Verhandlungen der verfassungsgebenden deutschen Nationalversammlung* (henceforward *NV*), cccxxix. 2475–80. For the National Service Law: *Reichsgesetzblatt*, 1916, 1333–9. Trans. of text in R. H. Lutz (ed.), *The Fall of the German Empire* (2 vols.; London, 1932), ii. 99 ff. For impact: P. Umbreit, *Der Krieg und die Arbeiterverhältnisse*, 262: quoted in A. Mendelssohn-Bartholdy, *The War and German Society* (Yale, 1937), 85. Text of Foreign Office Report: Lutz, ii. 106–11.

self-sufficient but had merely been deprived of her former export markets, which in 1913 had absorbed about a quarter of her total industrial production.[38]

Although exact figures are again not available, it is certain that the Allied blockade reduced Germany's imports during the war years to a much lower figure than the 1910–13 average of 10.2 billion gold marks. This reduction had a serious economic effect since nearly half of pre-war imports were raw materials for manufacture and another third consisted of livestock and foodstuffs. To make matters worse, Germany's agriculture was heavily dependent on nitrates imported from Chile; and her dairy cattle subsisted largely on imported forage. The effects of the blockade were mitigated somewhat by the unwillingness of the Allies to offend neutrals such as Holland, Denmark, Sweden, and Switzerland, which maintained considerable trading ties with Germany throughout the war. Yet there is ample evidence that a shrinkage of imports contributed substantially to the dearth of food and raw materials from which the economy suffered in both the war and post-war period.[39]

The methods used by the German government to offset its war expenditure could do little to delay or reduce the economic trauma of the war. They did, however, determine which section of the community would bear the brunt of the conflict. It was only to be expected that the Second Reich would devise a system of war finance which would minimize the sacrifice of the conservative militarists and capitalists it represented and off-load a disproportionate share of the burden of the war onto the shoulders of the broad masses of consumers. The inflationary effect of these policies was not fully apparent in November 1918, when the mark was no more depreciated than the currencies of the other major belligerents.[40] Yet violent price inflation had only been averted by the fortuitous and temporary restraint of German investors and consumers, the preparedness of the public to subscribe to government loans, and the confidence of international investors in the mark.

[38] For war-time trade dislocation: M. C. Siney, *The Allied Blockade of Germany, 1914–1916* (Michigan, 1957), 20–1, 131; L. Grebler and W. Winkler, *The Cost of the War to Germany and to Austria-Hungary* (Yale, 1940), 20–1; Keynes, *Economic Consequences*, 182–3. For the blockade and increased domestic consumption of materials: Siney, 125, 175, 270 (Appendix F); C. Rist, *Les Finances de guerre de l'Allemagne* (Paris, 1921), 202. For 'autarky': Lutz, ii. 89–90.

[39] Siney, *passim*; Lutz, ii. 107; Vincent, ch. 2.

[40] W. Lotz, *Die deutsche Staatsfinanzwirtschaft im Kriege* (Stuttgart, 1927), 96. The index of German wholesale prices (1913 = 100) had risen to 234 by Nov. 1918: C. Bresciani-Turroni, *The Economics of Inflation* (London, 1937), 25 and Appendix, Table V.

Rising prices were encouraged throughout the war by non-monetary influences such as the ever-increasing demand for war *matériel*, falling productivity, and production and transport bottlenecks. Price inflation was also aggravated by the inability of the government to impose effective controls. Laws were passed on 4 August and 17 December empowering the Bundesrat (Federal Upper House) to fix maximum prices for strategic commodities such as food, fodder, fuel, and raw materials. The Bundesrat was, however, both tardy and inept in imposing restrictions; and vested interests had little difficulty in circumventing attempts to fix maximum prices during the war. A flood of maximum price legislation was enacted in the autumn of 1915: but this was undermined by the sophisticated evasion techniques of the business community; and it was obvious by the spring of 1917 that the government's countermeasures had enjoyed only limited success.[41]

The chief source of the inflation which ultimately occurred was the purchasing power released in the community by the massive expenditure of the federal government. Although the technical measures taken to facilitate this expenditure were neither precipitant nor ill-conceived in the light of contemporary 'nominalist' monetary theory, which asserted that the value of money depended on the guarantee of the state rather than on gold, the whole exercise was based on the expectation of a short, victorious, and remunerative conflict such as had occurred in 1866 and 1870 and had been predicted once more by General Schlieffen.[42] In the event of a long war, countervailing measures to absorb excess purchasing power would clearly be needed

[41] K. Pribram, 'Zur Entwicklung der Lebensmittelpreise in der Kriegszeit', *Archiv*, 43 (May 1917), 773–6. For attempts at price control: H. Schacht, *The Stabilization of the Mark* (London, 1927), 20; Mary Stocks, 'The Attempt to Fix Maximum Corn Prices in Germany, November 1914', *EJ* 25 (June 1915), 274; eadem, 'German Potato Policy', ibid. 26 (Mar. 1916), 57; eadem, 'The Meat Problem in Germany', ibid. 26 (June 1916), 168–9; G. D. Feldman, *Army, Industry and Labor in Germany, 1914–1918* (Princeton, 1966), 97–117, 471–2.

[42] For technical measures: Gesetz vom 4 August betreffend die Änderung des Bankgesetzes, *Reichsgesetzblatt*, 1914, 347; J. M. Keynes, 'The Economics of War in Germany', *EJ* 25 (Sept. 1915), 444. Steps were also taken to liberalize credit in the private sector: Darlehnskassengesetz vom 4 August 1914, *Reichsgesetzblatt*, 1914, 340; J. Jastrow, 'Die Organisation des Kredits im Kriege', *Archiv*, 40 (Dec. 1914), 95 ff.; R. Stucken, *Deutsche Geld- und Kreditpolitik, 1914 bis 1953* (Tübingen, 1953), 25–6; Schacht, *Stabilization*, 31–2. For figures on the eight-fold increase in note circulation and the dilution of the metallic component of the Reichsbank's liquid assets during the war: Stucken, 16–17; Lotz, *Staatsfinanzwirtschaft*, 95. Such measures had been canvassed both privately and in the Prussian Finance Ministry before Aug. 1914: Mendelssohn-Bartholdy, *The War and German Society*, 63 (n.), 67; Rist, 30–2. Note particularly the writings of Jakob Riesser, the banker, financial publicist, and Reichstag

if inflation was to be avoided. The inadequacy of the German government's policy in this respect is revealed by the figures for its expenditure and revenue (Table 3) in the years 1914–18. The extraordinary lag in revenue did not have serious monetary repercussions in 1915 and 1916 because of the remarkable success of the government's

TABLE 3. *German Federal Revenue and Expenditure, 1914–1918* (million marks)

Year	Expenditure	Revenue	Deficit
1914	8,619.5	2,350.8	6,268.7
1915	25,693.8	1,735.2	23,958.6
1916	27,732.0	2,029.4	25,702.6
1917	52,002.7	7,830.3	44,172.4
1918	44,019.7	6,795.0	37,224.7
TOTAL	158,067.7	20,740.7	137,327.0

Source: Lotz, *Staatsfinanzwirtschaft*, 104.

war loans. Until the spring of 1916 loan subscriptions, encouraged by patriotic propaganda and facilitated by Germany's highly liquid financial institutions, exceeded the government's short-term borrowing from the Reichsbank (floating debt) by 6.6 billion marks. Thereafter, however, the massive expenditure occasioned by the Hindenburg Programme easily outstripped the loan yield and caused the floating debt to rise to 48 billion marks by the end of October 1918. This was eventually to cause grave financial instability, even though the immediate inflationary effect was cushioned because of the large sums retained by servicemen or kept in reserve by the business community as a hedge against rising costs and the approaching transition from war to peace.[43]

deputy: *Finanzielle Kriegsbereitschaft und Kriegsführung* (Berlin, 1909); *The German Great Banks and their Concentration* (trans. of 3rd German edn., National Monetary Commission, Washington, 1911), 21–6. On the influence of G. F. Knapp's 'nominalist' or 'Chartalist' monetary theory: H. S. Ellis, *German Monetary Theory, 1905–1933* (Harvard, 1937), 180. Note the subsequent testimony of Eugen Schiffer, a post-war Finance Minister: *NV*, 15 Feb. 1919, cccxxvi. 95. On the influence of the Schlieffen Plan: K. Helfferich, *Money* (trans. of 6th German edn., London, 1927), 229.

[43] For a discussion of different methods of computing Germany's wartime revenue and expenditure: Lotz, 98–105. For loan and floating debt figures: Rist, 76–9, 99–103; Lotz, *Staatsfinanzwirtschaft*, 32–3; Bresciani-Turroni, 439; Schacht, *Stabilization*, 14–15. For suppressed inflation: Helfferich, *Money*, 593–5; John G. Williamson, *Karl Helfferich* (Princeton, 1971), 147–8.

The indifferent fiscal performance of the government was due partly to the long-standing refusal of Prussian conservatives and Catholic particularists to transfer the right of direct taxation from the states to the federal government. As recently as 1909 the Conservative and Catholic Centre Parties, concerned to restrict the financial power of the democratically elected and relatively progressive Reichstag, had defeated a proposal by Chancellor Bernhard von Bülow for a Federal Inheritance Tax. The gains of the Social Democratic Party (SPD) at the 1912 elections had enabled Bülow's successor, Theobald von Bethmann-Hollweg, to push through, in the teeth of fierce opposition from the Conservatives, the so-called Defence Contribution (*Wehrbeitrag*) of 1913. However, despite the jubilation of the SPD, this 900 million mark levy on property was of such a special nature as to diminish its significance as a precedent.[44]

Apart from the strength of conservatism and particularism, the most important reason for the heavy dependence of the German government on borrowing was pressure from the German business community. The apprehensions of the commercial world had been aroused by the increasingly cogent predictions of the middle-class peace movement in Germany and Britain that a European war would cause severe economic dislocation and yield no worthwhile spoils. Instead, however, of promoting the cause of peace, German businessmen had sought to reconcile patriotism with self-interest by pinning their hopes on a short war and an indemnity and by insisting on measures to cushion the immediate financial impact of any conflict. The attitude of the business world on the eve of the war was reflected in the writings of Professor Heinrich Dietzel of Bonn, who recommended that government war expenditure should be covered by loans rather than taxes on the grounds that the former would do less to aggravate the recession which it was feared would be induced by the outbreak of hostilities. There were, it is true, advocates of increased wartime taxation among advisers of the Prussian Finance Ministry such as Dr Jakob Riesser, the president of the Hansabund and the chairman of the Central Association of Banks. Yet the blind insistence of the German business community that the war would be short and that it could be waged on the cheap was an important reason for the absence of adequate

[44] H. Booms, *Die Deutschkonservative Partei* (Düsseldorf, 1954), 71–2; C. E. Schorske, *German Social Democracy, 1905–1917* (Harvard, 1955), 148–9. On the significance of the *Wehrbeitrag*: V. V. Badulesco, *Le Prélèvement extraordinaire sur le capital dans l'empire allemand* (Paris, 1922), 7–25.

measures to absorb the excess purchasing power unleased in the community by the government's war expenditure. In March 1915 an SPD proposal for a tax on war profits was smothered by a Reichstag majority which, preoccupied with maintaining 'business confidence' and still hopeful of a quick victory and an indemnity, endorsed Finance Minister Karl Helfferich's slogan 'No new taxes'.[45]

By 1916 it was realized that the war would be long, that its cost would be immense, and that, if an indemnity were obtained, it would be insufficient to exempt the German people from increased post-war taxation. It was also obvious that the yield from war loans would not be enough to prevent a rapid increase in the floating debt. Yet, despite growing agitation in radical and academic circles for a levy on capital, the only significant gesture towards direct taxation for the remainder of the war was the War Tax on Capital Gains of 21 June 1916, which was designed to cover deficits in the ordinary budget (as opposed to the extraordinary *war* budget), and a law of 9 April 1917 directing firms to hold in reserve 60 per cent of their excess profits in the coming year. The rapidly widening gap between revenue and expenditure sparked off fresh discussion of radical financial reform in February 1918. One of the main arguments used to stifle this debate was the renewed assertion that Germany's war costs should be defrayed by an indemnity. Although such a view had not been advanced in the Reichstag since the adoption of its Peace Resolution renouncing annexations and indemnities in July 1917, it was now forcefully resuscitated by Stresemann and Roesicke, the spokesmen of the National Liberal and Conservative Parties. Encouraged by rising hopes of victory, they insisted that at least a part of Germany's outlays on the war should

---

[45] For an account of the peace movement which, in my opinion, underplays the growing concern of businessmen about the economic implications of a European war: R. Chickering, *Imperial Germany and a World Without War: The Peace Movement and German Society, 1892–1914* (Princeton, 1975), ch. 6. Cf. N. Angell, *After All: The Autobiography of Norman Angell* (London, 1951). For the impact of Angell's *The Great Illusion* in Britain: see above, n. 17. For German fears that war would cause an economic recession: H. Dietzel, *Kriegssteuern oder Kriegsanleihen?* (Tübingen, 1912). Cf. F. Y. Edgeworth, 'Some German Economic Writings about the War', *EJ* 27 (June 1917), 241–2; Mendelssohn-Bartholdy, *The War and German Society*, 65, 67 ff.; Stucken, 22–3. For the writings of Riesser: see above, n. 42. For his advisory activity: Mario Alberti, 'Le finanze della Germania e la Guerra', *Giornali degli Economisti (Roma)*, June 1915, summarized in *EJ* 25 (Sept. 1915), 486. For the best account of pre-war German thinking on war finance: Roesler, 12–34. For the debate of Mar. 1915: *Verhandlungen des Reichstags* (henceforward *RT*), 1 Mar. 1915, cccvi. 39 ff., 47 ff.; Badulesco, *Prélèvement*, 33; Williamson, 125–6. For subsequent inertia: Schacht, *Stabilization*, 17–18; Lotz, *Staatsfinanzwirtschaft*, 54; *RT*, 20 Dec. 1915, cccvi. 462; Williamson, 129–34.

be borne by the enemy. This provoked a partisan but perceptive retort from Vogtherr, an Independent Socialist opponent: 'Either an indemnity or national bankruptcy! That's the slogan one hears again and again in all Pan-German propaganda. They're afraid of direct taxes, they're afraid of capital levies. That's why Dr. Roesicke and Dr. Stresemann insist that "whatever happens, we must have an indemnity." ' The indemnity mirage, like the short-war illusion which it complemented and ultimately replaced, was clearly being exploited to prevent the war from damaging the interests of men of property or upsetting the financial balance of power between the federal government and the states. In a speech on 23 April 1918, Roedern, the Secretary of State to the Treasury, was candid enough to admit that the shortcomings of the government's fiscal policy were due to Germany's federal structure and what he referred to as the vulnerability of German commerce to war-induced disruption. Yet he merely reiterated his preference for loans over taxes and insisted that thoroughgoing reform of direct taxation should be deferred until after the war and left to the initiative of the states.[46]

The German government was even more insouciant about its external financial problems. The war, it will be recalled, did away with half of Germany's export markets, severely restricted her entry into others, and paralysed her merchant shipping. The resulting decline in foreign earnings was offset to some extent by a fall in spending abroad induced by the blockade. However, the emphasis of the trade which was maintained during the war with neutral neighbours was on imports rather than exports. Thus, even if no figures were available, it could be assumed that Germany's balance of trade was decidedly unfavourable. The financial implications were serious for a country which possessed relatively small reserves of gold and foreign securities, and which found it difficult to obtain foreign credits. It has been estimated that the total German trade deficit during the war was 15 billion gold marks; and that of this deficit only 5 billions were covered by exports

[46] For the growth of the public debt: Lotz, 56. The ordinary budget covered only normal administrative expenditure and debt charges. For reform proposals: E. Jaffe, 'Kriegskostendeckung und Reichsfinanzreform', Archiv, 43 (May 1917), 711 ff.; E. Dahlin, French and German Public Opinion on Declared War Aims, 1914–1918 (Stanford, 1933), 71–2; Badulesco, Prélèvement, 33–9; C. W. Guillebaud, 'The Cost of the War to Germany', EJ 27 (June 1917), 270; Verein für Sozialpolitik, 156 (1919). For the War Tax and Law of 9 Apr. 1917: Reichsgesetzblatt, 1916, 561; 1917, 351; Lotz, Staatsfinanzwirtschaft, 60, 63, 72. For the 1918 debate: RT, 27 Feb. 1918, cccxi. 4192 (Stresemann); 28 Feb. 1918, 4256–7 (Roesicke); 1 Mar. 1918, 4289 (Vogtherr); 23 Apr. 1918, 4734–7 (Roedern).

of gold and the sale of securities. Since only one-third of the remaining 10 billion marks appears to have been covered by credits, the rest must have been financed by selling mark notes. This meant that by the end of the war Germany had a sizeable external floating debt which was likely to exert downward pressure on the value of the mark.[47]

Germany's precarious external financial position was not eased by the belated and ineffective attempts of the government to impose trade controls and exchange restrictions. A list of forbidden imports was published in February 1916; and in the following January a system of import licensing was formally introduced. Over the same period a system of exchange control was set up which, although originally designed simply to regulate the use of foreign exchange for imports, was extended in February 1917 with a view to countering the flight of capital from Germany. But these measures had little effect on the basic imbalance of German trade or on the activities of speculators.[48]

It was, therefore, remarkable that the exchange rate of the gold mark expressed in paper marks declined only from parity in August 1914 to 1.77 in November 1918.[49] This relatively slight fall was, however, due to a number of artificial and temporary influences which could not be expected to operate for long after the war. One of these was the Allied blockade, which postponed a violent deterioration of the trade balance by preventing large-scale imports at a time when there was an overwhelming demand for goods within Germany. Another was the hope of victory, which dissuaded Germans and neutrals from speculating against the mark until well into 1918. Finally there were the irresponsible delusions of the victors about Germany's underlying financial strength which encouraged the Belgian government to redeem at an excessively generous rate of exchange some six billion marks of German currency which were circulating in Belgium, Luxemburg, and Holland on the eve of the armistice. Defeat, revolution, the lifting of the blockade, and the predictable refusal of the German government to support the mark at its wartime value soon set the stage for violent currency depreciation.[50]

---

[47] Siney, 125; Rist, 181; Otto von Glasenapp (vice-president of the Reichsbank), 'Germany's Balance of Payments with Other Countries', MGCRE, 20 Apr. 1922, 22. Cf. Statistisches Reichsamt, Deutschlands Wirtschaftslage unter den Nachwirkungen des Weltkrieges (Berlin, 1923): cited in Schacht, Stabilization, 23.

[48] Rist, 190–5.

[49] Bresciani-Turroni, 441.

[50] For Belgium's mark purchases: S. Marks, Innocent Abroad: Belgium at the Paris Peace Conference of 1919 (Chapel Hill, 1981), 178–80. For a discussion of the impli-

The war of 1914–18 had brought Germany to the brink of economic collapse and bankruptcy. The deterioration of the economy was the result of the ruthless mobilization of domestic resources, which culminated in the Hindenburg Programme, and the severing of Germany's ties with the greater part of the world. Financial instability was caused, not by the technical measures which were taken to expand credit, but by the failure of the government to absorb the increased mark holdings and credit balances created both inside and outside Germany by war-induced overspending both at home and abroad. This omission was to a certain extent the result of the chronic fiscal weakness of the federal government and the inevitable deterioration of an already passive balance of trade during the war. Yet Germany's financial problems were, like those of the other belligerents, compounded by undue sensitivity to pressure from conservatives and men of property.

The excessive dependence on the German government on the good will of the domestic and foreign lending community was to have serious consequences after the war. When deprived of the indemnity illusion and confronted with the liquidity problems associated with the transition to a peacetime economy, the German economic élite did not hesitate to use the threat of domestic revolution and a Carthaginian peace as an excuse for ceasing to subscribe to government loans. To make matters worse Germany's external credit was so undermined that her chief source of foreign exchange came to be the purchase of mark notes by international speculators. The leaders of post-war Germany were forced back on those sources of internal and external revenue—taxation and trade—which had been neglected during the war. In attempting to exploit these they were seriously handicapped by the economic repercussions of the conflict; and they were frustrated by the inadequate federal fiscal machinery and the ineffective system of trade and exchange controls which had been bequeathed to them.

In their efforts to swell revenues and restore credit republican leaders were also hindered by the political legacy of the war. The decision of the discredited ruling élite to thrust political power into the hands of the Majority Socialists and Centrists in October 1918 did not usher in a period of political accord. Conservatives unashamedly capitalized on their new opposition status by denouncing the ensuing revolution

cations of German war finance: Bruce Kent, 'Der Preis des Kriegs: wie Deutschland für den Ersten Weltkrieg bezahlte', *in* B. Hüppauf (ed.), *Ansichten vom Krieg: vergleichende Studien zum Ersten Weltkrieg in Literatur und Gesellschaft* (Meisenheim/Glan, 1984), 231–9.

as an unnecessary aberration which had cost Germany both the war and the peace; and the radical left wing, increasingly frustrated by the stand-pat policies of the SPD, complained with equal force that the revolution had not proceeded far enough. This polarization did much to impede financial and economic recovery. Right-wingers continued to be vocal advocates of financial conservatism and devolution, and they vigorously opposed the radical centralizing measures introduced by the federal government in its efforts to achieve financial stability. They were, moreover, sufficiently powerful to obstruct fiscal measures of which they disapproved and to undermine unacceptable projects for restoring internal and external credit. The extreme left, on the other hand, while theoretically sympathetic to confiscatory measures which would strengthen the financial position of the federal government, in practice added to the government's problems by aggravating social unrest and pressuring it into increased welfare expenditure. Extremists of both complexions also did their best to compromise Germany's delicate financial relations with her erstwhile enemies. The agitation of the right for a campaign of patriotic resistance to the Versailles Treaty and the appeal of the left for an international uprising to overthrow international capitalism were to be a constant source of embarrassment to the German government as it struggled both to fulfil and to deflate the financial demands which Allied political leaders now concocted in order to appease the expectations of their electorates.

2

The Division of the Spoils

THE preliminary reparation demands of the Allies during the armistice period were indirectly responsible for prolonging the starvation of the German civilian population into the early months of 1919; and they contributed directly, if marginally, to the general economic and political dislocation of post-war Germany. Paradoxically, however, the surrealism of the sums which the victors mooted at the end of 1918 prevented the inauguration of a full scale reparation scheme for several years. Because they were unwilling to disappoint the hopes that had been aroused, the statesmen at the Paris Peace Conference of 1919 quickly became deadlocked over questions of assessment and distribution. A dispute between the British Empire, which registered a tactical claim for enormous general war costs, and France, which had an interest in a more restricted demand for purely physical reparation, was finally resolved at Germany's expense by a compromise agreement that the pensions and separation allowances of combatants and their dependants should be admitted as categories of damage. The reparation terms were also prefaced by a provocative assertion of Germany's war guilt, which was inserted only because British leaders had raised the cry of German responsibility for the war in order to justify their bid for war costs. Yet the task of fixing the bill which was actually to be presented to Germany was delegated to a future Reparation Commission, which was directed to take into account the debtor's capacity to pay as well as the claims of the creditors. The Reparation Chapter of the Versailles Treaty was not, therefore, an effective blueprint for long-term economic exploitation, despite its offensiveness to German opinion. Its most important concrete demand was for a preliminary payment of 20 billion gold marks (£1,000,000,000) by 1 May 1921. This was to consist of relatively simple transfers of property in ceded territories, war *matériel*, railway rolling stock, shipping, and agricultural implements and to a lesser extent, of goods from current output such as coal. The burden of these deliveries, some of which began during the period of the armistice, was increased by predictable distributive haggling among the victors: but its relative significance was also reduced by the delay in implementing the treaty and by the general dislocation and political polarization of the aftermath.

REPARATIONS UNDER THE ARMISTICE

The November 1918 armistice and the various conventions which prolonged it were more concerned with winding up the war than making peace. For this reason their economic clauses did not deal with the long-term question of reparations but with immediate problems such as the restoration of economic activity in the invaded territories and the provisioning of Germany. The implementation of these clauses brought to the surface a conflict of interests amongst the victors which was to inflate their subsequent paper claims against Germany. Yet, apart from depriving the half-starved German masses of food imports until the end of March 1919, Allied policies made only a peripheral contribution to the financial, economic, and political chaos of Germany in the early post-war months.

As we have seen, the preoccupation of France with obtaining prompt compensation for physical damage was responsible for Article XIX of the original armistice, which registered the general Allied claim for 'reparation of damage' and directed the freezing of German gold and foreign securities as a pledge for reparations. The British had also pressed on the eve of the armistice for the immediate surrender of the German merchant fleet, even if they quickly bowed to the American view that such a matter ought to be determined by the forthcoming peace conference. This Anglo-French importunity was to have sorry consequences for Germany when the question of reparation became linked with that of food imports early in 1919. The Allies had obliquely assumed responsibility for the German food supply in Article XXVI of the armistice, which stipulated that the wartime blockade of Germany would be prolonged: but the issue of provisioning had by the end of 1918 become entangled in a power-play between the Allied blockade authorities and Herbert Hoover, who, for a mixture of commercial and humanitarian reasons, was advocating the speedy resumption of American food exports to Europe. The deadlock appeared to have been broken after Hoover's appointment as chairman of an inter-Allied Supreme Council of Supply and Relief which was set up early in January; and Article 8 of the Treves (Trier) Convention of 16 January (which marked the second monthly renewal of the armistice) duly achieved a tentative marriage of British and American policy by directing that, 'in order to secure the provisioning of Germany and the rest of Europe', the German merchant fleet should 'for the duration of the armistice be placed under the control and flags of the Allied powers and the United States'. This arrangement, however, immediately ran into opposition from the French when the German government requested, as a quid pro quo, that it should be permitted to use some of its gold and foreign exchange reserves to pay for the food imported. Germany, Klotz declared to the Supreme War Council on 13 January, should not 'pay for food in preference to paying off debts incurred for the restoration and for the reparation of damage committed elsewhere'. The initial response of the council to the impasse was to direct that the imports should be financed by foreign credits. This was, however, unrealistic in view of the financial isolationism of Germany's major potential source of food, the United States. Although it was anxious to unload the current American pork surplus on Europe and fearful that hunger would drive the German people to political extremes, the Wilson administration was unwilling to court domestic criticism by lending money to Germany. The German government therefore refused to hand over the ships on the grounds that the Allies had not honoured Article XXVI; and it was only after an inhuman delay of two months that France, bowing to overwhelming Anglo-American pressure, agreed that Germany could use up to one billion francs (US$200,000,000) of its gold and foreign securities to buy food. This incident, which was vividly described in a memoir by Keynes, the British Treasury representative in the negotiations, was a foretaste of how Britain and France were to wrangle over the spoils while the United States sought vainly to resume business with an exhausted Europe without picking up the tabs for its reconstruction.[1]

The impact of the various reparation deliveries under the armistice can only be accurately gauged if the depressed and dislocated con-

[1] For texts of armistice of 11 Nov. 1918 and the Trèves Convention of 16 Jan. 1919: H. W. V. Temperley (ed.), *A History of the Peace Conference of Paris* (6 vols.; London, 1920–3), i. 459–80; *FRPPC* ii. 1–15. For the best account of Hoover and the politics of the blockade: Vincent, 'The Post-World War I Blockade', ch. 4. For the shipping debate: Supreme War Council, 13 Jan. 1919, *FRPPC* iii. 516, 522–3; 8 Mar. 1919, iv. 274–93. For the American pork surplus: ibid. ii. 713–15. For American reluctance to extend credit to Germany: Miller, *My Diary*, i. 82–3. See also J. M. Keynes, *Two Memoirs* (London, 1949), 42–62; Elcock, 'J. M. Keynes', 165–8. For Klotz's version of the dispute: Sénat, CAE, 13 Aug. 1919, 1836–8.

ditions of the early post-war years are appreciated. Despite a gradual upswing in 1920, Germany's output of key heavy industrial goods such as coal, pig iron, and crude steel was still well below its 1913 level within her new frontiers. The position was even more serious in agriculture, where a painfully slow recovery of livestock holdings and crop yields was interrupted by the disastrous rye harvest of 1920. German foreign trade was also very sluggish, despite an upsurge of imports after the lifting of the Allied blockade in July 1919 and a short-lived and unhealthy boom in the export of German capital equipment, which was induced by the depreciation of the mark later in the year. The short-term result was a massive trade deficit of 4.7 billion gold marks in 1919. Although 1920 saw the revival of more normal exports to Britain, France, and the United States, as well as to Germany's neutral wartime trading partners, the value of both exports and imports was still much lower than it had been in 1913.[2]

The cost of interest payments on the public debt, demobilization, pensions, food subsidies, and unemployment relief kept federal government expenditure at 8.6 billion gold marks for the budgetary year 1919–20, or more than double its 1913 level of 3.8 billions. Since revenues trailed well behind at 2.6 billions, the floating debt, in the absence of long-term public loans, increased from 49 billion paper marks at the end of the war to 113 billions in June 1920. This enormous expansion of credit in the public sector made possible, as it had during the war, an increased amount of lending by private credit institutions whose deposits had been swollen by the abnormal spending of the government. The supply of credit in the private sector was still supplemented, moreover, by the advances of the War Credit Offices, the value of which rose from 14 billion marks at the time of the armistice to 30 billion marks by the end of May 1920. A by-product of all these forms of credit creation was that the face value of Reichsbank notes and War Credit Vouchers in circulation grew from 28 to 64 billion marks in the period under review. The purchasing power released in the community helped the index of wholesale prices (1913 = 100) to rise from 234 in November 1918 to 1380 in June 1920.[3]

[2] See below, Appendix I for: coal, iron, and steel figures, Table A; livestock, Table B; crop yields, Table C; foreign trade, Table D. Available statistics of wages, cost of living, and employment reveal that the index of German national income (1913 = 100) was 80 in 1919 and 84 in 1920: Laursen and Pedersen, 75–84. For comment on German trade fluctuations: *The Economist*, 29 Nov. 1919, 983–4; *Monthly Bulletin of Statistics*, 2, No. 3, vi–vii.

[3] For budget figures: Bresciani-Turroni, 437. For floating debt: *Deutschlands Wirt-*

Price inflation was also boosted by the imbalance of Germany's external finances. Official figures for imports were underestimated because of the smuggling which occurred through the 'hole in the west' created by Allied occupied territory; and export figures were exaggerated by the inclusion of the value of reparation deliveries. Germany's negligible invisible foreign earnings were, moreover, outweighed by her annual expenditure of 0.75 billion gold marks on the interest and amortization of post-war credits. Her total deficit on both visible and invisible account between January 1919 and May 1920 was, therefore, far greater than the official visible trade deficit of approximately 5 billion gold marks in this period. Efforts to mitigate the situation were hampered by the delay in imposing import and export controls in the occupied regions and, more importantly, by the government's inability to obtain foreign financial assistance, apart from stop-gap credits to facilitate imports of food and raw materials and arrangements whereby raw materials were supplied by foreigners in return for an interest in German businesses or a right to the finished goods produced by them. There was, as a result, an increase in Germany's external obligations in the form of either bank or book credits or mark notes held by foreigners. By August 1920 this foreign floating debt, which had been 6 billion paper marks at the end of the war, had increased to about 50 billions. It was hardly surprising that between November 1918 and June 1920 the dollar rate of the mark rose from 7 to 37, after having peaked temporarily at 100 in the preceding February.[4]

In view of the powerful internal and external monetary influences

schaft, Währung und Finanzen (Berlin, 1924), 29. For credit expansion: J.S. Davis, 'Recent Economic and Financial Progress in Germany', RES 3 (1921), 148; Stucken, 35. For wholesale prices: Bresciani-Turroni, 442.

[4] For balance of payments: Glasenapp, 'Germany's Balance of Payments', 22. Imports were also undervalued because of the inflexibility of official methods of valuation in periods of rapid depreciation of the mark. Monthly Bulletin of Statistics, 2, No. 2, v; No. 3, vii. On controls: General Report on the Industrial and Economic Situation in Germany in December 1920, ..., House of Commons Papers, Cmd. 1114, 1921, xxxi. 589, at 8–9; Stuart to Curzon, 17 Apr. 1920, DBFP I, ix. 416–18. Note German and British protests about the absence thereof: Gothein (DDP), 1 Oct. 1919, NV cccxxix. 2797–9; Erzberger, 2800–3; Pohlmann (DDP), 27 Feb. 1920, cccxxxii. 4550; Kilmarnock to Curzon, 31 Jan. 1920, DBFP I, ix. 27; Stuart to Waterlow, 4 Feb. 1920, ibid. 36–8. On credits: Stuart to Curzon, 25 Feb. 1920, DBFP I, ix. 96; Rist, 205. On foreign participation in German firms: General Report on ... Germany in December 1920, 6. For external floating debt figures: League of Nations, International Financial Conference, Paper No. III (rev. edn., London, 1921), 53–7. For the dollar rate: Die Entwicklung der Reparationsfrage (Berlin, 1924), 6, 13.

which were at work, it is perhaps superfluous to remark that the role of wages was entirely secondary in the inflationary process of this period. Real wages had fallen well below their 1913 level during the war except in the munitions industries. Although they recovered somewhat in 1919 as a result of the so-called Labour Magna Carta concluded on 15 November 1918 between employer and employee organizations, they never attained their former level and tended to lag behind prices in times of rapid depreciation. This lag was somewhat offset by the rise in employment which accompanied any depreciation-induced upsurge of industrial activity: but the size of the national wages bill was never a precipitating factor in the inflationary cycle.[5]

At first sight the stipulation of Article VII of the November armistice that Germany should surrender 5,000 of her 34,000 locomotives and 150,000 of her 780,000 goods wagons would appear to have made a significant contribution to this economic and financial chaos. But the efficiency of the German railway system was reduced far more by the disrepair into which all rolling stock had fallen during the war and the chronic maintenance lags of the aftermath. In August 1919 it was asserted in the National Assembly that almost half of Germany's locomotives were out of order as compared with 19 per cent in 1913 and 34 per cent in 1918. The post-war shortage of railway equipment was either ascribed solely to 'the human and material wear and tear caused by the war' or attributed jointly to the armistice deliveries and the decreased efficiency of equipment and personnel. Apart from poor maintenance, the reasons most commonly advanced for the latter were industrial unrest, the eight hour day, seasonal bottlenecks, and the lack of coal. In February 1920, Rudolf Oeser, the Federal Transport Minister, went so far as to predict that the restoration to Germany of the rolling stock delivered under the armistice would only temporarily relieve the current railway crisis, which was due chiefly to lagging maintenance.[6]

Care has to be exercised for somewhat different reasons in estimating

[5] Bresciani-Turroni, 300–8, 450 (Table XI).

[6] For text of armistice see above, n. 1. For figures: Mumm (DNVP), 15 Aug. 1919, NV cccxxix. 2500. Cf. Dr Weirauch, 'Railway Transportation in Germany', Annals, 92 (Nov. 1920), 88. Percentages for 1913 and 1918 derived from A. Sarter, Die deutschen Eisenbahnen im Kriege (Stuttgart, 1930), 163–5, 287. For comment: Hue (SPD), 15 Aug. 1919, NV cccxxix. 2479; Hugenberg (DNVP), 2467; Schirmer (Zentrum), 25 Oct. 1919, cccxxx. 3430; Deglerk, 17 Mar. 1921, RT cccxlviii. 3120. For Oeser's statement: FZ, 18 Feb. 1920, No. 130, 1. Cf. Francke, 405; Davis, 'Recent ... Progress in Germany', 159–60; Ministerialrat von Völcker, 'German Transport and Communication', Annals, 92 (Nov. 1920), 81–2; Report on Industrial and Commercial Conditions in Germany at

the impact of deliveries of merchant shipping. The Trèves Convention and Annexe III of the Reparation Chapter of the treaty directed that Germany should surrender (1) all her merchant ships of over 1,600 tons, (2) half of those weighing between 1,000 and 1,600 tons, and (3) a quarter of her steam trawlers and other fishing boats. In fulfilment of these provisions 2.6 million tons of shipping was eventually delivered. A large part of this (1.8 million tons) was handed over in 1919, and another 400,000 tons found its way to the Allies before May 1921. As a result of these deliveries and the loss of about 2.7 million tons during the war, the German merchant fleet was reduced from its pre-war size of over 5 million tons to about 500,000 tons at the end of 1919. Despite the gloomy predictions of the German government, the immediate impact of the deliveries was cushioned because the vessels were used for the duration of the armistice to transport food and raw materials to Germany, and their earnings were not appropriated by the Allies until after the treaty came into force in January 1920. By the end of 1919, moreover, the larger German shipping companies such as HAPAG and Norddeutscher Lloyd had begun to undertake agencies for lines running their former fleets. A year later the major lines had, by means of such arrangements and by chartering, resumed most of their pre-war services. The general dislocation of post-war trade and the recession of 1920 further reduced the short-term economic and financial significance of shipping deliveries. The long-term effect of replacing capital goods such as rolling stock and shipping was more serious, and will be discussed later.[7]

Deliveries of agricultural equipment must also be set in the context of the general derangement of the period. The persistence of poor crops in the early post-war years was partly due to the continuation of the wartime shortages of phosphates. According to a contemporary German agricultural expert, only 139,000 of an estimated demand of 500,000 tons of phosphate was satisfied in the year 1919–20. The low price of agricultural produce was also important, since it discouraged farmers from purchasing comparatively expensive fertilizers and agri-

the Close of the Year 1919, House of Commons Papers, 1920, xliii, Cmd. 752, 257, at 16.

[7] For text of Trèves Convention, see above, n. 1. For text of Annexe III: Temperley, iii. 225–7. For progress of deliveries: RC, *Report on the Work of the Reparation Commission from 1920 to 1922* (London, 1923) (henceforward RC v), Appendix XVIII, 225–6. For effects: *Report on ... Conditions in Germany ... 1919*, 22; W. Cuno, 'The Present Position and Prospects of the German Mercantile Marine', *MGCRE*, 18 May 1922, 87–8; *The Economist*, 18 Dec. 1920, 1081. See below, ch. 5 n. 1 and text thereat.

cultural machinery for the purpose of improving their land. Other inhibiting influences were the shortage of labour and the dearth of coal, which was vital to numerous phases of agricultural activity. The deliveries which were made under Article 3 of the Trèves Convention and Article 238 of the Treaty were, therefore, not of very great consequence. The loss of the 2,500 machines, 2,000 wagons, and 200,000 tools which were handed over may have disrupted agricultural activity when, early in 1919, deliveries consisted of the actual articles which had been removed from occupied territories during the war, But, according to the Reparation Commission, short-term dislocation was substantially reduced by the action of the French government in 'speedily compounding for the restitution of identified material by the delivery of new material'.[8]

The impact of the armistice deliveries on German politics is equally hard to unravel. Despite the unanimous condemnation of the original armistice by all political parties in November 1918,[9] the domestic tensions induced by the war and the revolution were such that animosity towards the victors was soon submerged in partisan manœuvring and recrimination. It has recently been pointed out that the work which was done by the German Foreign Office and Treasury in the early months of 1919 to prepare for the financial and economic peace negotiations was undertaken largely in order to prevent the more radical Economics Ministry from shaping the post-war German economy along collective lines. The primacy of domestic politics was also apparent during the debate on the armistice terms in the newly convened National Assembly in February 1919. Albert Vögler, a conservative industrialist who was managing director of the German-

[8] For the state of agriculture: Dr Hüber, 'Food Conditions and Agricultural Production', Annals, 92 (Nov. 1920), 135; Davis, 'Recent . . . Progress in Germany', 155; Report on . . . Conditions in Germany . . . 1919, 13. For text of Trèves Convention: see above, n. 1. For text of Article 238: Temperley, iii. 216–17. For progress of deliveries: RC v. 68; Appendix X, 204. The delivery of the 370,000 head of livestock of various descriptions prescribed by Para. 6 of Annexe IV of the Reparation Chapter did not begin until Mar. 1920, and proceeded quite slowly thereafter. Since the number of animals delivered did not amount to as much as 2% of total German holdings except in the case of cattle, the economic impact cannot have been very great. The number of German livestock was far more heavily influenced by the availability of fodder. RC, Statement of Germany's Obligations under the Heading of Reparations, etc., at 30 April 1922 (London, 1922) (henceforward RC i), 8; v. 133; Davis, 'Recent . . . Progress in Germany', 154.

[9] Even Freiheit, the organ of the Independent Socialists, which soon became highly critical of the exploitation of foreign affairs by the right wing, condemned the armistice terms. Die Freiheit, 15 Nov. 1918, No. 1, 2; 20 Nov. 1918, No. 10, 1. Cf. FZ, 11 Nov. 1918, No. 313, 1; 12 Nov. 1918, No. 314, 2 (citations).

Luxemburg Mining Company, part of the industrial empire of Hugo Stinnes, confronted Matthias Erzberger, the Centre Party spokesman who represented the radical non-socialist supporters of the revolution of November 1918, over his dealings with the Allies. As leader of the German Armistice Commission, Erzberger had, Vögler alleged, 'lost the peace' and crippled the economy by excluding the representatives of German industry from the negotiations. The republican majority and its press retorted by accusing Vögler of attempting to shift the onus for Germany's plight away from the old regime and onto the shoulders of the new government. Despite mounting distrust of Allied intentions, partisan recrimination of this sort was to dominate the debate on German foreign policy for a considerable time to come.[10]

Familiar conservative pressures were at work when the SPD Chancellor, Philipp Scheidemann, and the Democratic Party (DDP) Finance Minister, Eugen Schiffer, presented the National Assembly with a financial programme which referred only in general terms to the need for taxes on incomes, war profits, and property to reduce the public debt. Apart from lack of legislative time and the delay in drafting the new constitution which was to provide the federal government with increased fiscal power, the major reason for the failure of specific tax proposals to emerge during these months was continuing obstruction by right-wingers and states-righters. The inflationist ideas of 'nominalist' monetary theorists such as Friedrich Bendixen, Karl Elster, and Rudolf Dalberg, who denied any relationship between the quantity and the value of money, also appeared to have been vindicated by the relative stability of the mark during the war despite massive govern-

[10] For bureaucratic politics: P. Krüger, *Deutschland und die Reparationen 1918/19* (Stuttgart, 1973), 68–70, 79–80; id., 'Die Rolle der Banken und der Industrie in den deutschen reparationspolitischen Entscheidungen nach dem Ersten Weltkrieg', in H. Mommsen *et al.* (edd.), *Industrielles System und politische Entwicklung in der Weimarer Republik* (Düsseldorf, 1974), 568–82. For the ideas of Wichard von Moellendorf, Under-Secretary of State of the Economics Ministry: G. D. Feldman, *Iron and Steel in the German Inflation, 1916–1923* (Princeton, 1977), 100–8; D. E. Barclay, 'A Prussian Socialism? Wichard von Moellendorf and the Dilemma of Economic Planning in Germany, 1918–19', *CEH* 11 (1978), 50–82; id., 'The Insider as Outsider: Rudolf Wissell's Critique of Social Democratic Economic Policies, 1919 to 1920', in G. D. Feldman *et al.* (edd.), *Die Anpassung an Inflation* (Berlin, 1986), at 453–6. For the political debate: Vögler (DVP), 18 Feb. 1919, *NV* cccxxvi. 132; Erzberger, 142; Gröber (Zentrum), 148. The dispute over the conduct of the armistice negotiations between Erzberger and the north-western group of the Verein Deutscher Eisen- und Stahlindustrieller is summarized in: Memo of Jan. 1919, Nachlass Stresemann, ccii, Polit. Akten 1919/I. Cf. Stresemann to Vögler, 26 Feb. 1919, ibid.; *FZ*, 19 Feb. 1919, No. 135, 1. For distrust of Allies: Schiffer (DDP), 15 Feb. 1919, *NV* cccxxvi. 97; 9 Apr. 1919, cccxxvii. 910–11; Scheidemann (SPD), 26 Mar. 1919, 807–9.

ment expenditure and private credit expansion. More importantly, they were taken up by German industry, which saw inflation as the best means of making the transition from the wartime to the peacetime economy. The prevalence of these views in a financial hierarchy which had been remarkably unaffected by the revolution of 1918 prevented the discount rate of the Reichsbank from being raised above 5 per cent until July 1922. Nor could a radical financial policy have been expected, in the short term, from the first two Finance Ministers of the Weimar Republic, Eugen Schiffer and Bernhard Dernburg. The former, who held office from November 1918 to April 1919, had been on the right wing of the old National Liberal Party; and his successor, who served until he resigned in protest against the Versailles Treaty in June, was a prominent banker-politician who had been Secretary of State for the Colonies from 1907 to 1910. The presentation of the draft peace terms obviously precluded any coherent attempt at financial reform in May and June 1919. Yet the policies of these men in the first half of 1919 were, like those of their Allied counterparts, largely a response to pressure from right-wing vested interests.[11]

German external financial policy was just as ineffectual. An Order of 21 November 1918 and further measures in January and March 1919 sought to control the consignment of German securities abroad and to widen the government's wartime powers of appropriating German-owned foreign securities. Yet from the end of 1918 individuals who wished to export capital or to retain foreign bills managed to find ways and means of doing so, partly because of the government's inability to control foreign exchange transactions in the occupied territories. In July 1919, moreover, all restrictions on imports and on

[11] For financial programme: Scheidemann, 13 Feb. 1919, NV cccxxvi. 45; Schiffer, Memo of 12 Mar. 1919, ibid. cccxxxv, Annexe 158. Cf. budgetary debates: ibid. 27 Mar. 1919, cccxxvii. 827–62; Schiffer, 9 Apr. 1919, 904–12. On the time factor: Schiffer, 8 July 1919, ibid. 1395. On the increased federal fiscal power conferred by Articles 8 and 80–5 of the draft constitution: Preuss, 24 Feb. 1919, ibid. cccxxvii. 287. Cf. Schiffer, 9 Apr. 1919, cccxxvii. 910–11. For fiscal conservatism within the cabinet: Kabinettssitzung 15 Mar. 1919, Akten der Reichskanzlei: Weimarer Republik. Das Kabinett Scheidemann, 13. Februar bis 20. Juni 1919, ed. H. Schulze (Boppard-on-Rhine, 1971), 49–50, 56–9. For state opposition to increased federal tax power: A. Amt to Reichs-kanzlei, 4 Apr. 1919, ibid. 138–40; Kabinettssitzungen 2, 6 May 1919, ibid. 256 n. 10; 266. Cf. conservative and state opposition to a capital levy: Keil (SPD), 8 July 1919, NV cccxxvii. 1387; Stresemann to Bund der Industriellen, 30 Jan. 1919, Nachlass, cxiv, Industrie-Organisationen, 1916–1919; Badulesco, Prélèvement, 277; K. Epstein, Matthias Erzberger and the Dilemma of German Democracy (Princeton, 1959), 338. On the influence of nominalist theory: Schiffer, 15 Feb. 1919, NV cccxxvi. 91, 94; Ellis, 40–1, 180; Bresciani-Turroni, 42–3; H. Schacht, 'The Discount Policy of the Reichsbank', MGCRE, 7 Dec. 1922, 689–90.

the export of capital were removed with the lifting of the Allied blockade. German attitudes were certainly affected by the armistice terms and apprehension about the coming peace. But the government's authority had been undermined most of all by defeat, which had removed the motive for financial patriotism; by social and political unrest, which made the propertied classes afraid that their wealth would be confiscated; and by the falling value of the mark, which further encouraged them to send their assets abroad. A government which was committed to dismantling wartime controls was in no position to counter such behaviour on the part of the well-to-do.[12]

REPARATIONS AT THE PARIS PEACE CONFERENCE

While there was a haphazard element about the armistice terms, the Reparation Chapter of the Versailles Treaty faithfully mirrored the irresponsibility of all the peacemakers. Even the Americans, who made no reparation claims at Paris, were by no means above reproach. This was not due to any lack of competence amongst the reparation experts of the United States financial delegation. Vance McCormick, a newspaper publisher who had been the Democratic Party's campaign manager for the 1916 presidential elections, was the chairman of the United States War Trade Board. Bernard M. Baruch, who had entered public life after having made, lost, and recouped several fortunes on the New York stock exchange, was chairman of the War Industries Board and a member of the Allied Supreme Economic Council. Norman H. Davis, another affluent refugee from the world of business, where he was head of the Trust Company of Cuba from 1905 to 1917, had served as a Treasury consultant on foreign loans in 1917 and as a personal emissary of the President in 1918. Thomas W. Lamont, a partner of J. P. Morgan and Company since 1911 and proprietor of

---

[12] For measures: Hampe (DNVP), 16 Aug. 1919, *NV* cccxxix. 2507. See also *Reichsgesetzblatt*, 1918, 1325; Thelwall, *General Report on ... Germany in December 1920*, 8. No attempt was made to control either the price or the volume of exports until Dec. 1919. On effects: F. Urbig, 'The Practicability of Exchange Control', *MGCRE*, 20 Apr. 1922, 30; Schiffer, 8 July 1919, *NV* cccxxvii. 1395–6. For pressure to remove export controls in the early post-war period: G. D. Feldman, 'Economic and Social Problems of the German Demobilization, 1918–19', *JMH* 47 (1975), 9–11. For a complaint by Dernburg about the effect of the armistice terms: Ausführungen des Reichsfinanzministers ... über die finanzielle Leistungsfähigkeit des Reichs, 26 Apr. 1919, *Das Kabinett Scheidemann*, 233–43 at 241–3.

the *New York Evening Post* since 1918, had organized American loans to Britain and France before the entry of the United States into the war, and was the Treasury representative on the Peace Delegation. Finally, there was the 31-year-old New York international lawyer, John Foster Dulles, who had been McCormick's assistant in 1918 and acted as the legal adviser, draftsman, and spokesman of the financial delegation. Despite its impressive membership this group was to be hamstrung by the politically motivated refusal of the United States government to give any financial backing to co-operative European reconstruction and its insistence on the repayment of Allied war debts. This more than cancelled out the 'moral advantage' which Wilson subsequently alleged the United States had gained by not claiming reparations. The praiseworthiness of this restraint was in any case very much reduced by the relatively small amount of American civilian war damage and by the manageable size of the United States war debt. It is also worth recording that the United States had seized twice as many German merchant ships as she herself had lost, and had sequestrated German property in North America to the value of $425,000,000.[13]

The reparation experts of France and Britain laid no claim to moral detachment: but they were torn by conflicting impulses. The readiness of the French Finance Minister, Louis-Lucien Klotz, to arouse false reparation hopes in order to divert attention from France's budgetary plight was, if anything, increased by the storm of right-wing protest which greeted his short-lived proposal for a tax on capital in February 1919. The Napoleonic strategy of subjecting the Rhineland to military occupation pending Germany's fulfilment of virtually impossible

---

[13] For Wilson's claim: Senate Committee on Foreign Relations, 19 Aug. 1919, 66th Congress, 1st Session, Sen. Doct. 76, 9. Cf. Dulles in P. M. Burnett, *Reparation at the Paris Peace Conference* (2 vols.; New York, 1940), Foreword, vi. According to an American estimate of May 1919 the war-induced public debt and damage of the US amounted to 11.5% of her national wealth in 1919. The corresponding figure for France was 94.1% and for Britain 59.4%. See 'Comparison of the Post-War Financial Situation of the Principal Allied Nations', May 1919, Burnett, i. 1130–4. On shipping: Memo from Robinson to House regarding the Shipping Controversy and Agreement, 28 May 1919, ibid. ii. 49–51; G. A. R. Riddell, *Lord Riddell's Intimate Diary of the Peace Conference and After, 1918–1923* (London, 1933), 60. On sequestrated German property: A. A. Young, Tentative Valuation of Germany's Immediately Transferable Assets, n.d., Burnett, i. 525. The interest of American businessmen in the revival of trade with Germany, which had obtained 40% of her imports from the US in 1913, was a further reason for American reluctance to see Germany economically crushed or, worse still, driven into Bolshevism. See P. D. Cravath, Preliminary Suggestions regarding Indemnities, 12 Dec. 1918, ibid. i. 460; *FRPPC* ii. 559.

financial obligations also had its attractions for Clemenceau, especially after Marshal Foch's proposal for a French Rhine frontier had been rejected out of hand by Britain and the United States in March 1919. Yet despite the continuing clamour of sections of the French press for *réparation intégrale* (full war costs) in March and April, the representatives of France were kept in check by their distributive preoccupations. Albert Lebrun, the future President of the Republic, who was Minister for the Liberated Regions, and the industrialist-administrator Louis Loucheur, who was Minister for Reconstruction in 1919, ultimately opted to safeguard France's share of reparations by asserting as far as possible the priority of physical damage over general war costs. Because of this French restraint, the persistent tactical pressure of the British Empire for wider war costs was crucial in swelling the reparation bill presented to Germany. A desire to inflate the demands of Britain and her dominions at the expense of the continental victors appears to have encouraged Lloyd George to ignore the scepticism of the Imperial War Cabinet, the Treasury, and the Board of Trade about indemnities and to appoint well-known extremists such as Hughes and Cunliffe, not to mention Lord Sumner, an outspoken Germanophobe, to present the British reparation case at Paris. The Prime Minister's readiness to unleash such men was increased by Leo Amery, a Secretary of the War Cabinet who, in a barrage of letters and memoranda late in 1918, urged that, 'whatever the amount Germany does pay, we should get our fair share'. The resulting demand for costs in excess of physical damage in the shape of pensions and separation allowances, and the assertion of German war guilt with which it was linked, were to be the main reasons for the financial impossibility of the peace treaty and its moral unacceptability to Germany.[14]

British distributive concerns were evident well before the formal

[14] For the French press reaction to the Klotz proposal and to the negotiations of Mar. 1919: Miquel, *La Paix de Versailles*, 433–60. For the effect of the rejection of the Foch proposal for a French frontier on the Rhine: J. C. King, *Foch versus Clemenceau: France and German Dismemberment, 1918–1919* (Harvard, 1960), 44–8; J. Bariéty, *Les Relations franco-allemandes après la première guerre mondiale* (Paris, 1977), 62. For Hughes and Cunliffe: see ch. 1 nn. 25 and 29 and text thereat. For the scepticism of the Imperial War Cabinet: IWC, 46, 24 Dec. 1918, Min. 3, 16–17, CAB 23/42. For the isolation of Keynes, the Treasury's representative at Paris: R. F. Harrod, *The Life of John Maynard Keynes* (London, 1951), 235–40. Sumner, an eminent commercial lawyer, was a Lord of Appeal in Ordinary. For his Germanophobia: P. Mantoux, *Paris Peace Conference 1919: Proceedings of the Council of Four, March 24–April 18* (Geneva, 1964), 16. L. C. M. S. Amery (1873–1955), a tariff-reformer Unionist MP, was on the threshold of his long career as an imperial statesman. See Amery to Smuts, 26 Dec. 1918,

opening of the peace negotiations. On 30 December 1918 Lloyd George informed the Imperial War Cabinet that in preliminary discussions between heads of state he found Wilson more unyielding on reparations than on any other question. 'The utmost concession he seemed inclined to make', the Prime Minister reported, 'was that the claims for pure reparations should be tabled first, and that then other claims might possibly be considered afterwards.' Although Lloyd George had protested that this 'practically ruled the British Empire out in spite of the enormous burdens it had borne, and that France and Belgium, who had borne a lesser burden, would practically get everything', he had 'failed to make any impression on the President'. Another skirmish occurred a few weeks later when Lloyd George, acting on the decision of the inter-Allied conference at London early in December 1918, proposed that a commission be appointed to 'examine and report on the question of the amount of the sum for reparations and indemnity which the enemy countries should pay'. Wilson objected immediately to the use of the word 'indemnity'. 'The word reparation', he said, 'would meet the case. Bodies of working people all over the world had protested against indemnities, and he thought the expression reparations would be sufficiently inclusive.' Although Lloyd George deferred formally to the President's opinion, he only did so on the condition that the word 'reparation' was 'taken at its widest terms'.[15]

Efforts, particularly on the part of the British Empire, to widen the scope of reparations had an important effect on the discussion of the legal basis of Allied demands which began immediately after the Commission on the Reparation of Damage had been set up by the plenary session of the Peace Conference on 25 January. It was no accident that W. M. Hughes, the Australian leader of the British reparation team at Paris, whose country's vested interest in a swollen reparation bill has already been noticed, was vociferous in his efforts on the eve of the conference to saddle not only Germany's leaders but also the German people with the responsibility for the war. 'The Kaiser may have led Germany', he declared in London on 9 January, 'but she followed not only willingly, but eagerly. Upon the shoulders of all

W. K. Hancock and J. van der Poel (edd.), *Selections from the Smuts Papers* (4 vols.; Cambridge, 1966), iv. 33–4; Amery to Lloyd George, 24 Dec. 1918, Lloyd George Papers, F/2/1/32; Amery to Bonar Law, 26 Dec. 1918, PRO T 172/905.

[15] IWC, 47, 30 Dec. 1918, 5, CAB 23/42; Notes of a Conversation ..., 22 Jan. 1919, *FRPPC* iii. 682. For Colonel House's earlier objection to 'indemnity': Notes of an Allied Conversation ..., 2 Dec. 1918, IC 98, 1–4, CAB 28/5; *FRPPC* i. 340–2. See above, ch. 1 n. 30 and text thereat.

classes and all sections lies the guilt. They were drunk with bestial passion, with the hope of world conquest—Junker, merchant, and workman, all hoped to share in the loot. Upon the German nation, then, rests the responsibility for the war, and she must pay the penalty of her crime.' This rhetoric made Hughes well qualified to emerge on 10 February as the spokesman of the members of the Commission on Reparation who wished to establish a legal link between German 'aggression', in the widest sense of the term, and the 'absolute right' of the victors 'to demand the whole cost of the war'. Such legal sophistry was not acceptable to the American delegation, whose spokesman, Dulles, insisted that, however much the victors agreed about 'the enormity of the enemy's crime', the only legal basis for reparations was the pre-armistice agreements between the Allies and Germany. 'The Associated Governments were confronted not by a blank page', he declared, 'but by one covered with writing, to which were appended the signatures of President Wilson, Mr Orlando, Mr Lloyd George, and Mr Clemenceau.' In reply to Lord Sumner's rejoinder that the pre-armistice agreements were not binding, but merely furnished 'bases of discussion', Dulles referred to a German submission to the same effect on 4 October 1918. This, he said, had been rejected by Wilson, and the Germans had been forced to concede that there would be discussion only about the 'practical details of the application' of the agreement. Notwithstanding the arguments of Dulles and the temporary suspension of the debate pending a ruling by the Allied Supreme Council on the meaning of the word 'aggression' in the Lansing Note of 5 November 1918, the question of war guilt was bound to remain alive as long as the British Empire pressed for the payment of general war costs in addition to physical reparation. Nor was the cause of moderation likely to be advanced by the concentration of the commission from now onwards on the burning question of distribution.[16]

Although continuing to affirm Germany's theoretical liability for all

[16] For Hughes: *The Times*, 10 Jan, 1919, 6. For the creation of the commission: *FRPPC* iii. 176 ff. On 'principles of reparation' see Memorandum on Principles of Reparation for Damage Presented by the French Delegation, in Plenary Commission, Minutes (henceforward PC), 1, 3 Feb. 1919, Burnett, ii. 283–4. For minutes of the debate: PC, 4, 10 Feb. 1919 (Hughes); 5, 13 Feb. 1919 (Dulles, Sumner); 6, 14 Feb. 1919 (Dulles); 10, 24 Feb. 1919, ibid. 294–7, 309–12, 317–23, 339–40. For texts of the speeches of Hughes, Sumner, and Dulles: ibid. i. 553–7, 564–75. For the German suggestion of 4 Oct., Wilson's refusal of 8 Oct., and German compliance on 14 Oct. 1918: *FR*, 1918, Suppl. 1, i. 337–8, 343, 357–8. For the Lansing Note: see above, ch. 1 nn. 10 and 21 and text thereat. For the eventual resolution of the war guilt question: see below, n. 23 and text thereat.

the damage occasioned by the war, the French now intensified their somewhat forlorn agitation for the pooling of war costs until the United States Treasury curtly threatened early in March to cease granting credits to any Allied government making such proposals. Both France and Belgium were also well aware that, in the absence of an agreement over priorities, a general Allied claim for non-physical reparation would work to their detriment. As van den Heuvel of Belgium pointed out on 15 February, 'the Great Powers might weigh down Germany's debt with huge war costs'. A French memorandum therefore stressed the need to establish an order of priority for the distribution of reparations which gave precedence to the repair of material damage. The continental Allies were more than matched by Lloyd George. On 19 February he informed the British War Cabinet that the French 'would not press for indemnity, inasmuch as their bill for direct war damage would be made up to 4,000,000,000 l., or any figure they cared to name, and it would be very difficult to dispute their claim'. The Belgians, he added, were taking the same line. For this reason he had instructed Hughes to persist with the British claim for an indemnity and to resist the Franco-Belgian demand that reparation should have priority. A week later Hughes, Cunliffe, and Sumner were recalled from Paris to attend a meeting of the War Cabinet at which they were specially briefed along these lines.[17]

This manœuvring did not augur well for the work of the Sub-Committees into which the Commission on Reparation resolved itself late in February. The First Sub-Committee (Valuation of Damage) was so paralysed by a tactical dispute over admissible categories of damage that it could do no more than compile a list of everything for which Germany might conceivably be liable. Nor was it able to attach a provisional value to reparation claims, partly because of the genuine difficulty of making a rapid estimate, but also because of the distaste of some of its members for figures which might disappoint inflated

[17] On the American reaction to the pooling of war costs: Klotz, Sénat, CAE, 13 Aug. 1919, 1816–20; Trachtenberg, 'Reparation at the Paris Peace Conference', 29–30. See above, ch. 1 n. 32. For Franco-Belgian policy on priority: PC, 7, 15 Feb. 1919, Burnett, ii. 325–6; French Memorandum Regarding Priority, n.d., ibid. i. 637–46. For a report by Klotz on French tactics: Sénat, CAE, 27 Feb. 1919, 1707–8, 1762. Cf. the approving summary by *Le Temps* of Klotz's financial programme which began: '1. Réclamer à l'ennemi l'intégralité de sa dette; obtenir pour certaines créances, en raison de leur qualité, un rang privilégié ...', *Le Temps*, 20 Feb. 1919, 1. Cf. 1 Mar. 1919, 1; 9 Mar. 1919, 1. See also G. B. Noble, *Policies and Opinions at Paris* (New York, 1968, reprint), 194–6; Tardieu, 292. For British policy: War Cabinet Minutes, 534, 19 Feb. 1919; 536, 26 Feb. 1919, CAB 23/8.

expectations. As P. M. Burnett has suggested, the reticence of the French and Belgian delegates may have been increased by their growing desire to limit reparations to the making good of physical damage. An electorate which had been schooled to think a few months earlier in sums of 300–400 billion francs (£12–16 billion sterling) was unlikely to react favourably to figures in the region of 60–100 billion francs, which was the estimated cost of direct civilian damage in France. On the other hand, the British delegation, which persisted with its enormous demand for total war costs, had no qualms about supporting the American contention that at least provisional figures for reparation claims should be named.[18]

In the Second Sub-Committee (Germany's Capacity to Pay) only the British government's tactical interest in an inflated reparation bill and its reluctance to gainsay the promises of the previous December can explain the figures of Cunliffe, who doubled the sanguine estimate of Germany's financial capacity made by T. W. Lamont. Louis Loucheur was capable of taking a more realistic view because of his calculation that France would get the lion's share of a restricted claim for pure reparation. Yet even he was ultimately unwilling to incur domestic unpopularity by committing himself to a viable figure. It would be unwise to assign too much importance to the moderate recommendation presented on 15 March by the American financial expert Norman Davis on behalf of an *ad hoc* committee of three (consisting of himself, Loucheur, and Montagu), which had been set up to make an estimate of Germany's capacity for the American, British, and French heads of state. Although Loucheur acquiesced, and almost certainly believed in his colleagues' finding that Germany could not pay more than $30 billion, he was prepared to testify ten days later to the Council of Four that her total capacity was between a minimum of $30 billion and a maximum of $50 billion, and that it would not be 'absurd' to believe that she could afford the latter figure. The extravagance of British estimates, and the apparent reluctance of French leaders to lag too far behind them, made it impossible for the Second Sub-Committee to reach agreement. It therefore confined itself to recommending that Germany should make a preliminary payment of $5 billion (£1 billion, or 20 billion gold marks) and relinquished the

---

[18] For First Sub-Committee: Minutes, 24 Mar. 1919, Annexe I (categories of damage); 24 Feb. 1919 (British attitude to figures), Burnett, ii. 529–54, 385–6. For Burnett's comment: ibid. i. 33–4.

responsibility for deciding her long-term capacity to a future inter-Allied Commission.[19]

The heads of state of the four major Allies were unable to make any more headway when they began a series of special discussions on 24 March. At the first meeting of the so-called Council of Four Lloyd George stressed, in one of his periodic bouts of statesmanship, the need for a quick decision on the related issues of Germany's capacity to pay and distribution. 'The experts', he declared, 'will never find a solution if we do not make up our minds together and face the risks of our decisions.' Yet, within two days, Allied leaders found themselves evading the issue of Germany's capacity. On 26 March Lloyd George, who had been alarmed by Bela Kun's seizure of power in Budapest and had just circulated his apprehensive Fontainebleau Memorandum appealing for a moderate peace settlement, warned that the harsh reparation terms which had been proposed that day by Loucheur might provoke the Germans to refuse to sign the treaty and 'ally themselves with the Bolsheviks'. Clemenceau agreed that it would be unwise to kill the goose that laid the golden egg: but, because of his desire to placate French public opinion, he suggested that the best solution would be for the treaty merely to stipulate maximum and minimum annuities and to leave the assessment of Germany's total liability to a future commission. The latter idea, which was embodied in a formal proposal by Klotz on 28 March, was immediately opposed by Wilson on the grounds that it was tantamount to a demand for an 'unlimited credit' from Germany. Yet it was gratefully received by Lloyd George as a means of postponing the politically embarrassing decision he had so recently advocated.[20]

In the mean time the battle over the division of the spoils had been joined. On the afternoon of 26 March Lloyd George sought to enlarge Britain's share by pressing for the admission of pensions and separation

[19] For Second Sub-Committee: Minutes, 21 Feb. 1919 (Cunliffe versus Lamont); 24 Feb. 1919 (Loucheur); 18 Apr. 1919, Annexe (First Interim Report), ibid. ii. 621–4, 632, 745–70. See also T. W. Lamont, in E. M. House and C. Seymour (edd.), *What Really Happened at Paris* (New York, 1921), 277; Burnett, i. 47–50. For a revisionist account which stresses Loucheur's would-be moderation, but ignores his ultimate extremism: Trachtenberg, 'Reparation at the Paris Peace Conference', 33–6. For Loucheur's advice to the Council of Four: Mantoux, *Paris Peace Conference*, 26 Mar. 1919, 11 a.m., 11–13. For the Committee of Three: Burnett, i. 53–6.

[20] Mantoux, *Paris Peace Conference*, 24 Mar. 1919, 3 p.m., 1; 25 Mar. 1919, 11 a.m., 4; 26 Mar. 1919, 11 a.m., 11–16. *Memorandum Circulated by the Prime Minister on 25 March 1919, House of Commons Papers*, Cmd. 1614, 1922, xxiii. Text of Klotz proposal: Burnett, i. 726–54.

allowances as categories of damage. For the same reason he also proposed that reparation receipts should be divided according to a fixed ratio of 50 (France): 30 (Britain): 20 (the rest). The second proposal quickly ran aground when Loucheur refused to concede any more than 55: 25: 20, after declaring rhetorically that he would prefer to abide by the Fourteen Points, under which France and Belgium would divide 80 per cent of receipts between them and Britain receive 20 per cent. Lloyd George was therefore forced to stake everything on his claim for pensions, which he embodied in a revised draft of the Klotz proposal on 29 March. This worried Wilson, who considered that such a demand was inconsistent with the pre-armistice agreements; and it initially disturbed the French, who immediately entered reservations about priorities. By 31 March Lloyd George had managed to allay French fears by making detailed concessions to Klotz about categories of civilian damage. Although the Americans initially stood firm and insisted that doubtful categories should be referred to international arbitration, they succumbed after Wilson had been 'very much impressed' by a memorandum drafted, at the instigation of Lloyd George, by General Smuts of South Africa. On 1 April Wilson attempted to justify his capitulation by arguing that the naming of specific categories of damage would help to make Germany's obligations more precise. Yet he had, by conniving at the special pleading of Smuts on behalf of the British dominions, potentially doubled Germany's reparation bill. The silent agreement of the French delegation to the inclusion of pensions can be seen as a compromise between a politically popular demand for total war costs (which would not have been in the distributive interests of France) and a distributively advantageous (but politically unacceptable) claim for purely physical reparation.[21]

The huge demands which resulted from Anglo-French haggling and

---

[21] Mantoux, *Paris Peace Conference*, 26 Mar. 1919, 3.30 p.m., 17–23; 29 Mar. 1919, 4 p.m.; 31 Mar. 1919, 11 a.m., 57–60. For Lloyd George draft: Burnett, i. 754–6. For American opposition to pensions see clause 3 of Second American Proposed Modification of the Lloyd George Draft, 31 Mar. 1919, ibid. i. 764–5. See also Dulles's Memorandum Reporting Wilson's Decision on Pensions, 1 Apr. 1919, ibid. i. 775–6. For the Smuts memorandum: ibid. Cf. Smuts to Gillett, 31 Mar. 1919, Hancock and van der Poel, iv. 94–5. Text of memorandum: Burnett, i. 773–5. For its special pleading: Smuts to Gillett, 3 Jan. 1921, Smuts Archive, 24/376. For Wilson's attitude: Mantoux, *Paris Peace Conference*, 1 Apr. 1919, 4 p.m., 79. For French acquiescence: Tardieu, 291–2; Noble, *Policies*, 198–9. I am puzzled by Trachtenberg's insistence that the reason for British pressure for the inclusion of pensions was punitive rather than distributive. His thesis depends on a misreading of Lloyd George (who had been concerned since Nov. 1918 about the impact of an inflated reparation scheme on British trade), a misinterpretation

American complaisance had been virtually agreed upon before time-lagged rumours that the Allies were relaxing their demands on Germany had provoked a storm in the House of Commons, the French Chamber, and the press. The Commons debate of 2 April was, in fact, remarkable chiefly for a bland attempt by Bonar Law to let the public down lightly and a courageous plea for reason by a young Liberal barrister, Alexander Lyle-Samuel, who had been invalided out of the army in 1917. 'War', the former subaltern declared, 'is a bad bargain ... We have been engaged in a bad thing economically and we have got to cut our loss. I would ask this House not to send the impression out from the House that the Government is failing in its duty because it is not collecting the utmost demands, but to stand by their effort to get all they can, and to realize that one of the greatest blessings that will come out of this war will be that the world will be taught that, whether victors or vanquished, war is a bad game and does not pay.' As is well known, this common sense was submerged beneath the persiflage of Mr Kennedy Jones, Colonel Claude Lowther, and Brigadier-General Page-Croft; and a telegram signed by 370 Members was sent to the Prime Minister demanding that he should stand by his election promise to present 'the whole bill' to Germany. Yet the impact of the debate and of similar criticism in France should not be exaggerated. Quite apart from the fact that *The Times* came out on 3 April with a demand for physical reparation rather than an indemnity, the representatives of France and Britain had already indicated on 1 and 2 April their determination to press their demands when they resisted an American attempt to nullify the effect of the inclusion of pensions by imposing a thirty-year time limit. In view of the obvious reluctance of the Europeans to give the appearance of cancelling any part of Germany's obligation, Colonel House, who was deputizing for his ailing President in the Council of Four, finally agreed on 5 April that the time limit should be dropped.[22]

of the Smuts memo of 29 Mar. (which did not advocate that Germany should sign a blank cheque but that reparation should be limited to *direct* war damage), and failure to appreciate the significance of the deadlock over apportionment by a fixed ratio. See Trachtenberg, 'Reparation at the Paris Peace Conference', 44–7; Smuts to Lloyd George, 29 Mar. 1919, Hancock and van der Poel, iv. 93–4.

[22] *HC*, 2 Apr. 1919, cxiv. 1304–10 (Lowther); 1311–18 (Jones); 1322–5 (Lyle-Samuel); 1333–45 (Law); 1346–8 (Page-Croft). For the Kennedy Jones telegram and Lloyd George's contrite reply of 9 Apr.: Lloyd George Papers, F/30/3/43. For the British and French press reaction: *MP*, 1, 2, 3 Apr. 1919 (LA); *The Times*, 3 Apr. 1919 (LA); Noble, Current Intelligence Summaries, 3, 5, 7 Apr. 1919; Miquel, *Paix de Versailles*, 470–82. Cf. Mayer, *Politics and Diplomacy*, 627–32; McCallum, 40–5. For the waiving of the time limit:

This second American surrender, which has been aptly referred to by Burnett as the 'financial effectuation' of the pensions decision, coincided with an agreement over the hotly disputed legal basis of the claim for reparations. The 'Lloyd George Draft' of 29 March had begun with an assertion of the theoretical right of the Allies to claim total war costs and had continued with a statement that the bill actually presented to Germany would be more modest. This formulation had been supported by Clemenceau but it had been opposed by the American delegation, which persisted with its earlier refusal to join in any demand, however theoretical, for war costs. In support of their stand the Americans produced a revised draft which began, not with any positive assertion, but with a negative statement recognizing the limited capacity of Germany to pay reparations. This dispute was resolved by yet another American surrender to Franco-British pressure. After appearing unimpressed by Lloyd George's reference to the British parliamentary debate on reparations and to the state of French and British public opinion, House fell in with a suggestion of Norman H. Davis that a distinction should be drawn in the reparation clauses of the treaty between Germany's complete *moral* responsibility for the war and all its consequences and her limited *legal* liability for reparations. In this manner the war guilt clause (Article 231) came to be inserted as the preamble of the Reparation Chapter of the treaty. Such an assertion was in the short term designed to divert popular attention from the unreality of earlier promises about indemnities. Yet the issue would never have been dealt with in the treaty if the victors had restricted their reparation claims to the limits prescribed by the pre-armistice agreements. The importance of the manœuvring in the Commission on Reparation and the Council of Four is emphasized by the reticence of Robert Lansing's Commission on the Responsibility of the Authors of the War about the general question of war guilt, and its studied concentration on the prosecution of persons responsible for specific crimes committed during the course of hostilities. The distributive preoccupations of the first two bodies, on the other hand, blinded them to the historical untenability and explosive political implications of the blanket charge contained in Article 231.[23]

The capitulation of Wilson and House over the four vital questions

Burnett, i. 783–96; Mantoux, *Paris Peace Conference*, 5 Apr. 1919, 11 a.m., 121. Wilson had influenza.

[23] See paras. 1 and 2 of The Lloyd George Draft, 29 Mar. 1919, Burnett, i. 754–5. See also the remarks of Lloyd George in the Council of Four: Mantoux, *Paris Peace Conference*, 29 Mar. 1919, 4 p.m., 57. For Clemenceau's attitude: ibid. 31 Mar. 1919,

of Germany's total liability, pensions, the time limit, and war guilt reflected their reluctance to make the United States intervene positively and forcefully in the financial affairs of Europe. Moderation and precision could only have been obtained from France and Britain if American resources had been deployed to foster a co-operative approach to post-war reconstruction. The United States government had already refused to take the initiative by consenting to an adjustment of inter-Allied war debts, and Wilson had, according to Clemenceau, 'had a fit' when Klotz broached the subject of a Financial Section of the League of Nations in January 1919. The reaction of the American President was similar when, late in April 1919, Keynes submitted his 'Scheme for the Rehabilitation of European Credit and for Financing Relief and Reconstruction'. The aims of this proposal were to assist Germany to resume normal economic life and meet her preliminary obligations as well as speed the financial and economic recovery of the other European ex-belligerents. Yet, in order to succeed, it needed the formal backing of the United States government, which would have encouraged the international lending public, and above all the American investor, to take up German government bonds. Wilson acknowledged the need for measures to 'clear and improve' the confused economic conditions of Europe. Yet he rejected the scheme because he felt that it would be impossible 'to secure from the Congress of the United States authority to place a federal guarantee on bonds of European origin'. Quite apart from the desire of the United States Treasury 'to retire at the earliest possible moment from "the banking business" ', Wilson believed that the American public, from whom 40 billion dollars of loans and taxes had been extracted in the past two years, had 'reached, and perhaps passed, the point of complete saturation in respect of investments'. The President tried to justify the financial inertia of his government by launching an attack on the reparation proposals of the Allies. 'How', he asked, 'can your experts or ours be expected to work out a *new* plan to furnish working capital to Germany when we deliberately start out by taking away all Germany's present capital?' But this argument ignored the part that American financial isolationism had played in increasing the harshness of Allied reparation terms. Like European statesmen, Wilson was

11 a.m., 57. For American opposition: Minutes of the Experts, 1 Apr. 1919, 4 p.m. (Lamont), Burnett, i. 782. Cf. Para. 1 of Second American Proposed Modification of the Lloyd George Draft, 31 Mar. 1919, ibid. at 764. For the adoption of the 'war guilt clause': Mantoux, *Paris Peace Conference*, 5 Apr. 1919, 11 a.m., 116–17. For the Commission on the Responsibility of the Authors of the War: FRPPC iv. 332.

simply unprepared to admit to his people that most of the funds which had been raised to fight the war had been dissipated, and that further sacrifices and financial co-operation would be needed from all the belligerents if the European economy and world prosperity were to be restored.[24]

The desire of the United States government to wash its hands, both financially and politically, of Europe, and the domestic political sensitivities of the Europeans ensured that the financial terms of the peace settlement would not be revised before the treaty was signed by Germany late in June 1919. The violent reaction of the German government when the draft treaty was presented to it in May and a vigorous revisionist campaign launched by Smuts prompted Lloyd George to call four meetings of the British Empire Delegation and of the British War Cabinet in the last weekend of May. On 2 June the British Prime Minister even informed the Council of Four that, if the treaty was not modified and Germany refused to sign it, the Empire would not join in a resumption of hostilities. But the changes which Lloyd George envisaged in the Reparation Chapter were emasculated by his continuing desire to avoid financial precision. Much to the disgust of Smuts, he confined himself to the impractical suggestion that, in order to avoid naming Germany's total liability, unassessed damage should be repaired by German man-power. Failing this, Germany should be invited to propose within three months a sum which she considered herself capable of paying. Lloyd George's attitude ensured that Wilson's attempt to reopen the question of Germany's total liability in the Council of Four would founder on Franco-British opposition; and that a tentative and highly conditional German offer of 100 billion gold marks would be summarily rejected. An Allied Note of 22 June merely informed the German government that it could submit within four months of the signature of the treaty 'documents and proposals in order to expedite the work connected with reparation, and thus to shorten the investigation and to accelerate the decisions'. Although attempts were subsequently made to use this note as the basis for a negotiated rather than an imposed reparation settlement, it was hardly a significant contribution to the cause of treaty revision.[25]

[24] For Wilson and the Klotz proposals: A. Ribot, *Journal d'Alexandre Ribot et correspondances inédites, 1914–1922* (Paris, 1936), 261. See above: ch. 1, n. 32. The Keynes scheme involved an issue of German government bonds guaranteed by Switzerland and Holland and all the ex-belligerents. Text: Burnett, i. 1011–14. For its rejection: Wilson to Lloyd George, 5 May 1919, ibid. 1127–8.

[25] For the revisionist memos written by Smuts for Lloyd George on 5 and 22 May:

The paramount importance of politics was evident in other ways. Since war guilt had become a hot political issue once it had been formally alluded to in the treaty, the Allies responded to Germany's protests about Article 231 by reaffirming her responsibility for the war, and even insisting on the connection between 'guilt' and reparations. On the other hand the victors were embarrassed about the powers of the Reparation Commission, the body to which they had delegated the responsibility for fixing Germany's total liability and organizing the reparation scheme. It was impossible to deny that the commission would violate Germany's economic and financial independence through its control of imports of food and raw materials under Article 251. The Allies had, therefore, to content themselves with a vigorous disclaimer of any intention to pry into German trade secrets. A general assurance was also given that the commission would 'take into account the true maintenance of the social, economic, and financial structure of a Germany earnestly striving . . . to repair the loss and damage she has caused'.[26]

The Reparation Chapter nevertheless remained a specious document which threatened the stability of Europe. In order to expedite the work of treaty revision, Smuts, the only non-American statesman who had tried to mitigate the terms of peace, suggested to Keynes on 10 June that he should write 'a clear and connected account (not too long or technical) of what the financial clauses of the Treaty are and mean, and what their probable results will be'. A week later even Smuts had changed his mind about the advisability of an open attack on the treaty: 'Better to be constructive . . . You will find many opportunities to help the world, especially when the real trouble over the Reparation

---

Hancock and van der Poel, iv. 148–50, 183–9. Smuts was heavily influenced by Keynes at this time: Smuts to Gillett, 24 Apr., 7 May 1919, ibid. 127–8, 152–3. For British discussions: Peace Conference, British Empire Delegation, Minutes, 33, 34, 1 June 1919, 11 a.m., 5.30 p.m., CAB 29. See also Burnett, i. 136. For the negotiations of the Council of Four: P. Mantoux, *Les Délibérations du Conseil des Quatre* (2 vols.; Paris, 1955), ii. 266, 273, 284, 355–6; FRPPC vi. 139–42, 146, 240, 261–3. For the reaction of Smuts: Smuts to Lloyd George, 2, 4 June 1919, Hancock and van der Poel, iv. 215–16, 219–21. Note the rumblings of the *Morning Post*, 7 June 1919 (LA). For the rejection of the German offer: A. Luckau (ed.), *The German Delegation at the Paris Peace Conference* (New York, 1941), 446. For the Allied Note of 22 June: ibid. 478. Cf. Keynes to Smuts, 8 June 1919, Hancock and van der Poel, iv. 221–2.

[26] For insistence on 'war guilt': Allied Note of 20 May on Responsibility and Reparations; Allied Reply to the German Counterproposals, 16 June 1919, Luckau, 254, 438–41. For a definitive discussion of this topic: Burnett, i. 142–57. For reassurances about the Reparation Commission: Luckau, 443.

and Financial clauses begins with Germany.' But Keynes, who had already publicly expressed his indignation by resigning from the British Peace Delegation, rejected Smuts's tactic of waiting upon time. It was necessary, he considered, 'to get to work very quickly with action to make the Treaty, or much of it, a dead letter, if Europe is to pull through'. He therefore set about writing *The Economic Consequences of the Peace*, which was to do so much to crystallize revisionist thinking in 1920.[27]

It is difficult to gauge the precise impact of the peace negotiations on German financial politics. The short-term German reaction was summed up by the demonstrative, but futile, resignation of Scheidemann, and his replacement as Chancellor by Gustav Bauer, who represented the trade unionist wing of the SPD. The reparation terms certainly ranked as a major source of outrage, along with Germany's territorial losses and the honour clauses (Articles 227–231), which asserted Germany's war guilt and demanded the extradition and trial of the Kaiser and German war criminals. Much resentment was aroused by the insistence on war guilt as the legal basis for reparations, the refusal to fix her total obligation, the confiscation of her merchant shipping, coal, and other resources, and the extensive powers which were vested in the Reparation Commission. Yet a distinction must be drawn between the ultimate reaction of the National Assembly to the peace terms and that of the German Peace Delegation—and the Scheidemann cabinet, which it represented—to the fruitless exchange of notes between victors and vanquished at Paris in May and June 1919. All the German economic experts at Paris were members of the old industrial, commercial, and banking élite which had complained so vociferously a few months earlier about its exclusion from the armistice negotiations. Otto Wiedfeldt, a Krupp director, Wilhelm Cuno and Philipp Heineken, directors of the HAPAG and Norddeutscher Lloyd shipping lines, and Ewald Hilger, an Upper Silesian mining magnate, were bound to object violently to a treaty which, apart from ceding Alsace-Lorraine to France, mortgaged a considerable proportion of Germany's future coal production, surrendered most of her merchant fleet, and threatened to sever Upper Silesia from the Reich. They therefore advised the German government on 19 June that the consequences of refusing to sign the treaty, 'such as the

---

[27] Smuts to Keynes, 10 June 1919; Smuts to Gillet, 16 June 1919; Smuts to Keynes, 17 July 1919; Keynes to Smuts, 12 Aug. 1919, Hancock and van der Poel, iv. 222–3, 266, 279–80. For revisionism: see below, n. 44 and text thereat.

planned occupation of German territory and domestic unrest', were of 'minor importance' compared with those of capitulation.[28]

The government eventually decided to ignore this advice and sign the treaty under protest. Scheidemann's initial declaration on 12 May that the draft treaty was unacceptable (*unannehmbar*) was supported by all political parties except the Independent Socialists (USPD) who, while roundly condemning everything except the war guilt clause, disassociated themselves from 'the desperado policy of heroic gestures advocated by the right wing'. Yet even at this stage the cabinet reserved judgment about whether the treaty would eventually have to be signed. Within a few days Rudolf Wissell, the SPD Economics Minister, was comparing the outcry against the treaty to a grass fire which would be extinguished as soon as the Entente threatened to use force. A survey commissioned by the Supreme Command late in May also revealed that a renewal of hostilities would enjoy little popular support and provoke serious unrest in major cities and industrial regions. Yet another cause for concern was that an Allied invasion from the west would spark off secessionist movements in southern Germany. Erzberger, anxious to preserve national unity, was the first to plead for acceptance of Allied terms at cabinet meetings on 3 and 4 June. Support for the idea of capitulation finally became widespread, particularly in the vulnerable southern, western, and central regions of Germany, after the Allied Note of 16 June made it clear that further resistance would lead only to a resumption of the war. Although the minutes of the cabinet ceased to be kept in the traumatic third week of June, opinion was so evenly divided in a meeting which lasted until 3 a.m. on 19 June that President Ebert transferred the responsibility for the decision to the parties. Later that day the Democrats (DDP) decided unanimously to reject the treaty: but the SPD voted 75 to 35 for

---

[28] For German criticism of the treaty: German Notes of 13 May and 24 May 1919 on Reparations and Responsibility; German Note of 13 May 1919 on Economic Questions; German Counterproposals of 29 May 1919, Luckau, 241–2, 268–72, 348–9 (war guilt); 382–3 (unsettled total obligation); 243, 346, 351–4, 358 (economic demands); 356, 361, 382–5 (powers of the RC). For the final note exchange and report: Allied Reply of 16 June 1919; Final Report of the Financial and Economic Experts to the German Government, 19 June 1919, ibid. 411–72, 489–95. The other economic experts were: W. Beukenberg, managing director of Bergbau u. Hütten-AG Phoenix, a Rhenish-Westphalian iron combine; Georg Lübsen, a director of the Rhenish-Westphalian Coal Syndicate; Emil Georg von Stauss, a director of the Deutsche Bank; Franz Urbig, managing director of the Diskonto-Gesellschaft; Max Warburg, the Hamburg financier; Louis Hagen, the Cologne banker; and P. H. Witthoefft, president of the Hamburg Chamber of Commerce. *Der grosse Brockhaus* (Leipzig, 1928); *Neue Deutsche Biographie* (Berlin, 1952–).

acceptance, as did all but 16 of the Zentrum. After the resignation of Scheidemann, who had voted in the minority at the SPD meeting, the Bauer cabinet, which included no Democrats, was formed. On 22 June this obtained from the Assembly a vote of 237 to 138 in favour of signing the treaty with reservations about the honour clauses. The curt Allied rejection of these reservations prompted the Zentrum, which was afraid of becoming the victim of a nationalist witch-hunt, to reverse its vote. On 23 June, however, after the army had undertaken to remain loyal to the republic and the opposition parties had been requested to vouch for the patriotism of those who signed the treaty, it was agreed that the vote of the previous day should be allowed to stand as one for unconditional acceptance.[29]

The decision of the moderates to sign the treaty was taken primarily in order to avert the social upheaval, political extremism, and secessionist movements which an Allied invasion would have unleashed. Yet it was also encouraged by the hope that the peace terms would not be implemented. In an appeal which it addressed to the German people on 24 June and in subsequent declarations the Bauer cabinet expressed the conviction that if a sincere attempt was made to fulfil the treaty, it would be revised.[30] For as long as it survived, this optimism, and the domestic preoccupations of the National Assembly, did much to muffle the impact of the reparation question in Germany.

FROM PARIS TO SPA

What Smuts had described as 'the real trouble over the Reparation

---

[29] For the initial reaction of the cabinet and National Assembly: Schulze, *Das Kabinett Scheidemann*, 303–4, 314–15; *NV*, 12 May 1919, cccxxvii. 1081–1111. Cf. Haase (USPD), 1102–5; *Die Freiheit*, 9 May 1919, Nos. 220–1 (LA). For summaries of press reaction: ibid. 8, 9 May 1919, Nos. 219, 221, 1; *FZ*, 10 May 1919, No. 342, 1. For Wissell, the Supreme Command, and Erzberger: *Das Kabinett Scheidemann*, 349, 400–1, 417–21. For the swing of opinion: *FZ*, 17 June 1919, No. 440, 1; 19 June 1919, Nos. 444–6. For Berlin press opinion: ibid. 18 June 1919, No. 443, 1; 20 June 1919, No. 448, 1. For the ultimate behaviour of the cabinet, the parties, and the army: *Das Kabinett Scheidemann*, 476–507; *Akten der Reichskanzlei: Weimarer Republik. Das Kabinett Bauer, 21. Juni 1919 bis 27. März 1920*, ed. A. Golecki (Boppard-on-Rhine, 1980), 3–12; Luckau, 105–11; Epstein, 318. For the votes in favour of acceptance: *NV*, 22–3 June 1919, cccxxvii. 1136–40.

[30] Appeal of the German Government to the German People, 24 June 1919, Luckau, 496–7; *The Times*, 30 June 1919, 13.

and Financial clauses' did not begin for more than a year. Until January 1920, when ratifications were signed by all the signatories except the United States, relations between Germany and the Allies continued to be governed by the terms of the armistice. This meant that, except in the case of deliveries of coal and other less important items which began by special agreement, the provisions of the Reparation Chapter could not come into effect. Even in the early months of 1920 events moved very slowly. Apart from the second refusal of the United States Senate to ratify the treaty in March 1920, the most important development was the setting up of the Reparation Commission, to which the peacemakers had delegated the formal responsibility for implementing the reparation scheme. Yet Germany's creditors would not allow this body to exercise its most important functions of expediting preliminary payments and fixing the total bill. It was not until July 1920 that the Allied heads of state, having agreed to short-circuit the commission, broached these matters with the German government at the Spa Conference. The repercussions of the reparation problem were not, therefore, serious before the middle of 1920.

The relatively relaxed atmosphere immediately after Germany's signature of the treaty in June 1919 was evident during the negotiations about preliminary coal deliveries between the Commission on the Organization of the Reparation Commission (CORC), the German government, and the Rhenish-Westphalian Coal Syndicate, the cartel which, notwithstanding the German revolution, still controlled the production, pricing, transport, and marketing of all coal mined in the Ruhr district. Because the treaty had not yet been ratified the Versailles Coal Protocol of 29 August 1919 made no attempt to implement the Coal Annexe of the Reparation Chapter. On the contrary, it explicitly stated that, in order to prevent economic dislocation and political upheaval, Germany would 'begin deliveries only in accordance with the measure of increase of production'. Although the French electorate was placated with the stipulation that annual deliveries would gradually rise to 40 million tons after the treaty came into force, there was a verbal agreement that for the time being no more than 1 million tons a month would be insisted upon. Germany's domestic coal supply was further safeguarded by provisions exempting her from making compulsory deliveries to her eastern and south-eastern neighbours and guaranteeing her 100,000 tons a month from the Saar, which the treaty had placed under the control of the League of Nations for 15 years.[31]

[31] See Annexe V (Coal) of the Reparation Chapter: Temperley, iv. 229–31. The CORC

Apart from its belief that the repatriation of German prisoners of war would be expedited, a major incentive for the German government to agree to advanced coal shipments was the provision of Article 235 of the treaty that, after the costs of the armies of occupation had been met, the fund constituted by reparation deliveries could be used to finance imports of food and raw materials needed to fulfil treaty obligations. This had prompted Carl Bergmann, the German repara-tion negotiator, to ask the CORC on 28 August for a credit of 200 million gold marks to purchase food, clothing, and equipment for the Ruhr coal fields. Such a proposal was unacceptable to the French, the main recipients of reparation coal. Reaffirming the stand taken by his colleague Klotz during the armistice shipping negotiations in January, Loucheur declared to the CORC on 17 September that France refused 'to pay Germany for deliveries in kind' and insisted that she should use her remaining gold and foreign securities to obtain imports. As a result, the German government had to be content with the permission granted to it on 29 August to sell or pledge foreign securities worth £20 million (400 million gold marks) for food purchases. Since it was undesirable for Germany to diminish her reserves any further, the imports were in fact paid for, via the printing press, with foreign exchange acquired by the sale of paper marks.[32]

Although the German request for credits in return for reparation deliveries was to be blocked for another year by French opposition, the immediate political impact of the coal negotiations was reduced by the low level of deliveries envisaged. A right-wing (DNVP–DVP) interpellation on 31 July attributed the current German coal crisis jointly to the drop in Ruhr production, the dislocation of the railways, and the deliveries prescribed by the treaty. The Nationalist spokesman, Alfred Hugenberg, declared a fortnight later that the main threat to the coal industry was posed by strikers and agitators in the mines and on the railways; and he referred to Germany's reparation obligations merely as an incentive to higher production. After Schmidt, the

was set up by the Allied Supreme Council on 1 July: *DBFP* I, v. 60 (n.). On the Coal Syndicate: A.H. Stockder, *Regulating an Industry: The Rhenish-Westphalian Coal Syndicate, 1893–1929* (London, 1940), *passim*. For the coal negotiations: *DBFP* I, v. 335–9. On the verbal agreement: Stutz (German Commissioner for Coal Distribution) to Stresemann, 24 Jan. 1920, in Stresemann to Verband Sächsischer Industrieller, 29 Jan. 1920, A. Amt, Politisches Archiv, Nachlass Stresemann, ccxx, Polit. Akten 1920/I. The distribution of Upper Silesian coal was left to the discretion of the International Coal Conference until the future of the region was decided in 1921.

[32] On repatriation: *DBFP* I, ii. 458–61; v. 793. On credit negotiations: ibid. v. 401–3, 508, 535–6. For Klotz: see above, n. 1 and text thereat.

Majority Socialist Economics Minister, had reported that reparation deliveries would not initially exceed 20 million tons a year (as opposed to the 45 million tons stipulated by the treaty), the National Assembly refrained from any protest and confined itself to suggesting means of increasing output.[33]

The economic significance of coal shipments was relatively restricted in the months that followed. Between September 1919, when deliveries began, and mid-1920 they were, in fact, responsible for only one-third of a total lag of 12–13 per cent behind the 1913 level of coal distribution. Reparation deliveries were sometimes mentioned in the numerous petitions which were directed to the National Assembly by industries or regions suffering from the dearth of coal in the winter of 1919–20. Yet the main emphasis of the petitioners and of the government in its replies was invariably upon the low level of production, transport bottlenecks, and the difficulty of achieving equitable distribution. This was the case even in the Palatinate and south Germany, which had been heavily dependent on the Saar coal mines before their ownership was transferred to France under Articles 45–50 of the treaty. Because of the presence of the Allied armies of occupation in these areas both the Luxemburg Protocol of 28 February 1919 and the Versailles Protocol of August had initially guaranteed them a fixed amount of the Saar's output. By late 1919 the reduction of deliveries from the Ruhr had prompted the French authorities to limit shipments from the Saar to the rest of Germany to between 2,000 and 2,500 tons a day; and on 6 January 1920 they announced that all Saar deliveries to Germany would cease from 1 February. These measures certainly aggravated the crisis: but the main reasons for both the shortages in southern Germany and the inadequate flow of reparation coal from the Ruhr in the winter of 1919–20 were the transport bottlenecks caused by the severe flooding of the Rhine in December 1919 and a railway strike in the following month. After the transport crisis had eased in April, the shortage of coal in the areas bordering the Saar was no worse than in the rest of Germany.[34]

[33] Interpellation of Heinze, Arnstadt, and others (63 signatories), 31 July 1919, *NV* cccxxxviii Annexe 739; Resolution of 15 Aug. 1919, ibid. Annexe 878; *Das Kabinett Bauer*, 158–9, 182–3; debate of 15 Aug. 1919, ibid. cccxxix. 2467, 2471.

[34] For distribution percentages see Appendix II, below. For the coal shortage in the Düsseldorf area: Petition of Erkelenz and Jäcker, 11 Dec. 1919, *NV* cccx, Annexe 1746; in the Aachen area: Petition of Oertel, 18 Dec. 1919, ibid. Annexe 1844. See also petitions from the Rhenish-Westphalian smelting industry, 6 Dec. 1919, ibid. cccxli, Annexe 1946; and from the lime and cement industry: Petition of Dusche, 29 Dec. 1919, ibid. Annexe 1876; Petition of Astor, 15 Apr. 1920, ibid. cccxlii, Annexe 2580. Cf. Petition of Dietrich

The relative insignificance of the coal question helped to defuse reparations as a political issue during the second half of 1919. From July onwards the attention of the National Assembly was focused on the strenuous but ultimately unsuccessful efforts of Matthias Erzberger, the Finance Minister of the new Bauer government, to institute fundamental financial reform by imposing new taxes, curbing tax evasion, and reorganizing the federal fiscal system. In August Hugenberg tried vainly to score points off Erzberger by protesting that a Premium Loan scheme with which the government tried to resume borrowing from the public would be used partly to compensate German shipowners and overseas Germans for losses occasioned by the treaty. But Hugenberg's well-known connections with those who stood to benefit from the measure and the preoccupation of the Nationalist Party with vilifying Erzberger for his domestic policies blunted the attack.[35]

The restricted importance of the reparation question was further evidenced by the federal budget for 1919–20. In the estimates which were presented to the National Assembly in October 1919 an inflated sum of 17 billion paper marks was allocated to cover the cost of implementing the treaty. Yet actual expenditure of all sorts arising out of the treaty proved to be only 2 billion paper marks, a sum which was dwarfed by the government's total eventual outlay of 90 billion paper marks for the year. The unreality of the estimates perhaps explains why references to the reparation question were so low-key in the debates of October 1919. Speakers as far apart as the Majority Socialist, Scheidemann, and Stresemann of the People's Party certainly stressed that Germany could fulfil her obligations only if they were substantially revised. Yet a full-scale debate was pointless in the

and Löbe, 22 Nov. 1919, ibid. cccxxxix, Annexe 1522: answered, 5 Dec. 1919, ibid. cccxxxi. 3850. Note that 37% of the Saar's 1913 output of 12.2 million tons was consumed within Germany (excluding Alsace-Lorraine and the Saar itself). See L. G. Cowan, *France and the Saar, 1680–1948* (New York, 1950), 145, 148–51. For post-war distribution: Report on the Coal Situation in Occupied German Territories by the British Department of the Inter-Allied Rhineland High Commission, Feb. 1920, in Stuart to Curzon, 14 Feb. 1920, *DBFP* I, x. 184–95. For the diversion of Saar coal: Petition of Herr Pick, 19 Dec. 1919: answered 13 Feb. 1920, *NV* cccxl, Annexe 1855; cccxli, Annexe 2133. For transport bottlenecks: Petition of Herr Haussmann and others, 15 Jan. 1920: answered 13 Feb. 1920, ibid. Annexe 1950, 2135; Petition of Herr Pick, 3 Mar. 1920: answered 19 Apr. 1920, ibid. Annexe 2284, cccxliii, Annexe 2775.

[35] For the Premium Loan proposal: *Das Kabinett Bauer*, 197–8; Hugenberg (DNVP), 20 Aug. 1919, *NV* cccxxix. 2675–7; Dernburg (DDP), 5 Dec. 1919, cccxxxi. 3882. Note the press campaign which had been launched against Erzberger in June by Karl Helfferich, the wartime Secretary of State to the Treasury. K. Helfferich, *Fort mit Erzberger!* (Berlin, 1919); Williamson, 291–302; Epstein, 352.

absence of concrete Allied reparation proposals. Erzberger argued, to good effect, that it would be a tactical blunder to make detailed estimates of expenditures likely to be occasioned by the treaty until the Entente had presented its demands; and he was able to satisfy the Assembly with a general declaration that, although Germany sincerely wished to fulfil the treaty, she could not do so beyond the limit of her capacity.[36]

More heat was generated in December when the government introduced the important States Tax Law (*Landessteuergesetz*), which settled the distribution of tax receipts between the federal government and the states, and the Income and Capital Gains Taxes, which were expected to yield about ten billion marks of new revenue. It was also in this month that the controversial National Emergency Levy and Sales Tax were finally adopted after stormy discussion. The debate was marked by increasing financial pessimism, which was induced partly by the treaty: but domestic partisan recrimination and class antipathy were still the dominant themes.[37] As on previous occasions, the only measure which was opposed explicitly because of Allied reparation demands was the Emergency Levy, the proceeds of which, it was claimed, would be seized by the Entente. Members of the People's Party even argued that the Levy should be replaced by a Forced Loan on the grounds that the latter would be less vulnerable to confiscation. On 5 December Erzberger felt obliged to quote the National Assembly a legal opinion, which he had originally cited confidentially in committee on 18 October, that the treaty precluded any interference with Germany's domestic finances as long as she fulfilled her obligations. This did not satisfy the right-wing opposition, which seized upon a current dispute with the Allies over lagging

[36] Budget estimate of Oct. 1919: Erzberger, 30 Oct. 1919, NV cccxxxi. 3606–9. Final budget figures: League of Nations, *International Financial Conference, ... Paper No. IV* (rev. ed., London, 1921), 167. See also H. G. Moulton and C. E. McGuire, *Germany's Capacity to Pay* (New York, 1923), 170–1; Davis, 'Recent ... Progress in Germany', 144–5. For debate: Scheidemann, 7 Oct. 1919, NV cccxxx. 2891; Stresemann, 8 Oct. 1919, 2917; Müller, 23 Oct. 1919, 3357; Heinze, 24 Oct. 1919, 3393; Erzberger, 30 Oct. 1919, cccxxxi. 3610–11.

[37] For references to the treaty: Keil (SPD), 5 Dec. 1919, NV cccxxxi. 3859–60; Zehnter (Zentrum), 3868; Dernburg (DDP), 3878; Wurm (USPD), 6 Dec. 1919, 3911; Becker (DVP), 3904; Hugenberg (DNVP), 9 Dec. 1919, 3936. For partisan abuse: Keil (SPD), 5 Dec. 1919, 3860; Erzberger, 6 Dec. 1919, 3898; Düringer (DNVP), 3896; Hugenberg (DNVP), 9 Dec. 1919, 3936; Braun (SPD), 10 Dec. 1919, 3950. For class antipathy: Dernburg (DDP), 5 Dec. 1919, 3879; Düringer (DNVP), 6 Dec. 1919, 3889; Becker (DVP), 3900; Hugenberg (DNVP), 9 Dec. 1919, 3938; Erzberger, 3947; Gothein (DDP), 3929; Farwick (Zentrum), 3955.

armistice deliveries of shipping and dock material and prohibited exports of German aeronautical material. Taking up a threat of sanctions in an Allied Protocol of 1 November, Hugenberg provoked an uproar by challenging the Entente to occupy the Ruhr. Yet the situation was quickly defused by the relatively amicable resolution of the dispute with the Allies. Hugenberg's patriotism was, moreover, clouded by the continuing opposition of the right wing to the levy on the familiar grounds that it would diminish the working capital and credit-worthiness of private enterprise, raise prices, encourage capital flight, and reduce the yield from other taxes. This gave credibility to the republican riposte that the right wing was prepared to court an Allied invasion merely to protect the short-term interests of men of property.[38]

Despite the relatively muffled impact of the treaty and the formal discomfiture of Erzberger's opponents in the Assembly, the impotence of the government's external financial policy had by this time indicated that effective financial stabilization was highly unlikely. The phenomenon of capital flight, or what *The Economist* referred to in November 1919 as the tendency of the German mark to flow abroad in 'inexhaustible streams', indicated a deep-seated lack of confidence in Germany's financial future and a distaste for the federal government's tax programme. Efforts to counter this form of tax evasion and speculation against the mark by ordering that notes and securities should be consigned abroad only through banks met with determined opposition from liberals in the Assembly. The clearest pointer to the ineffectiveness of the government was, however, the apathy and partisanship of the debates on the external financial crisis in August, October, and December. The futility of the discussion was underlined on the last occasion when, after government and opposition had abused each other, the Assembly adjourned for want of a quorum.[39]

[38] For the Forced Loan (*Zwangsanleihe*) proposal: Becker (DVP), 6 Dec. 1919, NV cccxxxi. 3901; Riesser (DVP), 9 Dec. 1919, 3931. For texts: ibid. cccxl, Annexe 1682, 1799. For Erzberger's assurances: ibid. cccxxxi. 3876–7. Cf. Badulesco, 284–5. For the dispute over armistice deliveries: DBFP I, i. 805–8; ii. 109–11, 144–6, 474, 496–8, 533, 539–41, 643–5; v. 894; *Das Kabinett Bauer*, 349–51, 366–7, 424–5, 459–61. For its impact on German opinion: ibid. vi. 426–31, 486–8, 502; FZ, 5 Dec. 1919, No. 910 (LA); 6 Dec. 1919, No. 911, 1. For business opposition to the Levy: Becker (DVP), NV cccxxxi. 3901; 10 Dec. 1919, 3961; Riesser (DVP), 9 Dec. 1919, 3929; 17 Dec. 1919, 4117. For business petitions: ibid. cccxxxvii, Annexe 647; cccxxxviii, Annexe 753, 863; cccxxxix, Annexe 1171, 1287, 1429; cccxl, Annexe 1762; cccxli, Annexe 2112. For Hugenberg's outburst and government counter-charges: Hugenberg (DNVP), 9 Dec. 1919, ibid. cccxxxi. 3932–7; Erzberger, 3941; Braun (SPD), 10 Dec. 1919, 3949; Farwick (Zentrum), 3958; Petersen (DDP), 3959; Waldstein (DDP), 17 Dec. 1919, 4121–2.

[39] On capital flight: *The Economist*, 29 Nov. 1919, 983–4. Cf. Erzberger, 16 Aug. 1919,

In the early months of 1920 the desultory policies of the victors did little to disturb either the introversion of German financial politics or the economy. Allied irresolution was clearly reflected in the Reparation Commission, which was set up in February 1920 after the treaty had been ratified. Because of the calculated vagueness of the Reparation Chapter about Germany's total obligation and the manner in which it would be discharged, the potential power of the commission to fix the reparation bill and to enforce, postpone, or waive payments was immense. The status of the commission, not to mention its possible role as an instrument of treaty revision, was, however, quickly undermined by the successive refusals of the United States Senate to ratify the treaty on 19 November 1919 and 19 March 1920. These meant that the American seat on the commission could only be filled by an unofficial non-voting delegate; and, further, that France, by virtue of her chairmanship and casting vote, could get her way if any one of the other three countries with permanent seats (Britain, Italy, and Belgium) sided with her. The predictable British reaction was to short-circuit the commission by insisting on cabinet-level negotiations on all matters of importance. The diminution of the authority of the commission was such that by May 1920 its French delegate and chairman, Raymond Poincaré, had resigned in protest.[40]

Despite the resignation of Poincaré, neither of the major creditor powers had really wished to use the commission to settle Germany's obligations or otherwise implement the Reparation Chapter. The

---

NV cccxxix. 2512–14; Urbig, 30. On counter-measures: Gesetz gegen die Kapitalflucht, 8 Sept. 1919, *Reichsgesetzblatt*, 1919, 1540–2; Hampe (DNVP), 16 Aug. 1919, NV cccxxix. 2507; Riesser (DVP), 2510–11. For the tone of the National Assembly: ibid. Raschig (DDP), 2508; Braun (SPD), 2511. See also Interpellation ... betreffend die deutsche Valuta, 24 Sept. 1919, ibid. cccxxix, Annexe 1061; Erzberger, Memo 'Zur Valutafrage', 27 Sept. 1919, ibid. Annexe 1067; Interpellation ... betreffend Wirtschafts- und Steuerpolitik sowie ... Steigerung aller Preise, ibid. cccxl, Annexe 1792; Interpellation betreffend die Ein- und Ausfuhr, ibid. Annexe 1795; Hugo (DVP), 1 Oct. 1919, ibid. cccxxix. 2784–9; Erzberger, 2793–4; Schiele (DNVP), 2807; Bolz (Zentrum), 2808; Hugo (DVP), 19 Dec. 1919, ibid. cccxxxi. 4166–74; Mumm (DNVP), 4175; Erzberger, 4185–90.

[40] The powers of the RC are defined in Articles 233–4 and Annexes II–VII of the Reparation Chapter. Para. 2 of Annexe II provided that no more than five delegates could participate or vote at any one time; that the delegates of the United States, Great Britain, France, and Italy would have the right to vote 'on all occasions'; and that the Belgian delegate would have the fifth vote except when matters being considered related to either Japan or the 'Serb-Croat-Slovene state', the other two powers represented on the commission. For text: Temperley, iii. 215, 219–33. For Anglo-French manœuvring and Poincaré's resignation, see below, nn. 44–6 and text thereat.

French general election of November 1919 had resulted in a swing to the right which merely strengthened the rhetoric of French reparation policy at the expense of its precision. The emphatically anti-socialist platform of the victorious *Bloc National* ensured that the demand of the left for stern progressive taxation would be ignored; and Klotz was even encouraged to prolong financial illusions in December 1919 by deferring the submission of precise budget estimates for the following year and declaring to the Chamber that all of the government's outlays on reconstruction and war pensions would be covered in a special 'German budget' out of reparation receipts. This continuing unreality was bound to delay the achievement of a viable settlement.[41]

There were even difficulties about seemingly straightforward coal deliveries, in which France had a major interest. Although the smaller French industrialists and a vocal element in the Chamber wanted the government to extract as much coal from Germany as possible without delay, heavy industry preferred private arrangements with, or participation in, the Ruhr coal industry. It was also tacitly agreed that Germany still could not deliver sizeable amounts of coal in the spring of 1920. In January, when the monthly delivery rate prescribed by the Versailles Protocol was 1.6 million tons, German shipments amounted to 450,000 tons; and from 19 February, when the newly constituted Reparation Commission raised the schedule to over 2 million tons out of deference to the clamour for coal in France, the gap between Germany's performance and official demands became even more obvious. Yet the commission covertly acquiesced in the 6 million tons of coal which were delivered in the first seven months of 1920, even though this was only half the amount it had demanded and a quarter of what was prescribed by the treaty. Carl Bergmann, the German delegate to the Reparation Commission, later claimed that the Commission was deeply gratified when deliveries approached a million tons in May 1920. It was no wonder that Millerand, Clemenceau's successor as French premier, pinioned as he was between contradictory domestic pressures and the harsh realities of lagging German coal production and distribution bottlenecks, resorted from February onwards to blustering for an Allied occupation of the Ruhr. This was, however, a gesture of frustration for domestic political consumption or for

---

[41] E. Bonnefous, *Histoire politique de la Troisième République: III. L'Après-guerre, 1919–1924* (Paris, 1959), 59–73, 84–7; Brogan, 564–5, 589–90; C. S. Maier, *Recasting Bourgeois Europe: Stabilization in France, Germany, and Italy in the Decade after World War I* (Princeton, 1975), 91–109.

intimidatory purposes rather than a proposal designed to achieve rational economic, or even strategic, ends.[42]

France's continuing illusions about Germany as an exploitable source of coal and cash were evident when the Allied Supreme Council met in London in February for the first time since the Paris Peace Conference. Although this gathering was preoccupied mainly with drafting a peace treaty with Turkey, it was also concerned about the implementation of the German settlement and the related problems of inflation and exchange instability in Europe. On the second day of the conference, following a fruitless discussion of the question of the extradition and trial of the Kaiser and German war criminals, Millerand demanded an occupation of the Ruhr in retaliation for what he alleged to be Germany's deliberate evasion of her coal obligations. Lloyd George and the Italian Prime Minister, Nitti, who attributed the lag in deliveries to circumstances beyond Germany's control, temporarily parried this thrust by having the matter referred to the Reparation Commission. That afternoon, however, François-Marsal, the French Finance Minister, counter-attacked on a broad financial front by pressing for the immediate funding of sufficient of Germany's reparation obligations to enable her to transfer annuities of 3 billion marks. 'The reconstruction programme of France', he declared, 'necessitated the immediate liquidation of a substantial part of the reparation to which she was entitled.' A fortnight later, when the conference was able to concentrate its attention on financial and economic matters, there was considerable scepticism about the French claim that Europe's problems could be solved by German reparations. Nitti was particularly outspoken:

M. Marsal had suggested that assistance could be got by liquidating the German indemnity. For his part, he frankly stated that he was willing to sell his share in that indemnity at a heavy loss if he could find a purchaser in the United States. Whoever bought it would find himself faced with Germany, and only be able to realize by keeping Germany under something like a system of slavery. In the financial arrangements of Italy he had reckoned the indemnity at zero so that anything that came in would be surplus. The only sure asset, to his mind, lay in the resumption of work, and that was what he wanted to see.

[42] For disagreement in France over coal deliveries: Maier, *Recasting Bourgeois Europe*, 194–203. For amounts delivered: RC v. 95, 220; Germany, A. Amt, White Book, *Die Konferenz in Spa*, RT ccclxiii, Annexe 187, 65. Cf. C. Bergmann, *The History of Reparations* (London, 1927), 29; DBFP I, viii. 508.

Lloyd George, while declaring that it would be morally and economically indefensible to accept Nitti's view 'that the indemnity should
be written down to zero', insisted that because of her economic debil-
itation Germany should first of all be granted credits to purchase food
and restart her industries. 'Until that had been done', he maintained,
'it was neither businesslike nor humane to talk of borrowing on a
starving and bankrupt people.' No loan could in any case be floated
until Germany's liability had been fixed and her capacity to pay had
been gauged by the Reparation Commission. He therefore proposed
on 1 March that the commission should be directed (1) to extract from
Germany the reparation offer she had been invited to make by the
Allied Note of 16 June 1919, (2) to fix Germany's total liability as soon
as possible at a figure within her capacity, (3) to allow her to finance
essential imports out of preliminary reparation payments in accordance
with Article 235, and (4) to authorize, if necessary, a German foreign
loan, the service of which was to have priority over all other liabilities,
including reparations. Because of Franco-Belgian pressure, the Reparation Commission ignored this directive and simply instructed the
German government on 4 March to pay for its imports by liquidating
foreign securities in the possession of its nationals. The 'Declaration
... on the Economic Condition of the World', which the Supreme
Council issued a few days later, also contained only a watered down
version of Lloyd George's resolution. While conceding the desirability
of arriving at a prompt reparation settlement and enabling Germany
to obtain vital imports, it attached prime importance to the reconstruction of France and stressed the authority of the Reparation Commission to decide the amount and priority of any loan granted to
Germany.[43]

The desire of France to harvest the fruits of victory without even
providing Germany with working capital seemed to be unabated when
Millerand reiterated his demand for an Allied occupation of the Ruhr
at a further meeting of the Supreme Council at San Remo on 18 April.
Lloyd George, now determined to by-pass the Reparation Commission,
countered with the hitherto unthinkable suggestion that, instead of
persisting with their unproductive note exchange, the victors should

---

[43] For the London Conference: *DBFP* I, vii. 30–1 (Millerand, Lloyd George); 40–1
(Marsal); 276 (Nitti); 289–90 (Lloyd George); 336–8 (resolution of 1 Mar.). For the RC's
letter of 4 Mar.: ibid. 432–4 n. 3. For the Supreme Council's declaration of 8 Mar.:
House of Commons Papers, 1920, li, Cmd. 646, at 6, 8.

invite the German government to answer orally for its policies on coal and disarmament and also to submit a reparation proposal as requested by the Allied Note of 16 June 1919. This conciliatory gesture, which resulted in German attendance at the Spa Conference in July, cannot be attributed entirely to an upsurge of British financial revisionism. *The Economic Consequences of the Peace*, which Keynes had published late in 1919, had certainly added force and cohesion to the piecemeal criticisms of the treaty which were being voiced by a small group of Allied statesmen, economists, businessmen, and journalists. When the British Parliament reassembled in February 1920 the Liberal and Labour opposition in the House of Commons moved an amendment to the Address which regretted that the government had 'not recognised the impracticability of the fulfilment by our late enemies of many of the terms of the Peace Treaties nor shown an adequate appreciation of the grave dangers to our economic position at home and abroad by the continuance of the delay in the restoration of settled conditions in many parts of Europe and the Near East'. The ensuing debate, which, as Balfour observed, was little more than a discussion of Keynes's polemic, was notable for the declaration by Colonel Josiah Wedgwood (Labour) that the current reparation demands of the Allies were 'sheer, stark, staring lunacy'. It was also the occasion of a powerful revisionist speech by Lord Robert Cecil. However, the government, while admitting that the treaty was far from perfect, remained unsympathetic to a policy of immediate revision. Lloyd George's main concern at San Remo was not, therefore, to revise the treaty but to curb French expansionism which, he feared, might jeopardize the trade and diplomatic balance of Europe. British misgivings about France's desire for a Rhine frontier had been evident at the Paris Peace Conference in 1919. They had since been deepened by Millerand's sabre-rattling about the Ruhr and brought to fever pitch by the unilateral French occupation of Frankfurt, Darmstadt, and other towns on 6 April 1920. This action was projected as a means of guaranteeing the withdrawal of the German troops who had entered the demilitarized zone to suppress the left-wing uprisings in the Ruhr in the wake of the Kapp Putsch. Yet it was undertaken for a mixture of motives ranging from retaliation for German infringements of the treaty to encouragement of the federalist movement in south Germany. For this reason it provoked an outraged reaction from Britain, which manifested itself first of all in the suspension of British coal exports to France. It was in order to thwart France's short-sighted 'Napoleonic' policy which, he alleged, would drive the Germans into the arms of 'a powerful militarist or communist government' that Lloyd George proposed the admonitory-consultative meeting with the Germans at Spa.[44]

Millerand's acceptance of the idea of a conference did not reflect the growth of Keynesian revisionism in France, where the reception of *The Economic Consequences of the Peace* varied from indifferent to vitriolic. Yet, while maintaining its pressure for literal implementation of the treaty, if necessary by military force, the French government was embarking on a contradictory and equally illusory quest for a special economic relationship with Germany. It was initially propelled in this direction by German discrimination against French imports after the lifting of the blockade in July 1919. This, as Georges Soutou has shown, led to efforts by the French government to regain access to the German market culminating on 15 April 1920 with the suspension of France's own embargo on German imports. Another powerful incentive for Franco-German economic collaboration was that, when negotiating a sterling loan in London in December 1919, the French government agreed to the British demand that reparation receipts should be divided according to a fixed mathematical ratio. It was primarily in order to restore through the back door the priority of France's reparation claim that Millerand supported the somewhat quixotic attempts of Jacques Seydoux, the Deputy Director of Commercial Relations in the French Foreign Ministry, to obtain French participation in the German coal industry and to negotiate special agreements with German firms to supply reconstruction materials to France. Millerand's awareness of the tactical desirability of a working economic relationship with Germany, sharpened as it was by the abrupt cessation of British coal shipments in April 1920, obliged him to agree to the proposed discussions at Spa about coal and cash reparations. He was, however, afraid that the efforts of Lloyd George

[44] For San Remo: *DBFP* I, viii. 7–8, 14–15, 192–3. For slightly variant texts of the invitation to Spa: ibid. 209–10; *Protocols and Correspondence ... respecting the ... Treaty of Versailles ...*, House of Commons Papers, 1921, xliii, Cmd. 1325, 94; *Die Konferenz in Spa*, 22. For good surveys of Allied revisionism in 1919 and 1920: *FZ*, 1 Jan. 1920, No. 1, 4; 2 Apr. 1920, No. 249 (LA). For the British debate on treaty revision: *HC* cxxv. 265 (amendment); 314 (Wedgwood); 276–81 (Cecil); 297–300 (Balfour); 372–4 (Law); cxxvii. 663–7 (Lloyd George); 671 (Cecil); *HL* xxxix. 13–14 (Crewe); 24 (Curzon). For France and the Rhine: see above, n. 14. On the motives for the French occupation of Apr. 1920: McDougall, *France's Rhineland Diplomacy*, 110–11, 119–20. Cf. the exchange in Mar. 1920 between Cambon and Curzon at the London Conference: *DBFP* I, vii. 606–10, 683–5. For the British reaction: Curzon to Derby, 8 Apr. 1920, ibid. ix. 340–4.

and Nitti to achieve a rapid lump sum settlement (*forfait*) might lead to a politically unacceptable reduction of Germany's total obligation. Hence his insistence at San Remo that there could be agreement at Spa only on her immediate liability; and that the responsibility for settling the total reparation bill should rest with the Reparation Commission, which he assumed would be impervious to revisionist pressure.[45]

Although Millerand's reservations ruled out any definitive settlement, the Allies were obliged to agree on a provisional reparation scheme which they could use as a counter to any German proposal at Spa. To this end a conference was held at Hythe on 13–15 May and several British schemes involving sums of between 100 and 120 billion gold marks were discussed and referred to a panel of experts for further examination. Sufficient progress was made to precipitate Poincaré's resignation from the Reparation Commission on the grounds that, by discussing Germany's total obligation, Millerand and Lloyd George were usurping the commission's most important function. Efforts to reach agreement were hampered by the revival of the dispute over distribution after the French made their agreement to a *forfait* hinge upon temporary priority for their claims. This evoked a negative response from Lloyd George. 'It would be impossible', he declared during a second conference at Hythe on 20 June, 'to force public opinion in Great Britain and in the Dominions to accept any sort of arrangement which would deprive the taxpayers of any payment of annuity or capital.' The other formidable stumbling block to a rational financial settlement was the problem of inter-Allied debts, the resolution of which was precluded ultimately by the sensitivity of the United States administration to *its* taxpayers. For this reason, Lloyd George insisted that, although the British government 'would like to wipe out all debts', the question would have to be postponed until after the American elections in the coming autumn. As on previous occasions, the only way out of the impasse was to defer any decision about Germany's total liability. The extravagant schedule of 42 annuities totalling 269 billion gold marks which was approved by the Allied heads of state at Boulogne on 21 June 1920 was intended less as a practical settlement than as a means of bolstering the false hopes which had been aroused in France and the British Empire. To safeguard

[45] F. Crouzet, 'Réactions françaises devant *Les Conséquences économiques de la paix de Keynes*', *RHMC* 19 (1972), 6–26; G. Soutou, 'Problèmes', 580–90. For Franco-British Agreement of 13 Dec. 1919, *DBFP* I, ii. 780. For Millerand at San Remo: ibid. viii. 14–15. Cf. *Le Temps*, 5 May 1920 (LA).

against any accidents in the forthcoming discussions with the Germans it was agreed at Boulogne that no final decision would be made on any reparation scheme mooted at Spa until the Reparation Commission had been consulted.[46]

The continuing restraint of the Allies about coal and their reticence about the total reparation bill reduced the political effect of the treaty on Germany in the first half of 1920. Hopes of treaty revision were raised by the publication of *The Economic Consequences of the Peace*; and the German reaction to the forthcoming Spa Conference was not entirely unfavourable. The assurance of the Allies that they did not 'intend to insist upon a too literal interpretation of the treaty', and the long overdue recognition of the need for oral discussion of the reparation and disarmament terms between victors and vanquished, even prompted the liberal *Frankfurter Zeitung* to moot the possibility of a more co-operative era in international relations. The journal concluded, to be sure, that the conference would bring 'little immediate benefit' to Germany because of the persistence of popular delusions about her economic capacity and the apparent determination of French political leaders to achieve their financial goals through the use of military sanctions. Yet the hopes of German political moderates that the treaty would be revised were by no means extinguished.[47]

Despite the absence of external pressure Germany lurched further down the inflationary road. Her financial situation was not eased by the politically charged Erzberger–Helfferich lawsuit, which ran from 19 January to 12 March 1920. Erzberger had been provoked into bringing a libel action by a press campaign in which Helfferich had made vague allegations of offences against propriety, habitual untruthfulness, and mixing politics with business affairs. The litigation quickly developed into another slogging match between the old and the new

---

[46] For Hythe: *DBFP* I, viii. 258–79. For Poincaré's resignation: *Le Temps*, 20 May 1920 (LA). Despite this the French Chamber voted 501:63 on 28 May 1920 in favour of an active reparation policy as opposed to one which observed the letter of the treaty: ibid. 30 May 1920 (LA). For the problem of distribution and war debts at the second Hythe conference: *DBFP* I, viii. 315–17. Note Lloyd George's complaint at Hythe about a 'violent speech' delivered in London by W. A. Watt, the Treasurer of the Commonwealth of Australia: ibid. viii. 274. Report of speech: *The Times*, 14 May 1920, 10. For the Boulogne schedule: *DBFP* I, viii. 331–3. These annuities did not include the cost of the armies of occupation. For the ultimate powers of the RC: ibid. viii. 359–61.

[47] For the impact of *The Economic Consequences of the Peace*: FZ, 2 Apr. 1920, No. 249 (LA). Note the front-page review: ibid. 20 Feb. 1920, No. 135. For the reaction to the Spa invitation: ibid. 30 Apr. 1920, No. 314 (LA). The British chargé in Berlin considered that the invitation to Spa had raised the German government's domestic prestige. Kilmarnock to Curzon, 1 May 1920, *DBFP* I, ix. 458.

regimes. The conservative anti-Erzberger groups scored a notable popular triumph, for, although Helfferich technically lost the case, the verdict of the court was damaging enough to force Erzberger's resignation. The undesirable impact had been heightened by the publication in the press of Erzberger's tax returns, which appeared at first to provide evidence of tax evasion. Although the returns were subsequently proved to be in order, the immediate sensation caused Erzberger to resign on 24 February, pending the investigation of the charges made against him; and his suspension from office lasted until his formal resignation following the judgement in the libel suit a few weeks later.[48]

Early in April the left-wing Centrist, Joseph Wirth, who replaced Erzberger as Finance Minister, projected himself as a new broom who could stabilize the financial system. This prompted the Nationalist Party's *Kreuz-Zeitung* to remark sardonically that Wirth was embarking upon a Herculean labour without any chance of success. 'We have already seen', it went on, 'how in a controlled economy during the war (*Zwangswirtschaft*) the state came off second-best in its struggle against the economic self-interest of individuals. As a result of controls and the government's abuse of the law in the period since the revolution the moral sense of the whole community has been seriously undermined, and the new tax laws, with their heavy impositions, have placed a great strain on the morality of the tax-payer.' When, at the end of April, he introduced the budget for 1920/1, which involved a deficit of 25 billion marks, Wirth's major concern was not with the treaty, which accounted for only 5 billion marks of projected expenditure, but with the prevalence of tax evasion and the financial apathy which was reflected in the poor attendance in the Assembly. In order to combat these tendencies, which other speakers such as the former Finance Minister, Dernburg, attributed partly to recent right-wing press campaigns, Wirth went out of his way to reassure the middle classes that they would not be unduly harmed by federal taxation and appealed for a revival of the spirit of self-sacrifice (*Opferpflicht*) in the German nation.[49]

The scant reference to reparations in the financial debates at this

[48] Epstein, 354–66; Williamson, 312–27.

[49] For Wirth's aspirations: *KZ*, 10 Apr. 1920, 1. For budget debate: Wirth, 26 Apr. 1920, *NV* cccxxxii. 5439–51, 5476; Dernburg (DDP), 5462–6. Cf. Keil (SPD), 5460; Nacken (Zentrum), 5469; Posadowsky-Wehner (DNVP), 5474; Riesser (DVP), 27 Apr. 1920, 5494–5. The components of the deficit were extraordinary expenditures of 11.6 billions (which included treaty expenditures), the deficits of the railways and post office

time, and the growing conviction amongst both government and opposition speakers that Germany's obligations would be lightened before the treaty was actually implemented, are a pointer to the comparatively minor role of reparation deliveries in aggravating Germany's growing external financial problems. The 7.3 million tons of coal and coke which made up the bulk of payments out of current output to June 1920 had a potential export value (Table 4) of about 530 million

TABLE 4. *Export Value of Reparation Coal Deliveries to June 1920*

	Amount delivered (million tons)	Av. British export price (shillings per ton)	Value (million gold marks)
Jan.–Dec. 1919	2.5	60	150
Jan.–Jun. 1920	4.8	80	384
TOTAL	7.3		534

Sources: Figures for monthly deliveries: RC v. 229. Export prices for German coal in this period are unavailable. British export prices are a close enough guide in this rough calculation. They are drawn from *The Statist*, 24 Jan. 1920, 159; 29 Jan. 1921, 159. My figures are higher than those of the Reparation Commission and German authorities (see n. 50) since Germany was credited for the bulk of coal deliveries at artificially low internal prices under the terms of the treaty.

marks. Yet the shortage of coal made it unlikely that these deliveries would have been exported, and Germany's inability to import coal meant that reparation shipments did not deprive her of import substitutes. On the generous assumption that one-third of the coal in question would otherwise have been exported, the net balance of payments effect of deliveries of coal and of other items from current output would have been 180 million gold marks (for coal) plus (at the very most) 100 million gold marks for other items, or a total of 280 million gold marks during the period under review.[50]

(12 and 1 billion respectively), and the 2.9 billions by which ordinary expenditure exceeded ordinary revenue of 25 billions.

[50] German coal exports did not rise above 6 or 7 million tons p.a. in 1919 and 1920, as compared with 34 million tons in 1913. See Lübsen, 427; Appendix II, below. For opposition to increased coal exports: Petition of Schilger and Hagemann, 15 Dec. 1919, NV cccxl, Annexe 1783. According to a German estimate, deliveries of items from current output other than coal and coke were worth 181 million gold marks before May 1921. F. Schroeder, 'Germany's Payments under the Treaty and their Effect on the

Calculation of the 'invisible' balance of payments effect of deliveries of capital equipment such as shipping and railway rolling stock depends to an even greater extent on surmise. Early in 1921 a committee of experts appointed by the German government estimated the annual pre-war foreign earnings of the German merchant fleet at 400 million marks. It should, however, be recalled that a considerable amount of German merchant shipping had been either destroyed or captured during the war; that profits would have been considerably diminished by the post-war dislocation of trade and low freight rates; that Germany was not deprived of the earnings of the ships she surrendered until January 1920; and that there was a gradual increase in income from ships which were retained, chartered, or constructed by the German shipping lines from 1920 onwards. Thus the unfavourable balance of payments effect of shipping deliveries in the first half of 1920 could hardly have been as high as 100 million gold marks. If we add the annual loss of income from transit traffic as a result of deliveries of railway rolling stock (say 30 million gold marks)—even though much of this loss could be attributed to general economic dislocation and to the alteration of trade routes caused by the redrawing of the Polish frontier—and allow another 40 million gold marks for the annual income from German foreign securities surrendered to the Allies, the total invisible losses occasioned by the treaty may have been as much as 200 million gold marks before the middle of 1920. These, taken together with the losses on visible account of 280 million gold marks, bring the total unfavourable balance of payments effect for the period to about 480 million gold marks. Although this is a considerable sum, its significance is reduced by the immense visible trade deficit of 4.7 billion gold marks in 1919 and a further deficit of 240 million gold marks in January to May 1920. The relative importance of reparation deliveries is further diminished by the fact that the visible trade deficit was appreciably greater than the official figures suggest, largely because of the treatment of reparations as exports. It should also be noted that the indirect effect of reparations on the balance of payments via the level of economic activity did not bulk very large beside the war-

Budget of the Reich', *MGCRE*, 28 Sept. 1922, 474–6. The RC valued these deliveries at about 140 million gold marks: RC, *Statement of Germany's Obligations under the Heading of Reparations, etc. . . . at 31 December 1922* (London, HMSO, 1923) (hence-forward RC iv), 6. My figure of 100 million gold marks for deliveries before June 1920 is obviously an overestimate. As a counter balance, cash payments, valued by the RC at 90 million marks up to May 1921, have not been included because they represented in part credits extended for the value of property ceded under the treaty: RC i. 9.

induced economic exhaustion and social unrest and the natural calamities which have been referred to earlier.[51]

The most important way in which the reparation problem affected Germany's external financial position in the immediate post-war period was by making it more difficult for her to secure a substantial long-term international loan so as to limit the growth of her foreign floating debt. Until the conclusion of the Spa Agreement of July 1920 the German government was unable even to obtain credits under Article 235 of the treaty to finance urgently needed imports of food and raw materials. Moreover, although the flotation of an international loan on the security of future reparation payments was envisaged by the creditor powers, no progress could be made in this direction until Germany's total liability was fixed. Yet both the satisfactory settlement of the reparation question and the general financial reconstruction of Europe still depended ultimately upon the intervention of the United States government. The prospect for this had receded by mid-1920 because of the successive refusals of the Senate to ratify the treaty. The negative votes of November 1919 and March 1920 were, in the first instance, the result of partisan in-fighting and Wilson's inflexibility rather than of any irrevocable revulsion against the peace terms. Their financial implications were nevertheless grave. On 31 January 1920 Dresel, the American commissioner in Berlin, informed Erzberger that there would be no chance of an American loan for Germany until the treaty had been ratified by Congress. American policy was now proving a formidable obstacle to the resolution of Germany's financial problems.[52]

---

[51] For the pre-war earnings of the merchant fleet: *The Times*, 11 Feb. 1921, 9. American commentators, basing their calculations on a comparison with the pre-war earnings of the British merchant fleet, arrived at a figure of 500 million gold marks: Moulton and McGuire, 268. It is assumed that both these figures include earnings from German nationals (which are strictly exchange savings) as well as earnings from non-Germans. On the economic impact of shipping deliveries: see above, n. 7 and text thereat. On low post-war freight rates: Davis, 'Recent ... Progress in Germany', 144, 160. For tonnage launched in Germany in 1920 and 1921, see below, Table 6. The pre-war annual income from transit traffic on the German railways and inland waterways has been estimated at 100 million gold marks: Moulton and McGuire, 266. The figure of 40 million gold marks represents a 5% yield on securities with a face value of 800 million gold marks: ibid. 288.

[52] On Germany's credit difficulties: see above, n. 32 and text thereat. The general reparation scheme drawn up by the Allied financial experts on 21–2 June 1920 at the Boulogne Conference recommended that Germany should issue a series of loans with the support of the RC: *DBFP* I, viii. 338. On the reasons for American non-ratification of the treaty: W. S. Holt, *Treaties Defeated by the Senate* (Baltimore, 1933), 249–307.

None of the parties to the reparation dispute had been prepared to come to grips with financial reality in the first twenty months of peace. The British, despite the intermittent pleas of Lloyd George for short-term restraint, had pressed their long-term claims in such a way as to double the reparation bill and necessitate a declaration of war guilt which was to be a major impetus to future German revanchism. The French, while more moderate in their long-term demands because of their preoccupation with the restoration of physical damage, tended, for a mixture of strategic and distributive reasons, to subject Germany to harsh short-term pressures. Finally the Americans, who were the-oretically in favour of a responsible settlement, were prevented from restraining British bombast or tempering French aggression by their reluctance to increase the post-war burdens of the United States tax-payer. Even the preliminary deliveries of shipping and coal which Germany made under the armistice and Article 235 of the Versailles Treaty were impeded by the refusal of the creditor powers to advance any of the funds necessary to prime the German reparation pump. Only the increasing restiveness of the French electorate about the inability of its government to match illusion with reality, and growing British concern about the diplomatic implications of Millerand's sabre-rattling in the early months of 1920 made possible the convening of the Spa Conference, at which the victors sat down for the first time to discuss the implementation of the Reparation Chapter with the vanquished. Although this was to yield a more workable system of coal deliveries, the continuing legerdemain of Allied policy was to preclude any general reparation settlement.

Apart from encouraging the unforgivable prolongation of the food blockade in the early months of peace, the demands of the Allies had relatively little effect on Germany before the middle of 1920. The chaos of the aftermath was only marginally increased by armistice deliveries of capital equipment and the limited deliveries from current output which were made under the treaty. Even the traumatic armistice and peace negotiations culminating in the *Diktat* of June 1919 and the menacing vagueness of the Reparation Chapter about Germany's total liability were offset by the delay in implementing the treaty and the widespread expectation that it would be revised. The financial inertia of the Scheidemann cabinet between February and June 1919 was due

See also T. A. Bailey, *Woodrow Wilson and the Great Betrayal* (New York, 1945), *passim*. On the prospects for an American loan: Kilmarnock to Curzon, 31 Jan. 1920, *DBFP* I, ix. 26.

largely to its preoccupations in other areas and the delay in drafting the Weimar Constitution, which conferred increased fiscal powers on the federal government. The vigorous financial reform programme of Matthias Erzberger in the second half of 1919 was also handicapped less by Germany's still undefined reparation obligations than by domestic political divisions which had been evident during the war and had been deepened by defeat and revolution. The reparation problem certainly did not enhance the domestic credit of the government or improve fiscal morality. It also worsened the trade deficit, encouraged the flight of capital, and made it more difficult for Germany to contract loans abroad. Yet the most important influence at work on Germany, as on her creditors, was domestic politicking, which prevented the adoption of realistic internal and external policies.

3
Fixing the Bill
July 1920–May 1921

IN the summer of 1920 Allied statesmen and financial experts embarked on nine months of fitful negotiations with their German counterparts about implementing the reparation provisions of the treaty. Although the Spa Conference of July 1920 yielded a viable six-month agreement on the important side issue of coal, less success attended discussions on the central question of the total reparation bill. Progress was impeded by the unwillingness of all the creditor powers, including America, to dispel the financial illusions they had encouraged and by constant Anglo-French manœuvring over the distribution of the spoils. The situation was also complicated by the swing to the right at the Reichstag elections of June 1920 and, paradoxically, by the gradual restoration of normal economic and social conditions in Germany, which threw into sharper relief the increasing, but still by no means intolerable, burden of preliminary reparation payments and deliveries. Late in January 1921 Anglo-French haggling, growing apprehension that America would press for the repayment of war debts, and German evasiveness combined to wreck promising negotiations about a pro-visional five-year settlement similar to the Dawes Plan that was to be adopted three years later. As a result, Germany was suddenly con-fronted with a fanciful 'final' settlement involving payments of 226 billion gold marks over 42 years. This served only to strengthen further the hand of recalcitrant elements, and led quickly to the rupture of negotiations and the imposition of sanctions by the Allies in March 1921.

The responsibility for settling Germany's obligations now reverted, by default, to the Reparation Commission. Early in May this body, at the behest of the Allied Supreme Council, temporarily squared the circle. After naming a figure which did not disappoint popular expec-tations it succeeded in devising a schedule of payments which sur-reptitiously reduced Germany's total liability so that it was not, in the short term, beyond her capacity to pay. This sleight of hand was, however, largely the result of short-term pressure from Britain, which remained less concerned with a definitive resolution of the reparation question than with preventing France from increasing her military and economic sway over Germany. It remained to be seen how long, in the absence of any really viable settlement, France would be content with the shadow rather than the substance of reparations.

THE SPA COAL AGREEMENT OF JULY 1920

Because of the Reichstag elections in June 1920, there was a considerable interval between the Allied Note of 26 April inviting Germany to Spa and the opening of the conference on 5 July. In the mean time there were a number of developments which caused the participants to approach the conference in an aggressive frame of mind. The Allies had been annoyed by an interruption in the delivery of German horses to Belgium and by the elusiveness of some Dutch-owned, German-built merchant ships which had been claimed as reparation. Then, on 15 June, the German government, in response to a demand by the Reparation Commission for increased shipments of Upper Silesian coal to Poland, unilaterally reduced deliveries from the Ruhr. This led the commission on 30 June, five days before the negotiations began at Spa, to notify the Allied governments formally that Germany had defaulted. In the mean time the Reichstag elections had strengthened the right wing at the expense of the moderates. The Nationalist Party (DNVP) obtained 71 seats as compared with its bag of 44 in January 1919; the big business People's Party (DVP) recorded an even more spectacular improvement from 19 seats to 65; and the liberal republican Democratic Party (DDP) slumped from 75 to 35 seats. To judge from the election campaign as it was reflected in the German press, this swing to the right had little to do with the reparation question. Reparations were one of a number of issues which Nationalists such as Hergt and Helfferich, aided by the revelations of Keynes about the Paris Conference, used to embarrass the government. Yet the emphasis of the campaign was so much on domestic issues that the *Frankfurter Zeitung* felt constrained to remind its readers on the eve of the election that the coming poll would also affect Germany's relations with the outside world. In fact the main preoccupation of those who voted for the extreme right (and for the extreme left) was the continual left-

wing and right-wing disorders which had rocked Germany since the
Kapp Putsch of March 1920. These made credible the assertions of
extremists on both sides that the elections were a contest between
revolution and the forces of order.[1]

Despite its largely domestic origin, this shift in the balance of
political power in Germany had immediate diplomatic repercussions.
Because the DVP had replaced the SPD in the cabinet, Hugo Stinnes,
the bearded 'Christ of coal', who was to acquire a vast industrial
empire during the inflation years and was already the *bête noire* of the
German left because he owned more than sixty newspapers, was
included in the German delegation at Spa. Stinnes, who represented
the right wing of the DVP and was resolutely opposed to a foreign
policy of conciliation, made his presence felt on 9 July when, after five
days of tense disarmament negotiations, Millerand criticized Germany's failure to make the coal deliveries of 2.4 million tons a month
prescribed by the Reparation Commission and tabled a protocol
designed to ensure the 'complete execution' of her coal obligations
under the treaty. The aggressive retort of Stinnes—whom Harold
Nicolson, a member of the British delegation, likened disdainfully to
the biblical King Ahasuerus dressed in plus-fours—that the Allies were
'sick beyond recovery with the disease of victory' overshadowed the
more moderate reaction of other German spokesmen and strengthened
Millerand's outward resolve to coerce Germany. He therefore pressed
for the rupture of negotiations, the unilateral imposition of the protocol, and the resumption by the Reparation Commission of its control
over the coal question. It took several days of cajoling by Lloyd George
before Millerand, who was well aware that he would get less coal if
he resorted to force, agreed to submit to the German delegation a plan
for deliveries at the rate of 2 million tons for the next six months.[2]

[1] For the postponement of the conference: *DBFP*, I, viii. 253–6. For the disputes
over ships, horses, and coal, and the declaration of default: ibid. 398–9; Bergmann,
Reparations, 38–9; Maier, *Recasting Bourgeois Europe*, 202–3. For the Reichstag election
campaign: *FZ*, 3 June 1920, No. 401 (LA); 4 June 1920, No. 404 (LA); *Die Freiheit*,
4 June 1920, No. 208 (LA). Cf. Kilmarnock to Curzon, 25 May 1920, *DBFP* I, ix. 494–5.

[2] For two first-hand British portrayals of Stinnes: Viscount D'Abernon, *Portraits and
Appreciations* (London, 1931), 165–9; H. Nicolson, *Curzon: The Last Phase, 1919–1925*
(London, 1937 edn.), 227–8. For a German left-wing view: *Die Freiheit*, 30 May 1920,
No. 200 (LA). For French policy at Spa: Soutou, 'Problèmes', 590. For the Spa coal
negotiations: *DBFP* I, viii. 509–13 (Millerand); 520 (Simons, German Foreign Minister);
521 (Stinnes); 523 (Otto Hue, German miners' representative); 531–3, 564–73 (Millerand
and Lloyd George). See also *Die Konferenz in Spa*; Bergmann, *Reparations*, 32–43; M.
J. Bonn, *Wandering Scholar* (London, 1949), 251–7; W. Rathenau, *Tagebuch, 1907–
1922* (Düsseldorf, 1967), 236–9.

FIG. 2. The *Star*, London, 3 May 1921.

The decision of the Allies to discuss a coal delivery scheme with the Germans at first merely brought to the surface divisions of opinion reminiscent of those at the Paris Peace Conference. The main issue in dispute was whether Germany should be compelled to agree to the new delivery schedule by the threat of a Ruhr occupation or whether she should be given financial inducements to co-operate. In opposing Millerand's contention that Germany should, if necessary, be forced to fulfil Allied demands unconditionally Lloyd George reiterated his argument of the previous year in favour of priming the German reparation pump with credits for food and other essential imports. 'M. Millerand knew quite well', he declared, 'that coal was the only article of export which the Germans had to exchange for food for themselves. When we took away 2 million tons of coal from Germany it was the equivalent to the corresponding amount of food which Germany needed . . . We had promised to supply food to Germany and to help start her industries at San Remo. Our interest was to set Germany on her feet, and we could not get reparation without doing so.' Lloyd George's other major concern, apart from that of preventing a French occupation of the Ruhr, was to stop coal deliveries from working to France's advantage in the overall distribution of reparation receipts. Since Britain neither received, nor wished to receive, any reparation coal, the practice prescribed by the Versailles Treaty of crediting coal deliveries to Germany's reparation account at the artificially low German domestic price was, he complained, 'equivalent to presenting France with an annual sum of £33,600,000 for which she would be under no obligation to account to the Reparation Commission or to anyone else'. It was for this distributive reason as much as because of his concern for Germany that Lloyd George suggested, in the course of a private conversation on 14 July with the German Foreign Minister, Simons, that Germany should offer deliveries of 2 million tons a month in return for credits equal to the difference between the internal and external price of German coal.[3]

When the German delegation responded almost immediately with an offer along the lines suggested by Lloyd George, Millerand protested that any alteration of the price of reparation coal would constitute a revision of the treaty. The Italian Foreign Minister, Count Carlo Sforza, also objected to any substantial increase in the cost of the coal his country was receiving from Germany. The Allied Coal Experts at Spa therefore adopted Sforza's proposal that the advances granted to

[3] DBFP I, viii. 607, 620, 631–2.

Germany should not exceed 5 gold marks a ton; and recommended that any further funds for provisioning the mining population should be raised through the agency of a Mixed Commission which the Germans had suggested should be set up at Essen to enquire into conditions in the mining districts. The original Lloyd George credit scheme was, moreover, redrafted so that it did not appear to alter the price provisions of the Reparation Chapter. Instead it stipulated that Germany should be credited for coal deliveries at domestic prices; and added that, in order to ensure that the coal should be properly sorted, the recipients should pay a cash premium of 5 gold marks a ton.[4]

Even this modified scheme was dearly bought. Apart from the fact that Britain, who received no German coal, agreed to supply 24 per cent of any advances made to Germany over and above the premium of 5 gold marks, these advances were to be made only for coal which was delivered overland (or by internal waterway) and for which Germany was, in accordance with paragraph 6(a) of the Coal Annexe of the Reparation Chapter, credited at the low German internal price. This removed any incentive for the German government to increase deliveries by sea, which were credited at the higher world price. A German request for credits to finance imports needed by the population outside the mining region was, moreover, shelved after Millerand insisted that he had agreed 'to supply food for the coal miners and not for the whole of German industry'. The revised proposals, in short, discouraged any attempt by Germany to discharge her reparation debt on favourable terms and failed to resolve her overall credit difficulties. The premium of 5 marks per ton and the additional cash advances she received under the agreement were, however, a useful short-term source of foreign exchange, especially since the advances were never repaid but were debited to her reparation account.[5]

The German delegation at Spa, which included, apart from Stinnes, prominent industrialists such as Ewald Hilger, Georg Lübsen, and Otto Wiedfeldt, who had been members of the Committee of Experts at the Paris Peace Conference, recommended against signing this agreement. Their stand partly reflected their interest in restricting coal deliveries as much as possible and their disappointment at the limited credits which were provided by the Allied powers. Even more import-

---

[4] *DBFP* 1, viii. 623 (Millerand); 624, 626 (Sforza); 628 (German proposal); 634–5 (Allied proposal).

[5] Ibid. 629–35; *Die Konferenz in Spa*, 17. For earlier German efforts to increase coal deliveries by sea: *DBFP* I, v. 793–4. For the text of Coal Annexe: Temperley, iii. 229–31.

ant was the lack of any firm Allied undertaking about the distribution of Upper Silesian coal, which seemed likely to be removed from German control by the coming plebiscite about the future of the region. The industrialists and their DVP representatives might even have swung in favour of accepting the agreement if Lloyd George had vouchsafed anything more than a vague assurance of 'fair play' on this matter.[6]

As in June 1919, the German cabinet chose to ignore the recommendations of its representatives and accepted the terms of the Allies. In so doing it was influenced by Fehrenbach's Centrist Finance Minister, Joseph Wirth, who, in the opinion of one of his DVP cabinet colleagues, 'played a most unfortunate part'. The cabinet's decision was also in line with the views of a liberal internationalist coterie within the German corps of experts. This group included Moritz Bonn, the scholar-diplomat, who was an old friend of Philip Kerr, Lloyd George's Private Secretary, and Walther Rathenau, the industrial magnate, both of whom acted as intermediaries in the crucial negotiations of 14 July. The main concern of these men, and of their banker colleagues Bernhard Dernburg and Carl Melchior, was to avert the disaster of a Ruhr occupation. But the plea of *force majeure*, which was subsequently advanced by Fehrenbach in the Reichstag, was to a certain extent a shield against partisan attack. Before Lloyd George had suggested his credit scheme to Simons on 14 July, the German Foreign Minister had claimed to be unimpressed by the threat of a Ruhr occupation because he considered that its consequences would not differ from the economic chaos, default, and eventual imposition of sanctions which would have followed from acceptance of the Allied coal terms as they then stood. Lloyd George's credit proposals, mauled as they were, had made it worth while for the German government to attempt to avert a Ruhr occupation by fulfilling Allied demands. The government's hope that the Spa Coal Agreement could in fact be fulfilled was expressed by Fehrenbach on 26 July. After admitting that a number of experts considered the agreement impossible, Fehrenbach

---

[6] *DBFP* I, viii. 638–9, 647; *Die Konferenz in Spa*, 80. For the recalcitrance of the industrialists at Spa: Stresemann at DVP meeting, 26 July 1920, Nachlass, ccxiv, Polit. Akten, 1920/VIII. For their hopes about credits and Upper Silesian coal: Dr Ernst Scholz, DVP Minister for Economic Affairs, 21 July 1920, ibid. ccxix, Polit. Akten, 1920/VII. On the other German experts at Spa: Simons, 26 July 1920, *RT* cccxliv. 256. See also Bergmann, *Reparations*, 41; Maier, *Recasting Bourgeois Europe*, 204–6; D. Felix, *Walther Rathenau and the Weimar Republic: The Politics of Reparations* (Baltimore, 1971), 61–3. For the German experts at Paris: see above, ch. 2 n. 28.

claimed that there were many others who thought that the necessary
production could be attained 'by dint of the utmost exertion, and by
the fullest use of technical ingenuity'. In these circumstances, 'when
faced with the threat that non-acceptance of the Coal Agreement
would endanger national unity, every opportunity had to be seized to
avert the major catastrophe'. On the following day Fehrenbach listed
the detailed reasons for the government's optimism. In the first place,
Germany could expect to receive a substantial share of Upper Silesia's
coal output. Secondly, the provisions in the agreement for an improved
supply of food and clothing to the mining districts would give the
miners an increased will and capacity to work. Finally, the domestic
German coal supply could be improved by the increased use of brown
coal, stricter economies, measures against black-marketing, and
improvements in methods of distribution. Clearly the decision to
accept the agreement was not an act of passive compliance unrelieved
by any hope that fulfilment was possible. On the contrary, the Allies,
despite their disagreements, had managed to provide the Germans
with incentives and hopes which were, as in June 1919, just sufficient
to secure their grudging and conditional co-operation.[7]

TOWARDS A NEGOTIATED SETTLEMENT?

There was even less to worry the German government in the general
reparation negotiations at Spa, because uncertainty about the debtor's
future capacity and continuing Allied reluctance to deflate popular
illusions ensured that there would be no immediate settlement. The
preference of the Allies for vague provisional formulae had been
revealed in June when Bergmann and Melchior discussed with the
Reparation Commission the form of the German offer to be made at
Spa. The main suggestion which emerged was that, in order to prevent
any figure from appearing too low, there should be a scheme for
increasing Germany's payments in accordance with a 'prosperity

---

[7] For Simons at Spa: *DBFP* I, viii. 619. For the moderates: Stresemann to Warburg,
26 July 1920, Nachlass, ccxiv, Polit. Akten, 1920/VIII; Stresemann at DVP meeting,
26 July 1920, ibid. For the sympathy between Wirth and the moderates: Cremer at
DVP meeting, 27 July 1920, ibid. For the government's apologia: Fehrenbach, 26 July
1920, *RT* cccxliv. 254–5; 27 July 1920, 302–5. For the cabinet debate about acceptance
on 14 July: *Akten der Reichskanzlei: Weimarer Republik. Das Kabinett Fehrenbach,
25. Juni 1920 bis 4. Mai 1921*, ed. P. Wulf (Boppard-on-Rhine, 1972), 63–7. See particularly 63 n. 2 and 66 n. 4 for the role of Bonn and Rathenau.

index'. Flexibility, if not studied imprecision, therefore characterized the various memoranda which were laid before the Spa Conference by the German government. Figures were cited only to refer to the amount which, it was claimed, had already been paid under Article 235 of the treaty, and to indicate the thirty-year time limit which should be imposed upon reparation payments; and only general recommendations were made about a minimum annuity, Germany's total liability, and the use of a 'prosperity index'. Other memoranda which dealt with the organization of deliveries in kind and with the problem of reconstructing the devastated areas were of a similarly general character.[8]

When the Allies discussed the German proposals on 12 July, neither Lloyd George nor Millerand mentioned definite figures, the former for domestic political reasons and the latter because of his wish to avoid trespassing on the province of the Reparation Commission. Nor were the speeches of the German representatives on the following day any more precise. Bergmann submitted an incomplete summary of deliveries to the alleged value of 20 billion gold marks, which had already been made by Germany. Wirth then stressed the impossibility of an annuity of 3 billion gold marks, which, he pointed out, was equal to a year's 'ordinary' paper-mark expenditure by the German government. Finally, Melchior stated openly that it would be undesirable to risk an impasse by naming any specific figure; and emphasized that the shape of any reparation agreement would, in any case, depend upon the fate of Upper Silesia.[9]

There was no further discussion of the general reparation question at Spa. On 16 July, the last day of the conference, Delacroix, the chairman, opened the way for further negotiations by proposing that the German memoranda should be referred to a special commission, composed of Allied and German representatives, which should meet at Geneva within a few weeks. However, even this proposal proved to be over-ambitious. Although the British government continued to press for the discussions foreshadowed at Spa, the conference was postponed for several months, ostensibly because France and Belgium remained reluctant to sanction reparation negotiations outside the Reparation Commission. As Lloyd George remarked to Giolitti, the

[8] For the German delegation's preparations: *Das Kabinett Fehrenbach*, 1–5; *Das Kabinett Müller I*, ed. M. Vogt (Boppard-on-Rhine, 1971), Doc. 133. For preliminary Allied discussions on 2, 3, and 5 July: *DBFP* I, viii. 400–3, 406–9, 425–30. For memoranda: *Die Konferenz in Spa*, 89–93. See also Bergmann, *Reparations*, 37.

[9] *DBFP* I, vii. 566, 569–70, 586–7.

Italian Prime Minister, late in August, 'Germany was like a bankrupt who could not pay the whole claim against him. This would become clear at Geneva, and France would then, for the first time, have to face the position of having to accept something less than the full claim. M. Millerand could not face the Chamber with that.'[10]

By the autumn of 1920 there was evidence of increasing conflict between French and British policy. In October, out of concern for London's reputation as an international financial centre, the British government unilaterally waived its right to seize German bank balances in retaliation for any voluntary default on reparation payments. Although Britain's desire to opt out of the financial coercion of Germany provoked an angry French reaction, the French government was, for its part, becoming committed to policies detrimental to British interests. Spurred on by an Allied agreement of 16 July which reduced France's share of reparation from 55 to 52 per cent, and by the realization that a great deal of Germany's early payments would be absorbed by the costs of the armies of occupation, Millerand was increasingly attracted to the schemes of Seydoux for a bilateral agreement with Germany about deliveries in kind. Despite opposition within the French cabinet to any such arrangement before the Reparation Commission had fixed Germany's total obligation, Millerand gave his support on 23 October to a proposal to establish a Franco-German authority which would short-circuit the Reparation Commission and order deliveries in kind directly from German firms. Even if the motives behind this scheme were as enlightened as Seydoux made them out to be, its distributive implications were bound to arouse British opposition. The contradiction between France's preoccupation with obtaining immediate assistance for her reconstruction and Britain's reluctance to concede too much to France or jeopardize European financial stability was to complicate the task of Germany's creditors when they embarked on their first serious attempt to settle her obligations at Brussels in December.[11]

In the mean time the German government's attitude to financial

[10] For the Delacroix proposal: *DBFP* I, vii. 641. For British pressure: Curzon to the Belgian Ambassador, 10 Aug. 1920, ibid. x. 503. For Franco-Belgian policy: Derby to Curzon, 2 Sept. 1920, ibid. 508–9; Lloyd George, ibid. viii. 761. See the similar comments of Bradbury, the British delegate to the RC: Bradbury to Chamberlain, 8 Sept. 1920, ibid. x. 510–12. See also Derby to Curzon, 20 Sept. 1920, ibid. 531. For French opposition to a Geneva conference: *Le Temps*, 10 Sept. 1920 (LA).

[11] For the British waiver: Curzon to Seeds, 15 Oct. 1920, *DBFP* I, x. 533. For the French reaction: Derby to Curzon, 27, 28 Oct. 1920, ibid. 536–9; *Le Temps*, 27 Oct. 1920 (LA). For Seydoux and French policy: Soutou, 'Die deutschen Reparationen',

reform and treaty fulfilment was hardening. The ineffectiveness of its financial policy from the middle of 1920 is revealed by the budget

TABLE 5. *German Budget Estimates and Actual Budget, 1920/1921* (billion paper marks)

Estimates	Tax Revenue	Expenditure				
		Ordinary	Extraordinary			Total
			Treaty	Subsidies to public utilities	Other	
Apr. 1920	27.9	27.9	5.0	13.0	6.6	52.5
July 1920	27.7	27.7	5.0	16.0	6.6	55.3
Oct. 1920	39.9	39.9	41.4	19.2	11.2	111.7
Mar. 1921	44.5	44.5	42.8	20.5	48.0	155.8
Actual Budget	50.9	51.9	25.6	17.0	50.8	145.3

Sources: For April: Wirth, 26 Apr. 1920, *NV* cccxxxiii. 5439. For July: id. 1 July 1920, *RT* cccxliv. 89. For October: id. 27 Oct. 1920, ibid. cccxlv. 794–7. For March 1921 (including a May 1921 Supplement) and the actual budget: *Reichshaushaltsrechnung 1920*, ibid. ccclxxv, Annexe 4883, 46, 56–7.

estimates and the actual budget of 1920–1 (Table 5). None of the estimates made in April, July, and October 1920 and March 1921 contemplated tax revenues which covered more than 53 per cent of total expenditure; and only 35 per cent of this expenditure was ultimately recouped by taxes. The government was in fact concerned only to balance its ordinary budget, and it resorted to the printing press to finance all of its so-called extraordinary expenditure occasioned by the peace treaty (25.6 billions), the deficits of the public utilities (17.0 billions), and other items (50.8 billions), the most important of which were demobilization, the public debt, reconstruction, and food subsidies.

These figures support Professor Feldman's suggestion that one of the major obstacles to financial stabilization at this time was the continuing commitment of the government to outlays which were designed to smooth the transition from war to peace and maintain social and political order. Yet the extreme budgetary imbalance of these months cannot be satisfactorily explained without looking at the

243–7. For the agreement of 16 July 1920: *House of Commons Papers*, xxiii, Cmd. 1615 of 1922.

reasons for the inordinately low level of tax receipts. To a certain
extent this was due to the inability and occasional unwillingness of
the under-staffed local tax offices to achieve with sufficient rapidity
in a time of inflation the assessment and collection of the federal
government's various new direct taxes. Yet the fundamental explanation was that the Social Democrats, who had been the main supporters of the stern direct taxes introduced by Erzberger, had been
displaced from the cabinet by the DVP, the party of German heavy
industry. Although no taxes were actually repealed, increased pressure
was exerted both inside and outside the cabinet against any attempt
to adapt the tax system to inflation. This was particularly the case
with the War Levy on Capital Gains and the National Emergency
Levy, which had been assessed on property values at 30 June 1919 and
31 December 1919 respectively, and had hence been very much reduced
in value by the time they began to be collected in 1920. The only
measure which Fehrenbach's Finance Minister, Joseph Wirth, succeeded in carrying through was one which speeded up the collection
of these taxes rather than restored their original value. Despite their
membership of the government, the Democratic Party and the People's
Party joined the Nationalists in attacking even this proposal on the
grounds that a rapid confiscation of wealth might cause financial
dislocation. The DDP was soon persuaded to support the measure:
but the DVP remained adamant, and a cabinet crisis developed when
the Centre Party and DDP demanded that the DVP should either
concur or leave the coalition. The DVP was eventually won round,
but only because it did not wish to resign from the cabinet on the eve
of the elections for the Prussian Landtag. The opponents of the proposal were, in any case, amply compensated by their success in relaxing
the manner in which the Emergency Levy was assessed. A government
order of 4 September 1920 had directed that landed property was to
be valued according to its average yield in the years 1914–19. This had
aroused protests from the Nationalists, who claimed that wartime
land values were abnormally high and demanded that the valuation
period should be extended back to 1908–9. Ultimately, however, the
final decision about the basis of assessment was left to the local tax
authorities. This in effect made good the promise which the DVP had
extracted from the government that the provisions of the *Reichsnotopfer* would be applied in a 'liberal spirit'.[12]

---

[12] G. D. Feldman, 'The Political Economy of Germany's Relative Stabilization during

The stone-walling attitude of the middle-class parties towards direct taxation, above all property taxes, provoked a strong protest from the left-wing opposition. On 22 January the Independent Socialist, Paul Hertz, complained that the yield of the War Levy on Capital Gains had been reduced from 80 per cent to 20 per cent of the sums liable to taxation; and his Majority Socialist colleague, Wilhelm Keil, went so far as to allege that systematic sabotage *(planmässiger Abbau)* of property taxation had taken place. To the claim that direct taxes had been imposed to the limit and that only socially regressive indirect taxes on consumption could be increased, Keil retorted by declaring 'before the whole world' that 'German tax legislation ... was a deceptive piece of window-dressing which would not be carried out'. The government parties denied the existence of any plan to undermine Erzberger's taxes: but all of them, including the Centre Party, insisted more or less strongly on their right to work for the revision of any taxes which threatened the interests of business or agriculture. There was, in other words, sufficient opposition within the Reichstag to explain the relative inertia of the government about direct taxation. A contrary impression was momentarily conveyed by the Democrat, Pohlmann, who advocated that the fiscal committee of the Reichstag should become a standing committee with the responsibility of adjusting German tax law to changing financial conditions. Yet there is no indication that Pohlmann envisaged the tax committee as an organ for the stern implementation of Erzberger's direct taxes.[13]

The Reichstag's lack of fiscal dynamism made it highly unlikely that

---

the 1920/21 World Depression', in G. D. Feldman et al. (edd.), *The German Inflation Reconsidered: A Preliminary Balance* (Berlin, 1982), 180–206. On the difficulties of the German fiscal authorities: Memo of Glasenapp, 27 Nov. 1920, *Das Kabinett Fehrenbach*, 314–16; Keil (SPD), 22 Jan. 1921, *RT* cccxlvii. 2012; P.-C. Witt, 'Reichsfinanzminister und Reichsfinanzverwaltung', *VfZ* 23 (1975), 52–61. For the low yield of major federal taxes between July and Sept. 1920: Denkschrift über ... Reichssteuern, 25 Oct. 1920, *RT* cccixiv. Annexe 720. See also D'Abernon to Curzon, 30 July 1920, *DBFP* I, x. 501. Note the anti-tax pressures on Stresemann and Heinze at a DVP Conference at Hanover on 4 and 5 Oct. 1920: Nachlass Stresemann, ccxviii, Polit. Akten, 1920/XI. For Wirth's Entwurf eines Gesetzes zur beschleunigten Erhebung des Reichsnotopfers und der Kriegsabgabe vom Vermögenszuwachse, 13 Nov. 1920: *RT* cccixiv. Annexe 876. For the attitude of the DDP and DVP: ibid. 18 Dec. 1920, cccxlvi. 1859–83. For the dispute over the basis of assessment: Helfferich (DNVP), 1862; Roesicke (DNVP), 1881; Pohlmann (DDP), 22 Jan. 1921, ibid. cccxlvii. 2038. Cf. *Das Kabinett Fehrenbach*, 285–6, 318 n. 2; Badulesco, *Prélèvement*, 311–12.

[13] Keil (SPD), *RT* cccxlvii. 2018; Hertz (USPD), 2028; ten Hompel (Zentrum), 2026; Pohlmann (DDP), 2036–8; Becker (DVP), 2032; Helfferich (DNVP), 2023. Cf. *The Economist*, 15 Jan. 1921, 88–9.

the government would be able to raise domestic loans or to check tax evasion and capital flight. A half-hearted proposal for a forced loan had been made in November 1920 by right-wing groups who preferred such a measure to the government's project for the prompt collection of the National Emergency Levy. On 1 December 1920 the tax committee of the Reichstag, encouraged by the favourable testimony of the president of the Reichsbank, Rudolf Havenstein, had provisionally adopted a scheme which combined the Levy with a forced loan. Since, however, the loan was regarded by its advocates as an alternative rather than a supplement to the *Reichsnotopfer*, the passage of Wirth's original proposal caused discussion of the former to lapse. The possibility of any voluntary long-term lending to the government by the German public was obviously remote. So also was the prospect of any abatement of tax evasion or reduction of the rate at which German citizens were consigning their assets abroad. The entry of the DVP into the cabinet had in fact decreased the likelihood that the government would resort to measures to curb the latter evil, for in October 1920 its leadership cited the abolition of wartime controls (*Zwangswirtschaft*) as a major achievement since taking office.[14]

This growing financial inertia went hand in hand with mounting opposition to Germany's reparation obligations, even though the practical impact of these remained limited. During the period of the Spa Agreement (August 1920–January 1921) monthly reparation coal deliveries rose by almost a million tons to 1,825,000 tons. Because of the substantial financial incentives embodied in the agreement, this rise was more than offset (in all months except August 1920) by a sharp increase in production. There was as a result 3 per cent more coal available within Germany between August 1920 and April 1921 than there had been in the first seven months of 1920. Yet the residual lag of 10 per cent behind the 1913 level of distribution could now be attributed almost entirely to reparations. Hence the complaints in October 1920 from the iron and steel industry, and from members of government parties when the Reichstag reassembled after its summer recess, that, as a result of coal deliveries, some plants were being forced to slow down or even to cease production altogether.[15]

---

[14] On the forced loan: Badulesco, *Prélèvement*, 310. For references to the prevalence of tax evasion and capital flight: Wirth, 27 Oct. 1920, *RT* cccxlv. 798–9; Pohlmann (DDP), 19 Mar. 1921, cccxlviii. 3262. On DVP opposition to controls: DVP meeting in Hanover, 4, 5 Oct. 1920, Nachlass Stresemann, ccxviii, Polit. Akten, 1920/XI.

[15] For monthly delivery figures: RC v. Appendix XXI, 229. For the level of coal

These complaints may to a certain extent have reflected a long-term growth in the demand for coal resulting from increased production of capital goods which were to replace, amongst other things, reparation deliveries of shipping and railway rolling stock. Yet, to judge from the employment statistics of this period, the level of German industrial activity was ultimately determined at this stage more by the behaviour of the mark exchange than by the availability of coal. Any rapid currency depreciation tended to increase production both by stimulating foreign demand for German exports and by inducing an unhealthy domestic 'catastrophe boom', which resulted from panic purchases of goods by persons who expected the buying power of the mark to decline still further. On the other hand, any dramatic improvement in the mark could bring about industrial stagnation by discouraging foreign buyers and dampening the domestic demand for goods among consumers who anticipated that the mark would continue to appreciate. The economic repercussions of this monetary instability, itself a product of Germany's long-term external financial weakness rather than of the short-term trade deficit, are easy to distinguish.[16] Between April and June 1920 there had been something of an export boom and a quickening of industrial activity (reflected in falling unemployment figures) in response to the low, but gradually rising, value of the mark. A violent improvement of the exchange rate in May had been largely responsible for a time-lagged reversal of this trend and an increase in unemployment between June and August. Because of this stagnation a foreign observer reported that the coal shortage caused by deliveries in the first month of the Spa Agreement,

distribution: see below, Appendix II, and above, ch. 2 n. 34 and text thereat. The most authoritative of these complaints are summarized in: Thelwall, *General Report on...Germany in December 1920*, 14–16. For the text of a telegram addressed to the German government on 15 Oct. by Stinnes, Vögler, and Kirdorff: *Die Entwicklung der Reparationsfrage*, 15. Cf. *Iron Age*, 4 Nov. 1920, 1234; 2 Dec. 1920, 1483. For the Reichstag protest: Fehrenbach, 27 Oct. 1920, *RT* cccxlv. 787; Scholz, 29 Nov. 1920, cccxlvi. 1334; Resolution II(e) of the Committee for the Budget of the Ministry of Economic Affairs, 19 Nov. 1920, ccclxiv. Annexe 939. See also: Bericht des Reichswirtschaftsministers über die Wirtschaftslage im Oktober 1920, *Das Kabinett Fehrenbach*, 327–9.

[16] For the incomplete German trade statistics for 1920–1 see below, Appendix I, Table D. The unfavourable balance of payments effect of coal deliveries was, moreover, very much reduced by Allied payments made under the Spa Agreement totalling 390 million gold marks: RC iv. 20. On the assumption that half of the coal and coke delivered as reparations from July 1920 to Dec. 1921 would otherwise have been exported, the net loss of foreign exchange involved was under 500 million gold marks, most of which would have been incurred in 1921. See below, Appendix II.

before coal production had risen to the level of succeeding months, was less severe than anticipated. It was not until October, when the fall of the mark (which began late in July and accelerated early in September) had awakened fears of a 'catastrophe boom', that the same observer described the lack of coal as 'a distinctly limiting factor'. Finally, after the recovery of the mark in December–January and the simultaneous onset of the world industrial recession, the coal shortage dwindled in economic significance. As Thelwall, the British Commercial Secretary in Berlin, reported, 'the violent controversy concerning Germany's coal supply and coal deliveries which raged throughout 1920 died down almost completely' in 1921. Coal deliveries, he conceded, remained a burden, but they were by no means an excessive one, nor was it impossible to remedy their effect 'by judicious purchases on the world's coal markets and improved exploitation'.[17]

The imagined impact of Germany's obligations was again more important than their reality when the prospect of a settlement caused the general reparation question to be discussed in the Reichstag in October 1920. In his budget speech of 27 October Wirth predicted that the cost of implementing the treaty in the current financial year would be 41 billion paper marks, or more than the entire ordinary budget of the federal government. This proved to be an exaggerated estimate since actual treaty expenditure was 25.6 billion paper marks, or about 18 per cent of the government's total outlay. It was hardly surprising that Wirth's inflated figures, which he openly referred to as a 'propaganda weapon' for the forthcoming negotiations with the Allies, brought the reparation question to the centre of the German political stage for the first time and caused an upsurge of financial pessimism. 'Until recent months', Walter Simons, the Foreign Minister, observed, 'the erroneous opinion has prevailed in Germany that the treaty is not to be taken seriously. Now, however, a fuller awareness of the

---

[17] The mark was worth 73 to the dollar at the end of Apr., 50 in mid-May, and 37.25 on 31 May. It remained stable at this level until the end of July, then declined to bottom at 87 on 12 Nov., and recovered to 60 by mid-January 1921: *Die Entwicklung der Reparationsfrage*, 13–16. For the Apr.–June boom: J. H. Williams, 'German Foreign Trade and the Reparation Payments', *QJE* 36 (May 1922), 493. For the July–Aug. slump: Bericht des Reichswirtschaftsministers über die Wirtschaftslage im Juli 1921, *Das Kabinett Fehrenbach*, 168–71; Davis, 'Recent ... Progress in Germany', 165. For the Sept.–Dec. boom: *The Economist*, 18 Sept. 1920, 437; 25 Sept. 1920, 475; 13 Nov. 1920, 866; 1 Jan. 1921, 15; *Iron Age*, 23 Sept. 1920, 809; 7 Oct. 1920, 916; 21 Oct. 1920, 1062. For the 1921 recession: Davis, 'Recent ... Progress in Germany', 144; *The Economist*, 23 Apr. 1921, 825; Thelwall, *Report on ... Germany to March 1922*, 84. For unemployment figures: see below, Appendix I, Table E.

significance of the obligations undertaken by the German nation is gradually beginning to dawn on the German people.' Less temperate language was used by Karl Helfferich who, after spuriously attributing Germany's post-war financial malaise entirely to the treaty, flatly declared that any increase in taxation to meet the reparation demands of the Allies would be 'a complete and utter impossibility'. This outburst probably contributed to the short-lived slump of the mark in the second and third weeks of November; and it was undoubtedly a spur to tax evasion and capital flight. The financial paralysis of the government was still, however, largely domestic in origin. On 22 January 1921 Wirth mentioned the uncertain state of reparation negotiations as a reason for his failure to introduce a large-scale tax programme. But he admitted that the imminence of the Prussian elections had also hampered progress; and he appealed to the parties which were members of the cabinet 'to open the way for the measures which were needed to obviate further financial distress'. The treatment which the cabinet had accorded his proposals for speeding up the collection of the Capital Gains Tax and National Emergency Levy could hardly have made him optimistic that the necessary co-operation would be forthcoming.[18]

Even without the growing passive resistance of German conservatives to financial reform and fulfilment, the restrictions which were placed by the French government on the deliberations of the Brussels Conference of 16–22 December were certain to prevent it from yielding any tangible results. A niggling Anglo-French note exchange in October and November had established that Brussels would merely provide an opportunity for preliminary discussions between Allied and German financial experts. Only after the experts had reported to their respective governments, and after the future of Upper Silesia had been decided, would the Geneva Conference which had been foreshadowed at Spa be convened to settle the reparation question. Even the decisions of this gathering would then have to be submitted to the Reparation Commission, which was to retain its ultimate authority under the treaty to fix the amount and mode of German payments.[19]

[18] Wirth, 27 Oct. 1920, *RT* cccxlv. 790–802; Simons, 29 Oct. 1920, 857; Helfferich (DNVP), 4 Nov. 1920, 948–51. Cf. Quaatz (DVP), 962, 967; Dittman (USPD), 5 Nov. 1920, 988; Heim (Bäy. VP), 29 Oct. 1920, 897; Scholz (DVP), 29 Nov. 1920, cccxlvi. 1332; Wirth, 22 Jan. 1921, cccxlvii. 2025. For government expenditure: see above, Table 5. Expenditure on reparations, as opposed to other treaty obligations, amounted to just under 10% of total government outlay in 1920–1. See below, Appendix I, Table F.

[19] For the negotiations leading to the Brussels Conference: Curzon to Derby,

Although the German delegates to Brussels favoured a prompt reparation settlement because they reasoned that Allied terms would stiffen with the recovery of the German economy, they were happy to use the conference as a short-term propaganda pitch both to soften up the Entente and to encourage American intervention in the reparation dispute. On the opening day of the conference the inertia of German financial policy was justified by Franz Schroeder, a Secretary of State in the Finance Ministry with DNVP sympathies, who asserted the impossibility of any further increases in German direct taxation, and by Rudolf Havenstein, the ultra-inflationist president of the Reichsbank, who insisted that monetary developments in Germany were the inescapable consequence of her chronic balance of payments difficulties. On the following day, Carl Bergmann, the chairman of the German War Burdens Commission *(Kriegslastenkommission)*, presented a formidable shopping list of preconditions for a workable reparation settlement. It was in the first place essential that Germany's obligations should be settled as soon as possible at a figure which would not drive her to despair, that she should not be burdened with more than thirty annuities, and that payments should be made entirely in kind until financial stabilization had been achieved. In addition Germany should be permitted to float an international loan, enjoy economic equality with other nations, retain Upper Silesia, and keep sufficient merchant shipping to enable her to maintain her foreign trade. Finally the multifarious financial burdens imposed by the treaty should be lightened by reducing the cost of the armies of occupation, releasing confiscated German private property in Allied countries, and implementing less rigorously the system of clearing agreements under Article 296 of the treaty.[20]

Bergmann's representations were not without effect, since the Brussels experts eventually recommended in favour of restricting reparation payments almost entirely to deliveries in kind, waiving further deliv-

---

18 Sept. 1920; 26 Oct. 1920; Derby to Curzon, 29 Oct. 1920; 10, 11 Nov. 1920; Memo by Blackett, 4 Nov. 1920, *DBFP* I, x. 527–9, 535–6, 540–1, 549–50, 557–8. Cf. Ministère des Affaires Étrangères, *Documents relatifs aux réparations* (3 vols.; Paris, 1922), i. 69–70.

[20] For the German attitude to Brussels: *Das Kabinett Fehrenbach*, 33 _, bergmann, *Reparations*, 47–9; D'Abernon to Curzon, 9 Dec. 1920, *DBFP* I, x. 561. For Schroeder, Havenstein, and Bergmann: *Sammlung von Aktenstücken über die Verhandlungen auf der Sachverständigenkonferenz zu Brüssel* (Berlin, 1921), 13–17. For M. J. Bonn's report on the conference: *Das Kabinett Fehrenbach*, 379–86. Article 296 made the German government responsible for repaying through a monthly clearing system the pre-war debts of German private citizens to the nationals of other powers.

eries of merchant shipping, and limiting the cost of the armies of occupation to 240 million gold marks a year. Yet, despite this agreement on peripheral issues, the Brussels experts became deadlocked about the very nature of the reparation scheme. Apparently because of Millerand's influence, the French delegation was led, not by France's representatives on the Reparation Commission, but by Jacques Seydoux, who was preoccupied with alleviating France's immediate reconstruction problems by negotiating about how, rather than how much, Germany could pay. For this reason the French delegates devoted most of their energy during the conference to unsuccessful efforts to persuade the Germans to enter into side-deals about deliveries in kind. The British and Belgian delegates, on the other hand, who were worried about the distributive effects of any Franco-German sweetheart agreement, asserted that their first priority was to obtain a lump-sum settlement which would restore order to the European financial system and encourage the revival of international trade. They therefore sought, with equal lack of success, to obtain agreement on schemes involving total sums which were far too low to be politically acceptable in France. In a vain attempt to reconcile these conflicting policies Seydoux proposed on 7 January that his scheme of deliveries in kind should be combined with a suggestion of Lord D'Abernon, the chief British delegate, for a temporary settlement of five annuities of 3 billion marks. D'Abernon's aim was to postpone a final settlement until revisionist feeling had gained ground. Since the annuities he suggested were the same as the early years of the Boulogne schedule of payments and bore no relation to Germany's immediate capacity to pay, the chances of voluntary acceptance by the debtor seemed slim. Yet the idea of a temporary settlement was fleetingly endorsed by the British government in the second week of January; and it was vigorously supported by Millerand, whose personal influence was enhanced during the French cabinet crisis of mid-January. Joint Anglo-French pressure, and the assurance of Laurent, the French ambassador in Berlin, that the size of the annuities was negotiable, induced the German cabinet to empower Foreign Minister Simons on 15 January to discuss a temporary settlement. An important reason for this decision was, however, the desire to avert the formation of a hard-line Poincaré cabinet; and the government had by no means abandoned its hope of achieving, through American intervention, a final settlement based on Germany's currently reduced capacity.[21]

[21] For the recommendations of the Brussels experts: *Documents relatifs aux*

Briand   Lloyd George

"PERHAPS IT WOULD GEE-UP BETTER IF WE LET IT TOUCH EARTH"

Fig. 3. The *Star*, London, 24 January 1921.

Despite these German reservations, which were reinforced by the lack of interest of German heavy industry in economic collaboration with France, it was the creditors who torpedoed the Seydoux proposal ten days later at a time when, in D'Abernon's opinion, French and German experts were approaching a compromise about the size of the provisional annuities. On 24 January the Supreme Council met in Paris to discuss, in unfortunate juxtaposition, the questions of reparation, disarmament, and the trial of war criminals. Four days later, without referring to the Brussels experts or the German government, it adopted a reparation scheme which envisaged payments of 226 billion gold marks over a period of 42 years. These payments were to be made in annuities which rose after 11 years to the enormous figure of 6 billion marks. The basic annuities for the first five years began at 2 billion marks as did those of the amended Seydoux proposal: but an additional levy of 12 per cent of the annual value of German exports ensured that the amount demanded would in practice be much greater. What was more, the cost of maintaining the Allied armies of occupation and control commissions was not included.[22]

These impossible figures were partly a reflection of the embarrassment of the French government after the Chamber of Deputies had overthrown Georges Leygues, who had been president of the Council of Ministers since Millerand had translated himself to the presidency of the Republic in September 1920. Since an important reason for the dissatisfaction of the Chamber had been the delay in implementing the treaty, Briand, the incoming premier, had promised on 20 January that Germany's resources would be exploited forthwith in the interests of her creditors. Doumer, his Finance Minister, had also felt emboldened to lay before the Supreme Council on 26 January a reparation scheme which envisaged enormous annuities of 12 billion gold marks. Finally, when Lloyd George remarked that Doumer's proposal 'was not a serious contribution made to serious people', and refused to accept anything more than the Boulogne schedule, Briand dug his toes in. 'No

réparations, i. 72–6. For the text of the Seydoux proposal of 7 Jan.: ibid. 96–8. For its origins and fate: Soutou, 'Die deutschen Reparationen', 251–60; Jacques Seydoux, *De Versailles au Plan Young* (Paris, 1932), 37–40. For the German reaction: *Das Kabinett Fehrenbach*, 416–17; Simons, 1 Feb. 1921, *RT* cccxlvii. 2300; Bergmann, *Reparations*, 52–5. For D'Abernon and British policy: Hardinge to Curzon, 11 Jan. 1921; Kilmarnock to Curzon, 13, 14, 16 Jan. 1921; D'Abernon to Curzon, 19 Jan. 1921, *DBFP* I, xvi. 443–8.

[22] D'Abernon to Curzon, 20, 26 Jan. 1921, *DBFP* I, xvi. 449–51. For the text of the Paris Resolutions of 29 Jan.: ibid. xv. 101–4; *Weissbuch ... vom 1. bis 7. März 1921*, 6–24.

French government', he declared, 'could go before Parliament and justify the figure which, under the Boulogne Agreement, would go to France. This figure would be 65 milliard gold marks. France had incurred very heavy debts amounting to 25 milliard gold marks. The residue—40 milliards of gold marks—would go very little towards meeting her vast reparation claims.'[23]

Despite Briand's insistence on French claims, he clearly preferred to resolve the deadlock by postponing any final settlement and reaching agreement on a provisional reparation scheme. In this way, he asserted, 'the French people would gradually get informed as to the true position, and perhaps accept the necessity of accepting a lower figure than they would contemplate at present'. It was Lloyd George who, at this juncture, forced a prompt decision about Germany's liability, even though he knew that this would entail the announcement of a sum which would be beyond her capacity. The ostensible reason for Lloyd George's stand was his conviction that Germany's recovery would be impossible until her total liability was fixed. Yet the Prime Minister's readiness to juggle impossible figures indicates that he was, as ever, moved by short-term tactical considerations. His rejection of the idea of a temporary settlement was closely related to his refusal on 26 January to concede to Loucheur, Briand's Minister for the Liberated Regions, the practical priority of France's reparation claims which the Seydoux proposal involved. His preference for an inflated payments schedule was, furthermore, increased by the information conveyed to him on the eve of the Paris Conference by Sir Auckland Geddes, the British ambassador in Washington, about the determination of the new administration of President Harding to press for the repayment of American war loans. It was, therefore, for the familiar purposes of protecting Britain's share of the spoils and hedging against the repayment of her debts to the United States that Lloyd George insisted on his extravagant claims at Paris. Yet his behaviour reflected the continuing desire of all the victors to prolong the illusion that the problems of post-war reconstruction and international indebtedness could somehow be resolved by others.[24]

[23] For the fall of Leygues and the declaration of Briand: *Le Temps*, 15 Jan. 1921, 1; 22 Jan. 1921, 1. Note the heckling of the government by right-wing extremists such as Daudet, who advocated military sanctions as a means of forcing Germany to fulfil the treaty: ibid. 23 Jan. 1921 (LA). For the Supreme Council: *DBFP* I, xv. 41–2 (Doumer); 56–7 (Lloyd George); 70–1 (Briand). For the Boulogne schedule: see above, ch. 2 n. 46 and text thereat.

[24] *DBFP* I, xv. 71 (Briand); 71–2 (Lloyd George). For Lloyd George's concern about

The indignation aroused in Germany by the Paris Resolutions was such that it strengthened the hand of the extremists who had opposed any provisional reparation settlement. Although the cabinet, still hopeful of American intervention, wished to keep the negotiations alive rather than reject the Allied proposals out of hand, the growing firmness of German policy was expressed by Simons in the Reichstag on 1 February. After lamenting the confusion caused by the vacillation of the Allies between a provisional and final settlement, the Foreign Minister claimed that the Supreme Council had violated the Treaty of Versailles by transmitting the Paris Resolutions without consulting Germany and by demanding that the huge sum of 226 billion marks should be paid over an inordinately long period of 42 years. Simons also complained that the proposed export levy of 12 per cent and the projected use of customs receipts for reparations would be an invasion of German economic sovereignty. Finally he protested against Lloyd George's verbal threat at Paris that Germany's failure to accept the resolutions or to make suitable counter-proposals would lead to a further occupation of the Rhineland and the erection of a customs barrier between the occupied territory and the rest of Germany. Having taken this legalistic stand, Simons went on to declare that his government would submit counter-proposals which would take account only of Germany's limited capacity to pay. If these gave offence to Allied public opinion, it would, he asserted, be the fault of the Allied statesmen who had painted a misleading picture of Germany's capacity and had stunned the German people with their latest proposals.[25]

The determination of the German government to press for a prompt settlement of its total reparation obligation without regard to the reaction of the Allies was reflected in its refusal to allow preliminary contact between German and Allied experts before the conference at London at which its counter-proposals were to be presented. Pressure

---

fixing the bill and priority: Viscount D'Abernon, *An Ambassador of Peace* (3 vols.; London, 1929–30), i. 118. For the hurried departure of Geddes from Washington to brief the British government on the new administration's policies on disarmament, war debts, and other topics: *NYT*, 16 Jan. 1921, 1; 19 Jan. 1921, 17; 26 Jan. 1921, 1. For a discussion of Lloyd George's motives which concludes that he was genuinely concerned to fix Germany's liability: Soutou, 'Die deutschen Reparationen', 264–5. For the impact of American war-debt policy: G. Calmette, *Recueil de documents sur l'histoire de la question des réparations (1919–5 mai 1921)* (Paris, n.d.), Introduction, xcvii–xcix.

[25] *Das Kabinett Fehrenbach*, 440–5; Simons, 1 Feb. 1921, *RT* cccxlvii. 2299–305. Only the Independent Socialist, Georg Ledebour, and the Communist, Paul Levi, were critical of the reaction of the majority of the Reichstag: 2 Feb. 1921, 2312–19. Cf. D'Abernon, *Ambassador*, i. 121.

from the intransigent heavy industrialist wing of the DVP was again apparent. Before the London Conference began on 1 March a committee of experts whose members included moderates such as Rathenau and Melchior as well as Stinnes, Lübsen, Vögler, Wiedfeldt, and Cuno drew up a report which predicted that, in order to pay the maximum annuity of 6 billion marks envisaged in the Paris Resolutions, Germany would have to raise her exports from their estimated 1920 value of 5 billion gold marks to the unlikely level of 40 billion gold marks. However, although it was easy to demonstrate the absurdity of Allied demands, the committee was unable to agree on a counter-proposal. The scheme which was eventually proposed at London was in fact drawn up not by the committee but by Simons himself with the aid of a small group of 'very experienced and capable men', and was adopted by the German cabinet on 25 February before the experts had voiced their opinion. This occurred because the DVP insisted on the exclusion of all advisers from the conference in order to nullify the conciliatory influence of Rathenau and Moritz Bonn.[26]

The uncooperative posture of the German government, which was symbolized by Simons's public denials of Germany's war guilt during February, ensured that there would be little relationship between Allied demands and the German reparation offer of 1 March 1921. The Paris Resolutions had envisaged total payments of 226 billion gold marks over a period of 42 years in annuities ranging from 2 to 6 billion marks. Yet Simons proposed that the German obligation should be fixed at 50 billion marks. Twenty billions, he alleged, had already been paid through deliveries under Article 235. Of the remaining 30 billions, a third could be liquidated within five years by means of an international loan; and the residue, which was to bear interest at 5 per cent, could be amortized over the following 25 years. On the assumption that interest payments on the international loan would be at the rate of 5 per cent, the annual financial burden imposed upon Germany by this scheme would be about 1.5 billion marks.[27]

---

[26] For German behaviour before the conference: D'Abernon to Curzon, 4 Feb. 1921, DBFP I, xvi. 460–1; Seydoux, 43–4; Bonn, Wandering Scholar, 258. For the experts' report: Das Kabinett Fehrenbach, 485–91; Weissbuch ... vom 1. bis 7. März 1921, 32; Simons, 12 Mar. 1921, RT cccxlviii. 2841. For DVP pressure: Stresemann to Wagner, 31 Mar. 1921, Nachlass Stresemann, ccxxxvi, Polit. Akten, 1921/III. For Independent Socialist protests: Breitscheid (USPD), 5 Mar. 1921, RT cccxlviii. 2668–9; 12 Mar. 1921, 2868.

[27] For Simons and 'war guilt': RT cccxlviii. 2874–5. See also D'Abernon, Ambassador,

Although it was in keeping with the financial dishonesty which pervaded the reparation dispute, the unconvincing attempt of the German government to relate its offer to the Paris Resolutions was bound to give offence. The figure of 50 billions was derived by discounting the Paris annuities at the rate of 8 per cent in order to arrive at their 'present value'. Since, however, the German government did not intend to make an immediate lump sum settlement of reparations, this scaling-down was difficult to justify. The deduction of 20 billion marks on account of deliveries under Article 235 was also extremely tendentious. Simons produced no evidence to support this figure, even though the Reparation Commission had, as we shall see, just estimated the value of these deliveries at only 8 billions. Yet another objection to the German proposal was that, whereas the 'present value' of the Paris annuities had been calculated by discounting them at the rate of 8 per cent, it had suggested that interest of only 5 per cent should accrue on Germany's outstanding reparation obligations. Finally, the German offer was unsatisfactory to the Allies because it was conditional upon the retention of Upper Silesia and failed to stipulate that payments should be adjusted to increases in prosperity.

Since this sort of conjuring was a game reserved strictly for the victors, the Simons proposal merely provoked Lloyd George to issue on 3 March a brusque threat that sanctions would be imposed unless a more acceptable offer was received within four days. The united front of German protest against the Paris Resolutions had, in any case, begun to crumble. During a debate on 1 March Keil had criticized Wirth's misleading estimate of expenditure that would be occasioned by the treaty in the current financial year. The discrepancy between the 41 billion paper marks budgeted and the 17 billions actually spent up to 1 December 1920 would, he declared, destroy the confidence of the Allies in Germany's good faith. There was also, he added, widespread indignation in Germany at what even official circles were dubbing the 'grand fiasco' of property taxation. Further dissent, which Helfferich condemned as a 'stab in the back' to the German delegation in London, was voiced in the next few days. Even government spokesmen, while refraining from self-criticism, began to emphasize the desirability of a compromise settlement; and Stresemann declared that,

i. 126; G. Zwoch, 'Die Erfüllungs- und Verständigungspolitik der Weimarer Republik', Phil. Diss. (Univ. of Kiel, 1950), 17. For the text of the German counter-proposals: *Weissbuch ... vom 1. bis 7. März 1921*, 148–51. For Simons's speech at London on 1 Mar.: ibid. 136–44. See also *RT*, 12 Mar. 1921, cccxlviii. 2841; *DBFP* I, xv. 217–23.

irrespective of the outcome of the current negotiations, the day of reconciliation was approaching. This upsurge of moderation led the cabinet to ignore the opposition of the DNVP and the right wing of the DVP and to endorse a last-minute resumption of negotiations by Simons about a temporary settlement. By 6 March the cabinet was seriously considering Rathenau's imaginative suggestion that it should seek to resolve the deadlock by offering to take over the debts of the Allies to the United States. Yet, before a proposal along these lines could be formulated, the negotiations over a provisional payments plan had foundered because of the insistence of Simons on an international loan and the retention of Upper Silesia; and the conference broke up after the expiry of Lloyd George's four-day time limit.[28]

Despite the short-lived truculence of the German government, the rupture of the London Conference and the imposition of sanctions on 8 March were caused mainly by the more aggressive attitude of the Allies since the end of January. The superficial attraction of such a policy for France had been increased by disturbing reports about the slow progress of German disarmament. Yet *Le Temps* rejected with some justification the allegation of Keynes in the *Manchester Guardian* that the Allies were simply seeking to achieve the French strategic objective of detaching the Rhineland from Germany. 'France', protested the Parisian journal, 'does not dream of dismembering Germany. She wants only one thing: that the Allies should collectively seize pledges for payment.' French policy was, in fact, genuinely confused. 'The French', Lloyd George remarked to D'Abernon on 1 March, 'can never make up their mind whether they want payment or whether they want the enjoyment of trampling on Germany, occupying the Ruhr, or taking some other form of military action.' Lloyd George's distaste for French bluster ensured that the military sanctions of 8 March were restricted to the occupation of the Rhine ports of Duisburg, Ruhrort, and Düsseldorf. Yet nothing could have revealed more clearly the unreality of Britain's own reparation policy than Lloyd George's insist-

[28] For Lloyd George's ultimatum: *Weissbuch ... vom 1. bis. 7 März 1921*, 152–67. For the Reichstag debate: Keil, 1 Mar. 1921, *RT* cccxlvii. 2563; Helfferich (DNVP), 2571; Müller (SPD), 5 Mar. 1921, cccxlviii. 2657, 2660; Breitscheid (USPD), 2668–70; Stoecker (KPD), 2681; Trimborn (Zentrum), 2661; Schiffer (DDP), 2677; Stresemann (DVP), 2671–7. For subsequent negotiations: *Das Kabinett Fehrenbach*, 515–18, 525–40, 564–78; Simons, 12 Mar. 1921, *RT* cccxlviii. 2844–6; *DBFP* I, xv. 286–324, 327–31. For the right wing of the DVP: DVP meeting, 8 Mar. 1921, Nachlass Stresemann, ccxxxvii, Polit. Akten, 1921/II. For the Rathenau proposal: Rathenau, *Tagebuch*, 241–2. Cf. *Das Kabinett Fehrenbach*, 540 n. 1.

ence that, as a quid pro quo for French military action, the Allies should impose 50 per cent tax on German exports. Despite its short-term distributive advantages for Britain, such a proposal made it virtually impossible for Germany to earn the foreign exchange she needed to fulfil her reparation obligations.[29]

Allied policy inevitably provoked an upsurge of nationalist feeling in Germany. Simons predicted in the Reichstag on 12 March that the sanctions would inhibit future reparation negotiations. He was firmly supported by the Majority Socialist, Otto Wels, who absolved the German delegation from any blame for what had occurred at London; and the Centrist spokesman, Karl Trimborn, even declared that all previous German reparation offers were void. Not to be outdone, the Nationalist leader, Count Kuno von Westarp, welcomed the break-down of the conference as 'a stroke of luck—perhaps better luck than we deserve', and called for a campaign of passive resistance until the sanctions were revoked. In this atmosphere a USPD motion criticizing German reparation policy was brushed aside, and a motion of con-fidence in the government was carried by 268 votes to 49. There was clearly little prospect for a negotiated reparation settlement.[30]

THE ORIGINS OF THE LONDON SCHEDULE OF PAYMENTS

Since government-to-government negotiations arising out of the Allied invitation of 16 June 1919 had foundered, the responsibility for fixing Germany's total liability fell once more, in accordance with Article 233 of the treaty, onto the shoulders of the Reparation Commission. The commission's first duty was to settle, or to appear to settle, the vexed question of Germany's preliminary 20 billion gold mark payment

[29] On French policy towards Germany: *DBFP* I, xvi. 630–1, 636–7; McDougall, *France's Rhineland Diplomacy*, 140–8; Nicolson, *Curzon*, 233; *MG*, 3 Mar. 1921; *Le Temps*, 9 Mar. 1921; D'Abernon, *Ambassador*, i. 127–8. On British policy: *DBFP* I, xv. 227–8, 257. Cf. *Weissbuch ... vom 1. bis 7. März 1921*, 164. A 50% tax on German exports to Britain was imposed by the British Reparation (Recovery) Act of 24 Mar. 1921. This was reduced to 26% from 13 May 1921. The yield was only £3,680,000 in 1921–2 but rose to over £8 million in the next two years. See Treasury Minutes of 24 Mar. and 17 May 1921, *House of Commons Papers*, Cmd. 1251, 1329, 1921, xix. 205–7; and Statements for 1922–4, ibid. Cmd. 1664, 1922, xi; Cmd. 1861, 1923, xiii; Cmd. 2116, 1924, xiii.

[30] Simons, 12 Mar. 1921, *RT* cccxlviii. 2847–8; Trimborn (Zentrum), 2849–50; Wels (SPD), 2851; Westarp (DNVP), 2863–4; Breitscheid (USPD), 2869–70. For the USPD motion: 2882–3.

under Article 235. An incomplete summary of deliveries submitted to the Spa Conference in July 1920 had been supplemented by a German claim on 20 January 1921 that payments already amounted to 21 billion gold marks. On 26 February the commission replied that this figure was an exaggeration of 13 billion marks, and that an additional payment of 12 billions was therefore necessary. Subsequent negotiations did little to close the gap between these estimates. In his speech on 1 March at the London Conference Simons made no reference to the commission's valuation, and a German Note of 14 March disputed it. A demand by the commission on 15 March for payment of the outstanding 12 billions (the first billion by 23 March: the remainder to be raised through an international loan) was ignored by the German government. Accordingly, on 24 March, the commission declared that Germany was in default in respect of her obligations under Article 235. However, since both the demand and the declaration were intended largely as a belated justification for the imposition of sanctions on 8 March, they did not lead to any positive action. On 16 April the commission made the more realistic demand that the Reichsbank's gold and silver reserves should, on pain of confiscation, be transferred to its branches at Cologne and Coblenz. On 22 April the government refused this request but offered instead that the commission's control over the export of gold from Germany should be prolonged from 1 May to 1 October 1921. This concession did not satisfy the commission, which on 25 April reverted to its earlier demand for a prompt payment of one billion marks—this time before 30 April 1921. The government was ready in principle to comply with this more limited request and stated that such a payment was part of a scheme which it had transmitted to President Harding on 24 April. However, the commission would brook no further delay, and on 3 May it announced that Germany had defaulted on both the immediate payment which had been demanded of her and on a further sum of 11 billion marks. But this declaration of default, like that of 24 March, was regarded by the commission more as a formal justification for future disciplinary measures than as a prelude to an attempt to collect the sums outstanding. The ultimatum which was transmitted to Germany on 5 May with the London Schedule of Payments advanced the default under Article 235 as a reason for the threat of further sanctions: but it suggested no way of remedying this default. Moreover, although a demand for the payment of one billion gold marks within 25 days was included in the London Schedule, the balance of Germany's obligations under Article 235 was tacitly 'assimilated' into her total reparation bill.[31]

The negotiations which led to the so-called settlement of Germany's total obligation were similarly marred by the preoccupation of all parties with political histrionics. The creditors, anxious to be seen to comply with the stipulation of Article 233 that Germany should be given a 'just opportunity to be heard', submitted to the German War Burdens Commission for its comment in March and April 1921 all the reparation claims that had been filed to that date. The German government duly protested on 22 April that this consultation had been inadequate; and, in the mean time, embarked on its own public relations exercise. After seeking in vain the mediation of the League of Nations Council, the Vatican, and Warren Harding, it finally resorted on 24 April to transmitting a proposal through the new American head of state, who had agreed to act as an intermediary. The main reason for this manœuvre, as Simons admitted to the Reichstag, was that Germany's recent pessimistic estimates of her financial and economic position had 'antagonized everybody in the world'. The apparent imminence of further sanctions therefore made it necessary for her to strengthen her moral position by making an attractive offer. The desire to appease Allied and neutral (above all, American) opinion was reflected in the open-ended character of the scheme. In the counter-proposals which Simons had presented at London on 1 March, the main concern had been to establish a maximum figure which Germany could, in her present condition, be sure of paying. By contrast, the offer of 24 April did not mention a fixed sum, but suggested a flexible system of annuities which would vary with Germany's economic capacity and with the amount she could borrow abroad. It also assumed optimistically that the interest rate on a long-term international loan would be 4 per cent, and that any uncovered balance would be met from Germany's own resources. 'It was', Simons confessed, 'something of a leap in the dark and the cabinet's decision to make this leap was governed more by political than by technical considerations.'[32]

---

[31] This paragraph is derived from RC v. 14–23 and A. Amt, Büro des Reichsministers, Reparation, i–ii. Cf. A. J. Toynbee, *Survey of International Affairs, 1920–1923* (London, 1925), 137–140. A law prolonging the RC's control of German gold exports under Article 248 of the treaty was passed on 28 Apr. 1921: *RT* cccxlix. 3461–2. The offer of 24 Apr. and the London Schedule will be dealt with below.

[32] For the German appeals to the League of Nations: Memo by Sir Eyre Crowe, *DBFP* I, xvi. 512–13; to the US: *FR*, 1921, ii. 38–9, 41, 44–5, 46–8, 54–5; to the Vatican: Simons,

Even though this eleventh hour proposal gave Stresemann the opportunity to make an appeal to French and German businessmen such as Loucheur, Eugène Schneider (of Schneider-Creusot), and Stinnes to short-circuit their governments and discuss current economic problems, it came far too late to make a negotiated reparation settlement possible. On 27 April the Reparation Commission announced that it had fixed Germany's total obligation at 132 billion gold marks. This figure was decided upon during informal discussions of which there is no record in the official minutes of the commission: but it is clear that it bore no precise relation either to Germany's capacity to pay or to the claims of her creditors. On the contrary, because of the difficulty of gauging Germany's future economic strength and assessing the exact value of the damage which had been sustained, the members of the Reparation Commission relapsed ultimately into crude bargaining among themselves. Bemelmans, the Belgian delegate to the commission, revealed at the time in a letter to Logan, the American assistant unofficial delegate, that the combined reparation claims of France, Great Britain, Italy, and Belgium had amounted to 152.2 billion francs for damage to persons and 176.8 billion francs for damage to property. These figures had, however, been translated into gold marks by arbitrarily dividing the claim for personal damage by 2.5 and that for property damage by 3.0, and then by adding 10 per cent to both these amounts to cover the claims of the minor Allies. The result of this computation was 67.2 billions (persons) plus 64.9 billions (property) = 132 billion gold marks.[33]

While these transactions had been taking place in the Reparation Commission, the Allied governments, concerned at the deadlock over Article 235, had resumed direct control of the negotiations. During

26 Apr. 1921, *RT* cccxlix. 3417. For Simons on world opinion: 22 Apr. 1921, ibid. 3378. For Simons on offer of 24 Apr.: 26 Apr. 1921, ibid. 3415, 3418, 3420, 3423. For USPD criticism of the offer for its insincerity: Breitscheid, ibid. 27 Apr. 1921, 3445–50. For Nationalist claims that it was an act of 'excessive self-denial' *(Selbstüberbieten)*: Helfferich (DNVP), ibid. 3437–9. The cabinet minutes for 23 and 24 Apr. have not survived. For the notes of Koch, the Minister of the Interior, on the debate in the cabinet whether the offer of 24 Apr. should be made with an eye to domestic or overseas opinion: *Das Kabinett Fehrenbach*, 651–4.

[33] Stresemann, 28 Apr. 1921, *RT* cccxlix. 3468–9. For RC: Bemelmans to Logan, 28 Apr. 1921, Secret Letters of James A. Logan, jun. The Reparation Question (10 vols.; typescript, Hoover Institution, Stanford), v. Annexe 34. The 132 billions did not include the value of restitutions which had been or were to be made under Article 238 of the Versailles Treaty; nor did it include the Belgian Debt to the Allies which Germany had been obliged to assume under para. 3 of Article 232 of the treaty: RC v. 34–5. For a good scholarly analysis: Marks, 'The Myths of Reparations', 236.

discussions with Lloyd George at Lympne on 23–5 April Briand had referred to the deepening conviction of the French government that it was necessary to occupy the Ruhr in order to ensure German fulfilment of the reparation and disarmament provisions of the treaty. This course of action was opposed by Lloyd George, whose cabinet had just expressed 'considerable misgiving' about French policy and urged that pressure should be brought to bear upon the French government 'to retard decisive action and . . . to persuade them to disillusion French public opinion as to the amount which it was possible to recover from Germany by way of reparation'. More significantly, Lloyd George informed Briand of the widespread British belief that the current unemployment problem stemmed from the disturbance of world peace occasioned 'by the French desire for occupation and the demand for reparation'. He therefore concluded that 'better terms could be obtained by a threat than by immediate action'. Despite this discouragement, Briand, under pressure from the French right wing, virtually promised the Chamber of Deputies on the following day that the Ruhr would be occupied on 1 May. French action was, moreover, only temporarily staved off when, on a Belgian suggestion, it was agreed to proclaim that military sanctions would be imposed upon Germany if she refused to accept forthwith both the Reparation Commission's recent assessment of her total liability and a forthcoming decision of the commission about modes of payment and guarantees.[34]

Even before this decision had been taken, a diplomatic campaign had been launched by Britain to ensure that any reparation programme presented to Germany would be sufficiently realistic to preclude German non-acceptance and the consequent imposition of sanctions. The remarkable success which attended British efforts was to be recorded in the so-called London Schedule of Payments, which, although presented to Germany by the Reparation Commission on 5 May, was in fact adopted as a virtual *fait accompli* by that body after having been drawn up by the Supreme Council with the aid of an

[34] Cabinet 24 (21), 19 Apr. 1921, Min. 5, CAB 23/25. A week later Churchill, who was Secretary of State for the Colonies, asked for his opinion to be recorded that 'the British Government were still trying to extract from Germany, in the way of reparations, more than it was possible to obtain'. Cabinet 29 (21), 27 Apr. 1921, Min. 3, ibid. For Lympne: *DBFP* I, xv. 463, 484. For Briand: *CD* 26 Apr. 1921, 1732–4. For samples of right-wing pressure: ibid. 1734–5 (Tardieu); *Le Matin*, 19, 26 Apr. 1921, 1; *AF*, 24 Apr. 1921, 1. For the deferment of sanctions: *DBFP* I, xv. 511–23.

inter-Allied committee of financial experts.[35] The aims of the British
government had been evident from the first meeting of the financial
experts, which had been convened at the daunting hour of ten o'clock
in the evening on 30 April. After squashing a protest from Loucheur
that, by deliberating on annuities and modes of payment, the committee was trespassing on the domain of the Reparation Commission,
the British experts, Worthington-Evans and Bradbury, had laid before
the meeting a very moderate draft scheme of annuities which had been
drawn up by Sir Basil Blackett, the Controller of Finance at the
Treasury. When George Theunis, the Belgian premier, had complained
with some justice that this would yield less than the schedule envisaged
by the Paris Resolutions of January 1921, he had been curtly advised
by Churchill 'not to cry for the moon'. Although neither Loucheur nor
Theunis had initially succumbed to this revisionist onslaught, the
representatives of France and Belgium in the Supreme Council ultimately agreed to the British suggestion that Germany's annuities
should be fixed at the relatively low figure of 2 billion gold marks
payable in quarterly instalments on the fifteenth day of January, April,
July, and October plus a payment equal to 26 per cent of the value
of German exports, to be remitted in February, May, August, and
November. In addition, because of the obvious impossibility of extracting anything more from Germany, they took no real action to remedy
the alleged deficit of 12 billion gold marks in her payments under
Article 235. The only financial allusion made in the London Schedule
of Payments to the dispute over Article 235 was the almost meaningless
distinction which was drawn in Article 2 between Series A bonds
(amounting to 12 billion gold marks) and Series B bonds (for the sum
of 38 billion gold marks), both of which were to be delivered to
Germany's creditors in 1921 and were to bear interest and amortization
charges of 6 per cent. There was, admittedly, a direction in Article 5
that, in the year beginning 1 May 1921, the two quarterly payments
of 500 million gold marks due in July and October should be replaced
by a single instalment of 1 billion gold marks payable on 31 May. But
even this penalty was counterbalanced by the exemption of Germany
from any payments of her variable annuity (based on the value of her

[35] The RC arrived at London at 10.30 a.m. on 4 May, after having been summoned
by the Supreme Council on the preceding afternoon. *DBFP* I, xv. 562. See also a letter
written to *Le Matin* in 1924 by Dubois, who was French delegate to, and chairman of,
the RC in May 1921. *Le Matin*, 20 Sept. 1924, 1. For the rubber-stamping activities
of the RC at the Carlton Hotel on 4 and 5 May: RC, Minutes, No. 184, 4 May 1921;
No. 185, 5 May 1921.

exports) until 15 November 1921. This meant that, if Germany's exports were worth 5 billion gold marks, her total burden in the first year of the schedule's operation would be 2.65 billion gold marks. Such an obligation, although exceedingly onerous unless the debtor received financial assistance, was a considerable reduction on previous Allied estimates of Germany's capacity to pay.[36]

When the French and Belgian representatives gave way about the size of Germany's annuities, they appear to have assumed that the whole of Germany's reparation debt, and not just the 50 billion gold marks represented by Series A and Series B bonds, would bear interest. Such an assumption was encouraged by an opinion given on 2 May by the Legal Service of the Reparation Commission. It was, however, vigorously contested on the same day by the British and Italian governments, who pointed out that the accumulation of interest charges on the 82 billion gold marks of Series C bonds which represented the balance of Germany's liability would swell her obligations to an impossible sum. The turning point in the crucial struggle over interest payments came after Lloyd George delivered one of his periodic lectures on statesmanship. By demanding sums which could never be paid the Allies were, he said, endangering the viability of the whole schedule and thus threatening to deprive France of substantial reparation payments in the current year. This, he declared, must be patent to reasonable men. He quite realized that

there might be unreasonable men in the French Chamber as there were in the Parliaments of other countries, but in the main men were reasonable beings, and were content to grasp the substance rather than to pursue elusive shadows which would lead them into a morass. The decision in this matter was so important that he (Mr. Lloyd George) would regard it as a vital and acid test of statesmanship. It was the duty of a statesman to be courageous, and if the Allied Parliaments declined to endorse the decisions reached by the Conference then the responsibility should rest with the Parliaments. On the other hand, if the statesmen assembled together inserted something in the document which

---

[36] For the authorship of the London Schedule: P. J. Grigg, *Prejudice and Judgment* (London, 1948), 64–8. For the text: RC, *Official Documents Relative to the Amount of Payments to be Effected by Germany under Reparations Account, I, 1 May 1921–1 July 1922* (London, 1922) (henceforward RC iii), 4–9. For the Allied discussions: Séance des Experts tenue aux Treasury Chambres, 30 Apr. 1921 at 10 p.m. Typescript minutes in Louis Loucheur Papers, Box 7, Folder 4. The idea of 'assimilating' the outstanding 12 milliards into Germany's total debt had already been accepted by the RC. RC, Minutes, No. 181, 29 Apr. 1921, 7–8.

they knew to be wrong in the end the countries to which they were respectively responsible would condemn them.[37]

The subsequent agreement of the French and Belgian delegations that interest should not accrue on the last 82 billion gold marks of Germany's indebtedness was facilitated partly by the sops which had been thrown to the French extreme right wing. The British and Italian governments had already agreed that the London Schedule should be accompanied by a six-day ultimatum, and that Briand should, in order to save face with the Chamber of Deputies, proclaim on 2 May the mobilization of the French class of 1919. However, if Britain and Italy were ready to tolerate some costly French sabre-rattling, which was unlikely, in view of the moderation of the London Schedule, to develop into military action, they would not consent to the imposition of economic and financial controls upon Germany which might infringe her political and economic sovereignty. This reluctance had been clearly expressed when proposals for effective Allied control of German public revenues and for the imposition of a coal tax were laid before the committee of experts by Loucheur on 1 May. Such proposals were resisted by Worthington-Evans and Bradbury on the grounds that they would lead to 'the Ottomanization of Germany'; and Churchill expressed the view that 'the sole guarantee for the execution of the present terms was the good will of Germany and the armed strength of the Allies'. As a result of this pressure, considerable restrictions were placed upon the powers of the Committee of Guarantees, a sub-committee of the Reparation Commission which was set up at the request of France under Articles 6 and 7 of the London Schedule. This body was directed, somewhat unspecifically, to *supervise* the collection of the three types of revenue which were to be used as a security for reparation payments, namely (a) customs receipts, (b) the 26-per-cent levy on German export earnings (except on exports to Great Britain, which were already taxed under the provisions of the British Reparation Recovery Act), and (c) the proceeds of any direct or indirect taxes suggested by the German government and approved by the committee. It was also the general duty of the committee to ensure that, in accordance with Articles 241 and 248 and paragraph 12(b) of Annexe II of the Reparation Chapter, reparation payments were

---

[37] For the debate over interest: Opinion of the Legal Service, 2 May 1921, RC, Annexe 883(b); DBFP I, xv. 537–9. Note the dissenting opinion of J. Fischer Williams, the British member of the Legal Service of the Reparation Commission: RC, Annexe 883(a). For Lloyd George: DBFP I, xv. 556–7.

treated as a first charge upon revenue and that the level of German taxation was at least as high as in Allied countries. However, the role of the committee was limited in practice to an advisory one by the clear stipulation that it was not 'to interfere in the German administration'.[38]

The moderation of the London Schedule of Payments was such that even Keynes felt constrained to refer to it publicly as 'a signal triumph for the spirit of justice', and advised the German government to accept its terms. Keynes, it is true, considered that even Germany's reduced obligations would soon prove to be beyond her capacity. But he conceded that the schedule did not 'call on her to do immediately— that is to say in the course of the next six months—anything incapable of performance'. He therefore hoped that, if Germany accepted the schedule and attempted to fulfil it, further revision of her obligations would follow. In the mean time Germany should believe 'that the whole world is not unreasonable and unjust, whatever the newspapers may say, that time is a healer, that time is an illuminator, and that we must still wait a little before Europe and the United States can accomplish in wisdom and mercy the economic settlement of the war'.[39]

Although Keynes can be forgiven his wishful thinking, the behaviour of Germany and her creditors in the preceding year did not give much ground for hope. The Spa Agreement, under which the Allies had traded short-term credit assistance for larger coal deliveries, had almost been torpedoed by the increased influence of conservative industrialists over German policy after the Reichstag elections of June 1920; and much of the impetus to the agreement had, in any case, derived from Britain's desire to restrain France militarily and reduce her share of reparations rather than from any recognition of the need for treary revision. The passivity of German financial policy in the second half of 1920, the irresponsibility of the Allies in opting for the Paris Resolutions rather than a provisional five-year settlement in January 1921, and the intransigence of the German government at the London Conference in March had revealed the continuing predilection of all parties for play-acting. The onset of the international recession in the

---

[38] For Anglo-Italian agreement to French sabre-rattling: DBFP I, xv. 522–6. For British opposition to controls: French minutes of the meeting of 1 May in 'La Politique des réparations de gouvernement français au cours de l'année 1921', 8–10, in Louis Loucheur Papers, Box 5, Folder 11. For the Committee of Guarantees: DBFP I, xv. 534–5. For text of Reparation Chapter: Temperley, iii. 217, 221, 234.

[39] MG, 6 May 1921, 6. Keynes's judgement of the London Schedule was still the same late in Aug. 1921. See his article: Sunday Times, 21 Aug. 1921.

early months of 1921 had encouraged something of an upsurge of revisionism in Britain by demonstrating in a practical manner the threat posed to employment by a large-scale reparation scheme in a *laissez-faire* world. Yet the most compelling reason for the relative moderation of the London Schedule of Payments had been Britain's strategic concern to prevent the military coercion and financial Otto-manization of Germany by France. The sleight of hand of the schedule would not lead to a resolution of the reparation dispute unless it gave rise to an attempt by all the nations involved, including the United States, to grapple realistically with the problems of domestic and international indebtedness.

PART TWO
Making Germany 'Pay'

4
'Fulfilment'
May 1921–January 1922

NOTHING revealed more clearly the unreality of Allied reparation demands and the unlikelihood of any effective, or even genuine, German attempt to fulfil them than the brief history of the London Schedule of Payments. The failure of the creditors to charge interest on the bulk of Germany's notional obligation of 132 billion marks was a tacit admission of the financial impossibility of their demands; and their refusal to vest adequate powers in the Committee of Guarantees, the sub-committee of the Reparation Commission which was set up to supervise the collection of interest and amortization on the remaining 50 billion gold marks, showed that, despite their Germanophobic posturing, the bourgeois liberal governments of the victors were ultimately unwilling to assert sufficient control over the German economic and financial system to obtain the required transfer of wealth. Statesmen who had condoned the cry for an indemnity largely in order to shield their own propertied classes from stern post-war taxation could hardly expect a government such as that of Joseph Wirth, which depended for its survival on the support of the German middle classes, to carry through of its own accord the confiscatory taxation of wealth which was needed if Germany was to meet her obligations. Wirth managed to enlist the support of German industry for a short-lived 'offensive of fulfilment' in the autumn of 1921. Yet the co-operation of the tycoons was proffered largely in order to defuse moves by the radical Ministry of Economics to institute an 'appropriation of real values' (*Erfassung der Sachwerte*); and it was quickly withdrawn at the end of October in response to the decision of the League of Nations to partition Upper Silesia. Thereafter the only way of salvaging something from the wreck of the London Schedule would have been a substantial reduction of its annuities. Yet, notwithstanding their awareness that one nation could not bear the entire burden of post-war reconstruction, Britain, France, and the United States refused to renounce any of their reparation claims or their loans to each other. The slate-wiping which the situation demanded in the summer and autumn of 1921 was discouraged by Anglo-French friction over the Near East, French intransigence at the Washington Disarmament Conference, and further disputes over sanctions and distribution. Growing concern about the effect of reparations on trade provoked the British cabinet to toy with schemes of debt renunciation which would have induced France to relax her pressure on Germany in December 1921. Yet Lloyd George baulked, as usual, at any tangible British initiative. After Poincaré had assumed power there was little to stop the reparation illusion from becoming a menace to the peace of Europe as well as to its prosperity.

THE BREAKDOWN OF THE LONDON SCHEDULE

Although the economic significance of reparation deliveries of items such as coal was reduced in 1921, the combined financial effect of cash payments and deliveries in kind now reached its peak. In the budgetary year 1 April 1921–31 March 1922 reparations were responsible for almost a third of German government expenditure (2.0 billion out of 6.7 billion gold marks) and over half of the budget deficit. This was clearly an intolerable burden in the long run. Yet the deficit was much larger than it need have been, since 1921–2 revenues of 3 billion gold marks compared unfavourably with those of 1913, when the tax powers of the federal government had been far more restricted. Allied demands also placed an immense strain on the balance of payments at a time when, notwithstanding the incompleteness of official trade statistics, imports appear to have exceeded exports. It should, however, be borne in mind that from the autumn of 1921 Germany's adverse trade balance was due increasingly to imports of iron ore and coal to meet the needs of an inflation-induced heavy industrial boom. The impact of reparation payments on the mark exchange could, moreover, have been cushioned by more effective methods of raising the necessary funds abroad.[1]

The possibility of any serious attempt to cope with the burdens of

---

[1] For the diminished impact of coal deliveries in 1921: see above, ch. 3 n. 17 and text thereat. See below, Appendix I for budget figures, Table F; trade figures, Table D; increased heavy industrial production, Table A. Note the rapid decline in unemployment from the summer of 1921: Table E.

the London Schedule was diminished by the hostile reception it was accorded when it was transmitted on 5 May. There was, symbolically, not even a government to receive the Allied terms, since the Fehrenbach cabinet, undermined by its failure to achieve a negotiated settlement and powerless in the face of Polish incursions in Upper Silesia, had resigned on the previous day. Although there was no debate on 6 May when Fehrenbach, still acting provisionally as Chancellor, informed the Reichstag of the Allied communications, press comment was highly unfavourable. Even Walther Rathenau, who was shortly to join a cabinet committed to fulfilment of the schedule, declared in the *Berliner Tageblatt* that the 'remnants of German honour' demanded 'that we do not promise what we cannot possess'. One reason for the outcry was the mistaken but widespread belief that the whole sum of 132 billion gold marks would bear interest, and thus represented only the present, or uncapitalized, value of Germany's obligation. Another was the arbitrary manner in which the schedule was drawn up and the threat of sanctions which accompanied it. This recreated the *Diktat* atmosphere of June 1919 and decreased the willingness of the parties, above all those which had borne the brunt of the earlier crisis, to shoulder the responsibility for acceding to Allied demands. 'No section', the British Ambassador observed, 'wished to bell the cat.'[2]

As on the previous occasion, the only parties prepared to accept Allied terms within the time limit prescribed by the ultimatum were the SPD, Zentrum, and DDP, which formed a coalition under the leadership of Wirth with the support of the USPD. The Reichstag debate of 10 May, which yielded a 220:172 vote of confidence, revealed the unanimous conviction that Germany would be ruined unless her obligations were reduced. Yet the government parties argued that a sincere attempt at fulfilment would prompt further revision of Allied demands. The hope that the March sanctions would be lifted and that the Upper Silesian question would be adjusted in Germany's favour also influenced a few members of other parties to vote in the affirmative. On 9 and 10 May Stresemann sought, and received, assurances from the British government, which was anxious to avert military action by France, that it favoured the lifting of the March sanctions,

---

[2] Fehrenbach, 6 May 1921, *RT* cccxlix. 3623–4. For citation of Rathenau's article: Brauns (DNVP), 2 June 1921, ibid. 3735. For the strident reaction of the conservative and industrial press: *BLA*, 6 May 1921, No. 210, 1; *DAZ*, 6 May 1921, No. 209 (LA). For confusion about 'present value': W. von Rheinbaben, *Von Versailles zur Freiheit* (Hamburg, 1927), 37–8. For sensitivity about acceptance: D'Abernon, *Ambassador*, i. 170.

the reduction of the British levy on German exports from 50 per cent to 26 per cent, and the limitation of German participation in Allied reconstruction solely to the restoration of war damage. The DVP leader told the Reichstag on 10 May that only his failure to obtain a firm British assurance about Upper Silesia prevented a group within the DVP from giving active support to an attempt to fulfil the London Schedule. As it was, however, only 6 members of the DVP and 17 Democrats voted for acceptance. The cabinet was strengthened some-what when Rathenau, the DDP industrial magnate, joined it as Min-ister for Reconstruction at the end of May. Yet, despite the publicly expressed eagerness of Stresemann to join the coalition, the DVP remained aloof throughout the summer because of the continuing failure of the Allies to give ground on the issues of sanctions and Upper Silesia.[3]

The tentative and conditional nature of the support of the financially influential parties, and the outspoken opposition of the extreme right and left wing, explain the distinct lack of enterprise of the government in collecting and transferring the first billion gold marks due under the schedule. The operation began in the second half of May when advantage was taken of the temporary improvement in the mark brought about by the acceptance of the Allied ultimatum in order to buy gold and foreign exchange with paper marks. On 31 May, the date prescribed by the schedule, the yield from these purchases—150 million gold marks—was remitted to the Reparation Commission together with three-months treasury bills to cover the remaining 850 million gold marks. In order to honour these bills when they matured on 31 August the government simply continued to buy foreign exchange and gold within Germany. Because of the scarcity of these assets and the unwillingness of Germans to part with them in a time of monetary instability, the dollar rate rose by the end of the first week of June to 66 (its level before the acceptance of the ultimatum), and

---

[3] For the affirmative voters: Wirth (Zentrum), 10 May 1921, *RT* cccxlix. 3629–30; Wels (SPD), 3630; Ledebour (USPD), 3637–8. For the voting behaviour of the DVP and DDP: 3652–4. Cf. Haas (DDP), 3640; Stresemann (DVP), 3631. For the latter's account of his negotiations with the British cabinet: *DAZ*, 31 July 1921, No. 354, 1. See also D'Abernon, *Ambassador*, i. 164–6; *DBFP* I, xvi. 664–6; Cabinet Minutes 36 (21), 10 May 1921, Min. 1, CAB 23/25. For Rathenau's appointment: *BLA*, 3 June 1921, No. 257, 1; *DAZ*, 30 May, 3 June 1921, Nos. 247, 1; 254 (LA). For Stresemann and DVP entry into cabinet: ibid. 28, 30 May 1921, Nos. 245, 247, 2. For DVP resentment at lack of Allied concessions: Stresemann, 3 June 1921, *RT* cccxlix. 3760–5; Interpellation of 30 June 1921, ibid. cccl. 4235; 1 July 1921, 4258 ff. Note DVP abstention in vote of confidence on 4 June 1921: *BLA*, 4, 5 June 1921, Nos. 259, 261, 1.

thence to 75 on 30 June, 81 on 31 July, and 86 on 31 August. This development in turn increased the desire of German citizens to hoard foreign exchange. The result was that, as 31 August approached, the government found itself in need of 400 million gold marks in foreign currency, which could only be purchased at the risk of violent depreciation. This sum was raised at the last moment by drawing upon 68 millions of the Reichsbank's gold reserves, by pledging 58 millions of its silver, and by obtaining short-term high-interest foreign credits, the largest of which was a Dutch credit of 270 million gold marks. The latter procedure merely postponed until September and October further purchases of foreign exchange, which contributed to the continued fall of the mark in those months.[4]

The first cash instalment under the London Schedule had been financed simply by increasing the government's floating debt at the Reichsbank, by obtaining short-term foreign credits, and, ultimately, by buying foreign currency with paper marks. This hand-to-mouth procedure inevitably caused further depreciation of the mark, which was already highly vulnerable because of the huge external floating debt accumulated in preceding years and the continuing imbalance of German trade. Such haphazard behaviour, which effectively undermined the London Schedule, was made easier by the impotence of the Committee of Guarantees, which was established under Articles 6 and 7 of the schedule to supervise the raising of 'the funds assigned as security for the payments to be made by Germany'. The two most important sources of foreign exchange which the German government was directed to tap were its customs receipts and the proceeds of a 25-per-cent levy on the value of exports. In its efforts to ensure the exploitation of these revenues, the committee was hamstrung both by the general directive of the London Schedule that it should not 'interfere' in the German administration and by the specific provision that the government could suggest taxes or funds 'in addition to or in substitution for' customs revenues and the export levy. As a result of these loopholes, the German War Burdens Commission retained effective control over financial policy affecting reparations; and Schroeder, the Secretary of the Finance Ministry, was able to declare

---

[4] For the opposition of the extreme right and left: Hergt (DNVP), 10 May 1921, *RT* cccxlix. 3632–6; Koenen (KPD), 3650. For the buying operations: Wirth, 1 June 1921, ibid. 3709; Schmidt (Minister of Economics), 8 Nov. 1921, cccli. 4879. For the dollar rate: *Die Entwicklung der Reparationsfrage*, 18–19. For short-term credits: Bergmann, *Reparations*, 82; Bresciani-Turroni, 95–6. For critical comment: *DAZ*, 31 July 1921, No. 354, 1.

to the Committee when it visited Berlin on 17 and 18 June that, because an export levy would raise 'political and economic difficulties', the German government preferred alternative sources of funds which, apart from a proposed tax on dividends and interest, consisted entirely of indirect taxes on consumption. The response of the committee to this evasive behaviour was to refuse on 28 June to accept as substitutes 'resources which still exist only in the form of proposals'. Yet it was not until 29 July that the *Kriegslastenkommission* reluctantly agreed to take steps to exact the export levy on the condition that it could consult further with the committee about the matter. The delaying tactics of the German negotiators, not to mention their prolonged dispute with the committee about whether the level of exports was an appropriate determinant for the variable component of Germany's annuities, virtually ensured the premature demise of the London Schedule.[5]

The passivity of the government's financial policy in the summer of 1921 was reflected in the budget which Wirth, who was Finance Minister as well as Chancellor, presented to the Reichstag on 6 July. Expenditure for the budgetary year 1921–2 would, he predicted, amount to between 145 and 150 billion paper marks. Of this sum, 49.5 billions were classified as ordinary expenditure, 59 billions extra-ordinary expenditure, and a further 40 to 45 billions reparation expenditure. Since 26.6 billions of the extraordinary budget was earmarked for treaty expenditures other than reparations, the total budgetary outlay occasioned by the treaty would be between 67 and 72 billion paper marks. Against these expenditures was set an estimated revenue of only 80 billion paper marks, of which some 30 billions were to be raised by new taxation. Although this revenue was not much greater in real terms than that of 1913, the idea of a deficit of between 60 and 70 billion paper marks dissuaded everyone in the Reichstag, apart from the two socialist parties, from calling for a more energetic financial policy. Even Keil, the Majority Socialist, now conceded that much

[5] For text of London Schedule: RC iii. 4–9. Note the restrictive interpretation of the powers of the Commitee of Guarantees by its French chairman Mauclère: Comité des Garanties: Délégation Française. Procès-Verbaux. Minutes No. 4, 17 and 18 June 1921; Minutes No. 20, 14 Sept. 1921. AN AJ[5]3. For relations between Committee of Guarantees and *Kriegslastenkommission*: RC iii. 10–24; *Akten der Reichskanzlei: Weimarer Republik. Die Kabinette Wirth I and II*, ed. I. Schulze-Bidlingmaier (2 vols., Boppard-on-Rhine, 1973), i. 72 n. 2, 97–114, 158–68. For Briand's subsequent complaint about the ineffectiveness of the Committee of Guarantees: Chambre des Députés, CAE, 26 Dec. 1921, 136–8. For a good discussion: Trachtenberg, *Reparation in World Politics*, 224–6.

would depend on the prompt abrogation of sanctions and the retention of Upper Silesia.[6]

The non-co-operation of the bourgeois parties soon led to the mooting of confiscatory tax schemes which were favoured by the left wing of the Centre Party, the SPD, and the USPD. Plans for an 'appropriation of real values' (*Erfassung der Sachwerte*) which had been drawn up by the Ministry of Economics in mid-May were mentioned by Wirth in an address at Essen on 19 June and in his budget speech of 6 July. Significantly, however, details of the scheme were revealed to the Reichstag not by Wirth, but by Keil. The government would, Keil declared, confiscate a portion of all land, property, houses, machinery, and raw materials, which were the sole repositories of real wealth in a time of monetary inflation. This would enable it to balance the budget and strengthen Germany's credit abroad and, at the same time, make the propertied classes bear more of the fiscal burden. Such a proposal, Keil stressed, would not have been preferred to a more expeditious loan scheme if the wealthy had voluntarily supported financial reform. As one would expect, such a measure was welcomed by the Independent Socialists as a step towards socialism. Yet Wirth had already opposed it within the cabinet, both because of his sensitivity as Finance Minister to the wishes of a conservative department which preferred to adjust existing taxes, and because, as Chancellor, he feared that the 'appropriation of real values' would be rejected by the Reichstag. Wirth's reservations had prompted him to submit to the cabinet on 27 June an alternative proposal for speeding up the collection of the National Emergency Levy; and two days later, in order to preserve cabinet unity, the rival projects of the Ministries of Economics and Finance had been consigned to the limbo of an interdepartmental committee. A similar fate awaited another Economics Ministry proposal late in July for advanced payments of the Corporation Tax. The objections voiced in the cabinet were the same as those of its DVP critics in the Reichstag, who denounced such levies as socialistic and vulnerable to seizure by the Entente. The consensus was that it would be undesirable to resort to such drastic financial expedients before the outstanding issues of sanctions and Upper Silesia had been resolved in Germany's favour.[7]

[6] Wirth, 6 July 1921, *RT* cccl. 4468–73; Keil (SPD), 4482; Crispien (USPD), 4492–8; Geyer (VKP), 4500–3; Keinath (DDP), 4498. Cf. Helfferich (DNVP), 4474–6; Becker (DVP), 4487–91.

[7] For scheme of 'appropriation of real values': Denkschrift des Wirtschaftsministers,

This stonewalling did not immediately evoke a hostile French response. Partly, no doubt, because of its unfavourable reception in Germany, the London Schedule at first enjoyed a good press in France. There was bound to be discontent in extreme nationalist circles, if only because liberal Anglo-Saxons such as Keynes had hailed the Reparation Commission's deliberations as a triumph for revisionism and Lloyd George. The 68 billion gold marks to which France's share of the spoils had now shrunk also compared very unfavourably with Briand's February 1921 estimate of the cost of French civilian damage at between 100 and 110 billion gold marks. Yet even *Le Matin*, perhaps reassured by the prominently reported comment of the American reparation expert, Thomas W. Lamont, that the London Conference had resulted in a 'victory for France', uttered no real criticism of the schedule for several months. On the contrary it gave firm support to Briand while he was extracting his 390: 162 vote of confidence from the Chamber; endorsed his argument that France would have gained no reparations and destroyed the Entente by taking unilateral action in the Ruhr; and published a front page photograph of the first bonds to be delivered by Germany under the complacent caption 'L'Allemagne paye'.[8]

It was not, in fact, until September that *Le Matin*, alarmed by the recent rapid depreciation of the mark, began to express misgivings about 'the new danger' of a self-inflicted German bankruptcy. By this time, however, negotiations between Rathenau, Wirth's Minister of Reconstruction, and Louis Loucheur, his French ministerial counterpart, appeared to be promising Franco-German economic collaboration along the lines which Jacques Seydoux had been advocating. On the initiative of Rathenau and Charles Laurent, the French ambassador in Berlin, the two men had met secretly in June at Wiesbaden, in the political no-man's-land of occupied Germany, to talk 'as one businessman to another' about converting as much as possible of

---

19 May 1921; Die Belastung der Sachwerte als Teil des Reparationsprogramms, 27 June 1921, A. Amt, Wirtschafts Reparationen, Ausführung des Londoner Ultimatums ... (henceforth A. Amt, Ausführung). Cf. *Die Kabinette Wirth*, i. 7–13. For cabinet discussion on 29 June and 4 Aug.: ibid. 115–19, 187–9; *BLA*, 29 June 1921, No. 286, 1. For Reichstag debate: Keil, 6 July 1921, *RT* cccl. 4484; Crispien (USPD), 4494; Becker (DVP), 4489–90; Helfferich (DNVP), 4479–80. For good accounts: Laubach, *Die Politik der Kabinette Wirth*, 61–6; Felix, 92–3; *Die Kabinette Wirth*, Introduction, xlvii–xlix.

[8] For right-wing criticism: *AF*, 5, 6, 8 May 1921 (LA, Daudet); 20 May 1921, 1 (Daudet, Maurras). Cf. Tardieu, 19 May 1921, *CD*, 3–10. For Briand's Feb. estimate: 4 Feb. 1921, ibid. 225. *Le Matin*, 15, 25, 27, 31 May, 1.

Germany's reparation obligation into deliveries in kind. The fruit of their discussion was the well-intentioned but impractical Wiesbaden Agreement of 6 October 1921. This stipulated that between 1 October 1921 and 1 May 1926 France should receive from Germany deliveries of machinery and other items referred to in Annexe IV of the Reparation Chapter to the value of 7 billion gold marks. The superficial attractions of the scheme were that it provided for direct contact between German industry and the French recipients; that deliveries were to be made only to the devastated regions and only in so far as they did not overtax the German economy; and that valuation was to be entrusted to a committee of three composed of a Frenchman, a German, and a neutral arbitrator acceptable to both parties. Another advantage was that only 35 per cent of the value of these deliveries was to be credited to Germany's reparation account, and that the remainder was to be treated as an advance to France which would be repaid between May 1926 and December 1937. It was further stipulated that the value of *all* types of deliveries in kind to France credited to Germany's reparation account should not exceed one billion gold marks a year. Thus, if goods delivered to France under the other annexes of the Reparation Chapter (III, V, and VI) were worth 1 billion marks by themselves, the entire value of deliveries under the agreement would be treated as an advance to France.[9]

The viability of the agreement was extremely doubtful. It would, as Loucheur pointed out to Rathenau, encounter formidable opposition from French businessmen who had no wish to be deprived of lucrative reconstruction contracts by a flood of reparation deliveries. Nor was it likely to please France's established trading partners and Germany's other creditors who were concerned about their share of the rapidly crumbling reparation cake. From Germany's point of view, moreover, the immediate financial advantages of the scheme were minimal. Rathenau appears to have realized that deliveries in kind would only relieve the strain on the German balance of payments in so far as they were neither potential exports nor imports substitutes and were not

[9] For French qualms about the mark: *Le Matin*, 10 Sept. 1921 (LA). Cf. *Le Temps*, 17 Sept. 1921 (LA); Meyer to A. Amt, 20 Sept. 1921, A. Amt, Ausführung. For the origins of the Wiesbaden talks: Laurent to Affaires Etrangères, 4 June 1921; Laurent to Loucheur, 3 June 1921, Louis Loucheur Papers, 7/7. For Loucheur's views on deliveries in kind see his interview with *Le Journal*, 18 Feb. 1921, ibid. 5/12. For the text of the Wiesbaden Agreement of 6 Oct. 1921: RC, *Agreements Concerning Deliveries in Kind to be Made by Germany under the Heading of Reparation* (London, 1922) (henceforward RC ii), 3–11. For the ideas of Seydoux: see above, ch. 3 n. 21, and text thereat.

manufactured from imported raw materials. Yet he was concerned to prevent a repetition of the short-term 'buyers' strike' (*Kauferstreik*) against the mark which occurred in the summer of 1921 when the government sold paper marks to obtain the foreign exchange needed to cover its cash reparation obligations. Rathenau's preoccupations were also diplomatic. In the first place, he hoped that the rapid repair of war damage would remove a visible source of French anti-German feelings; and he even made the suggestion, which was rebuffed by Loucheur, that he should embark on a goodwill tour of the devastated regions. More broadly, he expected that the negotiations leading to the agreement would generate a Franco-German *rapprochement* and a consequent reduction of the London Schedule. This prompted the observation of the German reparation expert, Carl Bergmann, that the Wiesbaden Agreement was an unworkable piece of 'political window dressing'. A similar conclusion was drawn by D'Abernon. As a rigid adherent of the 'quantity theory of money', the British Ambassador disapproved of the potentially inflationary effect of the agreement on the level of German government expenditure: but he conceded that, although it was 'a swindle based on a fallacy', it might 'pacify Europe'.[10]

Yet the Wiesbaden Agreement was more than a crude public relations exercise. Rathenau calculated, like Brüning a decade later, that a massive transfer of goods between Germany and her creditors would immediately demonstrate the absurdity of the London Schedule of Payments. It would have been bad enough for Germany's creditors, he said in July 1921, if they had been forced to receive a flow of German gold. 'But it would be even less bearable for them to see all the world's markets flooded with an unhealthy over-production of

---

[10] For Loucheur's record of the Wiesbaden talks: Entrevue à Wiesbaden, 12, 13 June 1921, Louis Loucheur Papers, 7/7, at 11–12, 17–18. Cf. L. Loucheur, *Carnets secrets, 1908–1932*, ed. J. de Launay (Brussels, 1962), 85–92. For Rathenau's views see his speeches to the Provisional Federal Economic Council: Reichswirtschaftsrat (henceforward RWR), Reparations Ausschuss, 27 July 1921, 121; 9 Nov. 1921, 52–84. Cf. J. A. Neumann, 'Rathenaus Reparationspolitik', Phil. Diss. (Univ. of Leipzig, 1930), 17–18; J. Ruppel, 'Deliveries in Kind from Germany under the Wiesbaden and Subsequent Agreements', *MGCRE*, 28 Sept. 1922, 477. For French opposition: *CD*, 5 Dec. 1921, 994 (Bouvet, Girod); E. Weill-Raynal, *Les Réparations allemandes et la France* (3 vols.; Paris, 1947), ii. 59–62. This prevented the Chamber from ratifying the agreement until 6 July 1922: Neumann, 56; Ruppel, 477. For British objections: see below, n. 23. It was not until 31 Mar. 1922 that the RC approved a modified version of the agreement: RC, Minutes, No. 276, 31 Mar. 1922, 7–13. For comments: Bergmann, *Reparations*, 94; D'Abernon, *Ambassador*, i. 214.

German goods.' The net result of this would be that 'the amount of tribute they obtained from Germany would be just sufficient to support their unemployed'. And that, he concluded, 'did not make sense economically'. These facts were already beginning to be recognized abroad, and with this recognition would come the realization that Germany's obligations must be revised before there could be any 'solution of the current world crisis of consumption and production or any co-operative economic reconstruction'. In short, Rathenau regarded the Wiesbaden negotiations as the first phase of what was soon to be referred to in Germany as an 'offensive of fulfilment'. This policy sought the reduction of Germany's obligations not, as heretofore, by protests and passive resistance, but by a genuine, if short-lived, attempt to fulfil them.[11]

It appeared that a section of the German economic élite was adopting this more positive strategy in September when the Federation of German Industry (RDI) offered to underwrite a government overseas reparation loan to cover the January and February instalments of the London Schedule. This 'credit offer' was in part a tactical response to further talk by Wirth and the Federal Economic Council about 'the appropriation of real values'. It may also have been precipitated by concern about a possible swing to the left during the widespread revulsion against the assassination of Erzberger on 24 August. Yet the authors of the credit offer were certainly influenced by Rathenau's notion of achieving treaty revision either by generating good will or by demonstrating in a practical way Germany's inability to pay, and her creditors' inability to receive, the huge sums envisaged by the London Schedule. Hans Kraemer, who represented the RDI in its September discussions with Wirth, considered that Germany would be unable to keep up her payments under the London Schedule for more than a year. He also cited to the Federal Economic Council the opinion of influential British financiers such as Reginald McKenna that the effect on British trade of such payments would be disastrous.[12]

The more co-operative attitude of the leaders of industry was briefly

[11] Rathenau, RWR, Reparations Ausschuss, 27 July 1921, 126. For Brüning: see below, ch. 9 n. 8 and text thereat.

[12] For the origins of the credit offer: RWR, Reparations Ausschuss, 10, 15 Sept. 1921, 202–3, 274. For Kraemer's denial that the RDI had been stampeded by the confiscatory proposals of the left-centre: ibid. 262. Note, however, the subsequent statement by Dr Sorge, the president of the RDI, that such proposals had been 'ruled out' in the initial negotiations between Wirth and the representatives of industry: DAZ, 11 Nov. 1921, No. 522, 2. Cf. Laubach, 84–6; Albertin, 580–1. For McKenna's views: Melchior to Wirth, 29 July 1921; Dufour to A. Amt, 8 Sept. 1921, A. Amt, Ausführung. Note the

reflected in the behaviour of the DVP and its supporting press. In September 1921 the *Deutsche Allgemeine Zeitung* gave prominence to a series of declarations by Stresemann that the DVP wished to enter the cabinet in order to increase the confidence of overseas financiers in Germany and to ensure that industry would be adequately represented in the government. Negotiations which began late in September about broadening the coalition were hailed enthusiastically by Rathenau when he addressed a conference of the Federation of German Industry at Munich on 28 September. Progress was, however, halted within a few days by familiar differences between the DVP and SPD over fiscal policy. The insistence of the Social Democrats on stern property taxation and their demand for the speedy collection of another third of the National Emergency Levy were acceptable to the DVP only on the condition of a longer working day. Since such an idea was anathema to the SPD, the discussions reached a deadlock on 3 October.[13]

When hopes for a broader coalition faded, the DDP became anxious to leave the cabinet. As Rudolf Breitscheid subsequently observed, the DDP and Centre Party had wished to draw the DVP into the government 'before the storm of new tax proposals broke'. When they were unsuccessful, and when, in addition, it became clear that Upper Silesia was to be partitioned, the Democrats became immoderately eager to divest themselves of cabinet responsibility, and they forced Wirth's demonstrative, but pointless, resignation on 22 October, two days after the partition had been officially announced. Since both the DDP and the DVP subsequently persisted with their patriotic rhetoric about Upper Silesia, Wirth had no alternative but to form a Zentrum–SPD coalition on 26 October which was committed to acceptance of the League of Nations decision and depended heavily on the support of the USPD.[14]

Notwithstanding the new government's insistence that it would continue to fulfil the treaty, even if at a reduced rate, effective reparation and financial policies were now hampered by lack of support

subsequent references of Stinnes and Silverberg, who represented German industry in the negotiations about the credit offer in Nov., to the idea of achieving revision of Germany's obligations by means of a 'trade offensive'. *Die Kabinette Wirth*, i. 368–9, 372. For a brief treatment of the credit offer: Feldman, *Iron and Steel*, 285–6.

[13] *DAZ*, 4, 19 and 23 Sept. 1921, Nos. 414, 1; 439, 2; 446, 2. For text of Rathenau's speech: ibid. 5 Oct. 1921, No. 446, Suppl. 1–2. For the dispute over fiscal policy: Laubach, 86–9; Albertin, 587–90.

[14] Breitscheid (USPD), 26 Oct. 1921, *RT* cccli. 4757; Schücking (DDP), 4760. Albertin, 590–9.

in the Reichstag and the violent depreciation of the mark. The exchange rate had slipped from 120 to 150 to the dollar between 10 and 15 October when the decision of the League of Nations Council had become known in broad outline, and thence to 310 to the dollar on 8 November, after the Allied Supreme Council's formal announcement on 20 October. Although it eventually settled at 180, the net depreciation was sufficient to play havoc with the tax system. The budgetary plight of the government was revealed on 4 November when Andreas Hermes, who had temporarily replaced Wirth as Finance Minister, predicted an enormous deficit of 110 billion paper marks, of which 60 billions were attributable to the treaty. Hermes and his SPD supporters steadfastly dismissed ideas of internal bankruptcy and external default. Yet their continuing optimism was based solely upon the possibility of domestic credit assistance and treaty revision. There was, in this respect, little to distinguish the government from the right-wing opposition, although Karl Helfferich, never to be outdone, juggled figures so as to predict a deficit of 300 billion paper marks (280 billions occasioned by the treaty) which, he alleged, would be greater than Germany's national income. Clearly neither the government nor the majority of the Reichstag was in a mood to introduce harsh taxation. The most radical measure which Hermes could manage was a property tax (*Vermögenssteuer*) to be levied on the shares of joint-stock companies. Even this provoked allegations from the DDP, DVP, and DNVP that it threatened private property and would be confiscated by the Entente. The conservatism of the Reichstag was, moreover, so powerful that valuation provisions which had sought to base the tax on the increased market value (*Gemeinwert*) of shares rather than on their depreciated dividends (*Ertragswert*) were watered down so as to diminish appreciably the revenues which accrued.[15]

In the general retreat from financial responsibility the Reichstag was outpaced by German industry. Early in October the RDI had appointed a powerful committee, whose members included Hugenberg and

[15] For the debate on Wirth's policy statement: Wirth, 26 Oct. 1921, *RT* cccli. 4734–6; Müller (SPD), 4738; Breitscheid (USPD), 4760; Hergt (DNVP), 4746; Kahl (DVP), 4750; Schücking (DDP), 4764–5. For mark depreciation: *Die Entwicklung der Reparationsfrage*, 21; *The Economist*, 15 Oct. 1921, 566. For the budget debate, *RT* cccli: Hermes (Zentrum), 4 Nov. 1921, 4823–4; Herold (Zentrum), 7 Nov. 1921, 4832; Braun (SPD), 4827–32; Dietrich (DDP), 4838–42; Helfferich (DNVP), 4851, 4856–8; Schmidt (SPD), 8 Nov. 1921, 4879; Becker (DVP), 4882, 4885–6; Hertz (USPD), 4895. For successive drafts of the Property Tax: ibid. ccclxxi, Annexe 3728, 3834–7. For the watering down of the notion of *Gemeinwert*: ibid. 3802; ibid. ccli: Dietrich, 4841; Herold, 4834; Helfferich, 4855–6; Becker, 4890.

Stinnes, to negotiate with the government about its credit offer. The storm of protest about Upper Silesia and the discomfiture of the Wirth Ministry had, however, emboldened some of the less co-operative industrialists such as Hugenberg either to disassociate themselves from the offer or to attach strings to their aid. A meeting of the RDI on 4 and 5 November ruled that the continuation of credit negotiations with the government would depend upon 'the introduction of strict economy in the entire budget of the Reich, on the relief of economic life from all restraint upon its operation and development, and on the immediate transfer of all public utilities then in government hands to private enterprise, in order that their operation might produce sufficient revenue to meet interest and amortization charges on the proposed foreign loan instead of being a burden on the government as heretofore'. Despite its avowed purpose of reassuring foreign lenders, the domestic implications of such a programme of denationalization were all too clear. Dr Sorge, the president of the RDI, in fact stated explicitly a few days later that German industry was anxious to make public utilities such as the railways disgorge large numbers of their employees into the open labour market. The proposal may also have been a response to pressure from Stinnes, whose grandiose plans for taking over the eastern European railway system hinged upon first acquiring control of the German network. Whatever the reasons for the demand, the unacceptability of denationalization, even to the moderate left, placed Wirth in an impossible position and doomed the negotiations. In the Reichstag on 7 November both Braun (SPD) and Schmidt, the Socialist Minister of Economics, deplored the attachment of such conditions to the 'credit offer'. The extreme left claimed that the industrialists' only concern had been to divert the government from a confiscatory tax programme; and it pressed that property taxes should be collected immediately, that the government should participate in the capital of industry, that foreign exchange accruing from exports should be confiscated, and that there should be import and export controls. The uncompromising attitude of the right wing was revealed when Becker, the spokesman for the DVP, and Helfferich retorted that, if German industry was to assist the government at all in the present financial emergency, it should do so in its own time and on its own terms. Although the credit negotiations were prolonged for a few more weeks, their failure was a foregone conclusion. The immediate financial fate of Germany now depended on the response of overseas financiers to a final half-hearted appeal by the German government for aid. As

Wirth remarked in an address to the Berlin Press Club on 4 December, the decision whether money should be consigned to 'the bottomless bucket of reparations' now rested neither with the German government nor with German industry but with foreigners.[16]

It took some time for this financial paralysis to dissipate the atmosphere of *détente* which had been built up between Germany and France in the autumn. Early in October the leader writer of *Le Temps* had praised the Wiesbaden Agreement as 'a milestone in Franco-German relations'. Other indicators of *rapprochement* had been the removal of the Rhineland customs barrier erected in March as part of the Allied sanctions programme, and a speech by Briand at Saint-Nazaire on 9 October in which he referred sympathetically to Germany's difficulties and emphasized the need for financial co-operation. The outcry in Germany over the partition of Upper Silesia had started the French right-wing press baying again for an occupation of the Ruhr and a Rhine frontier: but the policy of the government towards Germany had remained moderate. On the eve of his departure for the Washington Disarmament Conference, Briand confronted his right-wing critics in the Chamber by declaring that the policy of single-handed coercion of Germany which they advocated would be both expensive and fraught with danger for France. He also squashed the protest of Maurice Barrès against the removal of the Rhineland customs barrier by pointing out that France could not expect both to impede the efficiency of the Germany economy and to obtain reparations.[17]

The Chamber expressed its approval for Briand's restraint both by its 338 to 172 vote of confidence in the government's foreign policy on 26 October and by the tone of the prolonged financial debates which

[16] For the negotiating committee of the RDI: *DAZ*, 5 Oct. 1921, No. 466, 1. For Hugenberg's attitude: Bernhard, 4 Nov. 1921, RWR, 1253–61. Cf. the more co-operative attitude of German light industry: Kraemer, 25 Nov. 1921, RWR, Reparations Ausschuss, 253–60. For the RDI's conditions: *DAZ*, 6 Nov. 1921, No. 513, 1; 11 Nov. 1921, No. 522, 2 (Sorge); Bergmann, *Reparations*, 101. For the interest of Stinnes in the German railways: see below, n. 25. For the Reichstag debate: Braun (SPD), 7 Nov. 1921, *RT* cccli. 4828; Schmidt (SPD), 4846–7; Helfferich (DNVP), 4860; Hertz (USPD), 8 Nov. 1921, 4898–900; Hollein (KPD), 4912–13; Becker (DVP), 4886. For trade-union protests: *DAZ*, 11 Nov. 1921, No. 521, 1. Cf. Georg Berhard's comment: *VZ*, 13 Nov. 1921, No. 525 (LA). On the ultimate failure of the credit negotiations: Wirth, 22 Nov. 1921, 11th Committee, *RT* ccclxxi, Annexes 3728, 3789–90; Wirth, *VZ*, 5 Dec. 1921, No. 572, 1–2; Laubach, 120–6.

[17] *Le Temps*, 8 Oct. 1921 (LA); 10 Oct. 1921, 1 (Briand at Saint-Nazaire). For removal of customs barrier: Hardinge to Curzon, 29 Sept. 1921, *DBFP* I, xvi. 777–8. For the extreme right on the Ruhr: *AF*, 14, 18, 19 Oct. 1921, 1 (Maurras). Cf. R. J. Schmidt, *Versailles and the Ruhr: Seedbed of World War II* (The Hague, 1968), 31–2; Briand, 18, 19 Oct. 1921, *CD* 17, 32.

occurred during his absence in November. The latter were distinguished not only by increasing appreciation of Germany's inability to procure unlimited amounts of foreign exchange for reparation payments but also by a belated and tacit admission that the French left wing had been justified in its long-standing demand that France should take drastic steps, independently of Germany, to set her financial house in order. This new realism had been foreshadowed in the budget for 1922, which had been laid before the Chamber by Doumer in July 1921, and was noteworthy as the first post-war French budget voted on schedule. By November 1921 a more reasonable attitude was being adopted even by Charles de Lasteyrie, the rapporteur of the special reparation budget of 'expenditures recoverable from Germany', who had just returned from a fact-finding visit to Berlin. De Lasteyrie informed the Chamber that Germany was about to succumb to a virtually self-inflicted bankruptcy which was 'purely and exclusively' monetary and not warranted by her economic strength. However, ignoring the demands of Léon Daudet and the Bonapartist, Pierre Taittinger, for an immediate occupation of the Ruhr, the speaker advocated more sophisticated counter-measures such as the imposition of rigid financial controls. He went on to suggest that Germany should obtain foreign financial assistance to meet her obligations, and concluded by demanding that France's allies should also help 'by conceding priority to the reparation claims of countries which were, like France, accepting deliveries in kind'.[18]

By the end of November 1921, influential French politicians were not only unsympathetic to plans for the military coercion of Germany but were even beginning to doubt the efficacy of de Lasteyrie's proposal for the establishment of a virtual receivership over the bankrupt German government. Despite the outspoken support of Poincaré for such a plan, a confidential memorandum of 23 November which American financial representatives in Paris received 'through the most reliable French sources', and which was said to represent the views of 'Loucheur and in fact most of the French Government', was extremely sceptical about the feasibility of using military force against Germany or controlling her finances. Instead it recommended that Germany

---

[18] For Briand's speeches of 21 and 26 Oct. and the vote of confidence: CD 70–82, 153–7, 160–1. For Doumer's draft budget of 8 July 1921: Annales de la Chambre des Députés. Documents parlementaires, 1921, Doc. No. 3068, 2274. See also Haig, 72–7. In Nov. 1921 the slogan 'la Boche payera' was condemned even by non-socialist speakers for having encouraged a reckless financial policy in post-war France. CD, 9 Nov. 1921, 321–2 (Tixier); 10 Nov. 1921, 360 (Roux-Freissineng); cf. de Lasteyrie, 325–7.

should fulfil her obligations by means of increased deliveries in kind after the manner envisaged in the Wiesbaden Agreement (which implied an adjustment of priorities in favour of France), and by means of an international loan (to be serviced by Germany) which was to provide cash for needy Allied treasuries. That such flexible and far-reaching proposals were in the air in France was also indicated by Jules Sauerwein, who proclaimed in *Le Matin*, early in December, that France was 'ready to enter into negotiations to adjust the reparation problem within the world economy'.[19]

The same moderation was discernible in the behaviour of the Committee of Guarantees, which, as we have seen, had been set up by the Reparation Commission to supervise fulfilment of the London Schedule. After deliberating in Berlin between 23 September and 14 October its members reserved final judgement about German financial policy pending the outcome of efforts to raise a foreign loan with the assistance of the RDI's 'credit offer'. It was not for another month that the Reparation Commission itself, having followed in the footsteps of its committee to assess the situation in Berlin at first hand, cast doubt on the sincerity of the RDI and *a fortiori* on the possibility that the international banking fraternity would lend money to Germany. Havenstein, the president of the Reichsbank, had in fact been informed late in October by Montagu Norman, the governor of the Bank of England, that the procurement of funds to make reparation payments 'was not a banking matter which would be undertaken by either of us'. Hopes for a British loan to Germany had only been kept alive in November because the Treasury had inclined to the more balanced view of Sir John Bradbury, the British representative on the Reparation Commission, that in order to avert 'drastic action' by France the German government should 'bleed' German industry by making it responsible for the repayment in foreign exchange of the credits necessary for the next two reparation instalments. However, by the beginning of December the circumspection of Bradbury had been overruled by the belief of the City that any loan to Germany would be a bad business proposition and that, therefore, a moratorium, including the postponement of the January and February payments, was an absolute necessity. Hence, when Havenstein applied to the Bank of England on 25 November for a long-term advance of 500 million gold marks, it

[19] See Poincaré's articles in *Revue des deux mondes*, 1 Nov. 1921, 238; 15 Nov. 1921, 470–5; *Le Matin*, 5 Dec. 1921 (LA). Memo of 23 Nov. 1921, enc. in letter of 2 Dec. 1921, Secret Letters, V, Annexe 44; *Le Matin*, 1, 8 Dec. 1921, 1.

was certain that his application would be rejected. The anticipated negative reply from Threadneedle Street was cited when, on 14 December, Wirth informed the Reparation Commission that Germany would be unable to pay the reparation instalments which fell due on 15 January and 15 February 1922.[20]

ANGLO-FRENCH RELATIONS AND THE FALL OF BRIAND

The London Schedule of Payments had been undermined by the passivity of German financial policy and by the consequent wariness of British bankers. The German request for a moratorium might, however, have been rendered superfluous, or its political impact upon France might have been softened, if there had been more effective financial liaison between Germany's erstwhile enemies. It was too much to expect that British bankers would lend money to enable a virtually bankrupt government to make reparation payments which were now believed by the Federation of British Industries, a leading advocate of vast indemnities two years earlier, to be the cause of Britain's current economic crisis. There had, however, been suggestions since October 1921 that Britain might safeguard her own trading interests and, at the same time, afford relief to Germany and France by renouncing both her share of German reparations and her wartime loans to her continental Allies. The proposal that the British government should, by waiving its claim to reparation payments for pensions and allowances, effectively opt out of the reparation scheme, had been aired by Keynes on 13 October at an 'Economic Recovery Conference' in London. Such an action would, he argued, both increase the proportion of the indemnity due to France and reduce Germany's total obligation to a manageable figure. The benefit of this to Britain was not immediately apparent even to such an ardently pro-Keynesian

[20] Report from the Committee of Guarantees concerning its visit to Berlin (Sept.–Oct. 1921), RC, Annexe 1145, 14–15; RC, Minutes, No. 237, 19 Nov. 1921, 2–8. Cf. the comments of Boyden, the unofficial American delegate to the RC: Boyden to Hughes, 22 Nov. 1921, Dept. of State, 462.00 R296/1307. See also: RC to the German government, 2 Dec. 1921, RC ii. 49. For Havenstein and Norman: H. Clay, *Lord Norman* (London, 1957), 197–8. For Bradbury's attitude: Bradbury to Blackett, 21 Nov. 1921, *DBFP* I, xvi. 817–19, at 819; Blackett to Crowe, 22 Nov. 1921, ibid. 817. See also Boyden to Hughes, 1 Dec. 1921, Dept. of State, 462.00 R296/1285. For the City's veto: Memo by S. P. Waterlow, 30 Nov. 1921, *DBFP* I, xvi. 826–7. On the rejection of the German loan application: Clay, 200–1; letter from Dr Wirth to the RC, 14 Dec. 1921, RC iii. 50. See also Sthamer to Curzon, 15 Dec. 1921, *DBFP* I, xvi. 851–2; Bergmann, *Reparations*, 101.

journal as the *Manchester Guardian*, which could not refrain from the observation that, 'on Mr. Keynes's proposal, France and Belgium would get whatever reparations remain to be paid and we should get next to nothing'. The *Guardian* concluded, however, that British commerce would stand to gain because renunciation would encourage the restoration of normal international trade and stem the flow of cheap goods which Germany would have to pour onto the world's markets in order to meet her obligations.[21]

An even more radical suggestion was soon to emanate from Reginald McKenna, the chairman of the London Joint City and Midland Bank, who had been Asquith's Chancellor of the Exchequer in 1915 and 1916, but had retired from politics after losing his House of Commons seat in December 1918. In the autumn of 1921, while on a personal visit to the United States, McKenna declared that Britain would be 'selfishly wise, having regard only to her industrial economic position', to write off the advances she had made to her allies during the war. This was in part an oblique appeal to the United States to renounce its loans to Britain; and the British government was careful to disassociate itself from McKenna's views. Yet McKenna had sufficient financial stature to be offered, and to refuse, the post of Chancellor of the Exchequer in 1922; and his views were commended by liberal statesmen such as Asquith, journals such as the *Manchester Guardian* and *Daily News*, and the British National Committee of the International Chamber of Commerce. More significantly they won the support of the Francophile *Daily Mail* and the *Morning Post*, even if the latter insisted that Germany's reparation obligations should remain the same.[22]

It seemed unlikely in November 1921 that the British government would rise to such heights of apparent self-denial. As the *Manchester Guardian* subsequently remarked, the political leaders of Britain and France were at this time behaving less like 'statesmen concerned for the welfare of Europe' than like 'dogs yapping over a bone which was quite obviously going to slip into the river'. The Allies had, in short,

[21] For a memo of the Federation of British Industries blaming reparations for the recession then current: *The Times*, 24 Nov. 1921, 5. For the Keynes proposal: *MG*, 14 Oct. 1921, 9 and LA.

[22] For McKenna: *NYT*, 26 Oct. 1921, 26; 2 Nov. 1921, 26. For liberal reaction: *MG*, 27 Oct. 1921, 8; 28 Oct. 1921 (LA); 4 Nov. 1921, 7. See also *NYT*, 29 Oct. 1921, 11 (citations from *Daily Mail* and *Morning Post*); *MP*, 28 Oct. 1921 (LA). For British disavowal of McKenna: Horne (Chancellor of Exchequer), 20 Oct. 1921, *HC* cxlvii. 244.

become involved in a sordid dispute over the distribution of Germany's first remittances under the London Schedule of Payments. From July onwards there had been mounting concern in the British Treasury and Foreign Office about the Franco-German negotiations which led to the Wiesbaden Agreement because it was feared that the strain imposed upon Germany by additional deliveries in kind to France would prejudice Britain's reparation claims. The French government had also discovered cause for complaint after Doumer, Briand's Finance Minister, had agreed during talks in August that Germany's first cash payments should be distributed along the lines laid down by the Spa Agreement of July 1920. Since this meant that the eagerly awaited yield of the London Schedule would be used either to defray the costs of the Allied armies of occupation (which were proportionally higher for British than for French troops) or to satisfy Belgium's prior claim to reparations, there was much dissatisfaction in France. The end result was that the French government flatly refused to ratify the convention of 13 August and that Britain insisted with equal firmness on such ratification as a preliminary to her recognition of the Wiesbaden Agreement.[23]

Despite this deadlock and serious Anglo-French friction, both in the Near East and at the Washington Disarmament Conference, Britain and France came tantalizingly close to a resolution of the reparation problem in December 1921. This occurred because, after it had become clear that the City was unwilling to help Germany to meet her obligations or to stabilize her finances, the schemes of McKenna and Keynes for the unilateral renunciation of Britain's claims against her Allies appear to have gained favour with the British Treasury. When Loucheur visited London on 8 and 9 December to prepare the way for discussions of the reparation question between Briand and Lloyd George, he brought with him clear demands that Germany should be both constrained and encouraged by international loans, presumably of British origins, to reform her finances and to provide security for

---

[23] MG, 13 Dec. 1921 (LA). For Britain and Wiesbaden: Blackett to Crowe, 14 July 1921, DBFP I, xvi. 707–15. For the hostile French reaction to a report by Bradbury summarizing British objections to the Wiesbaden Agreement (pub. 26 Oct. 1921 as Cmd. 1547 of 1921): Hardinge to Curzon, 9 Nov. 1921, DBFP I, xvi. 804. See also Weill-Raynal, ii. 53–6. For the convention of 13 Aug.: Documents relatifs aux réparations, i. 164–70. See also Hardinge to Curzon, 17 Aug. 1921, DBFP I, xvi. 735. For French dissatisfaction: Le Temps, 16 Sept. 1921 (Tardieu); Le Matin, 20 Sept. 1921 (Lauzanne). For the British view: Curzon to Saint-Aulaire, 9 Dec. 1921, Louis Loucheur Papers, Box 5, Folder 6. See above, n. 10 and text thereat.

reparation payments. He could, however, only have welcomed an alternative proposal by Sir Basil Blackett, the Controller of Finance at the Treasury, that Britain should ease the financial strain on continental Europe by the unilateral annulment of her wartime loans to France and by renouncing her 22 per cent share of German reparations.[24]

Discussions with Lloyd George soon revealed that Blackett's proposal had been too good to be true. In the first place the Prime Minister stressed that his government's offer of renunciation was conditional upon a corresponding American waiver of British war debts to the United States. Secondly, it was clear that Lloyd George was reluctant to grasp the nettle of reparations and war debts and preferred to air a less tangible, but more appealing, scheme for 'reconstructing' Russia and eastern Europe through a consortium of British, German, French, and, hopefully, American capitalists. Although general proposals of this nature had already been canvassed, this particular project had apparently crystallized in his mind after discussions late in November 1921 with Hugo Stinnes and Walther Rathenau, who were interested in expanding their industrial and commercial empires via the eastern European railway system. Such a means of solving western Europe's economic problems, and the reparation problem into the bargain, was far more attractive than the act of financial statesmanship advocated by Blackett.[25]

The preference of the British cabinet for unlikely schemes of European reconstruction was confirmed after 'tentative enquiries ... in responsible quarters' had revealed that the United States government

[24] For Anglo-French friction: G. Suarez, *Briand, sa vie—son œuvre, avec son journal* (6 vols.; Paris, 1938–1952), v, chs. 7–9. For the renunciationist ideas of the British Treasury: Grigg, 80. For Loucheur's demands: Memo of 8 Dec. 1921, Louis Loucheur Papers, Box 7, Folder 4. Loucheur had been directed by the French Council of Ministers to draw up this plan for the contingency of a 'fraudulent German bankruptcy'. Réunion chez le Président de la République, 27 Oct. 1921, Box 5, Folder 13. For Blackett's proposal: Notes of a conversation with Blackett at Chequers, 8 Dec. 1921, Box 5, Folder 6.

[25] For Lloyd George's attitude: Report of a conversation at Chequers ..., 8 Dec. 1921, Loucheur, 185–8. Cf. Comte de Saint-Aulaire, *Confession d'un vieux diplomate* (Paris, 1953), 449–53. For the origins of the reconstruction scheme: R. Himmer, 'Rathenau, Russia and Rapallo', *CEH* 9 (1976), 146–83; *The Times*, 25 Nov. 1921, 10; 30 Nov. 1921 (LA). For references in the cabinet to the proposals of Stinnes and Rathenau: Cabinet 93 (21), 16 Dec. 1921, Min. 2, CAB 23/27. Cf. the comments of Blackett on the scheme of 'Herr X' (almost certainly Stinnes) to finance Germany's next two reparation instalments by transferring the German railways to private ownership. Blackett to Grigg, 24 Nov. 1921, Lloyd George Papers, F/27/6/52.

was, if anything, more resolutely opposed than ever to discussion of inter-Allied indebtedness. The Blackett proposal, which might have induced France to reduce her reparation claims on Germany and shamed the United States into relaxing its throttling grip on Europe, was quietly shelved. The less dramatic French idea that Britain should 'pay Germany's reparation' by lending her the money for the next two instalments of the London Schedule was also rejected out of hand; and the cabinet quickly relapsed into a discussion of the distributive implications of the convention of 13 August and the Wiesbaden Agreement. This led in turn to criticism of France for failing to balance her budget, and thence to condemnation of her foreign policy of 'maintaining a very expensive army, fleet, and air service and engaging in costly ventures in the Near East'. It was felt that, so long as France refused to economize, it would be a mistake 'to deal tenderly with her on the reparation question'. All that she could be offered was the doubtful privilege of participating in a scheme of eastern European reconstruction which, it was hoped, would create the markets needed by Germany to generate an export surplus with which to pay reparations. The cabinet therefore resolved, somewhat fatuously, that 'in the conversations with M. Briand and M. Loucheur, the Prime Minister should be perfectly free to examine all aspects of proposals for dealing with the problem of German reparations and *inter alia* a scheme for the formation of a syndicate of the Western Powers (and possibly the United States) for the economic reconstruction of Russia'. The improbable nature of such a project was, however, indicated by the stipulation of the cabinet that its feasibility depended upon Bolshevik recognition of Tsarist debts, western European control of Russian railways and customs, and the diplomatic recognition of the Soviet government by the West.[26]

The attitude of the British government made it highly unlikely that the discussion between Lloyd George and Briand which began in London on 18 December would yield any result acceptable to the Chamber of Deputies. The divergence between the commercially orientated policy of Britain and the short-term budgetary preoccupations

---

[26] Cabinet 93 (21), 16 Dec. 1921, Min. 2, CAB 23/27. The State Department had rejected schemes for veiled American debt renunciation in Sept. 1921: D. B. Gescher, *Die Vereinigten Staaten von Nordamerika und die Reparationen, 1920–1924* (Bonn, 1956), 98–100. The opposition of Congress to debt cancellation had stiffened in Dec. 1921 as a result of French recalcitrance about naval disarmament at the Washington Conference: J. C. Vinson, *The Parchment Peace: The United States Senate and the Washington Conference, 1921–1922* (Athens, Ga., 1955), 170.

of France was underlined on the second day of the conference. '... In England', Lloyd George explained to Briand, 'people were so concentrated upon the problem created by the low state of trade and the high state of unemployment that they judged everything by that point of view.' However, in France, Briand pointed out, the situation was 'extremely calm from a social point of view. Financial circles felt a certain amount of uneasiness but this was not shared by the people in general. Their sole preoccupation was with the question "Will Germany pay?" '[27]

It was understandable that any proposals made by Briand and Loucheur at London would be concerned less with the mirage of Russian reconstruction than with practical financial programmes such as had been outlined by Blackett on 8 December. They in fact suggested that there should be a temporary reduction of Germany's cash reparation obligations on the dual condition that she should carry through stringent financial reforms (which included the suspension of interest payments on her domestic public debt) and that Britain should make considerable financial concessions. It was agreed that, pending corresponding sacrifices by the United States, Britain might defer any final decision about the distribution of German reparations and about waiving loans to her Allies. However, in the mean time, France was to be accorded practical priority to German reparations. Germany's total liability was to be reapportioned into 53 billion gold marks of first priority payments (of which France was to receive 45 billions), and 83 billion gold marks of second priority payments, which included the bulk of Britain's reparation claim and would almost certainly be written off in due course.[28]

The hardening of the British government's short-term reparation policy, which coincided with its new interest in long-term reconstruction schemes, created an unbridgeable gap between these proposals and the reparation plan submitted by Blackett on the same day. Concerned as it was with distributive matters and the terms and conditions under which a partial and temporary moratorium might be granted to Germany, the British document contained nothing that would resolve the reparation deadlock. By 20 December Lloyd George, having summarily rejected the French scheme because of the non-co-operation of the United States, was diverting the attention of the

[27] DBFP I, xv. 764.
[28] Note remise officieusement par M. Avenol à Blackett, 19 Dec. 1921, Louis Loucheur Papers, Box 5, Folder 11.

conference away from the immediate reparation impasse to more remote vistas. The major achievement of the next two days was the adoption of a memorandum outlining plans for a syndicate intended mainly 'to undertake the organization of transport and harbour facilities' in eastern Europe. Only secondary importance was attached to a further memorandum 'dealing with the immediate problem of German reparations', which resembled in form, if not in its detailed concessions to French views, the plan submitted by Blackett on 19 December.[29]

Towards the end of the London conversations Briand, anxious to prepare the ground for a reduction of French arms expenditure and to extract some quid pro quo from Lloyd George, broached the subject of an Anglo-French defensive alliance. Such a project had been discussed for some weeks in the French and English press. It was also the subject of a desultory diplomatic exchange between Curzon and Saint-Aulaire, the French ambassador in London, in the first half of December; and was casually mentioned in the British cabinet on 16 December as a possible means of inducing France to spend less on armaments. Yet serious differences of opinion about the scope of such an alliance emerged during the discussion between the two premiers on 21 December. It was, moreover, doubtful whether a defensive pact, however watertight from France's point of view, would be sufficient to induce the French public to accept Lloyd George's promise of future European reconstruction in lieu of immediate German reparation payments.[30]

Misgivings had already been expressed in France, particularly after the visits of Stinnes and Rathenau to London, about the softening of British policy. When Briand returned to Paris he was confronted with charges that he had been swept along the path of revisionism by Lloyd George without obtaining any worthwhile compensation for France.

[29] Plan for temporary arrangement pending an International Financial Conference, presented on 19/12/21 by Blackett to Avenol, ibid. For successive drafts of the reconstruction scheme: DBFP I, xv. 797–800. For text of reparation memorandum: ibid. 800–4. For Briand's report on the London negotiations: Chambre des Députés, CAE, 26 Dec. 1921, Audition de Monsieur Aristide Briand, 67–73.

[30] For the alliance proposal: DBFP I, xv. 785–7. See also: Minutes of a Conference of Ministers, 21 Dec. 1921, Min. 7, CAB 23/29. For the Curzon–Saint Aulaire note exchange: Suarez, v. 346. See also Papers Respecting Negotiations for an Anglo-French Pact, House of Commons Papers, Cmd. 2169, 1924, xxvi, No. 31. For the British attitude: Cabinet 93 (21), 16 Dec. 1921, Min. 2, CAB 23/27. Lloyd George wanted the pact to apply only to an unprovoked German attack on France, whereas Briand originally envisaged an alliance with much broader ramifications. Suarez, v. 349–51.

Klotz, the ex-Finance Minister, declared to the Chamber that the French government should, instead of becoming involved in grandiose discussions about the future of Europe, 'concern itself a little about the situation of the French taxpayer'. Two days later Poincaré referred in similar vein in Le Temps to the coming 'touche-à-tout' conference at Cannes. 'Under the pretext of "restoring in a general way the well-being of peoples", and making heaven on earth, the whole Treaty of Versailles, approved by the House of Commons, approved by the French Parliament, and the law of the land in both countries, [was]', he asserted, 'going to be put back into the melting pot.'[31]

In the brief period before the meeting of the Allied Supreme Council at Cannes on 6 January 1922 Briand remained relatively unaffected by this criticism. His position could not, however, have been strengthened by the disagreements of Allied experts when they met at Paris at the end of December to discuss the financial structure of the projected reconstruction syndicate. Nor could he have been much encouraged when on 4 January Lloyd George offered France a security pact which guaranteed British support only in the event of an unprovoked German attack. The Cannes Conference opened with something of a flourish when it unanimously adopted a resolution in favour of summoning an economic and financial conference in February or early March 'to which all the Powers of Europe, including Germany, Russia, Austria, Hungary, and Bulgaria, should be invited to send representatives'. A co-operative effort by the economically stronger powers was necessary, it was asserted, in order to achieve the reconstruction of central and eastern Europe. Yet the failure of the Allies to grapple with the reparation problem could not be concealed indefinitely. Modifications introduced into the moratorium scheme which had been approved at London, notably an increase in Germany's cash obligations for 1922 from 500 to 720 million gold marks, were not in themselves highly significant. Yet, when Lloyd George attributed Germany's failure to meet her obligations primarily to the weakness of her financial policy, Rathenau retaliated with a three-hour speech which placed the blame squarely on balance of payments difficulties for which there was no rapid cure and budgetary problems which, he asserted, could not be resolved by an increase in current revenues. Although he stated that for political reasons he was ready to accept, with certain reservations,

---

[31] Revue des deux mondes, 15 Dec. 1921, 955–6 (Poincaré); CD, 24 Dec. 1921, 1594 (Klotz); Le Temps, 26 Dec. 1921, 1 (Poincaré).

the Allied programme of reparation payments and budgetary reform for the coming year, the Foreign Minister made it clear that the demands of the Allies would be impossible to fulfil unless Germany was given considerable assistance.[32]

Even before this renewed exposure of the reparation deadlock, there had been an outcry in the French right-wing press about the illusory nature of the benefits which would accrue from the rumoured Anglo-French Alliance and 'European reconstruction'. Saint-Aulaire, the French Ambassador in London, who subsequently claimed the credit for raising this storm, regarded the alliance proposal as 'fraudulent and dangerous' because of its narrow scope, and dismissed Lloyd George's reconstruction scheme as an electioneering stunt. These views were shared by Millerand, the President of the Republic, who bombarded Briand with admonitory notes from the beginning of the Cannes Conference. In the meantime, doubts about German good faith had been crystallized in the Chamber by the inaugural address of Jules Siegfried, its octogenarian president, on 10 January 1922. Fears that Briand was in some way compromising France's right to reparation were also recorded in resolutions on 10 and 11 January by the Finance Commission of the Chamber and the Foreign Affairs Commission of the Senate. These, and a further telegram from Millerand, prompted Briand to return from Cannes on the night of 11–12 January, without his bags or his valet, in order to rally parliamentary support. His abrupt resignation on 12 January came after he had made a convincing defence of his policy and before any vote had been taken. The words he used as he stalked out of the Chamber ('D'autres feront mieux') indicate that he aimed to call the bluff of Poincaré and the right wing, who had been demanding a policy of sternness to Germany and of diplomatic independence from Britain. Yet Briand would not have resorted to such a dangerous tactic if his diplomacy of conciliation had been rewarded with tangible financial gestures either by Germany or by the Anglo-Saxon powers. On 19 January, Poincaré, his successor, announced to the Chamber with chilling simplicity that his sole ambition was 'to uphold the treaties which had regulated the peace'. It was gradually to emerge that, unlike Briand, Poincaré was prepared

---

[32] For the resolution of 6 Jan.: German White Book, *Material über die Konferenz von Genua*, RT ccclxxiii. Annexe 4378, 6 ff.; *DBFP* I, xix. 35–6. For the text of the Allied reparation proposal of 10 Jan. 1922: *Aktenstücke zur Reparationsfrage vom Mai 1921 bis März 1922*, RT ccclxxii. Annexe 4140, 185–8. For Lloyd George's statement and Rathenau's reply: ibid. 39–44; *DBFP* I, xix. 112–26.

to implement such a policy by coercion rather than conciliation, and by single-handed action rather than inter-Allied co-operation.[33]

Although the London Schedule of Payments would have been impossible for Germany to fulfil for any length of time without considerable assistance, it had provided a breathing space in which the reparation problem could have been resolved. Despite initial French reluctance to accept the schedule, there was increasing awareness that large reparation payments were as undesirable for the creditors as they were for the debtor. Readiness to accept the shadow rather than the substance of reparations was reflected in the Wiesbaden Agreement of October 1921, a public relations exercise which neither Rathenau nor Loucheur believed would really be carried out. Increasing realism also encouraged the more responsible nature of French budgetary policy. It was unfortunate that progress should have been halted by the uncooperative behaviour of the German government in the autumn of 1921 in response to pressure from the conservative German industrial and commercial élite. Although it was not represented in the cabinet formed by Wirth to fulfil the schedule, this group was able to determine the success or failure of the 'offensive of fulfilment' which Rathenau tried to launch in September by attaching unacceptable political strings to its offer of financial support. Wirth's rejection of such terms and the decision of the Allied Supreme Council to partition Upper Silesia put paid to any hopes of collaboration by the financial establishment and necessitated his premature request for a reparation moratorium in December 1921. All hopes for a settlement now rested on a British initiative. Yet a far-sighted Treasury proposal for Britain to save the situation by renouncing both her war loans to her Allies and her share of reparations came to nothing because of the refusal of the American government to be party to any scheme of debt cancellation and, more importantly, because of the British cabinet's continuing reluctance to shatter the reparation illusion. At a time when a statesmanlike gesture might have had a profound impact Lloyd George and his colleagues allowed themselves to be inveigled into the unlikely schemes of Rathenau and Stinnes for the exploitation of Soviet Russia. This quixotic behaviour and the passivity of Germany reversed the moderate trend which had just begun in France, and led to the

[33] Saint-Aulaire, 558–9; 590. For Millerand's notes: Suarez, v. 364–6, 371–3. For the commissions: Le Temps, 12, 13 Jan. 1922, 1. See also Siegfried, 10 Jan. 1922, CD, 1–2. For Briand's defence: ibid. 12 Jan. 1922, 17–22; Le Temps, 14 Jan. 1922, 1–2. Cf. Poincaré, CD, 19 Jan. 1922, 37.

replacement of Briand by Raymond Poincaré, who had revived the false prophecy of 1919 that France's financial salvation lay in the literal implementation of the treaty. As Carl Bergmann, the head of the German War Burdens Commission, remarked, the reparation negotiations now had entered 'the blind trail of the moratorium' which was to lead into 'the jungle' of the Ruhr struggle.[34]

[34] Bergmann, *Reparations*, 104–12; Memorandum of a Conference between Mr Karl Bergmann and Messrs Ruben Clark and A. N. Young (US Dept. of Commerce), 2 Nov. 1921, Arthur N. Young Papers, Box 1, Folder 1.

5
From Cannes to the Ruhr

INSTEAD of precipitating a renegotiation of the post-war financial settlement, the collapse of the London Schedule led only to a makeshift adjustment of Germany's reparation obligations. The granting of a partial moratorium in January 1922 reduced the budgetary and balance of payments burden of reparations to a level which might have been tolerable in optimum conditions. The prospect of obtaining an international loan also encouraged the Wirth government to prolong a half-hearted attempt at financial reform until the middle of the year. Yet a settlement was prevented by the regressive inertia of French budgetary policy under Poincaré and the persistent refusal of the German industrial élite to countenance an effective stabilization policy which would jeopardize their inflation profiteering. Tension was increased when Lloyd George's European reconstruction pipe-dream was rudely shattered by the signature of a pact of mutual financial renunciation by the two debtor powers, Germany and Soviet Russia, at Rapallo on 16 April. The imposition of sanctions by France was prevented in the first half of 1922 by Britain's exploitation of the imprecision of the punitive provisions of the Reparation Chapter, and by the lingering hope that the reparation problem might be resolved by an international loan. After June 1922, when the loan negotiations had foundered, and it had become clear that the United States and Britain intended to press for the repayment of their war loans to the Allies, the French government once more began to hound Germany. Coinciding as it did with the assassination of Rathenau, the apostle of fulfilment, this renewed friction sparked a violent depreciation of the mark and an accompanying boom in the capital goods sector of the German economy. These developments so incensed the French that, when the German government requested a further stay of time in August, they were only restrained from retaliatory action when Belgium, under pressure from Britain and the United States, agreed that the transfer of the next reparation instalments, which had been allotted to her, could be post-poned for six months. In October, French hopes that a settlement might be achieved by British concessions were briefly revived by the fall of Lloyd George. However, Bonar Law, the new British Prime Minister, failed to offer a settlement which was sufficiently generous to resolve France's imminent financial crisis. In the mean time the French government had taken advantage of the defection of Belgium from the Anglo-Saxon camp in the Reparation Commission to push through resolutions which legalized an occupation of the Ruhr. Poin-caré's motives for actually launching this operation in 10 January 1923 were mixed: but his unwillingness to deflate the financial expectations of the French electorate was far more important than sensitivity to economic and chauvinist pressure groups.

THE GERMAN ECONOMY AND REPARATIONS IN 1922

By 1922 production in the heavy industrial sector of the German economy had virtually attained its 1913 level. Despite the partition of Upper Silesia in May 1922, output of pig iron and crude steel was either approaching or above its pre-war figure in the same area. A lag of about 10 million tons in black coal (anthracite) production was balanced by a sharp rise in the yield of lignite (brown coal), which was used more and more as a substitute for the former. Boom con-ditions were most noticeable in the ship-building industry where by

TABLE 6. *German Shipping Launched in 1913 and 1920–1922* (000s of tons)

1913	459
1920	326
1921	446
1922	625

Source: Bresciani-Turroni, 194 n.

1922 the tonnage launched (Table 6) was well above its 1913 level. A further indicator was the rapid fall in the number of unemployed receiving assistance to fewer than twelve thousand by the summer of 1922. Finally, German foreign trade, although still only 60 per cent of its 1913 value, was considerably greater than in preceding years.[1]

---

[1] For figures: see below, Appendix I, Tables A–F. For the 1913 output of Polish Upper Silesia: R. Machray, *The Problem of Upper Silesia* (London, 1945), 118; Lübsen, 427–9.

Despite these impressive statistics, Germany's national income appears to have been lower in 1922 than in 1921 because of the miserable performance of the agricultural sector and the lop-sided growth of the commercial, financial, and industrial infrastructure. The latter occurred because large-scale enterprises took advantage of their easy access to credit to make huge inflation profits which were ploughed back into industrial and commercial expansion. Such heavy investment was ultimately achieved at the expense of small rentiers and wage-earners, whose purchasing power was rapidly diminished by the reduction in the real value of interest on securities, savings bank deposits, and wages. The reduced living standards, social distress, and economic distortion caused by this process had become palpable by 1922. It is, of course, arguable that some such process was necessary if Germany was to recover her productive strength without external assistance under the handicaps imposed by the lost war. Yet the extreme suffering and the violence and wastefulness of much of the structural change which occurred as a result of this investment orgy were to scar German society for a generation.[2]

The direct contribution of reparation payments to these developments was secondary. The government's reparation expenditure of 1.1 billion gold marks in the budgetary year 1922–3 was responsible for 44 per cent of the total deficit of 2.5 gold marks. Yet this deficit was mainly due to the inflation-induced shrinkage of government revenue to the unheard-of figure of 1.5 billion gold marks. The cash payments of 720 million gold marks and deliveries in kind of 680 million gold marks which were made in the calendar year 1922 also placed a considerable strain on the balance of payments when the value of imports (6.3 billion gold marks) still marginally exceeded that of exports (6.2 billion gold marks). Germany could, however, have

[2] Recent commentators on the period have estimated German national income (1913 = 100) at 92 in 1921 and 84 in 1922: Laursen and Pedersen, 84, Table 10. Cf. Bresciani-Turroni, 192. On Germany's unfavourable terms of trade: ibid. 249–52; on inefficiency: ibid. 214–220; on the amalgamation of firms and the production of capital equipment: ibid. 192–212; on the increased financial power of industry and the eclipse of the credit banks: ibid. 212–14; on the fate of rentiers, savings bank depositors, and wage-earners, and the fall in the standard of living: ibid. 196, 305–8, 328–33. Cf. Great Britain, Dept. of Overseas Trade, *Report on the Economic and Financial Conditions in Germany to March 1923, by Mr. J. W. F. Thelwall* ... (London, HMSO, 1923), 9, 119–20. For an interesting attempt to weigh the complex socio-economic effects of the inflation: P. Czada, 'Ursachen und Folgen der grossen Inflation', in H. Winkel (ed.), *Finanz- und wirtschaftspolitische Fragen der Zwischenkriegszeit* (Schriften des Vereins für Sozialpolitik, 73, Berlin, 1973), 32–8; id., 'Grosse Inflation und Wirtschaftswachstum', in H. Mommsen *et al.* (edd.), *Industrielles System*, 386–95.

enjoyed a trade surplus in this period, notwithstanding the large imports of foodstuffs necessitated by the poor harvest of 1922, had it not been for excessive imports of raw materials by firms engaged in the capital goods boom, and foreign purchases by individuals who were hedging against inflation. The effect of the boom was particularly noticeable in the case of coal imports. In January–May 1922 Germany was a net exporter of 2.5 million tons of coal exclusive of reparation shipments. Yet in the following seven months she became a net importer of 10.3 million tons. This increase was not due to Allied reparation demands. Because of increased production the amount of coal available for domestic distribution (after reparation shipments had been made) had risen to almost its pre-war level in the first five months of 1922. Nor were supplies diminished appreciably by the partition of Upper Silesia in May 1922, since the region ceded to Poland was a considerable consumer of its own coal. Between June and December 1922 ten million more tons of coal were, in fact, distributed within Germany's reduced frontiers than had been available in the same area and over a comparable period in 1913. This increased consumption reflected the heightened demand for iron and steel occasioned by the feverish production of capital equipment. As an American observer remarked in January 1923, German complaints of a coal shortage now reflected 'increased productive requirements rather than reduced supplies or increased deliveries on reparation account'.[3]

The reparation question was, in fact, important chiefly for its psychological impact in 1922. The evaporation of the real value of government revenue and the lop-sidedness of German economic growth were both closely linked to the rapid depreciation of the mark. This in turn, although ultimately due to the long-term inadequacy of Germany's internal and external financial policy, was frequently precipitated by unfavourable twists in the reparation wrangle. Reparations were, in short, an important catalyst, even if they cannot be blamed simplistically for Germany's quickening progress towards financial collapse in 1922.

---

[3] For reparations and the budget: see below, Appendix I, Table F; for trade figures: ibid. Table D; for reparation payments in 1922: RC iv, Table X; for food imports: Thelwall, *Report on ... Germany to March 1923*, 16. On coal distribution: see below, Appendix II. For coal imports and the capital goods boom: Bresciani-Turroni, 197–200; J. S. Davis, 'Economic and Financial Progress in Europe', *RES* 5 (1923), 105.

MORATORIUM, JANUARY–AUGUST 1922

The breakdown of the Cannes Conference, like that of the London Conference in March 1921, caused the responsibility for the reparation dispute to devolve from the Supreme Council to the Reparation Commission. The initial effect of this was anticlimactic, since, notwithstanding the stern declaration of Poincaré about the rigid implementation of the treaty, the commission was bound by the provisions of the Reparation Chapter, and was therefore prevented from acting with the same expedition as the heads of state. On 13 January it confined itself to granting a provisional, partial, and conditional postponement of the reparation instalments due on 15 January and 15 February. In return for this concession Germany was to make cash payments of 31 million gold marks every ten days and was to submit within fifteen days a scheme of budgetary and monetary reform and a programme of cash payments and deliveries in kind for 1922. On 28 January the German government duly responded with a long memorandum undertaking to levy new taxes and impose a forced loan so as 'to meet its reparation payments at least for 1922 with the least possible recourse to the printing press'. In view of the difficulty of restricting the floating debt, the plan of reparation payments submitted to the commission was more a plea for reduction than a formal schedule. The memorandum insisted that the fulfilment of Allied demands would depend ultimately on the availability of domestic and foreign credit; and that this in turn would hinge on the restoration of confidence in Germany's solvency.[4]

Notwithstanding the manner in which this offer was hedged, the hope generated by the moratorium and the apprehension induced by Poincaré prompted the German government at least to go through the motions of a more active financial policy. The reform programme referred to on 28 January had been drawn up during five-party negotiations in the second half of January between the Social Democrats, the Centre Party, the Democrats, the Bavarian People's Party, and the all-important DVP. The resulting *Steuerkompromiss* (tax compromise), which included both a forced loan and increased indirect taxation, was hailed by Centrists and Democrats as evidence of a more co-operative trend in German politics. Yet the DVP's support for the deal had been motivated partly by its desire to avoid an election on

---

[4] Decision of 13 Jan. 1922 ..., RC iii. 55; Report submitted by Germany ..., ibid. 56–112. See also *DBFP* I, xix. 135–6.

the tax issue; and its approval of the forced loan had been secured only by other tax concessions, quite apart from the understanding that its proceeds would be devoted exclusively to the compensation of German industry for deliveries in kind to the Allies. The Social Democrats, on the other hand, were sensitive to charges that increased indirect taxation was socially regressive and that the forced loan was an inadequate substitute for earlier proposals to appropriate 'real values'; and they were forced to justify their support for the compromise on the grounds that it would be undesirable to force an election on the eve of the Genoa Conference.[5]

Given this uncertain backing and the conservative interpretation subsequently put upon the tax compromise in committee, the deterioration of Anglo-French relations and the hardening of French policy which now occurred did not augur well for the future. On 18 January, the British cabinet, upset by French hostility during the Cannes Conference, decided to suspend negotiations about the projected Anglo-French defensive alliance. Poincaré quickly reciprocated by insisting that decisions about Germany's obligations in 1922 should continue to be the exclusive responsibility of the Reparation Commission, and by vetoing discussions of the reparation question at the forthcoming Genoa Conference. He also went out of his way to ridicule Lloyd George's European reconstruction scheme when testifying to the Foreign Affairs Committee of the Chamber on 8 February. The resulting coolness between Britain and France, which was reflected in a glacial encounter between Lloyd George and Poincaré at Boulogne on 25 February, coincided with ominous trends in French domestic politics. Although Poincaré had retained half of Briand's cabinet in one capacity or another, he had taken care to replace Paul Doumer, the first post-war French Finance Minister to betray any enthusiasm for budgetary reform, with Count Charles de Lasteyrie. The latter had attracted attention late in 1921 as rapporteur of the reparation budget: but he was either unable—Léon Daudet referred to him as a 'zozo'— or unwilling to tackle France's financial problems, and was soon dubbed even in right-wing circles as 'le comte déficitaire'. The relapse of France into financial inertia was also indicated by the appointment of Charles Reibel, a young protégé of Poincaré, as Minister of the

    [5] Wirth, 26 Jan. 1922, *RT* ccclii. 5561; Müller (SPD), 27 Jan. 1922, 5580–1; Marx (Zentrum), 5584–5; Breitscheid (USPD), 5590–2; Becker (DVP), 5595–9; Petersen (DDP), 5601; Levi (KAPD), 5608. Cf. Laubach, 146–7. For continuing trade union and SPD pressure for the 'appropriation of real values': *Die Kabinette Wirth*, i. 506–9, 513–14, 520–2.

Liberated Regions in place of Loucheur, Briand's distinguished financial ambassador-at-large. By February, de Lasteyrie was to be heard
during a debate on France's reparation budget for 1922 (which was
clearly going to involve uncovered expenditure of at least ten billion
francs) expressing the financial sentiments that had earned Klotz popularity in 1919. 'We consider', he declared, 'that the problem of reparations today dominates our entire financial situation, I will even say,
our entire political situation.' De Lasteyrie's unwillingness to sanction
any increase in French taxation before Germany began to pay reparations was clearly expressed on 31 March when he submitted his
draft budget for 1923 to the Chamber of Deputies. Although he
predicted a deficit of 4 billion francs in the *ordinary* budget (which
was caused both by the increased burden of interest payments on the
public debt and by the shrinkage of extraordinary revenues accruing
from war taxes and from the sale of war material), he refused to
impose any new taxes before Germany had taken steps to pay for the
destruction she had caused.[6]

The regression of French policy may not have influenced the first of
the two notes which were, in consequence of the newly enhanced
authority of the Reparation Commission, transmitted by that body to
the German government on 21 March. This document, which had in
fact been drawn up early in March at a conference of Allied Finance
Ministers in Paris, simply confirmed the proposal of 10 January that
Germany's obligations for 1922 should amount to 720 million gold
marks in cash and 1450 million gold marks in kind. Since cash payments of 282 million gold marks had already been made in 1922, it
was directed that there should be further instalments of 18 millions in
April, 50 millions a month from May to October, and 60 millions in
November and December. It was further stipulated that cash payments
and deliveries in kind were to be used to cover the costs of the Allied
armies of occupation, and that only the balance should be reckoned

---

[6] On the fate of the alliance proposal: Cabinet Minutes, 2 (22), 18 Jan. 1922, Min. 2,
CAB 23/29. Note Derby's unsuccessful attempt to revive the negotiations in Feb.: Derby
to Lloyd George, 18 Feb. 1922, Lloyd George Papers, F/14/5/38. On the role of the RC:
Saint-Aulaire to Curzon, 2 Feb. 1922, PRO, FO371/7474/C1645; Curzon to Saint-
Aulaire, 15 Feb. 1922, ibid. 7474/C2044. For Poincaré and reconstruction: Chambre des
Députés, CAE, 8 Feb. 1922, Audition de M. Poincaré, at 203. On Genoa: Cabinet
Minutes, 13 (22), 24 Feb. 1922, Min. 2, CAB 23/29. For the meeting of 25 Feb.: *DBFP*
I, xix. 170–92. On French financial policy: de Lasteyrie, 23 Feb. 1922, *CD*, 498; 31 Mar.
1922, 1329; Chambre des Députés, *Doc. parl.*, 1922, Doc. 4220, at 525; L. Daudet,
L'Agonie du régime (Paris, 1925), 137; Hardinge to Curzon, 30 Mar. 1922; Memo
concerning the French Budgetary Situation, 4 Apr. 1922, *DBFP* I, xx. 24–5, 27–9.

as a credit against Germany's total reparation obligation under the London Schedule of Payments. The tone of the note accompanying this schedule was, however, clearly affected by a French memorandum of 15 March to the Reparation Commission accusing Germany of bad faith. This peremptorily ordered the German government to enact legislation by 31 May 1922 which would yield an extra 60 billion paper marks of revenue in the budgetary year 1922–3. It also recommended, for good measure, that steps should be taken to reduce public expenditure, float domestic and foreign loans, and check the flight of capital; and directed that Germany's financial administration should be more rigorously controlled by granting autonomy to the Reichsbank and allowing the Committee of Guarantees wider supervisory powers.[7]

Such demands were bound to provoke an uproar in Germany. The cabinet indignantly rejected the notion that its problems were caused by the budget deficit rather than the balance of payments, and that the Reparation Commission had the right to dictate its fiscal policy. Wirth, therefore, protested publicly in the Reichstag that the burdens which had been prescribed, and the resulting slump in the mark to over 330 to the dollar, would completely undermine the *Steuerkompromiss*. It would, in any case, be out of the question to raise an extra 60 billions in taxes within the time limit stipulated. Even the socialist parties, who still insisted that the tax compromise had let the propertied classes off too lightly, considered that the Reparation Commission's demands were technically and politically impossible. Rathenau and Stresemann went further and agreed with the claim of the Nationalists that the *Steuerkompromiss* represented the limit of Germany's taxable capacity. Resentment was also heightened amongst the patriotic middle-class parties by the extended competence of the Committee of Guarantees. The storm was, however, briefly lulled by the decision of the Reparation Commission on 4 April to appoint a committee of French, German, British, American, and neutral experts to investigate the possibility of raising an international loan for Germany. The revival of hope which this encouraged caused the German reply of 7 April to be a remarkable blend of intransigence and

---

[7] Letter from the RC to the German Government, 21 Mar. 1922, RC iii. 118–21. Cf. Horne to Lloyd George, 14 Mar. 1922, Lloyd George Papers, F/27/6/55; Memo of 15 Mar. 1922, RC, *Official Documents Relative to the Amount of Payments to be Effected by Germany under Reparation Account, II. . . .* (London, 1923) (henceforward, RC vi), 4–30; letter from RC to German Chancellor, 21 Mar. 1922, ibid. iii. 113–18. For increasing French pressure on the RC to impose tighter financial controls on Germany and the British response: Trachtenberg, *Reparation in World Politics*, 241–2.

conciliation. After flatly rejecting the commission's payments schedule and tax programme, and condemning any strengthening of the Committee of Guarantees, the government pointed out that the forced loan would bring about a substantial increase in revenue, and offered to provide the committee with any information it required. The same restraint was evident in the rejoinder of the Reparation Commission on 13 April. While careful to assert its ultimate authority, the commission's anxiety lest it prejudice the deliberations of the Loan Committee prompted it to leave the door open by inviting 'any practicable suggestions' from the German government for coping with its difficulties. The procedural reason for this flexibility was that Dubois, the French chairman of the commission who had previously sought to have Germany declared in default, now agreed with Bradbury, the British representative, that such a declaration should be delayed until 31 May, the deadline for the reforms demanded in the notes of 21 March.[8]

The first few days of this breathing space were occupied by the Genoa Conference, which was memorable chiefly for demonstrating the absurdity of Lloyd George's contention that European reconstruction could precede a provisional resolution of the reparation problem. The conference was hamstrung from the outset by the non-participation of the United States, which was made easier to justify by Poincaré's insistence on the exclusion of the reparation question from the agenda. The members of the new Loan Committee who happened to be among the delegates at Genoa took the opportunity to have informal discussions. Their initiative in drawing up a four-year reparation scheme in conjunction with a plan for an international loan of 4 billion gold marks would almost certainly have been vitiated by the objection of both France and Germany to any provisional reparation settlement. Their deliberations were, in any case, interrupted by the

[8] Wirth, 28 Mar. 1922, *RT* ccccliii. 6613, 6616, 6621; Hergt (DNVP), 6627; Stampfer (SPD), 6635; Marx (Zentrum), 29 Mar. 1922, cccliv. 6642; Stresemann (DVP), 6647; Rathenau (DDP), 6655; Breitscheid (USDP), 6660–2. For criticism of the Committee of Guarantees: Wirth, at 6617; Hergt, at 6624; Rathenau, at 6655. For the cabinet deliberations before this debate and the moderating effect of the establishment of the Loan Committee: *Die Kabinette Wirth*, i. 623–41; ii. 694–6; Laubach, 165–8. The dollar rate had risen, in response to Germany's continuing cash reparation payments, from 200 at the end of Jan. to 289 on 21 Mar., and thence to 332 on 24 Mar. In Apr. it fell back to 280. See Economics Ministry Memo of 24 Mar.: *Die Kabinette Wirth*, ii. 660 n. 4. For the Loan Committee's terms of reference: *Documents relatifs aux réparations*, i. 241–2. See also: Reply from German government to RC, 7 Apr. 1922; letter from RC to German government, 13 Apr. 1922, RC iii. 121–6. On the Apr. note exchange: Bergmann, *Reparations*, 123; Secret Letters, vi, 14 Apr. 1922.

signature of the Rapallo Treaty between Germany and Russia on 16 April.[9]

There is good reason to discount Wirth's subsequent claim in the Reichstag that the Treaty of Rapallo, which caused the virtual break-up of the Genoa Conference, owed its origin simply to the re-establishment of commercial ties between Russia and Germany, which had been proceeding since the Russo-German Trade Treaty of 6 May 1921. The most significant clauses of the Rapallo agreement were not those which renewed full diplomatic and consular ties between the signatories but those in which the two financial pariahs of Europe thumbed their noses at their western creditors by renouncing all their claims on each other, to wit, Germany's pre-war investments in Russia and Russia's entitlement to claim reparations from Germany under Article 116 of the Versailles Treaty. This gesture of bilateral financial renunciation was, on the Russian side, a reaction to the insistence of Entente statesmen, in their conversation with Chicherin and Litvinov on 14 and 15 April, that the Bolsheviks should honour Tsarist Russia's pre-war and wartime foreign debts as a precondition for having the benefits of reconstruction conferred upon them. For the German delegation at Genoa the immediate impetus to Rapallo was resentment at being excluded from the conversations of 14–15 April and the entirely unwarranted apprehension—no doubt fostered by the Bolsheviks—that the creditor powers would succeed in concluding a separate agreement with Russia. This momentarily allowed Baron Ago von Maltzan, an advocate of more intimate German relations with Russia, to assert his influence over Rathenau, the westerner, whose susceptibility may have been increased by pique at not being a party to negotiations in which he had a personal commercial interest. Rathenau's impulsive decision to sign the Rapallo Treaty early on Easter Sunday was clearly an overreaction which served the immediate interests of nobody but the Bolsheviks, whose major preoccupation at Genoa was not to have themselves 'reconstructed' by the West but to prevent an economic or political *rapprochement* between their capitalist foes.[10]

[9] For the American refusal to attend Genoa: Sec. State to the Italian ambassador, 8 Mar. 1922, *FR*, 1922, i. 392–4. Cf. Geddes (Washington) to Curzon, 7 Mar. 1922, *DBFP* I, xix. 198–9. For Poincaré's attitude: Hardinge to Curzon, 20 Jan. 1922, ibid. xx. 3–4. For the activities of the Loan Committee at Genoa: Bergmann, *Reparations*, 126–8.

[10] For the text of the Rapallo Treaty: *Reichsgesetzblatt*, 1922, ii. 677. For the side-negotiations with Chicherin and Litvinov at Genoa: *DBFP* I, xix. 380–402. For the German delegation's isolation: *Die Kabinette Wirth*, ii. 705–6, 710–12. Note, however,

Despite a chorus of protest from Germany's creditors and the hopeful assertion of the German right wing that Rapallo marked the end of fulfilment and the beginning of an 'active' foreign policy, the impact of Rathenau's aberration was muffled by the continuing discussions of the Loan Committee. As Logan, the American observer, remarked early in May, France's representatives on the Reparation Commission were still acutely aware that they would obtain 'quick hard cash' only 'through the medium of a German foreign loan'. The German government was so worried about the effect of Rapallo on its financial relations with the West that it vainly tried to persuade Chicherin to abrogate the treaty. Then, after some initial confusion caused by Wirth's absence at Genoa, it proceeded to mend its fences with the Reparation Commission by undertaking on 9 May to transmit a complete scheme for balancing its budget before 31 May. It also gave a general undertaking to comply with the demands of 21 March, although it stressed that some of these were impossible and requested further discussion along the lines foreshadowed by the commission's note of 13 April.[11]

Ten days of intense negotiations in Paris in mid-May between the German Finance Minister, Andreas Hermes, and the Reparation Commission re-emphasized the fundamental divergence of opinion about the reasons for Germany's financial instability. While the commission insisted that the root of the problem was the wildly unbalanced German budget, Hermes and his reparation expert, Carl Bergmann, argued with equal conviction that stabilization would be impossible until the balance of payments deficit was counteracted by an inter-

the evidence for the *Waffenbrüderschaft* between Wirth and Maltzan, the leading 'easterner' in the German Foreign Office: H. von Helbig, *Die Träger der Rapallo-Politik* (Göttingen, 1958), 54–82. For Rathenau's commercial designs on Russia: see above, ch. 4 n. 25. For an off-the-record criticism of Rathenau's behaviour at Genoa by Bergmann, the German reparation expert: Secret Letters, vi, 28 Apr. 1922. For recent scholarly appraisals of Rapallo: Laubach, ch. 5; Felix, ch. 8; Himmer, 'Rathenau, Russia and Rapallo'. See also L. Kochan, *Russia and the Weimar Republic* (Cambridge, 1954), 41–2, 51–2; E. H. Carr, *German–Soviet Relations between the Two World Wars* (London, 1952), ch. 3.

[11] For a summary of the British and French press reaction to Rapallo: *NYT*, 18, 19 Apr. 1922, 1–2. The hostility of the French nationalists was tempered by their satisfaction that Germany and Russia could now be blamed, instead of France, for wrecking the Genoa Conference. For Poincaré's reaction: *Le Temps*, 25 Apr. 1922, 4. Cf. Bergmann, *Reparations*, 128–9. For the reaction of the German right wing: Hoetzsch (DNVP), 30 May 1922, *RT* ccclv. 7710; Becker (DVP), 7723; Bohm (Bäy. VP), 7734. For the cabinet's concern about the impact of Rapallo, and the lead up to the note of 9 May: *Die Kabinette Wirth*, ii. 719–25, 758–60, 763–5, 769–71. For text: Letter ... to RC, 9 May 1922, RC iii. 128–9. For Logan's comments: Secret Letters, vi, 5 May 1922.

national loan. Only the undesirability of an open disagreement on the eve of the deliberations of the Loan Committee produced a compromise formula which prescribed restriction of the floating debt as well as access to international financial assistance as the cure for the disease. This line of thought was eventually embodied in a note of 28 May in which the German government undertook to balance its budget by increasing revenues, abolishing subsidies, and reducing administrative expenditure. A guarantee was given that, if a foreign loan were obtained, the floating debt would not be allowed to rise for more than a limited period above its level on 31 March 1922. The government also agreed to the supervision demanded by the Reparation Commission on the understanding that this would 'in no way affect the sovereignty of the German Government, ... disturb the working of the admin- istration, and ... violate the secrecy of the fortune or of the private affairs of taxpayers'. Finally, although it pleaded that there had so far been insufficient time to devise measures against the flight of capital, it reported that the Reichsbank had been made independent by a law of 25 May 1922, and that orders had been given for the publication of statistics in the pre-war manner. The widening gap between promise and performance was, however, revealed by an appended copy of the draft budget for 1922. This predicted a surplus on ordinary account of 71 billion paper marks, but forecast treaty expenditure of 213 billion paper marks (calculated at the rate of 70 paper marks to 1 gold mark). The resulting deficit of 142 billion marks would, together with additional extraordinary domestic expenditures of 23 billion paper marks, be covered by borrowing. Since a supplementary note of 30 May indicated that the proceeds of the proposed forced loan would be absorbed entirely in defraying ordinary expenditures, the clear implication was that the money to cover the extraordinary budget would have to come either from the printing press or from abroad.[12]

Although these proposals were approved by the Reparation Com- mission, thus enabling it, in Logan's words, to surmount 'the May 31 hump' created by the notes of 21 March, they were made in the teeth of growing opposition within Germany. In the last week of May a cabinet crisis had threatened because Wirth considered that Hermes should not have undertaken to restrict the floating debt; and agreement

[12] For the visit of Hermes to Paris: *Die Kabinette Wirth*, ii. 782–8, 791–821; Bergmann, *Reparations*, 130–1; Felix, 151–2. Reply from German government to RC, 28 May 1922, RC iii. 129–38. For the note of 30 May: Letter from Chancellor of the Commonwealth to RC, 30 May 1922, RC iii. 139–40.

was only reached with the Reparation Commission on this point after further pressure had been applied by the Loan Committee. There was also an upsurge of discontent in the Reichstag. Wirth and Müller pleaded to no avail that the unofficial text of the note of 28 May which had appeared in the press should not be discussed while negotiations were still in progress at Paris. On 30 May the Nationalist, Otto Hoetzsch, moved a no-confidence motion against the government for promising to balance its budget without insisting upon a definitive and reasonable settlement of Germany's total reparation obligation. The DVP and DDP refrained from voting on Hoetzsch's motion: but they registered their disquiet by demanding a fundamental re-examination of Germany's capacity to pay and urging treaty revisions which included the abrogation of the 'war guilt' clause upon which Germany's reparation obligation was commonly held to be based.[13]

The stiffening attitude of the German bourgeoisie was matched by the reaction of extremist groups in France to the Rapallo Treaty and the approach of the 31 May deadline. On 2 May, General Joseph Degoutte, commander of the French troops in the Rhineland, urged Maginot, the Minister of War, that it was an opportune moment to occupy the Ruhr in retaliation for Rapallo. On 28 May, Adrien Dariac, the vice-president of the Finance Committee of the Chamber, who had just returned from a tour of the occupied territories, presented a report which also advocated seizing the Ruhr as a reparations pledge and actively encouraging Rhineland separatism. On the following day, Degoutte's report was studied by an interdepartmental committee which included Foch and Paul Tirard, the head of the Inter-Allied Rhineland High Commission, both of whom were firm supporters of an independent Rhineland. Yet the existence of pressures and contingency plans does not indicate that the government had determined to act. Marc Trachtenberg has shown that Poincaré was making increasingly loud noises about the necessity for tighter financial controls on Germany. Yet in a discussion with the Foreign Affairs Committee of the Senate on 7 June the French premier clearly regarded a Ruhr occupation as a last resort and was mainly interested in using it as a threat to wring financial concessions from Britain and the United States. In the inter-Allied negotiations which would follow Germany's

[13] Letter from RC to Chancellor of the Reich, 31 May 1922, RC iii: 140–2; Secret Letters, vi, 26 May 1922. For an extended account of the cabinet crisis: Felix, 150–6. See also Bergmann, *Reparations*, 131–2; Laubach, 231–4. For the Reichstag debate: Wirth, 29 May 1922, RT ccclv. 7673; Müller (SPD), 7677; Hoetzsch (DNVP), 30 May 1922, 7704–8; Becker (DVP), 7721–8; Dernburg (DDP), 7731–3.

impending request for a total moratorium he did not wish, he said, 'to face Britain with empty hands'.[14]

With hawkish elements becoming more vocal on both sides of the Rhine, a negative report by the Loan Committee was certain to have dire repercussions. It is usual to attribute the unfavourable recommendations of the committee simply to the refusal of France to allow any reduction of Germany's obligations under the London Schedule of Payments. French obstinacy was, however, clearly related to the increasingly schizoid nature of American financial diplomacy. The original reason for the loan discussions was the hope of the Anglo-Saxon international banking fraternity, so powerfully represented on the committee by Sir Robert Kindersley, a director of the Bank of England, and by J. P. Morgan jun. himself, that it would be able to force the reduction of Germany's obligations to a financially realistic level. As Colonel Logan, the American observer on the Reparation Commission, remarked to Benjamin Strong, the governor of the Federal Reserve Bank, on 17 March, 'when the question comes up of Germany borrowing foreign money, the conditions and amount of such loan will not be dictated by the politicians but by the fellow who is going to lend the money.' Yet by the time the Loan Committee began its deliberations on 23 May, the tune was being called not by bankers but by American politicians who were demanding the prompt repayment of Europe's war debts to the United States. Although the new Republican administration had been warned of the threat that war debts posed to American commerce, Congress had even rejected an attempt in June 1921 by Andrew Mellon, the Secretary of the Treasury, to obtain power to vary debt repayments in order to cushion their impact on trade. This inflexibility, which was due—just as it had been in 1919—to a desire to minimize domestic taxation, was formalized in February 1922 by the setting up of the World War Foreign Debt Commission and subsequent requests to America's debtors in the second half of April that they should take steps to repay what they owed. This pressure increased French reluctance to reduce Germany's burden at a time when, according to Logan, the French Finance Ministry had just begun to be more malleable in this respect. On 7 June Poincaré reported to the Foreign Affairs Committee of the

<hr />

[14] On proposals for a Ruhr occupation: Bariéty, 'Les Réparations allemandes,' 21–35. For Poincaré: Sénat, CAE, 7 June 1922, 27–9, 40–6; D. Artaud, 'A propos de l'occupation de la Ruhr', *RHMC* 17 (1970), 1–21. McDougall, *France's Rhineland Diplomacy*, 206, does not refer to Poincaré's opposition to a Ruhr occupation at this stage.

Senate that he was opposed to the Loan Committee being empowered to make recommendations about Germany's total bill because 'American bankers had no ... mandate from their government to consider the question of inter-Allied debts'. The French government's determination not to give up any of its claims on Germany while the United States insisted on the repayment of its war debts prompted the French representative on the Reparation Commission to vote against that body's otherwise unanimous resolution on 7 June authorizing the Loan Committee to deal with any matter affecting Germany's ability to raise a foreign loan. The seemingly obstructive attitude of Germany's principal creditor in turn led the Loan Committee to conclude on 10 June that it would be pointless to continue its labours. Yet, in its final report, the committee insisted that the prerequisites for any future loan included a settlement of inter-Allied debts as well as the removal of uncertainty about Germany's obligations and a genuine effort on her part to achieve financial stability.[15]

Although the representatives of German heavy industry, reluctant to forgo their inflation profits, had been opposed to any international stabilization loan which was not associated with a final and favourable settlement of Germany's total reparation bill, the negative findings of the Loan Committee poisoned the three-day debate which began in the Reichstag on 21 June about reparations and other aspects of the treaty. The Nationalist Reichert set the pace with an indictment of the series of seemingly burdensome special agreements which had just been concluded for expediting deliveries in kind. Although the Wiesbaden Agreement of the previous October had proved to be a virtual dead letter because of opposition from French vested interests and from Britain, the emphasis of the new payments schedule of 21 March on deliveries in kind had made the Reparation Commission interested in improving delivery procedures. The Bemelmans–Cuntze Agreement of 2 June 1922 between the commission and the German government,

[15] For the origins and outlook of the Loan Committee: Link, 122–35. For its deliberations see the memo by Carl Bergmann, the German representative on the committee: *Die Kabinette Wirth*, ii. 855–65; RC, Minutes No. 293A, 6 and 7 June 1922; Rapport du Comité de l'Emprunt à la Commission des Réparations, *Documents relatifs aux réparations*, i. 243–50. For American war-debt policy: Artaud, *Question des dettes interalliées*, i. 337–58; M. Leffler, 'The Origins of Republican War Debts Policy, 1921–23', *J. of American History*, 59 (1972), 585–601. For the exchange between the Debt Commission and the French government: *FR*, 1922, i. 397, 404–5. For Poincaré's attitude: Sénat, CAE, 7 June 1922, 10–11; Artaud, 'A propos de l'occupation de la Ruhr', 8–9. See also H. G. Moulton and L. Pasvolsky, *War Debts and World Prosperity* (Washington, 1932), 82–3.

the Gillet–Ruppel Agreements of 15 March and 6–9 June between the French and German governments, and, later, the agreement between Hugo Stinnes and Lubersac, the chairman of the Union of the Co-operatives of the Devastated Regions, provided for direct ordering by French claimants from German producers, who were to be compensated for their deliveries by the German government. Although these arrangements were to yield deliveries worth only 7.4 million marks by the end of 1922 they were widely regarded in Germany as instruments of the French policy of encouraging Rhineland separatism. It is no accident, therefore, that an Anglo-French proposal some months earlier for the neutralization of the Rhineland was also the subject of a DVP interpellation, and that Centrist deputies voiced their opposition to the destruction of strategic railways in the Rhineland and their concern about the future of the Saar. Finally, the Independent Socialist, Paul Levi, joined in the chorus of complaint by entering reservations about the policy of fulfilment if it was to be achieved at the expense of the German proletariat.[16]

Although Rathenau replied in a calm and factual manner to this barrage of criticism, the only achievement which he and his supporters could claim was the condemnation of French reparation policy which seemed to be implicit in the negative report of the Loan Committee. Against this was to be set a clear DVP declaration that time was no longer on the side of fulfilment. The Nationalist spokesman, Karl Helfferich, also took the opportunity to pour scorn and partisan abuse upon a policy which, he claimed, had caused catastrophic depreciation of the mark, ruined the middle classes, driven countless people to despair and suicide, deprived Germany of much of her working capital, and shaken the foundations of the German economic and social system. Helfferich went on to demand that the government should be impeached for high treason for transmitting its notes of 9 and 28 May to the Reparation Commission. These, he maintained, had committed Germany to a budgetary programme and to infringements of her economic sovereignty which had been specifically rejected by the Reichstag at the end of March.[17]

---

[16] For the attitudes of German industry: Link, *Stabilisierungspolitik*, 127–30. For texts of the Bemelmans–Cuntze and Gillet–Ruppel Agreements, RC ii. 14–35. For their yield: ibid. iv, Table X. For the Stinnes–Lubersac Agreement: Ruppel, 477–8; Feldman, *Iron and Steel*, 329–30. See also *Die Kabinette Wirth*, ii. 274–5; Reichert (DNVP), 21 June 1922, *RT* ccclv. 7923–8; Moldenhauer (DVP), 7928–31; Lauscher (Zentrum), 7934–7; Bell (Zentrum), 7937–41; Levi (USPD), 7931–4. See below, n. 24 and text thereat.

[17] Rathenau (DDP), 21 June 1922, *RT* ccclv. 7941–5; Stampfer (SPD), 22 June 1922, 7948–51; Breitscheid (USPD), 7969–73; Gothein (DDP), 7953; Dauch (DVP), 7978; Helfferich (DNVP), 23 June 1922, 7992–7.

Neither the irresponsible rhetoric of Helfferich nor an unhappy confrontation with Hugo Stinnes at dinner that evening in the presence of a number of foreign diplomats was needed to bring home to Rathenau the bankruptcy of his policies. For this reason his assassination the next day at the hands of nationalist thugs was as redundant as it was brutal. He may, indeed, even have unconsciously courted martyrdom by his insistence on travelling to work in an open car. Yet neither the widespread revulsion against the right-wing authors of the assassination, which was summed up by Wirth's bitter condemnation of those who 'poured poison into the nation's wounds', nor the swift passage of the Ordinance for the Preservation of the Republic restored the financial vigour of the government. The dollar rate, which had slid from 280 to 300 after the Loan Committee's report, plummeted to 400 within a week of the murder. In the second week of July Germany requested a complete moratorium on cash reparation payments until the end of 1924 and a reduction of clearing payments under Article 296 of the treaty. On 13 July the Reparation Commission retorted with Olympian detachment that reparations were not the most important cause of the depreciation of the mark and that financial stability would be achieved only by domestic reform. Pending a report by the Committee of Guarantees, which had journeyed to Berlin in the second half of June, it directed that the cash instalment due on 15 July should be honoured. Although the German government complied, and also agreed on 21 July to a request by the Committee of Guarantees for more rigid financial controls, the inflexibility of France about clearing payments soon prompted it to refuse to pay either the 40 million gold marks of clearing debts due at the end of July or the 15 August reparation instalment of 50 million gold marks. On 3 August, when the mark was worth 762 to the dollar, German purchases of foreign exchange for reparation purposes were suspended in the teeth of renewed French threats of sanctions.[18]

---

[18] For an account of the Rathenau–Stinnes confrontation at dinner by Logan, who was the guest of honour: Secret Letters, vii, 26 June 1922. For Wirth's speech: 25 June 1922, RT ccclvi. 8056–8. For the text of the Ordinance: 24 June 1922, cclv. 8037–9. For its adoption on 18 July: ccclvi. 8739. For the dollar rate: Die Entwicklung der Reparationsfrage, 28–30. For the moratorium request of 12 July and the RC's reply of 13 July: Documents relatifs aux réparations, ii. 113–15. See Logan's description of the deliberations of the Committee of Guarantees in Berlin and texts of its memos of 18 July: Secret Letters, viii, 28 July, and Annexe 78. For the French government's refusal on 26 July to reduce clearing payments: Documents relatifs aux réparations, ii. 155–8.

The reparation deadlock had by this time begun to arouse considerable apprehension amongst responsible Frenchmen. On the eve of the parliamentary summer recess a remarkable interpellation had been moved in the Senate by Henry de Jouvenel, editor-in-chief of *Le Matin* since 1905, and François Albert, both of whom were to become members of Herriot's left-centre cabinet in 1924. De Jouvenel's speech was less an attack on Poincaré than an appeal to him to discard the Versailles Treaty and to engineer a genuine settlement based on the cancellation of inter-Allied debts, the granting of reparation priority to France, and the floating of an international loan. Such a sweeping programme was necessary, de Jouvenel asserted, if only for the sake of those deputies 'who had been elected on 16 November on the cry "la Boche payera", and who would face their electors in 1924 with an intact treaty but without a single *sou* in their hands'. The restricted vision of Poincaré was, however, only too apparent. 'MM. de Jouvenel and François Albert', he retorted, 'belittle this treaty. They consider it mediocre, they even regard it as evil. They believe that it is difficult to enforce, and they would be happy, if I understand their remarkable speeches aright, to replace it with some new agreement. I am afraid that I am unable to share their point of view. Notwithstanding what it is, the Treaty of Versailles is real; and this reality makes it superior to the alternatives suggested to us, which are admirable only because they are not on paper . . .' The premier went on to outline a programme of checks, guarantees, pledges, and sanctions which the Reparation Chapter entitled the Allies to impose upon Germany in order to ensure that she fulfilled these paper obligations. The order of the day submitted by de Jouvenel and Albert requesting the government to raise an international reparation loan was then withdrawn and replaced by one which simply expressed confidence in the government's ability 'to defend the rights and the interests of France'.[19]

The stubborn attitude of Poincaré was encouraged not only by American war-debt policy but also by the provocative behaviour of Lloyd George. After his European reconstruction scheme had evaporated at Genoa the British Prime Minister had adopted the view that France would only moderate her policies after experiencing the consequences of a single-handed attempt to impose her will upon Germany. His readiness to goad Poincaré into violent action was evident during a discussion with a group of British financial experts

---

[19] *Sénat*, 29 June 1922, 971–7 (de Jouvenel); 977–81 (Albert); 981–8 (Poincaré).

PUSH IN THE CORNER

Fig. 4. The *Star*, London, 3 August 1922.

on 15 July, three days after Germany had submitted her latest request for a moratorium. Having rejected out of hand the 'French idea' that 'everyone should surrender their reparations except France and Belgium', and having admitted that his plan 'was rather a dangerous one', he advanced the view that it was necessary to 'leave the French to become somewhat more frightened than they were at present'. In the subsequent discussion Sir John Bradbury pointed to the danger 'that if the matter were left alone and no action were taken, Germany might break up so badly that the situation would be irretrievable'; and Sir Robert Horne stressed that this was the last occasion upon which a reparation settlement might be arrived at. However, Lloyd George insisted 'the France was not ready to talk business on the subject', and concluded that 'he was not prepared to agree on any action at the moment'. The same view prevailed at a cabinet meeting three weeks later, where it was agreed that 'if, as seemed probable, M. Poincaré was determined to favour extreme measures it would on the whole be best to allow the French a free hand so that they might learn by experience'.[20]

The truculence of Lloyd George's policy towards France was complemented by his tactless handling of Britain's financial relations with the United States. Despite unequivocal advice through diplomatic channels that America was in no mood to discuss the cancellation of inter-Allied debts, he insisted, in the face of spirited opposition within the British cabinet from Chamberlain and Horne, that the Balfour Note should be dispatched on 1 August. In this skilfully wrought but ill-timed document, which the Prime Minister hoped 'would have important educational results on American opinion', the British government publicly repeated its confidential offer of the previous December to renounce its financial claims on the Allies and on Germany in return for a similar renunciation by the United States. The unfortunate effect of this manœuvre was reflected in a letter written to Louis Loucheur by Bernard Baruch, one of the most enlightened and influential financiers in the United States. The Balfour Note, Baruch wrote,

endeavoured to put the Americans into the position of being the offenders. First the English endeavoured to put the French in the position of being the offenders because they were militaristic. Now they are trying to put the

---

[20] Notes of a Conversation held at 10 Downing Street, 15 July 1922, CAB 23/26; Cabinet Minutes, 43 (22), 3 Aug. 1922, Min. 14, CAB 23/30.

Americans into the position of being the offenders because they are Shylocks. The English, because of their superior press work, put it over on the French; but they are not going to get away with making it appear that America is ungenerous.

Quite apart from the offence it gave in the United States, the note also restricted the financial manœuvrability of the British government vis-à-vis France, and armed Poincaré with the argument that, in the event of an American refusal to co-operate, France would be confronted with a rigid British demand for debt repayment.[21]

In view of the attitudes of Poincaré and Lloyd George there was little hope of an agreement between France and Britain when the Supreme Council met in London to consider Germany's request for a moratorium early in August 1922. Poincaré, who had become increasingly disturbed in July at France's budgetary position, and had been frustrated in his efforts to achieve prompt action through the Reparation Commission, had come to London seeking either a speedy all-round financial settlement or an Allied agreement to extract pledges from Germany. He had given up hope of the first alternative after the Balfour Note had made it clear that Britain wished for the time being to retain her loans to France and her other continental allies as a bargaining counter in her financial negotiations with the United States. Instead, therefore, of submitting to the conference a proposal for a reparation settlement which involved substantial British financial renunciation, he suggested that the Allies should take possession of a series of productive pledges in the Rhineland and the Ruhr district. These were to consist of (1) the control already exercised by the Rhineland High Commission over the granting of export licences; (2) a customs barrier between the occupied territories and the rest of Germany; (3) Allied exploitation of German state mines and forests; (4) Allied participation in 60 per cent of the share capital of German chemical industries on the left bank of the Rhine; (5) levies in the occupied territories; and (6) the German customs. Although Poincaré was unclear about how, given the low state of German trade, these

---

[21] Text of Balfour Note: *Despatch to the Representatives of France, Italy ... at London respecting War Debts, House of Commons Papers*, Cmd. 1737 of 1922. For the Cabinet discussions: Notes of a Conversation at 10 Downing Street, 5 July 1922, CAB 23/36; Cabinet Minutes, 38 (22), 7 July 1922; 42 (22), 25 July 1922, Min. 3, CAB 23/30. For the American reaction: Baruch to Tardieu, 11 Sept. 1922; Baruch to Loucheur, 16 Sept. 1922, Papers of Bernard M. Baruch. For American press reaction: *NYT*, 2 Aug. 1922, 16. On the implications of the Balfour Note for France: Trachtenberg, *Reparation in World Politics*, 257–8.

pledges would yield the required level of reparation receipts, he insisted that, unless they were taken, it would be impossible for France to consider any moratorium.[22]

Lloyd George proved just as reluctant to agree to these proposals as he was to chance his arm with unilateral financial concessions. This was not, as heretofore, because of his fear of the extension of French influence within Germany. Poincaré was, in fact, so anxious to extract some sort of agreement that he gradually jettisoned most of his demands and even agreed, during the dispute over the supervision of German state mines and forests which technically caused the break-up of the conference, to a form of indirect control identical with that which had been approved by British experts for exploiting the German customs. The revenue from these sources could, he conceded, be paid into a special fund which was only to be tapped by the Allies if Germany defaulted on her reparation payments. The immediate reason for the failure of Britain and France to reach agreement at London was not, as Marc Trachtenberg has suggested, Poincaré's lack of clarity about the precise function of the pledges. It was rather, as Bradbury remarked to Logan, the British government's desire 'to let M. Poincaré try out his policy in the face of their sulky disapproval in the hope that, when M. Poincaré had gone a little way on his independent policy, the French people, feeling consequently the weakening of the franc, increased taxation, etc., would rise in their wrath and oust M. Poincaré before too much harm was done'. Lloyd George, for whom time was running out, had clearly become obsessed with encompassing the downfall of the man who had, more than anyone else, undermined his European reconstruction scheme. The veteran French diplomat Paul Cambon considered that the London Conference had degenerated into 'une question d'amour-propre entre deux hommes qui se détestent'. Yet the evident antipathy between Lloyd George and Poincaré stemmed ultimately from the incompatibility of French and British reparation rhetoric. It was because neither government would, in the absence of massive American financial intervention, allow any diminution of its theoretical share of the illusory spoils, that the stage

---

[22] For the proceedings of the London Conference: *Documents relatifs aux réparations*, ii. 9–101 (esp. 12–16, for Poincaré's pledges scheme). For Poincaré's concern about the budget: Secret Letters, vii, 28 July 1922. For reference to his alternative slate-wiping plan: Cabinet Minutes, 46 (22), 14 Aug. 1922, 8, CAB 23/30. See also CD, 17 Nov. 1922, 3243 (Poincaré).

was now set for one of the most tragic years in the financial and economic history of western Europe.[23]

TOWARDS THE RUHR OCCUPATION

After the Supreme Council had dispersed on 14 August without deciding upon any reply to the German request for a moratorium, the Reparation Commission temporarily resumed control of the situation just as it had done on similar occasions before. Its first action was to send Bradbury and Mauclère, the British and French delegates, on a mission to Berlin to negotiate a scheme of productive pledges which would be acceptable to both the French and the German governments. However, the German attitude to the reparation question had now hardened. On 16 August, two days after the break-up of the London Conference, Wirth, alarmed at the catastrophic fall of the mark, and concerned about the increased food imports which would be made necessary by the poor harvest of 1922, had announced that Germany's food supply would henceforth have priority over reparation payments. It was now widely alleged in the German press, as it was in England, that France was using the reparation question in order to achieve the political subjugation of Germany. This prompted the German government to reject out of hand in the last week of August any proposal that state mines and forests should be used either directly or indirectly as pledges for coal and timber deliveries. Nor would it offer any greater guarantee of deliveries than a deposit of 50 million gold marks, and the promise of direct contracts between the Allied governments and German producers such as the agreement concerning deliveries of building materials to the devastated regions of France which Stinnes, now eager to reconcile patriotism with profit, was to conclude on 2 September with the Marquis de Lubersac.[24]

[23] For Lloyd George's negotiations with Poincaré: Cabinet Minutes, 44 (22), 10 Aug. 1922, 12–14; 45 (22), 12 Aug. 1922, Min. 2; 46 (22), 14 Aug. 1922, 8, CAB 23/30. For the dispute over supervision, see the differing British, Belgian, and French drafts of clauses 7 and 8 of a 'revise' of 12 Aug.: Secret Letters, vii. Annexe 80; *DBFP* I, xx. 206–10. See Trachtenberg, *Reparation in World Politics*, 253–5. For Bradbury's remark and for bad feeling between Lloyd George and Poincaré: Secret Letters, 8 Sept. 1922; P. Cambon, *Correspondance, 1870–1924* (3 vols.; Paris, 1940–6), iii. 413–15.

[24] For Wirth's statement: *Le Temps*, 17 Aug. 1922, 1. Cf. *Die Kabinette Wirth,*

In the face of this German intransigence, the Reparation Commission was strongly urged at the end of August 1922 by its French chairman, Dubois, to refuse Germany's request for a moratorium and to resort to coercive action. Such a procedure was only circumvented when the Belgian delegates, anxious to prevent an Anglo-French rupture, agreed to accept, in six-months German Treasury bills which the Reichsbank initially refused even to endorse, the reparation instalments due to their country for the remainder of 1922. In order to placate the Belgian public this gesture was preceded by a prearranged vote which rejected a motion by Bradbury that Germany should be granted a moratorium. The discontent of the Belgian electorate was not, however, to be assuaged for long by this stage-management, and the Belgian government was soon to be forced back into an alignment with France which would enable Dubois to gain a majority in the Reparation Commission in favour of Poincaré's policy of coercion.[25]

Belgium's sacrifice provided another respite which made possible a final round of general reparation negotiations between the Reparation Commission and the German government in the autumn of 1922. Early in October, when the mark had slumped to 2,000 to the dollar, the commission began unofficial discussions of a far-reaching proposal by Bradbury for a moratorium of between two and four years and the rehabilitation of German currency and credit. This scheme was so moderate that Logan considered it had only been submitted 'for the purpose of drawing out the French'; and it was duly rejected by

ii. 1047, 1072. His words 'Erst Brot für das deutsche Volk, dann Reparationen', were to become a slogan. D'Abernon, *Ambassador*, ii. 89. See also: E. Schiffer, 'Germany's Attitude towards the Reparation Problem', *MGCRE*, 28 Sept. 1922, 473. For the report of Bradbury and Mauclère to the RC: RC, Minutes, No. 214, 26 Aug. 1922. For the German government's opposition to pledges: *Die Kabinette Wirth*, ii. 1040–2, 1049–53; Bergmann, *Reparations*, 143; D'Abernon, *Ambassador*, ii. 84–5, 89, 96–7. This opposition was maintained by the German spokesman, Schroeder, when he presented his government's case for a moratorium to the RC on 30 Aug. 1922. RC, Minutes, No. 315, 30 Aug. 1922. For the Stinnes–Lubersac Agreement: see above, n. 16. For the meagre results of negotiations over special agreements for deliveries in kind: McDougall, *France's Rhineland Diplomacy*, 228–9.

[25] For the Belgian gesture: RC, Minutes, No. 316, 31 Aug. 1922; Decision of the RC ..., 31 Aug. 1922, RC, Annexe No. 1572. For similar Belgian efforts to prevent the break-up of the London Conference: Secret Letters, vii., 15 Aug. 1922; Notes of Conversations with M. Theunis, 12 Aug. 1922, CAB 23/36. For the prearranged vote: Secret Letters, vii, 8 Sept. 1922. Dubois, who wished to embarrass the Belgian delegates for adopting a soft line towards Germany, initially opposed this procedure. For the uncooperative attitude of the German cabinet and the Reichsbank: *Die Kabinette Wirth*, ii. 1071–6, 1081–2, 1098–1101.

the French delegation on 20–1 October because it made insufficient provision for controls and guarantees. However, on 24 October, when the mark stood at 4,000 to the dollar, the Reparation Commission decided to journey to Berlin for direct consultations with the German government. On 4 November the latter submitted a note which attributed the current depreciation to the diminution of domestic and foreign confidence in Germany's financial future, and proposed the stabilization of the mark by an international syndicate with a capital of 500 million gold marks. In reply to the commission's request for more details, both about this proposal and on the subject of controls, the government transmitted three reports by panels of foreign experts which it had recently invited to Berlin to give advice on questions of currency and credit. The first of these, which was drawn up by the British, Dutch, and Swiss bankers, R. H. Brand, G. Vissering, and L. Dubois, was a preliminary discussion of the German proposal for the short-term stabilization of the mark by an international syndicate. A second, signed by Brand, Gustav Cassel, the Swedish economist, Jeremiah Jenks, the American financier, and Keynes, stressed that if permanent stabilization were to be achieved stringent domestic reforms would be necessary as well as foreign financial assistance; while the third, by Vissering, Dubois, and Boris Kamenka, placed more emphasis upon international aid for Germany. All three reports emphasized that a moratorium of several years would be necessary prerequisite for both stabilization and budgetary balance. On 14 November the German government forwarded a plan for financial stabilization derived from all these reports which, while stressing that a permanent solution would be possible only after Germany's obligations had been fixed within her capacity, declared that the urgency of the financial situation warranted steps towards provisional reform. On the condition of a moratorium of three or four years on all payments except limited deliveries in kind to the devastated areas, this reform was to be achieved by means of a stabilization fund of one billion gold marks, of which half was to be provided by the Reichsbank and half by foreign bankers. Once internal and external confidence had been restored by using this fund to support the mark, the government would float a domestic and foreign gold loan to balance its budget. In the mean time, it undertook to reduce public expenditure, stimulate economic activity, and, if given equal trading rights, to improve the balance of payments.[26]

[26] For Bradbury's proposal: Secret Letters, vii, 13, 17, 27 Oct. 1922; ibid. Annexe 88;

Despite its theoretical soundness, Wirth's offer, which was transmitted just before his government fell on 14 November, was unlikely
to break the reparation deadlock or to bring about the financial
restoration of Germany because of the continuing non-co-operation
of the German industrial and financial élite. After the temporary
suspension of cash payments in August there had been renewed agitation in the liberal and socialist press for the Reichsbank to use its
newly granted autonomy under the law of 26 May 1922 to support
the mark with buying operations. This campaign coincided with efforts
by the radical Economics Ministry to introduce measures to counter
the flight of capital, check the repudiation of the mark in domestic
transactions, and introduce a currency which would be a stable reposi-
tory of value for the German public. Unhappily this initiative failed
because of opposition from the Finance Ministry and the Reichsbank.
Rudolf Havenstein, the president of the Reichsbank, testified to the
cabinet that any attempt to support the mark or to introduce a stable
currency would be pointless while Germany's balance of payments
remained unfavourable. This was consistent with the diagnosis of
inflation offered at the time by the 'balance of payments' school of
German monetary theorists. Yet the rigidity with which this diagnosis
was espoused by the German bureaucracy, despite the insistence of
authoritative contemporaries that inflation also had domestic monetary origins, suggests that its appeal was as much political as theoretical. Such a conclusion is encouraged by the assertion of Havenstein
that Germany's balance of payments problem (and hence the problem
of inflation) could only be cured by resorting to heavy industry's dual
prescription of a reduction of the reparation bill and an extension of
the German working day. Because of this opposition to stabilization,
the government's attempt to impose exchange controls was bound
to be ineffectual. Indeed, by depressing confidence in the mark, it

RC, Annexe No. 1614; *Documents relatifs aux réparations*, ii. 120–9. For the French
reaction: Mémoire de la délégation française . . ., ibid. 145–9; RC, Annexe No. 1617;
Minutes, No. 327, 6; Secret Letters, vii, 27 Oct. 1922. For the commission's visit to
Berlin: ibid. 13 Nov. 1922; Décision de la Commission des Réparations . . ., *Documents
relatifs aux réparations*, ii. 129. For the German proposal of 4 Nov.: Proposition du
gouvernement allemand . . ., ibid. 149–52. For the commission's reaction: RC, Minutes,
No. 329, 6 Nov. 1922. For the three reports of 7 and 9 Nov.: ibid. Annexes Nos. 1640
b, c, d; 1641 c, d. For the German proposal of 14 Nov.: Annexe No. 1641 d; Lettre du
gouvernement allemand . . ., *Documents relatifs aux réparations*, ii. 142–4; *Die den
Allierten seit dem Waffenstillstand übermittelten deutschen Angebote und Vorschläge
zur Lösung der Reparations- und Wiederaufbaufrage*, RT ccclxxix, Annexe 6138, 88–
98. Cf. *Die Kabinette Wirth*, ii. 1148–9, 1158–9, 1167–8.

encouraged the very practices of capital flight and the use of foreign exchange in domestic transactions which it sought to counteract.[27]

The fall of the Wirth cabinet, which was precipitated by the leftward swing of the SPD following its reunion with the USPD in September—and the consequent impossibility of broadening the coalition to include the financially influential DVP—had no decisive influence on German policy. The exclusion of the SPD from the non-party 'businessmen's cabinet' of Wilhelm Cuno, the managing director of HAPAG (Hamburg-Amerika Line), certainly diminished even further the enthusiasm with which the government contemplated financial reform. There were, moreover, grounds for the misgivings of the extreme left about the appointment of the DVP's Johannes Becker, one of the foremost opponents of the Forced Loan, as head of the radical Economics Ministry. Yet the change of government merely reinforced the financial paralysis which had been evident during Wirth's last months as Chancellor. The fiscal debates of December 1922 were distinguished less by any concern for monetary stabilization than by a desire to mitigate the immediate social distress and injustice caused by the dwindling value of the mark. The conservative Finance Ministry, whose influence was now unchallenged, rejected a proposal for the collection of taxes in gold marks or some other stable unit of value as an 'incomplete solution to the overall problem of monetary instability'. Discussion of a measure to amend the Income Tax centred around the relative injustice of wage-packet tax deductions during a period of hyperinflation. The Socialist, Paul Hertz, claimed that as a result of the fall of the mark, the proportion of the total yield of the Income Tax derived from wage deductions had risen from 57 per cent in April–July 1922 to 72 per cent in October. On the other hand, right-wing speakers played down the extent to which the burden of self-assessed taxpayers had been lightened. This preoccupation with adjusting the

---

[27] For Reichsbank autonomy: *Reichsgesetzblatt*, 1922, ii. 136. For the campaign to support the mark: *FZ*, 6 Oct. 1922, No. 712; 2 Nov. 1922, No. 784; *VZ*, 11 Oct. 1922, No. 481 (Bernhard); *Vorwärts*, 10 Oct. 1922, No. 478; 2 Nov. 1922, No. 518; K. Ackermann, 'Die Stellungnahme der deutschen Presse zum Stabilisierungsproblem der Mark, 1919–1923', Phil. Diss. (Univ. of Cologne, 1929), 56–7. For the Economics Ministry's proposals and the opposition of Havenstein, the Finance Ministry, and heavy industry: *Die Kabinette Wirth*, ii. 1117–20, 1123–7, 1139–44 (Havenstein at 1141–3), 1165–7; Laubach, 290–2; Feldman, *Iron and Steel*, 331–2. For the dispute amongst contemporary German monetary theorists about the sources of inflation: Ellis, chs. 12–14; L. A. Hahn, 'Handelsbilanz—Zahlungsbilanz—Valuta—Güterpreise', *Archiv*, 48 (1920–1), 596–614; id., 'Statische und dynamische Wechselkurse', ibid. 49 (1922), 761–79. For results: H. Schumacher, 'The New Exchange Regulations in Germany', *MGCRE*, 7 Dec. 1922, 666.

fiscal balance of power rather than with raising the diminished yield of the Income Tax precluded any effective attempt at stabilization.[28]

The same spirit pervaded a debate on 15 December on a proposal to amend the Forced Loan. When this measure had been approved by the Reichstag in July 1922, total subscriptions had been fixed at 70

TABLE 7. *Yield of the German Forced Loan, July–December 1922*

Month	Paper Marks	Gold Marks
July–Aug.	1,887,900,000	9,730,000
Sept.	584,900,000	1,670,000
Oct.	256,400,000	330,000
Nov.	108,500,000	60,000
Dec.	910,600,000	500,000
July–Dec.	3,748,300,000	12,290,000

Source: Thelwall, *Report on … Germany to March 1923*, 34–5.

billion paper marks. The actual yield between July and December 1922 is indicated by Table 7. The figures reveal not only that the real value of subscriptions was very much reduced by the depreciation of the mark, but also that there was a considerable decline in the yield in terms of paper marks, which could only have been the result of considerable tax evasion. The net effect was that after six months the yield amounted to 3.7 billion paper marks (12.9 million gold marks), which was a tiny fraction of the return originally envisaged.

The reaction of the Reichstag to the undermining of the Forced Loan was completely ineffectual. Despite left-wing pressure in favour of an increase in paper subscriptions to a level warranted by the diminished value of the mark, the majority would agree only to a negative stipulation that the total amount of the loan should not be limited to 70 billion paper marks. The passivity of the Reichstag was epitomized by the Democrat, Fischer, who, after noting that the mark

[28] Wirth resigned after he had tried unsuccessfully, at the prompting of Ebert, to form a DVP–SPD 'grand coalition': *Die Kabinette Wirth*, ii. 1169; Breitscheid (VSP), 24 Nov. 1922, *RT* ccclvii. 9106–7; F. Stampfer, *Die ersten vierzehn Jahre der deutschen Republik* (Karlsbad, 1936), 306; Laubach, 309–11. For the impact on financial policy: Koenen (KPD), 24 Nov. 1922, *RT* ccclvii. 9129. For the Income Tax debate: Hertz (VSP), 14 Dec. 1922, ibid. 9309; Helfferich (DNVP), 9310–12; *Akten der Reichskanzlei: Weimarer Republik. Das Kabinett Cuno, 22. November 1922 bis 12. August 1923*, ed. K.-H. Harbeck (Boppard-on-Rhine, 1968), 94, 96, 99.

had fallen to one-thirtieth of its July value, proposed not that the value of subscriptions should be raised but that contributions which had been made in July and August should be reckoned at double their face value. Although Fischer's proposal was rejected, the Reichstag's amendments of the Forced Loan deserved fully the criticism of Bernstein that they were conducive neither to financial stabilization nor to social justice, and that they were inconsistent with the terms of the 'fiscal compromise' of January 1922.[29]

The negative nature of German policy thrust the responsibility for the future of Europe back onto the creditor powers. On 18 October the French government had transmitted to Britain a proposal for further discussions which purported to be taking up a suggestion made by Lloyd George during the death throes of the London Conference in August, but was really a response to increased pressure from the Chamber for prompt action to resolve France's domestic financial problems. A batch of interpellations criticizing Poincaré's reparation policy for its intransigence or for its failure to produce results had been moved in the Chamber when it reassembled on 12 October. This was soon to be followed by an onslaught on the government in the debate on the budget for 1923. Maurice Bokanowski, the rapporteur of the Finance Commission of the Chamber, fired the first shot by declaring on 24 October that de Lasteyrie's budget proposal of the previous March, with its projected deficit of 4 billion francs, was no longer acceptable in view of the deterioration of France's domestic and external financial position. He also made it clear that, even if Germany fulfilled the demands of the London Schedule, the 78 billion francs which were France's share of the spoils would cover less than half of the past and future reparation expenditure by the French government. This point was emphasized by the Socialist spokesman, Vincent Auriol, who also flayed de Lasteyrie for the confused fiscal conservatism of a speech which he had made at a banquet of the Paris Chamber of Commerce on 5 October. The assault on the financial policies of the government culminated with speeches on 6 and 7 November by Léon Blum and Louis Loucheur. Although the Socialist and the industrialist differed in their ideas about budgetary reform, they were of one accord in their demand for an international financial agency which would adjudicate on the reparation question in the course of fulfilling its wider function of engineering the economic recovery of Europe.[30]

In replying to these attacks Poincaré and de Lasteyrie staked everything on the outcome of the projected inter-Allied conference. They would still, however, have welcomed a broad-ranging international financial settlement involving the United States. At this time Hughes, the American Secretary of State, and Herrick, the United States ambassador to France, were trying to organize talks between Poincaré and J. P. Morgan in order to achieve an impartial examination and realistic settlement of the reparation question. Yet French and American attitudes soon proved to be as far apart as they had been at the time of the Loan Committee's ill-starred deliberations in June. An effective intervention by the United States was still impeded by the inflexibility of its war-debts policy. On 23 October, Houghton, the American ambassador in Berlin, transmitted an eloquent plea to Hughes for the cancellation of war debts in return for a commensurate reduction of reparations. He conceded that Americans were disillusioned with Europe and feared that the former belligerents would resume hostilities with each other if they were relieved of their obligations to the United States. Yet he insisted that cancellation was necessary in order to counteract pessimism and to encourage the return of economic prosperity. 'Either course is open', he concluded. 'We can make the conditions under which millions of human beings in Europe must live almost infinitely better, or we can make them infinitely worse. It is for us alone to decide.' However, after consulting with Harding, Hughes rejected Houghton's appeal on 14 November on the familiar grounds that 'Congress alone has the power to remit debts' and that any such remission would be unlikely 'in the immediate future'. This intransigence meant that there would be no common ground for the proposed Franco-American negotiations. On 23 November Poincaré reported to his cabinet colleagues that Morgan's reply to de Lasteyrie's overtures 'couldn't have been worse', insisting as it did that American financial intervention would be conditional upon a five-year moratorium and the conclusion of a final reparation settlement at Brussels. The distance between American and French policy was indicated when Poincaré declared that an immediate settlement involving a reduction of Germany's obligations was out of the question. No French govern-

[30] *CD*, 12 Oct. 1922, 2591–6 (Albert–Favre); 13 Oct. 1922, 2641–6; 20 Oct. 1922, 2756–65 (Reynaud); 24 Oct. 1922, 2799–2807 (Bokanowski); 26 Oct. 1922, 2838–45 (Auriol); 6 Nov. 1922, 2954–66 (Blum); 7 Nov. 1922, 2976–87 (Loucheur).

ment, he added, would survive if it granted Germany a moratorium without extracting productive pledges as a quid pro quo. The unwillingness of the Americans and British to temper French policy by making financial concessions paved the way for a cabinet meeting on 27 November attended by Millerand, Foch, Tirard, and Maginot which approved contingency plans for an occupation of the Ruhr. Poincaré reassured the Foreign Affairs Committee of the Senate two days later that no decision to act had been taken and that he still preferred to use the threat of an occupation for bargaining purposes. With this objective in mind, a press communiqué was issued on the same day which stated that independent coercive action would be taken by France unless her financial problems were resolved at London by an international loan and a war-debt settlement. Yet the French premier was rapidly running out of room in which to manœuvre.[31]

The domestic plight of the Poincaré government and the blackmailing tactics to which it had resorted appear to have made little impression on Bonar Law when the premiers of France, Great Britain, Italy, and Belgium met in London on 9 December. The new British Prime Minister, who had taken office in October, had been advised both by his cabinet and by the influential Federation of British Industries (FBI) that he should refrain from making unilateral financial concessions in the forthcoming reparation negotiations. On 7 December the cabinet recommended that the question of inter-Allied indebtedness should be completely excluded from the agenda at Brussels on the grounds that 'at this Conference Great Britain would be the only large creditor country among a large number of debtor States'. A similar view was expressed in a declaration of the FBI which was published on the morning on which the London conversations began. While accepting the desirability of 'a general readjustment of inter-

---

[31] For the apologias of Poincaré and de Lasteyrie: de Lasteyrie, 26 Oct. 1922, ibid. 2845–51; Poincaré, 17 Nov., 1922, ibid. 3241–8. For the fullest analysis of American policy: Artaud, *Question des dettes interalliées*, i. 476–82. See Hughes to Herrick, 9 Oct. 1922; Herrick to Hughes, 13, 14 Oct. 1922; Hughes to Herrick, 17 Oct. 1922; Herrick to Hughes, 23, 27 Oct. 1922, 7 Nov. 1922, *FR*, 1922, ii. 165–70, 175, 177–8, 182–4. For the Houghton–Hughes exchange: ibid. 171–5, 180–2. For Poincaré on Morgan: Réunion chez le Président du Conseil, 23 Nov. 1922, MAE, Papiers Millerand, Allemagne XII. Réparation 16 Nov.–31 Dec. 1922, 3–4. For cabinet meeting of 27 Nov.: Bariéty, 'Les Réparations allemandes', 25; McDougall, *France's Rhineland Diplomacy*, 228–9. For Poincaré and Foreign Affairs Committee: Sénat, CAE, 29 Nov. 1922, 47–65. For Communiqué: Secret Letters, vii, 1 Dec. 1922; *Le Temps*, 29 Nov. 1922, 1. Artaud, *Question des dettes interalliées*, i. 445–8, argues that Poincaré was in fact set upon a Ruhr occupation by the end of Nov. 1922. I have difficulty in ascribing such fixity of purpose to any politician.

national indebtedness', the federation doubted that 'in the present circumstances' a 'unilateral sacrifice by this country would lead to any reciprocal sacrifices by other countries'. It considered, therefore, that 'the risk involved in cancelling any substantial portion of the debt owed to this country outweighed any possible advantage to be gained, since to cancel these debts would be to throw away our principal bargaining weapon in any future settlement'.[32]

These pressures clearly influenced the unenthusiastic response of Bonar Law when Poincaré reaffirmed at London his opposition to any reduction in France's claims, and reiterated the Loucher/Briand proposal of the previous December to reduce Germany's theoretical burden by transferring to Britain an amount of Series C reparation bonds equivalent to France's indebtedness to Britain. The British Prime Minister rejected this scheme because the immensity of Germany's total debt had rendered the Series C bonds almost valueless, and because he considered that Britain should get her fair share of the genuine reparation payments which were to be made by Germany. Like his predecessor, Lloyd George, he justified this demand by referring both to Britain's huge expenditure of £100 million a year on unemployment relief and to her indebtedness to the United States. As a protectionist he was also in a better position than Lloyd George to reject the liberal notion that Britain's interest lay not in reparations but in the restoration of German prosperity. Far from agreeing to Poincaré's proposal for what amounted to a unilateral British financial sacrifice, Bonar Law therefore conceded only that Britain might be prepared to 'run the risk' of paying somewhat more to the United States than she received from the Allies and from Germany. Although this appeared to be a retreat from the policy of the Balfour Note, which had tied Britain's receipts from her European creditors rigidly to her repayments to America, Poincaré was unimpressed and insisted, in Bonar Law's words, that 'the only reduction in the French claim on Germany would be the amount which Britain sacrificed to him'. The deadlocked atmosphere was momentarily relieved on 10 December by the summary and unanimous rejection by all parties of a reparation and stabilization proposal from the new Cuno government which was similar to that transmitted by Wirth on 14 November. But the situation quickly deteriorated when Poincaré insisted that, no matter what other arrangements were agreed upon by the Allies, it was necessary to

---

[32] Cabinet Minutes, 69 (22), 7 Dec. 1922, Min. 2, CAB 23/32. For the FBI Declaration: *Lloyd's List*, 9 Dec. 1922.

occupy Essen and Bochum forthwith. 'In three hours', he claimed,

without any mobilization, without any offensive militarism or imperialism, the Allied forces now in certain occupied towns would be established in the heart of the German industrial region in the centre of the mines and manufactures. They would be in the midst of the country of those very industrials who had put forward the proposals under consideration today ... By going to Essen and Bochum it would save Herr Stinnes the trouble to go to Paris. He [Poincaré] would be able to speak to Herr Stinnes on the spot, and probably the conversation would be much more effective at Essen than at Paris.

Although this declaration sealed the fate of the discussions, an open diplomatic break was postponed because Bonar Law was afraid that it would undermine the position of Curzon, his Foreign Secretary, in his negotiations with the Turks at Lausanne. Poincaré, who may also have been glad to blunt the effect of the left-centre interpellations he was due to face in the Chamber on 15 December, was therefore prevailed upon to agree to an adjournment. It was announced that 'definitive conclusions had been impossible in the limited time available', and that the conversations would be 'continued' at Paris on 2 January. This, it was stated, would give time for a subsequent plenary conference of the Allies at Brussels to come to a decision on the reparation question before 15 January 1923, when Germany's next payment under the London Schedule of Payments was due.[33]

As both Bonar Law and Poincaré had expected, the adjournment of the discussions at London in mid-December 1922 merely postponed a breach between France and England and its attendant diplomatic and domestic embarrassments. Although they both adopted a moderate tone when reporting to their respective parliaments, neither premier showed any sign of retreating from his entrenched position. On 14 December Bonar Law repeated to the House of Commons all the arguments he had used during his conversations with Poincaré to justify Britain's refusal to renounce either her reparation claims or

[33] Proceedings of the Meetings of Allied Prime Ministers, in London, Dec. 9 to 11, 1922, in *Inter-Allied Conferences on Reparations and Inter-Allied Debts, held in London and Paris, December 1922, and January 1923* (henceforward: *Inter-Allied Conferences*), *House of Commons Papers*, Cmd. 1812, 1923, xxiv. 32–3 (Poincaré); 34–5, 41 (Law); 51–3 (Poincaré); 60–6. For the rejection of Cuno's proposal: ibid. 43–51. For its text: ibid. 57–9; *Die den Allierten ... deutschen Angebote ...*, 104–6. For Bonar Law's desire to postpone a rupture: Cabinet Minutes, 70 (22), 11 Dec. 1922, Min. 1, CAB 23/32; Bonar Law to Curzon, 5, 7 Dec. 1922, Bonar Law Papers, 111/12/38, 40. For Poincaré's anxiety about the Chamber: Secret Letters, vii, 14 Dec. 1922. For the Loucheur/Briand proposal of Dec. 1921: see above, ch. 4 n. 28 and text thereat.

her war loans. On the following day Poincaré, after referring in a conciliatory manner to the attitude of Bonar Law at London, merely reaffirmed his proposal for the transfer of France's Series C bonds to Britain. He also foreshadowed his future policy and, at the same time, attempted to stifle right-wing criticism by appealing to the Allies to support France if she felt constrained to take action to ensure that Germany fulfilled her obligations. His sole concession to the growing misgivings of French moderates was to emphasize that any measures taken would 'not be military in character' but would involve 'engineers and customs agents'.[34]

The drift of French policy was indicated by the efforts of Barthou, who had replaced Dubois early in October as French delegate to, and chairman of, the Reparation Commission, to establish legal grounds for the imposition of sanctions upon Germany. Barthou was technically assisted by a lag which had occurred in German deliveries of timber and coal in the closing months of 1922. It mattered little that on 1 December 1922 the representatives of the German government explained to the Reparation Commission that the falling off in timber deliveries had been the result of confusion in the German timber trade caused by the depreciation of the mark. Nor was it considered important during a heated debate in the commission on 26 December— the minutes of which were expurgated by mutual consent—that the lag in question was insignificant compared with the deliveries in kind for 1922 which had not been 'called for' by France because her economy could not absorb them. Bradbury, the British delegate to the commission, referred darkly on this occasion to the allegation that Germany had defaulted in her timber deliveries as a 'trumpery charge' designed by France to prepare for 'an offensive in other fields'. He then made his celebrated declaration that 'since, in the tenth year of the war, Troy fell to the stratagem of the wooden horse, history recorded no similar use of timber'. 'The situation', he went on, 'was at present somewhat different, it was the fifth year of the peace, and the city under attack was not Troy, but Essen.' Yet the legalistic view of Barthou was now supported by a majority of the Reparation Commission because of the relatively uncompromising attitude which Bonar Law had adopted towards inter-Allied indebtedness—Mussolini, in particular, was concerned about Italy's debts to Britain—and

---

[34] For Bonar Law: *HC*, 14 Dec. 1922, clix. 3228–37. For right-wing criticism of Poincaré: Tardieu, 15 Dec. 1922, *CD*, 4213–23. For the opposition of French moderates: 4224–30 (Pierre Forgeot). Cf. 4201–5 (Poincaré).

because of Belgium's apprehension about her prior reparation rights if Britain's policy of reducing Germany's debt were adopted. Thus the commission decided, despite the abstention of Bradbury, that the lag in timber deliveries constituted 'a default by Germany in her obligations within the meaning of Paragraph 17 of Annex II' of the Reparation Chapter of the treaty; and that the word 'default' in Paragraph 17 had the same meaning as the expression 'voluntary default' in Paragraph 18 of the Annexe. This implied that the Allied and Associated Powers were entitled to take measures against Germany which included 'economic and financial prohibitions and reprisals and in general such other measures as the respective Governments [might] determine to be necessary in the circumstances'.[35]

Only an improbable eleventh-hour intervention by the United States could now have prevented Poincaré from launching his nation into a self-indulgent act of criminal folly. After the breakdown of the London Conference, Hughes, alarmed at the commercial and political chaos which a French invasion of the Ruhr would precipitate, had repeated to Jusserand, the French ambassador in Washington, his proposal for an international committee of experts to examine Germany's capacity to pay reparations. The refusal of the American government to involve itself in a meaningful way in the financial affairs of Europe was, however, signalled on 18 December when the Secretary of State fobbed off a despairing last-minute appeal from Bonar Law for the United States to join in the forthcoming negotiations in Paris. Although Hughes cited French opposition to American participation as the reason for his negative reaction, the underlying impediment to action was his insistence that the United States 'could not enter into discussion' of war debts. The refusal of the United States to admit the practical connection between reparations and war debts was to hamstring attempts to resolve the reparation problem for another decade.[36]

Although Hughes decided to air his proposal for an expert com-

[35] For Barthou's appointment: RC, Minutes No. 325, 10 Oct. 1922. For the German explanation about timber: ibid. No. 336, 1 Dec. 1922. See also RC v. 240–7. For the timber debate: RC, Minutes No. 343, 26 Dec. 1922, 7–8, 12 (Bradbury). See also RC v. 248–64. For the expurgation of the minutes: Secret Letters, viii, 5 Jan. 1923. For the vacillating attitude of Mussolini: ibid. vii, 14 Dec. 1922. For Belgian fears: ibid. viii, 1 Mar. 1923. For text of paras. 17–19 of Annexe II: Temperley, iii. 244.

[36] Memorandum by Hughes of a Conversation with Jusserand, 14 Dec. 1922; Memorandum by Hughes of an Interview with Geddes, 18 Dec. 1922, FR, 1922, ii. 187–95. For the best scholarly account of American policy in Dec. 1922: Artaud, Question des dettes interalliées, i. 482–90. Cf. Gescher, Die Vereinigten Staaten, 103. For an account

mittee in a public address at New Haven on 29 December, this did nothing to resolve the financial deadlock between the European creditors when the Allied Prime Ministers met again at Paris between 2 and 4 January. It was, paradoxically, only on the question of 'pledges' that France and Britain seemed to be approaching agreement. Poincaré now stated that as a precondition for any moratorium he would insist in the first instance only that the Allies should seize non-territorial pledges which would ensure deliveries of coal, timber, and cash. Any German resistance to these measures would, however, result in the military occupation of Essen, Bochum, and other parts of the Ruhr district, and the establishment of an Allied customs barrier on the eastern boundary of all the occupied territories. Bonar Law, on the other hand, who stressed the undesirability of interference with Germany's financial system if her credit was to be rehabilitated, suggested that adequate financial reform and guarantees might be obtained by setting up an International Foreign Finance Council in Berlin with wide supervisory powers. Only if Germany refused to acknowledge the authority of this body or failed to achieve financial stabilization along the lines laid down by the Experts' Report of 7 November 1922 was there to be resort to measures of the type suggested by Poincaré.[37]

Although the possibility of compromise in this area was entertained favourably by the British cabinet, Bonar Law and Poincaré remained at loggerheads on fundamentals. The British Prime Minister proposed that Germany's credit should be restored by granting her a four-year moratorium and by reducing her total liability to 50 billion gold marks. The Allies, he declared, could not both 'seize what they could get' and give German credit 'a chance of recovery'. By way of contrast, Poincaré was concerned not that Germany's recovery might be too slow but that, if her reparation burden was unduly diminished, she might recover so quickly as to be able within a few years to flout the provisions of the Versailles Treaty. Even more important than these differing economic and strategic perpectives was the nagging politically induced tactical dispute between the Allies. This was succinctly expressed by Bonar Law's dogged but unconvincing insistence at Paris that Britain 'needed

[37] For extracts from Hughes's New Haven speech: FR, 1922, ii. 199–202. For a detailed account of the Paris conference: Toynbee, Survey . . . 1920–1923, 192–201. For minutes: Inter-Allied Conferences, 75–6 (Poincaré), 77–9 (Law). For texts of the French and British proposals of 2 Jan. 1923: ibid. 95–101, 112–19.

reparations as much as any other country', and by the French government's equally determined refusal to countenance any reduction of Germany's total obligation unless France were accorded a greater share of what remained. This Anglo-French financial confrontation was intensified because Poincaré and Bonar Law were both more conservative in their domestic fiscal reactions than were their predecessors, Briand and Lloyd George. Nor was the situation eased by the tactics of British financial diplomacy which had been enunciated in the Balfour Note of August 1922 and were in practice continued by Bonar Law, despite his disavowals. Britain's willingness to make financial concessions to France was, in short, still restricted in January 1923 by her desire to retain her share of reparations and her French loans as both a bargaining counter and a hedge in the Anglo-American debt negotiations which were shortly to begin in Washington. Such a consideration undoubtedly induced Bonar Law to declare to the House of Commons in mid-December that the repayment of Britain's debt to the United States 'without receiving anything from outside sources would reduce the standard of living in this country for a generation'.[38]

Although the incompatibility of French and British economic and financial aims is sufficient to explain why the Paris discussions bore no more fruit than the talks which had preceded them in London in December, it does not explain why the Franco-Belgian Ruhr venture which was launched a few days later was either condoned by Britain or favoured by the French government as a practical policy. British diplomatic complaisance was caused not only by the 'hats off to France' sentiment of die-hard conservatives and their press but also by Bonar Law's continuing preoccupation with the problem of making peace with Turkey in Asia Minor. This made it impossible for him to take any action to restrain France which might have been construed by the Turks as an Anglo-French diplomatic rift. On the other hand, Poincaré, although emboldened by the diplomatic embarrassment of Britain, was propelled into the Ruhr largely by his own rhetoric. It is misleading to portray him as the tool of French militarists who desired a Rhine frontier or as the agent of big business interests whose dream of a

---

[38] For the British cabinet's attitude to pledges: Cabinet Minutes, 72 (22), 29 Dec. 1922, CAB 23/32. For the deadlock between Bonar Law and Poincaré: Inter-Allied Conferences, 77–8, 123–4, 142. See also: Memorandum communicated by the French Delegation ... on 2 Jan. 1923, ibid. at 102. For Bonar Law on inter-Allied debts: HC, 14 Dec. 1922, clix. 3233.

THE WRONG WAY

Fig. 5. The *Star*, London, 5 January 1923.

French-dominated Ruhr–Lorraine iron, steel, and coal complex had been expressed in Adrien Dariac's report in May 1922. In common with influential military planners such as Marshal Philippe Pétain, the vice-president of the *Conseil Supérieur de la Défense Nationale*, who opposed a long-term defensive strategy based on France's temporary presence in the Rhineland, Poincaré had no strategic desire for full-scale military occupation of the Ruhr; and he even pressed at the last moment for the dispatch of a skeleton military force whose role was to be limited to escorting a small group of engineers. As a Germanophobic Lorrainer he was also reluctant to encourage the intermeshing of the French and German economies envisaged by Dariac. The French premier authorized the Ruhr occupation because he was a middle-class anti-tax nationalist politician who had painted himself into a corner by recklessly promising to translate the reparation illusion into reality. He could only have honoured his promise in the unlikely event that he could cajole or bluff his political replicas in Britain, the United States, and Germany into making financial concessions which would disillusion and disadvantage their domestic supporters. After his bluff had been called, Poincaré embarked hesitantly on the Ruhr adventure without any precise idea of what he wished to achieve. Apart from his desire to maintain face and retain office, he was responding to emotions which had been described two months earlier in the Chamber of Deputies by Léon Blum, the Socialist leader. Poincaré had been swept into office at the beginning of 1922, Blum declared, primarily by France's general concern for her security. Besides this 'there was also another feeling, which is as painful for nations as it is for individuals, a feeling that justice has been violated and trampled upon (Hear! Hear!). In addition to this sense of outraged justice, there was also the feeling that circumstances had till then conspired to deprive us and frustrate us of what was our due, in consequence not of our victory but of our rights as human beings.' It was because he had ridden to power by playing on these feelings of fear, outrage, and frustration that Poincaré felt obliged to order the Ruhr invasion after the Paris Conference broke up on 4 January. The legal preliminaries were completed on 9 January when, after German representatives had been given a further hearing, the Reparation Commission ruled (Bradbury abstaining) that Germany had 'voluntarily defaulted' on her coal deliveries. Then, with evident misgivings, the French and Belgian governments announced the imminent dispatch of Engineering Commissions under military protection to the Ruhr area. The futile posturing of the Ruhr invasion, which was to yield very little to France and have such a traumatic effect on Germany, was to provide an apt conclusion to the first act of the tragic reparation farce.[39]

[39] For British pro-French feeling: *MP*, 12 Jan. 1923 (LA). For Britain's diplomatic paralysis: Cabinet Minutes, 1 (23), 11 Jan. 1923, Min. 3, CAB 23/45. See above, n. 33. For the reservations of French strategists and Poincaré: McDougall, *France's Rhineland Diplomacy*, 241–2, 244–9; Trachtenberg, *Reparation in World Politics*, 275; G. Bonnet, *Quai d'Orsay* (Eng. tr., London, 1965), 70. For Poincaré's economic Germanophobia: Artaud, 'A propos de l'occupation de la Ruhr', 12–13. Note his rejection of Paul Reynaud's proposal in Nov. 1922 for French participation in Ruhr industry: CD, 20 Oct. 1922, 2759–64 (Reynaud); 17 Nov. 1922, 3246–7 (Poincaré). See also Blum, 10 Nov. 1922, 2966; RC, Minutes, No. 346A, 8, 9 Jan. 1923; *Le Temps*, 10, 11, 12 Jan. 1923, 1. Trachtenberg, *Reparation in World Politics*, ch. 7, provides a penetrating analysis of the Anglo-French dispute over how to deal with Germany which paved the way for the Ruhr invasion. It is hard, however, to understand his refusal (at 285) to acknowledge the importance of Poincaré's precarious domestic political position. Artaud, *Question des dettes interalliées*, i. 490, gives a good summary of the international financial deadlock out of which the invasion arose. For a thoughtful recent discussion of French policy which, in my view, underestimates its incoherence: Jacobson, 'Strategies of French Foreign Policy', 88–95.

6

The Ruhr Struggle

APART from his overriding desire to ingratiate himself with the conservative majority in the Chamber of Deputies, Poincaré's main motives for advocating an occupation of the Ruhr in 1922 had been to frighten the German government into a more resolute approach to stabilization and fulfilment and to blackmail Britain and the United States into making financial concessions. When both the Germans and the Anglo-Saxons proved impervious to his threats the French premier still went ahead with the invasion in order to save his political skin. Although the Chamber was suitably impressed by his bravado, the operation was bound to be counter-productive because it reduced even further Germany's propensity to reform and her capacity to pay. It also eliminated entirely the possibility of British and American concessions, disrupted the French economy, and undermined the franc. Even the short-term visible spoils of the Ruhr venture were derisory. Exploitation of the district was impeded not only by the campaign of passive resistance which the German government orchestrated and financed but also by the initial dithering of the occupying authorities and their subsequent failure to assert effective economic control over the region for fear of offending local and international opinion. Since a great deal of energy was diverted to sealing off the Ruhr from the rest of Germany in an effort to force the Cuno government to its knees, it was only to be expected that the booty extracted from the district would compare most unfavourably with the level of reparation receipts in 1922.

The counter-productive trial of financial strength into which the Ruhr struggle degenerated could only have been brought to a timely halt by the intervention of the Anglo-Saxons. Such a happy issue was now, however, even more unlikely than before. The British government, largely because of its diplomatic embarrassment in the Near East, at first allowed France and Belgium a free hand in the Ruhr. Yet most Liberals and moderate Conservatives clung to the hope that the invasion would be a costly failure which would topple Poincaré. Unfortunately, even after it had become clear that the false prophet would survive long enough to wreak havoc with the trade and political stability of Europe, Britain's efforts to secure a Franco-Belgian withdrawal were foredoomed to failure by her uncompromising financial policy in the wake of her onerous debt-funding agreement with the United States in the spring of 1923. British attempts at mediation in fact served only to prolong the conflict by encouraging German resistance. An even deeper aversion to constructive financial and diplomatic involvement in Europe emasculated the policies, if such they can be called, of the United States. This Anglo-Saxon isolationism permitted the Ruhr tragedy to drag on until Germany had capitulated and France and Belgium had established their illusory reparation province.

The struggle ended late in September 1923 when the hyper-inflation caused by the decline in economic activity and the expansion of government expenditure forced Gustav Stresemann to proclaim the cessation of passive resistance. The threat of social revolution and national disintegration prompted previously òbstructive right-wing groups to put their full weight for the first time behind policies of financial reform and international co-operation. Their intervention at this stage also ensured that the propertied classes, having indulged in a patriotic rampage at everybody else's expense, would not be called upon to bear too much of the burden of stabilization and would be in a position to extract the maximum benefit from the resumption of reparation payments and the ensuing normalization of international financial relations.

INVASION AND PASSIVE RESISTANCE

Late in February 1923 Poincaré asserted to the Foreign Affairs Committee of the Senate that the piecemeal character of the Ruhr invasion had been necessary in order to forestall international criticism. A more likely reason for the improvisation of the operation was that it began as a gesture designed primarily for domestic political consumption rather than as a coherent attempt to exploit, cow, cripple, or dismember Germany. If the French and Belgians seriously believed that a simple administrative take-over of Essen would compel Germany to fulfil her obligations and stabilize the mark, they were quickly disillusioned. Indeed, it almost seemed that the Ruhr industrialists had seized the initiative when, on 10 January, they 'castled their king' by removing the headquarters of the all-powerful Rhenish-Westphalian Coal Syndicate from Essen to Hamburg. As a result, the 17,000 French and Belgian troops who escorted the ill-assorted engineers and administrators of MICUM (the Inter-Allied Factories and Mines Control Commission) into Essen on the following day with their pistols, cutlasses, and outsize cannon were deprived of their only meaningful objective. Similarly, the extension of the occupation to Dortmund and Bochum on 15 January was a retaliation for the cessation of reparation coal deliveries by the German 'chimney barons' and their refusal to remit to the occupying authorities the proceeds of the federal coal tax. Three weeks elapsed before steps of questionable legality were taken to seal off the Ruhr and Rhineland from the rest of Germany through the agency of the Inter-Allied Rhineland High Commission (the body responsible for supervising the original occupation of the region under the terms of the treaty). Exports of coal to the unoccupied territories were not forbidden until 30 January; and it was not until 15 February that a customs barrier restricted the eastward flow of other types of goods. During hearings of the Foreign Affairs Committee of the Senate and Chamber a few days later, Poincaré sought to confer retrospective rationality on the Ruhr imbroglio by describing it, in Foch's words, as a 'process of infiltration followed by the encirclement of the whole region'. He also claimed that nine-tenths of the productive enterprises of the district were now under Franco-Belgian control. Yet he seemed to be in two minds about his next move. Thoroughgoing exploitation of the area would, he predicted, be difficult because of the small number of technical personnel accompanying the troops. The best procedure would therefore be to exploit the area as much as possible while using the occupation mainly to apply economic pressure to the German government. This would, he declared with spurious assurance, 'have the advantage of demonstrating to the Germans that, quite apart from the suffering we inflict upon them, we are capable of achieving a long, stable and remunerative occupation'. By this time, however, it was clear that, even in the strategic area of coal distribution, the pressure that the occupying authorities could bring to bear was limited. Maurice Frère, the head of the Research and Intelligence Bureau of the Reparation Commission, estimated that in 1922 unoccupied Germany obtained 36 per cent of the 96.2 million tons of the coal it consumed from the Ruhr. Yet an immediate shortage was averted by the stocks which had been built up, not only in 1922 but also in January 1923, after reparation deliveries to France and Belgium had been discontinued. Later on, supplies were also to be eked out by increased imports from Britain, Czechoslovakia, and Poland and by the reduction of domestic consumption when the weather became warmer.[1]

Just as galling as their inability to coerce Berlin was the failure of the invaders to extract any substantial short-term returns. The difficulties encountered by MICUM in its attempt to exploit the Ruhr's coal resources did not arise at first from any reduction of work by the miners, whose initial protest was limited to a half-hour stoppage on 15 January. Logan, the unofficial American delegate to the Reparation Commission, estimated at the time that, of the 550,000 miners in the occupied area, 70,000 Poles were positive supporters of the Allies, 200,000 SPD voters were not actively hostile, 200,000 Christian Social-ists were openly opposed to the occupation, and 70,000 Communists condemned Entente imperialism and German capitalism alike. Coal nevertheless accumulated at the pitheads as a result of strikes and sabotage by the more nationalistic railway workers. The importation of French and Belgian railway personnel which began in February 1923 eased the situation for the invaders: but even by May, when most of the Ruhr–Rhineland railway system had been under the control of the Franco-Belgian *Régie* for two months, and when the number of occupying troops had risen to 100,000, the coal shipped from the Ruhr

---

[1] Valuable insight may be gained into the early weeks of the Ruhr struggle and the ineffectiveness of MICUM from the reports of Lord Kilmarnock, the British High Commissioner on the Inter-Allied Rhineland High Commission: Kilmarnock to Curzon, 19, 22, 23, 26, 27 Jan., 1 Feb. 1923, *DBFP* I, xxi. 44–7, 51–2, 55–7, 72–3, 76–80, 86–7. For a convenient chronicle: A. J. Toynbee, *Survey of International Affairs, 1924* (London, 1926), 268–86. For the actions of the Coal Syndicate: H. Spethmann, *Zwölf Jahre Ruhrbergbau* (5 vols.; Berlin, 1928–30), iv. *Der Ruhrkampf 1923 bis 1925: das Ringen um die Kohle*, 86. For the German protest note of 12 Jan. 1923: RC, Annexe No. 1732c. For Poincaré: Chambre des Députés, CAE, 19 Feb. 1923; Sénat, CAE, 24 Feb. 1923, 32, 54. Cf. Secret Letters, viii, 23 Feb. 1923; *Le Temps*, 21 Feb. 1923, 1. For Frère's figures on coal distribution: Secret Letters, ix, 20 Apr. 1923. Cf. Kilmarnock to Curzon, 27, 30 Jan. 1923, *DBFP* I, xxi at 78–81; D'Abernon to Curzon, 2 Feb. 1923, ibid. 87–8. For an interpretation of the Ruhr struggle as a more or less coherent attempt either to establish French political and economic hegemony or to precipitate an international financial settlement favourable to France: Bariéty, 'Les Réparations allemandes', 25–7; id., *Les Relations franco-allemandes après la première guerre mondiale, 10 novembre 1918–10 janvier 1925: de l'exécution à la négociation* (Paris, 1977), 118–120. For accounts emphasizing the improvisation of French policy: Trachtenberg, *Reparation in World Politics*, ch. 7; McDougall, *France's Rhineland Diplomacy*, 251–9.

amounted to only one-third of average monthly reparation deliveries in 1922.[2]

This virtual stalemate made it appear that a compromise settlement might be achieved in the spring of 1923. Notwithstanding a patriotic speech by Stresemann on behalf of the parties of the right and centre, Cuno's policy of passive resistance had been endorsed by a majority of only 248 to 12 in the Reichstag on 13 January because of the abstention of the SPD which, since its reunion with the USPD in the previous September, had become wary of nationalist gestures. The unwonted efforts of the bourgeois parties to reform taxes and to prop up the sagging mark soon proved, moreover, to be ineffectual. A law which sought to adjust the yield of fourteen different taxes to inflation was laid before the Reichstag on 13 January; and the Reichsbank began to support the mark two weeks later with heavy buying operations in Berlin, Amsterdam, and New York. As a result, government expenditure did not completely outstrip revenue until May, and the mark, which had slumped from 10,000 to 49,000 to the dollar during January, was restored to about 21,000 until mid-April. However, the persistence of tax loopholes for inflation profiteers and the government's continuing subsidies to Ruhr wage-earners engaged in unproductive work and industries occupied solely in building up stocks eventually forced the Reichsbank to suspend its buying operations and caused the mark to resume its downward plunge. On 16 April Rosenberg, Cuno's foreign minister, praised the heroic resistance of the Ruhr population and declared that France would achieve nothing until she ceased trying to humiliate Germany. Yet Stresemann, while ruling out any dealings with France and Belgium as long as they sought 'to annex the Ruhr and Rhineland', now emphasized that the reparation problem could only be resolved by negotiation and compromise. There was also mounting pressure from the trade unions and the moderate left wing that the government should, while continuing passive resistance, make some constructive proposal to demonstrate its good faith. These feelings, and some diplomatic prodding by Britain, prompted a German

---

[2] For the stoppage of 15 Jan.: Spethmann, 85–6. On the myth of passive resistance: A. Rosenberg, *A History of the German Republic* (Eng. tr., London, 1936), 181–2. Spethmann's compendious nationalist account exaggerates both the patriotism of the Ruhr inhabitants in the early stages of the struggle and the importance of the Communist 'stab in the back' in undermining resistance in the summer of 1923. For the attitude of the miners: Secret Letters, viii, 9 Feb. 1923. For coal shipments: C. Lloyd Jones (US Commercial Attaché at Paris) to A. N. Young, 23 Jan. 1924, Arthur N. Young Papers, Box 4, Folder 2; Kilmarnock to Curzon, 29, 30 Jan. 1923, *DBFP* I, xxi. 80–1.

overture to the Allies on 2 May. The purely tactical motives behind
this move ensured that it would not be well received. Yet it did reflect
the growing desire of the government to discover some basis for
negotiations.[3]

French policy had also become more flexible in March and April
1923. During a visit to Paris in March Lord Robert Cecil reported that
Poincaré was under pressure from Loucheur, de Jouvenel, Barthou,
and Millerand to declare France's intentions in the Ruhr. Although
the premier was reluctant to nail his colours to the mast for fear of
disillusioning his mixed bag of nationalist, militarist, and annexationist
supporters, the meagre yield of the operation and the recession which
the French iron and steel industry suffered during the dislocation of
January and February made him vulnerable to moderate pressure for
a speedy settlement involving co-operation with the Anglo-Saxons. He
therefore declared to the Foreign Affairs Committee of the Chamber
on 9 March that his objective was still, as it had been during the inter-
Allied conferences of 1922, simply to force the German government to
institute financial reform so that its reparation obligations could be
funded by an international loan. Although he took care to scotch
rumours that the conflict was about to be settled by mediation, and
reaffirmed to the Finance Committee of the Chamber on 28 March
that the occupation would be 'long, stable and remunerative', his
practical weakness was reflected in a brief flirtation with Britain at the
beginning of April. This was in distinct contrast to the diplomatic

---

[3] For the initial reaction of the Reichstag: Stresemann (DVP), 13 Jan. 1923, RT ccclvii.
9422–4; Müller (SPD), 9424–8. Only the Communists opposed passive resistance: Frölich
(KPD), 9433–4. On the reasons for the SPD abstention: Vorwärts, 14 Jan. 1923, No. 22,
I. Suppl., 1. Maier, Recasting Bourgeois Europe, 356–7 oversimplifies the SPD position.
For the tax reform of 13 Jan.: H. Jonuschat, 'Die Steuerpolitik der Parteien im Reichstag,
1920–1923', Phil. Diss. (Univ. of Berlin, 1926), 38. For tax loopholes: Hertz (VSP),
9 Mar. 1923, RT ccclviii. 10041. For government subventions and credits to Ruhr industry:
Feldman, Iron and Steel, 358–79. For the Reichsbank's buying operations: Bergmann,
Reparations, 186–8. For the mid-April debate: Rosenberg, 16 Apr. 1923, RT ccclix.
10539–46; Stresemann, 17 Apr. 1923, 10572–80 at 10578. For pressure from the German
Miners' Union (Verband der Bergarbeiter Deutschlands) and the German TUC (ADGB):
Spethmann, iv. 150–5. Cf. Müller (VSP), 16 Apr. 1923, RT ccclix. 10548; Breitscheid
(VSP), 10596–602. Cf. Secret Letters, ix, 3 May 1923. The Communist Party, which was
veering towards 'national Bolshevism', now opposed any quick settlement of the Ruhr
conflict at the expense of the German working class: Frölich (KPD), 18 Apr. 1923, RT
ccclix. 10621–7. Cf. O. E. Schüddekopf, Linke Leute von Rechts (Stuttgart, 1960), 139–
64. For the origins of the Note of 2 May: Kabinettsprotokolle, xxxvi, 30 Apr. 1923;
Bergmann, Reparations, 191–2; McDougall, France's Rhineland Diplomacy, 273–4; H. J.
Rupieper, 'Politics and Economics: The Cuno Government and Reparations', Ph.D.
thesis (Stanford, 1974), 277–96. For text: RC, Annexe No. 1834a; Die den Allierten ...
übermittelten deutschen Angebote ..., RT ccclxxix, Annexe 6138, 114–16.

froideur of the early weeks of the invasion, when Barthou had made a fruitless attempt to bludgeon Britain out of her semi-isolation by threatening a Franco-Belgian take-over of the German economy, and the British had reciprocated by refusing to support a Reparation Commission resolution declaring Germany to be in 'general default', not to mention using their position in the Rhineland High Commission to restrict the *Régie's* access to the railway network in their occupation zone. Far from making threats, as he had in January, Poincaré now acquiesced in an exploratory mission to London by Loucheur, Briand's Minister for the Liberated Regions, during which a more conciliatory financial and diplomatic line was adopted. Out of recognition that Britain had just been pressured into funding her American war debts, Loucheur conceded that she should not be expected to renounce all of her reparation claims against Germany or all of her loans to her former Allies. He also made the relatively moderate suggestion that the Rhineland should eventually become an autonomous neutralized province of Germany under the supervision of the League of Nations. Professor Artaud concludes from her exhaustive analysis of the London conversations that they were an exercise in self-advertisement by Loucheur. Yet the very fact that they were allowed to occur by Poincaré indicates either opportunism or temporary loss of nerve on his part.[4]

The apparent thaw in Anglo-French relations induced Curzon to overcome his scruples about the legality of the Ruhr venture and to advise the German government on 20 April to make an offer to France. However, even before the German Note of 2 May had been dispatched, this temporary Anglo-French solidarity had been undermined by the growing confidence of the French government that the invasion would not prove to be a complete fiasco. Increased quantities of coal and

---

[4] Cecil to Curzon, 11 Mar. 1923, Bonar Law Papers, 111/12/64. For Poincaré: Chambre des Députés, CAE, 9 Mar. 1923, 110–49; Secret Letters, viii, 16 Feb., 23 Mar. 1923; ix, 29 Mar. 1923; *Le Temps*, 29 Mar. 1923, 1. For the recession: see below, n. 5. For Barthou's take-over threat and British abstention on the 'general default' resolution: Draft Letter and Draft Decision, 23 Jan. 1923, RC, Annexe No. 1728 abc; RC, Minutes, No. 353, 26 Jan. 1923; Crewe to Curzon, 26 Jan. 1923, *DBFP* I, xxi. 73–4; Secret Letters, viii, 26 Jan. 1923, 2 Feb. 1923. For Britain and the *Régie*: see the exchanges between Curzon, Kilmarnock, Crewe, and D'Abernon in Feb. 1923: *DBFP* I, xxi. 95–8, 100–4, 114–17, 120–1, 130–1; Cabinet Minutes, 10 (23), 15 Feb. 1923, Min. I, CAB 23/45. For Loucheur's visit: Loucheur to Poincaré, 10 Apr. 1923, Louis Loucheur Papers, Box 7, Folder 2; Memorandum on the Neutralization of the Rhineland, 7 Apr. 1923; Memorandum by Sir W. Tyrrell, 12 Apr. 1923, *DBFP* I, xxi. 220–1, 206–9, n. 4. Note the conciliatory leading article in *Le Temps*, 10 Apr. 1923. For the fullest scholarly discussion: Artaud, *Question des dettes interalliées*, ii. 525–39.

coke had begun to be transported from the Ruhr by mid-April, and there was a related revival of activity in the French iron and steel industries. In mid-May Poincaré remained vulnerable to Socialist critics such as Blum and Auriol, who pointed out in the Finance and Foreign Affairs Committees of the Chamber that the occupation had still not begun to pay and that the mobilization of Germany's obligations would be possible only after peace had been restored. Yet he insisted that the operation was becoming increasingly effective as an instrument of coercion; and he was sufficiently confident by the end of the month to allow a debate on the Ruhr question in the Chamber, from which he emerged with an overwhelming vote of confidence. In the mean time, notwithstanding the displeasure of Baldwin and Curzon, he had exploited his new-found diplomatic strength by engineering, without consulting the British cabinet, a curt Franco-Belgian rejection of the German note of 2 May.[5]

The dispute which now developed between France and Britain was foreshadowed in the replies which the British and Italian governments transmitted to Germany on 13 May. Like the French and Belgian notes of the preceding week, these condemned the German offer because it envisaged a figure of only 30 billion gold marks and was hedged with unacceptable conditions. But, instead of concluding with a flat rejection, they invited the German government to reconsider and to expand its proposals. The conflict between the desire of Britain and Italy to negotiate a prompt settlement and the determination of Poincaré to humble Germany was to become increasingly pronounced, much to the embarrassment of Belgium which, although tied diplomatically to France, was extremely sensitive to the financial and political strain of the Ruhr struggle.[6]

The divergence of views between France and Britain was thrown into sharp relief after 7 June when the German government transmitted, in

[5] Curzon, *HL*, 20 Apr. 1923, liii. 797–806. For increased Ruhr coal shipments: *Le Temps*, 20 Apr. 1923, 1 (Maginot); Secret Letters, viii, 19 Apr. 1923. For the French industrial revival: 'Success of the Ruhr Occupation as Reflected in French Iron and Steel Manufactures', in Jones (US Commercial Attaché at Paris) to Young, 23 Jan. 1924, Arthur N. Young Papers, Box 4, Folder 2. For Poincaré in May: Chambre des Députés, CFAE, 17 May 1923, 24 (Poincaré); 32 (Blum); 40 (Auriol); *CD*, 29 May 1923, 2195–208. For British displeasure: *HC*, 8 May 1923, clxiii. 2161–3; *HL*, 8 May 1923, liv. 2–3. For the text of the Franco-Belgian reply of 6 May: RC, Annexe No. 1834b.

[6] For the British and Italian replies: ibid. Annexe No. 1834 cd. For the embarrassment of Delacroix, the Belgian Delegate to the RC: Secret Letters, ix, 31 May 1923. For Belgian reservations about Ruhr invasion: Grahame to Curzon, 24 Feb. 1923; Curzon to Grahame, 26 Feb. 1923, *DBFP* I, xxi. 122–3, 129.

response to the Anglo-Italian invitation of 13 May, a much more acceptable reparation proposal. This wisely omitted any reference to a specific sum, and proclaimed the desire of Germany for a full and impartial examination of her capacity to pay reparations. It also bowed to the Franco-Belgian demand for 'pledges' by taking up proposals which had been put forward recently in Belgian memoranda concerning the use of revenues from the German railways and from specific German taxes as security for reparation payments. In the diplomatic discussions which this note occasioned during the second week of June it was clear that the Allies, while in general agreement about pledges, were divided about both the conditions under which Germany should be required to abandon passive resistance and the terms of any general reparation settlement. The first dispute, which originated from Anglo-French dissension over the legality of the Ruhr occupation, was of less significance to the vital interests of France and Britain than it was to the *amour propre* of Lord Curzon and M. Poincaré. But the second issue, although temporarily obscured during the brilliant but futile diplomatic exchange which now began, remained an insurmountable obstacle to any Allied agreement and, *a fortiori*, to any negotiations with Germany.[7]

Even before the German Note of 7 June, the vague but temperate statements of Baldwin when he succeeded the stricken Bonar Law as Prime Minister had been answered by inflexible semi-official declarations in the French press. *Le Temps*, less amenable than it had been two months earlier, stressed that there could be no reparation negotiations until Germany ceased passive resistance, and that any future settlement should satisfy an irreducible French claim of 26 billion gold marks in addition to the sums required to repay France's debts to the United States and Great Britain. The equally uncompromising attitude of the British Treasury at this time was confirmed by an interview in the first week of June between Marcel Ray, a contact-man of Louis Loucheur, and Austen Chamberlain who, although no longer a member of the cabinet, had been both Chancellor of the Exchequer and Lord Privy Seal under Lloyd George. Because of the immense financial burden of American debt repayments and unemployment relief, the Treasury no longer admitted, said Chamberlain,

---

[7] For the proposal of 7 June: *Die den Allierten ... übermittelten deutschen Angebote ...*, 116–17. For Belgian proposals: Secret Letters, ix, Annexe 137; Grahame to Curzon, 1 June 1923, *DBFP* I, xxi. 309–10. See also Toynbee, *Survey, 1924*, 326.

that France had a prior right to reparation for the physical damage which she had suffered.[8]

It was highly unlikely that the discussion of the German offer which began in London on 11 June between Curzon and the French, Belgian, and Italian ambassadors would yield any agreement. When the French ambassador, Saint-Aulaire, demanded concerted Allied pressure on Germany to make her cease passive resistance, the British cabinet parried with a request that Curzon should seek a 'more precise definition' of France's future policy in the Ruhr in the event of a German capitulation. The British government was also unenthusiastic about a resuscitated French offer, which Bradbury denounced privately to Logan as 'blackmail', to trade Series C reparation bonds for inter-Allied debts. The rigidity of Britain's policy towards France was soon reasserted by Baldwin in the House of Commons. 'The position is', he declared on 12 July, '... that those who owed us money, owe us money still.' This ensured that the French government would recoil when on 20 July a British 'draft identic reply' to the German Note of 7 June was circulated which contained, amongst other proposals, a potentially revisionist scheme for the examination of Germany's financial capacity by an impartial body of experts. The Reparation Commission, Poincaré hastened to affirm on 30 July, bore the sole responsibility for decisions on such matters. The Belgians, seeking, as ever, some formula to break the financial deadlock between France and Britain, suggested in their reply of the same day that any downward revision of Germany's obligations should be accompanied by a redistribution of what remained in favour of the devastated regions. But agreement was prevented by the refusal of the British government to limit its financial claims against Germany and the Allies to a figure below its own indebtedness to the United States. The only direct result of two months of Allied negotiations was, in fact, that the British cabinet, annoyed at its inability to achieve a settlement, resolved to publish the text of the diplomatic exchange which had taken place.[9]

Since much of the verbiage of the Anglo-French war of notes in the

---

[8] For French inflexibility: *Le Temps*, 7 June 1923, 1; Secret Letters, ix, 8 June 1923. For the Treasury's attitude: Report of Marcel Ray, 6 June 1923, Louis Loucheur Papers, Box 7, Folder 2. For the best recent discussion of the financial deadlock between France and Britain: Artaud, *Question des dettes interalliées*, ii. 539–53.

[9] For British policy: Cabinet Minutes, 30 (23), 11 June 1923, CAB 23/46; Curzon to Crewe, 11 June 1923; Curzon to Grahame, 12 June 1923, *DBFP* I, xxi. 333–41; Curzon to Saint-Aulaire, 13 June 1923, in *Correspondence with the Allied Governments respecting Reparation Payments by Germany, House of Commons Papers*, Cmd. 1943, 1923,

summer of 1923 had been concerned with the legality of the Ruhr occupation and with the related question of the conditions, if any, upon which Germany should be asked to renounce passive resistance, the German government was naturally encouraged to prolong the conflict in the hope of a more active British intervention. The German tendency to gamble on British support was particularly noticeable after Baldwin's uncompromising speech on 12 July in the House of Commons in which he announced that, because of its concern about the social and commercial repercussions of the Ruhr struggle, the British government would proceed independently to draft an Allied reply to the German Note of 7 June. This encouraged the Cuno cabinet to spurn the good offices of John Foster Dulles when he arrived in Germany on 12 July armed with a proposal which had been drawn up after discussions in influential French and Belgian circles. Dulles suggested that Germany should renounce passive resistance and resume reparation deliveries unconditionally on the secret understanding that this action would immediately be reciprocated by Allied concessions in the Ruhr. Rosenberg objected to some of the pledges which were proposed as a substitute for the occupation. But the most important reason for his ultimate rejection of the scheme was that a British initiative appeared to have been foreshadowed by Baldwin's speech on 12 July. 'Germany should not attempt', Rosenberg told Dulles on 17 July, 'to influence the British line of action.' In the event, Curzon's Note of 11 August, which was the Parthian shot in his duel with Poincaré, was so diluted by the cabinet as to destroy German hopes of an immediate British intervention. It therefore helped to precipitate the fall of the Cuno cabinet, which had been teetering for some time because of mounting domestic discontent about its handling of Germany's deepening financial and economic crisis.[10]

---

xxv. 4–7 (see also *DBFP* I, xxi. 342–5); Secret Letters, ix, 29 June 1923; Baldwin, 4 July 1923, *HC*, clxvi. 580. For the 'draft identic reply': Curzon to Saint-Aulaire and others, 20 July 1923, Cmd. 1943 of 1923, 18–25 (see also *DBFP* I, xxi. 426–32). For the Franco-Belgian response: Saint-Aulaire to Curzon, 30 July 1923, Cmd. 1943 of 1923, 25–38; Moncheur to Curzon, 30 July 1923, ibid. 38–46. For British inflexibility: Curzon to Saint-Aulaire, 11 Aug. 1923, ibid. 48–63 (see also *DBFP* I, xxi. 467–82); Cabinet Minutes, 44 (23), 1 Aug. 1923, Min. 3, CAB 23/46.

[10] Baldwin, 12 July 1923, *HC*, clxvi. 1584–9; Cabinet Minutes, 37 (23), 12 July 1923, CAB 23/46. Memo of Conferences Had in Germany, July 12 to 17, 1923, at 4, 8–9, John Foster Dulles Papers, Category II. Cabinet Minutes, 46 (23), 9 Aug. 1923, Min. 2, CAB 23/46. For text of Note of 11 Aug.: Cmd. 1943 of 1923, 48–63.

CAPITULATION AND STABILIZATION

The plight of Germany was clearly reflected in key indices of economic activity. Net black coal production (130 million tons in 1922) fell to 62 million tons in 1923; and even the production of lignite, much of which was mined outside the Ruhr district, was reduced from 137 to 119 million tons. Output of iron and steel, at 4.9 million and 6.3 million tons respectively, was half that of 1922. Another indicator of economic disruption was that goods transported on the German railways fell from a monthly average of 32.3 million tons in 1922 to 20.8 million tons in 1923. Finally the volume of exports fell from 21.6 millions to 12.7 million tons, even if the value of exports and imports remained almost exactly equal. Unemployment statistics reveal a dramatic slump in industrial activity in the second half of the year. The worst month was December, when there were almost 3.3 million totally or partially unemployed people in unoccupied Germany and a further 2.5 million in the Ruhr and Rhineland. This situation, which was comparable to the depression of the early 1930s, was aggravated by the stabilization policies of the government. Yet it was the unchecked inflation of the preceding period which made the eventual cure so painful.[11]

The hyper-inflation and depreciation which occurred from mid-1923 can be traced at a glance in the statistics of the note circulation and the movement of the dollar rate (Table 8). This financial tarantella occurred largely because of the gross imbalance between government revenue and expenditure in the second half of 1923, which is illustrated by the percentage in the right hand column of Table 9. The enormous deficit was not caused by a depreciation-induced failure of revenue to keep pace with constant expenditure. On the contrary, expenditure expressed in gold, as opposed to paper, marks (Table 10) was noticeably above its 1922 level for all but three months of the Ruhr struggle. The government's outlays were swollen not only by its subsidies to Ruhr industry but also by compensation paid for goods confiscated by the occupying authorities, Franco-Belgian requisitioning of German currency, and misappropriation on the part of the inhabitants of the Ruhr themselves, whose morale sank appreciably during the course of 1923. The chaos was compounded by the huge volume of emergency

---

[11] For coal, iron, and steel production: see below, Appendix I, Table A. For railway goods traffic: Bresciani-Turroni, 194. For export figures: Thelwall, *Report ... to April 1924*, 46. For unemployment figures: see below, Appendix I, Table E.

TABLE 8. *Note Circulation and the Dollar Rate of the Mark, 1923*

Date	Notes in circulation (excluding 'emergency' issues) (thousand billion marks)	Dollar rate (marks)
Jan.	1.30	7,260
Feb.	2.01	41,500
Mar.	3.54	22,800
Apr.	5.54	21,152
May	6.60	31,779
June	8.64	74,932
July	17.39	160,400
Aug.	43.89	1,102,750
Sept.	668.80	11,027,500
Oct.	28,244.40	242,605,000
Nov.	2,504,995.70	130,325,000,000
Dec.	400,267,640.00	4,210,500,000,000

Source: Thelwall, *Report . . . to April 1924*, 111.

currency which was being printed by local government bodies and the larger industrial and commercial enterprises. Although a law of 17 July 1922 had restricted the right to issue such money, this had been ignored in 1923. It appears that at the height of the inflation about two thousand different currencies were in circulation, and that their gold value was approximately equal to that of regular Reichsbank notes.[12]

The Cuno cabinet's inability to cope with this situation caused its stocks to slump rapidly in the summer of 1923. The headlong depreciation of the mark from June onwards and the tendency for real wages to lag behind prices provoked considerable industrial unrest culminating in a wage strike involving 300,000 Berlin workers early in July. There were also frequent complaints from the left wing on the eve of the Reichstag's summer recess about the failure of tax rates to adjust to the declining value of money. Concern rapidly spread to the middle-class parties when it appeared that the misery of the German workers was putting them into a revolutionary frame of mind. 'We are sitting on a volcano', Stresemann warned the Central Committee

[12] For emergency money: Bresciani-Turroni, 342–3; Schacht, *Stabilization*, 105–6.

TABLE 9. *German Federal Revenue and Expenditure, January 1923–May 1924*

	Expenditure	Revenue	Revenue (%)[a]
1923[b]			
Jan.	162,480	46,375	28.5
Feb.	484,544	150,509	31.0
Mar.	848,311	41,289	4.9
Apr.	777,930	175,000	22.5
May	705,782	600,348	85.0
June	1,795,432	226,578	12.6
July	5,376,483	259,508	4.1
Aug.	61,191,000	1,791,000	2.9
Sept.	1,302,812,000	49,905,000	3.8
Oct.	43,230,293,800	393,366,434	0.9
Nov.	57,901,569,000,000	53,449,000,000	0.09
Dec.	179,898,893,000,000	32,786,037,000,000	18.2
1924[c]			
Jan.	443,425,770	437,871,555	99.0
Feb.	478,630,013	339,759,047	71.0
Mar.	485,472,028	526,983,881	109.0
Apr.	472,100,000	396,400,000	84.0
May	511,000,000	449,500,000	88.0

[a] Revenue expressed as percentage of expenditure.
[b] First ten days of month, expenditure and revenue in million paper marks.
[c] Whole month, expenditure and revenue in Reichsmarks.

Sources: Thelwall, *Report ... to April 1924*, 28, 109–10; id., *Report ... on Germany, 1925*, 33.

of the DVP on 8 July, 'and we are on the threshold of revolution unless we can ameliorate the situation through determined and wise action.' The discontent of the Centrist and Democratic press at the 'aimless, vacillating, and passive behaviour of the government' was given added point when, later in July, the Communists gained an overwhelming victory over the SPD in the Berlin Metal Workers Union elections. A proposal to introduce stable value taxes on 8 August came too late to appease the mounting demand for more energetic measures. The government's fate had, in any case, been sealed by its incompatibility with the SPD, whose participation in the cabinet was now regarded as essential in moderate circles if Germany was to be saved from

TABLE 10. *German Federal Expenditure,*
January–October 1922 and January–October
1923 (million gold marks)

	1922	1923
Jan.	388.2	204.6
Feb.	342.4	279.0
Mar.	346.5	698.9
Apr.	321.8	466.6
May	376.9	284.7
June	313.8	496.4
July	208.5	473.9
Aug.	205.1	1,013.1
Sept.	434.9	1,661.8
Oct.	269.5	881.8

Source: Bresciani-Turroni, 438.

complete financial and political collapse. For this reason the cabinet which was formed by Stresemann after Cuno had finally been unseated on 13 August by a Berlin printers' strike (aimed at halting the printing of paper money) contained four SPD members, including Rudolf Hilferding and Wilhelm Sollmann at the strategic Ministries of Finance and the Interior.[13]

As in October 1918 and May 1921, the entry of the SPD into the cabinet had surprisingly little effect on Germany's foreign and domestic policy. Instead of taking immediate steps to wind up the Ruhr struggle, Stresemann continued Rosenberg's policy of exploiting Anglo-French differences so as to extricate Germany by some means short of total capitulation. In his first speech to the Reichstag as Chancellor on

[13] Note the complaint on 17 June 1923 by Finance Minister Hermes to Cuno that he had lost control of government expenditure: *Das Kabinett Cuno,* 578–81. For the strike: *Vorwärts,* 4 July 1923, No. 306, 1. For the movement of real wages: J. Kuczynski, *Die Geschichte der Lage der Arbeiter in Deutschland von 1800 bis in die Gegenwart* (2 vols.; Berlin, 1947), i. 309–11. For tax complaints: *Vorwärts,* 7 July 1923, No. 312, Suppl., 3; Hertz (VSP), 6 July 1923, *RT* ccclx. 11653–9. For Stresemann: *Vorwärts,* 11 July 1923, No. 318, 1. For Communist gains: Leidig to Stresemann, 25 July 1923, Nachlass Stresemann, cclx, Polit. Akten 1923/V. For Cuno's tax programme: *Das Kabinett Cuno,* 675–9, 703–6; 8 Aug. 1923, *RT* ccclxi. 11749–60. For the moderates and the SPD: Schacht to Stresemann, 1 Aug. 1923, Nachlass Stresemann, cclx, Polit. Akten 1923/V. For the printers' strike and the formation of the Stresemann cabinet: H. A. Turner, *Stresemann and the Politics of the Weimar Republic* (Princeton, 1963), 108–9, 115–18.

14 August he even referred optimistically to the British Note of 11 August. 'Passive resistance', he declared, 'has its deepest roots in the consciousness of the German people of its incontestable rights, which are now also clearly recognized by the British government. Even though a solution of the Ruhr and Rhineland question cannot be expected immediately as a result of these British observations, one can assume that this expression of opinion will not remain without an echo in France and Belgium.' Stresemann's stonewalling tactics over the next few weeks showed that he was more sensitive to Nationalist criticism than to the pessimism of the Social Democrats in the Federal and Prussian cabinets. Yet he yielded eventually to the opinion of Hilferding, his Finance Minister, that prolongation of the struggle and continuing subventions to the Ruhr would undermine efforts to stabilize the mark and lead to financial and politicial anarchy. He therefore decided on 20 September to prepare the German people for unconditional surrender, which was eventually proclaimed on 26 September. A further reason for the Chancellor's decision was almost certainly his failure to obtain any tangible British support. The isolation of Germany had been emphasized on the preceding day when, after conversations at Aix-les-Bains, Baldwin and Poincaré announced with studied imprecision that 'on no question was there any difference of purpose or divergence of principle which could impair the co-operation of Britain and France'.[14]

The SPD also had difficulty in asserting its influence over financial policy. Hilferding demanded to no avail that a gold-backed currency should be established alongside the existing paper mark; that a new Gold Note Bank which was to issue this currency should be a government rather than a private organization; and that part of the gold and foreign securities needed to support the new mark should be subscribed

[14] For Stresemann's stonewalling: D'Abernon to Curzon, 17 Aug. 1923, *DBFP* I, xxi. 488–9; Stresemann, 14 Aug. 1923, *RT* ccclxi. 11839–42. For Nationalist pressure: Hergt (DNVP), 11843–4. For SPD views: Kabinettsprotokolle, xl, 23, 30 Aug. 1923 (Hilferding, 8); *Akten der Reichskanzlei: Weimarer Republik, Die Kabinette Stresemann I u. II*, 13. Aug. bis 6. Okt. 1923, 6. Okt. bis 30. Nov. 1923, ed. K. D. Erdmann and M. Vogt (2 vols., Boppard-on-Rhine, 1978), i. 75–83, 155–69. Cf. Hilferding's speech to the Reichswirtschaftsrat on 12 Sept.: *Vorwärts*, 15 Sept. 1923, No. 431, 1–2. For the decision to cease passive resistance: Kabinettsprotokolle, xl, 20 Sept. 1923; *Die Kabinette Stresemann*, i. 319–23; Stresemann to Crown Prince, 10 Oct. 1923, Nachlass Stresemann, cclxi, Polit. Akten 1923/VI. For British policy: Conversation between Maltzan and D'Abernon, 12 Sept. 1923; Conversation between Tyrrell and German Ambassador, 15 Sept. 1923, ibid.; D'Abernon to Curzon, 14 Sept. 1923; Memorandum by Tyrrell, 15 Sept. 1923, *DBFP* I, xxi. 521, 525–6. For Baldwin and Poincaré: Note on Conversation, 19 Sept. 1923, ibid. 529–35. Cf. Grigg, 165.

by German business enterprises. In the mean time, the paper mark should, he insisted, be supported both by buying operations and by a 'brutal' tax programme which would diminish the government's deficit. Such proposals were far more radical than those favoured by conservative financial interests, whose views were expressed by Karl Helfferich, the spokesman for the DNVP. Early in August Helfferich had submitted to the Cuno cabinet a scheme for the introduction of a 'rye mark' (Roggenmark). As the name suggests, this currency was not to be backed by gold and securities accumulated with the assistance of the German propertied classes. Instead, it was to be 'guaranteed' by a 5-per-cent mortgage on all German landed property and business enterprises, and its value was to be tied not to the price of gold but to that of rye, the staple German crop. The immediate objective of the Helfferich scheme was to create a currency which would retain the confidence of German farmers, who had become reluctant to exchange their vitally needed produce for paper marks. Helfferich also envisaged that his new currency should be controlled, independently of the government, by its 'guarantors', the landed and industrial interests.[15]

Because of the insistence of Stresemann and of the Federation of German Industry (RDI) that an interim currency of the sort suggested by Helfferich was necessary in order to avert complete financial collapse, Hilferding eventually agreed on 13 September to sponsor a compromise scheme for the introduction of a Rentenmark. This was, like the Roggenmark, to be backed not by precious metal, but by the guarantee of the German agrarian and business community, and was to serve as a stop-gap until a new and permanent gold mark could be introduced. The long-term problem of balancing the budget had still, however, to be resolved; and it was on this issue that the cabinet once more became divided at the end of September. Hilferding, who feared that the stern programme of direct taxation with which he hoped to underpin the new currency might be rejected by the Reichstag, asked for an Enabling Act which would confer extraordinary financial powers on the cabinet. As a quid pro quo, Stresemann's DVP insisted that the cabinet's powers should include authority to suspend the eight-hour day. The opposition of the SPD to this attempt to shift the financial burden of stabilization onto the shoulders of the workers caused the dissolution of the cabinet on 3 October and a government

---

[15] For Hilferding's policy: Kabinettsprotokolle, xl, 10 Sept. 1923, 5–6; Die Kabinette Stresemann, i. 224–5; Vorwärts, 23 Aug. 1923, No. 392, 1. For Helfferich's stabilization plan: H. Luther, Die Stabilisierung der deutschen Währung (Berlin, 1930), 20.

crisis which lasted until 6 October. The *grosse Koalition* was eventually reconstituted after it was agreed that the offending provision should be deleted from the Enabling Act: but the SPD in effect capitulated by allowing the eight-hour day to be suspended by ordinary legislation. A further concession was made to the non-socialist parties when Hilferding was replaced as Finance Minister by Hans Luther, a non-party politician who had been a director of the Rhenish-Westphalian Metal Works of Hugo Stinnes and Mayor of Essen from 1918 to 1922, and whose outlook was that of the heavy industrial wing of the DVP. As Food Minister both under Cuno and in Stresemann's first cabinet, Luther had become preoccupied with the problem of provisioning the towns and therefore had an additional short-term reason for being a firm supporter of Helfferich's stabilization plan. It was, therefore, only after a memorandum advocating a gold-based currency had been published on 10 October by the Central Association of Banks and Banking Enterprises (*Zentralverband des Banken- und Bankiergewerbes*) that Luther finally agreed to the Rentenmark being issued as an auxiliary currency rather than as a permanent replacement for the old mark. The Rentenmark legislation which was proclaimed on 15 October, two days after the Enabling Act was passed by the Reichstag, nevertheless remained conservative in character. This was ensured by conversations at the Finance Ministry on 13 October during which Helfferich and the representatives of German industry established, amongst other things, the private basis of the Rentenbank.[16]

The decision about the nature of the new currency had been taken out of the hands of the SPD and become a matter of technical dispute between the representatives of the German banking world and the captains of industry. In the month which intervened before the first Rentenmarks were issued the Socialists and the working classes they represented were deprived of influence over other aspects of policy. By the end of October the SPD was powerless to prevent the use of martial law against the left-wing governments of Saxony and Thuringia, even

---

[16] For Hilferding's acceptance of the Rentenmark and Luther's views: *Kabinettsprotokolle*, xl, 13 Sept. 1923; *Die Kabinette Stresemann*, i. 256–62. For the cabinet crisis: ibid. 454–62. *Vorwärts*, 4 Oct. 1923, No. 464, 1–2. For the campaign for the gold-based currency: *FZ*, 11 Oct. 1923, No. 754, 1; 12 Oct. 1923, No. 756, 2 (Schacht). Note also the 'metallist' views of another influential liberal journal: *VZ*, 22 Sept. 1923, No. 450. Cf. Ackermann, 77–8; Schacht, *Stabilization*, 81–2. For the Rentenmark legislation: *Reichsgesetzblatt*, 1923, i. 963–6. Cf. Luther, 24–5. For a good scholarly account: C.-D. Krohn, *Stabilisierung und ökonomische Interessen: die Finanzpolitik des deutschen Reiches 1923–1927* (Düsseldorf, 1974), 23, 25–7.

though the state of siege had originally been proclaimed by Stresemann at the end of September in response to Kahr's Bavarian right-wing secessionist movement. This, and mounting indignation at Luther's delay in introducing a stable currency which would alleviate the plight of the working classes, prompted the withdrawal of the SPD from the Stresemann cabinet on 2 November.[17]

While this domestic power struggle was in progress, Stresemann had become involved in a two-month dispute with Poincaré over what was, for two conservative politicians, a crucial question of face: whether cabinet-level negotiations should precede or follow the resumption of reparation deliveries and payments. As in August and September, the German Chancellor was encouraged to bargain by his hope of Anglo-Saxon intervention. The qualms of Britain about the deepening commercial disruption of Europe which had helped to prompt Baldwin's *démarche* of 12 July were now sharpened by the very specific fear of the British cabinet that France might exploit her victory in the Ruhr to the detriment of the British steel industry. Further pressure was put upon the cabinet at the opening session of the British Imperial Conference in London on 1 October by the South African premier, Smuts, who had been moved by an appeal from Woodrow Wilson and primed by a two thousand word cable from Bernard Baruch. 'Your hand', the American financier assured Smuts, 'is in every Article of the Covenant of the League Stop Your voice is one of high authority because your motives are unquestioned and your character and attainments eminent in your time Stop You have it in your power to state the world's case and to be heard and heeded Stop If anyone can bring about a realisation of the facts it is you ...' Few men could have resisted such telegraphic magniloquence; and the urgent plea which Smuts entered for a more active British reparation policy was sufficiently effective to draw praise the following day from *The Times*, which cited Gladstone's dictum of 1869 that Britain could not 'foreswear her interest in the common transactions and the general interests of Europe'. Yet the British government was also influenced by Poincaré's appeal for a brief period of grace in which to restart reparation deliveries from the Ruhr. It therefore delayed action, much to the disgust of the *Manchester Guardian*, which likened a speech by Curzon on 5 October to the gesture of a man who tamely put his hands in his pockets after having shaped up to fight. Nevertheless the

---

[17] For martial law: Turner, 124–9. For the grievances of the SPD, see the resolution of its Reichstag representatives of 31 Oct.: *Vorwärts*, 1 Nov. 1923, No. 511, 1.

position of Smuts was strengthened in the second week of October when there were signs that the United States, under its new President, Calvin Coolidge, might at last emerge from financial isolation.[18]

Hopes of American intervention in Europe were aroused less by the activities of Baruch and Wilson, who carried little weight with the Republican administration, than by a visit of Lloyd George to North America. The former Prime Minister who was, like Smuts, eager to salve his conscience, began his tour on 5 October with a prominently reported speech in which he referred effusively to America as the country which was 'recreating the hopes of humanity'. He then appealed to the American government to concern itself once more with the affairs of Europe; and lamented that the European Allies had not taken up the suggestion of Secretary Hughes in December 1922 that the reparation question should be examined by an international panel of financial experts. Further similar declarations finally provoked the White House to issue a statement on 9 October that 'President Coolidge, like President Harding, was in accord with the proposal advanced by Secretary Hughes'. Although the communiqué was sceptical about the readiness of France to accept a conference of the type envisaged by the Secretary of State, Lloyd George immediately proclaimed at Ottawa that the Hughes proposal had been renewed. Moreover, in response to this 'encouragement' from the United States, Curzon, under pressure from the delegates to the Imperial Conference, dispatched a telegram on 12 October informing the American administration that the British government intended to enlist 'the immediate cooperation of its Allies in Europe in an invitation to the United States government to assist' in an impartial enquiry into the reparation problem.[19]

[18] For British fears: Cabinet Minutes, 47 (23), 26 Sept. 1923, Min. 2; 48 (23), 15 Oct. 1923, Min. 4, CAB 23/46. For Smuts: *The Times*, 2 Oct. 1923, 7 and LA; Baruch to Smuts, 29 Sept. 1923, Papers of Bernard M. Baruch. See also Wilson to Baruch, 28 Sept. 1923, 3 Oct. 1923, ibid. For British inaction: Hoesch to A. Amt, 5 Oct. 1923, A. Amt, Büro des Reichministers, Reparationsfragen, xv; Sthamer to A. Amt, 6 Oct. 1923, ibid.; *MG*, 6 Oct. 1923 (LA). Coolidge had succeeded Harding after the latter's death on 2 Aug. For a good discussion of German policy: K. P. Jones, 'Stresemann, the Ruhr Crisis, and Rhenish Separatism: A case study of *Westpolitik*', *European Studies Review*, 7 (1977), 311–40.

[19] Dwight Morrow of J.P. Morgan and Co., who was popularly regarded as an intimate of the new President, advised Coolidge when he became President in August 1923 to intervene in Europe. There is no evidence, however, that Coolidge either heeded or even acknowledged this advice. H. Nicolson, *Dwight Morrow* (New York, 1935), 271. For the Lloyd George–Coolidge dialogue: *NYT*, 6 Oct. 1923, 1; 10 Oct. 1923, 1–2. Cf. J. Campbell, *Lloyd George: The Goat in the Wilderness, 1922–1931* (London, 1977),

The American government by now had good reasons of its own for taking a more active interest in Europe. Spurred by the heavy losses of customers who had speculated in paper marks, sections of the American banking industry had once more begun to exert pressure in favour of a rational settlement of inter-government indebtedness involving a more lenient administration attitude to war debts. Commercial groups, some of which had profited from the removal of German competition in the early months of the Ruhr struggle, were also becoming aware of their long-term stake in European prosperity and political stability. On 10 October the front page of the *New York Times* carried a report on Germany's political crisis alongside statistics showing that she was the principal purchaser of American cotton and a heavy buyer of American copper. Five days later Senator Reed Smoot, the chairman of the Senate Finance Committee, visited the White House after returning from the Continent to urge the immediate implementation of the Hughes proposal because 'there was danger of an outbreak which might involve all Europe'. The energetic steps which the German government was at last taking to achieve financial reform also encouraged American pro-European feeling. On 5 October a *New York Times* leading article had been sceptical about the desire of the German government to co-operate with the Allies and pay reparation. Ten days later, however, the Reichstag's adoption of an Enabling Act which was to pave the way for the stabilization of the mark drew unstinted praise from the same journal.[20]

All this made it easier for the United States administration, when it replied to Curzon's telegram on 15 October, to refer favourably to the idea of an American intervention, even if it emphasized that any such action would be jeopardized as in the past by 'lack of unanimity on the part of the European powers'. Unfortunately the only immediate effect of this exchange was to encourage Stresemann to be less submissive towards France and hold out for government-to-government negotiations. On 7 October a German proposal for a cabinet-level conference about the restoration of normal conditions in the Ruhr and the resumption of reparation deliveries was dispatched to Poincaré. Three days later the Chancellor administered a stern reproof to Otto

71. For Curzon's telegram: Cabinet Minutes, 48 (23), 15 Oct. 1923, Min. 5, CAB 23/46; FR, 1923, ii. 68–70.

[20] For American bankers: Artaud, *Question des dettes interalliées*, ii. 568–75. For commercial interests: W. Link, 'Die Ruhrbesetzung und die wirtschaftspolitischen Interessen der USA', *VfZ* 17 (1969), 572–82; *NYT*, 15 Oct. 1923 (LA 'Germany's Great Decision'), 16 Oct. 1923, 3.

Wolff, the Ruhr industrialist, for his independent overtures to MICUM about the resumption of reparation deliveries; and, with British encouragement, he temporarily undermined these sub-governmental negotiations by refusing financial backing for any arrangement which might result. On 14 October, however, after Poincaré had rejected his plea for cabinet-level negotiations, Stresemann responded to SPD pressure and took a more conciliatory tack. Having once more consulted the British government, he transmitted to the Reparation Commission on 24 October a Note which was originally drafted by Hilferding. This reported measures taken to stabilize Germany's finances since the cessation of passive resistance and requested a fresh examination of her capacity to pay in the new situation created by the Ruhr struggle.[21]

Real progress depended, as ever, on negotiations among the creditor powers. Although the French government at first maintained its long-standing hostility to the idea of an impartial committee of experts, it eventually decided to go along with the British initiative on 25 October. Professor Bariéty, who has made a valiant attempt to discover rational diplomatic objectives behind France's Ruhr policy, insists that this decision was taken not in response to Anglo-Saxon pressure but in the belief that there was about to be an all-round settlement of reparations and war debts. Such a belief, he contends, was encouraged by an assurance given on 22 October by Hughes to Laboulaye, the French chargé in Washington, that the United States would only demand repayment of its war debts in reasonable proportion (*dans une proportion équitable*) to what the European creditors were able to extract from Germany. Yet the guarded language of the Secretary of State hardly warranted Poincaré's assertion in his reply of 24 October that Hughes had at last conceded the justification of France's claim that 'the general problem of reparations was ... inextricably linked (*solidaire*) with that of war debts'. Professor Bariéty might also have pointed out that, in the course of his conversation with Laboulaye, Hughes had stressed that growing American disquiet about French

[21] For American reply of 15 Oct.: FR, 1923, ii. 70–3; Artaud, *Question des dettes interalliées*, i. 581–2. For Franco-German exchange: Stresemann to German representatives in Belgium and France, 7 Oct. 1923; Conversation between Stresemann and Otto Wolff, 10 Oct. 1923; Stresemann to Hoesch, 14 Oct. 1923, A. Amt, Reparationsfragen, xv; *Die Kabinette Stresemann*, Introd. lviii–lxii. For Stresemann and Wolff: Feldman, *Iron and Steel*, 405–8. For Poincaré's opposition to cabinet-level negotiations: Poincaré to French Chargé in Brussels, 16 Oct. 1923, MAE, Papiers Millerand, 31, Allemagne XIX Réparations. For origins of German Note of 24 Oct., *Die Kabinette Stresemann*, i. 472–3; ii. 576–7. For text: PRO, T 172/1376 No. 15.

policy might inhibit (*entraver*) any effort by the United States government to help its allies out of their financial difficulties. Poincaré and his colleagues may well have been self-indulgent in putting such an optimistic construction upon the words of Hughes, which were even less encouraging in the American version of the interview; and they certainly took their decision on 25 October in full knowledge of the unease which their policies had been generating in the United States.[22]

If Poincaré really believed that France's 'victory' in the Ruhr had made the Americans more malleable, he was quickly disillusioned by a cable from Laboulaye on 26 October informing him that the attitude of Hughes was more reserved than he had previously indicated and that any American concessions on war debts would depend upon progress achieved by the debtors in the field of disarmament. The fragility of France's position was underlined by the explicit instructions of Hughes to American representatives in Paris on 25 October that they 'should lose no opportunity to make it clear that the present European situation is causing great anxiety; [and] that it is deemed most important to adopt at once an adequate financial plan based on the capacity of Germany to pay'. In response to this unyielding and admonitory American attitude Poincaré now hedged his acceptance of the experts' committee in a circular of 27 October to all French diplomatic missions. This asserted that neither the committee nor the Reparation Commission to which it would be responsible could do more than vary the rate and method of payment of Germany's obligations, that the total of these could be reduced only by the unanimous decision of the creditor powers, and that France would not consent to any such reduction. When Hughes retorted that these restrictions would make the proposed enquiry into Germany's capacity pointless, Poincaré was willing to concede only that the committee should examine Germany's *capacité actuelle*, or her present, as opposed to her long-term, capacity to pay. The underlying incompatibility of the French and Anglo-Saxon positions quickly became apparent in the discussions which occurred in the first week of November about the

[22] For initial French hostility: MAE to French Ambassador, Brussels, 22 Oct. 1923, MAE, Papiers Millerand, loc. cit. n. 21 above; DBFP I, xxi. 581 n. 5. For Hughes, Laboulaye, and Poincaré: Hughes to Whitehouse, 24 Oct. 1923, FR, 1923, ii. 79–83; Laboulaye to MAE, 23 Oct. 1923; Poincaré to Laboulaye, 24 Oct. 1923, MAE, Papiers Millerand, loc. cit. n. 21. For French acceptance of British invitation: Poincaré to French Ambassador, London, 25 Oct. 1923, ibid.; Record by Sir E. Crowe of a Conversation ..., 26 Oct. 1923, DBFP I, xxi. 594–5 n. 1. For the impetus behind the French decision: Bariéty, *Relations franco-allemandes*, 261–5; Artaud, *Question des dettes interalliées*, ii. 583–91.

precise meaning of the phrase 'present capacity'. Although Poincaré eventually agreed to an examination of Germany's capacity during the next six years (up to 1930) he remained unsympathetic to the American (and British) view that no time limit at all should be imposed upon the scope of the enquiry. The American government therefore announced on 9 November that the lack of unanimity amongst the Allies and the futility of any enquiry into Germany's 'present capacity' precluded its representation on the proposed committee.[23]

The deadlock among the creditors, and the insistence of the Ruhr industrialists upon reaching an agreement with the occupying authorities which would make possible a resumption of normal economic life, forced Stresemann to consent to sub-governmental negotiations which produced the MICUM Agreement of 23 November 1923. This document, which served as a model for other subsequent arrangements with individual mining and industrial enterprises in the Ruhr, bound the German contracting parties to pay directly to MICUM both the arrears and the future instalments of the German Coal Tax. It also stipulated that from 1 January 1924 reparation coal deliveries should amount to 27 per cent of utilizable German production and that MICUM should control the general distribution of Ruhr coal. These and other similar provisions affecting metallurgical products ensured that France and Belgium now possessed the working 'productive pledges' which had been the most tangible objective of the Ruhr occupation.[24]

Once this 'triumph' had been achieved Poincaré's attitude towards Germany relaxed noticeably. The progress of the MICUM negotiations, the unabated international disapproval of French policy, and

[23] For American policy: Laboulaye to MAE, 26 Oct. 1923, MAE, Papiers Millerand, loc. cit. n. 21 above; Hughes to Whitehouse, 25 Oct. 1923, FR, 1923, ii. 83–4. For Poincaré: Poincaré to French Missions, 27, 31 Oct. 1923, MAE, Papiers Millerand, loc. cit.; Laboulaye to Hughes, 29 Oct. 1923; Memorandum by Hughes of Conversation with Laboulaye, 31 Oct. 1923, FR, 1923, ii. 86–9. Cf. Secret Letters, ix, 30 Oct., 2 Nov. 1923. For the discussion of *capacité actuelle*: Hughes to Herrick, 6 Nov. 1923; Memo by Hughes, 7 Nov. 1923, FR, 1923, ii. 90–4; Herrick to Hughes, 8 Nov. 1923, Secret Letters, x. For British opposition to any time limit: Curzon to Graham, 6 Nov. 1923, DBFP I, xxi. 640–2; Secret Letters, ix, 9 Nov. 1923. For the American refusal to participate: Hughes to Herrick, 9 Nov. 1923, FR, 1923, ii. 94–5; Chilton to Curzon, 9 Nov. 1923, DBFP I, xxi. 651–2; NYT, 10 Nov. 1923, 1. For the best discussion of French and American policy: Artaud, *Question des dettes interalliées*, ii. 592–601. Cf. Bariéty, *Relations franco-allemandes*, 271–3.

[24] Memo of a conversation between Stresemann and Stinnes, 19 Oct. 1923, A. Amt, Reparationsfragen, xv. For MICUM: Bergmann, *Réparations*, 213–15; Bariéty, *Relations franco-allemandes*, 276–8.

the related decline in the external value of the franc had, in fact, already given rise to more conciliatory behaviour. On 12 November it had been announced in the French press that Barthou, the French delegate to the Reparation Commission, had been instructed to propose that the German government should be heard and that a committee of experts should be appointed to examine the reparation question. The initial stipulation of Barthou that this committee should investigate Germany's capacity only over the next three years provoked Bradbury to remark that the French proposal 'belonged to the world in which a certain philosopher invented pills for the treatment of earthquakes'. Yet, if the commission reserved judgement about the value of a committee with restricted terms of reference, it was unanimous that the German government should be permitted to state its case. Accordingly, Secretary of State David Fischer, the head of the German *Kriegslastenkommission*, made a formal declaration to the commission on 23 November in which he painted a vivid picture of the economic dislocation, social upheaval, unemployment, and near-starvation of the German nation. After welcoming a recent Belgian scheme of financial pledges as a basis for negotiations, Fischer concluded with an impassioned plea for even-handed justice. 'History', he declared, 'will be the court of judgement of the Commission in its handling of Germany in the present situation.'[25]

The signature of the MICUM Agreement on 23 November and Poincaré's exultant declaration to the Chamber on the same day ensured that Fischer's pleas would not go entirely unheeded. 'We are now', Barthou wrote to Logan, 'in an hour of relaxation.' The transformed atmosphere in the last week of November enabled Bradbury, Barthou, and Delacroix of Belgium to collaborate in drafting terms of reference for the proposed committee of experts which would skirt the dangerous topic of Germany's capacity to pay. Yet this cooperation was achieved only by a private understanding with Barthou that France, although putting no restriction on the scope of the proposed enquiry, would not in practice be asked to support any proposal for the reduction of Germany's debt. Such a compromise, which was

[25] For the pressures on France: Artaud, *Question des dettes interalliées*, ii. 602–5. Note the concern of the French right-wing industrialist newspaper, *Journée industrielle*, about possible Anglo-Saxon pressure on the franc: *FZ*, 11 Nov. 1923, No. 839, 2. For Barthou and Bradbury: Barthou to Millerand, 13 Nov. 1923, MAE, Papiers Millerand, 31, Allemagne XX Réparations; Bradbury to Treasury, 13 Nov. 1923, *DBFP* I, xxi. 664–6; Secret Letters, x, 12, 13 Nov. 1923. For the Belgian scheme of pledges: RC, Annexe No. 1964. For Fischer: RC, Minutes, 23 Nov. 1923; Secret Letters, x, 24 Nov. 1923.

necessitated by the refusal of any of the Allies to reduce their financial claims upon Germany or each other, made possible one of the few cordial meetings in the history of the Reparation Commission. On 30 November 1923 a resolution was unanimously adopted which called for the appointment of two expert committees: the first to examine means of mobilizing German capital abroad for reparation purposes, and the second to study methods of stabilizing the mark and balancing the German budget.[26]

All that was now needed to make these committees a reality was the support of the mystified and suspicious American administration. In response to a request of the State Department for precise and formal proposals instead of vague and whispered suggestions, Logan forwarded on 6 December a letter from Barthou which, for obvious reasons, did little more than repeat the Reparation Commission's evasively worded resolution of 30 November. This was, however, accompanied by Logan's assurance that the terms of reference, as suggested, permitted the examination of 'any relevant topic', including the volume of German indebtedness. The advantage of the formula which had been arrived at, Logan emphasized, was that, by eschewing the phrase *capacité actuelle*, it eliminated any controversy over the temporal scope of the inquiry. The French government, Logan somewhat disingenuously assured his superiors, was aware of the broad implications of the inquiry. Because the insistence of the United States on its war debts precluded a more radical approach to the problems of international indebtedness, the Coolidge administration announced on 11 December that it would support the appointment of the proposed committees, and that, although it would not nominate any official delegation, it would view 'with favour' the participation of American private citizens in their deliberations. The way was thus cleared for the appointment of the Dawes Committees, which were in the following months to subject the twin problems of reparation and the German financial system to a thorough scrutiny and to make recommendations which were as enlightened as their restricted terms of reference would allow.[27]

While these negotiations were in progress the struggle over

---

[26] Poincaré, 23 Nov. 1923, CD, 3682. For Barthou: Secret Letters, x, 28 Nov. 1923. For the appointment of the committees: RC, Minutes, 30 Nov. 1923; Secret Letters, x, 30 Nov. 1923.

[27] Phillips to Herrick, 30 Nov. 1923; Herrick to Hughes, 6 Dec. 1923; Hughes to Logan, 11 Dec. 1923, FR, 1923, ii. 101–6. For a good discussion: Artaud, *Question des dettes interalliées*, ii. 605–9.

stabilization intensified in Germany. The cessation of the government's Ruhr and Rhineland subsidies and its initial refusal to finance MICUM deliveries if they were to be used, as MICUM demanded, to defray the costs of the occupation rather than credited to Germany's reparation account, gave the Ruhr industrialists an excuse to demand a longer working day. On 16 November, notwithstanding an unofficial government undertaking that the industrialists would, in fact, be compensated for the deliveries, the Secretary of the Iron and Steel Industry Association (*Verband der Eisen- und Stahlindustrie*) summarily proclaimed the end of the working day of three eight-hour shifts and the inauguration of two ten-hour shifts. The same official also remarked ominously that 30 per cent of the Ruhr work force was redundant and would have to be transferred to unoccupied Germany. Within a few months these lock-out tactics were to create a huge reservoir of two million unemployed in the Ruhr district. They also provoked industrial unrest in the coal industry and railways and helped the Communists to increase their Reichstag representation from 4 to 62 seats at the elections of May 1924.[28]

On 15 November the Reichsbank ceased to discount Treasury bills and to print mark notes and the Rentenbank began to issue Rentenmarks, which were generally accepted as the equivalent of gold marks, to supplement the paper currency already in circulation. Of a strictly limited total issue of 3,200,000,000 Rentenmarks, 1,200,000,000 were allocated to meet the immediate needs of the government and a similar number were allotted to the Reichsbank and the private banks for the provision of credits to businessmen and farmers. Although the value of the Rentenmark was initially maintained because it was hoarded, its long-term stability and that of the paper mark would obviously depend on the ability of both the German government and the German community to live sufficiently within their means to avoid further recourse to the printing press. The remarkable budgetary exertions of the government in the next few months are clearly reflected in the figures of its expenditure and receipts. A sudden reduction of expenditure

---

[28] For the employers' attitude to working hours: Feldman, *Iron and Steel*, 427–42; *Vorwärts*, 9 Oct., 15, 16 Nov. 1923, Nos. 472, 536, 538, 1. For the government's official unwillingness to finance MICUM deliveries: *FZ*, 17 Nov. 1923, No. 855, 1. For the unofficial compensation agreement: *Die Kabinette Stresemann*, ii. 773, 914–18, 941–4; G. Stresemann, *Diaries, Letters, and Papers*, ed. and trans. E. Sutton (3 vols.; London, 1937), ii. 377–8. For unemployment in the Ruhr: *Vorwärts*, 29 Jan. 1924, Nos. 47–8, 1; *The Times*, 3 May 1924, 11 (Rhineland Correspondent); Krohn, 37–8. For unrest: *Vorwärts*, 19 Jan. 1924, No. 32, 1; 22 Jan. 1924, No. 35, 4.

was achieved by discontinuing subsidies to the Ruhr and Rhineland, retrenching some 400,000 government employees, reducing by about 30 per cent the salaries of those civil servants who were retained, re-organizing the financial relations between the federal government and the *Länder*, and making the railway and postal services financially independent of the government. The equally dramatic increase in revenue which accompanied this retrenchment was made possible by the stabilization of the mark and was materially assisted by a series of Emergency Tax Decrees (*Steuernotverordnungen*). These were initially delayed by the fall of Stresemann, which occurred on 23 November because of the continuing dissatisfaction of the SPD with the pro-longation of martial law. However, on 7 December, Wilhelm Marx, who had succeeded Stresemann as Chancellor on 30 November, prom-ulgated the First Emergency Tax Decree. This measure used the powers of the President of the Republic under Article 48 of the Constitution to speed up payment of Cuno's Rhine–Ruhr Levy and the Turnover Tax (*Umsatzsteuer*). Although the yield from those two taxes provided over half of the government's vastly increased income of 312 million gold marks in December, even more radical measures followed, notably in the field of indirect taxation. The renewal of the Enabling Act on 8 December made possible the proclamation of the Second Emergency Tax Decree on 19 December, which raised the rate of the Turnover Tax from 2 per cent to $2\frac{1}{2}$ per cent. According to Luther, this decree also 'transformed' the Income Tax into a property tax by ordering businessmen and farmers to pay taxes based upon the potential 'profit-worthiness' (*Ertragswert*) of their enterprises, rather than upon the actual yield. However, the practical effect of this apparent capitulation to the long-standing demand of the left for the 'confiscation of real values' should not be overestimated. Nor was the yield very great from the tax on revalued mortgages and other debts in the Third Emergency Tax Decree of 14 February 1924.[29]

Contemporary left-wing press comment conveys the impression that a disproportionate share of the burden of Germany's financial

[29] On the Rentenmark: L. A. Hahn, 'Zur Einführung der Rentenmark', *FZ*, 25 Nov. 1923, No. 875, 3. For retrenchment: Luther, 31; Thelwall, *Report ... to April 1924*, 30–45; Bergmann, *Reparations*, 211. On the railways and postal services: *Vorwärts*, 1 Feb. 1924, No. 53, 1; 2 Feb. 1924, No. 55, 1. For the SPD and martial law: *Vorwärts*, 23 Nov. 1923, No. 549, 1. For the tax decrees and the Enabling Act: *Reichsgesetzblatt*, 1923, i. 1177, 1179, 1205–28; 1924, i. 74–90. The Rhine–Ruhr Levy had been imposed by Cuno on the eve of his resignation in Aug.: ibid. 1923, i. 774–6. See above, n. 13. For the yield of direct and indirect taxes: Luther, 34; *Vorwärts*, 25 Jan. 1924, No. 40, Suppl. 3. For a good analysis: Krohn, 36–43.

stabilization was borne by consumers and wage-earners. Late in March 1924 Luther claimed in a speech to the Saxon Industrialists' Association (*Verband sächsischer Industrieller*) that property taxes were providing 58 per cent of total fiscal revenue. *Vorwärts* replied, however, that the yield from property taxation had attained this level only in December 1923 and had been diminishing ever since. On the other hand, the socialist journal observed, the yield from Income Tax wage deductions, the Turnover Tax, customs, and other indirect taxes had increased from 39 to 56 per cent of total revenue between December 1923 and February 1924. The frequent charge of the left wing that property was being taxed relatively lightly seems to be vindicated by the figures for

TABLE 11. *Revenue from Major Taxes, 1 April 1924–31 March 1925*

(Reichsmarks)

Income Tax	
(a) Deductions from wages	1,329,095,472
(b) Deductions from unearned income	19,136,300
(c) Other sources	862,875,443
Corporation Tax	313,824,349
Tax on Wealth, plus surcharge	499,020,254
Tax on Turnover	
(a) General	1,794,474,423
(b) Luxury Tax	119,096,735
Tax on Capital Transactions	168,039,069
Traffic Tax	
(a) Tax on passenger traffic	157,819,389
(b) Tax on goods traffic	155,306,275
Customs Duties and Indirect Taxes	1,546,657,630
Sundry Direct and Indirect Taxes	346,402,920
TOTAL REVENUE	7,311,748,259

Source: Thelwall, *Report on ... Germany, 1925*, 32–3.

tax receipts in the year beginning 1 April 1924 (Table 11). These show that 63 per cent of the government's total income of 7.3 billion Reichsmarks was derived from the Turnover Tax, from wage-packet Income Tax deductions, and from customs and other indirect taxes.[30]

[30] *Vorwärts*, 20 Dec. 1923, No. 596, 1; 18 Jan. 1924, No. 29, 1; 14 Feb. 1924, No. 76, 1; 25 Mar. 1924, No. 143, 2. Suppl., 1 (Luther). 'The government has', complained *Vorwärts* on 14 Feb., 'retreated step by step in response to the pressure of the bourgeois parties in those few areas where any initiative in increasing the tax burden of property was visible.'

A further symptom of the social bias of the government's stabilization programme was the difficulty encountered by Hjalmar Schacht, Germany's financial dictator, in making the business community live within its means in 1923 and 1924. Schacht had, on 12 November 1923, accepted the invitation of Luther to become an emergency Currency Commissioner with responsibility for stabilizing the mark and, in particular, for introducing the Rentenmark. The considerable financial power thus conferred upon him was increased when, on 17 December 1923, he succeeded Havenstein as president of the Reichsbank, after the latter had died of a heart attack. Schacht, who subsequently recorded that he assumed office in 1923 because 'Germany was in danger of succumbing to Communism', was in some respects ruthless in sacrificing the short-term interests of individuals in order to achieve his goal of monetary and political stability. While Luther was implementing his programme of radical budgetary retrenchment and fiscal reform, Schacht collaborated with the Reichsbank to eliminate the independent note-printing and credit-creating agencies which had been established during the inflation. On 17 November the Reichsbank announced that its branches would, from 22 November, discontinue their practice of accepting emergency notes as the equivalent of ordinary currency. This, and a simultaneous directive that all emergency notes in the possession of the Reichsbank should be redeemed forthwith by their originators, caused, according to Schacht, 'immense excitement amongst the numerous elements which were deriving advantage from the emergency money system'. The Reichsbank's firmness on this issue and its continued refusal to print any more of its own notes caused such a shortage of circulating media that by mid-December German speculators against the mark were forced to disgorge their hoards of foreign exchange in order to repurchase mark notes at what was, at the time, the relatively high price of 4.2 trillion marks to the dollar, the rate at which the mark had been stabilized on 20 November 1923.[31]

If Schacht was prepared to deal severely with the speculators, he was less eager to curb the demand for credit of German businessmen and agrarian interests. This was partly because the latter controlled the food supply of the towns, and partly because of his sensitivity to

[31] For Schacht's appointment and powers: Schacht, *Stabilization*, 90–6, 121–6. For some critical appraisals of Havenstein: *FZ*, 20, 21 Nov. 1923, Nos. 863–4. For Schacht's fears: H. Schacht, *My First Seventy-Six Years* (London, 1955), 182. For his policy on emergency currencies: *Stabilization*, 102, 107, 110–12.

the threat of the Ruhr and Rhineland industrialists that they might secede from the German financial system unless their credit needs were satisfied. In December 1923 the agitation of Hugo Stinnes and Louis Hagen, the president of the Cologne Chamber of Commerce, for the establishment of an independent Rhineland Bank (with French financial backing) stirred Schacht to announce plans for a German Gold Discount Bank, for which backing was hastily obtained from the Bank of England a few weeks later. It was not until Schacht had assured the Ruhr magnates that capital for the formation of the bank was available and that the 'Rhenish-Westphalian industry would receive preferential treatment from the Bank in the matter of credit' that the schemes for the independent Rhineland Bank were shelved. In the meantime the Reichsbank's reluctance to raise its rate of interest above 10 per cent, despite the existence of much higher rates on the money market, was causing an expansion of credit which, on Schacht's own admission, very nearly undermined the newly stabilized currency in February and March. As a result of the natural preference of German businessmen for obtaining money through direct advances by the Reichsbank rather than by liquidating either their stocks or their holdings of foreign exchange, there was in the early months of 1924 a serious rise in domestic prices, a fall in the Reichsbank's holdings of foreign currency, and a considerable decline in the exchange value of the mark. Schacht, who somewhat disingenuously attributed his tardiness in imposing credit restrictions to his preoccupation with other matters, subsequently emphasized his courage in announcing on 7 April that the Reichsbank would forthwith limit credits to their existing level. He failed, however, to point out in the appropriate context that he took this action on the same day as his Gold Discount Bank opened its doors and on the eve of the publication of the Dawes Report, which recommended the granting of considerable foreign credit assistance to Germany. Even Schacht, therefore, seems to have held the traditional view that the role of the banks was to create credit obediently for German industry.[32]

The assumptions which underlay the financial policy of the government during the stabilization crisis were nowhere more clearly revealed than in the extended parliamentary debate which began after the

[32] For the Rhenish separatist and autonomist movement late in 1923: Bariéty, *Relations franco-allemandes*, 250–61, 278–81; McDougall, *France's Rhineland Diplomacy*, ch. 8. For the Rhineland Bank proposal: *Vorwärts*, 13 Dec. 1923, No. 583, 3; *FZ*, 17 Dec. 1923, No. 934, 1. For the Gold Discount Bank and credit restrictions: Schacht, *Stabilization*, 136–9, 151–9.

VULTURES

Fig. 6. The *Star*, London, 23 October 1923.

Reichstag reassembled late in February 1924. On 16 February Marx appealed to the Reichstag not to tamper with any part of the government's financial programme lest the stability of the currency should be undermined. This did not, however, deter the Social Democrat, Müller, from launching an immediate attack on several aspects of the measures which had been introduced. The retrenchment of civil servants had, he claimed, become a purge of republicans and democrats; and the Ruhr industrialists had exacerbated the class struggle by their 'starvation tactics'. In order to ease the plight of the man in the street Müller demanded that the assets of savings bank depositors and of government bond-holders should be revalued in the same way as mortgages had been in the Third Emergency Tax Decree. This attempt to uphold the interests of the consuming classes made very little impression on the government. Dr Heinrich Brauns, the Centrist Minister of Labour, attributed the sufferings of the Ruhr workers to the burdens imposed by the MICUM Agreements; and Erich Emminger, the Bavarian People's Party's Minister of Justice, rejected any notion of compensating small savers and investors for their inflation losses. All available credit should, he considered, be used to restart production rather than to reimburse consumers. The same concern for the credit needs of industry rather than for the suffering of the masses was evident in the speech of Luther on 29 February. 'The order in which reconstruction must proceed', he declared, 'if the nation is to resume normal economic life is that, first of all, capital must be provided which will immediately increase production ... Only after this has occurred should savings be allowed to accumulate.'[33]

Despite the disruption, misery, and political extremism for which they had been responsible, the groups which had been behind the Ruhr invasion and passive resistance remained at the helm at the end of 1923. The futility and costliness of Poincaré's victory was beginning to become apparent, as were the consequences of the time-serving policies of the Anglo-Saxon powers. The German industrial establishment had also been sufficiently shaken by the repercussions of hyper-inflation to lend its support to a stabilization scheme which did not in the short term depend on international financial assistance.

[33] Marx, 26 Feb. 1924, *RT* ccclxi. 12466–9; Müller (SPD), 12470–6; Brauns (Zentrum), 12480–2; Emminger (Bäy. VP), 27 Feb. 1924, 12498–505; Luther, 29 Feb. 1924, 12572. Under Article II of the Third Emergency Tax Decree of 14 Feb. 1924 the revalorization of government bonds was postponed until the German government had discharged its entire reparation debt. See above, n. 29.

Yet none of the statesmen of the creditor powers were willing to acknowledge publicly that their policies had been misguided or irresponsible, nor would German middle-class politicians countenance any financial reform which threatened the privileged position of property. The continuing reluctance to dissipate illusions or to offend vested interests would eventually vitiate the settlement which was about to be concluded.

PART THREE

Internationalization and Collapse

7
The Dawes Interlude

By dint of clever financial and political stage-management the Dawes Committee were able to set the scene for five years of relatively trouble-free reparation payments. In the course of 1924 the mark was stabilized with the aid of an American-backed international loan; Germany's multifarious financial obligations arising out of the treaty were con-solidated; and an interim schedule of five annuities was drawn up which was not immediately beyond the debtor's capacity. The French and Belgians also undertook to evacuate the Ruhr in return for a purely financial system of guarantees and controls; and the responsibility for supervising the day-to-day collection and transfer of reparations was taken away from the Paris-based Reparation Commission and del-egated to specialist commissioners who were stationed in Berlin under an American Agent-General for Reparation Payments. Despite all these achievements the Dawes experts were unable to usher in a definitive settlement because neither the French nor the Americans would consent to the formal reduction of reparations and war debts which this would entail. The future of the Dawes scheme therefore depended entirely on the financial co-operation of the German government and the support of the international investing public, neither of which could be relied upon except in the temporary boom conditions of the late 1920s.

The main virtue of the Dawes settlement was its provision of a transfer protection mechanism which enabled the suspension of re-paration payments if they threatened the stability of the German currency. It was unfortunate that a temporary influx of foreign loans into Germany prevented this machinery from coming into operation and demonstrating the necessity for a realistic revision of Germany's obligations. The initial impetus to the replacement of the Dawes Plan with a sensible final settlement came from the financiers of Wall Street who became concerned by the second half of 1927 about the effect of reparations on the security of snowballing American investments in

Germany. Yet the main function of the Young Committee when it was eventually appointed at the end of 1928 was not to devise a settlement which took any real account of Germany's capacity but to ensure the smooth repayment of Allied war debts to the United States. The German government only allowed itself to become involved in these specious negotiations because of its increasing impatience to secure an early evacuation of the Rhineland and its acute sensitivity to American financial pressure.

THE DAWES NEGOTIATIONS

The theatrical character of the Dawes settlement was reflected in the preoccupation of the American members of the Dawes Committees with winning the confidence of the American investor and humouring the French government. It was no accident that Dawes, Young, and Robinson, the principal American financial experts appointed to the committees, were drawn from Chicago, New York, and Los Angeles, the three major financial centres of the United States. Nor was it false modesty that prompted Dawes, in his first address to the Reparation Commission on 14 January 1924, to play down his considerable personal expertise in budgetary matters 'lest he put his reputation for common sense under suspicion'. The heavy emphasis of the general upon the fruitfulness of inter-Allied collaboration during the war, and his subsequent well-publicized reunions with French military leaders, were also distinctly thespian. A further sop to French opinion was provided by the second Dawes Committee's somewhat ritualistic investigation of the amount of German capital which had been exported and its anodyne recommendations about how to encourage its repatriation.[1]

[1] Logan to Hughes, Secret Letters, x. 14, 21 Dec. 1923. Charles Gates Dawes (1865–1951), had been president of the Central Republican Bank and Trust Company, Chicago (1902–21), Brigadier-General (1918), and first national director of the United States budget (1921). He was to become Vice-President of the United States (1924–8) and US ambassador to Britain (1929–32). Owen D. Young (1874–1962), lawyer and businessman, was chairman of the General Electric Company (1922–39). Henry M. Robinson (1868–1937), lawyer and banker, was chairman of the First National Bank of Los Angeles, and had been a member of the Supreme Economic Council during the Paris Peace Conference in 1919. For Dawes and public relations: C. G. Dawes, *A Journal of Reparations* (London, 1939), 21–31; Arthur N. Young Papers, Diary, 18 Mar. 1924. See also Link, *Stabilisierungspolitik*, 215–18. For Second Committee: RC, *Reports of the Expert Committees Appointed by the Reparation Commission* (London, 1924) (henceforward RC viii).

Despite the Francophile image which Dawes projected, the French government's commitment to an enquiry which was an implicit condemnation of its reparation policy was at first lukewarm. Contemporary observers detected evidence of this lack of enthusiasm in the limited independence of the French experts who were appointed to the two committees. Logan, for one, feared that Parmentier would be 'apt to bow to Poincaré's direction', and was worried about the potentially restrictive nature of the premier's instructions to his delegates. In practice, France's willingness to comply with the eventual recommendations of the Dawes experts followed less from any voluntary relaxation of her reparation policy than from the lunacy of her previous financial behaviour and the consequent vulnerability of the franc. The French currency had slumped so heavily by January 1924 that the government was at last forced to stoop to domestic financial reform. De Lasteyrie and Poincaré had continued to insist until early in January that the budget deficit was due solely to Germany's reparation default and that the accelerating depreciation of the franc was caused by German sabotage. However, after the failure of the Eighth Credit National Loan in January 1924, the demand for a responsible financial policy had become more vocal. Concern was reflected in a report published in the French press on 15 January by Émile Mireaux of the Comité Nationale d'Études des Finances Publiques, which ascribed the depreciation of the franc to a variety of causes including the size of the floating debt, the volume of franc credits held by foreigners, French purchases of British coal during the Ruhr struggle, and the British Treasury's sale of francs and other currencies to counteract the weakening of sterling following its debt repayments to the United States. Domestic and international confidence in the franc could only be restored, Mireaux concluded, if the government embarked upon a programme of fundamental fiscal and financial reform and ceased to depend so much on German reparation receipts. This did not mean that France should relax her efforts to make Germany pay. But, he insisted, 'we should not engineer our own ruin by vainly repeating that our financial salvation depends on Germany's future payments'. Similar reasoning prompted the French government to announce on 17 January that it would impose a 20-per-cent surcharge (*double décime*) on all taxes, that it would reduce its expenditure, and that it would take measures to combat tax evasion and capital flight. According to Maurice Bokanowski, the rapporteur of the budget in the Chamber, these measures were designed to yield an increased revenue of 6.2 billion francs, which would cover all recurring outlays on interest, pensions, and war orphans' allowances in the budget of recoverable expenditure.[2]

This domestic reforming zeal did not prompt either the French government or its experts to reduce their formal reparation claims upon Germany when the Dawes Committees began their deliberations in mid-January. On the contrary, Poincaré went out of his way on 18 January to dismiss a suggestion made by Herriot in the Chamber that the experts should be allowed to revise Germany's total liability in the hope that this would precipitate a reduction of inter-Allied debts. In rejecting such a strategy, which was to be adopted by MacDonald and Herriot when they finally rang down the curtain on reparations at Lausanne eight years later, Poincaré declared that the Anglo-Saxons were not yet willing to waive their claims against France. He therefore went on to reiterate France's long-standing demand for a minimum of 26 billion gold marks plus the balance she owed to her wartime Allies. Such obstinacy was justified by the inflexibility of American policy and the consequent inhibition of Young. During informal discussions early in February the latter canvassed a total reparation bill of 92 billion gold marks which would cover not only the Series A and Series B Bonds of the London Schedule of Payments but also the debts of the victors to each other. Germany's obligations were obviously to remain inflated so that the resolution of the intractable problem of inter-Allied indebtedness could be deferred. It is possible that Young's subsequent agreement to a standard annuity of 2.5 billion gold marks, which his advisers considered to be beyond Germany's capacity, was also encouraged by the desire of the American business interests he represented to maximize the short-term tax burden on their German competitors. He may, on the other hand, have calculated that such

[2] The French experts on the first committee were Jean Parmentier, former director of Mouvement Général des Fonds in the Finance Ministry and administrator of the Crédit Foncier de France, and Edgard Allix, Professor of Political Economy in the Faculty of Law, Paris. France was represented on the second committee by André Laurent-Atthalin, director of the Banque de Paris et des Pay-Bas. For Poincaré's instructions: Poincaré to Barthou, 11, 16 Jan. 1924, AN AJ[5] 361, 'Documents signalés à l'attention des Experts'. These documents are not referred to in the otherwise full account provided by Bariéty, Les Relations franco-allemandes, 307–13. See also Logan to Hughes, 18 Dec. 1923; Fletcher to Logan, 7 Jan. 1924, Secret Letters, x. For the best account of the crisis of Jan. 1924, S. A. Schuker, The End of French Predominance in Europe: The Financial Crisis of 1924 and the Adoption of the Dawes Plan (Chapel Hill, 1976), chs. 2–3. For the loan failure: Haig, 90–1. For the Mireaux Report: Arthur N. Young Papers, Box 4, Folder 1. For the double décime and projected revenues: Chambre des Députés, Doc. parl. 1924, Docs. No. 6972, 137; 6980, 151. Cf. Haig, 91–7.

sums would never in practice be remitted abroad because of the transfer protection provisions which the British and Americans were, as we shall see, incorporating into the Dawes Plan. Yet the major consideration underlying his willingness to entertain extravagant figures both in 1924 and again in 1929 was, as Lord D'Abernon observed, that 'if Germany does not pay France, France cannot pay America'.[3]

If the Americans colluded with the French to keep Germany's total reparation bill intact, they also collaborated, somewhat schizophrenically, with Kindersley and Stamp, the British members of the first Dawes Committee, to ensure that her immediate practical obligations would be tolerable. Although the British experts deliberately avoided any public confrontation with Poincaré over Germany's total liability, they insisted that her payments over the next five years would not jeopardize the committee's objective of achieving a balanced budget and a stable currency. Stamp exploited his international reputation as a tax expert and Kindersley's leading position in the City to bludgeon the other members of his committee into a relatively moderate estimate of Germany's budgetary capacity. His tactics are revealed in a letter to his wife at a crucial stage of the negotiations on 26 March:

The Latins have all gone back on last week's figures and are trying to run us up to totals I won't stand. So I've issued my ultimatum tonight that I went to the former totals to get unity, but if I divide I do so on much lower figures which I shall fully justify by a detailed report. They know what this means in British banking credit, and if K. [Kindersley] will sign it too, they ought to come to heel ...

Stamp's account of the effect of this blackmail on the discussion of the size of Germany's standard reparation annuity was recorded a few days later by Arthur N. Young, an economic adviser to the State Department who had been seconded to Paris to assist the American experts:

Parmentier talked for an hour and a half in favour of 3 billions and when he got thru Stamp said he could best give his views by reading the first few pages of his draft minority report. Then there was a pause: Pirelli [the Italian expert] finally broke in and said there must be unanimity.

[3] For France's reparation claim: Dawes, *Journal*, 40–8. For US policy: Arthur N. Young Papers, Diary, 3 Feb. 1924; D'Abernon, *Ambassador*, iii. 60. For Young's attitude to German taxation: Artaud, *Question des dettes interalliées*, ii. 626. Note a differing interpretation of American policy by Werner Link, who sees the US as an arbitrator in the reparation dispute rather than an interested party: Link, *Stabilisierungspolitik*, 246–55.

The upshot was that the French experts were obliged to back down over the size of Germany's annuities because, as they put it to Poincaré, the Americans had threatened to publish a report by 'technical experts' which recommended that even an annuity of 2.5 billion marks 'was unreasonable and unacceptable to the informed economic opinion of the world'. Apart from beating the French down, the Anglo-Saxons devised the fail-safe system of transfer protection, which the German reparation expert, Carl Bergmann, referred to as 'the fundamental innovation, the decisive forward step, in dealing with the reparation problem'. The effect of this was that the transfer of reparations to the creditor powers (as distinct from the collection of the necessary sums within Germany) was to be placed under the supervision of a Transfer Committee staffed by five international experts which was empowered to recommend the suspension of payments if the stability of the mark was threatened. This arrangement reflected acceptance of the view of the British Treasury and Wall Street that in the 'sticky' demand conditions of the post-war international economy, the most important limiting factor on Germany's capacity to pay was the size of her trade surplus rather than the extent of her budgetary exertions. Transfer protection had already been incorporated in a scheme for the financial reconstruction of Hungary which had been drawn up for the League of Nations by Sir Arthur Salter, a British public servant who had emerged as a leading authority on the problems of financial sta-bilization and economic recovery in eastern Europe. Salter, who was invited to give evidence to the Dawes Committees and maintained close personal contact with Young and Stamp throughout their labours, clearly played an important part in shaping the recom-mendations of the experts on this and other matters.[4]

---

[4] Sir Robert Kindersley was chairman of the Lazard Brothers Ltd., director of the Bank of England, governor of the Hudson Bay Co., and chairman of the National Savings Committee; and Sir Josiah (later Baron) Stamp was Secretary to the Nobel Industries, Ltd., and formerly Assistant Secretary to the Board of Inland Revenue. The Right Hon. Reginald McKenna, chairman of the Midland Bank and former Chancellor of the Exchequer (1915–16), was chairman of the Second Committee. For refusal to spar with Poincaré: Bradbury to Chamberlain, 27 Dec. 1923; Minute by Sir E. Crowe, 31 Dec. 1923, *DBFP* I, xxi. 740–5. For Stamp's tactics and their effect: J. H. Jones, *Josiah Stamp, Public Servant: The Life of the First Baron Stamp of Shortlands* (London, 1964), 227; Arthur N. Young Papers, Diary, 1 Apr. 1924; Report by Parmentier and Allix in Barthou to Poincaré, 2 Apr. 1924, AN AJ[5] 361, 'Comité d'Experts: Correspondance échangée entre la délégation française et le Président du Conseil'. For the transfer provisions: RC viii. XIII, and Appendix VI; Bergmann, *Reparations*, 242–6; Sir A. Salter, *Recovery: The Second Effort* (London, 1932), 126–7, 142–4; Lord Salter, *Memoirs of a*

In his original brief for the French experts Poincaré had insisted that France should maintain both her military presence in the Ruhr and the financial and economic pledges she had acquired during the occupation; and he had even put in a bid for the cession of the railways on the left bank of the Rhine and of coal mines which would ensure the supply of coke to Lorraine, not to mention Allied participation in the strategic German chemical and aviation industries. It soon emerged, however, that French economic and military domination of Germany would be both unacceptable to the other creditors and financially counter-productive. France's diplomatic position was not seriously affected by the short-lived resignation of the Theunis government after the Belgian Chamber had refused to ratify a Franco-Belgian Economic Convention. There was, however, more cause for concern when Ramsay MacDonald, Britain's new Labour Prime Minister, followed his initial exchange of diplomatic pleasantries with a protest against 'what appears ... to be the determination of France to ruin Germany and to dominate the Continent without consideration for our reasonable interests and future consequences to European settlement'. It was even more important that British misgivings about French economic expansion were shared by influential Americans such as Owen Young. Poincaré's position was finally undermined by his admission in the Senate on 13 March that the net yield of the occupation in 1923 had been a paltry 659 million francs, or about 130 million gold marks, and his prediction that it would be only 3 billion francs in 1924. Since even the latter figure represented a mere 600 million gold marks (of which France would receive only 52 per cent), it was clear that earlier indirect methods of exploitation had been preferable. On 29 February, Parmentier had conceded for the first time that all measures which hampered German economic activity should be discontinued or modified as soon as Germany had put into operation the plan suggested by the experts. There was added incentive for the French government to collaborate after it obtained a J. P. Morgan loan of $100 million early in March to bolster the sagging franc for the next six months. Although no explicit political strings were attached to the loan, France's financial vulnerability was pin-pointed by Dawes on 11 March. 'The loan', he wrote, 'will be for 90 days with one renewal. If our plan succeeds, returning confidence may save the franc. If it does not, and one hundred million dollars is withdrawn from the reserves of the Bank of France for payment of this note in six months, the outlook for French industry and finance is dark.' For all these reasons the French experts subscribed to a report which recommended that the occupation of the Ruhr should be gradually replaced by a system of financial guarantees which did less obvious violence to liberal commercial ethics. These guarantees were to consist principally of earmarked revenues from certain German taxes, and the yield from German state railway bonds and industrial debentures. The French experts were able to withstand the Anglo-Saxons only on the question of the military, as opposed to the economic, evacuation of the Ruhr. Their success was due in no small measure to Dawes himself, who on 11 February recorded his opinion that the 'military occupation of the Ruhr, as distinguished from economic control, must be conceded to France, not only in the interest of her proper protection, but also as safeguarding the performance of the entire programme in the future'. The importance of Dawes's influence was underlined in mid-March when Owen Young decided not to insist on military evacuation because 'it would split the report, with Dawes on the other side'. As a result, the experts refrained from expressing any opinion about the political guarantees and sanctions which would ensure Germany's fulfilment of their proposals. It proved impossible, however, to postpone the resolution of the question indefinitely.[5]

Despite some Anglo-American friction over whether Germany's new currency should be based on sterling or gold, the Dawes experts produced on 9 April 1924 a unanimous report which recommended the reconstruction of the German monetary system and formulated a provisional reparation scheme which did not flout too obviously the commercial principles and practices of the day. The report was attractive because of the relative moderation of. the amounts it initially demanded from Germany (1 billion gold marks in 1925 rising to 2.5 billion early in 1929) and because the sums nominated com-

[5] For Belgian policy: *The Times*, 28 Feb. 1924, 12. For British Francophobia: ibid. 3 Mar. 1924, 12 (MacDonald); 27 Mar. 1924 (LA); *HC*, 27 Mar. 1924, ccxxi. 1589–91 (Asquith); 1614–18 (Lloyd George). For Owen Young's fears: Arthur N. Young Papers, Diary, 5 Feb. 1924. For Poincaré's figures: *Sénat*, 13 Mar. 1924, 785–6; Arthur N. Young Papers, Box 4, Folder 2. For Parmentier, economic evacuation, and the Morgan loan: Dawes, *Journal*, 133–4, 159–60; Schuker, *End of French Predominance*, 108–15. For guarantees in the Dawes Plan: Dawes, *Journal*, 313–29. For military evacuation: ibid. 99; Arthur N. Young Papers, Diary, 18 Mar. 1924. For American policy: Link, *Stabilisierungspolitik*, 241–6.

prehended all charges arising from the treaty. A further attraction was its recommendation that an international loan of 800 million gold marks should be advanced to Germany to support the new mark and to reduce the immediate burden of reparation payments. Most important of all was the administrative distinction it drew between the collection and transfer of reparations. This was significant not only as a safeguard against monetary instability but also as a potential trigger for the revision of Germany's obligations in the seemingly likely event of persistent transfer difficulties.[6]

Because of the good sense of these proposals and the general desire for a settlement it appeared that the Dawes Plan would be adopted with a minimum of delay. By 16 April the German government had complied with the Reparation Commission's urgent request that it should accept the report as 'a practical basis for the rapid solution of the reparation problem'. Ten days later both the commission and the governments it represented had declared their approval in principle. Only the French reply, which had been drafted by Poincaré in the early hours of Good Friday morning, entered a specific reservation: that France would retain her pledges in the Ruhr until she was satisfied that the Dawes scheme could provide better ones. However, differences of opinion even on this point seemed likely to be resolved after visits to Paris and London by Theunis and his Foreign Minister, Hymans, at the end of April. Having urged Poincaré to restore the debtor's economic unity before, rather than after, the report was implemented, the Belgians then obtained a general assurance from MacDonald that Germany would be faced with a united Allied front in the event of any default.[7]

This progress was interrupted by the dramatic gains of the Nationalists in the Reichstag elections of 4 May. Increasing left-wing criticism and the mounting campaign of the DNVP against implementing financial reforms before, rather than after, Germany's treaty obligations had been revised had prompted Marx to have the Reichstag dissolved on 13 March. Although the ensuing campaign was fought centrally on

[6] For Anglo-American friction: Link, *Stabilisierungspolitik*, 223–40; Arthur N. Young Papers, Diary, 8 Apr. 1924; Dawes, *Journal*, 163–4. For texts: RC viii.

[7] For the English text of the RC note of 11 Apr. and the German reply of 15 Apr.: A. Amt, Büro des Reichsministers, Reparationsfragen, xviii. The members of the RC had informally agreed on 11 Apr. that, if the report was accepted by Germany, it would automatically be recommended to their governments. Arthur N. Young Papers, Diary, 11 and 17 Apr. 1924. For the French reply and Belgian mediation: ibid. 24–6, 30 Apr. 1924; *The Times*, 5 May 1924, 14.

the Dawes Reports after they were made public on 9 April, the swing to the right was principally a reflection of domestic tensions and did not, as is usually claimed, represent a clear vote against the recommendations of the experts. The Majority Socialists and moderate parties had already expressed concern at the polarization of politics at the end of March; and the alacrity with which they brandished the Dawes Plan as an electioneering weapon indicates that it may have improved rather than diminished their vote. 'The Reichstag election of 4 May', declared *Vorwärts*, 'will be a plebiscite over whether we shall progress further along the road of the Note of 16 April or shall leave this road and plunge into the abyss.' Marx and Stresemann followed the lead of the SPD with articles in the *Berliner Tageblatt* and *Die Zeit* which, while admitting the extent of Germany's burdens, emphasized the desirability of liberating the Ruhr and Rhineland. Marx even felt emboldened to condemn those who advocated rejection of the Reports as 'un-German firebrands, whose loud mouths and empty slogans are leading the German people into error, and whose criminal irresponsibility incites them from one disaster to another'.[8]

Because of the attractiveness of the Dawes scheme to the German business world, the attitude of the DNVP and the influential right-wing press of Berlin was in fact far more restrained than Marx implied. The only journal initially in favour of outright rejection was the agrarian *Deutsche Tageszeitung*, which concluded its condemnation of the reports on 10 April with the Nationalist suicide slogan 'Better a terrible end than an endless terror'. Yet, in its afternoon edition of the same day, even this paper called for a realistic appraisal of 'those elements in the Reports which could serve later as the basis for an agreement and those which, under the circumstances, had to be rejected, come what may'. The rest of the conservative press, although highly critical of the Reports, conceded from the outset that they

---

[8] For left-wing criticism: see above, ch. 6 n. 30. For a Nationalist attack: Helfferich (DNVP), 6 Mar. 1924, *RT* ccclxi. 12620–33. Cf. Stresemann's reply: 12633–40. For the Reichstag dissolution: Marx, 13 Mar. 1924, ibid. 12828–9. For claims that the DNVP's bag of 96 seats (compared to 71 in 1920) was attributable to its 'clear rejection of the Dawes Plan': W. Liebe, *Die Deutschnationale Volkspartei, 1918–1924* (Düsseldorf, 1956), 77; L. Hertzman, *DNVP: Right-Wing Opposition in the Weimar Republic, 1918–1924* (Lincoln, 1963), 208. Charles Maier, while correctly attributing the election result to domestic causes, errs, in my opinion, in writing of the 'brusque condemnation' of the Dawes Plan by the DNVP: Maier, *Recasting Bourgeois Europe*, 455. For moderates' concern about polarization: *Vorwärts*, 30 Mar. 1924, No. 153, 1; 5 Apr. 1924, No. 163 (LA). For their reaction to the Dawes Reports: ibid. 18 Apr. 1924, No. 185, 1; *BT*, 20 Apr. 1924, No. 189 (LA, Marx); *Die Zeit*, 20 Apr. 1924, No. 94, 1–2 (Stresemann).

provided a basis for negotiations. Attitudes hardened briefly in the third week of April when Helfferich, five days before his death in a Swiss railway disaster, published an article entitled 'The Second Versailles', in which he appealed to the German people not to assume impossible obligations as it had in 1919. Yet this trend was reversed after the Federation of German Industries, concerned at the supposed strain of the MICUM agreements on the Ruhr industrialists, and eager for the international loan recommended by the Dawes experts, declared itself in favour of conditional acceptance. By the end of April, Count Westarp, the former leader of the old Conservative Party, felt obliged to declare in the *Kreuz-Zeitung*, the official organ of the DNVP, that the Nationalists espoused the same view. On the eve of the election the right-wing press either followed suit or tried to evade the issue. The latter tactic was adopted most obviously by the *Deutsche Allgemeine Zeitung*, which represented the views of the anti-Stresemann 'managing directors'' clique of the DVP, the Nationalliberale Vereinigung. 'The issue on 3 May', it concluded, 'is not the acceptance or rejection of the Experts' Report, but whether in the future there will be a strong government which will honourably, conscientiously, and without disastrous dilettantism, protect Germany's national interests against a hostile world.'[9]

The DNVP's electoral success cannot, therefore, be attributed to its outspoken opposition to the Dawes Reports. On the contrary, its gains were possibly due, as the Communist *Rote Fahne* suggested, to its appearance of standing simultaneously for both acceptance and rejection. Yet the fruits, if any, of the DNVP's equivocation were soured by the debate over the implementation of the Reports in ensuing months. Immediately after the elections there was disagreement in the right-wing press about whether the Nationalists should participate in

[9] *DT*, 10 Apr. 1924, No. 171 (Baecker); No. 172 (Flack). Cf. *KZ*, 10 Apr. 1924, No. 171, 1–2; 12 Apr. 1924, No. 176, 1–2; *Der Tag*, 10 Apr. 1924, No. 87, 1–2; *DAZ*, 13 Apr. 1924, No. 177, 1–2; *BLA*, 10 Apr. 1924, No. 172 (LA). For Helfferich: *DT*, 18 Apr. 1924, No. 185 (Suppl.). Cf. *KZ*, 18 Apr. 1924, No. 185, 1–2; 19 Apr. 1924, No. 186 (Westarp); *DAZ*, 19 Apr. 1924, No. 186, 1; *Deutsche Zeitung*, 22 Apr. 1924, No. 175, 1–2; 28 Apr. 1924, No. 185, 1. Max Maurenbrecher's *volkisch Deutsche Zeitung* had been unable to condemn the Dawes Reports earlier because it had been banned from 10 to 20 Apr. for questioning the validity of the Reichswehr's oath of loyalty to the constitution. For the RDI's declaration: *KZ*, 25 Apr. 1924, No. 193, 1; *BLA*, 25 Apr. 1924, No. 197, 1; *DT*, 26 Apr. 1924, No. 195, 1. Cf. *Deutsche Zeitung*, 25 Apr. 1924, No. 180, 3. For Westarp's declaration: *KZ*, 1 May 1924, No. 203 (Suppl.), 1; 3 May 1924, No. 208, 1–3 (Westarp). For election eve opinion: *DAZ*, 3 May 1924, No. 207 (Suppl.), 1; *DT*, 2 May 1924, No. 206 (LA); *BLA*, 2 May 1924, No. 208, 1; 4 May 1924, No. 212, 1; *Der Tag*, 3 May 1924, No. 107 (LA).

a conservative coalition committed to acceptance. Although *Der Tag*, the *Berliner Lokal-Anzeiger*, and the *Deutsche Allgemeine Zeitung* favoured such a course, they were opposed by the more xenophobic *Deutsche Zeitung* and the *Deutsche Tageszeitung*, which feared criticism from *volkisch* groups. It appeared briefly that the counsels of the moderates would prevail: but negotiations with the government parties in mid-May over a middle-class (*bürgerlich*) coalition soon foundered on the reluctance of all sections of the DNVP to commit themselves openly and specifically to acceptance. The parties of the centre, despite their eagerness to draw the DNVP into the cabinet so that it would share the responsibility for foreign policy, were naturally loath to present the Nationalists with a blank cheque. Since, moreover, their relatively poor showing at the polls was an improvement on their performance in recent state and local government elections, they considered that the trend towards political extremism had been reversed and that the vote of 3 May had in fact been for Dawes and moderation. They therefore published a joint declaration on 21 May that they would support only a cabinet which accepted the Dawes scheme as 'a single and indivisible whole'. This made a *bürgerlich* coalition impossible; and the DNVP, after further feelers during the Marx government's short-lived resignation of 26–8 May, relapsed into its customary opposition role.[10]

Despite the vacillating attitude of the DNVP towards the Dawes Plan, the result of the Reichstag elections increased French reluctance to leave the Ruhr. Nor was the situation eased by the defeat of the *Bloc National* on 11 May and the resignation of Poincaré. Although

[10] *Rote Fahne*, 6 May 1924, No. 44 (LA). For disagreement over cabinet participation: *Der Tag*, 6 May 1924, No. 129 (LA); *BLA*, 5 May 1924, No. 213 (LA); *DAZ*, 6 May 1924, No. 211 (LA); *Deutsche Zeitung*, 5 May 1924, No. 198 (LA); *KZ*, 6 May 1924, No. 212, 1; *DT*, 6, 8 May 1924, Nos. 211, 215, p. 1. Note the embarrassment of the *Kreuz-Zeitung* and the capital made by the moderate press at the end of Apr. when the *Deutsche Tageblatt*, the organ of the *volkisch Deutsche Freiheits-Partei*, criticized the DNVP for its readiness to accept the Dawes Reports: *KZ*, 30 Apr. 1924, No. 202, 1; *BT*, 1 May 1924, No. 207, 1; *Vorwärts*, 2 May 1924, No. 205, 2; *Die Zeit*, 3 May 1924, No. 104 (LA). For a résumé of the cabinet negotiations: Memo by Maltzan, A. Amt, Büro des Reichsministers, Reparationsfragen, xviii. For the uncompromising attitude of even the moderate right-wing press to the Dawes scheme after the elections: *DAZ*, 23 May 1924, No. 241. Cf. W. Gubalke, 'Das Gruppeninteresse in der Berliner Tagespresse am Dawes-Plan, 1924', Phil. Diss. (Univ. of Berlin, 1936). For the attitude of the centre parties: Stresemann to Hembeck, 13 May 1924, in Stresemann, *Diaries, Letters, and Papers*, i. 342–3; *BT*, 12 May 1924, No. 225, 1; Declaration by the Middle Parties, in Stresemann to Houghton, 21 May 1924, A. Amt, Reparationsfragen, xviii. For the DNVP's feelers of 26 May: Maltzan to the German Embassies in Paris, London ..., 27 May 1924, ibid.

the electorate had already registered its disapproval of the meagre results of the Ruhr invasion and the falling value of the franc, the French press and parliament prevented the new Radical government of Eduard Herriot from straying too far from the course somewhat presumptuously charted for it by Poincaré in a letter to MacDonald three days after his electoral discomfiture. There would not even be an economic evacuation of the occupied territories, Poincaré warned, until the German government had implemented the suggestions of the Dawes experts 'in their entirety and carried out their instructions'. France and Belgium would, moreover, by their continuing military presence in the Ruhr, 'remain in a position to resume pledges' in the event of a German default. During conversations with MacDonald at Chequers on 21–2 June, Herriot was not averse to concessions which would enable Marx and Stresemann to circumvent Nationalist criticism on the 'honour question' of evacuation. There was, however, an outcry in France when it was learned that Herriot had 'agreed' at Chequers to an economic evacuation of the Ruhr within a fortnight of the German government's execution of all the legislation and other measures prescribed by the Dawes Committees. The new premier was also criticized for conceding that the determination of any default by Germany could be the responsibility of an authority other than the Reparation Commission. Herriot's embarrassment was so acute that MacDonald felt obliged to make a special trip to Paris on 8 July so that a Franco-British memorandum could be drafted which restored to the Reparation Commission the authority to decide when the Ruhr sanctions should be lifted and to judge whether any German default occurred in the future. It was only after the commission, thus fortified, had prescribed the legislative and administrative steps which were to be taken by the German government before the Dawes Scheme could be considered in operation that a full inter-Allied conference was convened in London to consider the implementation of the experts' proposals.[11]

Despite their sensitivity to right-wing pressure on questions of face,

---

[11] For the French elections: Maier, *Recasting Bourgeois Europe*, 472–9. For Poincaré's letter: Toynbee, *Survey, 1924*, 363–4. For Stresemann's plea about 'honour' questions: Logan to Barthou, 11 June 1924, in Dawes, *Journal*, 255–61; Memo of 4 June 1924; Stresemann to German Embassy, London, 18 June 1924, A. Amt, Reparationsfragen, xix. Cf. Stresemann, *Diaries, Letters, and Papers*, i. 347–9. For Chequers: MacDonald to Moncheur, 25 June 1924, *Correspondence Concerning the Conference which it is Proposed to Hold in London on 16 July 1924, to Consider the Measures Necessary to Bring the Dawes Plan into Operation, House of Commons Papers*, Cmd. 2184, 1924,

the financial vulnerability of the French and German governments ensured that the Dawes Scheme would not founder. The negotiations over the April and June renewals of the MICUM Agreements occasioned passionate German protests about intolerable financial hardship and answering threats from the MICUM authorities. Yet in both instances the continuing dependence of the franc on J. P. Morgan credits and the eagerness of German industry for the impending Dawes Loan ensured that a compromise arrangement would be hammered out involving concessions by MICUM and covert subsidies by the German government to the Ruhr industrialists. The same determination to reach agreement was evident during the London Conference in July and August. The parties involved, like the Dawes experts before them, were at pains to emphasize the technical nature of their deliberations and to smooth over any areas of political conflict which might disturb the confidence of the international investing public. The three committees into which the plenary conference resolved itself on 16 July were concerned with the procedures to be followed by the Reparation Commission in the event of a German default, the means of restoring Germany's fiscal and economic unity, and problems of deliveries in kind and transfers. The eagerness of the first committee to reassure American investors was reflected in its recommendation on 23 July that an American citizen should take part in the Reparation Commission's discussion of any alleged German default; and that, in the event of sanctions being imposed on Germany, the securities pledged to the service of the Dawes loan would be safeguarded. The second committee, aided by the explicit exclusion of the military evacuation of the Ruhr from its terms of reference, was guided by the same spirit; and by early in August was divided only over the minor question of whether 5,000 French and Belgian railwaymen should be retained on certain sections of the German railway system west of the Rhine. Finally, the third committee recommended, amongst other things, that an international arbitrator should be appointed if there was a division of opinion in the Transfer Committee over any alleged German attempt to undermine the transfer mechanism. This progress enabled direct discussions to begin on 5 August with the representatives of the German government. By 9 August the latter had

xxvii. For criticism of Herriot: *Le Temps*, 26 June 1924. See also *Franco-British Memorandum of 9 July 1924, Concerning the Application of the Dawes Scheme, House of Commons Papers*, Cmd. 2191, 1924, xxvii; RC Decision, 15 July 1924: *Proceedings of the London Reparation Conference, July and August 1924* (henceforward *London Conference*), ibid. Cmd. 2270, 1924, xxvii. 110–11.

obtained the approval of the Reparation Commission for the draft measures which it was to submit to the Reichstag in order to implement the scheme. These consisted of three laws affecting the reorganization of the German railways, the participation of the Allies in the income from German industrial debentures, the setting up of the new German Bank of Issue, and a protocol dealing with controls. A week later the conference wound up with two agreements between Germany and her creditors which interpreted the accord of 9 August with the Reparation Commission and spelled out a detailed programme for restoring Germany's economic and financial sovereignty.[12]

The smoothness of these negotiations over matters which had hitherto been a chronic source of disagreement meant that the only remaining obstacle to the adoption of the Dawes Plan was the issue of military evacuation. The position of influential German conservative journals such as the *Deutsche Allgemeine Zeitung* was that the Dawes protocol should be signed only if the evacuation was to begin immediately; and even moderates such as the *Berliner Tageblatt* and *Die Zeit* pressed for negotiations to be broken off on 15 August after Herriot had refused to concede more than the withdrawal of troops within a year of the agreed date. The German delegation only reluctantly signed the protocol on the following day after it had been given an unofficial undertaking that the evacuation would be speeded if Germany fulfilled her obligations punctually. This did not, however, satisfy the DVNP's Reichstag members, who announced on 21 August that they would oppose the ratification of the Dawes Plan.[13]

It became clear in the last two weeks of August that this declaration was a face-saving gesture, and that a considerable number of Nationalists were still prepared to vote for the Dawes scheme. *Der Tag* and the *Berliner Lokal-Anzeiger* obliquely indicated their readiness to capitulate by stating that the battle over the Dawes Plan had already

[12] For MICUM: Maier, *Recasting Bourgeois Europe*, 417–18; see above, ch. 6 n.24. For the report of the first committee: *London Conference*, 148–52. For the second and third committees: ibid. 120–31, 152–8. American diplomatic pressure was brought to bear on Britain and France: D. B. Goldey, 'The Disintegration of the *Cartel des Gauches* and the Politics of French Government Finance, 1924–1928', Ph.D. thesis (Oxford, 1961), 82–3. For the agreement of 9 Aug.: Secretary-General, RC, to Secretary-General, Inter-Allied Conference, 9 Aug. 1924, *London Conference*, 224–50; RC, Minutes, 9 Aug. 1924. For the agreements of 16 Aug.: *London Conference*, 226–38.

[13] For the evacuation negotiations of 13–16 Aug.: Maltzan to the German Embassies ..., 16 Aug. 1924, A. Amt, Reparationsfragen, xix. For the *Berliner Tageblatt* and *Die Zeit*: Hergt (DNVP), 25 Aug. 1924, *RT* ccclxxxi. 797 (citations). For the *Deutsche Allgemeine Zeitung* of 14 Aug. 1924: Gubalke, 114. For the DNVP decision: *KZ*, 22 Aug. 1924 (Morning), 1; Hergt, *RT* ccclxxxi. 804.

been lost by Germany's diplomatic representatives in London. The *Deutsche Allgemeine Zeitung* began, moreover, to advocate the relaxation of party discipline so that a sufficient number of deputies could vote for the Dawes Railway Bill, which required a two-thirds majority because it embodied a constitutional revision. Such views were not immediately heeded by the party leadership. On 27 August the DNVP State Presidents voted overwhelmingly for rejection, and the Reichstag, with the DNVP voting in opposition, passed the vital Railway Bill at its second reading only by a simple majority of 248 to 174. However, in the next two days the formal unanimity of the DNVP cracked, and on 19 August 48 Nationalists gave the Railway Bill its required majority by voting with the government at the third reading. Some of those who voted in the affirmative were attracted by the renewed prospect of participation in a conservative cabinet following discussions between DNVP leaders and representatives of the DVP and Centre Party on 28–9 August. Others calculated that, because of the attractiveness of the Dawes Plan, a negative vote would only bring about a dissolution of the Reichstag and new elections resulting in a swing to the left and the formation of a new *grosse Koalition* which included the Social Democrats. The underlying reason for the vote, was, however, the prospect of an American-backed loan to underpin the new currency and fuel economic recovery. This persuaded the political representatives of the conservative élite to mute their patriotism sufficiently to enable resumption of large-scale reparation payments.[14]

The disappointing yield of the Ruhr invasion and its damaging effect on their currencies had prompted Germany's major continental creditors, France and Belgium, to abandon their posturing attempt at direct exploitation and to agree to more indirect methods which were acceptable to the financiers of London and New York. The lure of Anglo-Saxon loans had also persuaded the German economic establishment to moderate its policies of blind resistance and irresponsibility. Yet no realistic settlement had been achieved because Britain and the United States, although willing to mediate in the

[14] *Der Tag*, 24 Aug. 1924; *BLA*, 24 Aug. 1924; *DAZ*, 22, 24 Aug. 1924 (Morning). See Gubalke, 119–20. For second reading: 27 Aug. 1924, *RT* ccclxxxi. 996. For the third reading: 29 Aug. 1924, ibid. 1086–7. For hopes of DNVP entry into the cabinet: *KZ*, 30 Aug. 1924 (Morning), 1; ibid. 2 (text of DVP Resolution of 28 Aug. 1924); 30 Aug. 1924 (Evening), 2. For fears of a dissolution: *DAZ*, 24 Aug. 1924 (Morning); and *DT*, 26 Aug. 1924 (Morning): quoted in Gubalke, 120. The *Kreuz-Zeitung* admitted the possibility of electoral losses, but denied that this was a worthy reason for accepting the Dawes Plan: 23 Aug. 1924 (Evening), Suppl., 1–2. Influential army circles were also afraid of a swing to the left. See Hertzman, 216–17.

reparation dispute to restrict French influence in Germany and prevent undue dislocation and unrest, were not prepared to make the necessary gestures of financial renunciation. The Dawes Plan, like the Young Plan which was to follow it in 1929, was a flimsy improvisation which depended for its survival on continuing financial and political fair weather within Germany and abroad.

THE OPERATION OF THE DAWES PLAN

Despite its shortcomings, the Dawes Plan provided a substantial breathing space and an institutional framework more suitable than that of the London Schedule of Payments for working out a viable long-term reparation scheme. The division of the collection and transfer of reparations into separate operations meant that the German government was given five years to improve its international image by making a serious attempt to raise the required funds within Germany. This would have given the internationally staffed Transfer Committee an opportunity to demonstrate the difficulty and danger of converting these sums into foreign currencies. It was unfortunate, if predictable, that in the first four years of the plan's operation Germany failed to retrieve her financial reputation by achieving either a balanced budget or an export surplus; and it was also regrettable that the intractable nature of the transfer problem was concealed by an artificially induced and short-lived inflow of foreign funds to Germany. As a result the Dawes scheme had not exerted any appreciable depoliticizing or educational influence by the time the question of a final settlement arose again in 1928. The likelihood of a definitive solution was at this stage further reduced by the diversion of funds from Europe to the speculative maelstrom of the American stock exchange boom. The consequent restriction of credit in Europe, coinciding as it did with increasing pressure from the conservative United States administration for the repayment of its war loans, reduced the manœuvrability of both Germany and her European creditors. The tightening grip of Poincaré on French policy, the growth of French financial power relative to that of Britain after 1926, and the impatience of the German government at the meagre fruits of the 'Locarno diplomacy' of international reconciliation ensured that the Young Plan of 1929 would be little more realistic or politically acceptable than its predecessors.

After a Draconian beginning, the budgetary performance of the

German government during the period of the Dawes scheme fell away sadly for familiar reasons. In the course of its drive to underpin the new Reichsmark in 1924–5, the Marx government achieved an excessive budgetary surplus, largely at the expense of the less affluent, who, according to an estimate by the SPD's fiscal watchdog, Paul Hertz, provided through the medium of the *Massensteuern* 70 per cent of total tax receipts instead of the 55 per cent predicted by Finance Minister Luther in February 1924. The deficits of the following years were subsequently attributed by Schacht to swollen expenditure on social welfare: but their size was also due to the persistently low yield of direct taxes and the inordinate share of tax receipts enjoyed by the states and municipalities. Under the tax distribution arrangement of August 1925 the federal government was entitled to only 25 per cent of the yield of the Income and Corporation Taxes and 70 per cent of receipts from the Turnover Tax. Although this was an improvement on the violently devolutionary provisions of the Third Emergency Tax Decree of February 1924, it was still a substantial retreat from the 33 and 90 per cent share of these three major sources of revenue which went to the Reich under Erzberger's more centralist States Tax Law (*Landessteuergesetz*) of March 1920. Any attempt to boost federal tax receipts at the expense of the states was precluded by the conservatism and 'states-rights' sympathies of the cabinets of the period. The presence of the DNVP in the coalition from February 1927 to May 1928 and the fact that the Centre Party Finance Minister, Heinrich Koehler, had been premier and Finance Minister of Baden earlier in the decade are sufficient to explain why an already overdue redefinition of federal–state financial relations was postponed in April 1927 for a further two years. Notwithstanding the sluggishness of the tax yield, decisions were taken to raise the salaries of public servants and to compensate Germans who had lost property abroad during the war. The supine nature of German fiscal policy, which was reminiscent of the inertia of the Fehrenbach cabinet in 1920 and early 1921, drew heavy criticism from Parker Gilbert, the Agent-General for Reparations, both in his biannual report of June 1927 and in a Memorandum transmitted to Koehler on 20 October 1927. Although Gilbert considered that the situation was not yet beyond repair, his strictures indicate why the government was so ill prepared to meet the financial crisis which was soon to break.[15]

[15] Hertz, 27 July 1925, *RT* ccclxxxvii. 3530–1. For Luther: see above, ch. 6 n. 30. According to Hertz's definition, *Massensteuern* consisted mainly of the Turnover Tax,

TABLE 12. *German Foreign Trade, Reparations and Foreign Borrowing,*
1924–1932
(millions of marks)

	Exports	Imports	Invisibles	Balance	Reparations	Foreign Borrowing
1924	7,810	9,626	+ 433	− 1,383	281	2,919
1925	9,546	11,990	+ 456	− 1,988	1,057	3,135
1926	10,677	9,884	+ 359	+ 1,152	1,191	607
1927	11,118	14,087	+ 300	− 2,669	1,584	3,792
1928	12,627	13,938	+ 109	− 1,202	1,990	4,123
1929	13,632	13,676	− 88	− 132	2,337	2,304
1930	12,175	10,617	− 462	+ 1,096	1,706	490
1931	9,733	6,955	− 750	+ 2,028	988	− 2,693
1932	5,384	4,782	− 635	+ 417	160	− 513

Sources: C. R. S. Harris, *Germany's Foreign Indebtedness* (London, 1935),
Appendix XII.

Even more ominous than this budgetary weakness was the chronic
imbalance of Germany's foreign trade (Table 12). Although exports
rose steadily they always lagged behind imports, except between June
1925 and May 1926 when the latter were temporarily reduced by a
domestic recession. The pronounced adverse trade balance of the
next two years reflected the heavy dependence of German industry in
periods of expansion on imported raw materials and semi-finished
products; and the trade gap only narrowed again during a further
recession in 1928. The consequent deficit on current account was not
bridged by invisible earnings but by a considerable inflow of foreign
loans. In the summer of 1927 Keynes observed that if Germany were

Wages Tax, Customs, and taxes on consumer goods. For subsequent budgetary policy:
H. Schacht, *Das Ende der Reparationen* (Oldenburg, 1931), 87–9; Landessteuergesetz
of 30 Mar. 1920, *Reichsgesetzblatt*, 1920, i. 402–16 (particularly paras. 17, 34, 37, 41);
Dritter Steuernotverordnung of 14 Feb. 1924, ibid. 1924, i. 82 (Article V); Gesetz über
Änderungen des Finanzausgleichs, 10 Aug. 1925, ibid. 1925, i. 254–6; E. Eyck, *Geschichte
der Weimarer Republik* (2 vols.; Erlenbach–Zurich, 1954–6), ii. 162–5; J. M. Keynes,
'The Coming Crisis in Reparations', *The New Republic*, 51 (3 Aug. 1927), 275–7. For
the domestic debate over the *Finanzausgleich*: Krohn, 49–52, 157–64. For Gilbert's
strictures: RC, *Report of the Agent-General for Reparation Payments, 10 June 1927*
(London, 1927) (henceforward RC xvi), 113–14; Memo for the German government,
20 Oct. 1927, in *Report of the Agent-General . . ., 10 Dec. 1927* (London, 1927) (henceforward RC xvii), 204.

to pay reparations otherwise than by borrowing from abroad she would have to convert her current import surplus of 1 billion marks into an export surplus of 2 to 3 billions a year. This would involve a 36-per-cent increase in the value of her exports or, allowing for the imported raw materials embodied in the added exports, an increase of between 40 and 50 per cent. Since well over half of Germany's exports consisted of coal, iron, steel, textiles, chemicals, and machinery, it was highly unlikely that her industrial competitors would allow this. The Dawes Plan, Keynes concluded, would break down 'according to schedule'. The only question was the price of its modification. 'How considerable a crisis will have to be provoked in Germany's internal affairs', he asked, 'before the facts are admitted?'[16]

The policies of the major creditor nations remained unconducive to a rational reparation settlement. Little could be expected from the United States government, which was committed first under Coolidge and then under Hoover to conservative financial policies of retrenchment, tax reduction, and rapid retirement of the public debt. American financial diplomacy was so penny-pinching in the mid-1920s that, not content with Owen Young's inflation of Germany's obligations so as to cover the repayment of Allied war debts, the American administration insisted on at least a token share of the Dawes annuities themselves. Although the anxiety of the American Dawes experts to preserve their impartial image prevented them from making a direct claim for reparations, they drafted Article XI of the Dawes Report so as to leave a loophole for a subsequent demand by the United States for a share of the spoils. When the American claim was duly registered in the second half of 1924, the French Government, which was negotiating another $100 million J. P. Morgan loan at the time, was prepared to support it. Not so, however, the British, who insisted with some justification that the reference in Article XI to the right of 'Associated Powers' to participate in deliberations over the apportionment of reparations did not remedy the disqualification of the United States from any right to reparations as a result of its refusal to ratify the Versailles Treaty. American face was only saved at a Paris conference of Finance Ministers in January 1925 when the ever-resourceful Colonel Logan induced the British government to withdraw its objections of principle in return for a financial formula which ensured that America's total reparation claim would amount to less than the

[16] Keynes, 'The Coming Crisis', loc. cit.

compensation already due to her for the costs of her army of occupation under the Wadsworth Agreement of 25 May 1923.[17]

The anxiety of the United States government to collect, or to appear to collect, such comparatively trifling sums indicated that there was no hope of any concessions on the larger issue of war debts. The Republican platform of 1924 proclaimed the party's 'steadfast refusal' to consider the cancellation of foreign debts; and that of 1928 proudly recorded that the amount funded thus far (including the sums involved in the as yet unratified French debt agreement) was more than $1.5 billion. Although the Republicans disclaimed any 'desire to be oppressive or grasping', this result had been achieved only by stern financial pressure in the form of embargoes on additional borrowing by recalcitrant debtors such as Italy and France. The uncompromising nature of American policy was further emphasized by the Republican Party's consistent support for protective tariffs 'as a fundamental and essential principle of the economic life of the nation'. This meant that the United States, while insisting on the repayment of its war loans, was denying its debtors the access to the American market which would have assisted them to discharge their obligations. The attitude of the American administration naturally increased the reluctance of the European victors to renounce their financial claims on each other and on Germany.[18]

British policy was even less enlightened in the period of the Dawes scheme than it had been in the early 1920s. Britain's return to the gold standard in April 1925 proved to be a major obstacle to the resolution of the reparation dispute. The move was designed by Churchill, the Chancellor of the Exchequer, and his supporters in the British banking fraternity to restore sterling to its pre-war standing as an international currency. But the overvaluation of the pound at its pre-war rate of $4.86 reduced the competitiveness of Britain's exports, increased her trade deficit, and made her more dependent on American loans to balance her international accounts. This increased external vulnerability coincided with five years of budgetary tight-rope walking

[17] For the drafting of Article XI: *FR*, 1924, ii. 1–8. For the subsequent American claim: ibid. 61–134. Text of Agreement of 14 Jan. 1925: ibid. 1925, ii. 145–65 at 150. Wandel, *Die Bedeutung*, 15–21.

[18] D. Burner, 'Election of 1924', in A. M. Schlesinger, jun., and F. L. Israel (edd.), *History of American Presidential Elections 1789–1968* (4 vols.; New York, 1971), iii. 2506–7; L. H. Fuchs, 'Election of 1928', ibid. 2627–8. For foreign loan supervision and high tariffs: J. H. Wilson, *American Business and Foreign Policy, 1920–1933* (Lexington, 1971), chs. 3–4. For a good discussion of the internal debates over American policy: Artaud, *Question des dettes interalliées*, ii. 699–710, 736–55.

TO-DAY'S BALANCING FEAT.

FIG. 7. The *Evening Standard*, 24 April 1928.

during Churchill's unhappy period at the Exchequer. The Chancellor's obsessive efforts to stimulate the British economy by lowering the tax burden on industrial and agricultural enterprises meant that regular revenues were almost invariably insufficient to cover expenditure. Since he was afraid to incur a deficit lest he should appear financially unorthodox or irresponsible, he frequently resorted to cavalier 'raids' on the capital of the Unemployment Insurance, Health Insurance, and Road Funds in order to balance his budgets. There was little likelihood that the British government, reduced as it was to such makeshift policies, would have either the strength or the inclination to engineer a more realistic reparation settlement. As Keynes observed in May 1928, Britain was by that time so concerned about the $100 million gap between the $166 million annuity it owed to the United States and the $64.2 million it was due to receive from its allies in 1928 that it had become intent upon making up the balance by claiming its share of the full Dawes annuity of 2.5 billion marks which would be payable from 1929.[19]

The French government had similar difficulty in coping with its financial problems between 1924 and 1928. After its electoral victory in 1924, the *Cartel des Gauches* jibbed at the proposals of the Socialist left for reducing the national debt by means of a capital levy or forced loan. The passing parade of Finance Ministers which began with the resignation of Clémentel in April 1925 (Caillaux, Loucheur, Doumer, Péret, then Caillaux again) failed to persuade the Chamber and Senate to accept even their less stringent proposals for heavier taxation. They therefore had recourse, *faute de mieux*, to the printing press with the result that the franc slid from 19.20 to 41.15 to the dollar between April 1925 and July 1926. This rapid depreciation prompted an emergency report on 3 July from a right-wing committee of enquiry composed of bankers and businessmen, the granting of special powers to a newly-formed Poincaré government on 24 July, and the official stabilization of the franc at about four centimes to the dollar. These measures were underpinned by a harsh financial programme heavily slanted towards indirect taxation, the logic of which was that the affluent classes of French society, like those of Germany in 1923–4, would only desist from exporting capital to evade taxes when the bulk of the fiscal burden was transferred to the shoulders of those who were

[19] D. E. Moggridge, *The Return to Gold 1925: The Formulation of Economic Policy and its Critics* (Cambridge, 1969); id., *British Monetary Policy, 1924–1931: The Norman Conquest of $4.86* (Cambridge, 1972). On Churchill's budgets: Hirst, 203–15; Grigg, 195–205. See also J. M. Keynes, 'A London View of War Debts', *The New Republic*, 55 (23 May 1928), 8–10.

least able to bear it. Poincaré's newly-awakened determination to cure the financial instability which he had done so much to induce drew ironical applause from Keynes:

One blames politicians not for consistency but for obstinacy. They are the interpreters not the makers of our fate. It is their job, in short, to register the *fait accompli*. In this spirit we all applaud M. Poincaré for not being hampered by a regard for consistency. After declaring for years that it would be an act of national bankruptcy and shame to devalue the franc, he has fixed it at about one-fifth of its pre-war gold value and has retorted with threats of resignation against anyone who would hinder him in so good a deed ... Since it removes an element of uncertainty from the money markets and stock exchanges of the world, and since French importers and manufacturers need hesitate no longer, a good deal of purchasing power, which had been lying idle, may be returned to active employment. M. Poincaré has therefore done something—perhaps for the first time in his career—to make the rest of us feel more cheerful.[20]

Although the inflationary policies and piecemeal fiscal reforms of Poincaré and his predecessors had effectively wiped out four-fifths of the French government's internal debt and raised revenue sufficient to service the remainder, France's external financial obligations remained formidable. The desire to forget about these in the hope that they would go away was reflected in Finance Minister Clémentel's failure to mention foreign debts in the 'balance sheet' which he presented to the Chamber of Deputies in December 1924. A retaliatory ban on American loans to France by the United States Treasury prompted the Briand government to agree, soon after it came to power in mid-1925, to the staging of Franco-American debt negotiations the following September. But the yawning gap between the token payment the French government was willing to offer and the sums the United States administration expected to receive soon caused the breakdown of these discussions and considerable ill feeling on both sides. Even the conclusion of an agreement in April 1926 between Andrew Mellon, the Secretary of the Treasury, and Henri Bérenger, the new French ambassador to the United States, did not lead to any real settlement. The compromise scheme of 62 annuities and an average rate of interest of 1.6 per cent proved unacceptable to the French Chamber, which

[20] For a good recent account of the Cartel's budgetary and monetary policies: Schuker, *End of French Predominance*, 126–40. See also Haig, 99–178; Goldey, 'The Disintegration of the *Cartel des Gauches*'; J. M. Keynes, 'The Stabilization of the Franc', *The New Republic*, 55 (18 July 1928), 218.

refused to ratify either this or an even less onerous agreement initialled by Caillaux and Churchill in July with respect to France's debts to Britain. The summer of 1927 witnessed demonstrations by French ex-servicemen against the Mellon–Bérenger Agreement, insults to American tourists, and increasing references to 'Uncle Shylock'; and the United States Treasury retaliated by maintaining its loan ban until the end of the year. Franco-American financial relations improved somewhat in 1928, even though Poincaré continued to give Coolidge and the Treasury heartburn by insisting until just before the presidential elections that any final reparation settlement should be associated with a downward revision of war debts. The Mellon–Bérenger Agreement was finally ratified in July 1929 for the short-term reason that a ten-year American credit of $407 million (for French purchases of American war surplus stores in 1919) would have had to be repaid unless it were absorbed in an overall debt settlement. More importantly, France had been given the financially unjustifiable but politically comforting assurance that her debts to the United States and Britain would be more than covered by the annuities she would receive from Germany under the Young Plan. The problem of France's external indebtedness had, in short, not been resolved but merely lumped onto the shoulders of Germany.[21]

Given the unenterprising financial policies of all the parties to the reparation dispute, the sporadic reparation negotiations of the mid-1920s were unlikely to achieve much. This was not for want of informed criticism of the Dawes Plan almost from its inception by leading authorities in the field of international finance. There was something of a sensation in June 1925 when Sir Josiah Stamp, acknowledged to be one of the most able of the Dawes experts, delivered a paper to the third congress of the International Chamber of Commerce in Brussels which stressed the virtually insuperable problems of transferring substantial reparations from Germany. Stamp went on, according to the New York Times correspondent's report, to 'astound and alarm' the American delegates at the conference by declaring that the United States was the nation most concerned in the payment of German reparations and suggesting that she should lower her tariffs if she really wanted the Dawes Plan to work. The creditor countries, he asserted, had to be 'prepared to make vital economic sacrifices, even to the extent

[21] For the fullest discussion: Artaud, *Question des dettes interalliées*, ii. 711–20, 755–878. Cf. B. D. Rhodes, 'Reassessing "Uncle Shylock": The United States and the French War Debt, 1917–1929', *J. of American History*, 55 (1969), 787–803.

of permitting extensive reduction of national industrial production, if the Dawes Plan were to be operated successfully'. Stamp's scepticism was shared by Maurice Desprets, a leading Brussels banker, who declared in his presidential speech to the congress that the belief in reparations as a means of repaying the money spent on repairing war damage and lightening the burden of taxpayers was 'a crude notion' which had been 'spread almost everywhere' for 'political reasons'. The equivocal reaction of Dawes and Young to Stamp's observations was also significant. Rather than making a full-scale defence of the Plan, the two Americans restricted themselves to stating that it was 'practical' and observing that the statesmen of Europe had accepted it as 'feasible and the best experimental program brought forth to meet the economic situation and aid Germany in meeting her obligations'.[22]

Stamp's strictures had no immediate effect because the Dawes Plan was still in its infancy and enjoyed the benefit of the doubt. Yet there was considerable justification for his insistence that the United States now had a controlling interest in the reparation scheme. The crucial role of the American financial élite in priming and maintaining the reparation pump was institutionally reflected in the virtual phasing out of the Reparation Commission and its replacement by the office of the Agent-General for Reparation Payments which the Dawes experts had established in Berlin as the day-to-day administrator of their plan. The eclipse of the commission coincided with the departure of the two most colourful personalities of the early years of the reparation saga. Sir John Bradbury, the commission's gangling wit, relinquished his position as British representative on 31 January 1925, and was soon to be heard celebrating his new-found independence by predicting with characteristic éclat to the Commercial Committee of the House of Commons that Germany would not pay more than half of the Dawes annuities. Shortly afterwards, his bulky American colleague, Colonel James Addison Logan, Junior, the taciturn behind-the-scenes negotiator who had represented his country in Paris in various capacities almost continuously since September 1914, also announced his retirement. He then disappeared briefly into the wings of international financial diplomacy via a trip to Poland to seek out investment opportunities for the American banking firm Dillon, Read, & Co. Into the shoes of these stalwarts stepped the austere

[22] NYT, 14 June 1925, 4 (Stamp); 22 June 1925, 1 (Desprets); 24 June 1925, 1 (Stamp); 27 June 1925, 1, 6 (Dawes and Young). For Young's privately expressed scepticism about the viability of the Dawes scheme: Wandel, Die Bedeutung, 24.

and youthful figure of Seymour Parker Gilbert, a graduate of the Harvard Law School, who had risen to be Under-Secretary of the United States Treasury in his late twenties and then spent a year with the New York legal firm of Cravath, Henderson, and de Gersdorff before becoming Agent-General for Reparations at the age of thirty-two. The circumstances surrounding Gilbert's appointment reflect the embarrassment of the United States about its emergence as the dominant power in the reparation question. Late in June 1924 the Reparation Commission, acting on behalf of the Franco-British banking establishment, had unanimously recommended that the post of Agent-General should be filled by Dwight Morrow, a partner of J. P. Morgan & Co., who was respected in European government circles for his part in co-ordinating the Allied war effort in 1917–18, and whose involvement was calculated to assist the flotation of a reparation loan in the United States. However, the United States government was sensitive to the advice of Logan (who had himself been passed over for the position because he was unacceptable to J. P. Morgan & Co.) that the appointment of an American banker would 'crystallise and confirm' the feeling in European political circles that the Dawes Plan represented the 'capitalistic dictation of Wall Street and the City of London'. Morrow was therefore prevailed upon to refuse the position for 'personal reasons' and was replaced by Gilbert, who initially enjoyed a much lower profile. Gilbert's close links with the Treasury and the fact that he was being groomed for a partnership in J. P. Morgan & Co. were, however, to have a crucial effect on his behaviour when the Dawes Plan began to creak at the joints late in 1927.[23]

Notwithstanding their efforts to remain unobtrusive, American financiers had a decisive influence over the outcome of reparation negotiations in the years that followed. An offer of American financial support and its withdrawal were the most important reasons for the occurrence and failure of the conversations between Stresemann and Briand at Thoiry in September 1926 about a package deal involving the evacuation of the Rhineland, the restoration to Germany of the Saar, and her repurchase of Eupen-Malmédy from Belgium in return for the commercialization of part of the reparation debt. The

---

[23] For Bradbury: *NYT*, 31 Jan. 1925, 2; 1 Feb. 1925, 1. For Logan: ibid. 8 Feb. 1925, iv. 4; 30 May 1925, 3; 31 May 1925, 14; 10 June 1925, 6. For Gilbert's career and appointment: ibid. 30 Oct. 1927, v. 9; *FR*, 1924, ii. 135–9; K. P. Jones, 'Discord and Collaboration: Choosing an Agent-General for Reparations', *Diplomatic History*, 1 (1977), 118–39; Nicolson, *Dwight Morrow*, 289–91. For Logan's unacceptability to J. P. Morgan & Co.: Artaud, *Question des dettes interalliées*, ii. 677–9.

negotiations would never have got off the ground if Logan, now combining principle with profit, had not offered on behalf of Dillon, Read, & Co. to underwrite the necessary bond sales in the United States after J. P. Morgan & Co. and the United States Treasury had thrown cold water on the project. The scheme came to nothing partly because France's need for foreign exchange, which had been one of the reasons for the proposed trade-off, ceased to be so urgent after the franc was stabilized in the summer of 1926. Stresemann also became concerned lest premature commercialization—the sale of reparation bonds to private investors—should prejudice future downward revision of Germany's obligations. Yet the major obstacle to the, advanced marketing of reparation bonds in return for a prompt revision of the territorial terms of the treaty—an arrangement which would have contributed substantially to the pacification of Europe—was Washington's current embargo on the flotation of French loans on the American market in retaliation for the non-ratification of the Mellon–Bérenger Agreement. As Parker Gilbert and Benjamin Strong, the governor of the Federal Reserve Bank, pointed out to Émile Moreau, the governor of the Banque de France, late in September 1926, this made it highly unlikely that American investors would be permitted to take up German reparation bonds, the proceeds of which were in large part destined for France.[24]

The interests of Wall Street and the United States Treasury determined in a more positive manner first the timing and then the scope of the efforts of Parker Gilbert in 1927 and 1928 to replace the Dawes Plan with a final reparation settlement. In his early years as Agent-General, Gilbert saw himself, and was regarded by others who had dealings with him, less as an American citizen than as an international civil servant whose duty it was to monitor Germany's capacity to pay and her creditors' ability to receive. In fulfilling this role he had, as we have seen, become concerned in 1927 about the rapid growth of Germany's imports and government expenditure. His memorandum of 20 October 1927 to Finance Minister Koehler had referred to 'over-spending and over-borrowing on the part of the German public authorities' which would, if unchecked, 'lead to severe economic reaction and depression and ... encourage the impression that Germany

---

[24] For an account of Thoiry which emphasizes the role of Wall Street and Washington: Wandel, *Die Bedeutung*, 42–77. For the best account in English: J. Jacobson, *Locarno Diplomacy: Germany and the West, 1925–1929* (Princeton, 1972), 84–90. For Gilbert, Strong, and Moreau: Émile Moreau, *Souvenirs d'un gouverneur de la Banque de France: Histoire de la stabilisation du franc (1926–1928)* (Paris, 1954), 113–14.

was not acting with due regard to her reparation obligations'. Yet in his annual report of 10 December 1927 Gilbert exceeded his monitoring brief and, without bothering to consult either the Reparation Commission or the creditor governments it represented, recommended the suspension of transfer protection and the fixing of Germany's total obligation. The stated reason for such a proposal, when the fourth year of the Dawes scheme had only just begun and it had been impossible to establish the feasibility or otherwise of the current annuity of 1.75 billion marks, was that the German government would not set its finances in order until it knew how much it owed and was given sole responsibility for discharging its debts. Yet Gilbert's sudden desire for a settlement was also a response to the renewed fears of influential denizens of Wall Street that reparations constituted a threat to American investments in Europe and an impediment to world trade.[25]

This sort of anxiety had been reinforced in the second half of 1927 by predictions that reparations would take precedence over interest payments on the considerable number of American private loans which had been extended to Germany in recent years. Concern had been expressed about the 'priority question' within the Department of State and the Department of Commerce from the inception of the Dawes Plan. One of the first to sound the alarm again in 1927 was the seasoned revisionist Bernard M. Baruch, who, on returning to New York after a summer vacation in England and France, warned that under the Dawes scheme interest on private loans could not be transferred from Germany if the Transfer Committee considered that such remittances would jeopardize reparations. This problem, Baruch declared with tongue in cheek, had evidently not been taken into account by the Dawes Committee and would necessitate a 'complete revision' of the Dawes programme and 'force the making of a definite figure to be paid by Germany'. Baruch's concern was shared by the Department of State, which advised an American banking firm early in October to be wary about investing in a Prussian State Loan because of the 'serious complications in connection with interest and amortization payments by German borrowers [which might] arise from possible future action by the Agent-General and the Transfer Committee'. Such fears had been compounded by the prediction of Keynes in August that Germany

[25] For Gilbert's conception of his role, and his activities late in 1927: Lindsay to Chamberlain, 27 Oct. 1927; Lindsay to Tyrrell, 23 Nov. 1927, DBFP IA, iv. 69–72, 121–3. See also n. 15 above. For his cavalier treatment of the RC: Lindsay to Tyrrell, 9 Dec. 1927; Sargent to Phipps, 5 Jan. 1928; Goodchild to Phipps, 14 Jan. 1928, DBFP IA, iv. 175–7, 209–10, 220–3.

would be unable to meet her future reparation obligations without a continuing influx of foreign loans. By late October the *New York Times* was carrying nervous reports about the recent decline of American lending to Germany and the doubts of Washington officialdom as to whether she would be able to pay the fifth Dawes annuity of $625 million (due in 1928–9) as well as service her billion dollar borrowings from the United States. It was a measure of American financial apprehension that in November George P. Auld, a former Accountant-General of the Reparation Commission who had been Owen Young's assistant in 1924, published a polemic entitled *The Dawes Plan and the New Economics*, the avowed aim of which was to persuade American investors to ignore Keynes and continue lending to Germany.[26]

These circumstances, and the anxiety of Benjamin Strong about possible exchange instability in Europe because of its increasing indebtedness to the United States, clearly moved Gilbert, the aspiring partner of J. P. Morgan & Co., the underwriters of the Dawes Loan, to call for the suspension of transfer protection and the fixing of Germany's obligations. Although he was careful to refrain from any reference to the problem of Germany's credit-worthiness in his published report of 10 December, Gilbert addressed himself explicitly to the subject both in a conversation with Poincaré on 18 January and in a confidential memorandum of 24 February 1928 which summarized for the mystified and indignant Reparation Commission his reasons for single-handedly advocating a final reparation settlement. The theoretical question of 'the relative rank of private capital and reparation debts' had, he wrote, 'been the subject of increasingly active public discussion during the past year, and sooner or later [might] prove to be a serious deterrent to the inflow of the additional foreign capital which [was] needed for the reconstruction of Germany'. There was, he advised, no satisfactory solution to the 'priority question' except 'a final determination of Germany's reparation liabilities', which would place Germany in the same position as any other country owing foreign debts and enable foreign investors 'to make up their own minds in the usual way as to how far existing debts, in view of their nature or amount, make it wise to extend additional loans or credits'.[27]

[26] For American concern about priority: Artaud, *Question des dettes interalliées*, ii. 881–6; Link, *Stabilisierungspolitik*, 389–96; Wandel, *Die Bedeutung*, 87–96. For Baruch: *NYT*, 3 Aug. 1927, 1. Cf. Sec. State to Messrs Sullivan and Cromwell, 11 Oct. 1927, *FR*, 1927, ii. 727–30; *NYT*, 24 Oct. 1927, 5. For Keynes: see above, n. 15.

[27] For Strong's anxiety: Artaud, *Question des dettes interalliées*, ii. 88–9. For Gilbert's

Because of Gilbert's sympathy for the Wall Street view that reparation payments should be restricted within the bounds of commercial
reality, the sort of settlement he originally envisaged involved a genuine
writing down of both reparations and war debts. Although he subsequently denied that he espoused any specific plan, the scenario that
he sketched to French political and financial leaders in January 1928
was that Germany should, in return for an early evacuation of the
Rhineland, raise $4 billion by selling railway bonds and industrial
securities, the interest of which was to be guaranteed by Britain and
France. The yield from this operation would be used by Germany's
European creditors to make an advanced repayment of their American
war debts, the value of which would be heavily discounted. Britain,
relieved of her obligations to the United States, would then be in a
position to honour her undertaking in the Balfour Note and waive
both her reparation claims on Germany and her war loans to France.
A further issue of reparation bonds secured only by the goodwill of
the German government could then be made to provide cash payments
to defray part of the reconstruction expenditures of France and
Belgium.[28]

The trouble with this scheme, as Gilbert, an ex-Treasury official,
must have known, was that, whatever its attractions to Wall Street,
it was anathema to Washington because it involved a substantial
reduction of Allied war debts to the United States. The reservations
of the American Treasury were quickly made public on 19 December
1927 when Secretary Mellon, after commending the idea of a final
reparation settlement, reaffirmed his view that there was no connection
between reparations and war debts. Although the European parties to
the reparation dispute were aware that this declaration did not reflect
the personal convictions of Mellon and other members of the American
administration, most of them soon concluded that the unlikelihood of
any relaxation of American war-debt policy until after the forthcoming
presidential elections made a viable reparation settlement impossible
in the immediate future. It was this calculation that was primarily
responsible for the cool response of both the British and German

conversation with Poincaré: France, Ministère de l'Économie–Ministère du Budget:
Archives Économiques et Financières (henceforth AEF), F30, 1283, Notes prises au cours
de conversations entre M. Poincaré ... et M. Gilbert. For his memorandum of 24 Feb.
1928: *ADAP* viii. 242–9.

[28] AEF F30, 1282, Dossier 'Notes Seydoux', Visite de Mr Parker Gilbert, 17 Jan. 1928;
F30, 1283, Notes prises ..., Conversation 18 Jan. 1928; Moreau, *Souvenirs*, 475–7;
Sargent to Lindsay, 26 Mar. 1928, *DBFP* IA, iv. 320–1.

governments to Gilbert's proposal in the first half of 1928, although the British Treasury in any case inclined to the view that it would be unwise to attempt a final settlement until the Dawes Plan had been given a more extended trial, and the German Foreign Office, for its part, considered that it would be tactically preferable to postpone final reparation negotiations until the Rhineland had been cleared of foreign troops.[29]

Despite the opposition of Germany, Britain, and the minor creditors, Gilbert's suggestion bore stunted fruit in the summer of 1928 when it became a means of resolving the long-standing deadlock between France and the United States over the ratification of the Mellon–Bérenger Agreement. Since his return to office in July 1926 Poincaré, while sanctioning on a year-to-year basis the war-debt repayments prescribed by this agreement, had adopted a stonewalling policy towards its formal ratification. The objective of French policy, to judge from a memorandum drafted by Jacques Seydoux in July 1926, was to play for time until France's obligations were further reduced by her creditors or until the Dawes annuities had risen sufficiently to demonstrate the feasibility of a final reparation settlement in which Germany would foot the bill for France's outpayments to her allies as well as her domestic reconstruction costs. In the first half of 1928 Gilbert's advocacy of a staggered commercialization and scaling down of reparations and war debts seemed to indicate that the first alternative might be within reach, even if Poincaré was wary of the Agent-General's insistence that the liquidation of war debts should follow rather than accompany any reparation settlement. As the year progressed, however, the preoccupation of American investors with domestic stock exchange speculation made it unlikely that sufficient funds would be forthcoming for Gilbert's commercialization scheme to be realized. With the approach of the presidential elections the American administration also became extremely reluctant to discuss war-debt remission and began instead to step up the pressure on the French government to ratify the Mellon–Bérenger Agreement. By the summer

---

[29] For Mellon: *NYT*, 20 Dec. 1927, 45. For his personal views and his reluctance to act before the elections: Gilbert to Mellon, 7 May 1928; Mellon to Gilbert, 24 May 1928, David E. Finley Papers, Box 6, Files 'Foreign Debts owed to U.S.' and 'Gilbert, Seymour Parker'. For British reaction: Minute by Sargent in Howard to Chamberlain, 30 Dec. 1927; Lindsay to Chamberlain, 14 Jan. 1928; Sargent to Lindsay, 2, 10 Apr. 1928, *DBFP* IA, iv. 202, 219–20, 338–9 n. 2, 347–8. For German reaction: memo by Vallette, 27 Dec. 1927; Circular by Ritter, 27 Dec. 1927; Circulars by Stresemann, 30 Jan. 1928, 18 Apr. 1928, *ADAP* vii. 571–3, 576–8; viii. 108–13, 504–11.

of 1928 Gilbert was acting less as Agent-General for Reparations than as a conduit pipe for the views of his former superiors in the United States Treasury. In conversations with Poincaré on 23 July and with representatives of the Banque de France on 16 August he transmitted Secretary Mellon's plea for prompt ratification and confirmed that France would be expected to repay the American war stocks credit of $406 million in August 1929 if ratification had not been achieved by that date. All that he could suggest to Poincaré was that he should persuade the Chamber to ratify the agreement by holding out the prospect of a subsequent general liquidation of war debts. Yet this made him vulnerable to the retort that ratification would be pointless if it were a mere prelude to liquidation; and he was forced to concede that it would be simpler if Germany were made responsible for France's debt repayments over the next sixty-two years. In the next few months Gilbert continued to pay lip service to the idea of a commercialized settlement and Poincaré intermittently advocated a general liquidation of reparations and war debts. Yet both became increasingly committed in practice to an *ad hoc* settlement which would resolve, at Germany's expense, the Franco-American financial impasse.[30]

Despite the growing confluence of French and American interests, the other parties to the reparation dispute had still to be convinced of the desirability of an early settlement. Paradoxically, it was Germany, the nation with most to lose, that was most open to persuasion in the summer of 1928. To a certain extent this was because of the diplomatic expectations which had been brought to a pitch by the elections of May. The Social Democrats, who ended up with twice as many seats as any other party in the Reichstag and held key portfolios in the middle-of-the-way 'cabinet of personalities' which took office in June, had campaigned strongly for Stresemann's policy of immediate unconditional evacuation of the Rhineland. They had also declared, with the encouragement of Poincaré, that a socialist-led government would be more likely to obtain territorial treaty revision than the reigning right-of-centre *Bürgerbloc*, whose Nationalist Party members aroused the suspicion of Germany's former enemies. For these reasons Hermann Müller gave pride of place to the evacuation issue in his inaugural speech to the Reichstag as Chancellor on 3 July. Although he was guarded about the timing and nature of a final adjustment of

---

[30] AEF, F30, 1282, Dossier 'Notes Seydoux', Note 64–26, 15 July 1926; F30, 1283, Notes prises ..., Conversation 18 Jan. 1928, 23 July 1928; F30, 1282, Dossier 'Notes Seydoux', Moret to Poincaré, 18 Aug. 1928.

reparations, the campaign for immediate evacuation which he now launched was bound to precipitate discussion of Germany's obligations because the French government was adamant that its troops would not be withdrawn until its financial claims against Germany had been put on a secure basis.[31]

That this discussion developed into provocative play-acting about a final resolution of the reparation problem was due in no small measure to the duplicity of Gilbert in working both to secure the short-term interests of France and the United States and to persuade the German government that a commercially viable settlement was still possible. The alleged imminence of such a settlement was used by the Agent-General to scotch Stresemann's attempt early in 1928 to revive the Thoiry scheme of partial commercialization of Germany's obligations in return for an immediate evacuation of the Rhineland. The dubious objection which Gilbert advanced against this proposal, which would have assisted the pacification of Europe by achieving the speedy removal of foreign troops from German soil and obviating the traumatic Young negotiations of the following year, was that the American market would be unable to absorb bonds issued in the course of a partial mobilization if it was known that a final settlement was just around the corner. Yet the real reason for American opposition to such a scheme was still, as Gilbert was well aware, that by providing ready cash for France it would take the pressure off her to ratify the Mellon–Bérenger Agreement. Apart from his efforts to torpedo any attempt at a partial mobilization of Germany's obligations, the Agent-General used two contradictory arguments in favour of a 'final' settlement. The first, which appears to have made an impression on Schacht, the president of the Reichsbank, was that to delay a settlement until there was a transfer crisis (as the British government urged) would be damaging to German credit and to American investments in Germany. The second, which he used after German credit had recovered in the middle of 1928, and evidently appealed to Julius Curtius, Müller's DVP Economics Minister, was that the expected improvement in the

---

[31] For SPD election promises: Wels, 29 Mar. 1928, RT cccxcv. 13880–1; Breitscheid, Vorwärts, 1 May 1928, No. 205, 2. Note interview between Victor Schiff, the editor of Vorwärts, and Poincaré on 20 Apr.: Schiff to Stresemann, 5 June 1928, enc. at 12, Nachlass Stresemann, lxvii. For Müller's declaration: RT cdxxiii. 38–9. For French insistence of tying evacuation to a financial settlement: Memo by Schubert, 6 Mar. 1928; Hoesch to A. Amt, 3 Apr., 12 July 1928, ADAP viii. 293–6, 431–4; ix. 328–9. Cf. Phipps to Sargent, 19 Mar. 1928, DBFP IA, iv. 300–1.

German trade balance would cause any settlement arrived at in later years to be more onerous. Yet the undoubted influence which Gilbert wielded over German policy in the second half of 1928 arose less from his conflicting prognostications than from the hopes which were inspired by his Wall Street connections. The vision of a financially realistic settlement dictated by the bankers of New York was what prompted Schacht to throw in his lot with Gilbert and become the most powerful German advocate of definitive reparation negotiations. 'The bankers of the world', Schacht told Ambassador Lindsay in June, 'would see to it that Germany did not offer to pay too much; they knew what could be floated and how much Germany could afford to pay for the service of commercialized loans.' Schacht, whose international banking affiliations sat somewhat awkwardly with his Nietzschean desire to 'smash the Dawes Plan', was also attracted to a bankers' settlement because he believed it would involve freeing Germany from all foreign controls. In a letter to Stresemann on 20 September, a few days after the conclusion of the Geneva Agreement, he argued that the psychological moment had arrived for a completely new settlement (*um aufs Ganze zu gehen*). 'Almost more important than the sums involved', he went on, 'is the restoration of our absolute diplomatic freedom. The last vestiges of restraints, controls, and unresolved questions must be swept away. Only in this way can the confidence be created in the money markets of the world which will make a large-scale funding operation possible.'[32]

Having done so much to promote the idea of a final as opposed to a partial reparation settlement amongst Germany's financial leaders, Gilbert took advantage of his physical presence in Berlin to help stage-manage the necessary diplomatic preliminaries. Throughout July and August he pressed the German government to let it be understood that, after formally demanding immediate unconditional evacuation of the Rhineland, it would be prepared to agree to parallel negotiations on the evacuation and reparation questions. Not without some prompting by Gilbert via Schacht and Curtius, this tactic was followed by Müller when he raised the evacuation issue during a League of

---

[32] For Gilbert's opposition to a Thoiry-style partial settlement: Memo by Schubert, 28 Feb. 1928, *ADAP* viii. 264–5. For his arguments in favour of a prompt 'final' settlement: ibid. 267–8; Memo by Schubert, 18 Aug. 1928, ibid. ix. 585–8. For Curtius: J. Curtius, *Der Young-Plan: Entstellung und Wahrheit* (Stuttgart, 1950), 22–3. For Schacht: Lindsay to Chamberlain, 23 June 1928, *DBFP* IA, v. 130–3; Schacht to Stresemann, 20 Sept. 1928, *ADAP* x. 119–22. For observations on Schacht's 'rather Nietzschean personality': Lindsay to Chamberlain, 14 Jan. 1928, *DBFP* IA, iv. 219–20.

Nations Council meeting in Geneva in September. As a result, an agreement in principle was reached between Germany and her five major creditors on 16 September to inaugurate 'official negotiations in regard to the early evacuation of the Rhineland' and to appoint a committee of financial experts to devise 'a complete and final settlement of the reparation problem'.[33]

After Germany had taken this initiative Gilbert's overriding concern was to ensure that the coming negotiations would not embarrass the American administration by impinging on the war-debt question. Poincaré, never a man to throw away a useful card, had dismayed the Agent-General by advocating a settlement involving a reduction of both reparations and war debts during a campaign speech to a radical socialist audience at Carcassonne on 1 April; and he had kept the idea alive by stressing the common interest of France and Germany in a downward revision of war debts during conversations with Hoesch, the German ambassador to France, and Stresemann during the latter's visit to Paris late in August on the occasion of the signature of the Kellogg Pact. This accounted for Gilbert's reaction in September when, in response to American press reports that Müller and Briand were concerting a Franco-German *démarche* on the war-debt question at Geneva, he got Schacht to warn Müller to desist from such a course. To judge from his conversation with Gilbert on 20 September, Poincaré did not finally relinquish this option until he announced formally in a speech at Chambéry on 30 September that he wanted a reparation settlement which would produce annuities sufficiently large to cover France's outpayments to her allies plus an unspecified *indemnité nette* to defray her reconstruction expenditure. The election-eve anxiety of the American government was such that even this declaration was misconstrued as yet another attempt to link war debts and reparations to the detriment of the former. Renewed protests by Coolidge and Mellon made it necessary for Poincaré and Gilbert to reassure the Agent-General's former Treasury superiors that France was not making an oblique appeal to the United States for financial

[33] For Gilbert's pressure: Memo by Kiep, 6 July 1928; Memo by Schubert, 27 July, 18 Aug. 1928, *ADAP* ix. 288–90, 448–55, 585–8. For preliminary discussions between Müller and Briand at Geneva on 5 Sept. 1928: *Akten der Reichskanzlei: Weimarer Republik. Das Kabinett Müller II, 28. Juni 1928 bis 27. März 1930*, ed. M. Vogt (2 vols.; Boppard-on-Rhine, 1970), i. 77–84. For prompting via Schacht and Curtius: *ADAP* x. 18–19 n. 4; Curtius, *Der Young-Plan*, 26–7. For subsequent discussions between Germany and her five major creditors: *ADAP* x. 42–5, 53–61, 73–82; *DBFP* IA, v. 294–303. For declaration of 16 Sept. 1928: Cushendun to Lindsay, 18 Sept. 1928, ibid. 335.

clemency but merely setting the lower limit on her demands upon Germany.[34]

After Poincaré had come into line, Gilbert turned his attention to the British, who remained intractable opponents of any settlement which did not involve a reduction of war debts. Churchill's response to the Agent-General's initial overtures in April had been simply to administer 'a little dose of the Balfour Note'. A flicker of cupidity had been aroused in the Treasury early in June when Gilbert, after attacking the stand-pat policies advocated by Walter Layton, the editor of *The Economist*, and leading authorities in Treasury and Bank of England circles such as Otto Niemeyer and Josiah Stamp, asserted that Britain was seriously underestimating Germany's capacity to pay and that he 'would be prepared to advise the German government ... to accept as a total liability a payment which, expressed in terms of an annuity, would be ... very nearly the equivalent of the present maximum payment under the Dawes Plan'. However, a memorandum of 19 June by Leith-Ross, Churchill's Treasury adviser on reparations, insisted that a final settlement yielding the sums envisaged by Gilbert would be technically impossible. After pointing out Gilbert's inconsistency in pressing for the mobilization of Germany's obligations a few months after he had warned that the market was in danger of saturation with German securities, Leith-Ross predicted that the bankers might take up 8 or 10 billion marks (approximately $2 billion) of reparation bonds over an extended period. But they would do so only 'at a yield and subject to a commission so usurious that all the Allied governments will be unanimous in rejecting their offers as tending to impoverish Germany without enriching us'. It would be far better, he concluded, for Britain to persist with the Dawes Plan if she wished to achieve the aim of the Balfour Note, which was to balance her outpayments to the United States with reparation receipts and debt repayments from her allies. In a further memorandum endorsed by Churchill late in September, Leith-Ross, after rehearsing the same arguments, surmised that Gilbert's eagerness for a final settlement was

[34] For Poincaré's Carcassonne speech: Jacobson, *Locarno Diplomacy*, 162. For Gilbert's dismay: Moreau, *Souvenirs*, 526–8. For Poincaré on a Franco-German united front against the United States: Interview with Victor Schiff, 20 Apr. 1928, loc. cit. n. 31 above; Hoesch to A. Amt, 12 July 1928; Memo by Stresemann, 27 Aug. 1928, *ADAP* x. 327–31, 640; AEF, F30, 1283, Notes prises ..., 20 Sept. 1928. For the Müller–Briand conversation of 5 Sept: *Das Kabinett Müller II*, i. 77–84. For Schacht's note of 6 Sept. 1928: *ADAP* x. 19 n. 4. For Chambéry and American scepticism: *NYT*, 1 Oct. 1928, 1; 2 Oct. 1928, 28 (Mellon); 3 Oct. 1928, 1 (Coolidge); 4 Oct. 1928, 28 (Poincaré).

'perhaps influenced by his desire to get back as soon as possible to the United States with the reputation of having finally settled reparations on a basis which enables the United States Government to justify the maintenance of their debt-collecting policy'. Although Gilbert subsequently rejected suggestions that he wished to wind up his European activities, Leith-Ross was correct in emphasizing his preoccupation with protecting American war-debt claims.[35]

The unyielding attitude of the British Treasury was reflected in Churchill's misgivings about the Geneva decision of 16 September and his instructions to Lord Cushendun, the British representative at the negotiations, to have the appointment of the proposed committee of experts delayed for as long as possible. Soon, however, the Chancellor himself had succumbed to Gilbert's persuasion. During a tête-à-tête at Chartwell on the weekend of 12–13 October, Gilbert, as Churchill informed the cabinet a few days later, 'shed some new light on the question' and declared that Germany would be both able *and willing* to pay an annuity of 2 billion marks for a sufficient number of years to enable the Allies to discharge their debts to America. Reassured that Germany's willingness to borrow and the international banking community's propensity to lend would be twice as great as Leith-Ross had forecast, the gallant, but highly susceptible, Chancellor sallied forth to Paris with Gilbert to see Poincaré. There he had little difficulty in reaching an agreement with the French premier on 19 October about a scheme of reparation annuities which would underpin the structure of the war debts of Britain and France both to each other and to the United States. P. J. Grigg, Churchill's Private Secretary, who was the only other person present at these discussions apart from Gilbert and an interpreter, subsequently recorded that Poincaré was 'unusually amiable'.[36]

Having tailored the coming settlement to the immediate political requirements of the United States and France, and having short-circuited the British Treasury, Gilbert returned to Berlin—via Brussels,

---

[35] For Gilbert's unsuccessful overtures: Sargent to Lindsay, 10 Apr. 1928; Lindsay to Chamberlain, 30 May 1928, 15 June 1928, *DBFP* IA, iv. 347–8; v. 78–82, 114–15. For the Leith-Ross memo of 19 June 1928: F. Leith-Ross, *Money Talks* (London, 1968), 103–5. Cf. Memo by Dutton, 9 July 1928, enc. in Nicolson to Chamberlain, 24 July 1928; Memo by Churchill, 28 Sept. 1928, *DBFP* IA, v. 195–202, 354–64.

[36] For Churchill's uneasiness: Birkenhead to Cazalet, 15 Sept. 1928, ibid. 311–12. For Chartwell and the cabinet meeting: ibid. 385–6 n. 2; Cabinet Minutes, 47(28), 17 Oct. 1928, CAB 23/59. For Paris discussions: Memo by Churchill, 19 Oct. 1928, enc. in Tyrrell to Cushendun, 20 Oct. 1928, ibid. 391–4. See also: Jacobson, *Locarno Diplomacy*, 203–6, 216–17; Grigg, 208–9.

where he had little success in allaying the fears of the Belgians—to sell his package to the Germans. When reporting to Müller, Schacht, and Hilferding, the Finance Minister, on 25 October Gilbert did not hesitate to trade on the trust which Germany's financial leaders placed in him. Although he stressed that the creditor powers had defined 'their minimum requirements and were all proceeding on the assumption that ... no further concessions were to be expected from the United States in respect of their war debts', he refrained from mentioning the minimum annuity of 2 billion marks which had been agreed upon in his discussions with Churchill and Poincaré. Similarly, while referring to a 'difference of opinion' about whether the experts were to be truly independent or bound by their governments, he declared, somewhat equivocally, that 'the present trend of sentiment was in favour of an unofficial as distinguished from an official committee'. The impression Gilbert created was reflected in Müller's remark at the end of the discussion that no agreement about figures could be expected at this stage 'since it was the object of the committee to examine the capacity of Germany and arrive at its own conclusions'. Calculated wishful thinking may have played its part: but such insouciance, in the face of warnings from an incensed Leith-Ross about what had been transacted at Paris, also indicated a misplaced faith in the desire of Gilbert and the American financial establishment to engineer a commercially rational settlement.[37]

This faith, which was forcibly expressed in a letter from Schacht to Müller on 26 October, underlay the decision of the German cabinet on the same day to call formally for the drawing up of a 'definite and complete settlement' by a committee of 'independent financial experts enjoying international reputation and authority in their own countries and not tied by any instructions of their respective governments'. A foreign office circular of 27 October to all German diplomatic missions confidently asserted that any attempt to control the independence of committee members would preclude effective American participation and thereby prejudice the sale of reparation bonds in the American market. The unreal insistence of the German government that the coming negotiations were to be the preserve of bankers rather than politicians was responsible for the deadlock which now developed between Germany and her European creditors. In response to the

[37] For Gilbert at Brussels: Granville to Cushendun, 25 Oct. 1928, *DBFP* IA, v. 417–19. For his report to Berlin: unsigned memo of 25 Oct., *ADAP* x. 208–13. For Leith-Ross's warning: Dieckhoff to A. Amt, 19 Oct. 1928, ibid. 188–90.

F𝚒𝚐. 8. The *Evening Standard*, 7 January 1929.

German note, which was duly presented on 30 October, about the setting up of the committee, Poincaré and Churchill not only reserved the right to instruct French and British experts as they thought fit, but also added insult to injury by insisting that the committee should be formally appointed by the Reparation Commission and that its terms of reference should be more narrowly defined than in the Geneva declaration of 16 September. German resistance finally collapsed only when it was confirmed that the United States government, far from being an impartial and moderating influence, was solely interested in ensuring the smooth collection of its war debts. The preoccupation of American policy was made clear when Gilbert informed Hilferding during discussions on 27–8 November that the more restrictive terms of reference which he had devised instead of the Geneva communiqué were needed in order to defuse the allegations of the Hearst press in the United States that the war-debts question would be raised during the forthcoming deliberations. German disillusionment was complete when Mellon declared on 9 December that the United States was not particularly concerned about who formally nominated American experts, but was keenly interested that the committee should meet promptly so as to 'expedite the ratification of the Mellon–Bérenger Agreement and provide clarification about France's future payments'. Stresemann derived little comfort from Briand's assurances during a League of Nations meeting at Lugano on the same day that the nomination of experts by the Reparation Commission would be a pure formality and that, notwithstanding Poincaré's refusal to depart from the terms of his Chambéry speech, the committee of experts would be 'composed of practical men in search of a practical solution'. Both Stresemann and Schubert had already taken Gilbert to task in mid-November for having prearranged a settlement which would not be based on a realistic investigation of Germany's capacity. Gilbert had on this occasion admitted that annuities of between 2 and 2.5 billion marks would be demanded. Yet all that he could say in defence of such an imposition was that an onerous settlement would be preferable to the alternative of waiting for the economy to collapse under the strain of the Dawes Plan; and that Germany's co-operation would enhance her credit-worthiness and her moral standing. The Agent-General betrayed the ruthlessness of American financial policy when commenting to Rowe-Dutton on 7 November about the protests which Schacht had also been making about the straightjacketing of the proposed committee:

Dr. Schacht would blow off steam whatever happened. In the end, however, his devotion to German credit would keep him within bounds ... If Dr. Schacht in particular and the German Government in general said too much they would find themselves in a very difficult position. They would be very badly off if they failed to settle and in doing so impaired German credit ...

Because it was aware of its absolute financial dependence, for good or ill, on the United States, the Müller government ultimately had no alternative but to accept the face-saving but meaningless concessions which Poincaré made about the terms of reference of the committee and the method of appointment of its members in the agreement which he formally concluded with Hoesch, the German ambassador to France, on 19 December and which was made public on 22 December. Yet the evident preoccupation of the creditor powers with serving their short-term political interests rather than the cause of stabilization and pacification ensured that the coming negotiations would produce a settlement which would help to shake the financial and political structure of the western world to its foundations.[38]

[38] Schacht to Müller, 26 Oct. 1928, *Das Kabinett Müller II*, i. 176–7; Minister-besprechung 26 Oct. 1928, ibid. 177–80; Circular of 27 Oct. 1928; Hoesch to A. Amt, 3 Nov. 1928; Dieckhoff to A. Amt, 5 Nov. 1928; Stresemann to Hoesch, 5 Nov. 1928, *ADAP* x. 224–31, 266–77. Cf. Cushendun to Rumbold, 30 Oct. 1928; Cushendun to Tyrrell, 1 Nov. 1928, *DBFP* IA, v. 424, 433–6. For Gilbert's conversations with Hilferding on 27 and 28 Nov.: *Das Kabinett Müller II*, i. 242–3, 258–9. For Mellon: Prittwitz to A. Amt, 9 Dec. 1928, *ADAP* x. 474–5. For Lugano: Memo by Stresemann, 9 Dec. 1928, ibid. 476–82. For Gilbert's conversations with Stresemann and Schubert on 13 and 14 Nov. 1928: ibid. 315–22, 376–83; and with Rowe-Dutton: Rumbold to Cushendun, 7 Nov. 1928, *DBFP* IA, v. 444–8. For agreement of 19 Dec. 1928: Ritter to Prittwitz, 19 Oct. 1928, *ADAP* x. 550–2.

8

The Young Plan

TRUE to its makeshift origins, the Young Committee proved more concerned to shore up the creaking structure of inter-Allied indebtedness than to devise a genuine final reparation settlement. For this reason its recommendations enjoyed the powerful, if schizophrenic, support of the United States, the arch-creditor nation. The Young Plan was also welcomed, after some initial misgivings, by France and the minor European creditors because it recommended that their foreign-debt repayments should henceforth be covered by reparation receipts. It was not, however, well received in Britain, whose prolonged efforts to obtain the cancellation of inter-Allied debts had suffered a serious setback, and whose relative share of the spoils was appreciably diminished under the new dispensation. British disapproval was mild by comparison with that of Germany, whose financial capacity had never really been taken into account by the Young experts. The dissatisfaction of Britain and Germany was responsible for the protracted and acrimonious struggle over the ratification of the Plan at the Hague Conferences of August 1929 and January 1930.

THE DELIBERATIONS OF THE YOUNG COMMITTEE

Because of the tactical manœuvring of all parties, the labours of the Young Committee to achieve a 'complete and final settlement' of reparations were foredoomed to failure. It mattered little that the committee was composed of outstanding financial experts, most of whom had been steeped in the complexities of the reparation problem by service on the Reparation Commission, the Dawes Committee, or the supervisory bodies created by the Dawes Plan. Nor did the reinforcement of its ranks by leaders of the international banking fraternity such as J. P. Morgan, junior, and Lord Revelstoke, the head of Baring Brothers, have any significant effect. Both men played an important part as intermediaries, even if Morgan, accustomed to delivering *ex cathedra* judgments, was initially disconcerted by the cut and thrust of the proceedings. Yet, far from injecting a note of financial realism, the presence of the two moguls tended, if anything, to pre-empt the healthy criticism which had been levelled at the Dawes Committee by Anglo-American bankers in 1924. The false position in which Morgan and Revelstoke were placed almost certainly contributed to the latter's sudden death on 19 April after he had spent the previous day in a vain attempt to bridge the politically-induced gap between Germany and her creditors. Morgan's professional irrelevance was symbolized more frivolously by his departure on an extended Adriatic cruise in his private yacht with the archbishop of Canterbury at a crucial stage of the committee's negotiations.[1]

Morgan, in fact, accepted from the outset that the attention of the Young Committee would be focused not on the technical problem of mobilizing Germany's debt at a level which was within her capacity but on the essentially political question of the number and size of the annuities she would be asked to pay. This was only partly because, as Gilbert reported to Kellogg in January 1929, the demand for money created by the American stock exchange boom had made the commercialization of Germany's obligations impossible. Commercialization,

[1] On the reasons for Morgan's appointment: Stuart M. Crocker Papers, Memoirs from the Young Plan Days, 7–8. The members of the Young Committee were: *Belgium*: Émile Francqui, banker, vice-president of Société Générale de Belgique; Camille Gutt, banker, Minister of Finance, 1920–4, 1934–5. *Alternates*: Baron Terlinden; Henri Fabri, vice-president of the Belgian National Bank. *France*: Émile Moreau, governor of the Bank of France; Jean Parmentier, director, Crédit Foncier de France. *Alternates*: C. Moret, formerly director, Mouvement Général des Fonds, Ministry of Finance; deputy governor of the Bank of France; Edgar Allix, Professor of Law, University of Paris. *Germany*: Dr Hjalmar Schacht, president of the Reichsbank; Dr Albert Vögler, chairman of directors, Vereinigten Stahlwerke, AG. *Alternates*: Dr Carl Melchior, partner of M. M. Warburg & Co., Hamburg; Dr Ludwig Kastl, executive director, RDI. *Italy*: Dr Alberto Pirelli, president of Pirelli Cable and Rubber Co., president of International Chamber of Commerce; Fulvio Suvich, former Under-Secretary, Ministry of Finance, vice-president of Italian Petroleum Co. (AGIP). *Alternates*: Giuseppe Bianchini, banker, editor *Rivista Bancaria*; Bruno Dolcetta. *Great Britain*: Sir Josiah Stamp, president of LMS Railway Co.; director of the Bank of England; Lord Revelstoke, partner of Baring Bros., Bankers; director of the Bank of England. *Alternates*: Sir Charles Addis, chairman of London Committee of Hongkong-Shanghai Bank; director of the Bank of England; Sir Basil Blackett, former Controller of Finance, HM Treasury; Chairman, Communications Co. *Japan*: Kengo Mori, president of Japan Gas Co.; Takashi Aoki, director, Imperial Bank of Japan. *Alternates*: Saburo Sonada; Yasumune Matsui. *United States*: Owen D. Young, chairman, General Electric Co.; chairman, board of directors, Federal Reserve Bank; J. P. Morgan, jun., head of J. P. Morgan & Co. of New York, and Morgan, Grenfell, & Co. of London. *Alternates*: Thomas N. Perkins, corporate lawyer; Thomas W. Lamont, partner, J. P. Morgan & Co.

as Morgan and Gilbert were well aware, was also ruled out because the recommendations of the Young Committee, like those of earlier reparation experts, were to be based not on an honest appraisal of the German economy but on the amount of damage the creditors had sustained during the war and, more importantly, the extent of their indebtedness to each other. The conclusions of the experts were also significantly affected by the haggling which continued, particularly among the minor creditors, over the distribution of the reparation receipts. Because of her entitlement to 52 per cent of the total and the committee's readiness to grant her the lion's share of non-postponable payments, France could afford to be relatively accommodating about the size of Germany's annuities, even if she was insistent that they should be spread over the same fifty-eight-year period as her out-payments to the United States and Britain. The British government, on the other hand, whose share of the spoils was only 22 per cent, had an interest in a larger annuity, just as it had in 1919. The same was true, *a fortiori*, of the other minor European creditors and the United States, although the latter swelled Germany's obligations mainly by pressing her former allies to repay their war loans.[2]

In its early sessions the Young Committee created the impression of embarking on a serious investigation of Germany's capacity. Although Moreau insisted on staking out France's claim to fifty-eight annuities when the negotiations began on 11 February, Young ruled from the chair that it would be pointless to discuss the duration of Germany's obligations before their amount had been determined; and he allowed the rest of the week to be devoted to disquisitions by Schacht and his colleagues about the state of the German economy. Schacht chose as his point of departure Gilbert's report of December 1928, which, he claimed, exaggerated the extent of Germany's recovery and her ability to pay reparations. The Agent-General's desire to boost Germany's international credit standing was, Schacht conceded, understandable on the eve of an attempt to arrive at a definitive commercialized settlement. He had, however, created a misleading impression by using as a base for comparison her condition during the crisis of 1924 instead of the more normal situation of 1913. Another contestable source of Gilbert's optimism had been the trade statistics for September 1928, which showed a favourable visible balance for the first time since 1926.

---

[2] For Morgan's views: Lacour-Gayet to Poincaré, 27 Oct. 1928, AEF, F30, 1302, Mobilisation du Plan, Dossier 'Plan Dawes: son remplacement par le Plan Young'. For Gilbert on commercialization: Prittwitz to A. Amt, 9 Jan. 1929, *ADAP* xi. 24–5.

The trade gap had, however, reopened in November and December, and Germany had, he claimed, finished the year with an overall deficit of almost two billion marks. Since invisible exports, which yielded only 500 million marks a year, did little to offset the additional 1.25 billion marks needed to service foreign loans, it was easy for Schacht and Melchior to demonstrate, as Keynes had done in August 1927, that exports would need to increase from their current level of 11.7 billion marks to 19 billions in order to cover a reparation annuity of 2.5 billions. Because this would be intolerable for her trade competitors, Schacht suggested that Germany's only way out was to cut her bill for imports of food and raw materials. Yet, as he knew full well, this raised by implication the delicate questions of access to colonial primary products and the effect of the Polish corridor on the level of German grain production. A further major obstacle to assuming a large long-term reparation burden was, as Schacht's colleague Albert Vögler pointed out, the difficulty of curbing domestic living standards indefinitely. While the real wages of some sections of the workforce had risen since 1913, those of the urban middle classes and rural population had been depressed. Any further reduction of consumption for the sake of honouring excessive reparation obligations would, Vögler predicted, have grave political repercussions.[3]

This review of Germany's economic situation, which was couched in purely technical economic terms and avoided making explicit territorial demands, made such an impression on the rest of the committee that the German experts were buoyed up with a false sense of euphoria by the end of the first week. They were, however, quickly brought to earth when figures began to be discussed. Schacht's tentative offer during informal discussions on 16 February of a non-postponable annuity of 800 million marks evoked a strong negative reaction, particularly from Stamp, the leading British expert, who declared on 19 February that the creditors had previously been under the impression that Germany would be prepared to pay between 2 and 2.5 billion marks. The discovery that the difference between creditor and debtor expectations was far greater than Gilbert had led everyone to believe prompted the committee to veer off into a discussion of modes of

---

[3] *Report of the Agent-General for Reparation Payments, 22 December 1928* (London, 1929) (henceforward RC xix), 4; Vögler to Stresemann, 15 Feb. 1929; Schacht to Stresemann, 16 Feb. 1929, *ADAP* xi. 143–5, 161–6; M. Vogt, *Die Entstehung des Young-plans* (Boppard-on-Rhine, 1970), 177–86. Schacht's figures were exaggerated. See above, p. 263, Table 12.

payment instead of amounts. Three informal sub-committees were established under Revelstoke, Stamp, and Perkins to examine unconditional (hopefully commercialized) payments, conditional payments (and the safeguards to which they would be subject), and deliveries in kind. At the same time negotiations began outside these sub-committees about the establishment of a permanent international financial agency. The Bank for International Settlements, as this eventually came to be called, originated from the confluence of Schacht's desire for a body to foster international (particularly German) trade and Franco-Belgian pressure for a successor to the Transfer Committee which would, in the absence of a truly final settlement, supervise the transfer of Germany's obligations, organize their gradual mobilization, and earn profits which could eventually be applied to the satisfaction of the creditors' demands. Yet the bank's creation, which was perhaps the only constructive legacy of the entire reparation dispute, could not by itself bring about a realistic settlement. When, therefore, the committee wound up its technical discussions in mid-March and returned, in the sixth week of its labours, to the question of figures it swiftly arrived at an impasse.[4]

Although Young and Morgan prided themselves on their independence of the United States government, they were remarkably optimistic about Germany's capacity to pay and firmly committed to the Gilbert–Poincaré thesis that the new reparation settlement should facilitate the repayment of Allied war debts to the United States. For this reason the bulk of the fifty-eight annuities averaging between 2.15 and 2.2 billion marks which they proposed in mid-March were earmarked to cover inter-Allied outpayments. As Vögler reported to the German cabinet, almost 32 billion of the total 'present value' of the 39 billion marks which they suggested Germany should pay would go to the United States. The German experts, who considered both the amounts involved and the duration of the scheme excessive, and were confident that the creditors could be beaten down, quickly countered on 21 March with a proposal for only 37 annuities averaging 1.65 billion marks. In order to prevent the gap between these schemes from becoming unbridgeable during the committee's Easter recess

[4] Vogt, Entstehung, 186–9; Schacht to Müller, 19 Feb. 1929; Report by Kastl, 1 Mar. 1929; Report by Schacht, 12 Mar. 1929, Das Kabinett Müller II, i. 439–40, 455–9, 483–8; Memo by Ritter, 12 Mar. 1929, ADAP xi. 265–8. Stuart M. Crocker Papers, Memoirs from the Young Plan Days, 38–61. Wilson to Sec. State, 21, 26 Feb., 5, 12, 14 Mar. 1929, Dept. of State, 462.00 R296/2723, 2729, 2735, 2741, 2742; Herrick to Sec. State, 5, 12 Mar. 1929, ibid. 2719, 2730; Young to Sec. State, 3, 8 Mar. 1929, ibid. 2768–9.

(which began on Friday 29 March) two working papers were tabled on 28 March by the four major European creditors and Young. The first, while admitting that claims for reparation proper could be pared down, tried to achieve a realistic figure mainly by juggling with the outpayments component of the annuities, which, it claimed, could be reduced by 480 million marks in the immediate future because of the relatively small sums due initially to the United States. It also suggested that the funds required for the thirty-eighth to fifty-eighth annuities could be drawn largely from Germany's share of the accumulated profits of the Bank for International Settlements. Young's proposal, on the other hand, which was drawn up with the assistance of Gilbert, whom Melchior at this stage referred to as the 'evil genius' (*böse Geist*) of the conference, treated outpayments as sacrosanct and reparation claims as negotiable. The latter, it suggested, should include 40 billion francs for the French, a 'reasonable additional sum' for the Italians to make up for their inability to extract adequate reparation from Germany's former allies, and compensation to the Belgian government for the mark notes which it had redeemed at the end of the war. The relatively small share of the cake which this scheme allotted to reparation proper was sure to cause friction over distribution and to lead to pressure for higher annuities. Such, however, was the financial dominance of the United States that Young's proposal was to serve as the basis of the eventual settlement.[5]

The conference came perilously close to breaking point soon after it resumed on Thursday, 4 April. The crisis was precipitated when Young gave the European creditors their head and allowed them to embark on separate discussions with Schacht about their individual claims. Within a few days Schacht made the embarrassing announcement that these demands would entail an annuity of 2.9 billion marks, or 400 million more than the standard annual Dawes payment. There followed what the Germans sardonically referred to as 'the week the weather was so bad that we couldn't leave the hotel', during which the conference almost foundered because of the deadlock over distribution. Eventually the creditors turned in desperation to Young and invited him to make a proposal along the lines he had foreshadowed on

[5] Vogt, *Entstehung*, 199–202. For the American proposal and German counter-proposal: Crocker, Memoirs, 56–67; Bericht der beiden deutschen Hauptdelegierten . . ., 22 Mar. 1929, *Das Kabinett Müller II*, i. 508–17. For the working papers of 28 Mar.: Herrick to Sec. State, 28 Mar. 1929, *FR*, 1929, ii. 1034–8. For Gilbert's influence: Crocker, Memoirs, 74; Report by Melchior and Kastl, 29 Mar. 1929, *Das Kabinett Müller II*, i. 520–4.

28 March. Yet his suggestion on 8 April that the first ten annuities should remain below 2 billions, that the first 37 should average 2.1 billions, and that the last 21 should correspond to outpayments immediately gave rise to new bickering. The main reason for dissatisfaction was that, in order to accommodate Belgium's mark claim and increase Italy's receipts, he had made a disproportionate reduction in the share of the British Empire. As Stamp subsequently complained in a memorandum for Churchill, Young's scheme, while reducing the total annuity by 16 per cent and France's share by 15 per cent, slashed the receipts of Britain and her dominions by 24 and 68 per cent respectively. On the other hand, the amount payable to Italy and Belgium remained virtually unaltered in absolute terms. Young's proposal provoked three days of discussion during which the annuity for the first thirty-seven years was first of all raised to an average of 2.345 billions in order to satisfy competing claims and then lowered, on Young's insistence, to 2.198 billions. At this stage, according to Stamp, France and Italy had still made insufficient concessions to the British; and it was only after a threat to torpedo the conference that the dominions were given back their previous share of the spoils. The British experts were, however, forced to abandon their claim for 'arrears' (the sum by which their reparation receipts had hitherto fallen short of their outpayments to the United States); and they had to console themselves for the time being with an increased share of the capital which the German government was to provide for the Bank for International Settlements.[6]

This haggling, which was reminiscent of the behaviour of the victors at the Paris Peace Conference a decade earlier, evoked a histrionic reaction similar to that of the German Peace Delegation in 1919. The creditors, hard-pressed to achieve agreement among themselves, referred to the proposal which they presented to Schacht on 13 April as embodying their 'minimum requirements'. The hint of another *Diktat* gave nationalists such as Schacht and Vögler the excuse they had been seeking either to provoke a breakdown of negotiations or to disassociate themselves from any agreement which might be concluded. The German counter-proposal of 17 April, which was drawn up without reference to Berlin, in fact bore a striking resemblance to the Peace Delegation's Memorandum of 13 May 1919, which asserted that

[6] Crocker, Memoirs, 77–94; Memo by Stamp, 30 Apr. 1929, enc. in Memo by Churchill, 5 May 1929, *DBFP* IA, vi. 274–85. For the eventual text of the creditors' proposal presented to Schacht on 13 Apr.: Wilson to Sec. State, 16 Apr. 1929, Dept. of State, 462.00 R296/2827. Cf. Young to Sec. State, 13 Apr. 1929, ibid. 2786.

an onerous reparation scheme would only be feasible if the colonial and territorial provisions of the treaty were revised and Germany was not subjected to commercial discrimination. Although these arguments had been advanced in purely economic form by Schacht at the beginning of the conference, they had taken on political colouring after being publicly aired in March, with his connivance, by Richard von Kuhlmann, a former Secretary of State of the German Foreign Office. They therefore added to the furore which arose when the proposal of 17 April reiterated the view that, because of her chronic trade deficit, it would be impossible for Germany to transfer annuities which averaged more than 1.65 billions or lasted longer than thirty-seven years without jeopardizing her current standard of living.[7]

The outcry which greeted the German memorandum was such that Young was forced, in order to save the conference, to appoint a sub-committee under Revelstoke to examine the possibility of a provisional ten- or fifteen-year settlement. The deliberations of this group quickly foundered on the following day when Schacht remained impervious to Stamp's entreaties to improve his offer of 1.65 billions. A rupture therefore seemed inevitable when the sub-committee made its negative report to a plenary session scheduled for noon on Friday 19 April. It is usually asserted that the situation was retrieved only because Revelstoke suffered a stroke and died in his sleep during the preceding night. The German government had, however, taken last-minute action to save the conference even before this occurred. Müller and the ministers concerned with the reparation question—Stresemann, Hilferding, Curtius, and Wirth—had been following the course of events in Paris closely. On 17 April Hilferding, who was worried by Schacht's intransigence, had pressed unsuccessfully for intervention in favour of a provisional settlement. However, when telegrams received during the night of 18 April indicated the seriousness of the deadlock, it was decided early the following morning to telephone Schacht directing him to seek an adjournment of the plenary session until Monday, 22 April. It was only after Schacht had agreed to this course of action 'on the condition that it did not compromise the position of the experts' that the news of Revelstoke's death and the adjournment of the session was received in Berlin. Hilferding reported to the cabinet in the evening

[7] For Paris Peace Conference: see above, ch. 2 n. 28. For a vivid first-hand description of the impasse of 16–17 Apr.: Crocker, *Memoirs*, 117–47. See also Vogt, *Entstehung*, 220–8 and 204–16 (Kuhlmann's *démarche*). For text of German proposal of 17 Apr.: Ruppel to Ritter, 18 Apr. 1929, *ADAP* xi. 408–12.

that he was uncertain whether the adjournment had occurred because of Schacht's request or Revelstoke's death. The important fact was, he declared, that the cabinet had through its intervention committed itself to achieving some sort of settlement.[8]

The manner in which this would be concluded remained unclear even after Schacht and Vögler had returned to Berlin for discussion with the cabinet on Sunday 21 April. Both experts insisted that the conference was being wrecked by the subservience of the European experts to their governments' wishes and their consequent refusal to take account of Germany's economic capacity. The biggest obstacle to the success of the negotiations was, according to Schacht, that the repayment of inter-Allied debts was regarded as an article of faith. Young, he reported, had privately conceded that what was needed most of all was a 'large-scale gesture of cancellation' by the United States; but neither he nor Morgan had received any encouragement on this score from Washington. In these circumstances neither Schacht nor Vögler were willing to make any meaningful financial concessions, even if they agreed to the publication of a conciliatory communiqué declaring that the counter-proposal of 17 April was not intended as a political document and was designed merely to provide a basis for discussion. As in 1919, a settlement was clearly going to depend on the preparedness of the German government to overrule its expert advisers.[9]

On his return to Paris the following day Schacht made a last attempt to frustrate Franco-American efforts to convert the conference into an operation for reinforcing the framework of inter-Allied indebtedness. With the approval of Young he started discussions with Pierre Quesnay, director of the Economics Department of the Banque de France, about a settlement which relegated outpayments to the end of the plan and gave priority to reparations. Such a manœuvre appealed to French right-wing nationalists who were still struggling to prevent the ratification of the Mellon–Bérenger Agreement: but its fate was sealed when Poincaré reiterated on the same day in a speech at Bar-le-Duc his demand for annuities covering France's debt repayments as well as her reparation expenditure. On the following morning Schacht's parley with Quesnay was interrupted by Moreau, who

[8] For the work of the Revelstoke Committee: Crocker, Memoirs, 117–47. See also Besprechungen über Reparationsfragen, 17, 19 Apr. 1929; Ministerbesprechung 19 Apr. 1929, Das Kabinett Müller II, i. 552–66.
[9] Kabinettssitzung 21 Apr. 1929, Das Kabinett Müller II, i. 569–75.

angrily accused the former of conspiring with Poincaré's enemies and using delaying tactics. Schacht was in any case soon brought to heel by Germany's financial vulnerability. At the beginning of the last week in April Pierre Jay, the American representative on the Transfer Committee, attributed the growing pressure on the mark to the high interest rates which were being paid in New York and the consequent withdrawal of 'a large amount of short-term money which was previously on loan in Germany'. Withdrawals were also encouraged by 'an adverse general estimate of the security now offering' in Germany resulting presumably from the deadlock in the Young negotiations and the prospect that the onerous Dawes annuities might continue. On 23 April Gilbert estimated to Crocker, Young's secretary, that Germany had lost a billion marks in foreign exchange since January, 'that 600 millions of the total had been lost in the last month and that the losses during the last few days might reach 250 millions'. These developments prompted the Reichsbank, notwithstanding the prevailing recession in Germany, to counter the drain of its gold and foreign exchange reserves by raising its discount rate from $6\frac{1}{2}$ to $7\frac{1}{2}$ per cent on 25 April. On the previous day, however, fresh impetus had been given to speculation against the mark by press reports—which Schacht claimed were inspired by Moreau—that a meeting of the Transfer Committee had attributed the exodus of funds from Germany to the irresponsible discount policy of the Reichsbank. The ensuing haemorrhage of gold and foreign exchange was only stanched after Young had prevailed upon Gilbert to issue a denial of the report on the afternoon of 26 April; and after Wall Street and London, anxious to preserve the German goose, rallied to the support of the Reichsbank. On 27 April, Schacht, having seen the writing on the wall, made a tentative agreement with Ferdinand Eberstadt, another assistant of Young's, about a schedule of annuities averaging 2.05 billion marks. In an effort to evade responsibility, however, he kept the agreement secret and transmitted once more to Berlin Gilbert's allegation that senior members of the German cabinet had sold the pass by agreeing to annuities in the region of 2 billion marks before the committee met.[10]

---

[10] For the Schacht–Quesnay discussions: Besprechung über reparationspolitische Angelegenheiten, 29 Apr. 1929, *Das Kabinett Müller II*, i. 589–91; Memo by Schubert, 26 Apr. 1929, *ADAP* xi. 449–51. For Jay: Schurmann to Sec. State, 24 Apr. 1929, Dept. of State, 462.00 R296/2842. For discount policy of Reichsbank: id. to Sec. State, 30 Apr. 1929, ibid. 2870. For Gilbert and the Schacht–Eberstadt negotiations, which began on 24 Apr.: Crocker, Memoirs, 171–4. For Schacht's tentative agreement: Curtius, *Der Young-Plan*, 44.

It would be an oversimplification to attribute the outcome of events in this week to deliberate collusion between Poincaré, Moreau, Gilbert, and the United States Treasury. Yet, apart from causing concern in Wall Street by undermining the stability of the mark and the security of American investments in Germany, the deadlock was seen by both the United States and the French government as a threat to the ratification of the Mellon–Bérenger Agreement, and thereby to the whole international debt structure. It was a measure of Franco-American anxiety that Gilbert, who had had little or no contact with the German government since the previous November, now hastened to Berlin to urge capitulation. During discussions on 1 May with Schubert, the Secretary of State for Foreign Affairs, he resorted to the dubious arguments that acceptance of the creditors' terms would be good for German credit and that 'after the reparation question was settled, a great boom would begin which would enable Germany to fulfil her obligations'. It was hardly surprising that, in an interview with Hilferding on the following day, he dispensed with the kid gloves and threatened that the failure of the Young Committee to reach agreement would 'seriously undermine' the German economy.[11]

The Agent-General's pressure was not needed since the German cabinet had already been reduced into a state of submission. There must, indeed, have been a depressing element of *déjà vu* during the first three days of May for Müller and Wirth, who had also been forced to assume responsibility for accepting the Versailles Treaty in 1919 and the London Schedule of Payments in 1921. As on these previous occasions the cabinet did not believe that the terms were fair or reasonable, and it was motivated primarily by fear of the consequences of non-acceptance, hope of future amelioration, and territorial considerations. Curtius certainly emphasized that the initial payments which were now envisaged were much lower than the standard Dawes annuity and that acceptance of Young's scheme would free Germany from the financial controls to which she had been subjected under the Dawes Plan. Hilferding also pointed out that annuities starting at 1.8 billions might not prove to be all that much worse than Schacht's maximum of 1.65 billions. Yet none of the cabinet considered that a scheme of 58 annuities averaging over 2 billion marks would be viable in the long term. On the other hand,

---

[11] For the anxiety of Wall Street: Prittwitz to Haas, 29 Apr. 1929, *ADAP* xi. 457–60. For Gilbert's conversations with Schubert and Hilferding: Memo by Schubert, 1 May 1929, ibid. 467–74; Ministerbesprechung 3 May 1929, *Das Kabinett Müller II*, i. 632–7.

the advice of Schacht to break up the conference and provoke a transfer crisis by reverting to the Dawes scheme was rejected because of the grave financial dislocation, economic hardship, and political disorder which would ensue. The susceptibility of the German financial system to Franco-American pressure and the fragility of the domestic political situation, so amply demonstrated by the May Day disturbances which were rocking Berlin while the cabinet was deliberating, meant that there was little or no room for manœuvre.[12]

Both the cabinet and the two principal German experts were by this time concerned mainly to evade responsibility. Schacht, after making his impossible recommendation on 1 May, had taken care to put on record his willingness to follow any instructions given to him; and the cabinet, although making it clear that an agreement would eventually have to be achieved, had declined to issue any formal directive to Schacht before he departed for Paris. This shuffling continued on the following day when the cabinet telegraphed Schacht merely that its opinion remained the same as it had been on the previous evening. But the latter, not to be outwitted, immediately requested more precise instructions; and the cabinet, afraid that Schacht might call its bluff and wreck the conference, was forced to reply after a further meeting on 3 May, that acceptance was 'unavoidable' if economic and political disaster was to be averted. Having covered his flank, Schacht transmitted a note to Young on 5 May which, while stressing the impossibility of the proposed schedule of payments and disavowing responsibility for the success of any attempt to fulfil it, nevertheless announced German acceptance because of 'the desirability of the conference achieving some result'. A number of conditions were, however, attached including the establishment of machinery for moratoria on internal collection and external transfers, a renewed proposal for covering the last twenty-one annuities from the profits of the Bank for International Settlements, and a guarantee of the lifting of all controls and the revocation of all the provisions for sanctions and pledges in the Versailles Treaty.[13]

The success of the conference was by no means assured by this

[12] Besprechung über die Reparationslage, 1 May 1929; Fortsetzung der Aussprache über die Reparationslage, 1 May 1929; Ministerbesprechungen 2–3 May 1929, *Das Kabinett Müller II*, i. 612–37.

[13] For Schacht and the German cabinet: Ministerbesprechungen 2–3 May 1929, ibid. 624–37; Stresemann to Hoesch, 3 May 1929, *ADAP* xi. 486–7. For Schacht's proposal of 5 May: Schacht to Müller, 6 May 1929, ibid. 509–12. See also Curtius, *Der Young-Plan*, 46–7; Crocker, Memoirs, 211–12.

ON REPARATIONS ISLAND.

Fig. 9. The *Evening Standard*, 13 May 1929.

grudging and conditional German retreat. In proposals which he presented on 6 and 7 May Young managed to pare down Allied claims from 2.198 billions to 1.998 billions, or 2.050 billions including the cost of servicing the Dawes loan. Yet, because of the privileged position accorded to outpayments, he achieved this only by eliminating once more the claims of the British dominions, and thus reducing the British Empire's overall share of the spoils from the 22.8 per cent which it enjoyed under the Spa Agreement of 1920 to a mere 19.4 per cent. Coming on top of the rejection of Britain's claim for arrears, this unleashed a storm in the British press which forced Churchill to reassure the House of Commons on 9 May that such a sacrifice would be unacceptable. The British government, he added for good measure, would be in no way bound by the recommendations of the Young Committee. British discontent led to a further ten days of haggling and a new proposal on 22 May in which the creditors sought as usual to resolve their differences at Germany's expense by requiring her to keep paying the higher Dawes annuity of 2.5 billion marks until 31 December 1929. This demand, and a further request that unconditional annuities—the only ones the creditors could be sure of receiving—should be increased by biennial increments of 25 million marks from the fifth annuity onwards, were unacceptable to the German delegation; and Vögler was presented with the opportunity for which he had been waiting to tender his resignation. Schacht also made an ominous reference to Crocker about pressure from German industrialists 'to make no settlement at all on the theory that a deflation [sic] movement in Germany, although difficult for the German public, would help to weed out unnecessary small competition [and] reduce the standards [sic] of living'. Since the Belgians, the Italians, and the British were insufficiently moved by this threat to reduce their claims, everybody, including Young, who had by this time become very depressed, resigned themselves to failure. On 25 May, however, there was a partial breakthrough when Schacht agreed that the Dawes Plan could continue until 31 August 1929 in return for an American undertaking to have the Belgian mark claim settled in concurrent but separate negotiations between Belgium and Germany. Four days later discussions between Schacht, Quesnay, and Sarnoff, yet another of Young's factotums, led to a tentative agreement that the first annuity under the new scheme would run for seven months from 1 September 1929 to 31 March 1930 and amount to only 742.8 million marks, or the sum due for reparation proper (as opposed to outpayments) in the twelve months 1 April 1929–31 March 1930. To counterbalance this concession, it was agreed that, since Germany's payments between 1 April and 31 August 1929 at the full rate would more than cover the outpayments of the creditors in the year ending 31 March 1930, the resulting surplus would be made available to resolve the deadlock between Britain, Belgium, and Italy.[14]

Although this arrangement enabled an agreement to be reached on figures by adjourning the distributive dog-fight between the creditors, several obstacles still had to be surmounted. With Young close to physical collapse and Schacht maintaining as low a profile as possible in the seclusion of the Hotel Trianon at Versailles, negotiations continued between alternate delegates about side-issues such as the size of the unconditional annuities and the form of Germany's obligations during the last two decades of the scheme. Even when agreement was reached on these matters on 31 May, Moreau refused to sign anything on behalf of the French government until the Belgian mark claim was settled. The German government, having treated this matter as outside the terms of reference of the committee, had empowered Schacht to negotiate with Émile Francqui, the Belgian representative, a side-settlement involving the return of Eupen-Malmédy to Germany. The Belgians, who were on the eve of an election, refused to entertain any such quid pro quo and insisted, with the support of the French government, that they would sign the Young Committee's report only after their claim had been satisfied. Agreement was not reached until 4 June, when Stresemann side-stepped more bullying by Gilbert and Moreau and persuaded the French cabinet, through the good offices of Briand, to support a compromise whereby Germany dropped her territorial demands and undertook to negotiate a settlement with Belgium before the Young Plan came into operation. The way was at last clear for the signature of the report on 7 June. 'Thank God it's

[14] For Young's proposals of 6 and 7 May: Young to Sec. State, 6 May 1929; Armour to Sec. State, 9 May 1929, Dept. of State, 462.00 R296/2875½, 2868½. For British reaction: Undated Note, DBFP IA, vi. 286–90; Churchill, 9 May 1929, HC ccxxvii. 2309–12. For creditor proposal of 22 May: Dept. of State, 462.00 R296/2905; Crocker, Memoirs, 281; Memo by Stamp, enc. Henderson to Tyrrell, 9 Nov. 1929, DBFP IA, vii. 101–2; Schacht to Müller, 24 May 1929, ADAP xi. 574–7; Das Kabinett Müller II, i. 683 n. For the reaction of Schacht and Vögler: Schubert to Stresemann, 16 May 1929; Hoesch to A. Amt, 18 May 1929; Memo by Ritter, 22 May 1929; Circular by Stresemann, 23 May 1929, ADAP xi. 531–4, 549–51, 553–6, 563. Cf. Crocker, Memoirs, 278–9. For the final negotiations about figures and the resulting 'surplus': ibid. 285–300; Armour to Sec. State, 25, 29 May 1929, Dept. of State, 462.00 R296/2918, 2930; Das Kabinett Müller II, i. 712 n. 1; Report of the Committee of Experts on Reparations 1929 (London, 1929) (henceforward RC xx), Part 8, Para. 4.

over,' said Addis to Kastl. 'We'll see each other in three years, and get rid of all the plunder.'[15]

An appraisal of the result of this horse-trading depends upon the yardstick which is employed. It has been usual to compare the Young Plan favourably with the Dawes scheme because it freed Germany from foreign controls, virtually eliminated the threat of political sanctions, and reduced annuities by an average of 18 per cent, or almost 29 per cent in the first five years. Yet the new settlement did not fulfil the original hopes of Benjamin Strong and the Wall Street banking establishment that it would depoliticize and commercialize the reparation problem. The shortcomings of the Young Plan are reflected in the functions of the Bank for International Settlements, its institutional embodiment. Although the Bank was initially conceived as a mere conduit pipe for the receipt and distribution of reparation payments, it was ultimately made responsible, like its predecessors, the Reparation Commission and Transfer Committee, for adjusting Germany's burdens in the likely event that they would prove intolerable. The limitation of unconditional payments to 700 million marks a year (including the servicing of the Dawes loan) also prevented the bank from achieving the commercialization of the greater part of Germany's obligations. The improvised and essentially political character of the plan was emphasized most of all by the way in which the size and number of Germany's annuities were determined by her creditors' debts to each other rather than by her financial capacity. The arbitrary insistence of the Young experts on a settlement which would cover, or appear to cover, creditor outpayments for fifty-eight years made the scheme vulnerable to right-wing and left-wing protests that it would enslave the German people for two generations. It was difficult enough for the creditors to persuade their own legislatures to sanction the repayment of war debts to erstwhile allies. To demand that Germany should mortgage her future for the benefit of her former foes was unrealistic and provocative.

Although the political preoccupations of the creditors undermined the viability of the Young Plan, the behaviour of the German govern-

---

[15] For the condition of Young and Schacht; Schacht to Müller, 27 May 1929, *ADAP* xi. 579–80; *Das Kabinett Müller II*, i. 690–2; Poole to Castle, 31 May 1929, Dept. of State, 462.00 R296/3034; Crocker, *Memoirs*, 290, 308. For the Belgian mark claim: Memo by Stresemann, 31 May 1929; Stresemann to Hoesch, 31 May 1929; Memo by Stresemann, 3 June 1929; Hoesch to A. Amt, 3 June 1929, *ADAP* xi. 579–80, 598–600, 602–3; xii. 7–9, 11–12. Cf. RC xx, Annexe VI. For Addis: R.E. Lüke, *Von der Stabilisierung zur Krise* (Zurich, 1958), 176–7.

ment also contributed to its speedy collapse. Germany's original agreement to participate in a new reparation enquiry had been motivated as much by a desire to expedite the evacuation of the Rhineland as by hopes of a genuine bankers' settlement. After the early sessions of the Young Committee had confirmed that it would merely produce yet another questionable financial improvisation, German tactics were, on the one hand, to use the impossibility of the scheme to promote the cause of territorial treaty revision and, on the other, to reduce the proportion of future annuities which would be non-postponable and hence subject to commercialization. The protestations of financial incapacity which were made by German spokesmen in pursuit of these objectives did much to sap the confidence of the international investing community upon which the short-term fulfilment of the Young Plan depended.

RATIFICATION

It was a measure of the fragility of the Young Plan that only its American instigators gave it unequivocal support in the next few months. In a short-lived burst of enthusiasm, Young predicted to the *Chicago Daily Tribune* that the Bank for International Settlements would lubricate the machinery of international capitalism and prevent the spread of Bolshevism. A system which was already letting 'wheat rot in Dakota and men starve in China' was, he declared, sorely in need of overhaul if it was to withstand the additional strain of reparation payments. Two weeks later during discussions with the newly installed Hoover and his Secretary of State, Stimson, who were both inflexible about war debts, he adopted a more hard-nosed approach. Because it would maintain the international monetary stability which was necessary if Germany was to boost her exports and pay reparations, the plan would, he maintained, ensure the regular repayment of war debts to the United States. It was this self-interest rather than any idealism which prompted the heavy pressure which the United States now brought to bear to achieve the smooth ratification of the scheme.[16]

Although France, like the United States, stood to gain a great deal on paper from the Young Plan, there was considerable initial

---

[16] For Young: Wilson to Sec. State, 4 June 1929, Dept. of State, 462.00 R296/3000; T. W. Lamont's Memo of 25 June 1929, ibid. R296/3036½. For Hoover's attitude: Artaud, *Question des dettes interalliées*, ii. 891, 900.

opposition in the Chamber of Deputies to the way in which the new settlement subordinated reparations to war debts. Even before the Young Committee had presented its report, Socialist deputies were urging the government to continue to give priority to the restoration of the devastated regions. Despite the subsequent efforts of Poincaré and his Finance Minister, Henry Chéron, to win over the Foreign Affairs Committee of the Chamber, the deputies were unimpressed. The end of June saw the adoption of a right-wing resolution requesting the postponement of the maturity of the $406 million American war stocks credit (which was due to be repaid on 1 August) so as to remove the pressure for the ratification of both the Mellon–Bérenger war-debt agreement and the Young Plan. This tactic foundered on 29 June when Briand reported to the Foreign Affairs Committee the tearful, but resolute, refusal of Stimson (who had served in France during the war) to grant a financial reprieve to his former comrades in arms. Yet the Chamber adopted the Mellon–Bérenger Agreement on 21 July by only 300 to 292 votes after a prolonged debate peppered with right-wing proposals for the internationalization of war debts and further Socialist demands that priority should be given to reparations. The subsequent approval of the Senate was also subject to a rider that France's debt repayments to the United States should be formally tied to her reparation receipts from Germany.[17]

Once the Mellon–Bérenger Agreement had been ratified the prompt implementation of the Young Plan naturally became vital to the French government. This, however, merely raised new difficulties for the Chamber since the inauguration of the plan would entail the evacuation of the Rhineland as part of the general liquidation of the war foreshadowed by the Geneva Declaration of September 1928. Briand, who assumed the leadership of Poincaré's right-centre cabinet after the latter's health gave way on 27 July, was to be torn between the demand of Stresemann, not to mention that of the new British Labour cabinet and the French Socialist Party, for a speedy evacuation, and the insistence of the conservative groups upon which his government depended

---

[17] For French opposition to the Young Plan: Chambre des Députés, CAE, 25 Mar. 1929. For Socialist resolutions: ibid. 24, 27, 31 May 1929. For Poincaré, Chéron, and the Foreign Affairs Committee: Armour to Sec. State, 20, 21, 22, 27, 29 June, 1 July 1929, Dept. of State, 462.00 R296/3002, 3010, 3014, 3036, 3042, 3090. For the Franklin–Bouillon Resolution of 27 June and Briand's report of 29 June: id. to Sec. State, 28 June 1929, ibid. R296/3052; Chambre des Députés, CAE, 29 June 1929. For the Mellon–Bérenger Agreement ratification debate: Tyrrell to Henderson, 18 July 1929, *DBFP* IA, vi. 433–5; Armour to Sec. State, 17, 21, 26 July 1929, Dept. of State, 462.00 R296/3113, 3126, 3144.

that adequate means of coercing Germany should be retained. To resolve this dilemma Briand referred increasingly to the need for a European federation which would both facilitate economic co-oper-ation and guarantee the territorial status quo. In view, however, of the emergence of the German extreme right wing Briand's domestic critics were unlikely to be mollified by such a vision.[18]

If the French had misgivings about the Young scheme, the British regarded it as a completely inadequate substitute for the general liqui-dation of reparations and war debts which they had been advocating. To add insult to injury, the Empire's slice of the reparation cake was reduced from 22 to 20 per cent, while France was given the lion's share of the unconditional annuities; and the system of deliveries in kind which was so damaging to British trade was prolonged for another ten years. The Foreign Office conceded that ratification of the Report would help to pacify Europe by speeding up the evacuation of the Rhineland. Yet its advisers shared the scepticism of Snowden, the Chancellor of the Exchequer of the new Labour government, about the financial viability of the plan. As the latter observed in a memorandum foreshadowing his campaign at the first Hague Conference to restore Britain's share of reparation receipts to its former level,

there might be something to be said for making a final sacrifice now if there were any real prospect that the recommendations in the Report did represent an absolutely final and definitive settlement of the whole problem; but there can be no certainty of this, and, in the opinion of many well able to judge the probabilities, the present scheme is not likely to last more than a few years.

The degeneration of Britain's quest for a rational general financial settlement into the feckless pursuit of its short-term interests did little to ease the implementation of the plan. Nor did the deepening financial crisis make it likely that the British government would be capable of greater enlightenment in the future.[19]

[18] For Briand and European Federation: P. J. V. Rolo, *Britain and the Briand Plan: The Common Market that Never Was* (Keele, 1972), 11–12; W. Lipgens, 'Europäische Einigungsidee 1923–1930 und Briands Europaplan im Urteil der deutschen Akten', *HZ* 203 (1966), 46–89, 316–63; R. W. D. Boyce, 'Britain's First "No" to Europe: Britain and the Briand Plan, 1929–30', *European Studies Review*, 10 (1980), 17–45. For Briand's reference in the Chamber on 16 July to the need for a 'more general agreement' among the powers to secure the future peace of Europe: *The Times*, 17 July 1929, 16. See below, ch. 9 n. 2.

[19] For British reaction: Sargent to Wigram, 7 June 1929; FO Memo, 17 June 1929; Memo by Mr Carr, 17 June 1929; Memo by Mr Snowden, 15 July 1929, *DBFP* IA, vi. 333–4, 344–52, 420–6.

The political character of the Young Plan and its consequent failure to take any real account of the debtor's long-term financial capacity ensured that it would generate far more heat than warmth in Germany. The initial outward reaction of the German government was, it is true, relatively favourable. To a certain extent this was because, as Hilferding, the SPD Finance Minister, pointed out on 18 June, the windfall gain from reduced reparation payments would offset the 150 million mark deficit which had developed in the 1928–9 budget as a result of the declining revenues and increased outlays associated with the depression of the preceding winter. There were also political, pyschological, and diplomatic reasons for the government to put the best possible construction upon the new settlement. When the subject of the plan was, somewhat inauspiciously, broached in the Reichstag on the eve of the tenth anniversary of the signature of the Versailles Treaty, government spokesmen were acutely aware that Alfred Hugenberg had fired the first salvo of his campaign against the Young *Diktat* at Marburg University three days earlier. Hugenberg's appeal to German youth to resist the enslavement of themselves and their children forced Stresemann to devote much of his speech to emphasizing the short-term advantages of acceptance and ridiculing Hugenberg's proposal to induce a financial showdown by rejecting the plan and insisting that the Dawes scheme should remain in operation. Stresemann's concern to preserve what remained of Germany's foreign credit also explains his relatively restrained remark that it was 'a trifle rash' for the Young Committee to predict Germany's financial capacity even ten years hence. Finally, the delicacy of the forthcoming negotiations over the implementation of the plan precluded any discussion of the timing of the Rhineland evacuation or other territorial treaty revisions. For this reason Stresemann contented himself with condemning a proposal to establish a Conciliation Commission to regulate affairs in the Rhineland after the evacuation and making a resounding, if diplomatically unspecific, declaration that the Saar 'was German, is German, and will remain German'. The strident agitation of the Nationalist-Nazi Campaign Against the Enslavement of the German People would continue to inhibit the government tactically for some time. Yet the rapid deterioration of its budgetary position in the second half of 1929 and the additional financial and political demands of the creditors during the first and second Hague Conferences soon robbed the Young Plan of whatever attraction it originally possessed. The collaboration of the debtor would soon come to depend almost exclusively on fear of offending those foreign investors who still had funds committed in Germany.[20]

The First Hague Conference

Most of the time and energy of the first Hague Conference of August 1929 was consumed in futile haggling among the creditors over the highly problematical annuities of the later decades of the Young scheme. Apart from the manner in which the Americans and French had manipulated the plan, the immediate impetus to the dispute was an electioneering duel in April 1929 between Churchill and Philip Snowden, at that time Labour's shadow Chancellor of the Exchequer. The latter, who was not averse to a little financial jingoism in a period of economic stringency, had criticized the over-generous terms of Churchill's debt settlements with France and Italy and proclaimed himself to be 'sufficiently of an Englishman not to be content to see my country and my people bled white for the benefit of other countries who are far more prosperous than ourselves'. When the Labour Party was swept into office in the following month Snowden was, like Hilferding in Germany, faced with the prospect of substantial budgetary outlays to prop up his sagging Unemployment Insurance Fund. This gave him added reason to project himself as one who would garner the maximum yield from the coming reparation settlement for the benefit of the British taxpayer. In his memorandum of 15 July Snowden indicated the three aspects of the Young Report which were 'open to criticism':

(i) that we are asked to accept a reduction, on the average, of £2,400,000 a year of the amount we would be entitled to receive under the existing inter-Allied agreements . . . ;

(ii) that five-sixths of the unconditional Annuity . . . is given to France . . . ;

(iii) that the system of Deliveries in Kind is to be continued, on a reducing scale, for 10 years, and may be resumed on a larger scale if any transfer difficulties occur.[21]

---

[20] For statements by Müller and Schacht: *Das Kabinett Müller II*, i. 737–41; Vogt, *Entstehung*, 272–3; *KZ*, 29 June 1929, No. 229. For Hilferding: *RT*, 18 June 1929, cdxxv. 2590. For Hugenberg at Marburg: *KZ*, 23 June 1929, No. 215. For Stresemann: *RT*, 24 June 1929, cdxxv. 2810–15.

[21] For Snowden's brush with Churchill, *HC*, 16, 17 Apr. 1929, ccxxvii. 119–21, 311–15; P. Snowden, *An Autobiography* (2 vols.; London, 1934), ii. 748–53. For his memo of 15 July 1929: *DBFP* IA, vi. 420–6.

F<small>IG</small>. 10. The *Evening Standard*, 12 August 1929.

A collision over these matters was foreshadowed by the friction which occurred in July even over the venue of the conference. Poincaré professed to be offended by Snowden's claim during his exchange with Churchill that France had 'bilked' on her international obligations; and he was afraid that Britain would dominate the Bank for International Settlements. He was therefore unresponsive to Anglo-German pressure in favour of London. The British and German governments, on the other hand, rejected the Franco-Belgian suggestion of Brussels. Sparks quickly began to fly at the hastily arranged compromise location, The Hague, when Chéron refused to entertain Snowden's demand that Britain's share of reparations should be restored to 22 per cent. The two-week deadlock which ensued was initially enlivened by a set-to on the weekend of 10–11 August, when Snowden referred to the views, and implicitly the physique, of his rotund French adversary as 'grotesque and ridiculous'. An important reason for the prolonged impasse was the suspicion of the continental creditors that Snowden, who was *persona non grata* with the Americans, did not have the unqualified support of the British cabinet. An impression of disunity was certainly created when MacDonald, in response to pressure exerted by Dawes, Gilbert, and Lamont via Montagu Norman, dispatched a cautionary telegram to the British delegation which was accidentally transmitted to the Hague uncoded. MacDonald quickly sought to retrieve the situation by sending another *en clair* telegram expressing his full support for Snowden. Yet the damage done to the Chancellor's credibility reinforced the reluctance of the Financial Sub-Committee of the conference to make any concessions to the British viewpoint. Eventually, because of France's uneasiness about delaying the implementation of the Young Plan for too long after the Chamber had ratified the Mellon–Bérenger Agreement, some progress was made towards a settlement on 20 August when the French and Belgian delegates agreed to satisfy approximately half of Britain's demand (24 million marks) by allocating to her their share of the surplus from the last five months of the Dawes scheme. Since the Americans refused to 'put anything in the hat [the French and British] were passing around for Snowden', pressure was next brought to bear on the Italians. Although Pirelli was initially forbidden by Mussolini to make any concession, the total offered to Britain was raised to 28.6 million marks on 25 August when Italy contributed part of the liberation debt annuities she received from the successor states of eastern Europe. Since, however, the British delegation was convinced that this offer had been reduced at the last moment because of renewed press reports that the Labour cabinet was getting cold feet, it insisted that a further attempt to reach agreement should be made on 27 August. Snowden's nerveless stonewalling eventually increased his bag to 36 million marks, or 40 million counting the gains accruing from an arrangement whereby Britain would be advanced her instalments from the Bank for International Settlements at six-monthly rather than monthly intervals.[22]

The British Chancellor's remarkable success in persuading the other creditors to disgorge part of the spoils and, in addition, to make concessions about unconditional annuities and deliveries in kind, was due ultimately to their fear that he might try to engineer a genuine reparation settlement by undermining the Young negotiations and causing a short-lived reversion to the Dawes scheme. When Rudolf Breitscheid, the SPD Reichstag deputy, told him on 26 August that the German government was acutely concerned about the outcome of the conference and the fate of the Young Plan, Snowden merely retailed to him the British Treasury view that, if the Dawes Plan remained in operation, there would soon be a crisis which would trigger the transfer protection mechanism, and that, as a result, 'Germany would in a few months time be better off than she was at present'. Britain was, in short, able to extract concessions from her fellow creditors because she was far less interested in implementing the plan than they were.[23]

Concern to humour the British Labour Cabinet may also have encouraged the dangerously conciliatory attitude of Briand towards the evacuation of the Rhineland. In an effort to reassure the Chamber of Deputies about the advisability of surrendering France's military foothold in Germany, Briand had on 16 July spelled out stringent

---

[22] For the dispute over the venue of the conference: Henderson to Tyrrell, 5, 12, 17 July 1929; Tyrrell to Lindsay, 16 July 1929; Nicolson to Lindsay, 21 July 1929; Knatchbull-Hugessen to Henderson, 25 July 1929, *DBFP* 1A, vi. 401–3, 418, 430–1, 442–3, 449–50. For Snowden and Chéron: Henderson to Lindsay, 6, 7, 8, 10 Aug. 1929, ibid. 481–8, 494–6, 512–14. For American pressure: Sargent to Phipps, 9 Aug. 1929; MacDonald to Snowden, 11 Aug. 1929; Lindsay to Snowden, 11 Aug. 1929, ibid. 511–12, 515–16; Snowden, *Autobiography*, ii. 799–800; S. Roskill, *Hankey: Man of Secrets* (3 vols.; London, 1970–4), ii. 485–7. For Financial Sub-Committee: Jaspar to Snowden, 16 Aug. 1929; Snowden to Jaspar, 16 Aug. 1929, *DBFP* IA, vi. 537–47. For French anxiety: Armour to Sec. State, 20 Aug. 1929, Dept. of State, 462.00 R296/3246. For American and Italian policy: Tobin to Sec. State, 21 Aug. 1929; Wilson to Sec. State, 22 Aug. 1929, ibid. 3223, 3227, 3229. For subsequent negotiations: Jaspar to Snowden, 25 Aug. 1929; Phipps to Lindsay, 27 Aug. 1929; Hankey to MacDonald, 28 Aug. 1929, *DBFP* IA, vi. 587–91, 595–600; Snowden, *Autobiography*, ii. 813–21.

[23] For Snowden and Breitscheid: Pünder to A. Amt, 27 Aug. 1929, *ADAP* xii. 505–7.

criteria for judging when the Young Plan would be deemed to be in operation and the evacuation could begin. After he arrived at the Hague, however, there seemed to be very little divergence between his views and those of Arthur Henderson, the new British Foreign Secretary, who was committed to prompt and unconditional evacuation. By the end of the second week of the conference he had dropped the French demand for a Conciliation Commission to adjudicate any future disputes over the Rhineland; and Stresemann had reciprocated by waiving further German financial claims under the Rhineland Agreement so long as the British and Belgian evacuation was completed by the end of the year and the French by 1 April 1930. By 22 August the only dispute between Briand and Henderson was whether the last troops should be withdrawn by 30 June or 31 May 1930; and a week later even the niggling residual question of the allocation of the costs of the occupying armies after 1 September 1929 had been amicably settled. Such compliance can only have been a response to the dual pressure exerted by the ratification of the Mellon–Bérenger Agreement and the apparent unpredictability of British policy. But the consequent vulnerability of Briand to right-wing criticism meant that the days of his ministry were numbered.[24]

Partly because of the anxiety aroused by Snowden's behaviour, the eventual success of the first Hague Conference initially produced a favourable reaction in Germany. Although the German delegates scarcely received the hero's welcome which was accorded to Snowden on his return to London, they were publicly received and congratulated by Hindenburg. The prospect that the Third Occupation Zone of the Rhineland would be cleared of foreign troops five years earlier than the treaty stipulated took some of the sting out of the right-wing press, even if Westarp, the Nationalist spokesman, still found cause for complaint in the continuing demilitarization of the region. Much was also made by the moderate parties of the 20-per-cent reduction in Germany's annuities and the dismantling of the financial controls of the Dawes scheme. This relative euphoria was, of course, hard to sustain for long because the duration of Germany's obligations provided the Nationalists and Nazis with highly combustible material. As Poole, the American Counsellor in Berlin, observed early in September, Germany's obligations were

[24] For Briand's speech: Tyrrell to Henderson, 18 July 1929, *DBFP* IA, vi. 433–5. For the Hague negotiations: ibid. 556–60, 566–8; Wilson to Sec. State, 29 Aug. 1929, Dept. of State, 462.00 R296/3262.

appalling possibly not so much on account of their size, which the ordinary mind can hardly grasp, but on account of their duration. That two generations are to be burdened is easily understood ... The weight and duration of the burden which Germany is now to accept voluntarily certainly presents the Nationalists with strong matter for popular agitation.

Hitler had lost no time in proclaiming to his newly galvanized cohorts at Nuremberg on 2 August that their prime task would be 'the organization of general patriotic resistance (*eines allgemeinen Volkswiderstandes*) against the new Paris *Diktat*'; and a few weeks later Hugenberg's National Committee published its Draft Law Against the Enslavement of the German People.[25]

The role of the Nationalists and Nazis in crystallizing opposition to the Young Plan should not, of course, be exaggerated. Their campaign always lacked cohesion because of the refusal of more respectable Nationalists to support the demand for the impeachment of ministers who implemented the Young Plan. Yet the disunity of the movement and the overwhelming rejection of the Draft Law in the referendum of 22 December was counterbalanced by growing discontent in more responsible German circles in the closing months of 1929. To a certain extent this was generated by a memorandum published on 6 December by Schacht which protested at the way in which Germany's overall burden had been increased in recent months. The Hague Conference, Schacht complained, had forced Germany to increase her unconditional annuities and to renounce any claim to the surplus funds accruing from her last five monthly payments under the Dawes scheme; and additional obligations had subsequently been imposed upon her by the settlement of the Belgian mark claim and the continuing liquidation of Germany property in Britain. The most important reason for the deepening opposition to the Young Plan was, however, the growing budgetary embarrassment of the government. As Gilbert was at pains to point out in his final report as Agent-General a few months later, the long-term cause of the deficit was the chronic inability of the federal government to conclude a more favourable tax-sharing agreement with the states. Yet the immediate source of difficulty was the diminished revenue and increased expenditure on unemployment

---

[25] For the initial German reaction: Schurmann to Sec. State, 30 Aug., 9, 17 Sept. 1929, ibid. 3258, 3323, 3352; Poole to Sec. State, 4 Sept. 1929, ibid. 3311; *KZ*, 6 Sept. 1929, No. 290. For Hitler and Hugenberg: ibid. 4 Aug. 1929, No. 257; 13 Sept. 1929, No. 297. For the Hugenberg–Hitler campaign: Schurmann to Sec. State, 11 Nov. 1929, 1 Dec. 1929, Dept. of State, 462.00 R296/3461, 3466.

relief which resulted from the economic downturn in the last quarter of 1929. For this reason Schacht's memorandum of 6 December was an attempt to prod the government into drastic conservative financial reform as well as an attack on the behaviour of Germany's creditors. During the next few months German political leaders were to become embroiled in a dispute over which section of the community was to bear the brunt of the crisis. The reluctance of Finance Minister Rudolf Hilferding and Chancellor Hermann Müller to introduce measures which would increase the burden on the German lower classes was to precipitate the resignation of Hilferding in December and the ultimate downfall of the Müller cabinet in the spring of 1930. It was only to be expected that the deepening deadlock in German financial politics would have an inhibiting effect on the residual negotiations over the Young Plan.[26]

The Second Hague Conference

As in the winter of 1921–2, the dissipation of the reparation mirage provoked a swing to the right in France. The concessions which had been made to Britain in August and French apprehension, fuelled by the gathering momentum of the Hugenberg–Hitler campaign, that Germany would be less likely to fulfil her obligations after the Rhineland had been evacuated, precipitated the fall of Briand and the formation of a more conservative cabinet under André Tardieu. Yet the options open to the new administration were far more restricted than they had been for Poincaré in 1922. The use of military sanctions was now ruled out both by the insistence of the British Labour government on prompt evacuation of the Rhineland and by the high level of American investment in Germany. Tardieu therefore refrained from any attempt to prolong the occupation and sought to extract relatively innocuous financial and political guarantees from Germany. The satisfaction of these largely rhetorical demands was to absorb most of the energies of the Second Hague Conference when it assembled early in the new year.

[26] For Schacht: Schurmann to Sec. State, 6, 7, 10 Dec. 1929, Dept. of State, 462.00 R296/3472, 3474, 3507. For Gilbert: *Report of the Agent-General for Reparation Payments, 21 May 1930* (London, 1930) (henceforward RC xxii), 144. For the German budget: Transfer Committee, Economic Service, Germany's Financial Position at the Turn of the Year 1929–1930, Dept. of State, 462.00 R296/3630.

The kid-glove approach of Tardieu at the Hague was indicated when, in an effort to circumvent the reparation problem, he invited the German delegates to breakfast at the outset of the conference and proposed a scheme of Franco-German economic collaboration. This was, however, rejected out of hand by Curtius, the new German Foreign Minister, because of his unwillingness to jeopardize his country's economic independence. Tardieu was therefore forced to prop up the façade of reparations by insisting that everything possible should be done to commercialize Germany's debt. Since the Müller cabinet was wary of any positive long-term commitment, Tardieu had to settle for a negative arrangement whereby neither the German government nor its major public utilities such as the railways and post office would compete with the forthcoming Young Loan by floating issues in the international capital market in the 1930–1 financial year. This was, however, no great imposition since the $300 million Young Loan was designed to commercialize only a small fraction of Germany's total reparation obligation and the German government had an option to use one third of its proceeds for its own purposes. There was a similar futility about the objections which the French delegation registered against the $125 million German loan which had recently been negotiated with the Swedish Match Company and Kreuger and Toll of Amsterdam. Although Kreuger, the Swedish match king, was duly summoned to the Hague and persuaded both to postpone the flotation of his loan and, if necessary, to cede priority to the servicing of the Young bonds, this did not enable Germany to commercialize a significant proportion of her reparation debt. The harsh reality of her financial position was indicated a few months later when the government was forced to arrange a short-term credit with the American banking firm Lee, Higginson, & Co. in order to bridge the period until the Kreuger and Toll loan was floated.[27]

French efforts to obtain political, as opposed to financial, guarantees from Germany were equally gestural. Tardieu did press at first for the retention of the sanctions provisions of the Versailles Treaty to cover a possible German default. Yet he made it clear to the British government, which considered these provisions to have been superseded by

[27] For Tardieu's breakfast: Curtius, 68. For the suspension of German long-term borrowing: *Agreements Concluded at the Hague Conference, January 1930, House of Commons Papers*, Cmd. 3484, 1929–30, xxxii. 135–7. Cf. *Das Kabinett Müller II*, ii. 1362, 1377–9. For the Lee, Higginson credit: Gilbert to Sec. State, 22 Mar. 1930, Dept. of State, 462.00 R296/3691.

the Young Plan, that no French government would actually 'exercise the right to reoccupy the Rhineland'. His concern, he stressed, was that 'he could not admit that the German government should be in a position to repudiate the Young Plan with impunity, and it was essential to him for political purposes to be able to show that he had not abandoned the ultimate rights of France in this matter'. Such was Tardieu's scepticism about the feasibility of sanctions that he retreated after a few days of discussion with the German delegation to a far vaguer formula than that in the peace treaty. It was eventually agreed that if any creditor suspected Germany of working to undermine the Young Plan the matter could be referred to the Permanent Court of International Justice; and that if the decision of this body was unfavourable to the debtor the aggrieved party or parties would be entitled simply to 'resume their full liberty of action'. The purpose of this equivocation was not to establish a meaningful system of sanctions but, as Léon Blum observed in Le Populaire on 16 January, to encourage the French public to believe that, in the event of a German default, France would be entitled to fall back on her rights under the treaty, while leading Germans to assume exactly the opposite.[28]

The same ambivalence was evident in the formulae adopted by the conference about the finality of the Young settlement. Article I of the eventual agreement with Germany proclaimed that the new plan was 'definitely accepted as a complete and final settlement, so far as Germany is concerned, of the financial questions resulting from the war'; and it recorded 'the solemn undertaking' of the German government 'to pay the annuities for which the New Plan provides in accordance with the stipulations contained therein'. Yet, a few paragraphs later this certainty was dispelled by a reference to the possibility that, notwithstanding the German government's sincere efforts to fulfil its obligations, the threat to Germany's currency and economic life posed by some or all of the postponable annuities could justify a unilateral declaration of postponement.[29]

Despite the covert moderation of the Hague Agreements, French rhetoric about commercialization and sanctions produced reverberations in German nationalist circles. These were, somewhat predictably, relayed to the conference by Schacht, whose eagerness to

[28] For Tardieu's views: Leith-Ross to Lindsay, 4, 8 Jan. 1930, DBFP IA, vii. 335–6, 347–57. For sanctions formula: Agreements Concluded at the Hague Conference, January 1930, 28–9. For Léon Blum: MG, 17 Jan. 1930.

[29] Agreements Concluded at the Hague Conference, January 1930, 18, 21.

parade his patriotism in the international arena had been increased by the upsurge of right-wing extremism in Germany. The Reichsbank president had been excluded from the main German delegation because of the criticism which he had levelled at both the creditors and the German government in his memorandum of 6 December. He had, however, made his presence felt when the organizational committee of the Bank for International Settlements of which he was a member gathered to report to the conference in its second week. There was a sensation on 13 January when the committee received a letter from Schacht attaching political strings to German participation in the new bank. The collaboration of the Reichsbank and the eventual fate of the settlement would, he insisted, depend on 'whether the final Hague Conference [subjected] Germany to further political and economic pressure, whether German private property [continued] to be discriminated against, particularly in England, and whether the provisions of the Versailles Treaty for military and political sanctions [would] remain in force or be annulled after the adoption of the Young Plan'. The original purpose of Schacht's letter, which had been leaked to the press soon after it had been drafted on 31 December, was to bluff the creditors into moderating their positions; and it may have had a salutary effect on the negotiations in the first week of the conference. Its subsequent impact was, however, counter-productive since by mid-January agreement had already been reached on sanctions and the fate of German property in England. Schacht's persistence has led some observers to conclude that, because of Germany's deteriorating financial position, he was still trying to engineer the breakdown of negotiations, a reversion to the Dawes Plan, and the implementation of its transfer protection provisions. Yet his readiness to agree to the proposal of the German delegation that special legislation should be passed directing the Reichsbank to collaborate with the BIS indicates that, as in the previous May, his primary concern was to divest himself of personal responsibility for Germany's involvement in the Young Plan. Schacht's subsequent insistence that the plan had been undermined by the anaemic sanctions provisions of the Hague Protocol confirms the impression that he was playing to the ultra-nationalist gallery, no doubt with a view to future employment. Such a conclusion is also encouraged by the remark of Hermann Müller to Sir Horace Rumbold on 15 January that Schacht was 'attempting to wash his hands of all responsibility for the Young Plan and that he had purposely manœuvred himself into the position of being forced to come into line as regards participation of the Reichsbank in the organisation of the Bank for International Settlements.[30]

Of far more practical significance than Tardieu's bogus guarantees or the posturing of Schacht was the settlement of eastern European indebtedness. This was precipitated by the recommendations of the Young Committee that Germany should no longer be held responsible for the debts of her former allies, Austria and Hungary, and the consequent necessity to determine the obligations of those powers. Such a determination in turn involved adjudicating upon a mass of claims and counter-claims between the erstwhile 'master races' of the Habsburg Empire and the successor states. Since it became clear in the early days of the conference that nothing much could be extracted from Austria, hopes centred mainly on Hungary. The problem was, however, that the Hungarian government insisted on claiming more from Czechoslovakia, Yugoslavia, and Romania in compensation for the losses sustained by its citizens who were residents in the successor states than it was willing to pay in reparations. This prompted the three would-be creditor states to refuse to pay more to Hungary than they received from her. Their position was strengthened because they enjoyed the support of their French patrons. It was also important that the distributive dispute which had threatened to break up the first Hague Conference had been resolved partly at the expense of Czechoslovakia, whose liberation debt repayments to Italy had been transferred to Britain in order to satisfy Snowden's demands. It was poetic justice that the deadlock between Hungary and the Little Entente was only resolved in mid-January when the British government was cajoled by Loucheur—who apparently revelled in his job as chairman of the Committee on Eastern Reparations—to help establish a number of financial 'pools' out of which Hungarian counter-claims could be met. Sensing his power, Beneš, the Czech Foreign Minister, took a leaf out of Snowden's book by blackmailing Britain and France into paying part of the Czech liberation debt to Italy on the final day of the conference. As Hugh Dalton, at that time Parliamentary Under-

[30] For Schacht's exclusion: Chefbesprechung 28 Dec. 1929, *Das Kabinett Müller II*, ii. 1327–8; Curtius, 78–9. For Schacht and the BIS: Schacht to de Sanchez, 31 Dec. 1929, in H. Schacht, *Das Ende der Reparationen* (Oldenburg, 1931), 111–12; E. Wandel, *Hans Schäffer: Steuermann in wirtschaftlichen und politischen Krisen* (Stuttgart, 1974), 124; Lüke, 252; E. N. Peterson, *Hjalmar Schacht: For and Against Hitler* (Boston, 1954), 95–8. For his change of tune: *Das Kabinett Müller II*, ii. 1361–70. For his claims about sanctions: *Das Ende*, 119, 130. For Müller's verdict: Rumbold to Henderson, 16 Jan. 1930, *DBFP* IA, vii. 378 n. 2.

Secretary of State for Foreign Affairs, remarked, Britain was 'surrendering a small fraction of the financial gains of the First Hague Conference in order to buy a settlement in Eastern Europe'. Beneš, he concluded, was a 'clever little blighter'.[31]

Despite its success in unravelling the financial affairs of eastern Europe, the Second Hague Conference had merely papered over the cracks in the Young Plan. The unreality of the settlement was emphasized by the rancorous and protracted debate which it occasioned in the Reichstag and the histrionic resignation of Schacht on 7 March after he had failed to persuade Hindenburg to veto ratification. There was, of course, never any doubt that the plan would be adopted by a substantial majority. Yet, as on similar occasions in the past, this was simply because the Reichstag feared the domestic and international financial consequences of rejection. Müller and Curtius certainly advocated acceptance for the sake of fringe benefits such as the evacuation of the Rhineland, and they also referred to the additional incentive of Germany's reduced burden and the desirability of obtaining some relief for the hard-pressed economy. Yet both were at pains to reserve judgement when pressed by the extreme right about the plan's long-term viability. 'Neither the German government nor the experts nor anybody else', declared Müller on 12 March, 'could honestly predict with any degree of certainty about the impact of the Young Plan.' Even more important was the outspoken language of Heinrich Brüning, the parliamentary leader of the Centre Party. Since the Young Committee had admitted in its report that it had been influenced by political as well as economic considerations, the plan was, Brüning declared, a *Diktat*. Its economic irrationality would ultimately mean that continuing fulfilment would jeopardize the interests of private foreign investors in Germany. Until that situation brought about its revision the settlement would only be tolerable if disputes over implementation were settled by international arbitration and the standard of living of the German people was adequately safeguarded.[32]

The prospects for the Young Plan were clouded further by the

---

[31] For good analyses of eastern European financial relations see FO Memo of 11 Dec. 1929 (by Sargent) and 31 Dec. 1929 (by E. H. Carr): *DBFP* IA, vii. 237–40, 294–6. For the Hague negotiations: Phipps to Henderson, 6, 9, 11, 16, 17, 18, 19, 20 Jan. 1930, ibid. 336–41, 353, 369–70, 389–90, 392–3, 397–400, 411–14, 416–19. For subsequent remarks by Beneš about his achievement at the Hague: Livesey to Ratshetsky, 22 Mar. 1930, Dept. of State, 462.00 R296/3662.

[32] Curtius, 11 Feb. 1930, *RT* cdxxvi. 3902–5; Müller, 12 Mar. 1930, ibid. cdxxvii. 4352–7; Brüning, ibid. 4370–1.

political and social regression which gathered momentum as the German propertied classes sought to resolve the deepening financial crisis at the expense of the lower orders. The trend had been initiated by Schacht when he prevented Hilferding from covering the ballooning budget deficit with a loan from the American bankers Dillon, Read, & Co. Fortified by the opposition of Gilbert and Tardieu to any foreign borrowing which might prejudice the Young Loan, Schacht had persuaded the cabinet to steer through the Reichstag on 24 December a law providing for a credit of 350 million marks from a German banking consortium on the condition that a matching sinking fund would be established out of current revenue by 15 April 1930. The cabinet's rejection of its Finance Minister's more humane tactic of long-term borrowing precipitated the resignation of both Hilferding and his Secretary of State, Johannes Popitz, whose strategies of financial reform and tax reduction were now in tatters. The new complexion of German policy was reflected in their successors, Paul Moldenhauer of the DVP and Hans Schäffer, both of whom were firm believers in balancing the budget by traditional conservative methods. By February Moldenhauer had drawn up a budgetary reform programme which envisaged increased indirect taxation and the cessation of government subventions to the unemployment insurance fund. This drew immediate protests from the SPD that too much of the burden of the crisis was being borne by the broad masses of consumers. The demand of the left for a counterbalancing surcharge on the income tax was, however, flatly rejected by the DVP on the grounds that it would aggravate the shortage of funds for investment and encourage capital flight. In the compromise which was arrived at on 5 March only minor concessions were made to the SPD on the funding of unemployment insurance and new demands were registered for income tax reductions in the following year. The shape of things to come was also indicated by the appointment of Hans Luther as Schacht's successor. Although he styled himself as a non-party expert, the new Reichsbank president had been noted for the expedition with which he reduced wages and dismantled social welfare when he was Finance Minister in 1923 and 1924. Once the ratification of the Young Plan had removed the need for further collaboration between the DVP and SPD, the stage was therefore set for financial blood-letting. By 25 March the gap between the two parties had become even wider because of the insistence of the DVP that both unemployment benefits and direct taxes should be cut. On the following day the position of the SPD became untenable when Brüning and his party, drifting with the right-wing tide, deserted their Social Democratic colleagues and put forward a compromise proposal which threatened the maintenance of unemployment relief payments at their existing level. Although Müller and the SPD ministers still wished to prolong the coalition, they were, with good reason, overruled by the rank and file of the parliamentary party. The Chancellor's manœuvrability was also restricted by his awareness that Hindenburg and the Reichswehr were now angling for a conservative cabinet and that the President would be unlikely to support any attempt to force a radical financial programme through the Reichstag with the aid of the emergency powers provisions in Article 48 of the constitution. He therefore tendered his resignation on 27 March and was speedily replaced by a conservative coalition which had been waiting in the wings for some time. The brutally simplistic retrenchment programme of the new government was spelled out by Brüning when he addressed the Reichstag for the first time as Chancellor on 1 April. The only sure way of stimulating the economy and reducing unemployment was, he declared, to lighten the burdens of the business world by overhauling the budget and reforming the financial system.[33]

The growing tension in Germany over financial policy and the consequent fall of the Müller cabinet had a perceptible impact on the debate over the ratification of the Young Plan in France. Concern had been expressed on 22 March in the Finance and Foreign Affairs Committees of the Chamber about Germany's failure to achieve financial reform; and Le Figaro remarked a week later on the irony of the Müller cabinet's resignation because of its inability to agree upon a financial programme at the very moment when the Chamber was about to ratify the plan. Tardieu's response was to try to gloss over the difficulties by emphasizing the finality of the settlement and by pressing for speedy ratification so as to expedite the commercialization of the first tranche of bonds in May. Yet he found it necessary to reassure the Chamber that a German default would lead to the suspension of France's war-debt remittances to the United States. Léon Blum also extracted an undertaking that, even in the event of a wilful

---

[33] For the financial policy of the Müller cabinet: I. Maurer, *Reichsfinanzen und grosse Koalition: zur Geschichte des Reichskabinetts Müller (1928–1930)* (Frankfurt-on-Main, 1973), 102–39; Wandel, *Hans Schäffer*, 133–41. For Moldenhauer's proposal: *Das Kabinett Müller II*, ii. 1422–6, 1436–43, 1495–1500. For DVP/SPD conflict and the compromise: ibid. 1502–9, 1512–23, 1535–9. For letter: ibid. 1550–4. For the government crisis: Parteiführerbesprechung 25 Mar. 1930, ibid. 1594–8. For Müller's attitude: ibid. 1608–10. For Brüning's speech: *RT*, 1 Apr. 1930, cdxxvii. 4729.

German default, France would not have recourse to unilateral reprisals but would act in accordance with Article 13 of the League of Nations Charter. It was a measure of Tardieu's embarrassment that he ultimately fell back on the rhetoric of Franco-German *rapprochement*. 'The men who governed Germany up to yesterday and who will govern her tomorrow', he declared, 'are animated by the firm intention to put an end to a state of affairs between two of the greatest countries of Europe which has done them both much harm.' The Chamber was, in any case, locked into the Young Plan by its newly acknowledged financial commitments to the United States. It therefore voted overwhelmingly (527 to 38) in favour of ratification on 30 March; and the Senate quickly followed suit with an affirmative vote of 283 to 8 on 5 April. Its wishful thinking was, however, indicated by the report of its Foreign Affairs Committee. Having criticized the failure of the Hague Agreements to establish a juridical link between war debts and reparations, and having expressed concern about the impact of the early evacuation of the Rhineland and the dismantling of the Reparation Commission, the committee nevertheless went on to express pious hopes about European federation and Franco-German reconciliation. 'One world has finished and another is beginning', it declared. 'European Federation, essential for the equilibrium of Europe, can only be obtained by Franco-German *rapprochement* within the framework of public law.' In view of the considerable tensions which were present in Franco-German relations, such rhetoric was as misleading to the French public as the original reparation claims which its political leaders had concocted.[34]

---

[34] For French concern about developments in Germany: Armour to Sec. State, 24, 28 Mar. 1930, Dept. of State, 462.00 R296/3714, 3721. For Blum and Tardieu's response: Armour to Sec. State, 31 Mar. 1930; Edge to Sec. State, 7 Apr. 1930, ibid. 3722, 3735. For report of Senate Foreign Affairs Committee of 1 Apr. 1930: No. 194, Sénat Année 1930, enc. in Edge to Sec. State, 7 Apr. 1930, Dept. of State, 462.00 R296/3735. For Senate vote: Edge to Sec. State, 7 Apr. 1930, ibid. 3715.

9
The Last Act

WITHIN two years of its formal inauguration the Young Plan had collapsed and reparations had been spirited off the international stage. In view of the violent economic contraction which occurred between 1930 and 1932 it is remarkable that a system which was premissed on an unlikely upsurge of international trade should have survived for so long. The explanation is to be sought, as ever, in the domestic financial politics of the parties to the dispute. Much of the responsibility for the lack of remedial action must be borne by the United States government which, by its unrelenting attitude to war debts, provided the European victors with an excuse for maintaining their own financial pressure on Germany. Such was the reluctance of the American administration to relinquish, or to appear to relinquish, its claims upon Germany's creditors that it remained relatively impervious to the resurgence of Wall Street's concern lest the continuing fulfilment of the Young Plan should jeopardize the substantial funds which American private citizens had invested in Europe. President Hoover's proposal in June 1931 for a one-year moratorium on inter-governmental debts, and the measures subsequently adopted to arrest the withdrawal of private credits from Germany, were certainly a response to the fears of the American banking fraternity. Yet the abrupt and high-handed manner in which this moratorium was proclaimed and the restricted scope of the 'stand still' arrangements betrayed the abiding concern of the American government with pre-empting any international negotiations which might prejudice the war-debt repayments of the European powers. The rearguard action which Hoover subsequently mounted in defence of the Young Plan also indicated that he ultimately preferred to pose as guardian of the taxpayer rather than as friend of the American foreign investor.

Because it was committed by the Mellon–Bérenger Agreement to regular repayment of its war debts to the United States, the French government had a common interest with the American administration in prolonging the flow of funds from Germany provided by the Young Plan. However, the relative financial stability and economic prosperity of France and her increasing concern about the growth of German revanchism, especially after the Allied evacuation of the Rhineland in mid-1930, led to a change in the emphasis of French foreign policy. In the early 1920s French governments had deployed military force in an effort to achieve illusory financial objectives. A decade later they sought to use their financial muscle in an equally vain attempt to secure German diplomatic and economic collaboration. It was unfortunate that in 1930 and 1931 Curtius, Stresemann's successor as Foreign Minister, was hankering for an 'active' foreign policy which ruled out any Franco-German *rapprochement*. By the autumn of 1931 Laval, who succeeded Tardieu as premier, had, therefore, reverted to the short-term expedient of colluding with Hoover in his efforts to steer the Young Plan through the shoals of the depression. The evident collapse of the tributary system in subsequent months reduced the French government, like the American administration, to futile attempts to salvage either political compensation or paper claims from the wreckage. Herriot, who came to power after the electoral success of the Radicals in May 1932, made a half-hearted attempt to persuade the final reparation conference at Lausanne to admit the distinction between Germany's current impoverishment and her future financial capacity. Such, however, was the general desire to get rid of reparations in order to expedite international recovery and pacification that he could not extract anything more than the promise of a token 3 billion mark lump-sum payment, which was unlikely ever to be effectuated.

Of the three major reparation creditors, the only single-minded revisionist was Britain. The MacDonald government was, however, unwilling until late in 1931 to take the initiative in proposing the necessary all-round cancellation of inter-governmental debts because it was reluctant to compound its mounting financial problems by giving offence to American opinion. It therefore confined itself to spotlighting the difficulties of Germany, adopting defensive international economic strategies which happened to undermine the reparation scheme, and urging the French to embark on a revisionist course. MacDonald's invitation of Brüning and Curtius to the Chequers conversations of June 1931 helped to precipitate the Hoover Moratorium and the ice-breaking international discussions which followed in the second half of 1931. The National government's decision to abandon the gold standard and erect protective tariffs in the autumn also underlined the impossibility of Germany achieving the export surplus which was needed if the Young Plan was to be viable. Finally, it was partly in response to Britain's ever-increasing pressure that Herriot agreed to take part in the Lausanne Conference which delivered the somewhat botched *coup de grâce* to the reparation problem in July 1932.

It goes without saying that the German governments of the early 1930s objected strenuously to the Young Plan. Yet this does not mean that the domestic and external financial policies of Brüning and Papen were rigidly subordinated to the aim of getting rid of reparations. It could indeed be argued that the tendency of Brüning and his ministers to exploit the reparation question for domestic political purposes and their propensity for diplomatic adventurism, particularly after the emergence of the Nazis as a major political force in 1930, did more harm than good to the revisionist cause. It is certainly misleading to characterize Brüning's harsh deflationary policies simply as the actions of a man engaged in a race against time to achieve the cessation of reparation payments at the risk of plunging Germany into social and political chaos. Brüning believed that ruthless retrenchment was necessary for its own sake in order to shore up Germany's external credit and to reduce the fiscal burden upon German industry. His desire to achieve these aims stemmed in turn from the conviction, shared by modern 'monetarists', that economic recovery could only be fuelled by increased investment. The Chancellor's deflationary obsession was such that he referred soon after he assumed office to Germany's reparation obligations merely as an added justification for retrenchment. His subsequent concern with arresting the outflow of foreign exchange and gold from Germany—which had been provoked largely by the rise of the Nazis and his increasingly demagogic responses thereto—meant that in his first year in office he shrank from any attempt to have the reparation scheme revised for fear of the short-term damage that such an initiative might do to what remained of Germany's foreign credit. The policies of Brüning and his successor cannot therefore be portrayed as a systematic effort to dismantle the Young Plan. They were, on the contrary, a product of financial conservatism, peppered with demagoguery and diplomatic adventurism designed to steal the thunder of the extreme right wing.

THE YOUNG PLAN: FROM HONEYMOON TO MORATORIUM, MAY
1930–JUNE 1931

If there was ever any ground for optimism about the future of the
Young Plan it existed in the first month of its operation. One initial
reason for hope was that on 17 May, the day on which the plan began
to operate, the Bank for International Settlements opened its doors for
business in Basle. Although it had been set up mainly to supervise the
collection and distribution of the Young annuities, the bank could also
regularize collaboration between central banks, promote international
trade, facilitate the international circulation of capital, and help to
prevent exchange instability. Its effectiveness as an international financial institution seemed, moreover, to be assured by the high calibre of
its staff. Gates W. McGarrah, its president, came to the position from
the chairmanship of the board of the Federal Reserve Bank of New
York and had also been a member of the Transfer Committee under
the Dawes Plan. His assistant was Leon Fraser, who had been the Paris
representative of Parker Gilbert, the Agent-General for Reparation
Payments; and the bank's general manager, Pierre Quesnay, was a
senior officer of the Banque de France who was widely regarded as the
French equivalent of J. M. Keynes and had played a leading part in
both the financial reconstruction of Austria in the early 1920s and the
deliberations of the Young Committee in 1929. With these men at the
helm and a board of directors made up of the governors of the major
central banks, it seemed likely that the new body would not only trim
the Young Plan to the prevailing economic winds but also make
a positive contribution to international financial stabilization and
economic recovery.[1]

Another sign that a new era might have dawned was the political
moderation of the French government. The high-water mark of this
trend was reached on 17 May, when Tardieu gave the go-ahead for
the evacuation of the Rhineland and Briand circulated his Memorandum on European Federal Union. The latter was admittedly
designed in part to allay fears aroused by France's abandonment of
her strategic foothold within German territory. It was, moreover,
given a cool reception by the British and German governments, who
suspected that the aim of the proposal was to perpetuate the diplomatic

[1] On the BIS: G. W. McGarrah, 'The First Six Months of the BIS', *Proc. of the Acad.
of Political Science, New York*, 14 (2) (1930–2), 235–46; *The Economist*, 12 Apr. 1930,
817–18; 26 Apr. 1930, 938–9; *The Economist Banking Supplement*, 11 Oct. 1930. On
Quesnay: *MG*, 24 Apr. 1930, 6.

status quo. Yet the very fact that Briand was pressing for institutionalized consultation between the European powers on matters of mutual political and economic concern seemed to augur well for the process of depoliticization which was at the heart of the Young Plan.[2]

The mild euphoria inspired by the plan may account for the flicker of enthusiasm with which the international capital market greeted the $300 million Young Loan when it was launched in the second week of June. The oversubscription of the somewhat misleadingly entitled German Government International 5 Per Cent Loan was, however, only made possible by the low rate at which its bonds were issued (92), the extensive publicity it received, and the measures taken to give it right of way on the New York, Paris, and London bond markets. When the bonds were traded on the world's stock exchanges a few days later they sold at an even greater discount and seemed likely to yield a profit only for the bankers who had marketed them in return for a handsome commission.[3]

The third week of June marked the end of the Young Plan's brief honeymoon and saw the development of a new deadlock over financial policy in Germany. In the previous week there had been a fresh 'break' on the New York stock market which rivalled the crash of the preceding October and further reduced the already questionable ability of Germany to commercialize her reparation obligations. The imposition of the Hawley–Smoot tariff by the United States government on 17 June also made it highly unlikely that Germany would be able to earn sufficient foreign exchange from her export trade to sustain the level of monetary transfers required by the plan. On the following day the resignation of the Finance Minister, Paul Moldenhauer, signalled that all was not well with the German budget. Although falling prices had increased the burden of the first Young annuity of 1.8 billion marks (payable from 1 April), the main reason for the budgetary crisis was the rapid growth of unemployment, which had occasioned extraordinary outlays on emergency relief and the sagging unemployment insurance fund and also a sharp reduction in tax revenue. Because of the undesirability of interrupting the inflow of foreign funds which had occurred after the inauguration of the Young Plan, any attempt to reduce Germany's reparation obligations was considered

[2] For Briand's proposal: F. Siebert, *Aristide Briand, 1862–1932: ein Staatsmann zwischen Frankreich und Europa* (Stuttgart, 1973), 542–7. See above, ch. 8 n. 18.

[3] On the marketing of the Young Loan: *The Times*, 13 June 1930 (LA); 14 June 1930, 18; 17 June 1930, 21; *NYT*, 12 June 1930, 1, 4 (LA); 13 June 1930, 10; *The Economist*, 14 June 1930, 1317–18.

to be out of the question. Brüning and Moldenhauer therefore wished to restore budgetary balance by purely domestic financial reform. What was more, as Brüning had warned the Standing Committee of the Reichsrat on 28 June, any delay in implementing this reform would undermine Germany's external credit and make her vulnerable to external pressure in future international financial negotiations. The problem was, however, that any fresh attempt to balance the budget was bound to revive the struggle between the left and right wing which had brought down the Müller cabinet. Contention centred at first around proposals in the cabinet's original reform package of 5 June for a $2\frac{1}{2}$ per cent Emergency Levy on higher income groups and special taxes on single persons and directors' fees. Although these measures were intended as a quid pro quo for wage reductions which the government and its supporters hoped to introduce, they were so repugnant to the right wing of the DVP, to which Moldenhauer belonged, that the Finance Minister was forced to resign on 18 June. His successor, Hermann Dietrich of the DDP, placated the moguls of the DVP by watering down the offending measures and introducing a more regressive poll tax (*Bürgersteuer*). This, however, merely set the cabinet on collision course with the SPD, upon whose support it depended for a parliamentary majority; and the new programme was duly rejected by the Reichstag on 16 July. Not to be deterred, Brüning, who was more confident of the backing of Hindenburg than Müller, his Social Democrat predecessor, immediately promulgated the measures as an emergency decree under Article 48 of the constitution. When an SPD motion disallowing this decree was carried by a vote of 236 to 221, Brüning's response was to dissolve the Reichstag on 18 July and call for the elections of September 1930, which were to do so much damage to Germany's external credit and shatter the fragile *détente* which Briand had been labouring to construct.[4]

While German domestic politics were sapping the foundations of

[4] For Wall Street: *The Economist*, 21 June 1930, 1375–6. For the Hawley–Smoot tariff: *NYT*, 18 June 1930, 1. For Moldenhauer's remarks on the German budgetary crisis: I. Maurer and U. Wengst (edd.), *Politik und Wirtschaft in der Krise, 1930–32: Quellen zur Ära Brüning* (2 vols.; Düsseldorf, 1980), i. 205–12. For his resignation: ibid. 243–6. For the financial programme of Dietrich: ibid. 264–8, 273–5 nn. 4 and 5. For the confrontation between Brüning and the Reichstag: ibid. 283 n. 6; 300–2. Ministerbesprechungen vom 9., 15., 16., 18., Juli 1930, *Akten der Reichskanzlei: Weimarer Republik. Die Kabinette Brüning I u. II: 30. März 1930 bis 10. Oktober 1931, 10. Oktober 1931 bis 1. Juni 1932*, ed. T. Koops (3 vols.; Boppard-on-Rhine, 1982), i. 289–93, 320–1, 324–5, 329–30; *RT*, 16 July 1930, cdxxviii. 6400 (Breitscheid); 18 July 1930, 6505 (Lansberg); H. Brüning, *Memoiren* (Stuttgart, 1970), 162–82.

the Young Plan, diplomatic developments had already begun to sour the attitude of France towards Germany. Perhaps the most bitter pill for the French government to swallow was the German reaction to the evacuation of the Rhineland when it was punctually completed on 30 June. Hindenburg's Manifesto of 1 July to mark the occasion on behalf of the German government did not acknowledge the work of moderate statesmen such as Briand and Stresemann but claimed that the German people had achieved the evacuation only 'by years of bitter suffering' and 'by accepting heavy burdens' and complained that the Saar still remained under foreign rule. Within a few weeks agitation by German nationalists for further concessions on such issues as the demilitarization of the Rhineland and the future of the Saar, Eupen-Malmédy, Danzig, and the Polish corridor had provoked Poincaré to condemn Germany's apparently insatiable appetite for treaty revision. The growing predilection of the German government for an 'active' anti-western foreign policy such as it had pursued in 1922 also influenced its unenthusiastic reply on 11 July to Briand's circular on European Federal Union. Convinced that Briand's proposal was merely a ploy to consolidate French influence, and concerned at the favourable response to it from Vienna, the cabinet declared flatly that it would be 'pointless to seek to build a new Europe on foundations which could not withstand fresh development'. The negative reaction of the German and British governments delivered a mortal blow to Briand's scheme, and it was only a matter of weeks before the proposal was, in the words of Beneš, accorded 'a first class burial' by being referred to a League of Nations committee on 17 September. This was, however, three days after the cause of Franco-German *rapprochement* had suffered an even more serious set-back as a result of the gains of the Nazis in the Reichstag elections.[5]

The catastrophic swing to the NSDAP is attributed by some historians almost solely to their exploitation of the Young Plan as an election issue. 'The use of the Young Plan for propaganda purposes by the National Socialists', Wolfgang Helbich has concluded, 'was of decisive importance for the party's success in the 1930 elections.' The Nazi campaign was certainly replete with denunciation of 'the Young government', 'the Young Chancellor', 'Young slavery', 'Young taxes', and 'Young misery'. Yet it would be wrong to under-estimate the

---

[5] For Hindenburg's manifesto: Rumbold to Henderson, 3 July 1930, *DBFP* II, i. 485–8. For Poincaré: Campbell to Henderson, 13 Aug. 1930, ibid. 493–4. For the fate of Briand's scheme: Siebert, 548–59.

:: LOW ON "UNITED STATES OF EUROPE" PLAN

The German reply to M. Briand's proposals for a European Federation hints that a revision of unsatisfactory Treaty settlements should be an essential accompaniment.

GERMANIA: "DONDT YOU HAF ANY ICES MITOUT DER VERSAILLES FLAVOUR?"

BRIAND: "MAIS, C'EST IMPOSSIBLE, MADAME! IT IS THE PRINCIPAL INGREDIENT."

FIG. 11. The *Evening Standard*, 7 August 1930.

extent to which the appeal of the NSDAP derived from its social radicalism as well as its patriotism. Brüning insisted, both at the time and subsequently, that the election was fought solely over his attempt to balance the budget by means of emergency decrees. What upset his opponents on the radical left and right was not just that he was doing this in order to pay reparations but also that his policies favoured the propertied classes. The unashamed conservatism of Brüning's financial policy and his obvious sensitivity to the wishes of big business and its party, the DVP, increased the attractiveness of a group such as the NSDAP, which was not only patriotic but also boasted a social programme based, as the conservative *Kreuz-Zeitung* observed, on hatred of property (*Besitzfeindschaft*). The expulsion of the Strasser group from the party in July 1930 does not appear to have diluted its 'socialist' image too much, since a great number of the left-wing rank-and-file retained their membership and Gottfried Feder had no compunction about proclaiming his confiscatory financial schemes in the Reichstag on 18 July. The social radicalism of many of those who voted for the Nazis in September 1930 was emphasized by contemporary observers of varying political persuasions. On the eve of the elections the SPD's *Vorwärts* sought to tar the KPD and the NSDAP with the same brush by referring to the former as 'National Bolsheviks' and the latter as 'Hitler Communists'; and it subsequently asserted that many former DNVP supporters who had drifted into the Nazi camp were people who had become alienated from the existing social order. 'A proportion of them', it observed, had become 'outspokenly anti-capitalist and were therefore not simply nationalists but national socialists.' Leading members of the traditional military and civilian élite also considered that the heavy vote for the Nazis had been a reaction to the economic crisis, that the NSDAP's radical social programme had to be taken seriously, and even that Hitler and his party were financed from Moscow.[6]

[6] For the Young Plan and the elections: W. J. Helbich, *Die Reparationen in der Ära Brüning: zur Bedeutung des Young-Plans für die deutsche Politik 1930 bis 1932* (Berlin, 1962), 16. Cf. Eyck, ii. 350–1. For another view: H. Bennecke, *Wirtschaftliche Depression und politischer Radikalismus 1918–1938* (Munich, 1970), 89–92, 345–8. On the issue of the emergency decrees: Brüning, *Memoiren*, 182. Cf. *FZ*, 7 Sept. 1930, No. 252, 2. The significance of Strasser's expulsion is emphasized by G. Schulz, *Aufstieg des Nationalsozialismus: Krise und Revolution in Deutschland* (Frankfurt-on-Main, 1975), 579, but played down by R. Kuhnl, *Die nationalsozialistische Linke, 1925–1930* (Meisenheim-on-Glan, 1966), 257–60. For Feder: *RT*, 18 July 1930, cdxxviii. 6520–1. For contemporary analysis of the NSDAP's appeal: *KZ*, 12 Sept. 1930, No. 257 (LA); *Vorwärts*, 9 Sept. 1930, No. 421, 4; 15 Sept. 1930 (spec. edn.); 16 Sept. 1930, No. 434, 3; Aufzeichnung des Generalmajors Liebmann über eine Besprechung im Reichswehrministerium ... 25 Oct. 1930, in Maurer and Wengst, i. 165–6; Robert Weismann,

Although the September elections set up domestic and international shock waves which were eventually to jeopardize the Young Plan, the revisionist aspirations of the Brüning cabinet in the closing months of 1930 should not be exaggerated. The Chancellor's primary pre-occupation was still to promote economic recovery by means of domestic deflation. The case for such a policy had, in his view, been strengthened by the outflow of gold and foreign exchange which the financial deadlock and the elections had precipitated and by the consequent decision of the cabinet to seek a bridging credit of $125 million from the American banking firm of Lee, Higginson, & Co. Deflation was also favoured by business interests close to the government who had become concerned about the competitiveness of German goods in a period of sagging international prices. It is true that after the elections Brüning stressed to Hitler and other leaders of the extreme right wing who were pressing for an immediate reparation *démarche* that his financial programme was a necessary preliminary to the long-term resolution of the reparation problem. Yet he shrank from taking any short-term initiative which might destroy what was left of Germany's foreign credit and would be unlikely to yield any satisfactory settlement because of the continuing vulnerability of the unreformed German financial system to creditor blackmail. As he insisted to Westarp, the DNVP veteran, no demand should be made for revision of the Young Plan until the economic and financial system had been rehabilitated (*saniert*), a process which he expected would take three years. Brüning's concentration on domestic financial reform and his related reluctance to rock the international financial boat were reflected in his programme of 30 September, which consisted simply of measures to restrict government expenditure, reduce the tax burden on industry, lower wages and prices, and prop up the ailing agricultural sector. He appears to have broached the question of foreign policy in the Reichstag on 16 October largely in response to pressure from the radical left and right wing and the trade union movement to have Germany's reparation obligations reviewed or cancelled. To the accompaniment of persistent heckling from Goebbels and Strasser, he obliquely canvassed the possibility of new reparation negotiations by referring not only to Germany's deepening economic crisis but also to the machinery of the Bank for International Settlements for adjusting

State Secretary in the Prussian Ministry of State, as reported by British ambassador: Rumbold to Henderson, 16 Sept. 1930, *DBFP* II, i. 510–11; Aufzeichnung des Staatssekretärs Pünder . . ., 15 Sept. 1930, *Die Kabinette Brüning*, i. 425–7.

Germany's obligations to her capacity to pay and, for good measure, to the view of the Young Committee 'that the solution of the reparation problem was not the sole responsibility of Germany ... and that it required the co-operation of all the parties involved'. The Chancellor then hastened to reaffirm, however, that 'the immediate responsibility of the German people was to do everything in its power to put its own house in order'; and he succeeded in defusing five resolutions calling for some sort of reparation initiative by having them referred to the Foreign Affairs Committee of the Reichstag. Before they were considered by this body Brüning tried to persuade party leaders to refrain from voting on them on the grounds that their adoption would compound Germany's financial difficulties and their rejection would convey the misleading impression that she did not object to the Young Plan. The committee was in the end won over by Dietrich and Curtius to the view of the Centre Party, the DDP, and the DVP that the resolutions would be financially and diplomatically counter-productive; and the thunder of the extreme right was diverted into a resolution calling for the disarmament of the rest of the world to a level of parity with Germany. Having blunted the attack of the revisionists, Brüning went on the offensive in an address on 27 November to the Central Committee of the Federation of German Industry. Those who asserted that everything that was amiss in German political and economic life could be attributed to the reparation problem were, he claimed, 'misleading the German people and clouding their self-awareness (loud applause)'. In so doing, 'they were hindering the prompt implementation of measures which would have been necessary even if there had been no reparations'.[7]

Brüning's stand-pat position on reparations was in line with the views of senior advisers such as Hans Schäffer, Secretary of State of the Finance Ministry, and Hans Luther, the president of the Reichsbank. The latter considered that reparation revision would be achieved

[7] For path-breaking studies which stress Brüning's revisionist intentions in 1930: E. W. Bennett, *Germany and the Diplomacy of the Financial Crisis, 1931* (Cambridge, Mass., 1962), ch. 2; Helbich, *Reparationen*, 20–2. For the best recent discussion: C.-L. Holtfrerich, 'Alternativen zu Brünings Wirtschaftspolitik in der Weltwirtschaftskrise?', *HZ* 235 (1982), 605–31. For Brüning's concern about Germany's foreign credit: *Memoiren*, 189–90; Schäffer's notes of a conversation with Brüning and Luther, 22 Sept. 1930, Maurer and Wengst, i. 397–401. For the anxiety of industry: Kastl's speech to the RDI, 19 Sept. 1930, ibid. 393–7. For Brüning's conversations with Hitler and Westarp: *Memoiren*, 192–5; Maurer and Wengst, i. 443–4. For his programme, *Memoiren*, 190; *RT*, 16 Oct. 1930, cdxliv. 19–22; Report of Meeting of Foreign Affairs Committee, 29 Oct. 1930, Maurer and Wengst, i. 446–56. For speech of 27 Nov.: ibid. 477.

not by mouthing Nazi and Communist slogans about unilateral cancellation but by launching an 'offensive of fulfilment', which would
make the Young Plan unpalatable to the creditor powers by flooding
the world with cheap German goods. This strategy, which was a
revival of that advocated by Walther Rathenau and others in the
second half of 1921, had been espoused by Finance Minister Dietrich
both in an election-eve declaration on 11 September and in his statement to the Foreign Affairs Committee on 29 October. It emerged again
as the theme of the speech of Kastl, the president of the Federation of
German Industry, on the occasion of Brüning's address to that body
a month later:

Now that the movement of international capital is in a completely different
direction to what it was during the operation of the Dawes Plan, it has become
obvious what the payment and receipt of reparations means for the world
economy ... It has become clear that the illusion which the creditors have
hitherto been labouring under, that it would be sheer joy [*eitel Freude*] to
receive reparations from Germany, has been shattered. The objective of
German financial policy should not, therefore, be to demand a moratorium
but to build up our overseas credit and to strengthen our currency, not only
so that we can survive in the international market-place but also so that we
can compete so fiercely with other exporting nations that they can really feel
the effect of the reparations they have demanded.

It remained to be seen how long Brüning could afford to be guided by
such counsels.[8]

In many respects, but not all, the policies of the creditors also
resembled those which they had pursued nine years earlier. As in 1921,
Briand, the apostle of Franco-German *rapprochement*, was becoming
increasingly beleaguered. His position had already been weakened by
the lukewarm reception of his proposal for European federation. Then
came the electoral gains of the Nazis, the impact of which has been
compared by one of his biographers to that of the news of Napoleon's
escape from Elba upon the Congress of Vienna. In September and
October Briand hastened to warn Curtius that any attempt to have
the Young Plan revised would merely lead to the revival of French
demands for the reimposition of financial controls upon Germany. It
would be wiser, he advised, for the German government to tide itself

---

[8] For Schäffer and Luther: Wandel, *Hans Schäffer*, 160–1; Schäffer's notes of a
conversation with Luther, 6 Nov. 1930, Maurer and Wengst, i. 460–1. For Dietrich:
ibid. 449–51; Rumbold to Henderson, 12 Sept. 1930, *DBFP* II, i. 507–8. For Kastl: Maurer
and Wengst, i. 475–6.

over its current difficulties by obtaining long-term credits from France. This remark indicated the fundamental change in French policy since 1921. Although the extreme right wing bemoaned the evacuation of the Rhineland in the Chamber in November, the nationalist press now advocated that Germany should be reined in by the withdrawal of French short-term loans rather than by military means. As Erich von Gelsa of the DVP observed at the time, people were now saying in Germany that they had got rid of visible enemy occupation only to have it replaced by an equally objectionable invisible occupation in the shape of short-term foreign indebtedness.[9]

The Anglo-Saxons were, if anything, less inclined to revise Germany's obligations than they had been in the autumn of 1921, when there had at least been a little uncertainty about the war-debts policy of the United States government. A major source of concern in late 1930 for both the British government and the American financial élite was the destructive effect that any new reparation negotiations might have on Germany's overseas credit. As George Harrison, the governor of the Federal Reserve Bank of New York, warned financial leaders in Berlin in November, American investors would be likely to confuse a government request for a reparation moratorium with the inability of European businessmen to honour their private debts. British and American observers were also impressed by Germany's sizeable trade surplus in 1930, even if this had been achieved by reduced imports rather than increased exports. Most important of all, however, was the continuing refusal of the American government to contemplate the reduction of war debts which the British cabinet insisted, as it had in December 1921, was a *sine qua non* for reparation revision. There had, of course, been a resurgence of concern about the security of American investments in Germany towards the end of 1930. Revisionist statements by American businessmen with European interests such as Owen Young, William C. Redfield, Albert H. Wiggin, Paul M. Warburg, and James Speyer had aroused considerable comment in the European press. The New York *Journal of Commerce* had also declared that international indebtedness would have to be restructured if normal conditions of trade were to return. The way the wind was blowing in Washington was, however, indicated by a strongly anti-revisionist article in the *Washington Herald* by Senator Reed Smoot,

---

[9] For Briand's domestic position: Siebert, 557–67; Bennett, 22–4. For his policy towards Germany: Bülow to Schäffer, 27 Sept. 1930, Maurer and Wengst, i. 400–1. See Gelsa to Reusch, 5 Dec. 1930, ibid. 484.

chairman of the Senate Finance Committee, at the end of December. President Hoover, for his part, politely ignored a speculative appeal from Brüning via Frederick M. Sackett, the American ambassador in Berlin, that he should organize a five-power conference to discuss ways of tackling the world economic crisis. To judge from the views of the American financial experts who were working for the Bank for International Settlements, the main preoccupation of Washington in the winter of 1930–1 was to discourage any talk of a German moratorium for fear that this would precipitate requests from France and Italy for relief from their war-debt repayments. The hope was, according to Leon Fraser, that if Germany survived the next three or four months 'the question of revision [might] be postponed for three or four years'. It was generally agreed that 'brave leadership would be required to get Congress to lighten the burden on alien debtors at this time and impose correspondingly heavier taxes on Americans'.[10]

If such leadership was lacking in Washington it could hardly be expected in Berlin. From the end of 1930 Brüning became less preoccupied with domestic deflation for its own sake and increasingly attracted to the idea of making some sort of gesture which would strengthen his position in the Reichstag, where the advocates of an active reparation policy enjoyed a majority. He was still, however, constrained in the early months of 1931 by the rigid opposition of Luther and his ministerial advisers to anything that might undermine Germany's external credit, especially when a further loan of $32 million was being negotiated with American and French banks. For this reason his budget speech in the Reichstag on 5 February sought primarily to dispel what he referred to as 'the crisis of confidence in the stability of the German political and economic system' and to ensure that the budget for 1931–2 was promptly approved by the normal parliamentary procedures. In an effort to appease his parliamentary critics, he added that 'the entire economic and financial policy of the government was designed to prepare the way for an over-all solution of the reparation problem'. Brüning's discomfiture was, however, evident in

[10] For British policy: Henderson to Rumbold, 2 Dec. 1930, *DBFP* II, i. 435–9; Conversation between Curtius and Rumbold, 10 Dec. 1930, Maurer and Wengst, i. 491. For American policy: Schäffer's minute of a conversation with Harrison, 24 Nov. 1930, ibid. 470–3; *NYT*, 4 Dec. 1930, 2 (Young); 23 Dec. 1930, 20 (German trade surplus); *Washington Herald*, 28 Dec. 1930 (Smoot), in *Congressional Record*, 21 Jan. 1931, lxxiv, Pt. 3, 3274–5. For Brüning, Sackett, and Hoover: Brüning, *Memoiren*, 222–4; Rumbold to Henderson, 4 Mar. 1931, *DBFP* II, i. 577–8; Pünder to Bülow, 3 Jan. 1931, Maurer and Wengst, i. 531 n.2; Bennett, 31–3. For BIS view: Cochran to Cotton, 14 Jan. 1931, Dept. of State, 462.00 R296, BIS Special Reports, I, Box 405.

a discussion with his cabinet colleagues two days later. Having insisted that the reparation question had to be 'tackled' to dispel the impression that the government was doing nothing, he went on to admit that no definite initiative could be taken in the current diplomatic context. The only course open to him, he concluded, was to take steps to have the reparation question 'canvassed'. Such a compromise strategy appears to have been approved by the Reichstag on 12 February when it rejected more radical reparation proposals which had been considered by the Foreign Affairs Committee in October, and adopted (by 314 votes to 56) a middle-of-the-way resolution of the Christlich-Sozial Volksdienst (a conservative splinter group) which called on the government 'to begin discussion of the tribute burden as soon as possible with the powers involved in the Young Plan and to take all domestic measures necessary to ensure a successful outcome'. It was with a view to initiating such preliminary general discussions that Brüning now put out feelers to the British government. Although the latter was, as ever, unwilling to bell the reparation cat for fear of giving offence to American opinion, MacDonald and Henderson were attracted to the suggestion of Rumbold, the British ambassador in Berlin, that they should invite Brüning and Curtius to spend a weekend at Chequers in order to raise the German cabinet's domestic prestige. However, between mid-March, when this invitation was issued, and early June, when the two statesmen arrived in Britain, a financial crisis for which the German government was in part to blame had made the continuing fulfilment of the Young Plan impossible.[11]

The revelation on 21 March that Germany and Austria had been secretly negotiating a Customs Union did much to undermine the Young Plan in the spring of 1931. It is, however, hard to say whether the political and financial reverberations of the disclosure should be attributed more to the provocative behaviour of the Germans than to the overreaction of the French. The project was certainly adventurist enough to make nonsense of any claim that Brüning's foreign policy was rigidly subordinated to creating conditions which would enable

[11] For Brüning's changed attitude and the opposition of his advisers: Schäffer's Diary Entry of 15 Dec. 1930; Bülow to Prittwitz, 20 Jan. 1931, Maurer and Wengst, i. 512–13, 531. For budget speech: 5 Feb. 1931, *RT* cdxliv. 678–82 at 679–80; Brüning, *Memoiren*, 225–7. For statement of 7 Feb.: Aktenvermerk ... über eine Besprechung in der Reichs-kanzlei ..., Maurer and Wengst, i. 555. For resolution of 12 Feb. 1931: *RT* cdxliv. 953. Cf. Helbich, *Reparationen*, 20. On the origins of the Chequers conversations: Henderson to Rumbold, 19 Feb. 1931; Rumbold to Henderson, 4, 6 Mar. 1931, *DBFP* II, i. 559–61, 573–81; MacDonald to Stimson, 8 June 1931, *FR*, 1931, i. 11–14.

SPRINGTIME IN EUROPE.

(Copyright in all countries.)

FIG. 12. The *Evening Standard*, 28 March 1931.

him to achieve a final reparation settlement from a position of financial and political strength. The initiative was not, on the other hand, a desperate attempt to placate the Nazis and Nationalists without regard to external repercussions. The Brüning cabinet was not feeling particularly beleaguered in March 1931: the economy was enjoying a short-lived remission, the adjournment of the Reichstag until the autumn had provided a political breathing space, revisionist feeling was slowly growing abroad, the British had made a crucial gesture of friendship, and there were even signs of financial *rapprochement* with France. In fact, as Brüning remarked to the cabinet on 16 March, the timing of the scheme was neither entirely fortunate nor of Germany's choosing. It was, in the first place, a natural outgrowth of the discussions about European federation which had been inaugurated by Briand in 1930 and of the long-standing concern of the German Foreign Office that Austria should not be absorbed into an alternative economic grouping such as a Danubian federation. It also reflected the impetus which the deepening economic crisis had given to the negotiation of bilateral trading agreements in eastern Europe. In selling his department's brain-child to a sceptical cabinet in mid-March, Curtius certainly predicted that it would defuse domestic tensions by providing the basis for a united front from the SPD to the Nazis. Yet his presentation of the proposal to both the cabinet and the world as part of the general movement towards European federation and economic co-operation indicates that it was a product of the international diplomatic and economic context rather than of a desire to play to the jingo gallery. In comparison with the Rapallo Treaty of April 1922, which was a calculated slap in the face to Britain and France, the Customs Union scheme was merely an ill-timed and clumsy exercise in constructive economic diplomacy.[12]

The violence of the French reaction to the proposal was clearly increased by the secrecy of the Austro-German negotiations and the press leaks which occurred before the creditor powers were formally notified of what was afoot. The underlying reason for the behaviour

[12] For somewhat Machiavellian interpretations of Germany's role in the Customs Union negotiations: Bennett, 40–58; F. G. Stambrook, 'The German–Austrian Customs Union Project of 1931: A Study of German Methods and Motives', *J. of Central European Affairs*, 21 (1961), 15–44. For a more balanced account: Ann Orde, 'The Origins of the German–Austrian Customs Union Affair of 1931', *CEH* 13 (1980), 34–59. For Brüning's assessment of the German political situation in Mar. 1931 and his lack of enthusiasm for the *Zollunion: Memoiren*, 263–70. Cf. Ministerbesprechung vom 16. März 1931, *Die Kabinette Brüning*, ii. 952–5. For Nationalist approval: Westarp, *RT*, 25 Mar. 1931, cdxlv. 1987–8.

of the French government was, however, that the Customs Union was interpreted as a prelude to political union (*Anschluss*), which was forbidden both by Article 88 of the Treaty of Saint-Germain and by the Geneva Protocol of October 1922, which vetoed 'any negotiations or ... any economic or financial engagement calculated directly or indirectly to compromise' Austrian independence. A less legalistic, but important, source of French disapproval was that Austria and Germany appeared to be upstaging Briand's efforts to achieve European federation. The chagrin of the French premier was increased by the unveiling of the proposal two weeks after he had assured the Chamber of Deputies that fears of an *Anschluss* were groundless, and two months before he was to present himself to the French parliament as a candidate for the presidency. His bitter denunciation of the Customs Union in the Senate on 28 March and his subsequent efforts to disassociate himself from it in the Chamber yielded the government a 419 to 43 vote of confidence on 9 May, but created an excessively hostile atmosphere. This in turn encouraged the German government to overcome its initial qualms about the project and to reject out of hand an alternative scheme of tariff concessions and financial assistance to Austria which was drawn up in April by François-Poncet. The upshot was that the German proposal was blocked by France in the League of Nations Council on 18 May and that the question of its legality was referred to the Court of International Justice at the Hague.[13]

Care must be exercised in determining the precise relationship between the deadlock over the Customs Union and the financial turmoil of ensuing months. There is no evidence that direct French financial pressure on Austria in the form of withdrawal of credits was responsible for the collapse of the leading Austrian bank, the Creditanstalt, on 11 May. It could even be argued that a more serious threat would have been posed to Austria's already teetering financial institutions if the Customs Union had been established and Austrian industry had been exposed to an influx of cheap German goods. The financial sins of France were, in fact, those of omission rather than commission or, more precisely, of withholding rather than withdrawing capital. France's representatives on the Board of Directors of

[13] For the French reaction: Bennett, ch. 4; Siebert, 584–9. For texts of Treaty of Saint-Germain and Geneva Protocol: *Treaty of Peace between the Allied and Associated Powers and Austria ...*, *10 September 1919, House of Commons Papers*, Cmd. 400, 1919, liii; League of Nations, *Official Journal*, Nov. 1922, Annexe 433, Protocol No. I, 1471–2. For comment: Akers-Douglas to Curzon, 6 Oct. 1922, *DBFP* I, xxiv. 364–7.

the BIS had dealt their most telling blow to the financial system of
central Europe three months earlier when they rejected a suggestion
by Montagu Norman that the BIS should establish an International
Corporation (a forerunner of the World Bank) which would assist
world economic recovery by channelling surplus American and French
funds to capital-starved countries such as Austria and Germany. The
French, according to Leon Fraser, objected to any proposal 'to draw
upon France for capital which was to be managed by outsiders'. This
reluctance to deploy financial resources except when it was to her
diplomatic advantage was evident when, *after* the collapse of the
Creditanstalt, France compounded Austria's difficulties by making her
participation in an international financial rescue operation conditional
upon the abandonment of the Customs Union.[14]

The contribution of the German government's financial policy to
the disorders of mid-1931 was more direct. Brüning had become aware
by the beginning of May that the deficit in the budget for 1931–2 had
blown out to 800 million marks and had concluded that another
Draconian emergency decree (*Notverordnung*) would be necessary.
The debate about which section of the community should pick up the
tabs was, therefore, renewed amongst the groups upon which the
government depended for its support. The industrialists declared
through the DVP that they would resist further taxation, that expenditure on social welfare and unemployment relief should be reduced,
and that wages should be lowered. The SPD and the trade unions, on
the other hand, insisted that there should be increased taxation of the
well-to-do, that social welfare expenditure should be maintained, and
that the working week should be shortened. Both groups objected
strenuously to the government's protection of agriculture, which was
raising the cost of living. With a new political crisis looming, Brüning
reiterated to his financial advisers on 7 May that it would be necessary
'to broach [*anzuschneiden*] the reparation question at the same time
as the next big emergency decree if the cabinet was not to be overthrown'. His idea was still, however, merely 'to create the impression
in Germany that revision had begun' while the rest of the world
continued to believe that she was 'doing everything she could to fulfil
her obligations'. No real steps would in fact, he predicted, be taken to

[14] For French behaviour in the BIS: Cochran to Cotton, 11 Feb., 11 Mar. 1931, BIS
Special Reports, I. Box 405, Dept. of State, 462.00 R296. For France's financial policy
towards Austria: K. E. Born, *Die deutsche Bankenkrise: Finanzen und Politik* (Munich,
1967), 56, 64–6.

revise Germany's reparation obligations until the following year. The
Chancellor's suggestion was strongly opposed by Luther and flew in
the face of a memorandum of 9 April by Schäffer advising against
premature reparation negotiations on the grounds that they might
prejudice a favourable settlement and not appease public opinion.
It was, however, noteworthy that Finance Minister Dietrich now
considered that the outflow of gold and foreign exchange which would
be precipitated by a pseudo-*démarche* such as Brüning envisaged could
be stemmed by raising the discount rate of the Reichsbank.[15]

The debate over whether the government should defuse opposition
to the impending emergency decree by beating the reparation drum
continued until the end of May. In the mean time, Germany's financial
position was weakened further by the withdrawal of almost 300 million
marks of short-term foreign credits from German banks in the wake
of the collapse of the Creditanstalt. Business confidence was also
undermined by reports of the difficulties of the Karstadt department
store chain and the Nordstern Insurance Company at the end of May.
In this atmosphere the promulgation of the Emergency Decree and the
Reparation Manifesto (*Tributaufruf*) in the first week of June was
little short of disastrous. The Emergency Decree's package of reduced
welfare expenditure and increased taxation of consumer goods provoked a storm of protest from the SPD which threatened to bring down
the government; and the introduction of an Income Tax Surcharge
(*Krisensteuer*) gave offence to the DVP and encouraged the social
groups it represented to export their capital. The situation was, if
anything, worsened by the *Tributaufruf*, the text of which was only
finalized by the vacillating cabinet on 5 June after the departure of
Brüning and Curtius to England for the Chequers talks and of Luther
to Switzerland for a BIS board meeting. Its general declaration that
'the limit of the privations which could be imposed upon the German
people had been reached' was a reasonable concession to popular
feeling: but the more alarmist assertion that Germany's 'extremely
precarious economic and financial situation' required 'the removal of
her intolerable reparation burdens' did unnecessary damage to her
external credit. Secretary of State Stimson, who was very disturbed by

[15] For Brüning's views: Memo of Conversation in Reich Chancelry, 7 May 1931,
Maurer and Wengst, ii. 620–1. For industry's opposition to the Emergency Decree:
Dingledey to Brüning, 18 May 1931, ibid. 632–7. For the trade unions: Leipart to
Brüning, 31 May 1931, ibid. 631–2. For Schäffer's memorandum: ibid. 583–96. For
disagreement about advisability of *Tributaufruf*: Luther's Memo of Conversation in
Reich Chancelry, 30 May 1931, ibid. 632–6.

the *Tributaufruf*, complained to Lindsay, the British ambassador in Washington, that it had cancelled out the good financial effect of the Emergency Decree and would 'harm Germany's situation by destroying her credit beyond any measures of relief that could conceivably be afforded in respect to reparations'. The Reichsbank's loss of 400 million marks of its gold and foreign exchange reserves in the four days following the *Tributaufruf* provided stark confirmation of Stimson's prediction.[16]

Neither Brüning nor Curtius expected or desired these traumatic developments, which merely deprived Germany of the financial muscle which they considered necessary for negotiating a satisfactory final reparation settlement. They therefore hastened to reassure the somewhat ruffled MacDonald and Henderson, who had been expecting to discuss disarmament rather than reparations at Chequers, that the *Tributaufruf* was merely a sop to domestic opinion and not an appeal for an immediate resumption of reparation negotiations. On his return to Berlin Brüning also insisted, in the face of growing impatience in his cabinet, that no reparation initiative could be undertaken until after a projected visit of Stimson to Europe late in July. The Chancellor's attempt to put the lid back on the reparation question was, however, quickly frustrated by domestic political and economic developments. In the second week of June the predictable storm blew up over the *Notverordnung*, when the SPD and DVP joined with the extremist parties in demanding that either the Reichstag or its Budget Committee be recalled to debate the measure. The five-day deadlock which ensued after Brüning refused to comply with this demand induced renewed financial haemorrhaging in the course of which the Reichsbank, even though it raised its discount rate from 5 to 7 per cent on 13 June, lost another 500 million marks in gold and foreign exchange. The run stopped briefly on 17 and 18 June after the DVP and SPD were bought off with amendments to the Emergency Decree. But it began again after the first reports that the giant Nordwolle textile concern, which had borrowed heavily from the Danatbank, had fallen victim to the contraction of the economy and its over-expansionist and shady business practices. On 19 June Brüning and Luther decided that the diminution of the Reichsbank's reserves was such as to warrant an appeal

[16] For financial developments in May 1931: Born, 66–8. For protests against *Notverordnung*: *Vorwärts*, 7 June 1931, No. 261, 1; Brüning, *Memoiren*, 277; Circular of RDI, 3 June 1931, Maurer and Wengst, i. 648–9. For text of *Tributaufruf*: ibid. 633 n. 2. For vacillation of Cabinet: *Die Kabinette Brüning*, ii. 1183. For Stimson: Lindsay to Henderson, 6 June 1931, *DBFP* II, ii. 70. For Reichsbank's losses: Born, 71.

within the next few days to the BIS for a suspension of Germany's reparation payments.[17]

Such an initiative was pre-empted by the proposal of President Hoover on the following day that there should be a one-year moratorium on all inter-government debt transfers. This sudden American intervention owed its original impetus to Hoover's general desire to restore international commercial confidence and the growing awareness of the American administration of the financial and political interdependence of the United States and Germany. The latter's financial condition had been anxiously monitored by both Wall Street and Washington in the second and third weeks of June. George Harrison, the governor of the Federal Reserve Bank of New York, was, according to Ogden Mills, the Assistant Secretary of the Treasury, 'in constant communication' with Montagu Norman; Stimson, the Secretary of State, discussed the German situation with Ramsay MacDonald by telephone on 13 June; McGarrah cabled his views from the Bank for International Settlements on 14 June; and Secretary of the Treasury Andrew Mellon, who happened to arrive in London on 16 June on the way to visit his son at Cambridge, relayed his impressions back to Mills by telephone on 18 June. Although McGarrah, no doubt influenced by the stand-pat views of Luther, considered that the Reichsbank had the situation under control, the information received from these sources was sufficiently pessimistic to strengthen the hand of Wall Street advisers such as Baruch, Gilbert, Morrow, and Young, who were pressing, as they had in 1928, for bold action to safeguard the substantial funds which American private investors had sunk in Germany in recent years.[18]

[17] For Chequers conversations of 7 June: Henderson to Yencken (Berlin), 13 June 1931, DBFP II, ii. 71–7: MacDonald to Stimson, 8 June 1931, FR, 1931, i. 11–14. For Brüning and the German financial and political situation: Ministerbesprechung vom 11. Juni 1931, Die Kabinette Brüning, ii. 1187–91; Luther's Diary Entry of 11 June, Maurer and Wengst, i. 650–2, 653–4, nn. 17 and 19; Born, 73–7; Brüning, Memoiren, 290–1. For discussion of BIS appeal: Chefbesprechung vom 19. Juni 1931, Die Kabinette Brüning, ii. 1218–25.

[18] For Hoover's original motivation: Bennett, 165; Link, Stabilisierungspolitik, 500–2; H. L. Stimson and M. Bundy, On Active Service in Peace and War (London, n.d.), 54–7; E. E. Morison, Turmoil and Tradition: A Study of the Life and Times of Henry L. Stimson (Boston, 1960), 345–50. See also R. H. Ferrell, American Diplomacy in the Great Depression: Hoover–Stimson Foreign Policy, 1929–1933 (New Haven, 1957), ch. 7; L. P. Lochner, Herbert Hoover and Germany (New York, 1960), ch. 6. Hoover's memoirs are unhelpful and chronologically inaccurate on this topic: The Memoirs of Herbert Hoover: The Great Depression 1929–1941 (London, 1953), 67–72. For the concern and activity of the American financial establishment in mid-June: Mills to

As on the previous occasion, however, countervailing pressures from the United States Treasury and Congress against any initiative which might interfere with the flow of war-debt repayments transformed what might have been an act of financial statesmanship into a mere stop-gap arrangement. Hoover's advisers insisted that, in order to be effective, any moratorium should run for two years and be preceded by consultation with France which would, after the United States, be the major loser from any such step. The President's reluctance to incur the wrath of Senator Borah and the American taxpayer prompted him, however, to halve the length of the moratorium. As Keynes pointed out at the time, this did not allow sufficient breathing space for the recovery which was the necessary prerequisite for a balanced reappraisal of inter-government indebtedness. Also important in detracting from the effect of Hoover's gesture was the inordinate haste with which he ultimately acted, and his consequent failure to have any prior discussion with the French. Stimson's subsequent attempt to rationalize this omission as a deliberate attempt to maximize the beneficial 'shock-effect' of the moratorium proposal is unconvincing. The explanation for Hoover's behaviour is again to be sought in his reluctance to jeopardize war debts. It was this which, on Stimson's own testimony, caused Hoover to vacillate about whether to act even after his return to Washington from a tour of the mid-west on the afternoon of 18 June. The argument with which Ogden Mills probably swayed Hoover—it was Mills who according to Stimson 'did most of the talking' in the crucial discussions at the White House on the evening of 18 June—was not that Germany was on the verge of collapse but that she had to be prevented from making a formal application for a moratorium lest this should throw the whole question of reparations and war debts into the melting pot. The memorandum which Mills laid before the President on 18 June reported Mellon's equivocal advice earlier that day that a moratorium was 'not absolutely necessary, but would be very reassuring' as long as the French were consulted first. Mills then went on to press for a moratorium on the quite new grounds that, although the crisis had peaked, the German government would 'definitely ... invoke the suspension provisions of the Young Plan at a comparatively early date'. In this event, Germany's creditors would in turn cease to pay their debts to the United States. This would, he

Mellon, 15 June 1931, Ogden Mills Papers, Official Correspondence, Container 19. For conversation between MacDonald and Stimson: Atherton to Sec. State, 15 June 1931, *FR*, 1931, i. 16–17.

predicted, present the United States with the unpalatable alternatives of either holding her debtors to their existing agreements and turning her back on Europe or getting involved in a new round of war-debt and reparation negotiations. These, he warned, would be damaging 'to the interests of our own people, for at such a conference we should stand alone'. Such an outcome, Mills advised, could only be avoided 'by the announcement before the situation arises of an American policy consistent with that followed in the past'. Although Mills recommended that the French should be sounded out first, it was obvious that meaningful Franco-American discussions would be precluded by the necessity of forestalling the feared German initiative. For this reason the only communication with the French occurred when Stimson called in Claudel, the French ambassador in Washington, on the following afternoon and advised him of the President's intentions. The subsequent press leaks from congressmen whom Hoover had been canvassing were not, therefore, as Hoover and Stimson subsequently claimed, the underlying reason for the haste with which the moratorium proposal was proclaimed on 20 June. Hoover's stickiness about war debts, which restricted the scope of his proposal and caused the precipitant action which was to raise French hackles, ensured that his moratorium would do very little to resolve the world economic crisis.[19]

Despite the fanfare with which it had been greeted, the Young Plan had clearly begun to disintegrate within a year of its inception because it was a fair-weather scheme which could not survive the rigours of falling prices, contracting trade, and sagging international confidence. Its collapse was hastened appreciably by the domestic politics of the major parties to the reparation dispute. Although Brüning genuinely tried to fulfil the plan, the conservative deflationary policies with which he sought to combat the depression exacerbated Germany's financial problems in the second half of 1930 by giving rise to the political extremism which expressed itself in the September elections. The unsympathetic response of Curtius to the conciliatory diplomacy of Briand also undermined the position of the French moderates; and the ill-timed, if not adventurist, Customs Union proposal increased the reluctance of French bankers to shore up the teetering central European financial system in the first half of 1931. An even more serious blow

[19] For Hoover's vacillation: Stimson and Bundy, 57–8. For the Mills memo: Mills to President, 18 June 1931, Ogden Mills Papers, loc. cit. For Keynes's observations to the Chicago Council on Foreign Relations: *NYT*, 1 July 1931, 18. For Stimson's interview with Claudel: Memo by Sec. State, 19 June 1931, *FR*, 1931, i. 28–9.

was dealt to the Young system by Brüning's attempt to placate the opponents of his Draconian financial policy with the gestural *Tri-butaufruf* of 6 June, and by the domestic political crisis which his programme subsequently provoked. The damage done to Germany's credit and the Young Plan would not have been irreparable if the whole system of inter-government indebtedness had been frozen for the duration of the world depression. It was unfortunate that the Hoover Moratorium, which was originally conceived as a means of achieving such an objective, was diminished in its ambit and marred in its presentation by the unwillingness of a conservative American President of offend domestic opinion on the subject of war debts.

THE ROAD TO LAUSANNE

In view of the improvised nature of Hoover's diplomacy it would be unfair to blame the French entirely for the two weeks of confidence-sapping haggling to which the moratorium scheme gave rise. Hoover's failure to consult effectively with Laval before 20 June deepened the unfounded fears of an Anglo-American side deal with Germany which had been aroused in France since the Chequers conversations. Laval, whose vulnerability was increased because the French parliament was sitting, could hardly have known that Hoover's behaviour had been dictated partly by his anxiety to forestall negotiations leading to a long-term reduction of war debts; and his suspicion could only have been heightened when the American administration omitted to alert him to what was afoot by means of the recently inaugurated trans-Atlantic telephone link. Even if Hoover had allowed himself sufficient lead time to put the French government in the picture, the imprecision of his proposal in certain key areas would have made the clarificatory discussions of late June and early July unavoidable. Given his embargo on any permanent waiver of war debts, and the consequent concern of France to ensure that her reparation receipts from Germany would resume after the moratorium had expired, there was a point to the seemingly convoluted French demand that Germany should continue to pay the unconditional portion of her reparation obligations during the moratorium year on the understanding that the funds so remitted would be immediately reloaned to her by the Bank for International Settlements. By falling in so rapidly with this proposal, the American administration was not simply humouring the French in order to

"BUT DON'T YOU SEE THAT WE MUST GET COMPLETELY OFF FOR A YEAR'S REST?"

"MON DIEU! WHY 'COMPLETELY'? I AM NOT SO TIRED."

"FRANCE AGREES —BUT—"

(Copyright in all countries.)

FIG. 13. The *Evening Standard*, 25 June 1931.

obtain quick agreement but acknowledging that, if reparations were eliminated from the German budget in 1931–2, it would be politically impossible to reinstate them in subsequent years. For Hoover, the apostle of disarmament, there was an equally compelling logic in French insistence that the budgetary savings accruing from the moratorium should not be diverted by the German government into increased arms expenditure. This did not mean that the Americans approved of Laval's suggestion that all the funds reloaned to Germany by the Bank for International Settlements should be channelled to private enterprise. The French point was, however, met squarely by an agreement that the amounts in question would be earmarked for the state-owned German railways and also by the extraction of an undertaking from Brüning on 3 July that his defence spending would not increase during the period of the moratorium. A third shortcoming of Hoover's proposal which was remedied in response to French pressure was its failure to cushion the impact of the moratorium on the small creditor states of central Europe. Here again the remedy agreed upon was not the French scheme of diverting to these states a proportion of the sums reloaned to Germany. But the financial stability of the minor creditors was safeguarded by means of a special fund which was to be established by the major central banks in collaboration with the BIS. Although there was considerable disagreement at first about the rate at which the BIS loan should be repaid by Germany, the French were really intransigent only on the issues of whether current contracts for deliveries in kind between individual French and German enterprises should be abrogated during the period of the moratorium. The obstinacy of Laval on this point, which reflected the continuing preoccupation of the Ministry of National Economy with fostering Franco-German economic integration, was certainly responsible for prolonging the negotiations on 4 and 5 July. Yet most of the time and effort of the French and American negotiators in the preceding period had clearly been expended on imparting sorely needed precision to Hoover's proposal.[20]

[20] For French suspicions and reservations: Edge to Sec. State, 21 June 1931, *FR*, 1931, i. 43–5. For American support in principle for the reloan scheme: Sec. State to Atherton, 24 June 1931; Memo of a Conversation between Stimson and Claudel, 25 June 1931; Acting Sec. State to Edge, 26 June 1931, ibid. 65–9, 77–82. For the US, German disarmament, and Brüning's undertaking: Memo by Acting Sec. State, 29 June and 1 July 1931; Sackett to Acting Sec. State, 2, 3 July 1931; ibid. 97, 109–10, 130–2. For allocation of reloaned funds: Castle to Edge, 30 June 1931; Edge to Castle, 2 July 1931; ibid. 112–17, 123–6. For dispute over rate of repayment of BIS loan: Sec. State to Atherton, 24 June 1931; Acting Sec. State to Edge, 26 June 1931; Edge to Castle, 27 June

Although the protracted Franco-American negotiations were occasioned largely by Hoover's fuzziness, the dissipation of the euphoria which he had induced was due less to the delay in implementing his proposal than to growing awareness of its underlying shortcomings. The price of Young Loan bonds, which was a good indicator of the international financial standing of the German government, had slumped from 78 in May to a low of $62\frac{1}{2}$ in mid-June, and had then recovered after 20 June to fluctuate in the low to mid-70s until the end of the first week of July. In was only after 6 July, when an agreement with France was concluded, that the bonds resumed their downward slide. In so far as this movement was still a response to Germany's reparation burdens, it probably reflected the dawning realization that the Hoover proposal would only take the pressure off the German government for a year. As Henderson observed in a circular memorandum on 10 July to British diplomatic missions, 'the arrangements proposed in [the] Franco-American agreement [had] not sufficed to restore confidence in [the] future economic position of Germany'. On the contrary, it was 'to be feared that [the] markets tend more to regard the year's moratorium as an opportunity to withdraw their remaining credits from Germany rather than as an inducement to leave them there, still less to increase them'.[21]

The financial crisis which now engulfed Germany was the product of her excessive dependence on short-term foreign credits and it was precipitated as much by domestic commercial contraction as by external pressure. Speculation about the stability of the German banking system, which had been kindled by the collapse of the Creditanstalt in May, had flared up again early in June with press reports about the difficulties of the Darmstadter und National Bank (Danatbank). The flight of capital in the two weeks following Brüning's *Tributaufruf* had so depleted the Reichsbank's gold and foreign exchange reserves that it was forced to foreshadow credit restrictions on the eve of the Hoover moratorium. During the short-lived upsurge of confidence induced by the President's gesture the Reichsbank had been able to moderate these restrictions and boost its reserves with a $100 million credit advanced on 24 June by the Bank for International Settlements in conjunction with the central banks of Britain, France, and the

and 2 July 1931, ibid. 65–8, 77–82, 85–7, 123–6. For deliveries in kind: Edge to Acting Sec. State, 4 and 5 July 1931; Acting Sec. State to Edge, 4 and 5 July 1931, ibid. 135–43, 150–7.

[21] For Henderson's Circular of 10 July: *DBFP* II, ii. 164–5.

United States. The credit was, however, too small to counteract the groundswell of anxiety amongst overseas investors about the heavy dependence of the German economy upon short-term high-interest foreign credits. The withdrawals which resumed in the last few days of June were given added impetus by the revelation on 22–3 June of the full extent of the losses of the Nordwolle group and the shadow which this cast over the future of the Danatbank, Nordwolle's major creditor. Such was the concern of the German government about the repercussions of the Nordwolle collapse that it sounded representatives of the business community about the feasibility of propping up the company. In a further effort to restore confidence Luther proposed that a business consortium should establish a 500 million mark fund to guarantee the credit-creating activities of the Golddiskontbank, an affiliate of the Reichsbank which had been set up by Schacht in 1924. Although Luther's scheme was projected by the leaders of the German business world as an antidote to the protracted moratorium negotiations, it was also privately acknowledged to be a defensive reaction to the Nordwolle scandal. The gravity of the crisis was, however, such that Luther's proposal received only partial support and, consequently, increased rather than allayed disquiet. The evaporation of domestic and external confidence also prompted Luther's equally counter-productive 'incognito' flights to London, Paris, and Basle on 9 and 10 July in search of rediscount credits from the Bank of England, the Banque de France, and the BIS. Montagu Norman justified his refusal to come to Luther's assistance on the grounds that the Bank of England had already over-committed itself to Austria and that Germany's financial problems could only be resolved in the long term by international negotiations. The French reaction was just as predictable. Although the Banque de France had sufficient resources to provide the credits requested by Luther, Moret insisted that any French aid would be subject to political conditions such as the abandonment of the Austro-German Customs Union scheme and the cessation of work on the pocket battleships. Since these terms were unacceptable to Brüning, Luther returned home singularly ill-equipped to deal with the mounting financial pandemonium in Berlin, which began on the weekend of 11–12 July with the collapse of the Danatbank and peaked with the closure of all German private banks on 14 and 15 July.[22]

[22] For the fullest accounts of the German banking crisis: Born, 68–109; Bennett, 218–40. For a contemporary SPD analysis and the views of Schäffer: Maurer and Wengst, i. 811–42. For the Nordwolle scandal: Brüning, *Memoiren*, 294; Wandel, *Hans Schäffer*,

The virtual paralysis of the German financial system in the third
week of July made some sort of initiative by the major creditor
powers necessary. It was symptomatic of the demilitarization of French
reparation policy since the early 1920s that, although troops on
France's eastern frontiers were put on the alert, the only serious
response of the French government to the second financial collapse of
Germany in a decade was to repeat its offer of a loan which would
enable her to resume payments in the following year and, for good
measure, induce her to make political concessions. A 1924-style rescue
operation was, however, no longer acceptable to the Anglo-Saxons.
The British government, for its part, would have nothing to do with
a vain repetition of the Dawes Plan. 'Any such loan', Vansittart advised
Tyrrell, the British ambassador in Paris, on 16 July, 'would involve
perpetuating the system which has led Germany into the present
situation. For five years she has been borrowing in order to pay
reparations and as long as that situation continues no restoration of
confidence can be fully effective ... We fear that public opinion in this
country could not be got to accept proposal to guarantee loan for
Germany which would be used to pay reparation mainly to France.'
The Bank of England adopted an even more radical line than the
Foreign Office when Norman insisted at a Bank for International
Settlements board meeting on 13 July that the Reichsbank's $100
million rediscount credit, which was due to expire on 15 July, should
be renewed for only three weeks instead of 90 days. The governor's
transparent efforts to force an immediate renegotiation of reparations
and war debts were, however, unacceptable to the United States
government, which was 'very strongly of the opinion that the time
[was] not right for such a general conference and that the results would
be disastrous'. On the other hand, the American administration, having
just waived war-debt repayments for a year, was unwilling to be
involved in the loan proposed by France.[23]

The attention of Washington had, in fact, switched from the

193–4; Schäffer's Diary, 1, 3 July 1931, Maurer and Wengst, i. 727–8, 730 n. 4. For
Luther's consortium proposal: RDI Circular, 1 July 1931; Meisner's Memo of 8 July
1931, ibid. 734–40; Discussions of 6, 7, 8 July 1931, *Die Kabinette Brüning*, ii. 1292–4,
1301–2, 1306–9, 1312–13.

[23] For the best account of creditor reactions to the German banking crisis: Bennett,
244–74. For the French loan proposal: Tyrrell to Vansittart, 16 July 1931, *DBFP* II, ii.
201–2. For British reaction: Tyrrell to Vansittart, 16 July 1931; Vansittart to Tyrrell,
16 July 1931, ibid. 203–5. For Bank of England: Dept. of State, 462.00 R296, BIS Special
Reports, I, Box 405, 18 July 1931. For American policy: Castle to Edge (for Stimson),
14, 15, 16 July 1931, *FR*, 1931, i. 256–7, 268–9.

budgetary difficulties of the German government to the problem of the German banking system, in which a number of American financial houses were heavily committed. It therefore insisted that the intervention of the creditor nations should be restricted to central bank action to discourage further withdrawal of credits from Germany. In an effort to have this sticking-plaster strategy implemented it suggested that the British government, which was also concerned about the heavy withdrawals of gold from London in the wake of the German panic, should summon a Conference of Ministers in London on Monday 20 July. As soon as the British had issued this invitation Stimson telephoned MacDonald from Paris on 17 July to obtain an assurance that he was not as revisionist as Norman and the Treasury and that he would not, on the other hand, agree to guarantee any German loan. The French were, however, still wedded to their loan scheme; and Brüning felt obliged to play along with them during discussions with Laval in Paris on 18 and 19 April, even if he once again rejected out of hand the notion of making countervailing political concessions. The Americans and MacDonald were therefore careful to give the impression to the French that the scope of the London discussions would not be restricted to matters in which they had little immediate interest in view of their lack of substantial investment in Germany. This accounted for Stimson's testy reaction when J. P. Morgan & Co. independently advised the French government on 17 July that no German loan could be floated in New York. Such advice, he complained to Pierre Jay, Morgan's Paris representative, was ill-timed since 'the safety of the banks in New York who had advanced money to Germany was dependent on the conference going to London'.[24]

Even when the representatives of the seven powers concerned with the reparation question were safely assembled on the other side of the Channel, things did not go altogether smoothly for the Americans. MacDonald, who was still working hand in glove with Stimson, used his position as Chairman to steer the attention of the delegates away from the underlying political and economic causes of Germany's problems and towards the short-term financial emergency. On 22 July a subcommittee of Finance Ministers duly suggested a number of palliative

[24] For British invitation and Stimson–MacDonald telephone conversation: Lindsay to Castle, 16 July 1931; Memo of 17 July 1931, *FR*, 1931, i. 263–4, 271–2. For the Franco-German discussions of 18–19 July: Brüning, *Memoiren*, 327–37; Lutz Graf Schwerin von Krosigk, *Staatsbankrott: die Geschichte der Finanzpolitik des Deutschen Reiches vom 1920 bis 1945* (Göttingen, 1974), 74–9. For Stimson and Jay: Memo by Stimson, 17 July 1931, *FR*, 1931, i. 278–9.

measures such as a 90-day renewal of the $100 million BIS credit, rediscounting of Reichsbank bills by other central banks, and steps to maintain the volume of credits to Germany at its current level. It was at this stage that Snowden made himself difficult by interposing the Treasury view that more radical steps would be needed to achieve the permanent rehabilitation of Germany. He was, however, promptly rebuffed by MacDonald who observed that 'whether we like it or not ... we will have to do the temporary thing.' As a result the conference contented itself with the soothing but tendentious assertion that 'the recent excessive withdrawals of capital from Germany' had not been 'justified by the economic and budgetary situation of the country'; and it referred the whole question of Germany's further immediate and long-term credit needs to a committee which was to be appointed by the BIS in consultation with the central banks of the interested powers.[25]

Although the London Conference had merely propped up Germany and sent her back into the ring, it was reasonable to expect that the Wiggin–Layton Committee, to which authority had now been delegated, would put a stop to the bout. Albert Wiggin, as chairman of the Chase Manhattan Bank, the American financial institution with the largest German investment portfolio, and Sir Walter Layton, the editor of the revisionist English weekly, *The Economist*, both favoured a radical restructuring of Germany's external financial relations. Such an initiative was, however, prevented by the French and Belgian members of the committee, Moreau and Francqui, who insisted that it was competent only to investigate means of remedying Germany's short-term credit crisis. Because of this deadlock over its powers, the committee devoted most of its energy to the humdrum task of ascertaining the extent of Germany's short-term borrowing and holding discussions with the foreign creditors with whom the German government was negotiating a *Stillstand* agreement to maintain the current level of foreign credits. Instead of referring the question of the committee's terms of reference back to the seven London Conference powers, Wiggin, bowing to the views of the American administration, took the less adventurous course of suggesting that Germany should

[25] For fullest account of London Conference: Bennett, 274–9. For the collaboration between Stimson and MacDonald: Memo by Stimson, 20 July 1931, *FR*, 1931, i. 299–300. For MacDonald's tactics as chairman of London Conference: Stenographic Notes, 21 July 1931, *DBFP* II, ii. 443. For the recommendations of the Committee of Finance Ministers and the exchange between Snowden and MacDonald: ibid. 457–63. For final resolution of Conference: MacDonald to McGarrah, 23 June 1931, ibid. 222–3.

appeal to the Bank for International Settlements to appoint the Special Advisory Committee provided for under Article 118 of the Young Plan to adjudicate upon her position. This move foundered, however, on the opposition of the German government, which was aware that the BIS Committee only had the power to recommend the suspension of conditional payments, and now wished to play for higher stakes. After the *Stillstand* agreement had been concluded on 18 August the Wiggin Committee therefore returned the buck to the creditor governments by advising them that Germany would only be able to obtain essential long-term credits if there was international political stabilization and a reduction of her external obligations.[26]

Despite the prompting of the Wiggin–Layton Committee there was no meaningful effort to resolve the reparation problem for several more months. Inertia was encouraged by the *Stillstand* agreements, which took the edge off Germany's short-term credit crisis for six months from 1 September. The reopening of her banks and the easing of the restrictions which had been placed on their operations also created an impression of financial recovery in August and September; and the favourable trade balance which she enjoyed in the summer and autumn of 1931, albeit as a result of reduced imports rather than increased exports, diminished the immediate pressure on her balance of payments. Finally, the failure of the extreme right's referendum to obtain the dissolution of the left-centre Prussian Landtag on 9 August seemed to indicate a degree of domestic political stabilization. Even the Young Loan, which had plummeted to $54\frac{3}{4}$ on 15 July, had climbed slowly back to 62 by mid-August. In this brief period of remission none of the parties to the problem, apart from the British, displayed any interest in prompt action; and even MacDonald and Henderson, when they made their return visit to Berlin late in July, seemed resigned to the unlikelihood of any progress before the 1932 American presidential election. The reaction of Wall Street to the Wiggin–Layton Report three weeks later was very favourable: but it was recognized that there would be formidable opposition to any further war-debt negotiations, especially since the Hoover Moratorium had still to be ratified by Congress. Senior members of the American administration such as Ogden Mills now acknowledged privately that reparations and

[26] For Wiggin: Dept. of State, 462.00 R296, BIS Special Reports, I, Box 405, 31 July 1931. For Layton's views see his address to Liberal Summer School at Cambridge: *MG*, 3 Aug. 1931, 7. For deliberations of Wiggin Committee: BIS Special Reports, 14, 20 Aug. 1931, loc. cit. See also: Report of the Committee Appointed on the Recommendation of the London Conference, 1931, *DBFP* II, ii. 485–94.

war debts would ultimately have to be written down substantially. Official American policy was, however, that if Germany felt unable to fulfil her obligations after the expiry of the moratorium she should appeal to the Bank for International Settlements to appoint the Special Advisory Committee which was empowered by the Young Plan to deal with such a situation. The attraction of such a procedure for the Americans was, as the Germans knew only too well, that the Advisory Committee could regulate, but not revise, the Young Plan. That the French government also wished to preserve the Young Plan was clear from the obstructive behaviour of Moreau on the Wiggin–Layton Committee. These stonewalling tactics were still not considered inconsistent with renewed efforts to promote the integration of French and German industry. At his first press conference after becoming French Ambassador in Berlin on 22 September, François-Poncet expatiated on the desirability of a marriage between French capital and German know-how; and a week later Laval, during a visit to Berlin with Briand, did not appear to perceive the contradiction between the veto he imposed upon any discussion of reparations and his initiative in setting up a committee to further Franco-German economic collaboration. His reasoning was, on the contrary, that such collaboration would be expedited by the retention of France's increasingly evanescent reparation claim as a bargaining counter.[27]

The devaluation of sterling following the British government's decision to abandon the gold standard on 21 September made further procrastination inadvisable. Quite apart from the shock waves which were felt throughout the international financial community, the more competitive exports of Britain and other countries who followed her lead posed a new threat to the German balance of trade and hence to

---

[27] For Germany's temporary financial stabilization: see J. W. F. Thelwall's Memo of 4 Aug. in Rumbold to Henderson, 4 Aug. 1931, *DBFP* II, ii. 246–8. For July–Sept. 1931 trade figures: Report of the Special Advisory Committee ..., 23 Dec. 1931, ibid. at 497. For the Prussian referendum: O. Braun, *Von Weimar zu Hitler* (Hamburg, 1949), 196–7; Brüning, *Memoiren*, 351–3; Rumbold to Henderson, 5, 14 Aug. 1931, *DBFP* II, ii. 248–51. For British policy: Meeting between MacDonald, Henderson, Brüning, and Curtius, 28 July 1931, ibid. 233–7. For American policy: Osborne to Henderson, 20 Aug. 1931; Osborne to Reading, 20 Sept. 1931, ibid. 253, 262–3; Dept. of State 462.00 R296, BIS Special Reports, I, Box 405, 3 Sept. 1931; Mills to Gerrard Winston, 3 Oct. 1931, Ogden Mills Papers, Container 109. For French policy: A. François-Poncet, *The Fateful Years: Memoirs of a French Ambassador in Berlin, 1931–1939* (London, 1949), 8–10; F. L. Ford, 'Three Observers in Berlin: Rumbold, Dodd, and François-Poncet', in G. A. Craig and F. Gilbert (edd.), *The Diplomats, 1919–1939* (2 vols.; New York, 1971), ii. 460–2. For Laval's attitude: Tyrrell to Lindsay, 21 Oct. 1931, *DBFP* II, ii. 301–2.

the already disintegrating international debt structure; and this was reflected in a slump of the Young Loan to a new low of 40 by the end of September. The visit of Laval to Washington late in October, which had originally been planned as an occasion for diplomatic fence-mending following the moratorium contretemps, was now used by the two major creditors to concert the next phase of their rearguard action. The Hoover–Laval meeting made it possible for French and American Treasury officials to compare notes about long-term contingency plans for a reduction of reparations and a settlement of war debts involving the turning over to the United States of German bonds issued to the reparation creditors. The immediate outcome of the talks between the two principals was, however, merely an agreement that Germany should be directed to activate the Special Advisory Committee.[28]

As we have seen, such a course was not favoured in Berlin because the committee did not have the power to vary Germany's unconditional annuities. The Hoover–Laval Communiqué of 25 October had, more-over, spelled out that only the extent of Germany's obligations during 'the period of the business depression' should be examined. Brüning's reaction was stiffened by the alarming gains of the Nazis and Com-munists in the Hamburg local government elections on 27 September. There had also been growing criticism of the deflationary export-boosting strategy with which he was seeking both to combat the depression and to undermine the reparation system. The government's policies, Schacht declared at the Hugenberg–Hitler Harzburg Front Rally on 12 October, had choked off a third of Germany's normal economic activity and created a reservoir of long-term unemployment. The programme which a 'national government' would have to implement would be that of Frederick the Great after the Seven Years War. This would be based, not on the expansion of international trade, but on the development of the domestic economy. In order to counter these political and theoretical challenges with some progress on the reparation front, Brüning seized on newly published figures which showed that Germany's total short-term foreign indebtedness

[28] For Britain's abandonment of the gold standard: Reading to HM Representatives at Paris, Washington, Berlin, etc., 20 Sept. 1931, *DBFP* II, ii. 263–6. For impact on Germany: Sackett to Stimson, 3 Oct. 1931, Dept. of State, 462.00 R296/5215½. For the origins of the Hoover–Laval conversations see the exchange of telegrams between Edge, the US ambassador in Paris, and Stimson between 19 and 25 Sept. 1931: *FR*, 1931, ii. 237–43. For discussions between French and American Treasury officials: Mills to Gerrard Winston, 27 Oct. 1931, Ogden Mills Papers, Official Correspondence, Container 109. For the directive to Germany: Stimson's Memo of a Conversation with Prittwitz, 26 Oct. 1931, Dept. of State, 462.00 R296/5243.

(including commercial credits which had not gone through the banking system) was about twelve billion marks, or over four billion marks more than the estimate of the Wiggin–Layton Committee. This emboldened him to declare to Rumbold, the British ambassador, on 30 October that Germany would be incapable of generating more than the £80–100 million in foreign exchange she needed each year to pay off her short-term credits. Even this undertaking would be made difficult by the devaluation of sterling and the likelihood of higher tariffs after the forthcoming British elections. In an interview with John Foster Dulles, who visited Berlin at this time, Brüning insisted, not altogether convincingly, that the inauguration of a new round of reparation negotiations before a schedule for the amortization of Germany's short-term credits was drawn up would precipitate the 'complete collapse' of her economy. So great was his preoccupation with Germany's short-term private debts—or his determination to make tactical use of them—that he instituted prolonged negotiations with the French government in an effort to have the problem of these debts included within the terms of reference of the Special Advisory Committee when it was appointed. The French were adamant, however, that no other obligations should take precedence over reparations; and the American administration was also afraid of being charged with sacrificing receipts from war debts for the benefit of Wall Street. The appeal which the German government finally made to the BIS on 20 November therefore contained both the required genuflection to the Young Plan—a request for deferment of the postponable reparation annuities—and a plea that the Advisory Committee should take into account that Germany would also have to conclude an agreement with her private creditors before the end of February.[29]

Despite Brüning's efforts to exploit the short-term credit crisis, the inflexibility of Franco-American policy made it highly unlikely that the Special Advisory Committee would make any more specific or far-

[29] For the Hoover–Laval communiqué: *FR*, 1931, ii. 252–3. For the Hamburg elections, domestic criticism of Brüning's economic policy, and Schacht: *KZ*, 28 Sept. 1931, No. 271; 12 Oct. 1931, No. 285; Brüning, *Memoiren*, 366, 435–6. For Brüning's interviews with Rumbold and Dulles: Rumbold to Reading, 30 Oct. 1931, *DBFP* II, ii. 311–14; Dulles to Sullivan and Cromwell, 8 Nov. 1931, David E. Finley Papers, Box 18, 'War Debts' Folder. For Franco-American negotiations over terms of reference of SAC: Helbich, *Reparationen*, 86; Brüning, *Memoiren*, 437–8; Interviews of Simon with Laval and Bülow in Paris, 17 Nov. 1931, *DBFP* II, ii. 322–7. For American policy: Newton to Simon, 18 Nov. 1931, ibid. 330; Mellon's Memo of Conversation with Monick of French Embassy, 17 Nov. 1931, David E. Finley Papers, loc. cit. For German appeal to SAC: Neurath to Simon, 20 Nov. 1931, *DBFP* II, ii. 332–4.

reaching proposals than the Wiggin–Layton Committee before it. The membership of the two committees was virtually the same, the one significant exception being that, in order to evade the charge that it was more interested in 'retrieving bad investments' than safeguarding war debts, the Federal Reserve Board substituted Walter W. Stewart for Wiggin as its nominee. Apart from his considerable private and central banking experience, Stewart's most attractive qualification was that, unlike Wiggin's Chase Manhattan Bank, his Wall Street firm of Case, Pomeroy, & Co., was not financially involved in Germany. The standing of the committee would not have been diminished by the substitution of Professor Charles Rist for Émile Moreau as the representative of the Banque de France. Yet Laval made it clear to the Chamber of Deputies on 26 November that, despite the compromise terms of reference which had been agreed upon with the Germans, he was determined to restrict the scope of the committee's deliberations. France would, he declared, regard any new financial arrangement as a temporary expedient to tide over the depression; she would never concede that Germany's private foreign debts should have priority over her reparation obligations; and she would agree to a permanent reduction of reparations only if there was a corresponding diminution of war debts. This statement raised the hackles of the American administration, not so much because it prejudiced the forthcoming deliberations as because it sought to make the resolution of the reparation problem dependent upon American financial concessions. Hence, in order to emphasize that reparations were a matter for the Europeans to settle among themselves, Stewart steadfastly refused to take the chair when the committee assembled at Basle on 7 December. It was clear that neither the French nor the Americans were prepared to give the committee any room to manœuvre.[30]

Because of the constraints which would be placed upon the committee's recommendations, the German government viewed it primarily as a forum in which to prepare international opinion for the total cessation of reparations at a later date. In a letter of 5 December Brüning instructed Melchior, the Reichsbank's nominee, that he should concentrate on 'establishing the facts' and only press for conclusions if they would expedite complete cancellation. Melchior duly occupied

---

[30] For Stewart's career: *NYT*, 21 Nov. 1931, 4. For Laval's speech and the American reaction: Stimson's Memo of Conversation with Claudel, 3 Dec. 1931, *FR*, 1931, i. 352–3; Dept. of State, 462.00 R296, BIS Special Reports, I, Box 405, 3 and 10 Dec. 1931. A note setting out French reparation policy was circulated to interested powers early in Dec.: Simon to Tyrrell, 4 Dec. 1931, *DBFP* II, ii. 355–9.

THE ELEVENTH YEAR OF IT.

(Copyright in all countries.)

Fig. 14. The *Evening Standard*, 8 December 1931.

the committee's first two working days (8 and 9 December) with an exhaustive account of Germany's current international financial position. After confirming that her short-term foreign indebtedness was closer to twelve than eight billion marks, he pointed out that, despite the *Stillstand* Agreement and her trade surplus in recent months, the Reichsbank's gold and foreign exchange reserves had been reduced by another 450 million marks between 31 July and 15 December. He added that the excess of exports over imports had been due to exceptional circumstances such as the extremely depressed price of imported raw materials, the lower volume of imports due to the contraction of the German economy, and the sale of goods abroad at unrealistically low prices by hard-pressed German producers. The November trade figures had already revealed a reduction in exports and the trend was certain to continue because of the fragility of Germany's external credit, the devaluation of the currencies of trade competitors such as Britain, and the mushrooming of tariffs and other restraints upon international trade. After Melchior had completed his exposé his colleague, Schwerin von Krosigk, the director of the German Finance Ministry, weighed in with another two-day disquisition upon the budgetary situation. This was designed to demonstrate that the absolute limit of cost-cutting and revenue-raising had been reached; and to this end made much of the strategically timed Emergency Decree of 8 December, which contained such spectacular measures as a 10–15 per cent reduction in salaries and wages and an increase in the rate of the regressive *Umsatzsteuer* (Turnover Tax) from 0.85 to 2 per cent.[31]

The preoccupation of the German government with playing for time in order to achieve complete cancellation accounts for its consternation when Layton suggested in the second week of the Basle Committee's discussions that a viable final settlement could quickly be achieved with a scheme of creditor participation in the profits of the German railways. At a cabinet meeting on 16 December, Brüning, who also considered that the proposal would infringe upon Germany's economic independence, directed that Melchior and Schwerin von Krosigk should have it watered down. Three days later the Chancellor reaffirmed to his colleagues that it was undesirable in the present

---

[31] For German tactics at Basle: Brüning to Melchior, 5 Dec. 1931, Maurer and Wengst, ii. 1182 n. 3. For Melchior and Schwerin von Krosigk: Dept. of State 462.00 R296, BIS Special Reports, I, Box 405, 10, 15 Dec. 1931. For the Emergency Decree: Brüning, *Memoiren*, 439; Schwerin von Krosigk, *Staatsbankrott*, 91–2; Helbich, *Reparationen*, 40–1.

circumstances for the Advisory Committee to recommend any final settlement. 'The best thing would be', he said, 'for the Committee to declare why it was unable to make any recommendation.' Having relayed the advice of François-Poncet that neither a comprehensive settlement nor any further tinkering with the Young Plan would be possible before the French elections in the spring, Brüning initiated a desultory discussion about whether a long moratorium would be more advantageous to Germany than a brief suspension of payments followed by negotiations while the depression was at its worst. Before any conclusion had been reached, the Chancellor abruptly changed the subject by remarking that 'the most important problem for Germany in the immediate future was the presidential elections'. A request from Schäffer for a decision on the moratorium question for the guidance of Melchior and his colleagues at Basle only elicited another evasion. The order of priorities was, Brüning declared, first the prolongation of Hindenburg's term of office, second the French elections in April or May, and third the Prussian elections in May. 'After that', he said wryly, 'I'll be pensioned off to Basle.' Brüning's awareness that there would be no reparation negotiations until the summer and his over-riding preoccupation with domestic survival were to shape his behaviour in the new few weeks.[32]

Although the data provided by Melchior and Schwerin von Krosigk were incorporated virtually intact in the Committee's Report of 23 December, the stalling tactics of the French and German governments ensured that any recommendations would be confined to yet another general appeal to the governments concerned to 'adjust all inter-governmental debts (reparations and war debts) to the existing troubled situation of the world'. This was frustrating to the British government, which was still anxious for a prompt definitive settlement. British hopes were kindled when Hoover, in a message to Congress on 10 December, recommended 'the recreation of the World War Foreign Debt Commission with authority to examine such problems as might arise in connection with those debts during the present economic emergency'; and further grounds for optimism were provided by Mellon's statement on the following day that war-debt contracts would have to be revised. It was clear, however, from an exchange between

[32] For the German cabinet's reaction to Layton's scheme: Schäffer to Schwerin von Krosigk, 16 Dec. 1931, Maurer and Wengst, ii. 1182–5. For Brüning's domestic preoccupations and reparation tactics: Schäffer's Diary, 19 Dec. 1931, ibid. 1189–92; Brüning, *Memoiren*, 485–91, 497–50.

Rist and Stewart at Basle on the weekend of 12–13 December that neither the French nor the American government had the political nerve to initiate an all-round settlement. According to Rist, no French cabinet would survive if it reduced its reparation claims on the off-chance of a matching reduction of its American war debts; and Stewart insisted that, notwithstanding Laval's assertions about what had been agreed during his visit to Washington, the American administration had not, and would not, make any commitment in advance on this point. It was, therefore, unlikely that Laval would react favourably to MacDonald's suggestion on 16 December that Britain and France should give 'a lead to the whole world by an agreed action'; and the French government's immobility was reinforced the next day, when the House of Representatives Ways and Means Committee, in the midst of its deliberations about ratifying the Hoover moratorium, adopted a resolution which expressly ruled out the cancellation or reduction of war debts. For this reason, discussions in Paris on 19 December between Leith-Ross and Flandin (following a British memorandum of 16 December stressing the 'urgent need of a solution of the whole question of intergovernmental indebtedness which is something more than makeshift') began badly with a flat French refusal to discuss anything more than 'a temporary arrangement covering the period of the depression'. Nor was Flandin any more forthcoming when Leith-Ross conceded that the American Congress had just made an immediate slate-wiping operation impossible and proposed that there should be a five-year moratorium instead. Because he was aware that such a prolonged suspension of payments would cause the budgets of the creditors to become adjusted to the absence of reparations, the French Finance Minister insisted that any moratorium should be limited to two years in the first instance. He also demanded that deliveries in kind for public works should continue during this period. Since both of these proposals were anathema to the British, the possi-bility of a joint Anglo-French initiative was remote.[33]

Since the Americans, the French, and the Germans all sought either

[33] Report of the Special Advisory Committee . . . 23 Dec. 1931, DBFP II, ii. 495–514 at 507. Text of Hoover's Message of 10 Dec. 1931: FR, 1931, i, at xxiii–xxv. For Mellon, Rist, and Stewart: Dept. of State, 462.00 R296, BIS Special Reports, I, Box 405, 15 Dec. 1931; NYT, 12 Dec. 1931, 1. For MacDonald's letter of 16 Dec. 1931: DBFP II, ii. 379 n. 2. For the Resolution of the Ways and Means Committee, which was adopted on 23 Dec. as a Joint Resolution of the Senate and House of Representatives: FR, 1931, i. 248–9. For British Memo of 16 Dec. 1931: Simon to Tyrrell, 16 Dec. 1931, DBFP II, ii. 367–71. For Leith-Ross and Flandin: Notes of a Conversation of December 19 . . ., ibid. 379–82.

to prevent or to defer a final settlement, the efforts of the British government to expedite matters after the Special Advisory Committee had published its report served only to provoke an upsurge of anti-revisionism in the winter of 1931–2. The attempt of the Foreign Office to organize a government-level conference at Lausanne in mid-January suffered a predictable setback when Stimson, responding to the war-debt backlash in Congress, declared at the end of December that American participation would be both 'impossible and undesirable'. The Secretary of State also took the opportunity to restate to both the British and the French representatives in Washington the well-worn American theses that there was no connection between reparations and war debts and that the Europeans should conclude a reparation settlement among themselves before attempting to renegotiate their American obligations. This unyielding attitude, which Lindsay, the British ambassador, characterized to Stimson as a policy of 'open your mouth and shut your eyes and see what I will give you', prompted the British Cabinet Committee on Reparations and War Debts to conclude on 6 January that the general cancellation at which it had been aiming was currently impossible. It therefore resolved 'in a spirit of helpfulness to consider a temporary solution' involving a total moratorium of about five years in the hope that this would pave the way for a permanent settlement as soon as circumstances permitted. Such an arrangement had, however, already been rejected by Flandin in his conversations with Leith-Ross in December, and the attitude of the French government was stiffened by Stimson's confirmation that a final reparation settlement or even an extension of the existing mora-torium was unlikely to be followed by a compensatory reduction of American war debts. When, therefore, Leith-Ross journeyed again to Paris in the second week of January, Flandin countered the British proposal with a variant of Layton's scheme for a settlement involving participation in the profits of the German railways. The distance between the French and British positions was increased when Brüning announced to François-Poncet and Rumbold that he intended to in-form the Lausanne Conference of Germany's inability to pay repara-tions for the foreseeable future. This *démarche*, which was leaked to the press and then formally confirmed on 9 January, was in a general sense a response to the upsurge of revisionist feeling which the Basle Committee's Report had encouraged in Germany. Yet its timing reflected two facets of Brüning's policy which were evident in December: a readiness to sabotage any premature meeting at Lausanne and a desire to curry favour with the German extreme right in order to secure the extension of Hindenburg's term as president. Despite MacDonald's placatory declaration on 10 January that Brüning's *cri de cœur* merely underlined the urgent need for the Lausanne Conference, French anti-revisionists were now provided with the argument that any concessions to Germany would encourage further unilateral assaults on the Versailles Treaty. The receptiveness of the French government to such views and its reluctance to go to Lausanne were increased by the conservative restructuring of the Laval cabinet on 13 January following the death of Maginot and the retirement of Briand due to ill health.[34]

Realizing that no progress could be made until after the French elections, the British government dropped its proposal for an immediate conference to discuss a long-term moratorium and suggested instead on 15 January that the creditor governments should grant an unconditional one-year suspension of payments from 1 July 1932 and at the same time announce their 'intention to arrive at a permanent settlement at a conference to be convened as soon as possible, perhaps next July'. This scheme quickly ran into the usual French objections. France, Laval declared, would extend the moratorium only if all the arrangements for the payment and reloaning of the unconditional annuities during the Hoover year remained in operation and if the United States continued its moratorium on war debts. In order to avoid any implication that the proposed conference would revise the Young Plan he also insisted that its labours should be directed at achieving a 'lasting' rather than a 'permanent' settlement. Finally, in an effort to involve the Americans, he demanded that the terms of reference of the conference should be extended to include the whole range of financial and economic problems, apart from reparations, which were contributing to the world depression. In the protracted negotiations which followed, the British were forced to abandon the

[34] For British efforts to organize a conference: Simon to Tyrrell, 16 Dec. 1931; Tyrrell to Simon, 19 Dec. 1931; Campbell to Simon, 28 Dec. 1931, *DBFP* II, ii. 367, 378; iii. 1. For Stimson and French Chargé: Conversation of 29 Dec. 1931, Dept. of State, 462.00 R296 A1/1. See also Lindsay to Simon, 28 Dec. 1931, *DBFP* II, iii. 1–3. For British cabinet decision of 6 Jan. 1932: ibid. 590–2. For discussions between Leith-Ross and Flandin: Cabinet Meeting 1 (32), 11 Jan. 1932, CAB 23/70; Tyrrell to Simon, 10 Jan. 1932; Simon to Rumbold, 12 Jan. 1932, *DBFP* II, iii. 14, 20. For Brüning's *démarche* and press statement: Rumbold to Simon, 8 Jan. 1932, ibid. 12; Bülow to Pünder, 8 Jan. 1932, Maurer and Wengst, ii. 1203–6; Brüning, *Memoiren*, 498–9. For German revisionism: Rumbold to Simon, 31 Dec. 1931, *DBFP* II, iii. 5–8. For Brüning's pre-occupations: see above, n. 32. For MacDonald's statement and French reaction: Statement Issued by HM Government, 10 Jan. 1932; Tyrrell to Simon, 11 Jan. 1932; Simon to Rumbold, 15 Jan. 1932, *DBFP* II, iii. 13–15, 28–9.

one-year moratorium because of the impossibility of obtaining German and American consent to the conditions which the French sought to attach to it. The formula which was finally adopted in mid-February therefore stated simply that the six principals to the reparation dispute had agreed that the Lausanne Conference should be postponed until June and that the object of the conference would be 'to agree on a lasting settlement of the questions raised in the Report of the Basle Experts and on methods necessary to solve other economic and financial difficulties which [were] responsible for and [might] prolong the present world crisis'. These words clearly represented an agreement to differ rather than consensus. Laval emphasized to Tyrrell, the British ambassador in Paris, on 11 February that, notwithstanding anything contained in the agreement, France retained her 'liberty of action'; and the British government continued to press for complete cancellation, irrespective of any immediate American counter-concessions.[35]

American policy also continued to be unhelpful to the British in the first half of 1932. On 20 January Ogden Mills expressed the hope to Julian Mason of the *New York Evening Post* that 'the integrity of international agreements [might] be maintained and that, while some modifications [were] clearly necessary, we [did not need to] forego all expectations of substantial payments in the future'. British hopes of war-debt revision were briefly aroused by the appointment of Mellon as ambassador to London in February. The former Secretary of the Treasury was, however, under strict instructions not to reopen the war-debt question. On 8 June, Stimson, at Mellon's instigation, even issued a statement to disabuse the British Treasury of its view that a complete cancellation of reparations followed by a joint Anglo-French appeal to the United States would have a favourable impact on American opinion. Stimson had, in fact, stressed to Lindsay a few days earlier that the most desirable outcome of Lausanne for the Americans would be some sort of compromise agreement which would give the inter-government debt system another lease of life. If a more radical solution was to be achieved at Lausanne it would not be through the good offices of the United States. Parker Gilbert advised Lindsay late in April that it would be up to the European powers to give the United

[35] For British proposal of 15 Jan. and subsequent Franco-British discussions: Tyrrell to Simon, 15, 17, 18 Jan. 1932; Simon to Tyrrell, 18 Jan. 1932, ibid. 29–32, 35–40, 42–4; Cabinet Meeting, 26 Jan. 1932, CAB 23/70. For American and German policy: Simon to Lindsay, 18 Jan. 1932; Simon to Rumbold, 19 Jan. 1932, *DBFP* II, iii. 32–3, 44–6. For text of Six Power Agreement: Patteson to Vansittart, 12 Feb. 1932, ibid. 96–7. For French reservations: Tyrrell to Simon, 11 Feb. 1932, ibid. 94–6.

States 'a lead over the fence'. He might well have added that the American administration would still be likely to baulk.[36]

A final obstacle to the cancellation so devoutly wished for by the British government was the radical revisionism of the Germans. Although Brüning had confided to MacDonald that he was prepared to make face-saving financial concessions to the French, his domestic political situation prompted him to refer again in the Reichstag on 11 May to the necessity for total cancellation. Notwithstanding the encouragement given to such a declaration by British pressure for a slate-wiping operation, it drew an immediate appeal from Simon that the Chancellor should refrain from 'restating in dogmatic fashion a point of view which was likely to provoke retort from other quarters, especially in view of the delicate position of French politics'. A month later, on the eve of the Lausanne Conference, Simon repeated his plea to Neurath, the German ambassador in London, who was about to become Minister for Foreign Affairs in the new Papen cabinet. Simon duly received an assurance from Neurath that he 'had no intention of going to Lausanne to bang his fist on the table'. Yet he overplayed his role as honest broker by pressing the German minister-elect to devise a political truce proposal which would not only lure the French down the path of financial moderation but also promote European paci-fication and disarmament. Events were to prove that, in the interests of achieving a final settlement, the British would have been wiser to encourage the exclusion of non-financial questions from the Lausanne agenda.[37]

The outcome of the Lausanne negotiations in fact depended almost entirely on the swing to the left at the French elections on 1 and 8 May and the formation of the Herriot cabinet. Tardieu, who had taken over from Laval as President of the Council and Minister for Foreign Affairs after the latter's defeat in the Chamber on 19 February, would

[36] Mills to Julian Mason, 20 Jan. 1932, Ogden Mills Papers, Official Correspondence, Container 110. For Mellon: Dept. of State 462.00 R296, BIS Special Reports, I, Box 405, 9 Feb. 1932, 2 May 1932. For American policy in June 1932: Mellon to Stimson, 3 June 1932, ibid. 462.00 R296 A1/158; Statement by Stimson, 8 June 1932, ibid. A1/157½; Conversation between Stimson and Lindsay, 1 June 1932, ibid. A1/157; Lindsay to Simon, 1 June 1932, DBFP II, iii. 147–8. For Gilbert: Lindsay to Simon, 25 Apr. 1932, ibid. 125.

[37] For Brüning and MacDonald: Record of a Conversation at Geneva, 23 Apr. 1932, DBFP II, iii. 123 n. 2. For Brüning's speech: RT, 11 May 1932, cdxlvi. at 2895; Rumbold to Simon, 12 May 1932, DBFP II, iii. 136–7. For British reaction and Neurath's assur-ances: Simon to Rumbold, 14 May 1932; Simon to Newton, 6 June 1932, ibid. 139–40, 152–4. For Simon's political truce proposal: Simon to Neurath, 9 June 1932, ibid. 161–2. Cf. Tyrrell to FO, 11 June 1932, ibid. 172–3.

almost certainly not have agreed to the Lausanne settlement had he remained in office. Whilst attending the Disarmament Conference in Geneva late in April he asserted to MacDonald that Germany's incapacity to pay was only temporary and that he favoured nothing more than 'suspension either for a fixed period or for a period to be determined by experts'. The settlement which the French government was canvassing at this time still centred, moreover, around schemes for milking the German railways. The situation was transformed after Herriot's assumption of power on 4 June. As Léon Blum put it, somewhat lyrically, a week later:

Everything has been transformed in France since the elections of 8 May. For Tardieu, for Laval, for Flandin, for all the leaders of the 'faithful majority', the danger was action; risk-taking and bold initiatives would have been condemned in advance as foolhardy. It was by declaring 'I have preserved ... I have resisted ... I have said no' that they aroused enthusiasm. For Herriot, the sole danger lies today in obstinacy, inertia and timidity. The Chamber, which embodies the will of the people, expects from him a simple-minded yes and is less concerned with conditions than results. Europe shares this expectation.

In practical political terms the elections, although not ushering in the regular co-operation between Herriot and the Socialists of the 1924–5 period, meant that the premier could at least count on the support of a left-wing majority in the field of foreign policy. This made possible the revival of the MacDonald–Herriot partnership which had engineered the French evacuation of the Ruhr in 1924. Fleuriau, the French ambassador in London, informed Simon on 6 June that 'M. Herriot attached great importance to finding some formula which would involve a recognition by Germany of her obligations even though in fact it worked out as a termination of payments'. A week later, during pre-Lausanne discussions with MacDonald and Simon in Paris, the new French premier emphasized that such sleight of hand would only be possible if the Germans exercised restraint. 'If Germany said that ... she would not pay reparations, she would turn what was really an economic into a political question. He would not be able to admit this. He himself would take care not to say that he intended to remain within the framework of the Young Plan ... Between these two extreme positions they could meet at Lausanne and obtain a result.' Apart from being prepared to fabricate a settlement, Herriot swept away the other hitherto insuperable obstacle to progress by agreeing that any arrangement arrived at would be contingent upon *subsequent*, as opposed to *simultaneous*, American concessions. 'There would', he said, 'be two operations: a European operation which would be subordinated to a later American operation.' Herriot was, in short, prepared to give the lead to the Americans rather than wait upon their initiative.[38]

Largely because of the more relaxed financial attitude of the new French government, the Lausanne Conference covered considerable ground in its first week. In a pace-setting opening address from the Chair on 16 June MacDonald stressed the necessity for 'coming to an agreement' about 'the financial inheritance of the war' which was exacerbating the current crisis; and he prepared the way for the necessary revision of the treaty by observing that change by mutual consent was preferable to default. This pragmatic tone was maintained when the five major reparation creditors declared on the following day that all payments due to them would be suspended for the duration of the conference. Papen immediately reciprocated by omitting any reference to the question of war guilt and the necessity for complete cancellation. Herriot, too, behaved well by declaring that he did not intend 'to insist at length on the respect for contracts the legitimacy of which is recognized', even if he added that complete cancellation would give Germany an undue economic advantage over her neighbours and would not cure the current economic crisis unless its other causes such as political insecurity, the 'regime of closed economic systems', and the low prices of agricultural produce were also remedied. After this auspicious beginning, side negotiations to bridge the gap between the Anglo-German desire for cancellation and the preference of the French (and the absent Americans) for a scaling-down operation proceeded rapidly. Herriot and his Finance Minister, Germain-Martin, at first insisted upon a long-term *relic* (residual claim) which was to be realized from the profits of the railways after Germany had recovered. In response, however, to the British complaint that this would prejudice the prompt restoration of German credit the French quickly retreated on 23 June to the idea of a *forfait* (final lump sum settlement). Within another two days MacDonald was canvassing with Neurath (Papen

[38] For Tardieu: Record of a Conversation at Geneva, 23 Apr. 1932: *DBFP* II, iii. 123 n. 2. For France and the German railways: Dept. of State, 462.00 R296, BIS Special Reports, I, Box 405, 2 May 1932. For the position of Herriot: L. Blum, *L'Oeuvre de Léon Blum, 1928–1934* (Paris, 1972), 419; G. Ziebura, *Léon Blum: Theorie und Praxis einer sozialistischen Politik, i. 1872 bis 1934* (Berlin, 1963), 435. For 1924: see above, ch. 7. n. 11 and text thereat. For Fleuriau: Simon to Tyrrell, 6 June 1932, *DBFP* II, iii. 157–9. For Herriot: Notes of a Meeting, 11 June 1932, ibid. 173–7.

having returned to Berlin for consultations) the formula which was to be adopted two weeks later, to wit, 'a capital sum, possibly in the form of bonds, which would not be presented until certain representative German securities reached a given quotation in the markets'. After having obtained a favourable reaction from Neurath, MacDonald agreed that it was 'a most promising idea'. 'The great thing was, of course', he added, 'to get the whole question of politics'.[39]

By this time, such a strategy had become very difficult to follow. A political flare-up had always been likely because of the over-heated condition of German politics and the ultra-conservative character of Papen's 'cabinet of barons'. The new German Chancellor, seeking to take the wind out of the sails of the Nazis, had come to Lausanne holding forth to the press about the desirability of a comprehensive Franco-German *rapprochement*; and he had been prompted by MacDonald on 20 June to offer the French a 'counter-contribution' in order to sugar the pill of complete cancellation. Herriot had been sceptical before the conference about the effectiveness of a political truce of the sort which Simon had been advocating. He was now, however, impressed by Papen's offer of economic and political compensations, particularly his proposal for a Franco-German military alliance, which could have been broached by the latter during a tête-à-tête on 24 June; and when he returned to Paris on the weekend of 25–6 June he persuaded his cabinet that political reconciliation was preferable to the prolongation of reparations. He was therefore flabbergasted to discover when he returned to Lausanne on the following Monday that Papen, whose back had been stiffened by his sojourn in Berlin, had watered down the concessions he was prepared to make. The ensuing deadlock was only resolved when MacDonald, assisted by American pressure on the Germans, extricated Herriot and Papen from the minefield into which he had encouraged them to venture and cajoled them onto the narrower but safer terrain of negotiations about the technical terms and conditions of the *forfait*.[40]

The success of the conference seemed assured when, at a meeting

[39] For MacDonald's address: Stenographic Notes . . ., 16 June 1932, ibid. 191–3. For the suspension of payments and the speeches of Papen and Herriot: Stenographic Notes, 17 June 1932, ibid. 194–207. For American opposition to formal cancellation: Prittwitz to A. Amt, 6, 13 June 1932, A. Amt, Wirt. Rep., Akten betreffend . . . Lausanne 1932, iii. For side negotiations: Notes of a Conversation . . ., 21 June 1932 (*relic*); 23 June 1932 (*forfait*), DBFP II, iii. 237–40, 257–9, 267–9. For MacDonald and Neurath: Notes of a Conversation . . ., 25 June 1932, ibid. 269–71.

[40] For Papen and the press: F. von Papen, *Memoirs* (tr. B. Connell, London, 1952), 172–3; Schwerin von Krosigk, 119. For Papen and MacDonald: Neurath to A. Amt,

of delegates of the six inviting powers on 29 June, MacDonald obtained assent to the propositions that reparations were 'the first thing' and that 'as regards disarmament, political agreements, and so on, the Lausanne Conference should ... make a general declaration upon those points ... but that we should not postpone the settlement of reparations until these understandings have been completely accomplished'. Yet the Bureau of Financial Experts which was now appointed to assist MacDonald in hammering out the details of the *forfait* quickly became deadlocked in a characteristic dispute. As in the April 1921 manipulation of Germany's total reparation bill, there was only token Franco-Belgian opposition to the crucial proposal of Britain that the final tranche of reparation bonds should bear no interest until it was marketed. It was also quickly agreed that these bonds would not be offered for sale at all until they could command an extremely unlikely price. Although Francqui, the Belgian reparation expert, remarked on 30 June that these conditions reduced the final payment to the level of monkey money (*monnaie de singe*), both he and Georges Bonnet, the principal French negotiator, bowed to the riposte of MacDonald and Leith-Ross that the doubtful value of the bonds reflected the reality of Germany's present and future capacity to pay. The rapidity with which this grudging consensus was achieved contrasted with the prolonged dispute which occurred first of all between Britain and France and then between Germany and her creditors about the nominal value of this illusory final obligation. By 5 July, Herriot was refusing to go below 4 billion marks (the equivalent of two Young Plan annuities) for fear of incurring the wrath of the Finance Committee of the Chamber of Deputies; and Papen was insisting that anything more than 2 billion would be unacceptable to the Reichstag. In an effort to persuade the Germans to bridge the gap, MacDonald again took the risky step of offering them political compensations in the form of the abrogation of Article 231 (the war guilt clause) of the Versailles Treaty, together with an expression of intent to achieve an 'equitable' disarmament settlement and the conclusion of a consultative pact between the six inviting powers. This merely encouraged Papen to

20 June 1932; Papen to MacDonald, 21 June 1932, A. Amt, Wirt. Rep., Akten betreffend ... Lausanne 1932, iii; *ADAP* xx. 327, 333–6; Notes of a Conversation ..., 20 June 1932, *DBFP* II, iii. 228–32. For Papen's version of his tête-à-tête with Herriot: Bülow to A. Amt, 24 June 1932, A. Amt, loc. cit. iv; *ADAP* xx. 354–5. For Herriot's initial scepticism: Notes of a Meeting ..., 11 June 1932, *DBFP* II, iii. 176–7. For the contretemps between Herriot and Papen: Notes of a Conversation ..., 27 June 1932, ibid. 271–2. For American pressure: Prittwitz to A. Amt, 26 June 1932, A. Amt, loc. cit.

return later the same day with an offer of 2.6 billion marks (consisting of one Young Plan annuity plus the reloaned Hoover moratorium unconditional payment of 600 million marks) and a political shopping list which included expunging *all* references to Germany's war guilt, a commitment to *equality* of armaments, the elimination of all foreign influence over the Reichsbank and the German railways, and provisions to make it even less likely that the *forfait* bonds would ever be marketed. The reaction of Herriot to these demands was bitter. 'The German Delegation', he declared, 'was trying to settle the Reparations Question and the Disarmament question and the question of the responsibility for the War all for a payment of 2.6 milliards of marks.' It was to take a prodigious effort on the part of the exhausted Mac-Donald and Neville Chamberlain, the British Chancellor of the Exchequer, before agreement could be reached on 8 July on a compromise figure of 3 billion marks and an anodyne declaration referring to 'the establishment and development of confidence between the nations in a mutual spirit of reconciliation, collaboration, and justice'. Herriot's acceptance of this formula was facilitated by MacDonald's last-minute offer of a bilateral Anglo-French consultative pact which was to be announced after the conclusion of the conference; and the Germans were also swayed by the British Prime Minister's counterbalancing undertaking that he would refer in his final declaration as chairman to the necessity for political *détente* in the wake of the financial settlement.[41]

Although MacDonald kept his word by sounding a clarion call for disarmament and international reconciliation at the final plenary session of the conference on 9 July, the nub of his address was a somewhat hyperbolical celebration of the demise of the reparation system:

No more Reparations! They have gone. No more attempting in a blind and thoughtless way to heap burdens and burdens on anybody's shoulders. Have you not had your warning of that since 1919? Those great payments of sums which represent no transfer of goods have not been a punishment upon one nation, they have been an affliction on all nations, and it is from this transfer

---

[41] For the negotiations of 28–9 June and MacDonald's statement of priorities: *DBFP* II, iii. 275–97 at 296. For discussions of Bureau: Notes of a Meeting . . ., 30 June 1932, ibid. 308–15 (Francqui at 309; Leith-Ross at 312). For deadlock on 5 July: Notes of a Conversation . . ., 5 July 1932, ibid. 363–7. For political negotiations and Herriot's protest: Notes of a Conversation . . ., 8 July 1932, ibid. 415–20. For Anglo-French consultative pact: ibid. 418–19; Simon to Tyrrell, 11 July 1932, ibid. 437–8. For negotiations over final declaration: Notes of a Conversation . . ., 8 July 1932, ibid. 420–3.

of sums which upset the world's economy that the whole world is suffering so much today.

Reparations were not the sole cause of the world depression or the supervening international financial crisis of 1931, even if their abolition had come to be regarded in many quarters as a prerequisite for economic recovery and financial stabilization by the middle of 1932. Nor had the Lausanne Conference completely severed the Gordian knot of inter-government indebtedness. Because of the unwillingness of the United States to formally relinquish war debts the entire settlement was made subject to a separate 'gentlemen's agreement' among the European creditors that ratification would depend upon a subsequent arrangement with the Americans. No such arrangement was ever achieved; and within a year the Europeans had effectively defaulted on their war debts rather than revive the Young Plan. The meaningless 'gentlemen's agreement', like the worthless *forfait*, was an appropriate conclusion to the charade which the political leaders of the western world had inflicted on their long-suffering electorates for fourteen years.[42]

[42] For MacDonald: Stenographic Notes ..., 9 July 1932, ibid. at 434. For the fate of war debts: Leith-Ross, *Money Talks*, ch. 13; E. Johnson (ed.), *The Collected Writings of John Maynard Keynes. xviii. Activities, 1922–1932: The End of Reparations* (London, 1978), 380–90.

Conclusion

THE intractability of the reparation and war debt problem arose less from any systematic attempt by the former belligerents to punish, emasculate, or impoverish each other than from the concern of political leaders in all the countries involved to obscure and, if possible, evade the domestic financial consequences of the war. The network of inter-governmental financial claims which was established and maintained after the war of 1914–18 was, in other words, designed by the conservative statesmen of the day largely to deflect a widespread popular demand for genuine post-war reconstruction and to pre-empt confiscatory direct taxation. When reparations and war debts are viewed primarily as a diversionary smokescreen their history falls into four phases. During the first thirty months of peace the demands of the victors upon the vanquished and each other were overwhelmingly rhetorical, notwithstanding the deliveries made under the Armistice and the Spa Coal Agreement of July 1920; and the plight of Germany derived more from the traumatic domestic impact of war, defeat, and revolution than from harassment and exploitation by her former foes. On the other hand, in the period following the inauguration of the London Schedule of Payments in May 1921 the European creditors, prompted partly by their own rhetoric and partly by the increasing likelihood that the United States would insist on the repayment of its war loans, made a clumsy attempt to bleed Germany; and the German financial élite responded in an increasingly recalcitrant and self-serving manner. This friction developed into the pointless and counter-productive Ruhr conflict and the hyper-inflation of mid-1923. The resulting chaos was such as to provoke the intervention of the Anglo-Saxons and the inception of a third phase, in which reparations were propped up by the American-backed Dawes Plan and Germany's conservative élite sold their patriotic birthright for a mess of high-interest short-term foreign loans. Since, however, the Dawes scheme was only a provisional, and initially very moderate, five-year settlement which did not determine the crucial question of Germany's long-term capacity to pay, it was replaced in 1930 by the Young Plan. This new scheme, which was misleadingly proclaimed as the definitive settlement of reparations, ushered in a final two-year period, at the end of which the system of inter-government indebtedness, which had become more trouble than it was worth in a time of international economic depression, was surreptitiously dismantled by the moderate politicians who had come to the helm in Britain and France.

In the immediate post-war years the leading actors in the reparation dispute were Britain and France, while the United States and Germany filled minor roles. It seems remarkable that British politicians should have set the pace with extravagant reparation demands, since their country had sustained far less physical damage than France, and Lloyd George and his colleagues feared that a large indemnity would unleash a flood of German exports onto the world's markets. The explanation is not, of course, that the British man in the street was more vindictive than his continental counterpart but simply that, in the course of the general election campaign of November–December 1918, the budget-ary and commercial consequences of Britain's wartime financial prodi-gality were subjected for the first time to public scrutiny. Discussion of the long-term financial implications of the conflict had hitherto been pre-empted first by the short war illusion, then by the McKenna principle of restricting taxation to the level necesssary to service the ballooning public debt, and, finally, by the United States government credits advanced in 1917 and 1918. It was only to be expected that Lloyd George and Bonar Law should have preferred at the end of 1918 to indulge in rhetoric about indemnities rather than to confess to an electorate which was expecting increased expenditure on social services after the war that the blood-bath over which they had presided had also been a financial disaster for which the British taxpayer would have to foot the bill. Misleading declarations that Germany should 'pay' for the war were also attractive to representatives of the City of London such as Cunliffe who were anxious about Britain's future as an international financial centre, especially after it became clear that the United States was unlikely to make any gesture which would enable British international commercial pre-eminence to be restored. As a concession to financial rationality the indemnity slogans mouthed by government spokesmen were at first hedged with references to Germany's limited capacity to pay and the undesirability of triggering a German export boom which would ruin British industry. Following pressure from partisan dominion statesmen such as Hughes and press barons like Northcliffe the dominant cry soon became, however, that the question of Germany's capacity was secondary and that a claim for general war costs was necessary in order to prevent France and

Belgium from monopolizing the spoils. The British Empire's distributive preoccupations were ultimately to blame for both the enormous sums which were canvassed at the Paris Peace Conference and the provocative assertion of German war guilt with which the reparation terms of the Versailles Treaty were prefaced. British bombast also helped to warp the discussions of Germany's total reparation obligation which dragged on between the Peace Conference and the early months of 1921. Paradoxically, however, Lloyd George's underlying concern lest excessive indemnity demands should damage British trade and his growing fear that they would be exploited by France to dominate the Continent ensured that Britain would moderate the practical short-term pressures that were placed upon Germany in the immediate post-war period.

If British reparation demands were verbally extreme but practically restrained, the reverse was true of French policy. The relative moderation of French claims did not stem from a more responsible financial policy than that of Britain: French war budgets were far less adequate and candid than those brought down on the other side of the Channel. The restraint of France arose in the first instance from a myopic preoccupation with the restoration of physical damage; and it was subsequently underpinned by a growing awareness that a narrow definition of reparations was in her distributive interest. The problem for French leaders in 1918–19 was that, in view of the shambles into which their government finance had degenerated, the British cry for general war costs was bound to be taken up locally; and it was eventually in order to balance short-term domestic popularity against long-term national interest that France fell in with the British suggestion during the peace negotiations that non-material war damage as represented by pensions and separation allowances should be included in the bill presented to Germany. This tactical moderation was in distinct contrast to the manner in which Germany was hounded by her neighbour from the time of the armistice to disgorge the wherewithal for the immediate restoration of the devastated areas. In their efforts to extract something tangible, French policy-makers oscillated between the contradictory and equally ineffectual gambits of threatening military sanctions and fostering Franco-German economic collaboration and integration. The first of these courses was favoured in the early months of 1920 after the electoral victory of the conservative *Bloc National*: but it foundered on British insistence during the protracted coal negotiations of this period that, if Germany were to survive, let alone generate a meaningful amount of reparation, she would have to be provided with a financial breathing space rather than harassed. Having deferred to Britain on the immediate question of coal deliveries, the French now sought to obtain privileged access to reparations by means of bilateral negotiations with Germany. Although they had agreed at the Spa Conference of July 1920 that Britain should receive a fixed 22-per-cent share of reparations, French experts such as Jacques Seydoux began to devise schemes for deliveries in kind which were to be effected by special arrangements between German suppliers and French claimants. These proposals were to bear little fruit because of the opposition they aroused from French businessmen who were interested in reconstruction contracts. Yet their possible distributive implications were unacceptable to the British, whose attitude was hardened at the end of 1920 by indications that the new Republican administration in the United States would dun the Europeans for their war debts. In order to resolve the deadlock, Briand and Lloyd George brushed aside the proposal of Seydoux for a temporary five-year reparation settlement involving substantial deliveries in kind which was canvassed at the Brussels Conference of December 1920. They then squared the circle at Germany's expense by inflating her total obligation and presenting her with an impossible schedule of payments. The Paris Resolutions of January 1921 which embodied these unilateral decisions were bound to provoke a negative German reaction; and French policy consequently swung back briefly to that of securing German compliance by imposing military sanctions in the form of the occupation of Düsseldorf, Duisburg, and Ruhrort in March 1921. Briand was, however, realistic enough to recognize that military action was financially futile, and sufficiently liberal to be averse to the 'Ottomanization' of Germany through the imposition of rigid financial controls upon her. He therefore bowed to the British view that the annuities eventually prescribed by the London Schedule of Payments of May 1921 should not be so high as to invite outright German rejection and physical Allied retaliation; and he also yielded to British pressure in favour of watering down the powers of the Committee of Guarantees, which had been appointed by the Reparation Commission to supervise the collection of revenues earmarked for reparations.

Until the end of 1920 the leaders of the United States were, unlike their French and British opposite numbers, moderates whose international financial sins were those of omission rather than commission.

In view, however, of the immense potential of the United States for good or ill in the early post-war years even this delinquency was of crucial importance. The Wilson administration demonstrated its good intentions in the dispute over the lifting of the food blockade on Germany in March 1919. Yet it quickly became obvious that it lacked the budgetary muscle to prime the pump of international economic recovery by reducing its financial claims on the victors or underwriting reconstruction loans. This weakness, which was induced by the insistence of the Republican majority in Congress that the unprecedented federal expenditures of 1918 and 1919 should be discontinued, made it impossible for Wilson and his colleagues to engineer a genuine *peace* settlement at Paris: on the contrary, the possibility that the United States would collect its debts encouraged the presentation of exaggerated financial claims to Germany by the Allies. The subsequent refusal of the Senate to ratify the Versailles Treaty, which set the diplomatic seal on American financial isolationism, also meant that the United States would not have a determining influence upon the manner in which the vaguely drawn financial terms of peace were implemented. The absence of an official American representative from the Reparation Commission did not leave the French with an entirely free hand because of Lloyd George's insistence upon transferring decision-making to cabinet level. The fitful deliberations in 1920 and 1921 about the total reparation bill nevertheless lacked the ingredient of financial realism which formal American participation would have provided. The problems of Europe were, in any case, compounded by the less constructive policies of the Republican administration which was installed after the presidential elections of November 1920. Although the excessive Paris Resolutions of January 1921 were produced largely by the Anglo-French deadlock over distribution, they were given seeming justification by reports that President Harding was bent upon retrieving the war loans of the United States to the European victors. Since, moreover, the American administration now had an interest in a substantial reparation scheme which would enable the Allies to service their war debts, the appeal of the German government to Harding to mediate in the spring of 1921 was misplaced. Far from being a possible source of moderation the Americans were fast becoming an aggravating factor in the reparation problem.

Although Germany was largely a passive party to the reparation dispute before the middle of 1920, an understanding of what happened to her during the war and the early months of peace is essential. The

original Allied demand for reparations is thrown into perspective by
the way in which the German ruling élite, which was more privileged
and hence more politically vulnerable than its Allied counterparts,
decided at a relatively early stage in the war that an indemnity campaign was necessary in order to deflect moves for radical financial
reform. The other point that emerges is that, notwithstanding the
inhumanity of the Allies in prolonging the food blockade early in
1919, Germany's daunting problems during the aftermath were largely
domestic rather than external in origin. In this context it is essential
to distinguish between the Carthaginian rhetoric of Allied policy,
which served both a demagogic and a tactical purpose, and the practical
restraint which was enjoined both by the delay in framing and implementing the treaty and by the undeniable frailty of the goose that was
to lay the golden egg. The trauma associated with the acceptance of
the Allied armistice and peace terms may well have made it more
difficult for moderates such as Erzberger to achieve the vital task
of financial reform. Yet even here the stonewalling tactics of the
conservative opposition and the *sauve qui peut* behaviour of the
German business community were usually projected as a defence
against the confiscatory designs of the Socialists rather than those of
the Entente. The domestic preoccupations of Erzberger's opponents
would also have been encouraged by the widespread belief that the
financial peace terms were impossible and would never be implemented
in their original form. The primacy of domestic politics became somewhat less marked in the second half of 1920 when the Allies began to
fumble their way towards enforcing the Reparation Chapter. The Spa
Coal Agreement of July 1920, which was the first somewhat meagre
fruit of their endeavours, and the subsequent negotiations about Germany's total liability at last provided something specific for critics of
the treaty to get their teeth into. The accession to power of the right-
centre Fehrenbach cabinet after the Reichstag elections of June 1920
also enabled the conservative DVP to exert more influence on domestic
and foreign affairs. As a result, the government reacted more aggress-
ively to Allied pressure and became less committed to financial reform.
This tendency became most pronounced during the London Conference of March 1921 when the German delegation made an almost
frivolous response to the extravagant claims registered in the Paris
Resolutions. In the wake of the hostile international reaction to their
behaviour, particularly in the United States, Fehrenbach and his colleagues soon became more conciliatory. They were unable, however,

to prevent the unilateral imposition of the London Schedule of Payments by the Allied Supreme Council and the Reparation Commission early in May; and they had accordingly resigned by the time the Allied terms had been transmitted to Berlin.

The acceptance of the new *Diktat* by the more moderate government which Joseph Wirth formed on 10 May with the aid of the SPD ushered in a bizarre period during which Germany made spasmodic and decreasingly effective attempts at fulfilment and financial reform and the French devised piecemeal and equally ineffectual measures to coerce her. It was no coincidence that throughout this phase of partial fulfilment and haphazard coercion which culminated in the Ruhr fracas of 1923, the French and Germans occupied centre stage while the British, after a few flourishes, retired to join the Americans in the wings. The debilitating trial of strength in which France and Germany became engaged in 1923 could not, in fact, be permanently halted until the Anglo-Saxon powers decided to assume sufficient responsibility to enable the international banking fraternity to moderate the behaviour of the continental parties to the reparation dispute.

Although the London Schedule of Payments quickly proved impossible to fulfil in the commercial and diplomatic context of the 1920s, there were fleeting grounds for optimism in the second half of 1921 because Lloyd George and Briand had contrived that Germany's initial payments would not be beyond her capacity. This meant that a short breathing space was provided in which a more rational long-term settlement might have been negotiated. Such an outcome depended, however, on conciliatory behaviour on both sides of the Rhine followed by a decisive intervention on the part of the Anglo-Saxons to achieve all-round debt reduction. In view of the failure of the creditors to vest effective financial control of Germany in the Committee of Guarantees, it was of crucial psychological importance that the debtor should demonstrate her good faith by making a convincing attempt to meet her immediate obligations. Such a gesture was, however, unlikely from Wirth and his colleagues, who did not enjoy sufficient support from the German business world and had, in any case, accepted the London Schedule not because they thought it was feasible but largely in the hope of obtaining a favourable Upper Silesian settlement. In these circumstances it was almost inevitable that Germany's first instalment of a billion gold marks would be transferred in a manner which would undermine the value of the mark and arouse concern among the creditors. The belated 'offensive of fulfilment', which the Wirth government launched in the autumn of 1921 in an effort to cover the instalments due in January and February 1922, also quickly ground to a halt because of the lukewarm and highly conditional backing it received from German industry, especially after the League of Nations decision to partition Upper Silesia was announced late in October. Germany's co-operative image was finally shattered in December when the rapid depreciation of the mark induced by middle-class tax evasion and capital flight prompted Wirth's diplomatically premature request to the Reparation Commission for a moratorium.

The French reaction to this German passivity was time-lagged because the reparation illusion was prolonged by the Wiesbaden Agreement, which was concluded by Rathenau and Loucheur in October. This blueprint for Franco-German economic collaboration involving massive deliveries in kind was, as Rathenau foresaw, bound to be unacceptable to French businessmen who would be harmed by an influx of German goods and services; and it also raised the distributive hackles of the British government. Thus, although sufficient good will was generated to enable Briand to declare to the Chamber in mid-October that the coercion of Germany would be a *pis aller*, the liberal internationalist position of the French premier quickly became vulnerable to the impracticable, but politically resonant, assertions of Poincaré that the treaty terms should be more rigorously enforced.

If Briand's days were numbered after Wirth had transmitted his moratorium request, his fall was actually precipitated by Lloyd George. After the City of London had put a temporary stop to the London Schedule by refusing to tide the German government over with a loan at the end of November 1921, the British Treasury advised the Prime Minister to resolve the problem of inter-government indebtedness by taking the lead in an international slate-wiping operation which would have reduced British and possibly American financial pressure on France and eased the position of Germany. In justifying his refusal to follow such a forthright course of action Lloyd George cited further reports that the Republican administration in the United States was preparing to collect its war debts. Yet he was in any case attracted to an electorally more appealing idea of subsuming the reparation problem into a general European reconstruction scheme. Since the viability of this proposal was very dubious—hinging as it did on the willingness of the Bolshevik government to recognize Tsarist debts and to countenance the renewed exploitation of Russia by the West—it is difficult to regard the project as much more than a face-saving gambit by a statesman whose earlier rhetoric had overtaken him. It was certainly insufficient to save the political skin of Briand, who announced his resignation in the middle of discussions of the reconstruction scheme at the Cannes Conference of January 1922 in response to growing domestic criticism of his failure to extract any real concessions from either Germany or Britain.

Briand's resignation, which he obviously hoped would discredit Poincaré by forcing him to assume power and moderate his behaviour, did not lead to an outward hardening of French policy in the early months of 1922. Restraint was, in the first place, enjoined by the reform programme which Wirth introduced in return for the partial and temporary moratorium granted by the Reparation Commission on 13 January. Even, moreover, by May when Wirth had succumbed to the right-wing pressures that were responsible for both the rapidly deteriorating budgetary situation and the provocative Rapallo Treaty with the Soviet Union, Poincaré was still constrained by the deliberations of J. P. Morgan's bankers' committee about an international loan for Germany. He had, however, narrowed his diplomatic options by reversing the trend towards greater budgetary responsibility which had been evident in France under Briand's leadership. The establishment of the World War Foreign Debt Commission and subsequent American requests for the repayment of war debts also made his attitude to Germany more rigid. When, therefore, the bankers, reacting in turn to French inflexibility, decided against a German loan in June, Poincaré had no alternative, if he were to remain in power, but to reiterate the empty slogan of 1919 that Germany should be made to 'pay'. His problem was that France could neither single-handedly achieve effective control of Germany nor hope to gain the collaboration of the conservatives who had come to power there by the end of 1922. The coercive measures he proposed were therefore bound to be financially counter-productive, no matter how much applause they earned him from French right-wing groups. It should be emphasized that Poincaré was not the tool of militarists or annexationists but merely, like Lloyd George, a demagogue who had been hoisted with his own petard. There is even reason to discount his repeated claims to his colleagues that in advocating and actually launching the occupation of the Ruhr he was trying to blackmail the Anglo-Saxons into making financial concessions. There was little love lost between Poincaré and Lloyd George, especially after the former had pointedly refused to take part in the discussions of the European reconstruction scheme at Genoa in April; and, far from being impressed by French threats, the British Prime Minister was, by the summer of 1922, deliberately seeking to encompass his French antagonist's downfall by manœuvring him into rash unilateral action against Germany. Lloyd George's successor, Bonar Law, was even less likely to make financial concessions to France; and the Americans were clearly unimpressed by French posturing. Having brought France to the brink of bankruptcy with his irresponsible fiscal conservatism, Poincaré was, therefore, trying to save face rather than pursuing attainable financial or diplomatic objectives when he pressed on with his Ruhr venture. Having crossed the Rubicon, moreover, only to be confronted with the Cuno cabinet's predictable campaign of passive resistance, he inevitably became absorbed with the task of bringing Germany to her knees rather than with the long-term exploitation of her resources. Even the formal capitulation which he eventually extracted from the Stresemann government and the Ruhr industrialists in the autumn of 1923 was significant chiefly for its short-term political impact in France and did nothing to resolve France's financial problems by increasing the future level of French reparation receipts.

The aggressive irrationality of French policy was encouraged by the decreasingly co-operative behaviour of the Germans. In the course of 1922, and more particularly after the fall of Wirth in November, the influence of moderates who sought to balance the budget and achieve treaty revision through fulfilment came to be outweighed by that of conservatives, so powerfully represented in the Reichsbank and Ministry of Finance, who attributed Germany's financial problems solely to her external burdens and opposed any budgetary reform until these were removed or substantially reduced. These violently inflationary policies were motivated less by patriotism than by the desire of powerful business interests to evade heavy direct taxation and divert the German economy into a lopsided capital goods boom: but they acquired a patriotic veneer which was unjustified in view of the self-serving behaviour of many tycoons during the heavily subsidized campaign of passive resistance which the Cuno cabinet waged against the French and Belgians in 1923. Only after this posturing had brought Germany to the verge of social and political collapse was there a return, under the leadership of Stresemann, to more moderate policies of financial stabilization and international co-operation which, although imposing inordinate burdens upon the German masses, at least precluded the continuation of Poincaré's coercive measures.

The contribution of Britain and the United States to the Franco-German reparation impasse of 1922–3 was indirect but crucial. From late in 1921 the British and American international banking fraternity, who were the ultimate arbiters of Germany's capacity to pay, frequently gave her reason to hope that her obligations would be reduced to a financially feasible level. The Bank of England's refusal to lend money for reparations in November 1921 and the negative report of J. P. Morgan's Loan Committee in June 1922 were both unequivocal condemnations of the excessive demands that were being made upon Germany; and even the abortive proposal of Secretary of State Hughes in December 1922 for the appointment of an expert committee to examine Germany's capacity to pay could only have strengthened the position of opponents of fulfilment in Germany. On the other hand, the policies of the British and American governments did much to encourage French extremism in 1922. Lloyd George's failure to initiate a round of debt cancellation in December 1921 was a virtual political death warrant for Briand. The setting up of the World War Foreign Debt Commission in February 1922 by the United States helped to queer the pitch for the Morgan Loan Committee and strengthened Poincaré's case for adopting a tough line with Germany. Lloyd George's Balfour Note of August 1922, which made the waiving of Britain's claims on Germany and her continental Allies conditional on the unlikely event of a commensurate cancellation of Britain's American war debts, had a similar effect; and the hardening of British policy after Bonar Law came to power obviously increased the French premier's desire to vent his frustration in the Ruhr. Finally, the adamant refusal of the United States administration at the end of 1922 to participate in any international discussion which might involve the war debt question put paid to the desperate last-minute effort of Bonar Law to dissuade Poincaré from his adventurist escapade.

After the Ruhr struggle had begun, the limitations of British policy contributed appreciably to its prolongation. Despite its profound disapproval of French and Belgian behaviour, the British government's opposition was at first muted by its problems with the Turks and by the expectation, which Bonar Law shared with Lloyd George, that Poincaré would quickly encompass his own downfall. When this desirable outcome receded into the future, Curzon made known Britain's deepening concern about both the legality and the continuation of the conflict. Yet, because it had just concluded an onerous debt-funding agreement with the United States, Britain was in no position to offer sufficient financial inducement to France to leave the Ruhr. The sad result of this diplomatic activity was that, instead of resolving the conflict, it merely encouraged the Germans, whose hopes of British intervention had been aroused, to persevere with their resistance in the summer and autumn of 1923. The winding up of the Ruhr imbroglio had, in fact, to await Poincaré's hollow and costly, but domestically essential, victory over the German government and the conclusion of the short-lived MICUM agreements with the Ruhr industrialists.

The third phase of the reparation problem was inaugurated by the intervention of the United States, whose financial and commercial interests were threatened by the growing political and economic disorder of Europe. With the assistance of the British, the Americans were able to deploy sufficient financial power to orchestrate a return to moderation in France and Germany by levering the French out of the Ruhr and underpinning a stabilized German currency. Yet, because they were, like the French and British, too afraid of their taxpayers to reduce their overseas claims to a reasonable level, they were unable to engineer a realistic reparation settlement. The Dawes Plan which was drawn up in 1924 provided Europe with a substantial breathing space in which to recover from the Ruhr disaster. Yet it also left the structure of reparations and war debts intact. This contradictory achievement was possible because Germany's obligations were reduced during the first three years of the scheme to less than half their level under the London Schedule of Payments. The budgetary sting was also removed from her early payments by arrangements for them to be covered by foreign loans and earmarked extra-budgetary revenues; and the transfer problem was eased by making provision for payments to be temporarily suspended if they appeared likely to jeopardize the stability of the mark. Finally, an attempt was made to defuse the reparation question politically by transferring the responsibility for the day-to-day administration of the system from the Reparation Commission in Paris to a low-profile American Agent-General for Reparation Payments who was based in Berlin. The success of the Dawes Plan in its first three years depended on this feather-bedding and an accompanying upsurge of foreign lending to Germany; and no indication was provided of the feasibility of a full-scale reparation scheme. The policies of the major parties to the reparation dispute were not, moreover, such as to make substantial payments possible in the future. Although the conservatives who helped to rule Germany in the mid-1920s had swallowed their patriotism and accepted the Dawes Plan for the sake of American loans, their insistence on revenue-paring and devolutionary tax-sharing arrangements with the states made the Reich government ill-equipped to shoulder increased obligations. The right-wing governments of the major creditors, moreover, not only espoused similar hand-to-mouth budgetary policies which predisposed them against the necessary downward revision of inter-government debts but also displayed protectionist tendencies which would militate against any attempt by Germany to finance larger payments by expanding her exports. As it was, Germany's chronic adverse trade balance in the 1920s meant that her ability to meet her modest Dawes Plan obligations, let alone anything more onerous, depended on the continuing availability of foreign credit.

Because American private investors were a major source of the funds which enabled Germany to survive and, indeed, prosper in the early Dawes period, American financial policy became an increasingly important influence on the development of the reparation problem. A considerable number of influential Americans subscribed to what has been loosely described as the Wall Street view that reparations and war debts ought to be substantially reduced in order to prevent them from prejudicing the security of the large sums which American citizens were lending to Germany. It was to this current of opinion that Seymour Parker Gilbert, the young American Agent-General for Reparation Payments, who was aspiring to a partnership in J. P. Morgan & Co., originally responded when he surprised European reparation officialdom at the end of 1927 by suggesting that the time had come for a final commercialized and, by implication, revisionist settlement. There was, however, an even more formidable school of thought amongst political leaders and Treasury officials in Washington that the first priority of the government was to protect the interests of the American taxpayer by expediting the collection of war debts. Although the advocates of this policy refused, with good reason, to admit any legal or moral connection between reparations and war debts, the practical consequence of their position was that they opposed any reduction of Germany's obligations which might undermine the ability of former Allies such as Britain, France, and Italy to honour their American obligations. Unfortunately for Europe and the world, this was the view to which Gilbert, who had begun his career as a Treasury official, ultimately deferred in 1928 when he colluded with the American administration and Poincaré to resolve the hitherto intractable problem of France's indebtedness to the United States at Germany's expense. It was for this reason that the Agent-General cajoled, misled, and finally bludgeoned the sceptical British and the vulnerable, if somewhat importunate, Germans into participating in negotiations which he had prearranged to produce the excessively onerous and seemingly interminable annuities which came to be embodied in the Young Plan.

The deliberations of the Young Committee in the first half of 1929 and the Hague Conferences which considered the implementation of its recommendations in subsequent months were bound to be bitter and prolonged. The most aggrieved parties to the Young Committee's four months of sordid and exhausting haggling were the Germans, who protested vainly against the failure of the creditors to take any real account of their country's financial capacity and their pre-occupation with shoring up the structure of inter-Allied indebtedness. Despite its vigorous protests, the Müller government was ultimately forced by creditor financial pressure to accept a 58-year schedule of payments which, although on average about 20 per cent lower than the standard Dawes annuity of 2.5 billion gold marks, still imposed far too great a burden on the German budget and balance of payments in the absence of a dramatic expansion of world trade. The Germans were given some short-term inducement to co-operate by the creditors' undertaking to evacuate the Rhineland and their usual tactic of making the initial annuities sufficiently low to preclude immediate default. Yet the excessive duration of the plan, which arose from Franco-American insistence that it should be co-extensive with inter-Allied debt-funding arrangements, made it an explosive issue for any German government, as Hugenberg and Hitler quickly demonstrated late in 1929. Germany's budgetary difficulties after the depression began in 1929 also ensured that even the relatively modest sums demanded of her at the outset would be socially and politically insupportable.

Next to the Germans, it was the British who had most cause for complaint about the Young Plan. The new Labour cabinet, which had attained power after the Young Committee had submitted its report, would have preferred the radical reduction of inter-government indebt-edness which the British Treasury had been advocating for so long. Since, however, nothing of the kind was envisaged by the Americans, Snowden, the incoming Chancellor of the Exchequer, concentrated his energies mainly on restoring the British Empire's share of reparations, which had been appreciably diminished by the Young Committee's efforts to make Germany's annuities slightly more acceptable to her.

Snowden's opposition to the sacrifice which Britain had been called upon to make was strengthened by the budgetary problems which had been posed for Britain, like Germany, by the depression. His ability to wring concessions so dramatically from the other creditors at the first Hague Conference in August 1929 was, however, due less to any recognition of the justice of Britain's case than to apprehension lest the Labour cabinet, if it were not appeased, might be encouraged to break up the conference and scrap the Young Plan so as to precipitate a genuine reparation settlement.

Even the French, who had been accessories to American manipulation of the Young Plan, were very uneasy about it. Both the left and the extreme right wing disapproved of the way in which payments for reparation proper had been subordinated to outpayments for war debts. There was also understandable concern about how little of Germany's obligation was to be commercialized (that is, converted into bonds taken up by the international capital market) in the manner which Gilbert had envisaged at the end of 1927. The refusal of the creditors to reduce their claims to manageable proportions and the tightness of credit both before and after the Wall Street crash meant that reparations had not been transformed from a political into a technical financial question. This had been recognized by the Young Committee when it recommended that only 700 million marks, or less than half, of each annuity should be categorized as 'unconditional', and that the Bank for International Settlements, which was created to channel Germany's remittances, should be responsible for organizing the adjudication of any disagreement about the feasibility of transferring the 'conditional' residue. Since these provisions indicated that the Young settlement was no more final or definitive than its predecessors, the question naturally arose as to how, after the Rhineland had been evacuated, Germany could be persuaded to honour her commitments. The manner in which the problems of commercialization and guarantees were glossed over by Tardieu, Briand's conservative successor, at the second Hague Conference shows that even French right-wing circles were virtually admitting that the Young Plan was neither viable nor enforceable. It was their growing awareness that the financial and political preconditions for an effective reparation scheme were rapidly disappearing that encouraged so many French leaders to indulge in Briand's wishful thinking about European federation in the early months of 1930.

The Young Plan was able to survive for two years mainly because of the determined rearguard action which the Hoover administration mounted in its defence with the assistance of the conservative Laval and Tardieu cabinets. Yet its life was also prolonged by the diplomatically inhibiting financial vulnerability of its most resolute opponents, Britain and Germany. Although MacDonald and his colleagues were consistently revisionist, their ability to bring about a sensible settlement was restricted because of their reluctance to add to Britain's growing financial embarrassment by giving offence to American opinion. They therefore confined themselves to making muted gestures of solidarity with the Germans, endorsing the pleas for radical inter-governmental action which were made by a series of expert committees in the second half of 1931, and, finally, seizing the opportunity provided by the long overdue change of government in France in June 1932 to ensure that the Lausanne Conference cut the Gordian knot. Germany enjoyed even less room to manœuvre because of her heavy dependence on short-term overseas loans and the consequent unwillingness of the Brüning government, especially after the September 1930 elections, to make diplomatic initiatives which might undermine even further her foreign credit. Brüning's difficulties were, however, compounded by the rigid conservatism of his financial policies. His strategy of vigorous deflation was designed both to promote recovery via the export industries which were his political base of support and to achieve reparation revision by means of an 'offensive of fulfilment' which would flood the world's markets with German goods. However logical such a policy was in theory, it was difficult to sustain in practice because of the opposition it aroused from those who preferred a more direct attack on Germany's domestic and external problems. From the beginning of 1931, therefore, Brüning was forced to condone initiatives such as the Austro-German Customs Union proposal and to resort to pseudo-*démarches* like the *Tributaufruf* of June in order to contain the jingoes and divert attention from the Draconian financial measures he was instituting. Yet these gestures only accelerated the withdrawal of funds from Germany which his harsh fiscal programme and a series of business scandals had set in train. As a result, Brüning had virtually decided by the middle of June to resort to an appeal to the Special Advisory Committee of the BIS, even though he regarded such a move an an unsatisfactory half-measure which could not yield more than a temporary suspension of conditional annuities.

At this point the initiative was taken away from Brüning by the Americans and the French, who feared with some justification that a new enquiry into Germany's position by the Special Advisory Committee might lead to the dismantling of the whole Young Plan structure. In order to pre-empt such an outcome, Hoover abruptly proclaimed his one-year moratorium on inter-government debt repayments on 20 June and then, when Germany's financial condition continued to deteriorate, pressured the London Conference in July to prop her up with short-term credits and a temporary freeze on the withdrawal of private funds. These stopgap measures were not sufficient to deflect the growing pressure from Britain and the American banking fraternity for a thoroughgoing review of the situation. The American and French governments, however, took care to emasculate both the Wiggin–Layton Committee, which was set up by the London Conference, and its successor, the Special Advisory Committee, by restricting them to an examination of Germany's immediate, as opposed to her long-term, problems. These obstructive tactics, and the understandable desire of Brüning to postpone any fundamental reappraisal of the reparation question until after the forthcoming French elections, meant that Britain's unremitting efforts to organize a final reparation conference did not bear fruit until the Lausanne Conference assembled in June 1932.

The key to the success of this gathering was the readiness of Mac-Donald and Herriot, the new French premier, to break the Young Plan's nexus between reparations and war debts and to conclude a final reparation settlement without reference to the United States. Once this step had been taken, the European creditors were free to get rid of a system which was increasingly regarded as an impediment to economic recovery. It was, however, an indication of the residual strength of those forces which had produced the reparation problem that even the moderate politicians who stage-managed its demise contrived to convey the impression that Germany would still be required to 'pay' something. The reparation myth, like the war debt illusion, was never finally scotched, but left in limbo.

The sorry reparation story might encourage a casual observer to conclude that the peace settlement of 1919 was the embodiment of the financial and commercial imperialism which Lenin claimed was endemic to mature capitalism. Conservative political leaders who were sensitive to the views of big business were, it is true, largely to blame for the aggressive reaction of the major belligerents to their post-war financial difficulties. Yet the demands which the victors made upon Germany and each other were not part of a coherent programme of economic or geopolitical aggrandizement. They represented, on the contrary, a reckless attempt by frightened right-wingers and lapsed moderates to divert attention from unprecedented budgetary problems and forestall proposals for confiscatory direct taxation. The insistence of these elements that at least a substantial part of the cost of the war could be borne by the vanquished was both economically and diplomatically quixotic in the liberal capitalist world of the inter-war years. The persistence of such rhetoric for over a decade was understandable in France because of her chronic budgetary weakness and her fear of a resurgent Germany. It was, however, remarkable that myopic fiscal conservatism remained so powerful in Britain and, more particularly, in the United States, where prominent members of the financial and commercial élite complained repeatedly that reparations and war debts were destabilizing and bad for trade. That the tributary system survived for so long bears witness to the tendency of liberal democracies to respond to economic crises by protecting the short-term interests of the wealthy taxpayer rather than promoting balanced long-term recovery.

Similar observations can be made about the reaction of Germany to creditor demands. Although military defeat had made it impossible for Germany to 'export', in the same direct way as the victors, the financial problems accruing from the war and the aftermath, conservative political leaders subsequently pursued policies of hyper-inflation and ruthless deflation which transferred a disproportionate share of their country's burdens onto the shoulders of the masses of consumers and workers. Both the heavy industrialists who favoured inflation in the early 1920s and the export industries which supported Brüning a decade later projected their policies partly as a patriotic attempt to rid Germany of her external obligations. But German financial behaviour is best seen as an illustration of the way in which the propertied classes can manipulate the liberal state to their advantage in periods of stringency. The history of the reparation dispute serves to remind us of the anarchic *bellum omnium contra omnes* which lies just beneath the surface of domestic financial politics and international economic relations.

APPENDIX I

German Economic Statistics to 1922

TABLE A. *Coal, Iron, and Steel Production* (million tons)

	Black coal	Lignite	Pig iron	Crude steel
1913	190	87	12.9	15.9
1913[a]	173	87	10.9	11.9
1913[b]	140	87	10.3	10.9
1918	160	101	9.2	12.9
1919	108	94	6.3	8.5
1920	131	112	6.4	8.5
1921	136	123	7.9	10.1
1922	130	137	9.4	11.7
1923	62	118	4.9	6.3

[a] Post-war frontiers.
[b] Frontiers after May 1922.

Sources: Iron and steel production figures: Bresciani-Turroni, 193 n.; coal and lignite production figures: Davis, 'Economic and Financial Progress', 105. For the 1913 output of Polish Upper Silesia: Machray, 118; Lübsen, 427–9.

TABLE B. *Number of Livestock* ('ooo head)

Date	Horses	Cattle	Sheep	Pigs	Goats
1/12/13	4,523	20,994	5,521	25,659	3,548
4/12/18	3,493	18,095	5,382	10,545	4,426
Post-war frontiers					
4/12/18	2,978	16,448	4,905	9,227	4,021
1/12/19	3,468	16,298	5,356	11,469	4,052
1/12/20	3,588	16,807	6,150	14,179	4,459
1/12/21	3,666	16,791	5,891	18,818	4,296
1/12/22	3,650	16,316	5,566	14,678	4,140

Sources: For figures up to 1/12/19: *Monthly Bulletin of Statistics*, i. No. 12, 30; ii. No. 4, 34. Summarized in: Davis, 'Recent ... Progress in Germany', 154. For 1920 figures: Thelwall, *Report on ... Germany to March 1922*, 184–5. See also *Statistisches Jahrbuch für das deutsche Reich*, 1926, 50–1.

TABLE C. *Crop Yields* ('ooo metric tons)

Year	Rye	Wheat	Barley	Potatoes	Oats
1913	12,222	4,656	3,673	54,121	9,714
1918	8,035	2,527	2,038	29,941	4,769
Post-war frontiers					
1918	6,676	2,337	1,850	24,744	4,381
1919	6,100	2,169	1,670	21,449	4,494
1920	4,970	2,250	1,800	28,250	4,870
1921	6,798	2,933	1,937	26,149	4,004
1922	5,234	1,958	1,607	40,661	4,015

Sources: *Statistisches Jahrbuch für das deutsche Reich*, 1926, 44–5; Bresciani-Turroni, 192 n.

TABLE D. *Overseas Trade*

Month	Value (million gold marks)			Volume ('ooo tons)	
	Imports	Exports	Balance	Imports	Exports
1913					
Monthly average	897	842	− 55	6,068	6,143
1919					
Jan.	204	83	− 121	200	323
Feb.	188	90	− 98	159	377
Mar.	178	118	− 60	249	583
Apr.	209	90	− 119	373	641
May	480	82	− 398	613	538
June	805	122	− 683	884	1,055
July	1,061	171	− 890	1,298	1,085
Aug.	824	158	− 666	1,531	1,202
Sept.	702	132	− 570	1,277	944
Oct.	832	175	− 657	1,240	1,231
Nov.	500	144	− 356	1,018	1,324
Dec.	489	392	− 97	1,081	2,762
TOTAL	6,472	1,757	− 4,715	9,923	12,065
1920					
Jan.	459	224	− 235	1,129	1,523
Feb.	269	193	− 76	1,475	1,923
Mar.	310	230	− 80	1,357	1,826
Apr.	328	379	+ 51	1,224	2,170
May	514	616	+ 102	1,485	2,895
June		562		1,737	2,680
July		544		1,739	2,004
Aug.		529		1,512	1,910
Sept.		468		1,680	1,837
Oct.		401		1,758	1,494
Nov.		430		1,757	1,768
Dec.		449		2,007	1,758
TOTAL	7,000	5,025	− 2,000	18,860	23,788

TABLE D. (cont.):

Month	Value (million gold marks)			Volume ('000 tons)	
	Imports	Exports	Balance	Imports	Exports
1921					
Jan.					
May	373	310	− 63	1,530	1,140
June	392	331	− 61	1,820	1,510
July	407	334	− 73	1,920	1,560
Aug.	463	328	− 135	2,110	1,830
Sept.	440	309	− 131	2,530	1,870
Oct.	396	276	− 120	3,000	1,970
Nov.	219	226	+ 7	2,530	1,910
Dec.	299	318	+ 19	2,080	1,930
TOTAL	2,989	2,432	− 557	17,520	13,720
1922					
Jan.	330	325	− 5	2,309	2,027
Feb.	360	298	− 65	1,475	1,747
Mar.	563	324	− 239	2,645	2,153
Apr.	508	327	− 181	2,889	2,176
May	565	416	− 149	3,810	2,093
June	565	428	− 137	4,029	1,879
July	684	336	− 348	4,798	1,636
Aug.	545	255	− 290	4,676	1,407
Sept.	422	291	− 131	4,289	1,587
Oct.	532	291	− 241	5,552	1,539
Nov.	536	255	− 281	4,551	1,551
Dec.	570	423	− 147	4,320	1,760
TOTAL	6,180	3,969	− 2,214	45,343	21,555

Sources: (a) For the volume of trade in 1919–20: Bresciani-Turroni, 448. (b) Figures for the value of trade between Jan. 1919 and May 1920: League of Nations, *International Financial Conference, Brussels, 1920*, iii. 34. Statistics of exports June–Dec. 1920: Supreme Economic Council, *Monthly Bulletin of Statistics*. Figures for the value of imports in this period are unavailable. (c) The value of exports and imports has been converted from paper marks to gold marks in accordance with the monthly average rates in: Bresciani-Turroni, 441. (d) Figures of both the value and volume of trade between Jan. and Apr. 1921 have never been published. Approximate figures for the value of trade in this period and also for the value of imports between June and Dec. 1920 have been derived from the global estimates of trade in 1920 and 1921 made by O. von Glasenapp, 'Germany's Balance of Payments with Other

Countries', *MGCRE*, 20 Apr. 1922, 22. (*e*) Figures for 1921–2: *The Economist, Monthly Supplement*, 23 June 1923, 6; Thelwall, *Report on ... Germany to March 1922*, 33; *Report on ... Germany to March 1923*, 41.

TABLE E. *Number of Unemployed Receiving Assistance*

	1920	1921	1922
1 Jan.	454,775	410,238	164,248
1 Feb.	430,766	423,164	202,594
1 Mar.	370,296	426,600	212,526
1 Apr.	329,505	413,321	115,845
1 May	292,307	394,262	64,708
1 June	271,660	357,352	28,626
1 July	322,923	314,475	19,648
1 Aug.	403,835	267,108	15,137
1 Sept.	414,601	232,057	11,671
1 Oct.	392,823	185,806	16,678
1 Nov.	361,311	150,104	24,813
1 Dec.	350,087	149,126	42,900

Source: *Statistisches Jahrbuch für das deutsche Reich*, 1921/2, 446–7; ibid. 1923, 428–9.

TABLE F. *Government Expenditure* (millions of gold marks)

	Income	Expenditure	Increase in floating debt
1919			
Apr.	306.5	1,439.4	1,132.8
May	330.0	1,346.3	1,016.2
June	299.7	1,212.6	914.0
July	320.2	1,063.7	743.5
Aug.	256.5	947.8	691.4
Sept.	207.8	635.3	426.0
Oct.	242.6	660.5	417.9
Nov.	140.3	418.8	278.5
Dec.	136.5	232.4	95.2
Jan.	116.4	239.2	122.5
Feb.	73.8	105.9	31.8
Mar.	128.8	257.8	129.2
TOTAL	2,559.1	8,559.7	5,999.0
1920			
Apr.	52.0	307.9	247.8
May	102.2	694.8	584.5
June	193.5	1,441.6	1,240.0
July	256.1	1,279.3	1,015.1
Aug.	191.7	791.7	591.9
Sept.	176.8	817.2	632.3
Oct.	197.8	348.8	142.9
Nov.	241.1	629.1	379.9
Dec.	411.3	722.7	303.3
Jan.	434.9	613.5	170.5
Feb.	460.3	899.4	431.9
Mar.	460.4	782.9	314.4
TOTAL	3,178.1	9,328.9	6,054.5

	Income	Expenditure	Increase in floating debt
1921			
Apr.	352.3	773.2	416.9
May	411.8	686.0	270.2
June	350.3	862.3	508.0
July	304.8	617.8	309.0
Aug.	256.3	863.2	602.9
Sept.	196.5	506.0	305.5
Oct.	173.0	384.5	207.5
Nov.	112.5	254.6	138.1
Dec.	175.3	626.5	447.2
Jan.	192.6	388.2	191.6
Feb.	194.2	342.4	144.2
Mar.	207.8	346.5	134.7
TOTAL	2,927.4	6,651.2	3,675.8
1922			
Apr.	190.3	321.8	129.8
May	254.9	376.9	120.3
June	235.1	313.8	77.0
July	183.4	208.5	23.4
Aug.	116.4	205.1	86.9
Sept.	90.8	434.9	342.5
Oct.	66.2	269.5	201.6
Nov.	60.6	199.8	137.5
Dec.	73.4	438.0	362.9
Jan.	65.9	204.6	137.0
Feb.	50.8	279.0	226.5
Mar.	100.3	698.9	596.9
TOTAL	1,488.1	3,950.8	2,442.3

Source: Bresciani-Turroni, 437–8.

APPENDIX II

German Coal Distribution in 1913 and 1919–1922

The level of reparation coal deliveries varied considerably between 1919 and 1922. From September to December 1919 the monthly average was 600,000 tons. This figure rose to 850,000 tons in the first seven months of 1920, and thence to a peak of 1,750,000 tons between August 1920 and April 1921. Between May 1921 and December 1922 deliveries declined to about 1,500,000 tons a month.[1]

In assessing the impact of deliveries on German coal distribution it is necessary to isolate the months following the partition of Upper Silesia in May 1922. Table G shows the amount of coal available for all purposes, including reparations, between September 1919 and May 1922; and Table H indicates the significance of reparation deliveries in the pre-May 1922 period.

TABLE G. *German Coal Production, September 1919–May 1922* (million tons)

	Net[a] black coal production	Brown coal[b] production (in terms of black coal)	Total	Exports[c]	Remainder
Sept.–Dec. 1919	35.7	7.5	43.2	1.8	41.4
Jan.–July 1920	63.9	13.7	77.6	4.5	73.1
Aug. 1920–Apr. 1921	89.1	20.1	109.2	4.5	104.7
May 1921–May 1922	129.0	30.7	159.7	6.0	153.7

[a] For monthly gross production of black coal and brown coal (lignite): Supreme Economic Council, *Monthly Bulletin of Statistics*; Thelwall, *Report on ... Germany to March 1922*, 85; *Report on ... Germany to March 1923*, 60. In the case of black coal, net production = gross production less pithead

[1] Monthly delivery figures: Sept. 1919 to 10 Jan. 1920: RC v. 95; Jan. 1920 to Jan. 1922: ibid. Appendix XXI, 229. Total deliveries May 1921 to Dec. 1922: RC iv. 12.

consumption. Before the war about 10% of gross production was consumed at the pits: Keynes, *Economic Consequences*, 81. Because of the larger number of miners employed this figure rose to 13% after 1918. See figures for Aug.–Sept. 1920 in Thelwall, *General Report ... in December 1920*, 73–6. Cf. Lübsen, 427–9.

  [b] Nine tons of brown coal was the calorific equivalent of two tons of black coal: Bresciani-Turroni, 192–3 n. There was little or no pithead consumption of brown coal.

  [c] No complete monthly figures for German coal exports in 1919–21 are available. The figures given here have been deduced from (1) monthly export figures for July 1919 to May 1920 in: *Die Konferenz in Spa*, 65; (2) average monthly export figures for 1920 and 1921 in: Thelwall, *Report on ... Germany to March 1923*, 44; and (3) figures for Aug.–Sept. 1920 in: Thelwall, *General Report ... in December 1920*, 73–6.

TABLE H. *German Coal Production and Reparation Deliveries, September 1919–May 1922* (million tons)

	Amount available before reparation	Reparation deliveries	Amount available after reparation
Sept.–Dec. 1919	41.4	2.5	38.9
Jan.–July 1920	73.1	6.0	67.1
Aug. 1920–Apr. 1921	104.7	15.8	88.9
May 1921–May 1922	153.7	19.0	134.7

In order to judge the significance of reparation deliveries as a cause of the post-war coal shortage, these figures must be compared with those for coal distribution in Germany in 1913 in Table J. For the purpose of comparison with the consumption of post-war Germany, these figures must be reduced by 25.5 million tons, the amount of black coal consumed in 1913 in territories ceded after the war (Alsace-Lorraine, 11.1 million tons; Saar Basin, 5.8 million tons; Schleswig-Holstein and Eupen-Malmédy, 0.6 million tons; Poznania, 2.6 million tons; Polish East Prussia and Danzig, 1.5 million tons; and Luxemburg, 3.9 million tons). Further deductions must be made in respect of the 3 million tons of black coal consumed in 1913 by the navy, the merchant marine, and war industries, and also the 0.3 million tons of brown coal (in terms of black coal) consumed in territories subsequently ceded. Thus the 1913 consumption of all types of coal in post-war Germany would have been: $160.6 - 28.8 = 131$ million tons a year *or* 11 million tons a month.[2]

TABLE J. *Coal Distribution in 1913* (million tons)

Net[a] black coal production	Brown coal[b] production (in terms of black coal)	Total	Net[c] exports	Remainder
171	23.6	194.6	34	160.6

[a] That is, gross production of 190 million tons, less 19 million tons pithead consumption. For gross production figures: see above, Appendix I, Table A.

[b] This figure includes imports of Bohemian brown coal: Thelwall, *General Report ... in December 1920*, 73–6.

[c] Figure for net exports in 1913: Lübsen, 427.

The following table (Table K) compares the amount of coal available in 1913 with that available in early post-war Germany, and shows the extent to which the discrepancy was due to reparation deliveries. The columns show:

(1) the amount of reparation coal deliveries;
(2) the amount of coal which was available in Germany after reparation deliveries had been made;
(3) the amount of coal which would probably have been available if there had been no reparation deliveries;
(4) the amount of coal which was available in the same area and over the same period in 1913;
(5) the percentage relationship between (2) and (4);
(6) the percentage relationship between (3) and (4).

In calculating (3) it has been assumed (*a*) that one-third of the coal delivered as reparations would otherwise have been exported, and (*b*) that German coal production would have been the same if there had been no reparation deliveries.[3]

---

[2] For pre-war consumption of black coal in ceded territories and by navy, merchant marine, and war industries: *Economic Review*, 1 Apr. 1921, 373. These deductions are almost certainly too large, especially in respect of the latter part of 1919, when the cessions of territory had not been formalized by the ratification of the treaty. For brown coal figures: Thelwall, *General Report ... in December 1920*, 73–6.

[3] Both of these assumptions are hard to justify. Because of the coal shortage in Germany there was strong opposition to increased exports, despite the fact that they were one of the few means by which foreign exchange could be earned: see above, ch. 2

TABLE K. *Impact of Coal Deliveries, September 1919–May 1922*

	$(1)^a$	$(2)^a$	$(3)^a$	$(4)^a$	$(5)^b$	$(6)^b$
1919						
Sept.–Dec.	2.5	38.9	40.6	44	88	92
1920						
Jan.–July	6.0	67.1	71.1	77	87	92
1920–1						
Aug.–Apr.	15.8	88.9	99.5	99	90	100
1921–2						
May–May	19.0	134.7	147.4	143	94	103

[a] Figures in millions of tons.   [b] Figures expressed as percentage.

Although a high degree of accuracy cannot be claimed for these figures,[4] and although they conceal month-to-month variations, they provide a reasonable guide to the impact of coal deliveries. In the first two sub-periods, that is, between September 1919 and July 1920, the severity of the coal shortage was due far more to the low level of production than to reparations. The latter were responsible for only one-third of a total lag of 12–13 per cent behind the 1913 level of coal distribution. Reparation deliveries became a major reason for the coal shortage between August 1920 and April 1921 when, although not increasing the overall deficiency, they were responsible for all of a 10-per-cent lag behind the 1913 distribution level. However, in the following year, they accounted for a lag of only 6 per cent behind peacetime consumption.

In the last seven months of 1922 more coal was distributed within Germany than at any time since the war. This was in spite of the partition of Upper Silesia which deprived Germany of 2 million tons

n. 50. The assumption that the level of German coal production would have remained the same is also unreal in view of the fillip given to output by the Spa Coal Agreement of July 1920: see above, ch. 3 n. 15. However, since the first assumption encourages an underestimate, and the second an overestimate, of the amount of coal which would have been available, it can reasonably be hoped that any error will be cancelled out.

[4] It is, in particular, difficult to estimate accurately the coal needs of post-war Germany by 1913 standards. The figure cited (132 million tons) is in danger of being an underestimate. This would tend to make the post-war shortage appear less serious than it really was, and hence exaggerate the relative significance of reparation deliveries. If, for example, in the period Sept.–Dec. 1919, the coal needs of Germany were 12 million tons a month rather than 11 million, as they were in 1913, then reparation deliveries would have been responsible for only one-fifth of a total lag of 19% behind the required distribution level rather than a third of a total short-fall of 12–13%.

of her monthly coal output after May 1922.[5] The main reason for the improvement was that Germany, which had in the first five months of 1922 been a net exporter of 2.5 million tons of coal, became between June and December 1922 a net importer of 10.3 million tons.[6] As Table L indicates, the amount of coal which was potentially available for distribution in these seven months was therefore 89.5 million tons. Since reparation deliveries in these months amounted to 10.5 million tons, the amount of coal in fact available was 79 million tons. This was 2 million tons above the 1913 distribution level of 77 million tons (11 million tons a month for 7 months). Since the cession of Polish Upper Silesia reduced the total coal consumption of Germany by a considerable amount, coal was in fact even more plentiful by 1913 standards. In 1913 the consumption of the ceded portion of Upper Silesia had been about 14 million tons a year, that is 8 million tons for 7 months.[7] Thus between June 1922 and December 1922 there were about ten million more tons of coal available within Germany than there had been for a comparable area and over the same period in 1913.

TABLE L. *Coal Production in Germany, June–December 1922* (million tons)

Net black coal production	Lignite production (in terms of black coal)	Net imports	Total
61	18.2	10.3	89.5

Sources: see Table G, note a.

[5] Davis, 'Economic and Financial Progress', 105.
[6] Thelwall, *Report on ... Germany to March 1923*, 44–5; *Report on ... Germany to April 1924*, 69.
[7] Lübsen, 427–8.

BIBLIOGRAPHY

A. UNPUBLISHED MATERIAL

Note: the following published works are indispensable guides to German and British archival materials relating to the reparation problem.

KENT, G. O., *A Catalog of Files and Microfilms of the German Foreign Ministry Archives, 1920–1945* (4 vols.; Stanford, 1962–72).

Übersicht über die Bestände des Deutschen Zentralarchivs, Potsdam: Schriftenreihe des Deutschen Zentralarchivs, No. 1 (Berlin, 1957).

The Records of the Cabinet Office to 1922, Public Record Office Handbooks, No. 11 (HMSO London, 1966).

Index to the Correspondence of the Foreign Office, 1920–1932 (London, 1969–).

(1) *France*

(*a*) Archives de l'Assemblée Nationale, Palais Bourbon, Paris
Chambre des Députés. Commission des Affaires Etrangères, Procès-Verbaux, 1921–9.

(*b*) Archives Économiques et Financières, Ministère de l'Économie–Ministère du Budget, Rue de Rivoli, Paris
F30, 1282 Exécution du Plan Dawes (1925–8).
        Dossier Notes Seydoux.
        Marche Générale du Plan Dawes.
    1283 Exécution du Plan.
        Rapports avec le CDR.
        Notes prises au cours de conversations entre M. Poincaré, Président du Conseil et M. Parker Gilbert, agent-general des paiements des réparations.
    1302 Mobilisation du plan.
        Dossier 'Plan Dawes: Son Remplacement par le Plan Young'.

(*c*) Archives Nationales, Paris
AJ^5 3, 4 Comité des Garanties: Procès-Verbaux, 1921–4.
     361 Documents signalés à l'attention des Experts.
        Correspondance échangée entre la Délégation Française et le Président du Conseil.
     370 Nouveau Comité des Experts 1928–30.
    533–6 Commission des Réparations: Procès-Verbaux.

(*d*) Archives du Sénat, Palais Luxembourg, Paris
Sénat. Commission des Affaires Étrangères, Procès-Verbaux, 1917–23.

(e) Ministère des Affaires Étrangères, Quai d'Orsay, Paris,
Papiers Millerands, Allemagne XII Réparations; XIX Réparations; XX Réparations.

(2) *Germany*

(a) Alte Reichskanzlei (Microfilm)
Kabinettsprotokolle. Aktenzeichen R. Min. 2b.

(b) Auswärtiges Amt. Büro des Reichsministers (Microfilm)
Spa, Aktenzeichen 4.
Reparationsfragen, Aktenzeichen 5.
Genf–Brüssel, Aktenzeichen 5a.
Paris, Aktenzeichen 5b.
Reparationen (secret), Aktenzeichen 5 secr.
London, Aktenzeichen 5c.
Sanktionen, Aktenzeichen 5d.
Massnahmen der Entente, bei Nichterfüllung der Reparationen, Aktenzeichen 5e.
Kredithilfe der Industrie, Aktenzeichen 5f.
Cannes, Aktenzeichen 5g.
Genua, Aktenzeichen 5h.
Haag, Aktenzeichen 5i.
Internationale Geschäftsleutekonferenz, Aktenzeichen 5k.
Deutsche-Englische Industrie-Cooperation, Aktenzeichen 5m.
Londoner Konferenz 1924, Aktenzeichen 5n.
England, Aktenzeichen 6.
Frankreich, Aktenzeichen 7.

(c) Auswärtiges Amt. Büro des Staatssekretärs (Mircofilm)
Die wichtigsten Gespräche mit den Reparationsagenten Parker Gilbert, i–vi, Aktenzeichen Cgil.

(d) Auswärtiges Amt. Wirtschafts Reparationen (Microfilm)
Ausführung des Londoner Ultimatums vom 5.5.21 und die allgemeine Reparationsfrage, Aktenzeichen 7.
Amerikanische Vermittlung in der Reparationsfrage, Aktenzeichen 7.
Frage der endgültigen Regelung des Reparationsproblems, Aktenzeichen 18.
Einsetzung einer Kommission von Finanzsachverständigen, i–x, Aktenzeichen 19.
Die Haager Konferenz 1929–30, i–xi; Frage der Ratifikation der Haager Vereinbarungen, i–viii, Aktenzeichen 20A.
Bank für Internationalen Zahlungsausgleich, i–ix, Aktenzeichen 21.
Die Reparationskonferenz in Lausanne 32 hierin auch die Vorbereitungsverhandlungen, i–x. Aktenzeichen 22.

(e) Auswärtiges Amt. Politisches Archiv (Microfilm)
Nachlass Stresemann.

(f) Vorläufiger Reichswirtschaftsrat
Stenographische Berichte über die Verhandlungen des Vorläufigen Reichs-
wirtschaftsrats. Deutsche Zentralarchiv, Potsdam, Archiv No. 6.
Reparations Ausschuss. Stenographische Berichte, 9 June 1921–2 Oct. 1922.
Deutsche Zentralarchiv, Potsdam, Archiv Nos. 611–14.
Arbeitsausschuss für die Beratung des Problems der Devisenbeschaffung für die
Reparationen. Sitzungsberichte. Deutsche Zentralarchiv, Potsdam, Archiv
No. 896.

(3) *Great Britain*

Cabinet papers
Lord Milner's Committee on Terms of Peace, Minutes, PRO CAB 21/71.
Report of Committee on Terms of Peace, 24 Apr. 1917, PRO CAB 21/78.
War Cabinet Minutes 1916–19, PRO CAB 23/1–17.
Cabinet Minutes and Conferences of Minister 1918–22, PRO CAB 23/18–39.
Imperial War Cabinet 1917–18, PRO CAB 23/40–4.
Cabinet Minutes 1923–32, PRO CAB 23/45–72.
Committee on Indemnity, PRO CAB 27/47.
International Conferences (IC), PRO CAB 28.
Peace Conference. British Empire Delegation. Minutes, PRO CAB 29.

(4) *Reparation Commission*

Minutes and Annexes, 1920–4, Hoover Institution, Stanford.

(5) *United States of America*

Department of State
Reparation from Germany in Accordance with the Terms of the Treaty of
Versailles, National Archives, Washington, 462.00 R296.

(6) *Private Collections*

Papers of Bernard M. Baruch, Princeton University Library.
Crewe Papers, Cambridge University Library.
Stuart M. Crocker Papers, Library of Congress.
John Foster Dulles Papers, Princeton University Library.
David E. Finley Papers, Library of Congress.
Lloyd George Papers, Beaverbrook Library, London.
William Morris Hughes Papers, Australian National Library, Canberra.
Keynes Papers, Marshall Library, Cambridge.

Stephane Lauzanne Papers, Hoover Institution, Stanford.
Bonar Law Papers, Beaverbrook Library, London.
Papers of James A. Logan, Hoover Institution, Stanford.
Louis Loucheur Papers, Hoover Institution, Stanford.
Ogden Mills Papers, Library of Congress.
Current Intelligence Summaries. Daily summaries of trends in French opinion relating to peace negotiations, chiefly as revealed to the press. Prepared by 1st Lieutenant G. Bernard Noble ... for the American Commission to Negotiate Peace, 15 December 1918 to 28 June 1919. Typescript, 1933. Hoover Institution, Stanford.
The Smuts Archive (typescript copies formerly in the possession of Sir Keith Hancock, Australian National University, Canberra).
Arthur N. Young Papers, Hoover Institution, Stanford.

B. OFFICIAL PUBLICATIONS

(1) *France*

(*a*) Assemblée Nationale 1871–1940
Annales de la Chambre des Députés. Débats parlementaires.
                                   Documents parlementaires.
Annales du Sénat. Débats parlementaires.

(*b*) Ministère des Affaires Étrangères
Documents diplomatiques français, 1871–1914 (Paris, 1929–59).
Documents relatifs aux réparations (3 vols.; Paris, 1922, 1924).

(*c*) République Française. Imprimerie Nationale
Conférence économique des gouvernements alliés tenue à Paris, les 14, 15, 16, 17 juin 1916 (Paris, 1916).

(2) *Germany*

(*a*) Auswärtiges Amt

White Books:

Die Konferenz in Spa vom 5. bis 16. Juli 1920, RT ccclxiii, Annexe 187.
Die Internationale Finanzkonferenz in Brüssel vom 24. September bis 8. Oktober 1920, RT ccclxiv, Annexe 922.
Weissbuch enthaltend eine Sammlung von Aktenstücken über die Verhandlungen auf der Konferenz zu London vom 1. bis 7. März 1921, RT ccclxvi, Annexe 1640.
Aktenstücke zur Reparationsfrage vom Mai 1921 bis März 1922, RT ccclxxii, Annexe 4140.

Material über die Konferenz von Genua, RT ccclxxiii, Annexe 4378.

Nachtrag zu dem Weissbuch 'Aktenstücke zur Reparationsfrage vom März 1922', RT ccclxxiv, Annexe 4484.

Die den Allierten seit dem Waffenstillstand übermittelten deutschen Angebote und Vorschläge zur Lösung der Reparations- und Wiederaufbaufrage, RT ccclxxix, Annexe 6138.

Aktenstücke zur Reparationsfrage vom 26. Dezember 1922 bis 7. Juni 1923, RT ccclxx, Annexe 6226.

Published separately:

Sammlung von Aktenstücken über die Verhandlungen auf der Sachverständigenkonferenz zu Brüssel (Berlin, 1921).

Akten zur deutschen auswärtigen Politik, 1918–1945, Serie B: 1925–1933, i–xx (Göttingen, 1966–1983).

(*b*) Bundesarchiv/Historische Kommission bei der Bäyerischen Akademie der Wissenschaften

Akten der Reichskanzlei: Weimarer Republik.

ABRAMOWSKI, G. (ed.), *Die Kabinette Marx I und II: 30. November 1923–3. Juni 1924; 3. Juni 1924–15. Jan. 1925* (Boppard-on-Rhine, 1973).

ERDMANN, K. D. AND VOGT, M. (edd.), *Die Kabinette Stresemann I u. II: 13. August bis 6. Oktober 1923, 6. Oktober bis 30. November 1923* (2 vols.; Boppard-on-Rhine, 1978).

GOLECKI, A. (ed.), *Das Kabinett Bauer, 21. Juni 1919 bis 27. März 1920* (Boppard-on-Rhine, 1980).

HARBECK, K.-H. (ed.), *Das Kabinett Cuno, 22. November 1922 bis 12. August 1923* (Boppard-on-Rhine, 1968).

KOOPS, T. (ed.), *Die Kabinette Brüning I u. II: 30. März 1930 bis 10. Oktober 1931, 10. Oktober 1931 bis 1. Juni 1932* (3 vols.; Boppard-on-Rhine, 1982).

SCHULZE, H. (ed.), *Das Kabinett Scheidemann, 13. Februar bis 20. Juni 1919* (Boppard-on-Rhine, 1971).

SCHULZE-BIDLINGMAIER, I. (ed.), *Die Kabinette Wirth I und II: 10. Mai 1921–26. Oktober 1921, 26. Oktober 1921–22. November* (2 vols.; Boppard-on-Rhine, 1973).

VOGT, M. (ed.), *Das Kabinett Müller I, 27. März bis 21. Juni 1920* (Boppard-on-Rhine, 1971).

—— (ed.), *Das Kabinett Müller II, 28. Juni 1928 bis 27. März 1930* (2 vols.; Boppard-on-Rhine, 1973).

WULF, P. (ed.), *Das Kabinett Fehrenbach, 25. Juni 1920 bis 4. Mai 1921* (Boppard-on-Rhine, 1972).

(*c*) Reichstag

Verhandlungen des Reichstags (1914–18, 1920–32), cccvi–cccxxv, cccxliv–cdlix.

Verhandlungen der verfassungsgebenden deutschen Nationalversammlung (1919–20), cccxxvi–cccxliii.

(*d*) Reichsverlagsamt
Reichsgesetzblatt (Berlin, 1914–32).

(*e*) Sozialisierungs-Kommission
Verhandlungen der Sozialisierungs-Kommission über die Reparationsfragen (3 vols.; Berlin, 1921–2).

(*f*) Statistisches Reichsamt

Statistisches Jahrbuch für das deutsche Reich (Berlin, 1918–26).

Deutschlands Wirtschaftslage unter den Nachwirkungen des Weltkrieges (Berlin, 1923).

(*g*) Zentral-Verlag, G.m.b.H.
Deutschlands Wirtschaft, Währung und Finanzen. Im Auftrage der Reichsregierung den von der Reparationskommission eingesetzten Sachverständigenausschüssen übergeben (Berlin, 1924).

(3) *Great Britain*

(*a*) *Department of Overseas Trade*

Report on the Economic and Financial Conditions in Germany to March 1922, by Mr. J. W. F. Thelwall ... assisted by Mr. C. J. Kavanagh ... (London, 1922).

Report on the Economic and Financial Conditions in Germany to March 1923, by Mr. J. W. F. Thelwall ... assisted by Mr. C. J. Kavanagh ... (London, 1923).

Report on the Economic and Financial Conditions in Germany Revised to April 1924, by Mr. J. W. F. Thelwall ... together with a Report on the Occupied Territories by Mr. C. J. Kavanagh ... (London, 1924).

Report on the Economic and Financial Conditions in Germany by Mr. J. W. F. Thelwall ... together with a Report on the Occupied Territories by Mr. C. J. Kavanagh ... (London, 1925).

Report on the Economic and Financial Conditions in Germany, 1925–6 by Mr J. W. F. Thelwall and Mr C. J. Kavanagh (London, 1926).

Report on Economic and Financial Conditions in Germany to July 1927 by J. W. F. Thelwall and C. J. Kavanagh (London, 1927).

Economic and Financial Conditions in Germany to June 1928: Report by J. W. F. Thelwall and C. J. Kavanagh (London, 1928).

Economic and Financial Conditions in Germany, 1928–1929: Report by J. W. F. Thelwall and C. J. Kavanagh (London, 1929).

Economic Conditions in Germany to July 1930: Report by J. W. F. Thelwall and R. P. F. Edwards (London, 1930).

Economic Conditions in Germany to September 1931: Report by Mr J. W. F. Thelwall and R. P. F. Edwards (London, 1932).

Economic Conditions in Germany to September 1932: Report by J. W. F. Thelwall (London, 1932).

(*b*) Foreign Office

Documents on British Foreign Policy, 1919–1939.

First Series: Woodward, E. L., and Butler, R. (edd.), i–vi; Butler, R., and Bury, J. P. T. (edd.), vii–viii; Butler, R., Bury, J. P. T., and Lambert, M. E. (edd.), ix–xv; Medlicott, W. N., Dakin, D., and Lambert, M. E. (edd.), xvi–xxi (London, 1946–78).

Series IA: Medlicott, W. N., Dakin, D., and Lambert, M. E. (edd.), i–vii (London, 1966–75).

Second Series: Woodward, E. L., and Butler, R. (edd.), i–iii (London, 1946–8).

(*c*) Parliament

House of Commons Debates. Fifth Series, 1916–32, lxxx–cclxxx.

House of Lords Debates. Fifth Series, 1916–32, xxi–lxxxv.

First Interim Report of the Committee on Currency and Foreign Exchanges after the War, 15 August 1918, House of Commons Papers, Cd. 9182, 1918, vii.

Treaty of Peace between the Allied and Associated Powers and Austria ... 10 September 1919, ibid. Cmd. 400, 1919, liii.

Supreme Council's Declaration of 8 March 1920, ibid. Cmd. 646, 1920, li.

Report on Industrial and Commercial Conditions in Germany at the Close of the Year 1919, ibid. Cmd. 752, 1920, xliii.

General Report on the Industrial and Economic Situation in Germany in December 1920, by Messrs. J. W. F. Thelwall and C. J. Kavanagh, ibid. Cmd. 1114, 1921, xxxi.

Protocols and Correspondence between the Supreme Council and the Conference of Ambassadors and the German Government and the German Peace Delegation, between 10 January 1920, and 7 July 1920, respecting the execution of the Treaty of Versailles of 28 June 1919, ibid. Cmd. 1325, 1921, xliii.

Reparations (Recovery) Act, 1921: Statement Showing the Amounts Paid during the Year ended 31 March 1922, into the Special Account under Section 1(3) of the Act, and the Application thereof, ibid. Cmd. 1664, 1921, xi.

Memorandum Circulated by the Prime Minister on 25 March 1919, ibid. Cmd. 1614, 1922, xxiii.

Decision of the Reparation Commission on the Subject of the Payments to be Made by Germany in 1922, ibid. Cmd. 1634, 1922, xxiii.

Despatch to the Representatives of France, Italy ... at London Respecting War Debts, ibid. Cmd. 1737, 1922, xxiii.

Inter-Allied Conferences on Reparations and Inter-Allied Debts held in London and Paris, December 1922 and January 1923, ibid. Cmd. 1812, 1923, xxiv.

Statement showing the Amounts Paid, during the Year ended 31 March 1923, into the Special Account under the German Reparation (Recovery) Act, 1921, and the Application thereof, ibid. Cmd. 1861, 1923, xiii.

Correspondence with the Allied Governments respecting Reparation Payments by Germany, ibid. Cmd. 1943, 1923, xxv.

Treasury Minute, 25 February 1924, relative to the German Reparation (Recovery) Act, 1921, ibid. Cmd. 2065, 1924, xiii.

Negotiations between Her Majesty's Government and the German Government, with the Decree (3 March 1924) issued in pursuance thereof by the German Government, ibid. Cmd. 2089, 1924, xiii.

Reports of the Expert Committees Appointed by the Reparation Commission, ibid. Cmd. 2105, 1924, xxvii.

Statement Showing the Amounts Paid during the Year ended 31 March 1924, into the Special Account under Section 1(3) of the German Reparation (Recovery) Act, 1921, and the Application thereof, ibid. Cmd. 2116, 1924, xiii.

Papers Respecting Negotiations for an Anglo-French Pact, ibid. Cmd. 2169, 1924, xxvi.

Correspondence Concerning the Conference which it is Proposed to Hold in London on 16 July 1924, to Consider the Measures Necessary to bring the Dawes Plan into Operation, ibid. Cmd. 2184, 1924, xxvii.

Franco-British Memorandum of 9 July 1924 Concerning the Application of the Dawes Scheme, ibid. Cmd. 2191, 1924, xxvii.

Minutes of the London Conference on Reparations, August 1922, ibid. Cmd. 2258, 1924, xxvii.

Treasury Minute of 29 August 1924, ibid. Cmd. 2263, 1924, xiii.

Proceedings of the London Reparation Conference, July and August 1924, ibid. Cmd. 2270, 1924, xxvii.

Agreements Concluded at the Hague Conference, January 1930, ibid. Cmd. 3484, 1929–30, xxxii.

(4) *United States of America*

(*a*) Congressional Record

(*b*) Department of State

Papers Relating to the Foreign Relations of the United States, 1918–1932 (Washington, 1933–9).

Papers Relating to the Foreign Relations of the United States, Paris Peace Conference, 1919 (13 vols.; Washington, 1942–7).

(*c*) National Monetary Commission

The German Bank Inquiry of 1908–1909 (2 vols.; 61st Congress, 2nd Session, Senate, Doc. No. 407, Washington, 1910).

(5) *League of Nations*

International Financial Conference, Brussels, 1920 (3 vols.; London, 1920).

(6) *Reparation Commission*

i. *Statement of Germany's Obligations under the Heading of Reparations, etc., at 30 April 1922* (London, 1922).

ii. *Agreements Concerning Deliveries in Kind to be Made by Germany under the Heading of Reparations* (London, 1922).

iii. *Official Documents Relative to the Amount of Payments to be Effected by Germany under Reparations Account, I, 1 May 1921–1 July 1922* (London, 1922).

iv. *Statement of Germany's Obligations under the Heading of Reparations, etc., . . . at 31 December 1922* (London, 1923).

v. *Report on the Work of the Reparation Commission from 1920 to 1922* (London, 1923).

vi. *Official Documents Relative to the Amount of Payments to be Effected by Germany under Reparation Account, II. Memorandum Presented by the French Delegation, 15 March 1922* (London, 1923).

viii. *Reports of the Expert Committees Appointed by the Reparation Commission* (London, 1924).

ix. *Regulations for Deliveries in Kind* (London, 1925).

x. *Report of the Agent-General for Reparation Payments, 30 May 1925* (London, 1925).

xi. *Report of the Agent-General for Reparation Payments, 30 November 1925* (London, 1925).

xii. *Report of the Agent-General for Reparation Payments, 15 June 1926* (London, 1926).

xv. *Report of the Agent-General for Reparation Payments, 30 November 1926* (London, 1926).

xvi. *Report of the Agent-General for Reparation Payments, 10 June 1927,* (London, 1927).

xvii. *Report of the Agent-General for Reparation Payments, 10 December 1927* (London, 1927).

xviii. *Report of the Agent-General for Reparation Payments, 7 June 1928* (London, 1928).

xix. *Report of the Agent-General for Reparation Payments, 22 December 1928* (London, 1929).

xx. *Report of the Committee of Experts on Reparations 1929* (London, 1929).

xxi. *Report of the Agent-General for Reparation Payments, 1 July 1929* (London, 1929).

xxii.   *Report of the Agent-General for Reparation Payments, 21 May 1930*
(London, 1930).

C. PRIVATELY PUBLISHED DOCUMENTARY COLLECTIONS, CHRONICLES,
AND DIARIES

BAKER, R. S., *Woodrow Wilson and the World Settlement* (5 vols.; New
York, 1921).

BANE, S. L., and LUTZ, R. H. (edd.), *The Blockade of Germany after the
Armistice, 1918–1919* . . . (London, 1942).

BURNETT, P. M. (ed.), *Reparation at the Paris Peace Conference* (2 vols.;
New York, 1940).

CALMETTE, G. (ed.), *Recueil de documents sur l'histoire de la question des
réparations (1919–5 mai 1921)* (Paris, n.d.).

CAMBON, P., *Correspondance, 1870–1924* (3 vols.; Paris, 1940–6).

D'ABERNON, E. V., LORD, *An Ambassador of Peace: Pages from the Diary
of Viscount D'Abernon, Berlin 1920–1926* (3 vols.; London, 1929–30).

*Die Entwicklung der Reparationsfrage: Chronik des wirtschaftlichen Nie-
dergangs in Deutschland. Zweite Ausgabe, abgeschlossen 31. März 1924*
(Berlin, 1924).

Dotation Carnegie pour la Paix Internationale, *Rapports faits aux Conférences
de la Haye de 1899 et 1907* . . . *avec une Introduction de James Scott Brown*
(Oxford, 1920).

HANCOCK, W. K., and VAN DER POEL, J. (edd.), *Selections from the Smuts
Papers* (4 vols.; Cambridge, 1966).

HOUSE, E. M., and SEYMOUR, C. (edd.), *What Really Happened at Paris*
(New York, 1921).

JOHNSON, E. (ed.), *The Collected Writings of John Maynard Keynes: xvi.
Activities, 1914–1919: The Treasury and Versailles* (London, 1971); *xvii.
Activities, 1920–1922: Treaty Revision and Reconstruction* (London, 1977);
xviii. Activities, 1922–1932: The End of Reparations (London, 1978).

JONES, T., *Whitehall Diary* (2 vols.; London, 1969).

LAUNAY, J. DE, *Secrets diplomatiques, 1914–1918* (Brussels, 1963).

LOUCHEUR, L., *Carnets secrets, 1908–1932*, ed. J. de Launay (Brussels, 1962).

LUCKAU, A. M. (ed.), *The German Delegation at the Paris Peace Conference*
(New York, 1941).

LUTZ, R. H. (ed.), *The Fall of the German Empire, 1914–1918* (2 vols.;
London, 1932).

MANTOUX, P., *Les Délibérations du Conseil des Quatre, 25 mars–28 juin
1919* (2 vols.; Paris, 1955).

—— *Paris Peace Conference 1919: Proceedings of the Council of Four (March
24–April 18)*, tr. J. B. Whitton (Geneva, 1964).

MAURER, I., and WENGST, U. (edd.), *Staat und NSDAP 1930–1932: Quellen
zur Ära Brüning* (Düsseldorf, 1977).

—— *Politik und Wirtschaft in der Krise, 1930–1932: Quellen zur Ära Brüning* (2 vols.; Düsseldorf, 1980).

MERMEIX (pseud. Terrail, Gabriel), *Les Négociations secrètes et les quatre armistices, avec pièces justificatives* (Paris, 1919).

MILLER, D. H., *My Diary at the Conference of Paris* (21 vols.; New York, 1924).

RATHENAU, W., *Tagebuch, 1907–1922* (Düsseldorf, 1967).

RIBOT, A. (ed.), *Journal d'Alexandre Ribot et correspondances inédites, 1914–1922* (Paris, 1936).

RIDDELL, G. A. R., *Lord Riddell's War Diary, 1914–1918* (London, 1933).

—— *Lord Riddell's Intimate Diary of the Peace Conference and After, 1918–1923* (London, 1933).

SEYMOUR, C. (ed.), *The Intimate Papers of Colonel House* (4 vols.; Cambridge, Mass., 1926).

STRESEMANN, G., *Vermächtnis: Der Nachlass*, ed. H. Bernard, W. Goetz, and P. Wiegler (3 vols.; Berlin, 1932–3).

—— *Diaries, Letters, and Papers*, ed. and tr. E. Sutton (3 vols.; London, 1937).

TAYLOR, A. J. P. (ed.), *Lloyd George: A Diary by Frances Stevenson* (London, 1971).

D. SECONDARY WORKS

ACKERMANN, K., 'Die Stellungnahme der deutschen Presse zum Stabilisierungsproblem der Mark, 1919–1923', Phil. Diss. (Univ. of Cologne, 1927).

ADLER, S., *The Uncertain Giant: 1921–1941. American Foreign Policy Between the Wars* (New York, 1965).

ANGAS, L. B., *Reparations, Trade, and Foreign Exchange, 1922* (London, 1922).

—— *Germany and Her Debts: A Critical Examination of the Reparation Problem* (London, 1923).

ANGELL, J. W., *The Recovery of Germany* (2nd edn., London, 1932).

ANGELL, N., SIR, *The Great Illusion: A Study of the Relation of Military Power in Nations to their Economic and Social Advantage* (London, 1910).

—— *The Peace Treaty and the Economic Chaos of Europe* (London, 1919).

—— *After All: The Autobiography of Norman Angell* (London, 1951).

ANGRESS, W. T., *Stillborn Revolution: The Communist Bid for Power in Germany, 1921–1923* (Princeton, 1963).

ARTAUD, D., *La Question des dettes interalliées et la reconstruction de l'Europe (1917–1929)* (2 vols.; Paris, 1978).

AULD, G. P., *The Dawes Plan and the New Economics* (New York, 1927).

BADULESCO, V. V., *Le Prélèvement extraordinaire sur le capital dans l'empire allemand* (Paris, 1922).

BAILEY, T. A., *Woodrow Wilson and the Lost Peace* (New York, 1944).
—— *Woodrow Wilson and the Great Betrayal* (New York, 1945).
BARIÉTY, J., *Les Relations franco-allemandes après la première guerre mondiale, 10 novembre 1918–10 janvier 1925: de l'exécution à la négociation* (Paris, 1977).
BARUCH, B. M., *The Making of the Reparation and Economic Sections of the Treaty* (New York, 1920).
—— *Baruch: The Public Years* (New York, 1960).
BECHTEL, H., *Wirtschaftsgeschichte Deutschlands im 19. und 20. Jahrhundert* (Munich, 1956).
BENNECKE, H., *Wirtschaftliche Depression und politischer Radikalismus 1918–1938* (Munich, 1970).
BENNETT, E. W., *Germany and the Diplomacy of the Financial Crisis, 1931* (Cambridge, Mass., 1962).
BERGMANN, C., *The History of Reparations* (London, 1927).
BERGSTRASSER, L., *Geschichte der politischen Parteien in Deutschland* (9th edn., Munich, 1955).
BERLAU, A. J., *The German Social Democratic Party, 1914–1921* (New York, 1949).
BEUMELBERG, W., *Deutschland in Ketten von Versailles bis zum Youngplan* (Oldenburg, 1931).
BINION, R., *Defeated Leaders: The Political Fate of Caillaux, Jouvenel, and Tardieu* (New York, 1960).
BLAKE, R., *The Unknown Prime Minister* (London, 1955).
BONN, M. J., *Die Stabilisierung der Mark* (Berlin, 1922).
—— *Wandering Scholar* (London, 1949).
BONNEFOUS, E., *Histoire politique de la Troisième République, III: L'Après-guerre, 1919–1924* (Paris, 1959).
BONNET, G., *Quai d'Orsay* (Eng. tr., London, 1965).
BOOMS, H., *Die Deutschkonservative Partei* (Düsseldorf, 1954).
BORN, K. E., *Die deutsche Bankenkrise: Finanzen und Politik* (Munich, 1967).
BORSKY, G., *The Greatest Swindle in the World* (London, 1942).
BOYLE, A., *Montagu Norman: A Biography* (London, 1967).
BRAUN, O., *Von Weimar zu Hitler* (Hamburg, 1949).
BRENTANO, L., *What Germany has Paid* (Berlin, 1923).
BRESCIANI-TURRONI, C., *The Economics of Inflation: A Study of Currency Depreciation in Post-war Germany* (London, 1937).
BROGAN, D. W., *The Development of Modern France (1870–1939)* (London, 1953).
BROOKS, S., *America and Germany, 1918–1925* (New York, 1927).
BRÜGELMANN, H., *Politische Ökonomie in kritischen Jahren: die Friedrich List–Gesellschaft E.v. von 1925–1935* (Tübingen, 1956).
BRÜNING, H., *Memoiren* (Stuttgart, 1970).

BUNSELMEYER, R. E., *The Cost of the War 1914–1919: British Economic War Aims and the Origins of Reparation* (Hamden, Conn., 1975).

BÜSCH, O., and FELDMAN, G. D. (edd.), *Historische Prozesse der deutschen Inflation, 1914 bis 1924* (Berlin, 1978).

CAMPBELL, J., *Lloyd George: The Goat in the Wilderness, 1922–1931* (London, 1977).

CARR, E. H., *German–Soviet Relations between the Two World Wars, 1919–1939* (London, 1952).

CARROLL, J. M., 'The Making of the Dawes Plan', Ph.D. thesis (Univ. of Kentucky, 1972).

CHALLENER, R. D., *The French Theory of the Nation in Arms, 1866–1939* (New York, 1955).

CHANDLER, L. V., *Benjamin Strong: Central Banker* (Washington, 1958).

CHASTENET, J., *Raymond Poincaré* (Paris, 1948).

CHICKERING, R., *Imperial Germany and a World Without War: The Peace Movement and German Society, 1892–1914* (Princeton, 1975).

CLARK, J. M., HAMILTON, W. H., and MOULTON, H. G. (edd.), *Readings in the Economics of War* (Chicago, 1918).

CLAY, SIR H., *Lord Norman* (London, 1957).

COWAN, L. G., *France and the Saar, 1680–1948* (New York, 1950).

CROFT, H. P., *My Life of Strife* (London, 1948).

CURTIUS, J., *Der Young-Plan: Entstellung und Wahrheit* (Stuttgart, 1950).

CZERNIN, F., *Versailles, 1919* (New York, 1964).

D'ABERNON, E. V., LORD, *Portraits and Appreciations* (London, 1931).

DAHLIN, E., *French and German Public Opinion on Declared War Aims, 1914–1918* (Stanford, 1933).

DAUDET, L., *L'Agonie du régime* (Paris, 1925).

DAWES, C. G., *A Journal of Reparations* (London, 1939).

DAWES, R. C., *The Dawes Plan in the Making* (Indianapolis, 1925).

DIETZEL, H., *Kriegssteuern oder Kriegsanleihen?* (Tübingen, 1912).

DILLARD, D., *The Economics of John Maynard Keynes* (London, 1958).

ELLIS, H. S., *German Monetary Theory, 1905–1933* (Cambridge, Mass., 1937).

EPSTEIN, K., *Matthias Erzberger and the Dilemma of German Democracy* (Princeton, 1959).

ERZBERGER, M., *Erlebnisse im Weltkriege* (Stuttgart, 1920).

EULER, H., *Die Aussenpolitik der Weimarer Republik 1918–1923* (Aschaffenburg, 1957).

EYCK, E., *Geschichte der Weimarer Republik* (2 vols.; Erlenbach–Zurich, 1954–6).

FEINSTEIN, C. H., *Statistical Tables of National Income, Expenditure and Output of the U.K.* (Cambridge, 1972).

FELDMAN, G. D., *Army, Industry, and Labor in Germany, 1914–1918* (Princeton, 1966).

—— *Iron and Steel in the German Inflation, 1916–1923* (Princeton, 1977).

FELDMAN, G. D., and MÜLLER-LUCKNER, E. (edd.), *Die Nachwirkungen der Inflation auf die deutsche Geschichte, 1924–1933* (Munich, 1985).

—— HOLTFRERICH, C. L., RITTER, G. A., and WITT, P.-C. (edd.), *The German Inflation Reconsidered: A Preliminary Balance* (Berlin, 1982).

—— —— —— —— *Die Erfahrung der Inflation im internationalen Zusammenhang und Vergleich* (Berlin, 1984).

—— —— —— —— *Die Anpassung an Inflation* (Berlin, 1986).

FELIX, D., *Walther Rathenau and the Weimar Republic: The Politics of Reparations* (Baltimore, 1971).

FERRELL, R. H., *American Diplomacy in the Great Depression: Hoover–Stimson Foreign Policy, 1929–1933* (New Haven, 1957).

FISCHER, R., *Stalin and German Communism* (London, 1948).

FITZHARDINGE, L. F., *William Morris Hughes: A Political Biography* (2 vols.; Sydney, 1964, 1979).

FLOTO, I., *Colonel House in Paris: A Study of American Policy at the Paris Peace Conference, 1919* (Copenhagen, 1973).

FRANÇOIS-PONCET, A., *The Fateful Years: Memoirs of a French Ambassador in Berlin, 1931–1939*, tr. J. Le Clercq (London, 1949).

GALBRAITH, J. K., *The Great Crash 1929* (London, 1955).

GEORGE, A. L., and GEORGE, J. L., *Woodrow Wilson and Colonel House* (New York, 1956).

GEROULD, J. T., and TURNBULL, L. S. (edd.), *Selected Articles on Interallied Debts and Revision of the Debt Settlements* (New York, 1928).

GESCHER, D. B., *Die Vereinigten Staaten von Nordamerika und die Reparationen, 1920–1924* (Bonn, 1956).

GEYER, C., *Drei Verderber Deutschlands* (Berlin, 1924).

GILBERT, C., *American Financing of World War I* (Westport, Conn., 1970).

GOLDEY, D. B., 'The Disintegration of the *Cartel des Gauches* and the Politics of French Government Finance, 1924–1928', Ph.D. thesis (Oxford, 1961).

GRAHAM, F. D., *Exchange, Prices, and Production in Hyperinflation: Germany 1920–1923* (Princeton, 1930).

GREBLER, L., and WINKLER, W., *The Cost of the War to Germany and to Austria-Hungary* (Yale, 1940).

GREER, G., *The Ruhr–Lorraine Industrial Problem* (London, 1925).

GRIGG, P. J., *Prejudice and Judgment* (London, 1948).

GUBALKE, W., 'Das Gruppeninteresse in der Berliner Tagespresse am Dawes-Plan, 1924', Phil. Diss. (Univ. of Berlin, 1936).

GUICHARD, L., *Histoire du blocus naval, 1914–1918* (Paris, 1929).

HAIG, R. M., *The Public Finances of Post-War France* (New York, 1929).

HANCOCK, W. K., *Smuts* (2 vols.; Cambridge, 1962–1968).

HARDEN, M., *Germany, France, and England, 1924* (London, 1924).

HARRIS, C. R. S., *Germany's Foreign Indebtednesss* (London, 1935).

HARROD, R. F., *The Life of John Maynard Keynes* (London, 1951).

HASTE, C., *Keep the Home Fires Burning: Propaganda in the First World War* (London, 1977).

HELBICH, W. J., *Die Reparationen in der Ära Brüning: zur Bedeutung des Young-Plans für die deutsche Politik, 1930 bis 1932* (Berlin, 1962).

HELBIG, H. VON, *Die Träger der Rapallo-Politik* (Göttingen, 1958).

HELFFERICH, K., *Der Weltkrieg* (3 vols.; Berlin, 1919).

—— *Fort mit Erzberger!* (Berlin, 1919).

—— *Money*, tr. of 6th German edn. (2 vols.; London, 1927).

HERTZMAN, L., *DNVP: Right-Wing Opposition in the Weimar Republic, 1918–1924* (Lincoln, 1963).

HIRST, F. W., *The Consequences of the War to Great Britain* (London, 1934).

—— and ALLEN, J. E., *British War Budgets* (London, 1926).

HOBSON, J. A., *The Economics of Reparation* (London, 1921).

HOLT, W. S., *Treaties Defeated by the Senate* (Baltimore, 1933).

HOLTFRERICH, C.-L., *Die deutsche Inflation, 1914–1923: Ursachen und Folgen in internationaler Perspektive* (Berlin, 1980).

HOOVER, H., *The Memoirs of Herbert Hoover: The Great Depression, 1929–1941* (London, 1953).

—— *The Ordeal of Woodrow Wilson* (London, 1958).

HORTZSCHANSKY, G., *Der nationale Verrat der deutschen Monopolherren während des Ruhrkampfes 1923* (Berlin, 1961).

HOWARD, J. E., *Parliament and Foreign Policy in France* (London, 1948).

HUDDLESTON, S., *Poincaré: A Biographical Portrait* (London, 1924).

HUDSON, W. J., *Billy Hughes in Paris: The Birth of Australian Diplomacy* (Melbourne, 1978).

JACOBSON, E. E., *A Life for Sound Money: Per Jacobson, his Biography* (Oxford, 1979).

JACOBSON, J., *Locarno Diplomacy: Germany and the West, 1925–1929* (Princeton, 1972).

JÈZE, G., and TRUCHY, H., *The War Finance of France* and *How France Met her War Expenditure* (New Haven, 1927).

JOHNSON, P. B., *Land Fit for Heroes: The Planning of British Reconstruction, 1916–19* (Chicago, 1968).

JOLLY, J. (ed.), *Dictionnaire des parlementaires français*, i–viii (Paris, 1960–77).

JONES, J. H., *Josiah Stamp, Public Servant: The Life of the First Baron Stamp of Shortlands* (London, 1964).

JONUSCHAT, H., 'Die Steuerpolitik der Parteien im Reichstag, 1920–1923', Phil. Diss. (Univ. of Berlin, 1926).

JORDAN, W. M., *Great Britain, France, and the German Problem, 1919–1939* (London, 1943).

KANIN, E., 'Inflation und öffentliche Meinung', Phil. Diss. (Univ. of Königsberg, 1930).

KESSLER, H., COUNT, *Germany and Europe* (New Haven, 1923).
—— *Walther Rathenau, his Life and Work*, tr. W. D. Robson-Scott and L. Hyde (London, 1929).
KEYNES, J. M., *The Economic Consequences of the Peace* (London, 1919).
—— *A Revision of the Treaty* (London, 1922).
—— *A Tract on Monetary Reform* (London, 1923).
—— *Two Memoirs* (London, 1949).
KEYNES, M. (ed.), *Essays on John Maynard Keynes* (Cambridge, 1975).
KINDLEBERGER, C. P., *The World in Depression, 1929–1939* (London, 1973).
KING, J. C., *Foch versus Clemenceau: France and German Dismemberment, 1918–1919* (Harvard, 1960).
KLASS, G. VON, *Hugo Stinnes* (Tübingen, 1958).
KLOTZ, L.-L., *De la guerre à la paix* (Paris, 1924).
KOCHAN, L., *Russia and the Weimar Republic* (Cambridge, 1954).
KOCKA, J., *Klassengesellschaft im Krieg: deutsche Sozialgeschichte, 1914–1918* (Göttingen, 1973).
KROHN, C.-D., *Stabilisierung und ökonomische Interessen: die Finanzpolitik des deutschen Reiches, 1923–1927* (Düsseldorf, 1974).
KRÜGER, P., *Deutschland und die Reparationen 1918/19* (Stuttgart, 1973).
KUCZYNSKI, J., *Die Geschichte der Lage der Arbeiter in Deutschland von 1800 bis in die Gegenwart* (2 vols.; Berlin, 1947).
KUHNL, R., *Die nationalsozialistische Linke, 1925–1930* (Meisenheim-on-Glan, 1966).
LANSING, R., *The Peace Negotiations: A Personal Narrative* (Boston, 1921).
LARNAUDE, F., BARTHÉLEMY, H., *et al.* (edd.), *La Réparation des dommages de guerre: Conférences faites à l'école des hautes études sociales, novembre 1915 à janvier 1916* (Paris, 1917).
LARY, H. B., *The United States in the World Economy*, US Dept. of Commerce, Economics Ser. No. 23 (Washington, 1943).
LAUBACH, E., *Die Politik der Kabinette Wirth, 1921–22* (Lübeck, 1968).
LAURSEN, K., and PEDERSEN, J., *The German Inflation, 1918–1923* (Amsterdam, 1964).
LEBOVICS, H., *Social Conservatism and the Middle Classes in Germany, 1914–1933* (Princeton, 1969).
LEITH-ROSS, SIR F., *Money Talks* (London, 1968).
LEOPOLD, J. H., *Alfred Hugenberg: The Radical Nationalist Campaign against the Weimar Republic* (New Haven, 1977).
LICHTENBERGER, H., *The Ruhr Conflict* (Washington, 1923).
—— *Deutschland und Frankreich in ihren gegenwärtigen Beziehungen* (Leipzig, 1924).
LIEBE, W., *Die Deutschnationale Volkspartei, 1918–1924* (Düsseldorf, 1956).
LINK, W., *Die amerikanische Stabilisierungspolitik in Deutschland, 1921–32: die Vereinigten Staaten von Amerika und der Wiederaufstieg Deutschlands nach der Ersten Weltkrieg* (Düsseldorf, 1970).

LLOYD GEORGE, D., *The Truth about Reparations and War Debts* (London, 1932).
—— *The Truth about the Peace Treaties* (2 vols.; London, 1938).
—— *War Memoirs* (2 vols.; London, 1938).
LOCHNER, L. P., *Herbert Hoover and Germany* (New York, 1960).
LOTZ, W., *Die deutsche Staatsfinanzwirtschaft im Kriege* (Stuttgart, 1927).
LÜKE, R. E., *Von der Stabilisierung zur Krise* (Zurich, 1958).
LUTHER, H., *Die Stabilisierung der deutschen Währung* (Berlin, 1930).
LYMAN, R. W., *The First Labour Government, 1924* (London, 1957).
MCCALLUM, R. B., *Public Opinion and the Last Peace* (London, 1944).
MCDOUGALL, W. A., *France's Rhineland Diplomacy, 1914–1924: The Last Bid for a Balance of Power in Europe* (Princeton, 1978).
MCFADYEAN, A., *Reparation Reviewed* (London, 1930).
—— *Recollected in Tranquillity* (London, 1964).
MACHRAY, R., *The Problem of Upper Silesia* (London, 1945).
MAIER, C. S., *Recasting Bourgeois Europe: Stabilization in France, Germany, and Italy in the Decade after World War I* (Princeton, 1975).
MANTOUX, E., *The Carthaginian Peace, or the Economic Consequences of Mr Keynes* (London, 1946).
MARKS, S., *The Illusion of Peace: International Relations in Europe, 1918–1933* (London, 1976).
—— *Innocent Abroad: Belgium at the Paris Peace Conference of 1919* (Chapel Hill, 1981).
MARWICK, A., *Britain in the Century of Total War* (London, 1968).
MAURER, I., *Reichsfinanzen und grosse Koalition: zur Geschichte des Reichskabinetts Müller (1928–1930)* (Frankfurt-on-Main, 1973).
MAYER, A. J., *Political Origins of the New Diplomacy, 1917–1918* (New Haven, 1959).
—— *The Politics and Diplomacy of Peacemaking: Containment and Counter-revolution at Versailles, 1918–1919* (New York and London, 1968).
MENDELSSOHN-BARTHOLDY, A., *The War and German Society* (Yale, 1937).
MENDERSHAUSEN, H., *Two Post-war Recoveries of the German Economy* (Amsterdam, 1955).
MICHELS, R. K., *Cartels, Combines, and Trusts in Post-war Germany* (New York, 1928).
MIDDLEMAS, K., and BARNES, J., *Baldwin: A Biography* (London, 1969).
MILLER, K. E., *Socialism and Foreign Policy: Theory and Practice in Britain to 1931* (The Hague, 1967).
MILWARD, A. S., *The German Economy at War* (London, 1965).
—— *The Economic Effects of World Wars on Britain* (London, 1970).
—— *The New Order and the French Economy* (Oxford, 1970).
—— *War, Economy, and Society, 1939–1945* (London, 1977).
MIQUEL, P., *Poincaré* (Paris, 1961).

MIQUEL, P., *La Paix de Versailles et l'opinion publique française* (Paris, 1972).

MITCHELL, B. R., and DEANE, P., *Abstract of British Historical Statistics* (Cambridge, 1962).

MOGGRIDGE, D. E., *The Return to Gold 1925: The Formulation of Economic Policy and its Critics* (Cambridge, 1969).

—— *British Monetary Policy, 1924–1931: The Norman Conquest of $4.86* (Cambridge, 1972).

MOMMSEN, H., PETZINA, D., and WEISBROD, B. (edd.), *Industrielles System und politische Entwicklung in der Weimarer Republik* (Düsseldorf, 1974).

MOREAU, E., *Souvenirs d'un gouverneur de la Banque de France: Histoire de la stabilisation du franc (1926–1928)* (Paris, 1954).

MORGAN, E. V., *Studies in British Financial Policy, 1914–1925* (London, 1952).

MORGAN, J. H., *Assize of Arms* (London, 1945).

MORGAN, K. O., *Consensus and Disunity: The Lloyd George Coalition Government, 1918–1922* (Oxford, 1979).

MORISON, E. E., *Turmoil and Tradition: A Study of the Life and Times of Henry L. Stimson* (Boston, 1960).

MOULTON, H. G., *The Reparation Plan* (New York, 1924).

—— and McGUIRE, C. E., *Germany's Capacity to Pay* (New York, 1923).

—— and PASVOLSKY, L., *War Debts and World Prosperity* (Washington, 1932).

MOWAT, C. L., *Britain Between the Wars, 1918–1940* (London, 1955).

MYERS, D. P., *The Reparation Settlement, 1930* (Boston, 1930).

Neue Deutsche Biographie, i– (Berlin, 1952–   ).

NEUMANN, J. A., 'Rathenaus Reparationspolitik', Phil. Diss. (Univ. of Leipzig, 1930).

NICOLSON, H., *Peacemaking, 1919* (London, 1933).

—— *Dwight Morrow* (New York, 1935).

—— *Curzon: The Last Phase, 1919–1925* (London, 1937 edn.).

NITTI, F., *The Decadence of Europe*, tr. F. Brittain (London, 1923).

NOBLE, G. B., *Policies and Opinions at Paris* (New York, 1968, reprint).

NORTHROP, M. B., *Control Policies of the Reichsbank, 1924–1933* (New York, 1938).

OSBORNE, S., *The Upper Silesian Question and Germany's Coal Problem* (London, 1920).

—— *The Problem of Upper Silesia* (London, 1921).

PAPEN, F. VON, *Memoirs*, tr. B. Connell (London, 1952).

PAUL, R. E., *Taxation in the United States* (Boston, 1954).

PETERSON, E. N., *Hjalmar Schacht: For and Against Hitler* (Boston, 1954).

PLAUT, T., *Deutsche Handelspolitik: ihre Geschichte, Ziele und Mittel* (Leipzig, 1924).

POUND, R., and HARMSWORTH, G., *Northcliffe* (London, 1959).

POUNDS, N. J. G., *The Ruhr: A Study in Historical and Economic Geography* (London, 1952).

RATNER, S., *Taxation and Democracy in America* (New York, 1967 edn.).

REICHERT, W., *Rathenaus Reparationspolitik* (Berlin, 1922).

REINHOLD, P. P., *The Economic, Financial, and Political State of Germany since the War* (New Haven, 1928).

RENOUVIN, P., *Les crises du XXᵉ siècle de 1914–1929* (Paris, 1951).

REPINTON, C. À C., *After the War* (Boston, 1922).

RHEINBABEN, W. VON, *Von Versailles zur Freiheit* (Hamburg, 1927).

RIESSER, J. *Finanzielle Kriegsbereitschaft und Kriegsführung* (Berlin, 1909).

―― *The German Great Banks and their Concentration*, tr. of 3rd German edn., United States National Monetary Commission Publications, xiv (Washington, 1911).

RIST, C., *Les Finances de guerre de l'Allemagne* (Paris, 1921).

ROBBINS, L., *The Great Depression* (London, 1934).

ROBERTS, A. (ed.), *Civilian Resistance as a National Defence* (London, 1969).

ROESLER, K., *Die Finanzpolitik des deutschen Reiches im ersten Weltkrieg* (Berlin, 1967).

ROGERS, J. H., *The Process of Inflation in France, 1914–1927* (New York, 1934).

ROLO, P. J. V., *Britain and the Briand Plan: The Common Market that Never Was* (Keele, 1972).

ROSENBERG, A., *A History of the German Republic*, tr. I. F. D. Morrow and L. M. Sieveking (London, 1936).

ROSKILL, S., *Hankey, Man of Secrets* (3 vols.; London, 1970–4).

RÖSSLER, H. (ed.), *Die Folgen von Versailles, 1919–1926* (Göttingen, 1969).

RUGE, W., *Die Stellungnahme der Sowjetunion gegen die Besetzung des Ruhrgebietes* (Berlin, 1962).

RUPIEPER, H. J., 'Politics and Economics: The Cuno Government and Reparations', Ph.D. thesis (Stanford, 1974).

SAINT-AULAIRE, A. F. C. DE B., COMTE DE, *Confession d'un vieux diplomate* (Paris, 1953).

SALIN, E. (ed.), *Das Reparationsproblem* (2 vols.; Berlin, 1929).

SALTER, A., *Recovery: The Second Effort* (London, 1932).

―― *Memoirs of a Public Servant* (London, 1961).

SARTER, A., *Die deutschen Eisenbahnen im Kriege* (Stuttgart, 1930).

SCHACHT, H., *The Stabilization of the Mark* (London, 1927).

―― *Das Ende der Reparationen* (Oldenburg, 1931).

―― *My First Seventy-Six Years: The Autobiography of H. Schacht*, tr. D. Pyke (London, 1955).

SCHEIDEMANN, P., *Memories of a Social Democrat*, tr. J. G. Mitchell (2 vols.; London, 1929).

SCHLESINGER, A. M. JUN., and ISRAEL, F. L. (edd.), *History of American Presidential Elections, 1789–1968* (4 vols.; New York, 1971).

SCHMACKE, E., 'Die Aussenpolitik der Weimarer Republik, 1922–1925, unter Berücksichtigung der Innenpolitik', Phil. Diss. (Univ. of Hamburg, 1951).

SCHMIDT, R. J., *Versailles and the Ruhr: Seedbed of World War II* (The Hague, 1968).

SCHORSKE, C. E., *German Social Democracy, 1905–1917* (Cambridge, Mass., 1955).

SCHÜDDEKOPF, O. E., *Linke Leute von Rechts* (Stuttgart, 1960).

SCHUKER, S. A., *The End of French Predominance in Europe: The Financial Crisis of 1924 and the Adoption of the Dawes Plan* (Chapel Hill, 1976).

SCHULTZE-PFAELZER, G., *Von Spa nach Weimar* (Leipzig, 1929).

SCHULZ, G., *Aufstieg des Nationalsozialismus: Krise und Revolution in Deutschland* (Frankfurt-on-Main, 1975).

SCHUMAN, F. L., *War and Diplomacy in the French Republic* (Chicago, 1931).

SCHWERIN VON KROSIGK, LUTZ GRAF, *Staatsbankrott: die Geschichte der Finanzpolitik des Deutschen Reiches vom 1920 bis 1945* (Göttingen, 1974).

SELIGMAN, E. R., *Essays in Taxation* (10th edn. rev., New York, 1931).

SERING, M., *Germany under the Dawes Plan*, tr. S. M. Hart (London, 1929).

SEYDOUX, J., *De Versailles au Plan Young* (Paris, 1932).

SIEBERT, F., *Aristide Briand, 1862–1932: ein Staatsmann zwischen Frankreich und Europa* (Stuttgart, 1973).

SIMON, H. F., *Reparation und Wiederaufbau* (Berlin, 1925).

SINEY, M. C., *The Allied Blockade of Germany, 1914–1916* (Michigan, 1957).

SNOWDEN, P., *Labour and National Finance* (London, 1920).

—— *An Autobiography* (2 vols.; London, 1934).

SPETHMANN, H., *Zwölf Jahre Ruhrbergbau* (5 vols.; Berlin, 1928–30).

STAMP, J., SIR, *Taxation During the War* (London, 1932).

STAMPFER, F., *Die ersten vierzehn Jahre der deutschen Republik* (Karlsbad, 1936).

STEVENSON, D., *French War Aims against Germany, 1914–1919* (Oxford, 1982).

STIMSON, H. L., and BUNDY, M., *On Active Service in Peace and War* (London, n.d.).

STOCKDER, A. H., *Regulating an Industry: The Rhenish-Westphalian Coal Syndicate, 1893–1929* (London, 1940).

STOLPER, G., *The German Economy 1870–1940* (London, 1940).

STUCKEN, R., *Deutsche Geld- und Kreditpolitik, 1914 bis 1953* (Tübingen, 1953).

SUAREZ, G., *Briand, sa vie—son œuvre, avec son journal* (6 vols.; Paris, 1938–1952).

SVENNILSON, I., *Growth and Stagnation in the European Economy* (United Nations Economic Commission for Europe, Geneva, 1954).

SWINTON, P., LORD, *Sixty Years of Power* (London, 1966).

TARDIEU, A., *The Truth about the Peace Treaties* (London, 1921).

TAYLOR, A. J. P., *English History, 1914–1945* (Oxford, 1965).

TEMPERLEY, H. W. V. (ed.), *A History of the Peace Conference of Paris* (6 vols.; London, 1920–3).

TILLMAN, S. P., *Anglo-American Relations at the Paris Peace Conference of 1919* (Princeton, 1961).

TOYNBEE, A. J., *Survey of International Affairs, 1920–1923* (London, 1925).

—— *Survey of International Affairs, 1924* (London, 1926).

—— *Survey of International Affairs, 1932* (London, 1933).

TRACHTENBERG, M., *Reparation in World Politics: France and European Economic Diplomacy, 1916–1923* (New York, 1980).

TURNER, H. A., *Stresemann and the Politics of the Weimar Republic* (Princeton, 1963).

VINCENT, C. P., 'The Post-World War I Blockade of Germany: An Aspect in the Tragedy of a Nation', Ph.D. thesis (Univ. of Colorado, 1980).

VINSON, J. C., *The Parchment Peace: The United States Senate and the Washington Conference, 1921–1922* (Athens, Ga., 1955).

VOGT, M., *Die Entstehung des Youngplans dargesellt von Reichsarchiv 1931–1933*, Schriften des Bundesarchivs, xv (Boppard-on-Rhine, 1970).

WANDEL, E., *Die Bedeutung der Vereinigten Staaten von Amerika für das deutsche Reparationsproblem, 1924–1929* (Tübingen, 1971).

—— *Hans Schäffer: Steuermann in wirtschaftlichen und politischen Krisen* (Stuttgart, 1974).

WARBURG, P. M., *The Federal Reserve System* (2 vols.; New York, 1930).

WEILL-RAYNAL, E., *Les Réparations allemandes et la France* (3 vols.; Paris, 1947).

WEISBROD, B., *Schwerindustrie in der Weimarer Republik: Interessenpolitik zwischen Stabilisierung und Krise* (Wuppertal, 1978).

WHEELER-BENNETT, J. W., *The Wreck of Reparations: Being the Political Background of the Lausanne Agreement 1932* (London, 1933).

—— and LATIMER, H., *Information on the Reparation Settlement: Being the background and History of the Young Plan and the Hague Agreements, 1929–1930* (London, 1930).

WILLIAMSON, J. G., *Karl Helfferich* (Princeton, 1971).

WILSON, J. H., *American Business and Foreign Policy, 1920–1933* (Lexington, 1971).

WITT, P.-C., *Die Finanzpolitik des Deutschen Reiches von 1909 bis 1913: eine Studie z. Innenpolitik d. Wilhelmin. Deutschlands* (Lübeck, 1970).

WRIGHT, G., 'Franco–Belgian Relations, 1918–1934', MA thesis (Stanford, 1935).

—— *Raymond Poincaré and the French Presidency* (Stanford, 1942).

WÜEST, E., *Der Vertrag von Versailles in Licht und Schatten der Kritik* (Zurich, 1962).

ZIEBURA, G., *Léon Blum: Theorie und Praxis einer sozialistischen Politik, i. 1872 bis 1934* (Berlin, 1963).

ZIMMERMANN, L., *Deutsche Aussenpolitik in der Ära der Weimarer Republik* (Göttingen, 1958).

ZWOCH, G., 'Die Erfüllungs- und Verständigungspolitik der Weimarer Republik und die deutsche öffentliche Meinung', Phil. Diss. (Univ. of Kiel, 1950).

E. ARTICLES

ALBERTIN, L., 'Die Verantwortung der liberalen Parteien für das Scheitern der Grossen Koalition im Herbst 1921', *HZ* 205 (1967), 566–627.

ALEXANDER, J. S., 'The Prospects of American Participation in an International Reparation Loan', *MGCRE*, 16 Nov. 1922, 610.

ARTAUD, D., 'A propos de l'occupation de la Ruhr', *RHMC* 17 (1970), 1–21.

BADULESCO, V. V., 'Le Prélèvement sur le capital comme moyen de liquidation des charges financières de la guerre en Allemagne', *Revue de science et de legislation financière*, 19 (Jan.–Mar. 1921).

BARCLAY, D. E., 'A Prussian Socialism? Wichard von Moellendorf and the Dilemma of Economic Planning in Germany, 1918–19', *CEH* 11 (1978), 50–82.

—— 'The Insider as Outsider: Rudolf Wissell's Critique of Social Democratic Economic Policies, 1919 to 1920', in G. D. Feldman *et al.* (edd.), *Die Anpassung an Inflation* (Berlin, 1986), 451–72.

BARIÉTY, J., 'Les Réparations allemandes après la première guerre mondiale: Objet ou prétexte à une politique Rhénane?', *Bulletin de la Société d'Histoire Moderne*, Ser. 15, No. 6 (May 1973), 21–35.

BÉCHER, H., 'Government Subsidies in Germany since the War', *MGCRE*, 27 July 1922, 288.

BERGMANN, C., 'Germany and the Young Plan', *Foreign Affairs*, 8 (July 1930), 583–97.

BERNHARD, G., 'Die Politik der Reichsbank im Kriege', *Archiv*, 40 (Dec. 1914), 43–87.

BONN, M. J., 'The Reparation Problem', *Annals* 104 (1922), 149–56.

——'The Levying of German Customs in Gold Marks', *MGCRE*, 27 July 1922, 309.

BOYCE, R. W. D., 'Britain's First "No" to Europe: Britain and the Briand Plan, 1929–30', *European Studies Review*, 10 (1980), 17–45.

CONZE, W., 'Brünings Politik unter dem Druck der Grossen Krise', *HZ* 199 (1964), 529–50.

CROUZET, F., 'Réactions françaises devant *Les Conséquences économiques de la paix* de Keynes', *RHMC* 19 (1972), 6–26.

CUNO, W., 'The Present Position and Prospects of the German Mercantile Marine', *MGCRE*, 18 May 1922, 87.

CZADA, P., 'Grosse Inflation und Wirtschaftswachstum', in H. Mommsen *et al.* (edd.), *Industrielles System*, 386–94.

—— 'Ursachen und Folgen der grossen Inflation', in H. Winkel (ed.), *Finanz- und wirtschaftspolitische Fragen der Zwischenkriegszeit* (Schriften des Vereins für Sozialpolitik, 73, Berlin, 1973).

DAVIS, J. S., 'Recent Economic and Financial Progress in Germany', *RES* 3 (1921), 141–65.

—— 'Economic and Financial Progress in Europe', *RES* 5 (1923), 79–113.

DELAISI, F., 'French Coal Policy and the Versailles Treaty', *MGCRE*, 7 Sept. 1922, 421.

DULLES, J. F., 'The Dawes Report and the Peace of Europe', *The Independent*, 112 (Apr. 1924), 218.

EDGEWORTH, F. Y., 'Some German Economic Writings about the War', *EJ* 27 (June 1917), 238–50.

—— 'Extracts from German Periodicals Relating to the War', *EJ* 27 (Sept. 1917), 420–8.

ELCOCK, H., 'J. M. Keynes at the Paris Peace Conference', in M. Keynes (ed.), *Essays on John Maynard Keynes* (Cambridge, 1975), 162–76.

ESHER, VISCOUNT, 'Pax Mundi', *The National Review* (Aug. 1917).

EULENBERG, F., 'Literatur über Kriege und Volkswirtschaft', *Archiv*, 43 (July 1916, May 1917), 302–47, 1041–95.

FAURE, F., 'La Fin de la guerre et les responsabilités de l'Allemagne', *Revue politique et parlementaire*, 97 (Nov. 1918), 113–41.

FELDMAN, G. D., 'Economic and Social Problems of the German Demobilization, 1918–19', *JMH* 47 (1975), 1–23.

—— The Political Economy of Germany's Relative Stabilization during the 1920/21 World Depression', in id. *et al.* (edd.), *The German Inflation Reconsidered: A Preliminary Balance* (Berlin, 1982), 180–206.

FISCHER, W., 'Die Weimarer Republik unter den weltwirtschaftlichen Bedingungen der Zwischenkriegszeit', in H. Mommsen *et al.* (edd.), *Industrielles System*, 26–50.

FORD, F. L., 'Three Observers in Berlin: Rumbold, Dodd, and François-Poncet', in G. A. Craig and F. Gilbert (edd.), *The Diplomats, 1919–1939* (2 vols.; New York, 1971), ii. 437–76.

FRANCKE, G., 'The German Railway System after the War', *MGCRE*, 7 Sept. 1922, 405.

GIDE, C., 'Des projets d'Entente Financière après la guerre', *Revue d'économie politique*, 32 (1918), 1–16.

—— 'Indemnity for Reparations', *Annals*, 104 (1922), 140–8.

GLASENAPP, O. VON, 'Germany's Balance of Payments with Other Countries', *MGCRE*, 20 Apr. 1922, 22.

GUILLEBAUD, C. W., 'The Cost of the War to Germany', *EJ* 27 (June 1917), 270–7.

HAHN, A., 'Von der Kriegs- zur Friedenswährung', *Archiv* (1918), Suppl. xiv.

HAHN, L. A., 'Handelsbilanz—Zahlungsbilanz—Valuta—Güterpreise', *Archiv*, 48 (1920–1), 596–614.

—— 'Statische und dynamische Wechselkurse', *Archiv*, 49 (1922), 761–79.

HELBICH, W. J., 'Between Stresemann and Hitler: The Foreign Policy of the Brüning Government', *World Politics*, 12 (Oct. 1959), 24–44.

HIMMER, R., 'Rathenau, Russia and Rapallo', *CEH* 9 (1976), 146–83.

HOLTFRERICH, C.-L., 'Alternativen zu Brünings Wirtschaftspolitik in der Weltwirtschaftskrise?', *HZ* 235 (1982), 605–31.

HÜBER, DR, 'Food Conditions and Agricultural Production', *Annals*, 92 (1920), 131–6.

JACOBSON, J., 'Strategies of French Foreign Policy after World War I', *JMH* 55 (1983), 78–95.

JAFFE, E., 'Kriegskostendeckung und Reichsfinanzreform', *Archiv*, 43 (1917), 711–41.

JASTROW, J., 'Die Organisation des Kredits im Kriege', *Archiv*, 40 (Dec. 1914), 88–117.

—— 'Wirtschaft und Verwaltung nach dem Kriege', *Archiv*, 43 (July 1916), 42–107, 397–437.

—— 'The German Capital Levy Tax', *QJE* 34 (May 1920), 462–72.

—— 'The New Tax System of Germany', *QJE* 37 (Feb. 1923), 302–41.

JOHNSON, H. G., 'The Classical Transfer Problem: An Alternative Formulation', *Economica*, 42 (1975), 20–31.

JONES, K. P., 'Discord and Collaboration: Choosing an Agent-General for Reparations', *Diplomatic History*, 1 (1977), 118–39.

—— 'Stresemann, the Ruhr Crisis, and Rhenish Separatism: A Case Study of *Westpolitik*', *European Studies Review*, 7 (1977), 311–40.

KENT, B., 'Der Preis des Kriegs: wie Deutschland für den Ersten Weltkrieg bezahlte', in B. Hüppauf (ed.), *Ansichten vom Krieg: vergleichende Studien zum Ersten Weltkrieg in Literatur und Gesellschaft* (Meisenheim/Glan, 1984), 231–9.

KEYNES, J. M., 'The Economics of War in Germany', *EJ* 25 (Sept. 1915), 443–52.

—— 'The Forward Market in Foreign Exchanges', *MGCRE*, 20 Apr. 1922, 11.

—— 'The Stabilization of the European Exchanges: A Plan for Genoa', *MGCRE*, 20 Apr. 1922, 3.

—— 'The Theory of the Exchanges and Purchasing Power Parity', *MGCRE*, 20 Apr. 1922, 6.

—— 'The Inflation of Currency as a Method of Taxation', *MGCRE*, 27 July 1922, 263.

—— 'Is the Settlement of the Reparation Problem Possible Now?', *MGCRE*, 28 Sept. 1922, 462.

—— 'Speculation in the Mark and Germany's Balances Abroad', *MGCRE*, 28 Sept. 1922, 480.

KEYNES, J. M., 'The Stabilization of the European Exchanges, II', *MGCRE*, 7 Dec. 1922, 658.

—— 'The Experts' Report', *Nation and Athenaeum*, 12, 19 Apr. 1924.

—— 'How Can the Dawes Plan Work? A British View', *New Republic*, 38 (23 Apr. 1924), 224–6.

—— 'The Dawes Scheme and the German Loan', *Nation and Athenaeum*, 4 Oct. 1924.

—— 'What the Dawes Plan Will Do', *New Republic*, 40 (22 Oct. 1924), 195–6.

—— 'The Coming Crisis in Reparations', *New Republic*, 51 (3 Aug. 1927), 275–7.

—— Review of works by C. Bergmann and H. Schacht, *New Republic*, 53 (25 Jan. 1928), 276–7.

—— 'A London View of War Debts', *New Republic*, 55 (23 May 1928), 8–10.

—— 'The Stabilization of the Franc', *New Republic*, 55 (18 July 1928), 218.

—— 'The German Transfer Problem', *EJ* 39 (1929), 1–7.

—— 'The Reparation Problem: a Discussion: II. A Rejoinder', *EJ* 39 (1929), 179–82.

—— 'Views on the Transfer Problem', *EJ* 39 (1929), 404–8.

KÖHLER, H., 'Arbeitsbeschaffung, Siedlung und Reparationen in der Schlussphase der Regierung Brüning', *VfZ* 17 (1969), 276–307.

KRÜGER, P., 'Die Rolle der Banken und der Industrie in den deutschen reparationspolitischen Entscheidungen nach dem Ersten Weltkrieg', in H. Mommsen *et al.* (edd.), *Industrielles System*, 568–82.

—— 'Das Reparationsproblem der Weimarer Republik in fragwürdiger Sicht: kritische Überlegungen zur neuesten Forschung', *VfZ* 29 (1981), 21–47.

KUCZYNSKI, R., 'German Taxation Policy in the World War', *JPE* 31 (1923), 763–89.

—— 'The Reconstruction of German Finances and the Reparation Problem', *JPE* 31 (1923), 561–72.

KULEMANN, W., 'Die prinzipielle Berechtigung der Höchstpreise', *Archiv*, 40 (1915), 784–9.

LAMONT, T. W., 'The Final Reparation Settlement', *Foreign Affairs*, 8 (Apr. 1930), 336–63.

LEBON, A., 'La Solution interalliée de la question des dommages de guerre', *Revue politique et parlementaire*, 97 (1918), 260–5.

LEFFLER, M., 'The Origins of Republican War Debts Policy, 1921–1923', *J. of American History*, 59 (1972), 585–601.

LEXIS, W., 'The German Bank Commission, 1908–9', *EJ* 20 (1910), 211–21.

LINK, W., 'Die Ruhrbesetzung und die wirtschaftspolitischen Interessen der USA', *VfZ* 17 (1969), 572–82.

LIPGENS, W., 'Europäische Einigungsidee 1923–1930 und Briands Europaplan im Urteil des deutschen Akten', *HZ* 203 (1966), 46–89, 316–63.

LOTZ, W., 'Special War Banks (Darlehnskassen)', in National Monetary Commission, *Miscellaneous Articles on German Banking* (Washington, 1910).

—— 'Direct Federal Taxation in Germany and its Administrative Reform', *MGCRE*, 27 July 1922, 287.

LOVEDAY, A., 'German War Finance in 1914', *EJ* 26 (Mar. 1916), 44–56.

LÜBSEN, G., 'The German Coal Situation and the Reparation Coal Deliveries', *MGCRE*, 7 Sept. 1922, 427–9.

McDOUGALL, W. A., 'Political Economy versus National Sovereignty: French Structures for German Economic Integration after Versailles', *JMH* 51 (1979), 4–23.

McGARRAH, G. W., 'The First Six Months of the BIS', *Proc. of the Acad. of Political Science, New York,* 14 (1930–2), 235–46.

MACHLUP, F., 'The Transfer Problem: Theme and Four Variations', in id., *International Payments, Debts, and Gold* (New York, 1964).

McINTOSH, D. A., 'Mantoux versus Keynes: A Note on German Income and the Reparations Controversy', *EJ* 87 (1977), 765–7.

MAIER, C. S., 'The Truth about the Treaties?', *JMH* 51 (1979), 56–67.

—— 'Inflation and Stabilization in the Wake of the Two World Wars: Comparative Strategies and Sacrifices', in G. D. Feldman *et al.* (edd.), *Die Erfahrung der Inflation,* 106–29.

MARKS, S., 'Reparations Reconsidered: A Reminder', *J. of Contemporary History,* 2 (1969), 356–65.

—— 'The Myths of Reparations', *CEH* 11 (1978), 231–55.

MAXSE, L. J., 'Can Downing Street Save Germany?', *The National Review,* Nov. 1918.

MELCHIOR, C., 'The Collapse of the Mark and the Problem of its Stabilization', *MGCRE*, 20 Apr. 1922, 26.

MENDELSSOHN-BARTHOLDY, A., 'The Literature of Economic Reconstruction in Germany', *MGCRE*, 4 Jan. 1923, 749.

MENGES, F., 'Die Reaktion der sozialistischen Parteien in Deutschland und Frankreich (S.P.D. und S.F.I.O.) auf die Ruhrbesetzung 1923', *Francia,* 4 (1976), 624–58.

MISES, L. VON, 'Zur Klassifikation der Geldtheorie', *Archiv,* 44 (Oct. 1917), 198–213.

OHLIN, B. G., 'The Reparation Problem: A Discussion. I. Transfer Difficulties, Real and Imagined', *EJ* 39 (1929), 172–8.

—— 'Mr. Keynes' Views on the Transfer Problem: II. A Rejoinder', *EJ* 39 (1929), 400–4.

ORDE, A., 'The Origins of the German–Austrian Customs Union Affair of 1931', *CEH* 13 (1980), 34–59.

OTT, Regierungsrat, 'The Proposed German Forced Loan', *MGCRE*, 27 July 1922, 290.

PRETE, R. A., 'French Military War Aims 1914–1916', *HJ* 28 (1985), 887–99.

PRIBRAM, K., 'Zur Entwicklung der Lebensmittelpreise in der Kriegszeit', *Archiv*, 43 (May 1917), 773–807.

REICHERT, W., 'The German Iron and Steel Industry and its Supplies of Ore', *MGCRE*, 7 Sept. 1922, 445.

RENOUVIN, P., 'Les Buts de guerre du gouvernement français, 1914–1918', *RH* 235 (1966), 1–38.

RHODES, B. D., 'Reassessing "Uncle Shylock": The United States and the French War Debt, 1917–1929', *J. of American History*, 55 (1969), 787–803.

RUEFF, J., 'Mr Keynes's Views on the Transfer Problem: I. A Criticism', *EJ* 39 (1929), 368–99.

RUPPEL, J., 'Deliveries in Kind from Germany under the Wiesbaden and Subsequent Agreements', *MGCRE*, 28 Sept. 1922, 477.

SCHACHT, H., 'The Discount Policy of the Reichsbank', *MGCRE*, 7 Dec. 1922, 689.

SCHIFFER, E., 'Germany's Attitude towards the Reparation Problem', *MGCRE*, 28 Sept. 1922, 473.

SCHROEDER, F., 'The German Budget', *MGCRE*, 27 July 1922, 284.

—— 'Germany's Payments under the Treaty and their Effect on the Budget of the Reich', *MGCRE*, 28 Sept. 1922, 474.

SCHUKER, S. A., 'Finance and Foreign Policy in the Era of the German Inflation: British, French, and German Strategies for Economic Reconstruction after the First World War', in O. Büsch and G. D. Feldman (edd.), *Historische Prozesse der deutschen Inflation, 1914 bis 1924*, 343–61.

—— 'American "Reparations" to Germany, 1919–1933', in G. D. Feldman and E. Müller-Luckner (edd.), *Die Nachwirkungen der Inflation*, 335–84.

SCHULZ, G., 'Reparationen und Krisenprobleme nach dem Wahlsieg der NSDAP 1930: Betrachtungen zur Regierung Brüning', *Vierteljahrschrift für Sozial- und Wirtschaftsgeschichte*, 67 (1980), 200–22.

SCHUMACHER, H., 'The Export Duties in Germany', *MGCRE*, 27 July 1922, 310.

—— 'The New Exchange Regulations in Germany', *MGCRE*, 7 Dec. 1922, 666.

SCHUMPETER, J. A., 'Das Sozialprodukt und die Rechenpfennige', *Archiv*, 44 (1918), 627–716.

—— 'The Crisis of the Tax State', tr. W. F. Stolper and R. A. Musgrave, *International Economic Papers No. 4* (International Economic Association, London, 1954).

SCHWABE, K., 'Comment on Trachtenberg and McDougall', *JMH* 51 (1979), 68–73.

SOUTOU, G., 'Problèmes concernant le rétablissement des relations économiques franco-allemandes après la première guerre mondiale', *Francia*, 2 (1974), 580–96.

—— 'Die deutschen Reparationen und das Seydoux-Projekt 1920/21', *VfZ* 23 (1975), 237–70.

STAMBROOK, F. G., 'The German–Austrian Customs Union Project of 1931: A Study of German Methods and Motives', *J. of Central European Affairs*, 21 (1961), 15–44.

STEVENSON, D. 'French War Aims and the American Challenge, 1914–1918', *HJ* 22 (1979), 877–94.

STOCKS, M., 'The Attempt to Fix Maximum Corn Prices in Germany, November 1914', *EJ* 25 (June 1915), 274–80.

—— 'German Potato Policy', *EJ* 26 (1916), 57–61.

—— 'The Meat Problem in Germany', *EJ* 26 (1916), 168–73.

STOEPHASIUS, VON, 'The Coal and Metallurgical Industries of Upper Silesia as affected by the Geneva Decision and the German-Polish Treaty', *MGCRE*, 7 Sept. 1922, 429.

TRACHTENBERG, M., 'A New Economic Order: Étienne Clémentel and French Economic Diplomacy during the First World War', *French Historical Studies*, 10 (1977), 315–41.

—— 'Reparation at the Paris Peace Conference', *JMH* 51 (1979), 24–55.

—— 'Reply', *JMH* 51 (1979), 83–5.

URBIG, F., 'The Practicability of Exchange Control', *MGCRE*, 20 Apr. 1922, 30.

VOGEL, E. H., 'Die inneren Anleihen der kriegführenden Staaten im zweiten Halbjahr 1914', *Archiv*, 40 (Mar. 1915), 742–56.

—— 'Die Anleihen der kriegführenden Staaten im Jahre 1915', *Archiv*, 43 (July 1916), 244–301.

VÖLCKER, VON, Ministerialrat, 'German Transport and Communication', *Annals*, 92 (1920), 76–86.

WEIRAUCH, W., DR, 'Railway Transportation in Germany', *Annals*, 92 (1920), 87–90.

WILLIAMS, J. H., 'German Foreign Trade and the Reparation Payments', *QJE* 36 (1922), 482–503.

WITT, P.-C., 'Reichsfinanzminister und Reichsfinanzverwaltung', *VfZ* 23 (1975), 1–61.

WRIGHT, G., 'Comment', *JMH* 51 (1979), 74–7.

F. NEWSPAPERS AND JOURNALS

L'Action française, Paris.

Berliner Lokal-Anzeiger, Berlin.

Berliner Tageblatt, Berlin.

Deutsche Allgemeine Zeitung, Berlin.

Deutsche Tageszeitung, Berlin.

Deutsche Zeitung, Berlin.

The Economist, London.

Le Figaro, Paris.

Frankfurter Zeitung, Frankfurt.
Freiheit, Berlin.
L'Indépendance belge, London.
Iron Age, New York.
Kreuz-Zeitung, Berlin.
Liverpool Daily Post and Mercury, Liverpool.
Manchester Guardian, Manchester.
Le Matin, Paris.
Morning Post, London.
New York Times, New York.
Le Petit Parisien, Paris.
Revue des deux mondes, Paris.
Die Rote Fahne, Berlin.
Statist, London.
Sunday Pictorial, London.
Sunday Times, London.
Der Tag, Berlin.
Le Temps, Paris.
The Times, London.
Vorwärts, Berlin.
Vossische Zeitung, Berlin.
Die Zeit, Berlin.

Index

DATE DUE

DEMCO, INC. 38-2931